TEXAS

Real Estate Contracts

FIFTH EDITION

Ralph Tamper, CREI, DREI, GRI

Dearborn™
Real Estate Education

President: Mehul Patel
Vice President of Product Development & Publishing: Evan M. Butterfield
Editorial Director: Kate DeVivo
Senior Development Editor: Tony Peregrin
Director of Production: Daniel Frey
Senior Managing Editor, Production: Jack Kiburz
Production Artist: Virginia Byrne
Creative Director: Lucy Jenkins
Director of Production Management: Melissa Kleeman

Published by Dearborn™ Real Estate Education
30 South Wacker Drive
Chicago, Illinois 60606-7481
(312) 836-4400
www.dearbornRE.com

Printed in the United States of America

08 09 10 9 8 7 6 5 4 3 2 1

The Library of Congress has cataloged the fourth edition as follows:

Tamper, Ralph.
Texas real estate contracts / Ralph Tamper.—4th ed.
p. cm.
Includes index.
ISBN-13: 978-0-7931-9625-8
ISBN-10: 0-7931-9625-6
1. Vendors and purchasers—Texas. 2. Real property—Texas—Forms. I. Title.
KFT1326.T36 2006
346.76404'3—dc22

2006002412

Fifth edition ISBN-13: 978-1-4277-6837-7
Fifth edition ISBN-10: 1-4277-6837-4

CONTENTS

PREFACE

Texas Real Estate Contracts was created to provide a clear, practical approach to one of the most important things a Texas real estate broker or salesperson will do for a Buyer or Seller: fill in the blanks on the purchase agreement. The book is not designed as a definitive legal text, nor does it provide legal advice to license holders or their customers and clients. Readers are advised that it is always desirable to read every word of a legal document carefully and understand it before signing. When unusual matters arise or a party does not understand what he or she is being asked to sign, legal counsel should be sought before proceeding. Real estate license holders may not give legal advice or write documents defining legal rights and remedies of the parties. License holders may only add business details desired by the parties.

At the conclusion of your study of the material in this edition, you will be able to

- professionally fulfill the role of the license holder by accurately setting down the wishes and intent of the parties and refrain from making decisions for them or imposing the broker's or salesperson's will upon them;
- clearly state the elements of a contract;
- explain and comply with the provisions of the Statute of Frauds, the Texas Real Estate License Act (TRELA), and the Rules of the Texas Real Estate Commission (TREC) as they relate to the creation of purchase contracts between Sellers and Buyers;
- write down a business detail and know the difference between a word or phrase that establishes a business detail and one that attempts to define the legal rights and remedies of the parties;
- select the correct form or forms that are appropriate to define the agreement of the parties;
- recognize potential legal problems and know when to encourage the parties to seek competent legal advice from a competent real estate attorney;

- explain to a Seller what is required by statute with regard to property disclosure requirements;
- assist Buyers and Sellers in gaining understanding of the options available to them when a breach of contract occurs; and
- estimate the bottom line accurately for the Seller and the Buyer.

The book is intended for use by both new license holders and seasoned practitioners. As you begin your study, remember that what others do and what is popular are not always correct, and what is correct is not always popular. Real professionals accept the responsibility of verifying and making certain that the approach being used is accurate and appropriate.

Learn what is correct and do not let others intimidate you or put you at risk just because they have been in the business longer than you have. Many practicing license holders have never carefully read the forms. A truly competent real estate broker or salesperson should be able to discuss in detail every one of the TREC-promulgated contracts and addenda. A competent license holder should know exactly when to use and when not to use each of the forms.

Great care has been taken to ensure that every detail about contracts that is covered on the state licensing exams has been thoroughly explored in these pages.

The Texas Real Estate Broker-Lawyer Committee and the TREC meet on a regular basis to review and modify the forms. The commission makes license holders aware of any changes and any newly adopted forms through *The Advisor*, the official publication of the TREC for the distribution of important information to license holders. Carefully read every word of a new form before you use it. Additionally, you can always obtain current, accurate information at the TREC Web site where back issues of *The Advisor* are available.

If necessary, a supplement will be added to this book that will give you current information about revisions and new forms that have been promulgated since the publication of this fifth edition. A visit to the TREC Web site at *www.trec.state.tx.us* offers the opportunity for you to download the latest version of the forms.

This book explores the TREC-published forms. Forms made available for use by members of trade organizations such as local REALTOR® associations and the Texas Association of REALTORS® (TAR) are referenced sparingly because they are available to TAR members only.

New features of the fifth edition include an extensive glossary and additional opportunities to apply what you are learning. Found in Appendix B are the answer keys for the chapter review questions, the Chapter 12 Settlement Statement, and the Appendix A Quick Study Review and Practice Exam. Abbreviated answers for financing scenarios and case studies are found in the answer key. Completed versions of the form can be accessed in the instructor resources section at *www.dearbornre.com*. Always complete the exercises before referring to the answer key.

ACKNOWLEDGMENTS

Appreciation is expressed to Rick Knowles, former Broker-Lawyer Committee member and president of Capitol Real Estate Training in Austin for his valuable insights and excellent suggestions to make this edition more useful to students of providers who offer correspondence as well as live classroom study. Also, thank you to Bobby Reynolds, Instructor at the University of Texas at San Antonio and San Antonio College, who has spent countless hours reviewing the material for accuracy and has contributed many excellent suggestions that have been incorporated into this edition. Appreciation is additionally expressed to Charles J. Jacobus, attorney-at-law and a current member of the Broker-Lawyer Committee, for his friendship and ever present willingness to answer the author's questions.

Gratitude is expressed to the following who have contributed to the first four editions of this book:

Lela Jo Barkley, Instructor at Kapaln Professional Schools

Charlotte Goeters, Instructor at Galveston Community College

Harold Grimes, Instructor at Tyler Real Estate College

Dan Hamilton, Instructor at Real Estate Career Training, Dallas

Lloyd Hampton, Instructor at Kaplan Professional Schools

Nanci Hawes, owner of Legends Real Estate School, Dallas

Charles A. Hutchinson, deceased, Instructor at The Real Estate School, Inc., Houston

Frankie Jefferson, Instructor at Houston Community College

Randy McKechnie, formerly with the University of Texas at Arlington

Kevin S. Morris, Head of the Real Estate Department, San Jacinto College

Marga Shefman, formerly with the Austin Board of REALTORS®

Ken Trussell, Continuing Education for Licensing, Inc. (CELI) and Texas A&M University–Commerce

George Wagner, former Broker-Lawyer Committee Member and Instructor at Kaplan Professional Schools

ABOUT THE AUTHOR

Ralph Tamper founded The Real Estate School, Inc., in Houston, Texas, in 1982. In 2005 the school was acquired by Kaplan Professional Schools. He received his real estate training at the University of Houston. He is the author of *Mastering Real Estate Math* as well as a series of four 3-hour mandatory continuing education (MCE) courses that meet the continuing education requirements to renew a Texas broker or salesperson license. He is in demand as a reviewer of real estate–related texts and computer software for real estate study.

For the last two decades Mr. Tamper has been active as a presenter of continuing education classes for real estate brokers and salespersons, attorneys, appraisers, and accountants. He has been a popular senior instructor for the Graduate REALTOR® Institute (GRI) program in which he taught legal issues, pricing property, contracts, and technology applications for REALTORS®; taxation; and investments. He has additionally authored several modules of the GRI curriculum and has contributed to the test bank used for the GRI program. He has also served as a senior instructor for both the Certified Buyer Representative designation course and the Accredited Buyer Representative courses.

Tamper holds the prestigious Distinguished Real Estate Instructor (DREI) designation awarded by the Real Estate Educators Association. He served on the Board of Directors, was program chairman of the 1998 Annual Conference, and was president of the Real Estate Educators Association for 2000–2001. Additionally, he has been a senior instructor for the Real Estate Educators Association's Instructor Development Workshops since 1999.

Tamper is a life member of the Texas Real Estate Teachers Association and has been awarded its Certified Real Estate Instructor (CREI) designation. He also holds memberships in the national, Texas, and Houston Associations of REALTORS®. He has served as a member of the Education Committee at the local, state, and national levels.

In 2000 the Texas Association of REALTORS® named Tamper Real Estate Educator of the Year. In the same year, two courses authored by him (a 7-hour CE course, "Preserving This Old House," and a 3-hour course for use by the Houston Association of REALTORS® for orientation of new members to the REALTORS® Code of Ethics) were recognized as Education Programs of the Year by the Texas Association of REALTORS®.

CHAPTER ONE

1

An Agreement or a Contract?

KEY TERMS

assignment
attorney-in-fact
bilateral contracts
breach
breach of contract
competent party
consideration
contain a legal description
contract
default
earnest money
executed contract
executory contract
forbearance
fraud
incompetent party
in writing and signed by the parties
lawful objective
liquidated damages
minor
money damages
mutual agreement
novation
performance
Statute of Frauds
unenforceable
unilateral contract
valid
void
voidable

ELEMENTS OF A VALID CONTRACT

Every day individuals enter into agreements to do or to refrain from doing specific acts. Some of these agreements can be classified as contracts; others are simply agreements. A **contract** is a legally enforceable agreement to do **(performance)** or not to do **(forbearance)** a specific thing. Texas statutes protect contractual rights. Those who enter a contract and fail to perform **(default** or **breach)** may be sued by the other party or parties to the agreement. The nondefaulting party may ask the court to enforce specific performance or the nondefaulting may try to prove to the court that economic damages were created by the default and seek money damages to compensate the loss.

To be considered a legally binding or enforceable contract, the agreement must meet certain requirements defined by Texas statute. Parties who enter into agreements that do not meet those requirements may not have legal recourse when the other party decides to ignore the terms and conditions of the agreement. While a contract is legally enforceable in a court of law, an agreement may not be. When creating contracts, the final agreement should be clear, and the promises exchanged should be definite and specific.

The six elements of a valid real estate contract include the following:

1. ***Competent Parties.*** A party who does not have legal capacity **(incompetent party)** may not be held to the terms of an agreement. To be legally competent, a party must have attained the age of majority, which in Texas is 18 years old. An individual younger than 18 may be emancipated only by a court of competent jurisdiction and declared an adult with contractual capacity. A contract signed by a **minor** (younger than 18) is classified as *voidable;* that is, it can be set aside at the sole option of the minor party. If the minor chooses to uphold and fulfill the terms of the agreement, the contract is binding. The parties must be in control of their mental faculties. Individuals are considered sane or mentally competent until declared otherwise by a court. The parties must also be sober and demonstrate contractual intent. Some people define a competent party as a person who is at least 18, sane, and sober. (See Figure 1.1.)

   Any person who meets the **competent party** test may, through a duly executed specific *power of attorney*, name and appoint another to act as an **attorney-in-fact.** The *attorney-in-fact* serves in a fiduciary capacity to the one who makes the appointment. The signature of the attorney-in-fact binds a party just as effectively as the party's own signature. It should be noted that a power of attorney granting authority to transfer title to real property must recite the legal description of the subject of the authority.

   License holders dealing with corporate-owned real estate should remember that only an officer named in a *corporate resolution* passed at a meeting of the board of directors may sign a contract for and on behalf of the corporation. It may be a waste of a licensee's time to attempt to market and negotiate corporately owned real estate prior to obtaining a copy of the corporate resolution for the licensee's file and subsequently for the title company that will be asked to close the transaction.

FIGURE 1.1

TREC 20-7, Paragraph 1

1. PARTIES: ______________________________ (Seller) agrees to sell and convey to ______________________________ (Buyer) and Buyer agrees to buy from Seller the Property described below.

2. ***Consideration.*** To be valid, a contract must specifically identify that something, usually money, is being given in exchange for something else. Texas courts have clearly provided that a promise given in exchange for a promise is adequate **consideration** to bind a purchase agreement. The promise to sell and the promise to purchase in paragraph 1 of the promulgated forms serve as adequate consideration to bind the contract: "Your promise exchanged for my promise is a thing of value, something that is sacred in the eyes of the courts."

Many people incorrectly believe that **earnest money** must be tendered to create a valid contract. This belief was undoubtedly fostered by the fact that license holders used to refer to real estate sales contracts as earnest money contracts. With regard to a purchase contract, the listing broker best fulfills the fiduciary duty to the seller by encouraging a substantial amount of earnest money. The earnest money can demonstrate the buyer's serious intent to purchase and may serve as **liquidated damages** in the event of a breach of contract as defined in paragraph 15 of the contracts promulgated by the Texas Real Estate Commission (TREC). Liquidated damages are monies paid to a nondefaulting party under the terms of a contract as opposed to money damages, which are determined and awarded by a court.

The one type of contract that requires a prospect to tender cash money to bind the agreement is an *option contract*—an *option to purchase* or an *option to terminate*. In an option contract the property owner gives a promise and the purchaser gives money to purchase a legal right and to bind the agreement.

3. ***Mutual Agreement*** *(mutual assent)*. **Mutual agreement** means that the parties must enter the contract freely and voluntarily. Their decisions must be based on truthful, accurate information. The presence of false information or fraud (a deliberate act of deception) by either acts of commission (telling a lie) or acts of omission (failing to reveal material facts about the property) precludes an enforceable agreement. License holders should take decisive action to ensure that full disclosure is made and that the parties to a purchase agreement are making their decisions based on truthful, accurate information.

4. ***Lawful Objective.*** **Lawful objective** concerns the provisions of an agreement, which must call for lawful activity. A provision that does not comply with federal, state, or local law cannot be upheld by a court. Suppose a tenant signs a lease stating that if the tenant fails to pay the rent, the landlord may enter the premises, seize all of the tenant's personal possessions, and immediately sell them to satisfy the rent obligation. Because this provision is in violation of the homestead law, it is unenforceable.

5. ***In Writing and Signed by the Parties.*** The **Statute of Frauds** requires that, to be enforceable, all agreements affecting title to or interest in real estate in Texas be **in writing and signed by the parties.** An oral agreement of sale is void and therefore unenforceable in Texas. It is inadvisable for license holders to conduct real estate negotiations orally. Offers and counteroffers should always be reduced to writing. One does not have a binding executory contract until (1) a written offer has been made; (2) a written acceptance has occurred; and (3) the offeror has been notified of the acceptance. The only exception to the *in writing* rule is a lease for one year or less. All other real estate agreements must be in writing to be enforceable.

6. ***Contain a Legal Description.*** A street address does not constitute an adequate description of the property for contract and conveyance purposes. The Statute of Frauds calls for the agreement to **contain a legal description** that is of such certainty and accuracy that one can go to and identify it. The two commonly used legal descriptions are (1) reference to a recorded plat (lot, block, section number, subdivision name); and (2) metes and bounds. If students of real estate and readers of this book have not previously taken a principles of real estate course, they will learn a great deal about legal descriptions if and when they do.

VALID/VOID/UNENFORCEABLE/VOIDABLE

If an agreement has all six of the elements described above, it is considered **valid** and will be upheld by Texas courts. If it does not have the elements, it is identified as a **void** (the absence of) contract. Due to a change in the law or the passage of time, a contract or certain provisions of a contract may become **unenforceable.** It is important to emphasize that there is a difference between void and unenforceable. An agreement that is a void contract is not a contract; *void* means the absence of something. An *unenforceable contract* is an agreement that had all the six elements at the time it became an executory contract but due to a change in conditions no longer meets the requirements of law and no longer can be upheld by a court of law. A void contract was never enforceable; an unenforceable contract was valid but is no longer so.

As mentioned earlier, contracts can also be **voidable** (set aside at the option of one of the contracting parties). Voidable contracts typically exist in the following five instances:

1. When entered into with a minor, the agreement is voidable at the option of the minor party.
2. When **fraud** by acts of commission or acts of omission can be proven, the agreement is voidable at the option of the nonfraudulent party.
3. When the seller fails to provide and the buyer of a previously occupied single-family residence fails to receive the Texas legislature-mandated TREC Form OP-H, Seller's Disclosure of Property Condition, as required by section 5.008 of the Texas Property Code, the contract may be terminated at the sole option of the buyer and is therefore voidable at the option of the buyer. If the form is presented after the agreement is signed, the buyer may terminate the contract within seven days after receipt of the disclosure.
4. When homeowners' association information and TREC Form 32-1, Condominium Resale Certificate, have not been provided to the buyer prior to creating an executory contract to purchase, the buyer has the unrestricted right to terminate the agreement per section 5.012 of the Texas Property Code.
5. When the property is situated in a utility district or other statutorily created district providing water, sewer, drainage, or flood control, chapter 49 of the Texas Water Code establishes the contract voidable by the buyer if the seller has not forwarded the appropriate notice prior to creating an executory contract to purchase.

PRESENTING OFFERS

All offers should be in writing and presented to the property owner as quickly as is reasonably practical. The TREC rules call for *immediate* presentation. No real estate broker or salesperson has the right to withhold an offer from a property owner. To do so may result in suspension or revocation of one's license under the provisions of the Texas Real Estate License Act (TRELA) or, worse, result in an unpleasant lawsuit for tortious interference. A *tort* is an act that damages another individual and gives rise to legal action. A property owner may consider the license holder's failure to present an offer in a timely manner a tortious interference with his or her ability to sell the property. The reader would do well to explore the possible consequences of this further before failing to present an offer in a timely manner.

Every license holder in Texas must successfully complete a 30-hour course in the law of agency to obtain a license. As taught in the law of agency, licensees must never lose sight of their fiduciary duties to their clients when helping them negotiate contracts. In addition to obedience (finding a buyer for the property); loyalty (putting the client's interest above all others, including the licensee's own); confidentiality (not revealing the client's personal information, although licensees have the duty to disclose all material facts about the property not specifically excluded by statute); reasonable care; and due diligence, licensees owe their clients disclosure and accounting. *Failure to present an offer* is certainly a breach of a licensee's fiduciary duties, as well as the possible basis for a tortious interference lawsuit. Unless instructed otherwise by the owner, all offers must be presented! A seller's instruction not to present backup offers must be given to the licensee in writing.

A seller presented with a written offer may

- accept it,
- reject it,
- counter it, or
- do nothing—that is, ignore it.

When an offer is unacceptable to the property owner, the owner's interest is best served when the owner gives written notice that the offer is unacceptable, thanks the offeror for the prospect's interest in the property, and invites the offeror to submit another offer. The owner should give the offeror information that will shed some light on what terms would be more acceptable to the offeree. A REALTOR® and his or her client might use the Texas Association of REALTORS® (TAR) Seller's Invitation to Buyer to Submit New Offer form, available to TAR members at *www.TexasREALTORS.com*. The form is specifically designed for this purpose. A REALTOR® who is not a member of TAR might simply create a letter to convey the message to the offeror. An example of a letter of nonacceptance is seen in Figure 1.2.

Although the majority of lawsuits against license holders are still brought by buyers dissatisfied with the condition of the property after the sale closes, each year more and more suits are being brought by clients or customers who feel that the selling agent breached one or more fiduciary duties or treated them unfairly.

Failure to present an offer can also result in disciplinary action against the license holder by the TREC. A licensee must present all offers unless specifically instructed otherwise by the client in writing.

FIGURE 1.2

Letter of Nonacceptance

> Dear Mr. and Mrs. Prospect:
>
> Thank you for your offer to purchase our home at 4321 Pine Hollow Drive. We cannot accept your offer as presented. We appreciate your interest and encourage you to submit another offer which will be more favorably considered if you will
>
> - offer a purchase price more in line with current market value,
> - close within 20 to 30 days,
> - purchase the property in its present condition, and
> - pay your own loan origination costs including the fee for the survey required by your lender.
>
> Although this is not a counteroffer, we look forward to hearing from you soon and wish you a very pleasant day.
>
> Sincerely,
>
> *Note: When using this letter, do not sign the offer.*

The offeror may withdraw an offer any time before the offeree's acceptance or the offeror's receiving notification of the offeree's acceptance. To create a solid paper trail, the notice of withdrawal should be given in writing just as the offer was presented in writing. A written offer should not be withdrawn with a verbal notice of withdrawal.

Other factors that may cancel an offer include:

- Lapse of reasonable time
- Destruction of the physical improvements
- Death or insanity of the offeror

Never submit an offer on a second home before withdrawing the offer on the first home.

PERFORMANCE

When an offeror has presented a written offer, the offeree has accepted the offer in writing, and the offeror has been notified of the acceptance, an executed (signed by both parties) or enforceable contract exists.

Generally, the parties have agreed to perform all acts called for in the agreement within 15 to 20 days and to go to closing. When all acts have been performed and the Seller has delivered and the Buyer has accepted the general warranty deed, the contract will become a fully executed contract.

Law dictionaries will contain the term **executory contract** and define it as an enforceable contract that is in the process of being performed or fulfilled. In 2005, the Texas legislature defined an executory contract as one that involves the sale of a residence in which closing will occur more than 180 days after the execution (signing by both parties) of the contract. In Texas, executory is a term limited in meaning to include only a contract-for-deed, lease-purchase, or lease-option transaction. Do not attempt to create an executory contract with any of the TREC-promulgated forms. Always refer customers or clients to a competent real estate attorney to draft an executory contract.

When closing and funding occur, the contract is considered a fully **executed contract.** An *executory contract* is one that is fully negotiated and signed by the parties. The parties still have obligations to fulfill before all things called for in the agreement have been performed. A fully *executed contract* is one in which all parties have fulfilled all promises made in the agreement. When the seller has delivered the deed, received the proceeds, and granted possession to the purchaser, a fully executed contract exists.

The term *executed* may also be used informally to identify an agreement that has been signed by all parties to the agreement. At the signature line on page 7 of the TREC-promulgated forms, the wording calls for the broker to enter the effective date of the contract after all parties have signed, as seen in the following:

EXECUTED the _______ day of _______________, 20____ (EFFECTIVE DATE).

(BROKER FILL IN THE DATE OF FINAL ACCEPTANCE.)

If one of the parties defaults or violates the agreement **(breach of contract),** the non-defaulting party may

- sue the defaulting party for specific performance and/or
- sue the defaulting party for **money damages,** or
- accept the earnest money as liquidated damages as the sole remedy.

The TREC-promulgated contracts specify that the acceptance of the earnest money as liquidated damages releases the parties from further obligations to each other. (See Figure 1.3.)

FIGURE 1.3

TREC 20-7, Paragraph 15

15. DEFAULT: If Buyer fails to comply with this contract, Buyer will be in default, and Seller may (a) enforce specific performance, seek such other relief as may be provided by law, or both, or (b) terminate this contract and receive the earnest money as liquidated damages, thereby releasing both parties from this contract. If, due to factors beyond Seller's control, Seller fails within the time allowed to make any non-casualty repairs or deliver the Commitment, or survey, if required of Seller, Buyer may (a) extend the time for performance up to 15 days and the Closing Date will be extended as necessary or (b) terminate this contract as the sole remedy and receive the earnest money. If Seller fails to comply with this contract for any other reason, Seller will be in default and Buyer may (a) enforce specific performance, seek such other relief as may be provided by law, or both, or (b) terminate this contract and receive the earnest money, thereby releasing both parties from this contract.

Please note that if either party accepts the earnest money as liquidated damages, the parties agree that the earnest money shall be the sole remedy available to the nondefaulting party. In Chapter 9 we will carefully examine the paragraphs in the TREC-promulgated contracts that address default. It is important for a license holder to always remember that advising the parties to take one of the possible remedies over another constitutes the unauthorized practice of law in the eyes of the TREC enforcement division.

BILATERAL VERSUS UNILATERAL

Purchase contracts are **bilateral contracts** that involve a promise in exchange for a promise. The seller in a purchase agreement agrees to deliver clear title and the buyer agrees to deliver money. A **unilateral contract** involves a promise in exchange for an act. The seller agrees to pay the listing broker when and if the broker produces a ready, willing, and able buyer.

Understanding what binds whom to what and when is very important. A bilateral contract binds both parties to do or to refrain from doing specific acts from the moment all have signed. Most real estate–related contracts are bilateral agreements. Examples of bilateral and unilateral contracts include but are not limited to the following agreements:

- **Independent Contractor Agreement**—a bilateral agreement that defines the working relationship between salesperson and sponsoring broker
- **Lease**—a bilateral agreement that defines what the tenant may and may not do during the term of the leasehold and what the property owner may and may not do during the term of the leasehold
- **Option to Purchase**—a unilateral agreement that binds the property owner and prevents the property owner from selling the property to another party but does not bind the prospective purchaser to purchase
- **Option to Terminate**—a unilateral agreement that binds the property owner to release the prospective purchaser from all obligations if the buyer elects to walk away during the defined option period
- **Listing Agreement**—may be either a unilateral agreement or a bilateral agreement although most listing agreements are for an exclusive-right-to-sell agency and involve an exchange of promises and obligations. Only a nonexclusive or open listing may possibly be a unilateral agreement.
- **Buyer Representation Agreement**—a bilateral agreement that defines the working relationship between a buyer and the buyer's agent and creates an exclusive agency relationship
- **Purchase Agreement**—a buy/sell agreement is always a bilateral agreement that calls for each of the parties to perform certain actions and/or fulfill certain promises defined in the agreement

INTERPRETING CONTRACTS

When a court is called upon to settle a dispute between the parties to a contract, the court examines the entire agreement in an attempt to discover the intent of the parties. The court reads the preprinted form and presumes that anything added to the preprinted agreement more clearly shows the intent of the parties. Something handwritten on a contract overrides anything typewritten or preprinted, and an addendum takes precedence over the preprinted form. Once a *contract* has been created, the court favors upholding the agreement and applies the parol evidence rule when called upon to make a decision. The *parol evidence rule* prohibits the consideration of later written or oral agreements unless those agreements clear up any ambiguity in the original agreement. For example, if the original agreement called for closing in *late July* and a separate written agreement called for closing on *July 28*, the court would accept the additional *evidence* as a more specific time to close. When parties wish to alter the provisions of an executory contract, they may execute a new contract in place of the existing agreement or amend the existing contract by using the TREC-promulgated amendment form. In legal terms, a replacement contract is known as a **novation.** A novation or new contract should clearly reference the original agreement and state that the old agreement is replaced by the novation.

Priority of Contract Provisions

- Preprinted, approved form
- "Typewritten" provisions take precedence over preprinted provisions
- Handwritten provisions take precedence over "typewritten" or preprinted provisions
- Addendum provisions take precedence over contract provisions

It is also important to note that there is a definite priority to considerations when interpreting the written provisions of a contract. Courts, in an effort to discover the intent of the parties, will look first to the preprinted form and the details filled in the blanks. A Texas licensed salesperson or broker will always make certain that he or she is following the rules established by the TREC when completing the approved forms.

During negotiations, the parties may add or modify provisions that do not agree with or alter the preprinted provisions. Since the modified provisions better demonstrate the intent of the parties, they will prevail over the preprinted wording.

If during negotiations the forms pass back and forth between the parties a few or several times, preprinted provisions may be crossed out and replaced with handwritten provisions. The courts will consider the handwritten over the preprinted when there is a conflict.

An addendum added to the contract and clearly referenced in the contract will take priority over the contract provisions. An addendum not specifically referenced in the contract is not considered a part of the agreement and will not be considered by the court.

REASONABLE TIME VERSUS TIME IS OF THE ESSENCE

With regard to time frames established in contracts, Texas courts always favor upholding the provisions of the contract when the parties have acted in good faith and have performed within a *reasonable time*. The court must hold the parties to exact performance within the time specified only when the agreement has incorporated the words, *time is of the essence*, or when an Option to Purchase or an Option to Terminate is the contract being interpreted. As you examine the text of the TREC-promulgated forms, you will find that only the Option to Terminate clause in the six promulgated contract forms and three addenda include those words: the TREC Form 10-5, Addendum for Sale of Other Property by Buyer, the TREC Form 11-6, Addendum for "Back-Up" Contract, and the TREC Form 40-3, Third Party Financing Condition Addendum.

A real estate broker or salesperson ***should never*** add the words *time is of the essence* to a contract or advise a customer or client to do so. If a party wants to add the words, that party and the other party should be advised to seek the counsel of a competent real estate attorney before doing so.

The TREC-promulgated contracts call for things to occur within a certain number of days *after* the effective date of the contract. The effective date is filled in above the signature lines by the broker after the last party, usually the seller, has signed, and the other party, usually the buyer, has been notified of the acceptance. It is very difficult to establish performance and nonperformance when a careless license holder fails to fill in the appropriate date before opening title. In fact, such carelessness can result in a significant dispute between the parties. The effective date will need to be established by the parties or perhaps by a court if the parties cannot agree.

It is important to note that all 365 days of the year (366 days in leap year) have equal status. It is also important to learn that the word *after* does not include the effective day of the contract. Therefore, if the effective date of the contract is June 14, and the time frame calls for seven days, the time period will end at midnight on June 21.

We will explore the time frames and related issues in much greater detail in Chapter 8. A thorough understanding of the time issues in a contract is important to ensure that the transaction moves smoothly from offer to acceptance to closing.

■ ASSIGNMENT VERSUS NOVATION

Once an executory contract has been created, a party may transfer his or her interest to another legal entity **(assignment)** unless prohibited by statute or written agreement of the parties. Purchase contracts are typically assignable. Leases, by statute, may not be assigned without the express written permission of the property owner. Most other real estate–related contracts may be assigned unless specific language prohibiting assignment has been included in the body of the agreement. The *assignor* is the party who transfers a right, and the *assignee* is the party to whom the right is assigned. The assignee takes on all of the rights and obligations of the contract being assigned. *However,* the assignor is not released from the obligations of the contract. A good example is the obligation of paying back money borrowed for the purchase of a property. When a new borrower assumes the existing loan obligation, the original borrower is not "off the hook" unless specifically released from the obligation by the lender. Of course, the loan documents may prohibit assumption; one must always examine the loan documents to determine if the obligations may be assigned.

The replacement of an existing contract with a new contract is known as a **novation.** The new contract must reference the contract that is being replaced. There can also be a novation of the parties. A novation releases all of the terms and obligations of the original agreement.

SUMMARY

For a contract to be valid, the parties involved must be competent and must have reached mutual agreement and have tendered consideration. The acts agreed to must be lawful, and the agreement must be in writing if it involves rights and interest in real estate. Once the agreement is signed, it can be valid, void, unenforceable, or voidable.

The license holder should present all offers as quickly as possible to avoid disciplinary action by the Texas Real Estate Commission or a possible suit for tortious interference brought by the property owner.

Texas courts favor upholding the provisions of contracts and apply the reasonable-time rule when interpreting contracts unless the parties have specifically stated that time is of the essence.

CHAPTER 1 REVIEW QUESTIONS

1. What kind of contract exists when a promise is exchanged for a promise?

   a. Unilateral
   b. Executed
   c. Bilateral
   d. Defaulted

2. When all parties have signed a contract and the offeror has been notified of the offeree's acceptance, what exists at the time the contract is deposited at the title company?

   a. Executed contract
   b. Expired contract
   c. Unenforceable contract
   d. Executory contract

3. When there is a default on the part of one party and the other party wants the defaulting party to do what was agreed in the contract, for what would the nondefaulting party sue?

   a. Money damages
   b. Specific performance
   c. Liquidated damages
   d. Injunctive relief

4. What word *BEST* describes a contract entered into with a minor?

   a. Void
   b. Voidable
   c. Valid
   d. Venued

5. Which would *ALWAYS* be identified as a unilateral contract?

   a. Contract for Sale
   b. Buyer Representation Agreement
   c. Listing Agreement
   d. Option to Purchase

6. An agreement that does *NOT* fulfill the statutory requirements of a contract is identified as

   a. valid.
   b. void.
   c. voidable.
   d. invalid.

7. An offer made in response to an offer is known as what?

   a. Contract
   b. Assignment
   c. Counteroffer
   d. Novation

8. The substitution of a new contract for an existing contract is known as what?

   a. Amendment
   b. Novation
   c. Cancellation
   d. Rescission

9. What is a deliberate act of deception for the purpose of inducing another to part with something of value or to enter into a contract?

   a. Innocent misrepresentation
   b. Duress
   c. Mistake
   d. Fraud

10. The transfer of a contracting party's rights to a third party without a release of liabilities is identified as a(n)

   a. cancellation.
   b. assignment.
   c. amendment.
   d. specific performance.

HOMEWORK QUIZ

The following quiz does not have an answer key included with the answer keys in Appendix B. Students who are using this book as the basis for a correspondence course should record and submit their answers to their course provider as instructed by the provider. The student will submit his or her answers for the Homework Quiz at the end of each chapter and for each transaction in Chapter 11.

True or False?

1. An option to purchase contract is always a bilateral contract.

2. A fully executed contract is the correct way to reference a contract for a transaction that has closed.

3. The amount of money damages to be paid upon default or a breach of contract is determined by the contracting parties.

4. An attorney-in-fact and an attorney-at-law are the same.

5. A Texas salesperson or a broker must present all offers to the Seller-client unless instructed otherwise by the client.

CHAPTER TWO

2

The Texas Real Estate License Act and the Rules of the Texas Real Estate Commission

KEY TERMS

Broker-Lawyer Committee
business detail
lease
legal right
promulgate
remedies
temporary lease

Under its police power, the State of Texas has the legal right to enact and enforce laws to protect the health, safety, and general welfare of the public. Since 1949 Texas has had the Texas Real Estate License Act (TRELA) (Chapter 1101 of the Texas Occupations Code) to regulate those who, for a fee or other valuable consideration, sell, exchange, procure, prospect, or inspect real property. The law holds brokers responsible for all professional and vocational acts performed by any real estate salesperson associated with or acting for the broker. Brokers must pay close attention to the activities of their licensed staff.

TRELA SECTIONS 1101.155; 1101.251; 1101.252; 1101.654

The TRELA specifically prohibits license holders from practicing law by giving opinions or counsel regarding the validity or legal sufficiency of an instrument that addresses real property rights or as to the status of title to real estate. Throughout the act, it is clearly established that, prior to signing a purchase contract, the license holder must give a Buyer written advice to have the abstract covering the property examined by an attorney of the Buyer's selection or to obtain an owner's title insurance policy prior to closing. Failure to do so may result in disciplinary action by the Texas Real Estate Commission (TREC).

Those who choose to become REALTORS® will subscribe to a REALTOR® Code of Ethics that demands a very high level of professional conduct. Article 13 of the National Association of REALTORS® Code of Ethics addresses the unauthorized practice of law and states the following:

> REALTORS® shall not engage in activities that constitute the unauthorized practice of law and shall recommend that legal counsel be obtained when the interest of any party to the transactions requires it.

The TRELA clearly establishes that it is illegal for the license holder to draw a deed, note, deed of trust, will, or other written instrument that transfers or may transfer an interest in or title to real property. However, the act goes on to give permission for a license holder to complete a contract form that may bind the sale, exchange, option, lease, or rental of any interest in real property as long as forms are used that have been prepared by or are required by the property owner or have been provided by the real estate commission, prepared by an attorney licensed by Texas, and approved by that attorney for a particular type of transaction.

> Sec. 1101.654. SUSPENSION OR REVOCATION OF LICENSE OR CERTIFICATE FOR UNAUTHORIZED PRACTICE OF LAW. (a) The commission shall suspend or revoke the license or certificate of registration of a license or certificate holder who is not a licensed attorney in this state and who, for consideration, a reward, or in a pecuniary benefit, present or anticipated, direct or indirect, or in connection with the person's employment, agency, or fiduciary relationship as a license or certificate holder:
>
> > (1) drafts an instrument, other than a form described by Section 1101.155, that transfers or otherwise affects an interest in real property; or
> >
> > (2) advises a person regarding the validity or legal sufficiency of an instrument or the validity of title to real property.
>
> (b) Notwithstanding any other law, a license or certificate holder who completes a contract form for the sale, exchange, option, or lease of an interest in real property incidental to acting as a broker is not engaged in the unauthorized or illegal practice of law in this state if the form was:
>
> > (1) adopted by the commission for the type of transaction for which the form is used;
> >
> > (2) prepared by an attorney licensed in this state (Texas) and approved by the attorney for the type of transaction for which the form is used; or
> >
> > (3) prepared by the property owner or by an attorney and required by the property owner.

The legislature created an advisory body to develop and recommend various contract forms to the TREC for use by license holders when performing the tasks for which they have been licensed. This body, the Texas Real Estate **Broker-Lawyer Committee,** does not **promulgate,** or publish, forms for mandatory use by license holders. Only the

TREC has been given rule-making authority. The Broker-Lawyer Committee develops forms and recommends their adoption, but it is the TREC that promulgates the forms for mandatory use. The act clearly establishes the responsibilities of the committee, composed of six brokers appointed by the TREC, six attorneys appointed by the president of the State Bar of Texas, and one public member appointed by the governor. Carefully review the following text of the act that is reproduced below.

SUBCHAPTER F
TEXAS REAL ESTATE BROKER-LAWYER COMMITTEE

Sec. 1101.251. DEFINITION OF COMMITTEE. In this subchapter, "committee" means the Texas Real Estate Broker-Lawyer Committee.

Sec. 1101.252. COMMITTEE MEMBERSHIP. (a) The Texas Real Estate Broker-Lawyer Committee consists of 13 members appointed as follows:

(1) six members appointed by the commission; and

(2) six members of the State Bar of Texas appointed by the president of the state bar; and

(3) one public member appointed by the governor.

(b) Appointments to the committee shall be made without regard to the race, creed, sex, religion, or national origin of the appointee.

The license holder also needs to be aware that the legislature has given the commission rule-making authority and that the rules of the commission have the full force and effect of law. That authority is established in the part of the TRELA that is reproduced in the following:

Sec. 1101.155. RULES RELATING TO CONTRACT FORMS. (a) The commission may adopt rules in the public's best interest that require license holders to use contract forms prepared by the Texas Real Estate Broker-Lawyer Committee and adopted by the commission.

(b) The commission may not prohibit a license holder from using for sale, exchange, option, or lease of an interest in real property a contract form that is:

(1) prepared by the property owner; or

(2) prepared by an attorney and required by the property owner.

(c) A listing contract form adopted by the commission that relates to the contractual obligations between a seller of real estate and a license holder acting as an agent for the seller must include:

(1) a provision informing the parties to the contract that real estate commissions are negotiable; and

(2) a provision explaining the availability of Texas coastal natural hazards information important to coastal residents, if that information is appropriate.

Before engaging in the business of completing any contract forms that bind the sale, **lease, temporary lease,** or rental of any real property, the license holder should become thoroughly familiar with what the rules do and do not permit.

TREC RULE 537.11

It is the TREC rule 537.11 that addresses the use of standardized forms. The first part of Rule 537.11 lists the forms that are currently promulgated, that is, published, for mandatory use by a license holder when the form fits a particular transaction. The following list gives the date on which the form was promulgated, as well as the name of the form and the TREC form reference number. Earlier versions of forms may not be used; to do so could be considered the unauthorized practice of law, an illegal act. Remember that you must use promulgated forms unless one of the four exceptions mentioned earlier comes into play.

Texas Real Estate Commission Forms [537.11 (a)]

Promulgated Contracts:

Number	Name	Adoption Date
9-6	Unimproved Property Contract	02/06
20-7	One to Four Family Residential Contract (Resale)	02/06
23-7	New Home Contract (Incomplete Construction)	12/07
24-7	New Home Contract (Completed Construction)	12/07
25-5	Farm and Ranch Contract	02/06
30-6	Residential Condominium Contract (Resale)	12/06

Promulgated Addenda:

10-5	Addendum for Sale of Other Property by Buyer	04/07
11-6	Addendum for "Back-Up" Contract	04/07
12-2	Addendum for Release of Liability on Assumed Loan and/or Restoration of Seller's VA Entitlement	04/07
15-4	Seller's Temporary Residential Lease	12/06
16-4	Buyer's Temporary Residential Lease	12/06
26-5	Seller Financing Addendum	12/06
28-1	Environmental Assessment, Threatened or Endangered Species, and Wetlands Addendum	04/07
33-1	Addendum for Coastal Area Property	04/07
34-3	Addendum for Property Located Seaward of the Gulf Intracoastal Waterway	12/07
36-4	Addendum for Property Subject to Mandatory Membership in an Owners' Association	02/06
40-3	Third Party Financing Condition Addendum	12/07
41-1	Loan Assumption Addendum	04/07
43-0	Addendum Containing Required Notices Under 5.016, 420.001, and 420.002 Texas Property Code	12/07

Promulgated Amendment:

39-6	Amendment	02/06

Promulgated Resale Certificates:

32-1	Condominium Resale Certificate	04/07
37-2	Subdivision Information, Including Resale Certificate for Property Subject to Mandatory Membership in an Owners' Association	02/06

Promulgated Notice:

38-1	Notice of Termination of Contract	10/01
42-0	Notice Pursuant to Third Party Financing Addendum	02/04

Promulgated Consumer Disclosure:

	Consumer Information Form 1-1	08/91

Optional/Voluntary Use Forms:

OP-C	Notice to Prospective Buyer	12/99
OP-H	Seller's Disclosure of Property Condition	09/07
OP-I	Texas Real Estate Consumer Notice Concerning Hazards or Repairs	04/02
OP-K	Information About Brokerage Services	01/96
OP-L	Addendum for Seller's Disclosure of Information on Lead-Based Paint and Lead-Based Paint Hazards as Required by Federal Law	02/04

After itemizing the current inventory of available forms, the commission establishes the do's and don'ts for the completion of those forms. A careful reading of the rules tells licensees all they need to know. The underlining in the following excerpt has been added for emphasis:

> 537.11 (b)
>
> (b) When negotiating contracts binding the sale, exchange, option, lease or rental of any interest in real property, a real estate licensee shall use only those contract forms promulgated by the Texas Real Estate Commission for that kind of transaction with the following exceptions:
>
> (1) transactions in which the licensee is functioning solely as a principal, not an agent;
>
> (2) transactions in which an agency of the United States government requires a different form to be used;
>
> (3) transactions for which a contract form has been prepared by the property owner or prepared by an attorney and required by the property owner;
>
> (4) transactions for which no standard contract form has been promulgated by the Texas Real Estate Commission, and the licensee uses a form prepared by an attorney at law licensed by this state and approved by the attorney for the

particular kind of transactions involved or prepared by the Texas Real Estate Broker-Lawyer Committee and made available for trial use by licensees with the consent of the Texas Real Estate Commission.

537.11 (c) and Following

(c) A licensee may not practice law, offer, give nor attempt to give advice, directly or indirectly; the licensee may not act as a public conveyancer nor give advice or opinions as to the legal effect of any contracts or other such instruments which may affect the title to real estate; the licensee may not give opinions concerning the status or validity of title to real estate; and the licensee may not attempt to prevent nor in any manner whatsoever discourage any principal to a real estate transaction from employing a lawyer. However, nothing herein shall be deemed to limit the licensee's fiduciary obligation to disclose to his principals all pertinent facts which are within the knowledge of the licensee, including such facts which might affect the status of or title to real estate.

(d) A licensee may not undertake to draw or prepare documents fixing and defining the *legal rights* of the principals to a transaction. In negotiating real estate transactions, the licensee may fill in forms for such transactions, using exclusively forms which have been approved and promulgated by the Texas Real Estate Commission or such forms as are otherwise permitted by these rules. When filling in such a form, the licensee may only fill in the blanks provided and may not add to or strike matter from such form, except that licensees shall add factual statements and business details desired by the principals and shall strike only such matter as is desired by the principals and as is necessary to conform the instrument to the intent of the parties. A licensee may not add to a promulgated earnest money contract form factual statements or business details for which a contract addendum, lease or other form has been promulgated by the commission for mandatory use. Nothing herein shall be deemed to prevent the licensee from explaining to the principals the meaning of the factual statements and business details contained in the said instrument so long as the licensee does not offer or give legal advice. It is not the practice of law as defined in this Act for a real estate licensee to complete a contract form which is either promulgated by the Texas Real Estate Commission or prepared by the Texas Real Estate Broker-Lawyer Committee and made available for trial use by licensees with the consent of the Texas Real Estate Commission. Contract forms prepared by the Texas Real Estate Broker-Lawyer Committee for trial use may be used on a voluntary basis after being approved by the commission. Contract forms prepared by the Texas Real Estate Broker-Lawyer Committee and approved by the commission to replace previously promulgated forms may be used by licensees on a voluntary basis prior to the effective date of rules requiring use of the replacement form.

(e) Where it appears that, prior to the execution of any such instrument, there are unusual matters involved in the transaction which should be resolved by legal counsel before the instrument is executed or that the instrument is to be acknowledged and filed for record, the licensee shall advise the principals that each should consult a lawyer of the principal's choice before executing same.

(f) A licensee may not employ, directly or indirectly, a lawyer nor pay for the services of a lawyer to represent any principal to a real estate transaction in which the licensee is acting as an agent. The licensee may employ and pay for the services of a lawyer to represent only the licensee in a real estate transaction, including preparation of the contract, agreement, or other legal instruments to be executed by the principals to the transactions.

(g) A licensee shall advise the principals that the instrument they are about to execute is binding on them.

(h) Forms approved or promulgated by the commission may be reproduced only from the following sources:

(1) numbered copies obtained from the commission, whether in a printed format or electronically reproduced from the files available on the commission's Internet site;

(2) printed copies made from copies obtained from the commission;

(3) legible photocopies made from such copies; or

(4) computer-driven printers following these guidelines:

(A) The computer file or program containing the form text must not allow the end-user direct access to the text of the form and may only permit the user to insert language in blanks in the forms or to strike through language at the direction of the parties to the contract.

(B) Typefaces or fonts must appear to be identical to those used by the commission in printed copies of the particular form.

(C) The text and number of pages must be identical to that used by the commission in printed proofs of the particular form.

(D) The spacing, length of blanks, borders and placement of text on the page must appear to be identical to that used by the commission in printed copies of the form.

(E) The name and address of the person or firm responsible for developing the software program must be legibly printed below the border at the bottom of each page in no less than 6 point type and in no larger than 10 point type.

(F) The text of the form must be obtained from a copy of the form bearing a control number assigned by the commission.

(i) The control number of each copy must appear on all forms reproduced from the copy, including forms reproduced by computer-driven printers.

(j) Forms approved or promulgated by the commission must be reproduced on the same size of paper used by the commission with the following changes or additions only.

(1) The business name or logo of a broker, organization or printer may appear at the top of a form outside the border.

(2) The broker's name may be inserted in any blank provided for that purpose.

The TREC and the Broker-Lawyer Committee are charged with serving the best interest of the public and have adopted the foregoing to accomplish that purpose. They are always willing to hear comments from the license holders whom they regulate. Licensees should address their suggestions for contract and addenda revisions to the following:

General Counsel
Texas Real Estate Commission
PO Box 12188
Austin, TX 78711-2188

From time to time *The Advisor, published by TREC*, will carry a message from the TREC enforcement division relating to the proper approach to structuring, presenting, and negotiating purchase agreements. Volume 9, No. 4 addresses the proper handling of *multiple offers*, a common challenge in a *Seller's Market*. In response to the commonly asked questions about the listing agent's duty to notify the Seller of multiple offers, the TREC responded as follows:

> TREC rule 535.156(a) specifically requires a licensee to "convey to the principal all known information which would affect the principal's decision on whether or not to accept or reject offers." Subsection 535.156(c) further provides that "a licensee has an affirmative duty to keep the principal informed at all times of significant information applicable to the transaction or transactions in which the licensee is acting as agent for the principal." Thus the rules require the listing agent to submit all written purchase offers to the seller until a buyer and the seller have a fully executed contract.

Although the general rule is that all offers must be communicated to the Seller by the listing agent, there are a few exceptions. These include instances where the Seller has specifically instructed the listing broker in writing not to bring the Seller any offers below a certain price, or situations in which a binding contract has been executed between a Seller and Buyer. A good business practice to follow is to always have such directives reduced to writing and retained in your permanent file on the property and/or client. In the latter situation, Rule 535.156(a) provides that "the license holder shall have no duty to submit offers to the principal after the principal has accepted an offer." Furthermore, the listing agent is prohibited from sharing any information about one Buyer's offer with another Buyer. Note, however, that in the end, it is always the Sellers' decision whether to accept or reject offers they receive. The listing should address the broker's duty regarding backup offers to avoid confusion on the issue. Also, trade association rules and standards of practice may affect the broker's duty.

Remember that the latest TREC forms are available and can be downloaded and printed from *www.trec.state.tx.us*. License holders are responsible for making certain that the forms that they are using to structure a transaction are the currently approved or promulgated forms. REALTORS® should also take note that the forms provided by the Texas Association of REALTORS® (TAR) for use by its members must be the currently approved forms. When the TAR revises a form, creates a new form, or retires a form, it gives notice to its members through local association newsletters and through its member-provided forms software, Zipforms. When in doubt about a TREC form, contact the TREC to verify that the form that you are planning to use is an approved form. When in doubt about a TAR form, call the TAR Legal Hotline to verify that it is a currently approved form. License holders who are not members of the TAR may not use the TAR's forms that are protected by federal copyright laws.

SUMMARY

The purpose of the license act and the rules of the commission are to protect the public. The provisions prohibit the unauthorized practice of law by real estate license holders both in the area of structuring instruments and in the area of giving legal advice and opinions as to the legal sufficiency of instruments or the status of title.

To assist license holders, the commission has promulgated various forms for use by license holders. These forms must be used for all transactions assisted by license holders unless the transaction meets one of the defined exceptions itemized in the TREC rule. Remember that you must use promulgated contracts and addenda. Do not write a **business detail** addressing the business detail into the Special Provisions paragraph when there is a promulgated addendum. A *business detail* states what someone will or will not do. The license holder may only fill in the blanks provided and may not add material to or strike wording from the forms except to add business details to conform the instrument to the intent of the parties. When the license holder describes what will happen if someone does or does not do a certain act (e.g., terminate the contract, refund earnest money), the license holder steps over the line and begins defining **legal rights and remedies.** A thorough discussion and examples of what is and is not acceptable wording for paragraph 11 is provided in Chapter 9.

The license holder may help a customer or client read the document but shall not give legal advice or opinions. Never discourage a customer or client from employing a competent real estate attorney. It is good practice to encourage Buyers and Sellers to carefully read any document before they sign it and seek legal counsel to clarify anything they do not understand. Encourage Buyers and Sellers to provide the information to complete paragraph 24 of the contract.

CHAPTER 2 REVIEW QUESTIONS

1. Which defines a legal right as opposed to simply stating a business detail?
   a. The Buyer will inspect the property again during the four hours immediately preceding closing.
   b. The Buyer will pay for the owner's title policy.
   c. The Seller will pay for all of the Buyer's normal closing costs.
   d. The Buyer may terminate the contract if the foundation needs to be repaired.

2. Which addendum is *NOT* a TREC-promulgated form?
   a. The TREC Form OP-L, Addendum for Seller's Disclosure of Information on Lead-Based Paint and Lead-Based Hazards as Required by Federal Law
   b. The TREC Form 15-4, Seller's Temporary Residential Lease
   c. The TREC Form 26-5, Seller Financing Addendum
   d. The TREC Form 33-1, Addendum for Coastal Area Property

3. Who *MUST* notify the Buyer to have the abstract examined by an attorney or obtain a policy of title insurance?
   a. Seller
   b. Real estate license holder
   c. Lender
   d. Buyer's attorney

4. A license holder may use a contract form that has been prepared by the property owner when instructed by the property owner to do so.
   a. True
   b. False

5. What should a license holder do when there are unusual matters involved in a transaction?
   a. Explain it to the best of his and her ability before letting the prospect sign the contract
   b. Ignore it and hope that the client understands it
   c. Have the client sign the form and then advise him and her to talk to an attorney
   d. Advise the client to seek legal advice before signing anything

6. For which is there *NO* TREC-promulgated form?

   a. Sale of an unimproved residential lot
   b. Contract for deed
   c. Lease for temporary occupancy by a Seller after the closing
   d. Request for information about an owners' association

7. As an added value to the service provided by a broker, may a broker retain and pay for the services of an attorney to prepare documents and to provide legal counsel to a client?

   a. Yes
   b. No

8. Which action *MIGHT* leave a license holder open to a charge of practicing law without a license?

   a. License holder advises the Seller that the property probably won't sell because it is overpriced.
   b. License holder advises the Buyer in writing that a title policy should be obtained as well as a survey.
   c. License holder advises both the Seller and the Buyer that, in his opinion, title to the subject property is encumbered.
   d. License holder adds factual statements and business details to a promulgated form as requested by the client.

9. Which is *TRUE* about the TREC-promulgated contract forms?

   a. They must be used by all real estate license holders and Texas attorneys handling real estate transactions.
   b. They must be used by real estate license holders in all transactions to which the forms are applicable unless one of the four exceptions apply.
   c. They contain suggested language that a license holder may include when writing an agreement of purchase between a Seller and a Buyer.
   d. They are promulgated by the Broker-Lawyer Committee after being approved by the TREC.

10. When no promulgated form meets the needs of a particular transaction, the license holder may use which of the following?

   a. Any standard form sold at the office supply store
   b. Any of the State Bar standard forms
   c. A form structured and approved by a licensed attorney at law
   d. A form created and approved for that type of transaction written by an attorney licensed in Texas

HOMEWORK QUIZ

The following quiz does not have an answer key included with the answer keys in Appendix B. Students who are using this book as the basis for a correspondence course should record and submit their answers to their course provider as instructed by the provider. The student will submit his or her answers for the Homework Quiz at the end of each chapter and for each transaction in Chapter 11.

True or False?

1. A promulgated form is published by TREC for mandatory use by a licensed real estate salesperson or broker when the form fits the transaction.

2. The Broker-Lawyer Committee has rule-making authority granted to it by the Texas legislature.

3. A licensed salesperson or broker may copy the wording of a promulgated addendum into the Special Provisions paragraph of a promulgated contract form rather than attaching the addendum.

4. A licensed salesperson or broker, functioning solely as a principal in a given transaction, does not need to use a promulgated form to structure that transaction.

5. There are currently six contract forms promulgated by the TREC and six forms approved and published for voluntary use by license holders.

CHAPTER THREE

Defining Terms, Exchanging Promises, and Heeding Notices

■ KEY TERMS

Buyer
Buyer's Expenses
Commitment
Exception Documents
Loan Fees
Seller
Seller's Expenses
Title
Title Policy
TREC

■ INTRODUCTION

Almost all of this chapter was authored by the Texas Broker-Lawyer Committee and promulgated by the TREC as Form 20-7, One to Four Family Residential Contract (Resale), the most frequently used of the TREC-promulgated forms. This chapter is formatted with the text of the TREC Form 20-7 on the left and a blank page on the right. (See Figure 3.1.) Use the blank page to make notes when reading, evaluating, and comprehending this form.

When reading the contract, do the following three things:

1. ***Find and write down the definitions for the key terms*** listed at the beginning of this chapter. Notice that each of the terms is *capitalized.* In contract law, these terms are called *defined terms*. Defined terms are always set off in parenthesis following a longer piece of text. Once the term has been defined in the contract, throughout the remainder of the contract only the shortened version of that term is found. For example, in paragraph 12 of the following contract, there is a list of various expenses that the parties agree are to be paid by the buyer at the closing. Some of those costs are related to obtaining the financing being used to acquire the Property. At 12A(2)(a) the contract reads, "Loan origination, discount, buy-

down, and commitment fees (Loan Fees)." From that point forward only the words *Loan Fees* will appear and only loan origination, discount, buy-down, and commitment fees are being referenced. With a careful reading of the form, all the terms in the key terms list are easy to spot.

In a few places, the Broker-Lawyer Committee has set down the defined term first and then defined it in parentheses following the term. A good example of this is at paragraph 3C, where you will see the following:

EXAMPLE: Sales Price (Sum of A and B)

Another inconsistency is found at the beginning of paragraph 6B, where you will see the defined term Closing Date. This defined term is used several times before it is finally defined in the first line of the text in paragraph 9A:

EXAMPLE: The closing of the sale will be on or before ____________, 20___, or within 7 days after objections made under paragraph 6D have been cured or waived, whichever date is later (Closing Date).

2. ***Make a list of the promises*** that the buyer is making to the seller and a list of the promises that the seller is making to the buyer. Remember that a contract is created when a legally enforceable promise is exchanged for a legally enforceable promise or a promise is exchanged for money such as in an option contract. For example: In paragraph 1 of the contract, the seller promises or agrees to *sell and convey* and the buyer agrees to *buy from seller. That exchange of promises fulfills the requirement that there be consideration exchanged, the seller's promise for the buyer's promise.*Look for the words *shall* and *agree to.*

3. ***Highlight all of the notices*** contained in the form. Sometimes a notice in capital letters is found at the top of the first page of the form.

   EXAMPLE: NOTICE: Not For Use For Condominium Transactions

   Many notices are more subtle and appear as instructions to the individual filling in the form. A good example of this type of notice is found at the end of the first line of text of paragraph 4.

   EXAMPLE: (Check applicable boxes below)

   Another notice is found at paragraph 7B.

   EXAMPLE: (Notice): (Check one box only)

   In other places the following instructions will be found in parentheses.

   EXAMPLE: (check all boxes that apply)

A competent, professional real estate practitioner should always take very seriously the task of correctly filling in the blanks provided on the forms. It is equally important to know what the words that connect the blanks say and mean.

To guide you through your initial reading of the most commonly used of the promulgated forms, TREC 20-7, the lines that contain notices are marked in the left column of the first page of the form. You will mark them for the remaining pages. The defined terms, promises made by the parties, and notices are extracted for you and listed on the template page opposite the contract page. You will extract and list this information for the remaining pages of the form.

FIGURE 3.1

Form 20-7

Notices:

EQUAL HOUSING OPPORTUNITY

02-13-06

PROMULGATED BY THE TEXAS REAL ESTATE COMMISSION (TREC)

ONE TO FOUR FAMILY RESIDENTIAL CONTRACT (RESALE)

NOTICE: Not For Use For Condominium Transactions

→ **1. PARTIES:** ______________________________ (Seller) agrees to sell and convey to ______________________________ (Buyer) and Buyer agrees to buy from Seller the Property described below.

2. PROPERTY:

A. LAND: Lot ______ Block ________, ______________________________ Addition, City of ______________________________, County of ____________________, Texas, known as ______________________________ (address/zip code), or as described on attached exhibit.

→ B. IMPROVEMENTS: The house, garage and all other fixtures and improvements attached to the above-described real property, including without limitation, the following **permanently installed and built-in items,** if any: all equipment and appliances, valances, screens, shutters, awnings, wall-to-wall carpeting, mirrors, ceiling fans, attic fans, mail boxes, television antennas and satellite dish system and equipment, heating and air-conditioning units, security and fire detection equipment, wiring, plumbing and lighting fixtures, chandeliers, water softener system, kitchen equipment, garage door openers, cleaning equipment, shrubbery, landscaping, outdoor cooking equipment, and all other property owned by Seller and attached to the above described real property.

C. ACCESSORIES: The following described related accessories, if any: window air conditioning units, stove, fireplace screens, curtains and rods, blinds, window shades, draperies and rods, controls for satellite dish system, controls for garage door openers, entry gate controls, door keys, mailbox keys, above ground pool, swimming pool equipment and maintenance accessories, and artificial fireplace logs.

D. EXCLUSIONS: The following improvements and accessories will be retained by Seller and removed prior to delivery of possession: ______________________________.

The land, improvements and accessories are collectively referred to as the "Property".

3. SALES PRICE:

A. Cash portion of Sales Price payable by Buyer at closing................. $__________

→ B. Sum of all financing described below (excluding any loan funding fee or mortgage insurance premium)... $__________

C. Sales Price (Sum of A and B).. $__________

→ **4. FINANCING:** The portion of Sales Price not payable in cash will be paid as follows: (Check applicable boxes below)

❑ A. THIRD PARTY FINANCING: One or more third party mortgage loans in the total amount of $__________ (excluding any loan funding fee or mortgage insurance premium).

→ (1) Property Approval: If the Property does not satisfy the lenders' underwriting requirements for the loan(s), this contract will terminate and the earnest money will be refunded to Buyer.

→ (2) Financing Approval: (Check one box only)

❑ (a) This contract is subject to Buyer being approved for the financing described in the attached Third Party Financing Condition Addendum.

❑ (b) This contract is not subject to Buyer being approved for financing and does not involve FHA or VA financing.

❑ B. ASSUMPTION: The assumption of the unpaid principal balance of one or more promissory notes described in the attached TREC Loan Assumption Addendum.

❑ C. SELLER FINANCING: A promissory note from Buyer to Seller of $__________, secured by vendor's and deed of trust liens, and containing the terms and conditions described in the attached TREC Seller Financing Addendum. If an owner policy of title insurance is furnished, Buyer shall furnish Seller with a mortgagee policy of title insurance.

5. EARNEST MONEY: Upon execution of this contract by both parties, Buyer shall deposit $__________ as earnest money with ______________________________, as escrow agent, at ______________________________

→ (address). Buyer shall deposit additional earnest money of $__________ with escrow agent within ______ days after the effective date of this contract. If Buyer fails to deposit the earnest money as required by this contract, Buyer will be in default.

6. TITLE POLICY AND SURVEY:

A. TITLE POLICY: Seller shall furnish to Buyer at ❑Seller's ❑Buyer's expense an owner policy of title insurance (Title Policy) issued by ______________________________ (Title Company) in the amount of the Sales Price, dated at or after closing, insuring Buyer

Defined Terms:

1. Seller—name of current title holder
   Buyer—name of prospective buyer/purchaser
   Property—not defined until paragraph 2
2. Property—land, improvements, and accessories
3. Sales Price—(sum of A and B) in paragraph 3C
6. Title Policy—owner policy of title insurance

   Title Company—name of the company selected by the parties to issue the owner policy of title insurance/Title Policy

Promises:

Buyer

1. Buyer agrees to buy described Property.

4C. Buyer shall furnish mortgagee Title Policy.

5. Buyer shall deposit earnest money.

   Buyer shall deposit additional earnest money.

Seller

1. Seller agrees to sell and convey.
6. Seller shall furnish a Title Policy.

Notices:

	Title section—not for use with condominium transactions
2.	(address/zip code)—tells what to enter in the blank
3B.	(excluding . . .)—tells what is not included in the number entered in the blank
3C.	(Sum of A and B)—defines Sales Price
4.	(check applicable boxes below)
4A.	(excluding . . .)—same notice as found in 3B
4A(2)(b).	(check one box only)
5.	(address)—tells what shouldbe entered in the line
6.	(Title Policy) and (Title Company) defines defined terms.

FIGURE 3.1 (CONTINUED)

Form 20-7

against loss under the provisions of the Title Policy, subject to the promulgated exclusions (including existing building and zoning ordinances) and the following exceptions:
(1) Restrictive covenants common to the platted subdivision in which the Property is located.
(2) The standard printed exception for standby fees, taxes and assessments.
(3) Liens created as part of the financing described in Paragraph 4.
(4) Utility easements created by the dedication deed or plat of the subdivision in which the Property is located.
(5) Reservations or exceptions otherwise permitted by this contract or as may be approved by Buyer in writing.
(6) The standard printed exception as to marital rights.
(7) The standard printed exception as to waters, tidelands, beaches, streams, and related matters.
(8) The standard printed exception as to discrepancies, conflicts, shortages in area or boundary lines, encroachments or protrusions, or overlapping improvements. Buyer, at Buyer's expense, may have the exception amended to read, "shortages in area".

B. COMMITMENT: Within 20 days after the Title Company receives a copy of this contract, Seller shall furnish to Buyer a commitment for title insurance (Commitment) and, at Buyer's expense, legible copies of restrictive covenants and documents evidencing exceptions in the Commitment (Exception Documents) other than the standard printed exceptions. Seller authorizes the Title Company to deliver the Commitment and Exception Documents to Buyer at Buyer's address shown in Paragraph 21. If the Commitment and Exception Documents are not delivered to Buyer within the specified time, the time for delivery will be automatically extended up to 15 days or the Closing Date, whichever is earlier.

C. SURVEY: The survey must be made by a registered professional land surveyor acceptable to the Title Company and any lender. (Check one box only)

❑ (1) Within ________ days after the effective date of this contract, Seller shall furnish to Buyer and Title Company Seller's existing survey of the Property and a Residential Real Property Affidavit promulgated by the Texas Department of Insurance (Affidavit). If the existing survey or Affidavit is not acceptable to Title Company or Buyer's lender, Buyer shall obtain a new survey at ❑ Seller's ❑ Buyer's expense no later than 3 days prior to Closing Date. If Seller fails to furnish the existing survey or Affidavit within the time prescribed, Buyer shall obtain a new survey at Seller's expense no later than 3 days prior to Closing Date.

❑ (2) Within ______ days after the effective date of this contract, Buyer shall obtain a new survey at Buyer's expense. Buyer is deemed to receive the survey on the date of actual receipt or the date specified in this paragraph, whichever is earlier.

❑ (3) Within ______ days after the effective date of this contract, Seller, at Seller's expense shall furnish a new survey to Buyer.

D. OBJECTIONS: Buyer may object in writing to defects, exceptions, or encumbrances to title: disclosed on the survey other than items 6A(1) through (7) above; disclosed in the Commitment other than items 6A(1) through (8) above; or which prohibit the following use or activity: ____.

Buyer must object not later than (i) the Closing Date or (ii) ____________ days after Buyer receives the Commitment, Exception Documents, and the survey, whichever is earlier. Buyer's failure to object within the time allowed will constitute a waiver of Buyer's right to object; except that the requirements in Schedule C of the Commitment are not waived. Provided Seller is not obligated to incur any expense, Seller shall cure the timely objections of Buyer or any third party lender within 15 days after Seller receives the objections and the Closing Date will be extended as necessary. If objections are not cured within such 15 day period, this contract will terminate and the earnest money will be refunded to Buyer unless Buyer waives the objections.

E. TITLE NOTICES:
(1) ABSTRACT OR TITLE POLICY: Broker advises Buyer to have an abstract of title covering the Property examined by an attorney of Buyer's selection, or Buyer should be furnished with or obtain a Title Policy. If a Title Policy is furnished, the Commitment should be promptly reviewed by an attorney of Buyer's choice due to the time limitations on Buyer's right to object.
(2) MANDATORY OWNERS' ASSOCIATION MEMBERSHIP: The Property ❑ is ❑ is not subject to mandatory membership in an owners' association. If the Property is subject to mandatory membership in an owners' association, Seller notifies Buyer under §5.012, Texas Property Code, that, as a purchaser of property in the residential community in which the Property is located, you are obligated to be a member of the owners' association. Restrictive covenants governing the use and occupancy of the Property and a dedicatory instrument governing the establishment, maintenance, and operation of this residential community have been or will be recorded in the Real Property Records of the county in which the Property is located. Copies of the restrictive covenants and dedicatory instrument may be obtained from the county clerk. You are obligated to pay

Defined Terms:

6B. Commitment

Exception Documents

6.C affidavit

Promises:

Buyer	Seller
6.C.1. shall obtain new survey	6B. shall furnish commitment
	6.C.1. survey and affidavit
	6.C.3. shall furnish new survey to buyer if no previous survey
	6.D. shall cure timely objections

Notices:

E.1. abstract or title policy

2. mandatory owners' association membership

C. (check one box only)

6.A. (including existing building + zoning ordinances)

FIGURE 3.1 (CONTINUED)

Form 20-7

Contract Concerning ____ Page 3 of 8 02-13-06
(Address of Property)

assessments to the owners' association. The amount of the assessments is subject to change. Your failure to pay the assessments could result in a lien on and the foreclosure of the Property. If Buyer is concerned about these matters, the TREC promulgated Addendum for Property Subject to Mandatory Membership in an Owner's Association should be used.

(3) STATUTORY TAX DISTRICTS: If the Property is situated in a utility or other statutorily created district providing water, sewer, drainage, or flood control facilities and services, Chapter 49, Texas Water Code, requires Seller to deliver and Buyer to sign the statutory notice relating to the tax rate, bonded indebtedness, or standby fee of the district prior to final execution of this contract.

(4) TIDE WATERS: If the Property abuts the tidally influenced waters of the state, §33.135, Texas Natural Resources Code, requires a notice regarding coastal area property to be included in the contract. An addendum containing the notice promulgated by TREC or required by the parties must be used.

(5) ANNEXATION: If the Property is located outside the limits of a municipality, Seller notifies Buyer under §5.011, Texas Property Code, that the Property may now or later be included in the extraterritorial jurisdiction of a municipality and may now or later be subject to annexation by the municipality. Each municipality maintains a map that depicts its boundaries and extraterritorial jurisdiction. To determine if the Property is located within a municipality's extraterritorial jurisdiction or is likely to be located within a municipality's extraterritorial jurisdiction, contact all municipalities located in the general proximity of the Property for further information.

(6) PROPERTY LOCATED IN A CERTIFICATED SERVICE AREA OF A UTILITY SERVICE PROVIDER: Notice required by §13.257, Water Code: The real property, described in Paragraph 2, that you are about to purchase may be located in a certificated water or sewer service area, which is authorized by law to provide water or sewer service to the properties in the certificated area. If your property is located in a certificated area there may be special costs or charges that you will be required to pay before you can receive water or sewer service. There may be a period required to construct lines or other facilities necessary to provide water or sewer service to your property. You are advised to determine if the property is in a certificated area and contact the utility service provider to determine the cost that you will be required to pay and the period, if any, that is required to provide water or sewer service to your property. The undersigned Buyer hereby acknowledges receipt of the foregoing notice at or before the execution of a binding contract for the purchase of the real property described in Paragraph 2 or at closing of purchase of the real property.

(7) PUBLIC IMPROVEMENT DISTRICTS: If the Property is in a public improvement district, §5.014, Property Code, requires Seller to notify Buyer as follows: As a purchaser of this parcel of real property you are obligated to pay an assessment to a municipality or county for an improvement project undertaken by a public improvement district under Chapter 372, Local Government Code. The assessment may be due annually or in periodic installments. More information concerning the amount of the assessment and the due dates of that assessment may be obtained from the municipality or county levying the assessment. The amount of the assessments is subject to change. Your failure to pay the assessments could result in a lien on and the foreclosure of your property.

7. PROPERTY CONDITION:

A. ACCESS,INSPECTIONS AND UTILITIES: Seller shall permit Buyer and Buyer's agents access to the Property at reasonable times. Buyer may have the Property inspected by inspectors selected by Buyer and licensed by TREC or otherwise permitted by law to make inspections. Seller at Seller's expense shall turn on existing utilities for inspections.

B. SELLER'S DISCLOSURE NOTICE PURSUANT TO §5.008, TEXAS PROPERTY CODE (Notice): (Check one box only)

❑ (1) Buyer has received the Notice.

❑ (2) Buyer has not received the Notice. Within ______ days after the effective date of this contract, Seller shall deliver the Notice to Buyer. If Buyer does not receive the Notice, Buyer may terminate this contract at any time prior to the closing and the earnest money will be refunded to Buyer. If Seller delivers the Notice, Buyer may terminate this contract for any reason within 7 days after Buyer receives the Notice or prior to the closing, whichever first occurs, and the earnest money will be refunded to Buyer.

❑ (3) The Seller is not required to furnish the notice under the Texas Property Code.

C. SELLER'S DISCLOSURE OF LEAD-BASED PAINT AND LEAD-BASED PAINT HAZARDS is required by Federal law for a residential dwelling constructed prior to 1978.

D. ACCEPTANCE OF PROPERTY CONDITION: Buyer accepts the Property in its present condition; provided Seller, at Seller's expense, shall complete the following specific repairs and treatments: ____
____

E. LENDER REQUIRED REPAIRS AND TREATMENTS: Unless otherwise agreed in writing, neither party is obligated to pay for lender required repairs, which includes treatment for wood

Initialed for identification by Buyer______ ______ and Seller ______ ______ TREC NO. 20-7

Defined Terms:

Promises:

Buyer	Seller

Notices:

Attention! Take special note of the 7 statutory Title notices in paragraph 6E. In the second notice, parties must make a decision. If they check "is," what does eacy party promise?

FIGURE 3.1 (CONTINUED)

Form 20-7

destroying insects. If the parties do not agree to pay for the lender required repairs or treatments, this contract will terminate and the earnest money will be refunded to Buyer. If the cost of lender required repairs and treatments exceeds 5% of the Sales Price, Buyer may terminate this contract and the earnest money will be refunded to Buyer.

F. COMPLETION OF REPAIRS AND TREATMENTS: Unless otherwise agreed in writing, Seller shall complete all agreed repairs and treatments prior to the Closing Date. All required permits must be obtained, and repairs and treatments must be performed by persons who are licensed or otherwise authorized by law to provide such repairs or treatments. At Buyer's election, any transferable warranties received by Seller with respect to the repairs and treatments will be transferred to Buyer at Buyer's expense. If Seller fails to complete any agreed repairs and treatments prior to the Closing Date, Buyer may do so and receive reimbursement from Seller at closing. The Closing Date will be extended up to 15 days, if necessary, to complete repairs and treatments.

G. ENVIRONMENTAL MATTERS: Buyer is advised that the presence of wetlands, toxic substances, including asbestos and wastes or other environmental hazards, or the presence of a threatened or endangered species or its habitat may affect Buyer's intended use of the Property. If Buyer is concerned about these matters, an addendum promulgated by TREC or required by the parties should be used.

H. RESIDENTIAL SERVICE CONTRACTS: Buyer may purchase a residential service contract from a residential service company licensed by TREC. If Buyer purchases a residential service contract, Seller shall reimburse Buyer at closing for the cost of the residential service contract in an amount not exceeding $_______________. Buyer should review any residential service contract for the scope of coverage, exclusions and limitations. **The purchase of a residential service contract is optional. Similar coverage may be purchased from various companies authorized to do business in Texas.**

8. **BROKERS' FEES:** All obligations of the parties for payment of brokers' fees are contained in separate written agreements.

9. **CLOSING:**

A. The closing of the sale will be on or before ______________________, 20____, or within 7 days after objections made under Paragraph 6D have been cured or waived, whichever date is later (Closing Date). If either party fails to close the sale by the Closing Date, the non-defaulting party may exercise the remedies contained in Paragraph 15.

B. At closing:

(1) Seller shall execute and deliver a general warranty deed conveying title to the Property to Buyer and showing no additional exceptions to those permitted in Paragraph 6 and furnish tax statements or certificates showing no delinquent taxes on the Property.

(2) Buyer shall pay the Sales Price in good funds acceptable to the escrow agent.

(3) Seller and Buyer shall execute and deliver any notices, statements, certificates, affidavits, releases, loan documents and other documents required of them by this contract, the Commitment or law necessary for the closing of the sale and the issuance of the Title Policy.

C. Unless expressly prohibited by written agreement, Seller may continue to show the Property and receive, negotiate and accept back up offers.

D. All covenants, representations and warranties in this contract survive closing.

10. **POSSESSION:** Seller shall deliver to Buyer possession of the Property in its present or required condition, ordinary wear and tear excepted: ❑ upon closing and funding ❑ according to a temporary residential lease form promulgated by TREC or other written lease required by the parties. Any possession by Buyer prior to closing or by Seller after closing which is not authorized by a written lease will establish a tenancy at sufferance relationship between the parties. **Consult your insurance agent prior to change of ownership and possession because insurance coverage may be limited or terminated. The absence of a written lease or appropriate insurance coverage may expose the parties to economic loss.**

11. **SPECIAL PROVISIONS:** (Insert only factual statements and business details applicable to the sale. TREC rules prohibit licensees from adding factual statements or business details for which a contract addendum, lease or other form has been promulgated by TREC for mandatory use.)

Defined Terms:

9. A. Closing Date

Promises:

Buyer

9. B. 2. shall pay Sales Price in good funds acceptable to the escrow agent

B. 3. shall execute + deliver any notices, loan docs, other docs, commitment/law necessary, issuance of title policy

Seller

7. F. shall complete agreed repairs + treatments prior closing date

H. shall reimburse buyer @ closing for cost of residential service contract

9. B. 1. shall execute + deliver general warranty deed

B. 3. shall execute + deliver any notices, loan docs, + other docs commitment & issuance of title policy

C. shall deliver to buyer possession of property in its present or required condition ordinary wear + tear excepted

Notices:

11. (insert only factual statements ...

FIGURE 3.1 (CONTINUED)

Form 20-7

12. SETTLEMENT AND OTHER EXPENSES:

A. The following expenses must be paid at or prior to closing:

(1) Expenses payable by Seller (Seller's Expenses):

(a) Releases of existing liens, including prepayment penalties and recording fees; release of Seller's loan liability; tax statements or certificates; preparation of deed; one-half of escrow fee; and other expenses payable by Seller under this contract.

(b) Seller shall also pay an amount not to exceed $ ____________ to be applied in the following order: Buyer's Expenses which Buyer is prohibited from paying by FHA, VA, Texas Veterans Housing Assistance Program or other governmental loan programs, and then to other Buyer's Expenses as allowed by the lender.

(2) Expenses payable by Buyer (Buyer's Expenses):

(a) Loan origination, discount, buy-down, and commitment fees (Loan Fees).

(b) Appraisal fees; loan application fees; credit reports; preparation of loan documents; interest on the notes from date of disbursement to one month prior to dates of first monthly payments; recording fees; copies of easements and restrictions; mortgagee title policy with endorsements required by lender; loan-related inspection fees; photos; amortization schedules; one-half of escrow fee; all prepaid items, including required premiums for flood and hazard insurance, reserve deposits for insurance, ad valorem taxes and special governmental assessments; final compliance inspection; courier fee; repair inspection; underwriting fee; wire transfer fee; expenses incident to any loan; and other expenses payable by Buyer under this contract.

B. Buyer shall pay Private Mortgage Insurance Premium (PMI), VA Loan Funding Fee, or FHA Mortgage Insurance Premium (MIP) as required by the lender.

C. If any expense exceeds an amount expressly stated in this contract for such expense to be paid by a party, that party may terminate this contract unless the other party agrees to pay such excess. Buyer may not pay charges and fees expressly prohibited by FHA, VA, Texas Veterans Housing Assistance Program or other governmental loan program regulations.

13. PRORATIONS: Taxes for the current year, interest, maintenance fees, assessments, dues and rents will be prorated through the Closing Date. The tax proration may be calculated taking into consideration any change in exemptions that will affect the current year's taxes. If taxes for the current year vary from the amount prorated at closing, the parties shall adjust the prorations when tax statements for the current year are available. If taxes are not paid at or prior to closing, Buyer shall pay taxes for the current year.

14. CASUALTY LOSS: If any part of the Property is damaged or destroyed by fire or other casualty after the effective date of this contract, Seller shall restore the Property to its previous condition as soon as reasonably possible, but in any event by the Closing Date. If Seller fails to do so due to factors beyond Seller's control, Buyer may (a) terminate this contract and the earnest money will be refunded to Buyer (b) extend the time for performance up to 15 days and the Closing Date will be extended as necessary or (c) accept the Property in its damaged condition with an assignment of insurance proceeds and receive credit from Seller at closing in the amount of the deductible under the insurance policy. Seller's obligations under this paragraph are independent of any other obligations of Seller under this contract.

15. DEFAULT: If Buyer fails to comply with this contract, Buyer will be in default, and Seller may (a) enforce specific performance, seek such other relief as may be provided by law, or both, or (b) terminate this contract and receive the earnest money as liquidated damages, thereby releasing both parties from this contract. If, due to factors beyond Seller's control, Seller fails within the time allowed to make any non-casualty repairs or deliver the Commitment, or survey, if required of Seller, Buyer may (a) extend the time for performance up to 15 days and the Closing Date will be extended as necessary or (b) terminate this contract as the sole remedy and receive the earnest money. If Seller fails to comply with this contract for any other reason, Seller will be in default and Buyer may (a) enforce specific performance, seek such other relief as may be provided by law, or both, or (b) terminate this contract and receive the earnest money, thereby releasing both parties from this contract.

16. MEDIATION: It is the policy of the State of Texas to encourage resolution of disputes through alternative dispute resolution procedures such as mediation. Any dispute between Seller and Buyer related to this contract which is not resolved through informal discussion ☐will ☐will not be submitted to a mutually acceptable mediation service or provider. The parties to the mediation shall bear the mediation costs equally. This paragraph does not preclude a party from seeking equitable relief from a court of competent jurisdiction.

17. ATTORNEY'S FEES: The prevailing party in any legal proceeding related to this contract is entitled to recover reasonable attorney's fees and all costs of such proceeding incurred by the prevailing party.

Defined Terms:	
12. A. 1. Seller's Expenses 2. Buyer's Expenses 2. a. Loan Fees B. PMI MIP	
Promises:	
Buyer	**Seller**
12. B. shall pay Private Mortgage Insurance Premium, VA loan funding fee or FHA Mortgage Insurance Premium required by lender 13. shall adjust prorations when tax statements for current year are available shall pay taxes for the current year	12. A. 1. b. shall also pay an amount not to exceed ___ applied in order: Buyer's Expenses 13. shall adjust prorations when tax statements for current year are available 14. shall restore property to its previous condition as soon as reasonably possible, but in any event by closing date
Notices:	

will will not promises

may - optional

FIGURE 3.1 (CONTINUED)

Form 20-7

Contract Concerning ______________________________ Page 6 of 8 02-13-06
(Address of Property)

18. ESCROW:

A. ESCROW: The escrow agent is not (i) a party to this contract and does not have liability for the performance or nonperformance of any party to this contract, (ii) liable for interest on the earnest money and (iii) liable for the loss of any earnest money caused by the failure of any financial institution in which the earnest money has been deposited unless the financial institution is acting as escrow agent.

B. EXPENSES: At closing, the earnest money must be applied first to any cash down payment, then to Buyer's Expenses and any excess refunded to Buyer. If no closing occurs, escrow agent may require payment of unpaid expenses incurred on behalf of the parties and a written release of liability of escrow agent from all parties.

C. DEMAND: Upon termination of this contract, either party or the escrow agent may send a release of earnest money to each party and the parties shall execute counterparts of the release and deliver same to the escrow agent. If either party fails to execute the release, either party may make a written demand to the escrow agent for the earnest money. If only one party makes written demand for the earnest money, escrow agent shall promptly provide a copy of the demand to the other party. If escrow agent does not receive written objection to the demand from the other party within 15 days, escrow agent may disburse the earnest money to the party making demand reduced by the amount of unpaid expenses incurred on behalf of the party receiving the earnest money and escrow agent may pay the same to the creditors. If escrow agent complies with the provisions of this paragraph, each party hereby releases escrow agent from all adverse claims related to the disbursal of the earnest money.

D. DAMAGES: Any party who wrongfully fails or refuses to sign a release acceptable to the escrow agent within 7 days of receipt of the request will be liable to the other party for liquidated damages of three times the amount of the earnest money.

E. NOTICES: Escrow agent's notices will be effective when sent in compliance with Paragraph 21. Notice of objection to the demand will be deemed effective upon receipt by escrow agent.

19. REPRESENTATIONS: Seller represents that as of the Closing Date (a) there will be no liens, assessments, or security interests against the Property which will not be satisfied out of the sales proceeds unless securing payment of any loans assumed by Buyer and (b) assumed loans will not be in default. If any representation of Seller in this contract is untrue on the Closing Date, Seller will be in default.

20. FEDERAL TAX REQUIREMENTS: If Seller is a "foreign person," as defined by applicable law, or if Seller fails to deliver an affidavit to Buyer that Seller is not a "foreign person," then Buyer shall withhold from the sales proceeds an amount sufficient to comply with applicable tax law and deliver the same to the Internal Revenue Service together with appropriate tax forms. Internal Revenue Service regulations require filing written reports if currency in excess of specified amounts is received in the transaction.

21. NOTICES: All notices from one party to the other must be in writing and are effective when mailed to, hand-delivered at, or transmitted by facsimile or electronic transmission as follows:

To Buyer at: ______________________	**To Seller at:** ______________________
______________________	______________________
______________________	______________________
______________________	______________________
Telephone: ( ) ______________	Telephone: ( ) ______________
Facsimile: ( ) ______________	Facsimile: ( ) ______________
E-mail: ______________	E-mail: ______________

Initialed for identification by Buyer______ ______ and Seller _______ ______ TREC NO. 20-7

Defined Terms:

Promises:

Buyer

20. shall withhold from the sales proceeds an amount sufficient to comply w/applicable tax law & deliver the same to the IRS together w/appropriate tax forms.

18.C. shall execute counterparts of the release & deliver same to the escrow agent.

Seller

18.C. shall execute counterparts of the release & deliver same to the escrow agent.

Notices:

18. E. [illegible] escrow agent's notices will be effective when sent in compliance w/paragraph 21.
Notice of objection to the demand will be deemed effective upon receipt by escrow agent.

21. All notices from one party to the other must be in writing & are effective when mailed to, hand delivered at, or transmitted by facsimile or electronic transmission as follows.

FIGURE 3.1 (CONTINUED)

Form 20-7

Contract Concerning ____ Page 7 of 8 02-13-06
(Address of Property)

22. AGREEMENT OF PARTIES: This contract contains the entire agreement of the parties and cannot be changed except by their written agreement. Addenda which are a part of this contract are (Check all applicable boxes):

- ❑ Third Party Financing Condition Addendum
- ❑ Seller Financing Addendum
- ❑ Loan Assumption Addendum
- ❑ Buyer's Temporary Residential Lease
- ❑ Seller's Temporary Residential Lease
- ❑ Addendum for Sale of Other Property by Buyer
- ❑ Addendum for Seller's Disclosure of Information on Lead-based Paint and Lead-based Paint Hazards as Required by Federal Law
- ❑ Addendum for Property Subject to Mandatory Membership in an Owners' Association
- ❑ Environmental Assessment, Threatened or Endangered Species and Wetlands Addendum
- ❑ Addendum for "Back-Up" Contract
- ❑ Addendum for Coastal Area Property
- ❑ Addendum for Property Located Seaward of the Gulf Intracoastal Waterway
- ❑ Addendum for Release of Liability on Assumption of FHA, VA, or Conventional Loan Restoration of Seller's Entitlement for VA Guaranteed Loan
- ❑ Other (list): ______________________________

23. TERMINATION OPTION: For nominal consideration, the receipt of which is hereby acknowledged by Seller, and Buyer's agreement to pay Seller $______________ (Option Fee) within 2 days after the effective date of this contract, Seller grants Buyer the unrestricted right to terminate this contract by giving notice of termination to Seller within _______ days after the effective date of this contract. If no dollar amount is stated as the Option Fee or if Buyer fails to pay the Option Fee within the time prescribed, this paragraph will not be a part of this contract and Buyer shall not have the unrestricted right to terminate this contract. If Buyer gives notice of termination within the time prescribed, the Option Fee will not be refunded; however, any earnest money will be refunded to Buyer. The Option Fee ❑will ❑will not be credited to the Sales Price at closing. **Time is of the essence for this paragraph and strict compliance with the time for performance is required.**

24. CONSULT AN ATTORNEY: Real estate licensees cannot give legal advice. READ THIS CONTRACT CAREFULLY. If you do not understand the effect of this contract, consult an attorney BEFORE signing.

Buyer's	Seller's
Attorney is: ______________________	Attorney is: ______________________
______________________	______________________
Telephone: ( ) ______________	Telephone: ( ) ______________
Facsimile: ( ) ______________	Facsimile: ( ) ______________
E-mail: ______________________	E-mail: ______________________

EXECUTED the _____day of ____________________, 20____ (EFFECTIVE DATE).
(BROKER: FILL IN THE DATE OF FINAL ACCEPTANCE.)

Buyer	Seller
Buyer	Seller

The form of this contract has been approved by the Texas Real Estate Commission. TREC forms are intended for use only by trained real estate licensees. No representation is made as to the legal validity or adequacy of any provision in any specific transactions. It is not intended for complex transactions. Texas Real Estate Commission, P.O. Box 12188, Austin, TX 78711-2188, 1-800-250-8732 or (512) 459-6544 (http://www.trec.state.tx.us) TREC NO. 20-7. This form replaces TREC NO. 20-6.

TREC NO. 20-7

Defined Terms:

21. Option Fee
24. Effective Date

Promises:

Buyer	Seller
23. shall not have unrestricted right to terminate this contract.	

Notices:

22. Check all applicable boxes
24. [illegible]

FIGURE 3.1 (CONTINUED)

Form 20-7

Contract Concerning ______________________________ Page 8 of 8 02-13-06
(Address of Property)

BROKER INFORMATION AND RATIFICATION OF FEE

Listing Broker has agreed to pay Other Broker ______________ of the total sales price when Listing Broker's fee is received. Escrow Agent is authorized and directed to pay Other Broker from Listing Broker's fee at closing.

Other Broker License No.	Listing Broker License No.
represents ☐ Buyer only as Buyer's agent ☐ Seller as Listing Broker's subagent	represents ☐ Seller and Buyer as an intermediary ☐ Seller only as Seller's agent
Associate Telephone	Listing Associate Telephone
Broker's Address	Listing Associate's Office Address Facsimile
City State Zip	City State Zip
Facsimile	Email Address
Email Address	Selling Associate Telephone
	Selling Associate's Office Address Facsimile
	City State Zip
	Email Address

OPTION FEE RECEIPT

Receipt of $______________ (Option Fee) in the form of ______________ is acknowledged.

Seller or Listing Broker ______________ Date ______________

CONTRACT AND EARNEST MONEY RECEIPT

Receipt of ☐Contract and ☐$______________ Earnest Money in the form of ______________ is acknowledged.

Escrow Agent: ______________ Date: ______________

By: ______________ Email Address

Address ______________ Telephone (____) ______________

City State Zip ______________ Facsimile: (____) ______________

TREC NO. 20-7

Defined Terms:	
Option Fee	
Promises:	
Buyer	Seller
Notices:	

CHAPTER 3 REVIEW QUESTIONS

1. How many notices required by Texas statute are included in Form 20-7?

   a. Six
   b. Three
   c. Seven
   d. Nine

2. Which kind of a deed does the Seller agree to use to transfer title at closing?

   a. Special warranty
   b. General warranty
   c. Quitclaim
   d. Bargain and sale

3. Which would *NOT* be included in the Sales Price as listed in paragraph 3C of Form 20-7?

   a. PMI
   b. Cash down payment
   c. Any note being assumed
   d. A new third party second lien

4. What is included in the contract's definition of the Property?

   a. Land
   b. Improvements
   c. Accessories
   d. All of the above

5. To whom *MUST* the survey be acceptable?

   a. Seller
   b. Buyer
   c. Lender and the title company
   d. Title company only

6. Restrictive covenants are recorded in the county in which the

   a. transaction is closed.
   b. Property is located.
   c. Buyer resides.
   d. greatest amount of ad valorem tax is collected.

7. How many promulgated exclusions are listed in paragraph 6A of Form 20-7?

   a. Eight
   b. Seven
   c. Six
   d. Five

8. What happens when the Seller is unable to cure objections to title or matters of survey raised by the Buyer?

   a. Buyer may collect treble damages from the Seller.
   b. Earnest money is returned to Buyer, and Buyer is released from the contract.
   c. Seller keeps the earnest money, and Buyer is released from the obligations of the contract.
   d. Earnest money is paid to the brokers and the contract ends.

9. For the purposes of inspections and reinspections after repairs are made, Buyer may have access to the Property

   a. during the option period only.
   b. until loan approval has been obtained.
   c. at reasonable times during the term of the executory contract.
   d. within ten days of the effective date of the contract.

10. When the Buyer defaults and the Seller accepts the earnest money as liquidated damages, the

   a. Seller may sue for additional money damages.
   b. money is split between the Seller and his or her broker.
   c. money is split between the Seller, his or her broker, and the selling broker.
   d. the parties are released from the obligations of the contract.

11. The party entitled to recover reasonable attorney fees in a suit resulting from the contract is the

   a. plaintiff.
   b. defendant.
   c. loser.
   d. prevailing party.

12. Which alternative dispute resolution process can the parties agree to use if they are unable to resolve any dispute by informal discussion between themselves?

   a. Binding arbitration
   b. Nonbinding arbitration
   c. Litigation
   d. Mediation

13. Which costs associated with Property repair are *NOT* addressed in paragraph 7?

   a. Lender-required repairs
   b. Specific repairs requested by the Buyer
   c. Repairs arising from a casualty loss
   d. All of the above

14. A party who wrongfully fails or refuses to sign a release acceptable to the escrow agent within seven days of receipt of the request will be liable to the other party for

   a. damages plus $100.
   b. provable damages only.
   c. liquidated damages equal to three times the amount of the earnest money.
   d. an amount determined by the court.

15. Which is *NOT* an acceptable method of delivery for notices from one party of the contract to the other?

 a. Facsimile
 b. Telephone
 c. U.S. mail
 d. Personal delivery

16. At closing, the earnest money will be first applied to

 a. closing costs.
 b. cash down payment.
 c. loan origination costs.
 d. prepaids.

17. Which is clearly defined in the contract as having *NO* responsibilities for performance or nonperformance of any party to the contract?

 a. Escrow agent
 b. Seller
 c. Buyer
 d. Broker

18. For which have the parties specifically *NOT* reached agreement when they sign the TREC-promulgated contract?

 a. Lender-required repairs
 b. Discount points
 c. Recording fees
 d. Fees for preparing legal documents related to the closing

19. A disclosure of known lead-based paint hazards by the Seller to the Buyer is specifically required for houses built prior to which date?

 a. 1975
 b. 1978
 c. 1985
 d. 1990

20. The funds paid by the Buyer at closing must be in a form acceptable to the

 a. lender.
 b. Buyer.
 c. escrow agent.
 d. lender's attorney.

HOMEWORK QUIZ

The following quiz does not have an answer key included with the answer keys in Appendix B. Students who are using this book as the basis for a correspondence course should record and submit their answers to their course provider as instructed by the provider. The student will submit his or her answers for the Homework Quiz at the end of each chapter and for each transaction in Chapter 11.

True or False?

1. *Closing Date* is a defined term that is used several times before it is eventually defined by the parties in paragraph 11.

2. A notice in paragraph 11 advises the salesperson or broker to refrain from attempting to create language that defines legal rights and remedies.

3. Improvements and accessories are included in the definition of the Property as defined in paragraph 2.

4. The Seller promises to provide a mortgagee policy of title insurance.

5. The term *Foreign Person* is defined by federal law.

6. The parties are notified in the contract that they should read the contract carefully and that, if they do not understand the effect of the contract, they should consult an attorney sometime before closing the transaction.

7. The Buyer promises to pay any PMI, MIP, or VA-funding fee as required by the lender.

8. On the Closing Date, the Seller promises to execute a special warranty deed to deliver title to the Buyer.

9. The Seller promises to complete all agreed repairs and treatments prior to the Closing Date.

10. In paragraph 4, Financing, there is a notice that instructs to check all boxes that apply, and then at 4A(2) is an instruction to check only one box.

CHAPTER FOUR

4

The Three Ps (Parties, Property, and Price)

KEY TERMS

accessories
consideration
fixtures
improvements
land
legal description
metes and bounds
recorded plat

In previous chapters, we discussed the requirements for creating a legally enforceable agreement between parties, examined the basic terminology of contracts, and read through one contract to identify *defined terms* and to recognize promises that the parties are making to each other. Now we can make an in-depth examination of the blanks of a TREC-promulgated form. Unfortunately, many license holders fail to take the time to read carefully and understand the content of many of the promulgated forms before attempting to use them to capture the wishes of the party or parties whom they represent. Now we are ready to consider what needs to be entered into the blanks of one form to assist Buyers and Sellers in creating a clear blueprint for closing.

COMMON CONTRACT ERRORS

Through extensive interviews with many escrow officers over a period of many years, the author identified and ranked the most commonly recurring errors made in the completion of the contract and addenda forms. It is interesting to note that the errors and rankings have not changed dramatically since the first time the author did the interviews. Unfortunately, many of the errors can lead to confusion, unhappy clients, and serious legal complications. Real estate practitioners might want to reproduce the following list of the ten most common contract errors and use it as a checklist to keep on track when completing forms for customers and clients:

1. No effective date was entered by the broker before opening title.
2. Signatures or initials were missing on the contract or on one or more of the addenda.
3. Addenda not listed in paragraph 22 of the contract were attached.
4. Legal descriptions were incomplete or incorrect because they did not provide a section number. Agents frequently fail to include the section number with the subdivision name.
5. Documents, such as the TREC Form OP-H, Seller's Disclosure of Property Condition, were attached and listed as addenda that should not have been listed as such.
6. The appropriate TREC temporary leases—when possession is to be granted before or after the funding of the transaction—were not used.
7. Time frames to accomplish all of the tasks needing to be done before closing were poorly coordinated.
8. Agents tried to define legal rights and remedies in paragraph 11, Special Provisions.
9. Agents failed to define where notices can be effectively delivered to the Buyer and to the Seller in paragraph 21.
10. Agents failed to complete the Broker Information and Ratification of Fee on the last page of the contract form.

INFORMATION NEEDED TO COMPLETE CONTRACT FORMS

The various paragraphs of the contract forms might be thought of as the building blocks of a solid transaction. The parties can choose the size and shape of the blocks to be used to build their transaction. Some of the blocks will need to be modified to create the transaction desired by the principals. The knowledgeable agent will help the parties identify the alternatives available to them and then let the parties choose the details of their transaction. The following checklist will enable the agent to guide the parties in the selection of the appropriate contract form for their situation and the needed addenda to clearly define the details of a particular transaction.

To complete paragraph 1

- Name(s) of Seller(s) as on deed or owner's title policy including marital status
- Name(s) of Buyer(s) as Buyers wish to take title; include marital status

To complete paragraph 2

- Legal description including:

  Lot number ____________________; Block number ____________________;

  Section number ____________________;

  Subdivision name ____

  County ____________________; City ______________________________

  Address __________________________________; Zip code __________

- Excluded fixtures and accessories ____________________________________

  ____

To complete paragraph 3

- Cash down payment $____
- Amount of 1st loan $____________________; 2nd loan $____________________
- Sales Price $____

To complete paragraph 4 and/or financing addenda

- Type of financing ________________ Addenda needed ____________________
- Term of loan 1st ____________________; 2nd ________________________
- Interest Rate 1st ____________________; 2nd ________________________
- Assumption of loan balance $____________________________________

To complete paragraph 5

- Earnest money amount $____
- Additional earnest money and date of deposit if any ____________________
- Escrow officer ____
- Address ____

To complete paragraph 6

- Who will pay for title policy? ____________________________________
- What company will issue the title policy? __________________________
- Survey: New or existing ________________ Who will pay ________________

  Who will furnish? ________________

- Number of days to furnish? ______________________________
- Possible reasons for objections ______________________________
- How may days for Buyer to raise title objections? ______________________
- Is property subject to mandatory membership in an HOA? ______________

To complete paragraph 7

- Has Buyer received Seller's disclosure notice? ______________________
- If not, how many days for Seller to furnish? ______________________
- Was house built prior to 1978? ______________________________
- Do you need to use the Lead Addendum? ______________________
- Are there specific repairs required by the Buyer? ______________________

  ____

  ____

- How much does the Buyer want the seller to contribute to the price of a residential service contract? $______________________________

To complete paragraphs 9 and 10

- By what date will closing hopefully take place? ______________________
- When will possession occur? ______________________________
- If possession is before or after closing, define the terms of the temporary tenancy on the appropriate TREC temporary lease. ______________________

  ____

  ____

To complete paragraph 11

- Are there any business details not addressed in other parts of the contract?

  ____

  ____

  ____

To complete paragraph 12

- How much will Seller contribute toward Buyer's Expenses? $________________

To complete paragraph 16

- Do the parties agree to submit disputes to mediation? ________________

To complete paragraph 21

	Buyer	Seller
■ Address:	________________	________________
■ Phone numbers:	________________	________________
■ Fax number:	________________	________________
■ E-mail address:	________________	________________

To complete paragraph 22

- What addenda will need to be added to the agreement?

  ____

  ____

  ____

  ____

  ____

To complete paragraph 23

- How much is the option fee? ________________
- How many days is the option period being purchased? ________________
- Will the option fee be credited to the Sales Price at closing? ________________

To complete paragraph 24

	Buyer's Attorney	Seller's Attorney
■ Name:	________________	________________
■ Phone numbers:	________________	________________
■ Fax number:	________________	________________
■ E-mail address:	________________	________________

In Chapter 3, we began to develop our mastery of the content of the contract. In this chapter, we developed a detailed checklist of the 24 paragraphs of the most commonly used of the TREC-promulgated contract forms, TREC 20-7, One to Four Family Residential Contract (Resale). Now we will focus on important details of each paragraph and make suggestions for the proper completion of the blanks on the form. We will also introduce various addenda that may be needed to add business details or create contingencies that may be desired by the principals. Remember when using this form and other forms that while many transactions will require the use of multiple addenda, a significant number will not require the use of addenda. Many license holders wrongly believe that every transaction requires the use of addenda. When something is required to be a part of a contract, it is placed in the text of the contract by the Broker-Lawyer Committee.

The remainder of this chapter is devoted to the three paragraphs, usually the first three, that will be found in every real estate purchase agreement:

1. Identification of the Parties
2. Identification of the Property
3. Establishment of the Price

Before we look at the three Ps, take just a moment to examine the beginning of the form, its title, and statement of intended use. (See Figure 4.1.) The forms may also carry a notice of purposes for which the form was not designed. Heed these notices and warnings.

FIGURE 4.1

TREC 20-7 Heading

02-13-06

EQUAL HOUSING OPPORTUNITY

PROMULGATED BY THE TEXAS REAL ESTATE COMMISSION (TREC)

ONE TO FOUR FAMILY RESIDENTIAL CONTRACT (RESALE)

NOTICE: Not For Use For Condominium Transactions

Note that the intended use of TREC Form 20-7 is identified in its title and in the notice below it. Also note the following prohibitions:

- Resale—not for use with new construction
- One to Four Family Residential—not for larger residential or commercial
- Notice—not for use with condominiums

In the upper right-hand corner of each form is the date of the real estate commission meeting at which the form was promulgated. Agents can make certain that they are using the correct forms by verifying current forms at the TREC Web site: *www.trec.state.tx.us*. If agents have forms with an earlier date than those found on the list at the

TREC Web site, they should not use those forms. Once an earlier version of a form has been retired, it is illegal for license holders to use it in structuring a transaction. To do so would constitute the illegal practice of law as defined by the TRELA.

The executory contract provides the escrow agent and all affected parties with definitive instructions for closing the real estate transaction. The executory contract serves as a blueprint for the closing. It should address every detail relating to what must be done to close the sale of the property and have a fully executed contract. There should be no reason for anyone to contact the license holder to interpret the phraseology of any filled-in blanks, or of any special provisions, if the license holder has filled out the blanks in the contract form competently.

When proceeding through the various provisions of the contract, remember that reasonable, realistic time frames need to be defined. The transaction cannot close in 15 days if it is going to take 25 days to get loan approval and 20 days to get the results of an environmental inspection. It makes no sense to structure an executory contract that is contingent upon obtaining a 97 percent loan-to-value (LTV) loan at 5 percent annual interest for 40 years if only 90 percent LTV loans at 6.5 percent annual interest for 30 years are currently available from lenders.

PARTIES

FIGURE 4.2

TREC 20-7 paragraph 1

1. PARTIES: ________________________________ (Seller) agrees to sell and convey to ________________________________ (Buyer) and Buyer agrees to buy from Seller the Property described below.

The Seller(s) and Buyer(s) must be identified in the first paragraph. (See Figure 4.2.) Because Texas is a community property state, it is important to include marital status. The following are acceptable ways to identify the marital status of parties.

Unmarried	NAME, **an unmarried person** **NOTE:** Widows and widowers are unmarried persons
Married	(When spouse is not joining in the conveyance) NAME, **as separate property**
Married	(Community property) NAME, **and spouse** NAME Husband's NAME **and wife** wife's NAME Wife's NAME **and husband** husband's NAME

Unmarried Persons Buying Together	NAME and NAME, **as tenants in common** **NOTE:** When parties wish to create rights of survivorship or fractional interests are involved, the parties should be advised to seek the advice of a competent real estate attorney *before* proceeding to prepare an offer to purchase.
Executor or Administrator of an Estate	Executor's or administrator's NAME, **executor (administrator) of the estate of (decedent's name), deceased**
General Partnership	Business NAME, **a Texas partnership** or Business NAME, **a Texas partnership composed of name, name, and name**
Limited Partnership	Business NAME, **a Texas limited partnership, name, as general partner acting for and on behalf of the partnership**
Corporation	Company NAME, **a Texas* corporation** *or the name of the state in which the corporation is chartered *Note:* A corporate resolution, issued by the board of directors, grants the authority to and identifies the officers who can sign on behalf of the corporation. A license holder should request a copy of the corporate resolution prior to the execution of any written agreements. It is to be retained in the transaction file.
Texas Limited Liability Company	Company NAME, **a Texas limited liability company** or Company NAME, **LLC**
Nonprofit	NAME, NAME, and NAME, **trustees for and on behalf of (corporate name)**

Make certain that all names are complete and spelled correctly. To verify Sellers' names, check the owner's title policy issued when title was taken or examine the name or names appearing on the deed used to convey title and recorded at the county courthouse of the county in which the property is located. Remember that the tax records often contain significant errors and should not be relied upon as the final authority in these matters.

It is in paragraph 1 that the first **consideration** to bind the contract is expressed. The promise to sell by the Seller and the promise to buy by the Buyer is adequate consideration to bind the contract.

PROPERTY

The Statute of Frauds requires that agreements affecting title to real property have a **legal description,** a description of such certainty and accuracy that one can go to the property and identify it. Most urban residential properties are described by reference to a **recorded plat** at the courthouse of the county where the property is located.

The TREC Form 20-7 provides a blank for the lot number, the block number, the name of the subdivision, the name of the city, and the informal street or post office address. (See Figure 4.3.) When the subdivision has multiple sections, it is important to include the section number either before or after the name of the addition.

EXAMPLE: Lot 3, Block 5, Section 2 of Shady Hollow Addition . . .

When the property is located in a city, include the name of the city. If the property is located in an unincorporated area, put *Unincorporated* or *None* in the blank for city. Be sure to provide the zip code as called for in the contract form.

FIGURE 4.3

TREC 20-7, Paragraph 2

2. PROPERTY:

A. LAND: Lot ______ Block_________, ______________________________________Addition, City of ________________________________, County of ___________________, Texas, known as ____ (address/zip code), or as described on attached exhibit.

B. IMPROVEMENTS: The house, garage and all other fixtures and improvements attached to the above-described real property, including without limitation, the following **permanently installed and built-in items,** if any: all equipment and appliances, valances, screens, shutters, awnings, wall-to-wall carpeting, mirrors, ceiling fans, attic fans, mail boxes, television antennas and satellite dish system and equipment, heating and air-conditioning units, security and fire detection equipment, wiring, plumbing and lighting fixtures, chandeliers, water softener system, kitchen equipment, garage door openers, cleaning equipment, shrubbery, landscaping, outdoor cooking equipment, and all other property owned by Seller and attached to the above described real property.

C. ACCESSORIES: The following described related accessories, if any: window air conditioning units, stove, fireplace screens, curtains and rods, blinds, window shades, draperies and rods, controls for satellite dish system, controls for garage door openers, entry gate controls, door keys, mailbox keys, above ground pool, swimming pool equipment and maintenance accessories, and artificial fireplace logs.

D. EXCLUSIONS: The following improvements and accessories will be retained by Seller and removed prior to delivery of possession:____ ____.

The land, improvements and accessories are collectively referred to as the "Property".

If the property description is by **metes and bounds**—a description referencing directions, degrees, minutes, seconds, point of beginning, and point of termination—put N/A in the blanks for lot and block. You may or may not have a subdivision name. Add the description as an attached exhibit to the contract.

Often town houses are located in a platted subdivision but are described by a metes-and-bounds description. Fill in any blanks that apply, put N/A in those that do not

FIGURE 4.4

Non-Realty Items Addendum to Contract

TEXAS ASSOCIATION OF REALTORS®

NON-REALTY ITEMS ADDENDUM TO CONTRACT

ADDENDUM TO CONTRACT BETWEEN THE UNDERSIGNED PARTIES CONCERNING THE PROPERTY AT

____

(Street Address and City)

A. Seller shall convey to Buyer at closing the following personal property *(specify each item carefully, include description, model numbers, serial numbers, location, and other information)*:

____
____
____
____
____

B. Seller represents and warrants that Seller owns the personal property described in Paragraph A free and clear of all encumbrances. Seller shall convey the personal property:

❑ (1) at no cost to Buyer at closing.

❑ (2) for an additional sum of $______________ as separate consideration for the personal property.

C. Seller does not warrant or guarantee the condition or future performance of the personal property conveyed by this document.

______________________ Buyer	______________________ Seller
______________________ Buyer	______________________ Seller

apply, and be sure to attach the metes-and-bounds descriptions as Exhibit A. If the legal description uses a building letter and unit number, use the TREC Form 30-6, Residential Condominium Contract (Resale).

After describing the **land** in 2A, you move on to 2B and 2C. Part 2B lists the **improvements** or **fixtures** and, in bold print, clarifies that the form references *permanently installed and built-in items*. Part 2C lists the **accessories** such as the curtains, draperies, and appliances that usually remain with the property upon the transfer of ownership. *Do not strike any words in this paragraph*. When any of these items are to be removed by the Seller, carefully list in 2D the items that do not remain. If there are no exclusions, be sure that you enter N/A, or None, in the space provided for the purpose of listing any exclusions in paragraph 2D.

It is important to verify that both Buyers and Sellers carefully read and understand what does and does not stay with the property at closing because this is no place for assumptions and guesswork. A clear understanding of the form, in addition to fostering realistic expectations, creates the atmosphere for happy Buyers and Sellers after closing. The best time to address with the Sellers which accessories are included or excluded in the sale is at the listing appointment.

In paragraph 2, it is not advisable to attempt to deal with personal property that might remain with the property. It is best to keep personal property completely out of the contract. The contract addresses the proposed transfer of real property. Personal property should be handled by a bill of sale as an entirely separate transaction between the parties. However, if the parties insist on putting personal property in the contract, it may be addressed in paragraph 11 or by using the appropriate TAR-1924, Non-Realty Items Addendum to Contract. (See Figure 4.4.) Use the TAR form only if you are a member of the TAR.

PRICE

Paragraph 3 is one of the easiest to complete correctly. (See Figure 4.5.) Enter the Sales Price on line 3C. Add all loans that will be used to finance the purchase and enter the amount on line 3B. Most of the time you will deal with one loan only. Sometimes you may have a Buyer assuming an existing loan and asking a Seller to carry back a second.

EXAMPLE: The Buyer is assuming a first lien note with an outstanding balance of $283,400, taking a home improvement loan with a balance of $21,680, and asking the Seller to carry back a note for $80,000. To get the correct number to enter in 3B, add $283,400 + $21,680 + $80,000 for a total of $385,080. To get the correct number to put in 3A, simply subtract 3B from 3C.

If the Sales Price in the above example is $560,000, line 3A would be $174,920 ($560,000 - $385,080). Make certain that the Buyer realizes that 3A represents only the cash portion of the Sales Price to be paid at closing by the Buyer. Prepaids, reserve impounds, and closing costs are not included in this number.

FIGURE 4.5

TREC 20-7, Paragraph 3

3. SALES PRICE:

A. Cash portion of Sales Price payable by Buyer at closing................. $__________

B. Sum of all financing described below (excluding any loan funding fee or mortgage insurance premium)... $__________

C. Sales Price (Sum of A and B)... $__________

For an all-cash transaction, enter the same number on line 3A and 3C, and then enter N/A, None, or -0- on line 3B.

When financing is involved and the transaction is subject-to or contingent upon receiving financing approval, one of the following two addenda will be used to establish these details:

1. TREC 40-3, Third Party Financing Condition Addendum
2. TREC 41-1, Loan Assumption Addendum

If the Seller is financing the purchase and receiving part of the consideration in the form of a promissory note secured by a deed of trust, the TREC Form 26-5, Seller Financing Addendum, will be used to define the details of the financing transaction.

Financing details will be discussed in Chapter 5.

CHAPTER 4 REVIEW QUESTIONS

1. An unmarried female might appropriately be identified by all of the following *EXCEPT*

   a. femme sole.
   b. an unmarried person.
   c. as separate property.
   d. a single woman.

2. The TREC Form 20-7, One to Four Family Residential Contract (Resale), can be used for all but which one of the following properties?

   a. Patio home
   b. Town home identified as Unit 16, Building H of Phase One, Easy Living Estates
   c. Town home identified as Lot 6, Block 2 of Section 1 of Carefree Living Estates
   d. Duplex with two garage apartments

3. A TREC contract form has the date on which it was promulgated printed on the form.

   a. True
   b. False

4. When property owned by a married couple is being sold, what is the *BEST* way to identify the Sellers?

   a. Mr. and Mrs. Thomas Bud Smith
   b. Thomas Bud Smith and spouse Mary Ann Smith
   c. Thomas Bud Smith and his wife
   d. Thomas Bud Smith et vir Mary Ann Smith

5. The loan amount listed as the *sum of all financing listed below* (paragraph 3B) includes PMI, MIP, or a VA-funding fee.

   a. True
   b. False

HOMEWORK QUIZ

The following quiz does not have an answer key included with the answer keys in Appendix B. Students who are using this book as the basis for a correspondence course should record and submit their answers to their course provider as instructed by the provider. The student will submit his or her answers for the Homework Quiz at the end of each chapter and for each transaction in Chapter 11.

True or False?

1. An unmarried person may be referenced by "as separate property" in the contract.

2. A correct way to identify a married couple purchasing a home with community funds is "John Paul Happy and spouse Molly Bea Happy."

3. Only the amount of a loan that will hold first lien position should be entered in paragraph 3B.

4. In addition to listing excluded fixtures in paragraph 2D, the salesperson or broker should be sure to strike any excluded items from paragraphs 2B and 2C and have all parties initial next to the strikeouts.

5. It is best to handle the transfer of personal property outside of the purchase agreement for a parcel of real estate.

CHAPTER FIVE

Buying with Borrowed Funds

KEY TERMS

- assumption
- escrow accounts
- FHA-insured loans
- financing approval
- loan approval
- loan fees
- mortgage insurance premium (MIP)
- private mortgage insurance (PMI)
- promissory note
- seller financing
- VA-funding fee
- VA-guaranteed loans

One of the significant roadblocks to the consummation of many real estate transactions is the buyers' inability to obtain a loan. Sellers are well advised to require evidence of the buyers' ability to obtain financing before entering into purchase agreements with them. Competent buyer agents should encourage their clients to become preapproved by a lender before proceeding with searching for the ideal property and attempting to convince the owner to enter into a purchase agreement subject to the buyers' ability to obtain financing approval.

Paragraph 4 of the TREC-promulgated Form 20-7, One to Four Family Residential Contract (Resale), describes the manner in which the transaction will be financed. (See Figure 5.1.) You will check no boxes nor fill in any blanks if line 3B is zero. (Refer to page 62.)

In paragraph 4, three choices are available and can be used alone or in combination with each other. You will notice that the form here requires all applicable boxes to be checked; in other places, the form requires only one box to be checked. Each of the three choices requires the use of an addendum to define the conditions, as explained in the following:

A. Third party financing requires the use of the TREC Form 40-3, Third Party Financing Condition, unless 4A2 is selected. The Third Party Financing Condition Addendum will be used when the borrower seeks conventional financing,

Federal Housing Administration (FHA) insured financing, or Department of Veterans Affairs (VA) guaranteed financing.

B. Assumption of existing financing requires the use of the TREC Form 41-1, Loan Assumption Addendum. If, as a condition of permitting assumption of existing financing, the Seller wants to make the assumption subject to the Seller being released from future liability for the loan, the parties will need to use the TREC Form 12-2, Addendum for Release of Liability on Assumed Loan and/or Restoration of Seller's VA Entitlement.

C. Seller financing requires the use of the TREC Form 26-5, Seller Financing Addendum.

FIGURE 5.1

TREC 20-7, Paragraph 4

4. FINANCING: The portion of Sales Price not payable in cash will be paid as follows: (Check applicable boxes below)

❑ A. THIRD PARTY FINANCING: One or more third party mortgage loans in the total amount of $_______________ (excluding any loan funding fee or mortgage insurance premium).

(1) Property Approval: If the Property does not satisfy the lenders' underwriting requirements for the loan(s), this contract will terminate and the earnest money will be refunded to Buyer.

(2) Financing Approval: (Check one box only)

❑ (a) This contract is subject to Buyer being approved for the financing described in the attached Third Party Financing Condition Addendum.

❑ (b) This contract is not subject to Buyer being approved for financing and does not involve FHA or VA financing.

❑ B. ASSUMPTION: The assumption of the unpaid principal balance of one or more promissory notes described in the attached TREC Loan Assumption Addendum.

❑ C. SELLER FINANCING: A promissory note from Buyer to Seller of $_________________, secured by vendor's and deed of trust liens, and containing the terms and conditions described in the attached TREC Seller Financing Addendum. If an owner policy of title insurance is furnished, Buyer shall furnish Seller with a mortgagee policy of title insurance.

The real estate professional needs to carefully read paragraph 4 and each of the addenda and encourage the Buyer and Seller to carefully read and understand the portions that are applicable to their transaction. As you read, be sure to make note of the details itemized and discussed in the following paragraphs.

Paragraph 4A provides for one or more third party loans and provides a blank for entering the total of multiple third party loans. Point out to the Buyer that the loan amount entered does not include a **mortgage insurance premium (MIP)**, **private mortgage insurance (PMI),** or a **VA-funding fee.** Loans with low down payments require borrowers to provide indemnification from financial loss for the top portion of the loan in the event of borrower default. **FHA-insured loans** protect the lender through MIP paid for by the borrower. **VA-guaranteed loans,** backed by the Department of Veterans Affairs, are guaranteed by the government with a portion of the cost being charged to the Buyer in the form of a fee rather than as an insurance premium. Conventional loans that are neither insured nor guaranteed by an agency of government are done entirely in the private sector. Buyers using conventional financing purchase insurance typically referred to as *private mortgage insurance (PMI)*. In all three instances, the cost of the lender protection is most frequently rolled into the loan amount rather than being paid in cash at closing. In the **promissory note,** the amount of the loan will be an amount greater that the amount shown in paragraph 3B or 4A.

The next two check boxes in paragraph 4A are very important; checking the wrong box could have far-reaching financial implications for both you and the parties.

Box one (1) establishes that the parties agree that the contract *is* subject to the Buyer's being approved for the financing described in the attached addendum. Box two (2) states that the contract *is not* subject to the Buyer's being approved. *Do not* attach the TREC Form 40-3 when box 2 is selected. Neither of these boxes establishes that the Property has been approved by the lender and is acceptable collateral to approve the loan.

Please note that **financing approval** and **loan approval** are two different things. *Financing approval* comes when the borrower is acceptable to and approved by the lender; when the Buyer's assets, income, and credit history are adequate to meet the lender's underwriting requirements. *Loan approval* comes when both the borrower and the Property being offered as collateral meet the lender's underwriting guidelines.

Never check box 2 when FHA or VA financing is being sought.

THIRD PARTY FINANCING

The TREC Form 40-3, Third Party Financing Condition Addendum, is the most used of the promulgated addenda. Its use creates a very significant contingency in the contract. It places a responsibility on the Buyer to apply promptly for the described financing, to furnish information and documents required by the lender, and to notify the Seller in a timely manner if the Buyer is unable to obtain the described loan. Time is of the essence for the purposes of performance and the giving of notice in this addendum. Failure to give the Seller notice that the Buyer is unable to obtain the loan removes the contingency and obligates the Buyer to complete the transaction without the loan.

Failure to close becomes an act of default under the terms of the contract. Upon said default, the Seller may invoke the remedies established in paragraph 15 of the contract. The parties must be encouraged to carefully read and understand the first paragraph in the text of the addendum; give particular attention to the bold print.

When the Buyer is unable to obtain financing approval, most Sellers will undoubtedly require documentation from the lender that the Buyer did indeed exercise good faith in the attempt to obtain the desired financing. Buyer agents must make certain that the Buyer client gives the required notice in a timely manner, as time is of the essence. Failure to do so will create great problems for most Buyers.

A discussion of the types of third party financing follows the addendum and notice forms. (See Figure 5.2 and Figure 5.3.)

FIGURE 5.2

TREC 40-3

12-10-07

EQUAL HOUSING OPPORTUNITY

PROMULGATED BY THE TEXAS REAL ESTATE COMMISSION (TREC)

THIRD PARTY FINANCING CONDITION ADDENDUM

TO CONTRACT CONCERNING THE PROPERTY AT

____

(Street Address and City)

Buyer shall apply promptly for all financing described below and make every reasonable effort to obtain approval for the financing (Financing Approval). Buyer shall furnish all information and documents required by lender for Financing Approval. Financing Approval will be deemed to have been obtained when (1) the terms of the loan(s) described below are available and (2) lender determines that Buyer has satisfied all of lender's financial requirements (those items relating to Buyer's assets, income and credit history). If Buyer cannot obtain Financing Approval, Buyer may give written notice to Seller within ____ days after the effective date of this contract and this contract will terminate and the earnest money will be refunded to Buyer. **If Buyer does not give such notice within the time required, this contract will no longer be subject to Financing Approval. Time is of the essence for this paragraph and strict compliance with the time for performance is required.**

NOTE: Financing Approval does not include approval of lender's underwriting requirements for the Property, as specified in Paragraph 4.A.(1) of the contract.

Each note must be secured by vendor's and deed of trust liens.

CHECK APPLICABLE BOXES:

❑ A. CONVENTIONAL FINANCING:

❑ (1) A first mortgage loan in the principal amount of $ ____________________ (excluding any financed PMI premium), due in full in __________ year(s), with interest not to exceed _______% per annum for the first ________year(s) of the loan with Loan Fees (loan origination, discount, buy-down, and commitment fees) not to exceed ________% of the loan.

❑ (2) A second mortgage loan in the principal amount of $____________________(excluding any financed PMI premium), due in full in __________year(s), with interest not to exceed ______% per annum for the first _____________year(s) of the loan with Loan Fees (loan origination, discount, buy-down, and commitment fees) not to exceed ________% of the loan.

❑ B. TEXAS VETERANS LOAN: A loan(s) from the Texas Veterans Land Board of $_____________ for a period in the total amount of _____years at the interest rate established by the Texas Veterans Land Board.

❑ C. FHA INSURED FINANCING: A Section _________________ FHA insured loan of not less than $___________________ (excluding any financed MIP), amortizable monthly for not less than ________years, with interest not to exceed ________% per annum for the first _______year(s) of the loan with Loan Fees (loan origination, discount, buy-down, and commitment fees) not to exceed __________ % of the loan. As required by HUD-FHA, if FHA valuation is unknown, *"It is expressly agreed that, notwithstanding any other provision of this contract, the purchaser (Buyer) shall not be obligated to complete the purchase of the Property described herein or to incur any penalty by forfeiture of earnest money deposits or otherwise unless the purchaser (Buyer) has been given in accordance with HUD/FHA or VA requirements a written statement issued by the Federal Housing Commissioner, Department of Veterans Affairs, or a Direct Endorsement Lender setting forth the appraised value of the Property of not less than $___________________. The purchaser (Buyer) shall have the privilege and option of proceeding with consummation of the contract without regard to the amount of the*

FIGURE 5.2 (CONTINUED)

TREC 40-3

Third Party Financing Condition Addendum Concerning Page 2 of 2 12-10-07

____

(Address of Property)

appraised valuation. The appraised valuation is arrived at to determine the maximum mortgage the Department of Housing and Urban Development will insure. HUD does not warrant the value or the condition of the Property. The purchaser (Buyer) should satisfy himself/herself that the price and the condition of the Property are acceptable."

NOTE: HUD 92564-CN "For Your Protection: Get a Home Inspection" must be attached to this Addendum.

❑ D. VA GUARANTEED FINANCING: A VA guaranteed loan of not less than $_______________ (excluding any financed Funding Fee), amortizable monthly for not less than_______years, with interest not to exceed________% per annum for the first _______year(s) of the loan with Loan Fees (loan origination, discount, buy-down, and commitment fees) not to exceed ________% of the loan.

VA NOTICE TO BUYER: "*It is expressly agreed that, notwithstanding any other provisions of this contract, the Buyer shall not incur any penalty by forfeiture of earnest money or otherwise or be obligated to complete the purchase of the Property described herein, if the contract purchase price or cost exceeds the reasonable value of the Property established by the Department of Veterans Affairs. The Buyer shall, however, have the privilege and option of proceeding with the consummation of this contract without regard to the amount of the reasonable value established by the Department of Veterans Affairs."*

If Buyer elects to complete the purchase at an amount in excess of the reasonable value established by VA, Buyer shall pay such excess amount in cash from a source which Buyer agrees to disclose to the VA and which Buyer represents will not be from borrowed funds except as approved by VA. If VA reasonable value of the Property is less than the Sales Price, Seller may reduce the Sales Price to an amount equal to the VA reasonable value and the sale will be closed at the lower Sales Price with proportionate adjustments to the down payment and the loan amount.

Buyer hereby authorizes any lender to furnish to the Seller or Buyer or their representatives information relating only to the status of Financing Approval of Buyer.

______________________	______________________
Buyer	Seller
______________________	______________________
Buyer	Seller

FIGURE 5.3

TREC 42-0

02-09-2004

EQUAL HOUSING OPPORTUNITY

PROMULGATED BY THE TEXAS REAL ESTATE COMMISSION (TREC)

NOTICE PURSUANT TO THIRD PARTY FINANCING CONDITION ADDENDUM

To: Seller(s)

In accordance with the Third Party Financing Condition Addendum attached to the Contract between ______________________ as Seller and ______________________ as Buyer dated ______________________, _____ for the Property located at ______________________ Buyer notifies Seller that Buyer cannot obtain financing approval.

______________________ Buyer	Date	______________________ Buyer	Date

01A

To complete the blanks in the addendum, you need to know which loan products are available. It makes no sense to structure an agreement that calls for a 10-day approval when it is taking 20 days to obtain approvals. It also makes no sense to cap the interest rate at 6 percent when nothing is available at less than 6.5 percent. Checking box A establishes a contingency of obtaining a conventional loan for a defined term at a maximum interest rate of not less than a certain amount. You must enter specific numbers in the blanks. Using the words *Market Rate* or *To Be Determined*, or its abbreviation, *TDB*, is never acceptable. Always be specific. Avoid vague or nonspecific words and terms.

Often a borrower will obtain two loans to avoid a PMI premium. A very popular approach is to obtain a first lien loan for 80 percent or less of the purchase price and a second lien loan for 10 percent or so.

EXAMPLE: The Buyers are purchasing a new home for $450,000. They want to finance $405,000 after paying $45,000 cash. For the purpose of this example let's say that the Fannie Mae conforming loan limit is $333,700. Note that the conforming loan limit is set each year and may be higher or lower than the amount used in this example in any given year. Check *www.fanniemae.com* or with a loan offer for the current limit. A loan for more than this amount will be a nonconforming loan that will generally be made at a higher interest rate. The Buyer has the following four alternatives to consider:

1. Pay $116,300 cash down payment and finance $333,700 at a favorable rate.
2. Pay $45,000 cash down payment and obtain a first lien at $333,700 at a favorable rate and a second lien for $71,300 at a rate about 2 points higher than the first.
3. Pay $45,000 cash down payment and obtain a first lien of $333,700 and ask the Seller to carry back a second lien for $71,300.
4. An eligible Texas veteran could use the Texas Housing Assistance Program Loan in concert with a first lien loan that conforms to Fannie Mae guidelines.

A challenge is faced when the Buyer wants to pay a large cash down payment and obtain a loan of significantly less than 80 percent. Most Buyers do not want to pay more than the amount the lender's appraiser indicates the Property is worth. If the LTV is 80 percent or greater and an appraisal is for less than the Sales Price listed in line 3B of the contract, the Buyer can back out of the purchase or attempt to renegotiate the Sales Price. This is not the case when dealing with a lower than 80 percent LTV.

One possible solution is for the Buyer to add as a business detail to paragraph 11, Special Provisions, a statement to the effect that the loan in 4B and the Third Party Financing Conditions Addendum is to be for an LTV as established by the lender's appraisal not to exceed _____ percent. To calculate the LTV, simply divide the amount entered on line 3B by the amount entered on 3C of the contract to get the LTV. If the lender's appraisal is less than 3B, the LTV will be higher.

EXAMPLE: 3 A $300,000
B $175,000
C $475,000

$175,000 ÷ $475,000 = 0.37, or 37% LTV

After the lender's appraiser does the appraisal, the indicated value is $456,000.

$175,000 ÷ $456,000 = 0.38, or 38% LTV

The parties may agree to renegotiate the Sales Price or to release the Buyer from the contract. Buyers in this type of situation will do well to consult competent legal counsel to write language that accurately defines their wishes.

License holders, especially Buyer's agents, would do well to become thoroughly familiar with all of the financing options open to their clients. An especially good loan program available to eligible Texas veterans is known as the Texas Veterans Housing Assistance Program Loan. It is box B on the Third Party Financing Addendum. Buyers and their agents can learn more about the program by calling 800-252-VETS or going to *www.TexasVeterans.com*. The interest rate can be as much as 2 percent below the going rate on other available loans. The current maximum loan amount can be verified by calling the above listed number. The program can be used alone or in combination with conventional, FHA-insured, or VA-guaranteed loans.

Frequently, Buyers with limited up-front cash use the FHA insurance program. Remember that FHA does not loan money; it insures loans with high LTV ratios and reduces the risk to the lenders loaning the money.

Early in 1999 the FHA greatly simplified the rules for FHA-insured loan amounts and down payment requirements. The maximum loan amounts are a percentage of Fannie Mae's maximum conforming loan amount in the highest cost areas. For the maximum insured loan for your county, check FHA's Web site, *www.fha.com*.

For current limits on high cost counties, visit the HUD Web site (*www.hud.gov*), which features the most recent numbers available. Most lenders can also quickly provide this information. Cordial relationships with a variety of loan officers, mortgage brokers, and mortgage bankers can provide immediate access to the most current rates and loan underwriting requirements.

Under current regulations, a Buyer obtaining an FHA insured loan must invest at least 3 percent in down payment and/or closing costs. If the Sales Price is $50,000 or less, the maximum LTV is 98.75 percent. The borrower must pay 1.25 percent down and costs equal to a minimum of 1.75 percent. When the Sales Price is more than $50,000, the maximum LTV is 97.75 percent. The borrower must pay 2.25 percent down and costs equal to a minimum of 0.75 percent. Any closing costs in excess of these amounts may be paid by the Seller who is willing to pay them.

For current information, refer to a finance text or check with the Buyer's loan officer.

HUD Form HUD-92564-CN (12/04) must be used when a Buyer is getting an FHA insured loan. (See Figure 5.4.) It is a notice to the FHA Buyer to carefully investigate the physical condition of the home being purchased. It is just one of many consumer protection considerations addressed when one obtains a loan insured by FHA. It offers good advice that should be heeded by any purchaser and would make an excellent addition to the wording in paragraph 7 of the TREC Form 20-7, One to Four Family Residential Contract (Resale), which will be discussed in later in Chapter 7.

The final choice on the Third Party Financing Condition Addendum is for VA-guaranteed financing. Before structuring a contract that calls for a VA loan, the borrower must contact the Department of Veterans Affairs to determine eligibility and the amount of available entitlement. VA guaranteed loans are often used when the eligible veteran has limited cash available. These loans can also be a good choice for a Buyer who is making a large cash down payment. The loans are assumable with VA approval. When assumed, the interest rate does not increase. If interest rates rise significantly in the future, the Seller might have a significant advantage by being able to offer a Buyer the opportunity to assume a loan with a lower interest rate.

ASSUMPTION

The second choice offered in paragraph 4 is for the financing to be the **assumption** of an existing loan or loans. One of the following two addenda (shown in Figure 5.5 and Figure 5.6) may need to be used:

1. TREC 12-2, Addendum for Release of Liability on Assumed Loan and/or Restoration of Seller's VA Entitlement
2. TREC 41-1, Loan Assumption Addendum

Unfortunately, the TREC 41-1, Loan Assumption Addendum, does not address when a Buyer must apply for assumption approval when assuming a conventional, FHA-insured, or VA-guaranteed loan. It would be prudent to address this important business detail in paragraph 11 of the contract. Simply state in paragraph 11 that the Buyer will apply to the lender for assumption approval within a specific number of days after the effective date of the contract.

Before completing the blanks on the TREC Form 41-1, Loan Assumption Addendum, check with the Seller for which documentation the seller will want to review and then make certain that both parties understand the time frames to which they are agreeing in the Credit Documentation and Credit Approval sections.

Be sure to obtain accurate information for the Assumption section and have the parties decide about adjusting the Sales Price or the Buyer's cash payable at closing. Give careful attention to the discussion of liens, securing of assumptions, and transfer of

FIGURE 5.4

HUD-92564-CN

U.S. Department of Housing and Urban Development (HUD)
Federal Housing Administration (FHA)

OMB Approval No: 2502-0538
(exp. 06/30/2006)

For Your Protection: Get a Home Inspection

Name of Buyer (s) ____________________

Property Address ____________________

____

Why a Buyer Needs a Home Inspection

A home inspection gives the buyer more detailed information about the overall condition of the home prior to purchase. In a home inspection, a qualified inspector takes an in-depth, unbiased look at your potential new home to:

- evaluate the physical condition: structure, construction, and mechanical systems;
- identify items that need to be repaired or replaced; and
- estimate the remaining useful life of the major systems, equipment, structure, and finishes.

Appraisals are Different from Home Inspections

An appraisal is different from a home inspection. Appraisals are for lenders; home inspections are for buyers. An appraisal is required to:

- estimate the market value of a house;
- make sure that the house meets FHA minimum property standards/requirements; and
- make sure that the house is marketable.

FHA Does Not Guarantee the Value or Condition of your Potential New Home

If you find problems with your new home after closing, FHA can not give or lend you money for repairs, and FHA can not buy the home back from you.

Radon Gas Testing

The United States Environmental Protection Agency and the Surgeon General of the United States have recommended that all houses should be tested for radon. For more information on radon testing, call the toll-free National Radon Information Line at 1-800-SOS-Radon or 1-800-767-7236. As with a home inspection, if you decide to test for radon, you may do so before signing your contract, or you may do so after signing the contract as long as your contract states the sale of the home depends on your satisfaction with the results of the radon test.

Be an Informed Buyer

It is your responsibility to be an informed buyer. Be sure that what you buy is satisfactory in every respect. You have the right to carefully examine your potential new home with a qualified home inspector. You may arrange to do so before signing your contract, or may do so after signing the contract as long as your contract states that the sale of the home depends on the inspection.

I/we understand the importance of getting an independent home inspection. I/we have considered this before signing a contract with the seller for a home. Furthermore, I/we have carefully read this notice and fully understand that FHA will not perform a home inspection nor guarantee the price or condition of the property.

______ **I/We choose to have a home inspection performed.**

______ **I/We choose not to have a home inspection performed.**

X ____________________ X ____________________

Signature & Date Signature & Date

form **HUD-92564-CN** (12/04)

FIGURE 5.5

TREC 41-1

PROMULGATED BY THE TEXAS REAL ESTATE COMMISSION (TREC) 04-23-07

EQUAL HOUSING OPPORTUNITY

LOAN ASSUMPTION ADDENDUM
TO CONTRACT CONCERNING THE PROPERTY AT

____

(Address of Property)

A. **CREDIT DOCUMENTATION.** To establish Buyer's creditworthiness, Buyer shall deliver to Seller within_________days after the effective date of this contract ❑ credit report ❑ verification of employment, including salary ❑ verification of funds on deposit in financial institutions ❑ current financial statement and ❑ ______________________________________.
Buyer hereby authorizes any credit reporting agency to furnish copies of Buyer's credit reports to Seller at Buyer's sole expense.

B. **CREDIT APPROVAL.** If the credit documentation described in Paragraph A is not delivered within the specified time, Seller may terminate this contract by notice to Buyer within 7 days after expiration of the time for delivery, and the earnest money will be paid to Seller. If the credit documentation is timely delivered, and Seller determines in Seller's sole discretion that Buyer's credit is unacceptable, Seller may terminate this contract by notice to Buyer within 7 days after expiration of the time for delivery and the earnest money will be refunded to Buyer. If Seller does not terminate this contract within the time specified, Seller will be deemed to have approved Buyer's creditworthiness.

C. **ASSUMPTION.** Buyer's assumption of an existing note includes all obligations imposed by the deed of trust securing the note.

❑ (1) The unpaid principal balance of a first lien promissory note payable to__________________ ______________________________which unpaid balance at closing will be $ _______________. The total current monthly payment including principal, interest and any reserve deposits is $ _______________. Buyer's initial payment will be the first payment due after closing.

❑ (2) The unpaid principal balance of a second lien promissory note payable to _____________ ______________________________which unpaid balance at closing will be $ _______________. The total current monthly payment including principal, interest and any reserve deposits is $ _______________. Buyer's initial payment will be the first payment due after closing.

If the unpaid principal balance of any assumed loan as of the Closing Date varies from the loan balance stated above, the ❑ cash payable at closing ❑ Sales Price will be adjusted by the amount of any variance. If the total principal balance of all assumed loans varies in an amount greater than $500 at closing, either party may terminate this contract and the earnest money will be refunded to Buyer unless the other party elects to pay the excess of the variance.

D. **LOAN ASSUMPTION TERMS.** Buyer may terminate this contract and the earnest money will be refunded to Buyer if the noteholder requires:

(1) payment of an assumption fee in excess of $ _________in C(1) or $ ____________in C(2) and Seller declines to pay such excess, or

(2) an increase in the interest rate to more than ______% in C(1) or_____% in C(2), or

(3) any other modification of the loan documents.

E. **CONSENT BY NOTEHOLDER.** If the noteholder fails to consent to the assumption of the loan, either Seller or Buyer may terminate this contract by notice to the other party and the earnest money will be refunded to the Buyer.

F. **SELLER'S LIENS.** Unless Seller is released from liability on any assumed note, a vendor's lien and deed of trust to secure assumption will be required. The vendor's lien will automatically be

Initialed for identification by Buyer______________ and Seller__________ TREC NO. 41-1

FIGURE 5.5 (CONTINUED)

TREC 41-1

(Address of Property)

released on delivery of an executed release by noteholder.

G. TAX AND INSURANCE ESCROW. If noteholder maintains an escrow account for ad valorem taxes, casualty insurance premiums or mortgage insurance premiums, Seller shall transfer the escrow account to Buyer without any deficiency. Buyer shall reimburse Seller for the amount in the transferred accounts.

NOTICE TO BUYER: If you are concerned about the possibility of future adjustments, monthly payments, interest rates or other terms, do not sign the contract without examining the notes and deeds of trust.

NOTICE TO SELLER: Your liability to pay the notes assumed by Buyer will continue unless you obtain a release of liability from the noteholders. If you are concerned about future liability, you should use the TREC Release of Liability Addendum.

Buyer	Seller
Buyer	Seller

This form has been approved by the Texas Real Estate Commission for use with similarly approved or promulgated contract forms. Such approval relates to this form only. TREC forms are intended for use only by trained real estate licensees. No representation is made as to the legal validity or adequacy of any provision in any specific transactions. It is not suitable for complex transactions. Texas Real Estate Commission, P.O. Box 12188, Austin, TX 78711-2188, 1-800-250-8732 or (512) 459-6544 (http://www.trec.state.tx.us) TREC No. 41-1. This form replaces TREC No. 41-0.

FIGURE 5.6

TREC 12-2

EQUAL HOUSING OPPORTUNITY

PROMULGATED BY THE TEXAS REAL ESTATE COMMISSION (TREC) 04-23-07

ADDENDUM FOR RELEASE OF LIABILITY ON ASSUMED LOAN AND/OR RESTORATION OF SELLER'S VA ENTITLEMENT

TO CONTRACT CONCERNING THE PROPERTY AT

____

(Address of Property)

☐ **A. RELEASE OF SELLER'S LIABILITY ON LOAN TO BE ASSUMED:**

Within ____________ days after the effective date of this contract Seller and Buyer shall apply for release of Seller's liability from (a) any conventional lender, (b) VA and any lender whose loan has been guaranteed by VA, or (c) FHA and any lender whose loan has been insured by FHA. Seller and Buyer shall furnish all required information and documents. If any release of liability has not been approved by the Closing Date: (check one box only)

☐ (1) This contract will terminate and the earnest money will be refunded to Buyer.

☐ (2) Failure to obtain release approval will not delay closing.

☐ **B. RESTORATION OF SELLER'S ENTITLEMENT FOR VA LOAN:**

Within ____________ days after the effective date of this contract Seller and Buyer shall apply for restoration of Seller's VA entitlement and shall furnish all information and documents required by VA. If restoration has not been approved by the Closing Date: (check one box only)

☐ (1) This contract will terminate and the earnest money will be refunded to Buyer.

☐ (2) Failure to obtain restoration approval will not delay closing.

NOTICE: VA will not restore Seller's VA entitlement unless Buyer: (a) is a veteran, (b) has sufficient unused VA entitlement and (c) is otherwise qualified. If Seller desires restoration of VA entitlement, paragraphs A and B should be used.

Seller shall pay the cost of securing the release and restoration.

Seller's deed will contain any loan assumption clause required by FHA, VA or any lender.

______________________	______________________
Buyer	Seller
______________________	______________________
Buyer	Seller

This form has been approved by the Texas Real Estate Commission for use with similarly approved or promulgated contract forms. Such approval relates to this form only. TREC forms are intended for use only by trained real estate licensees. No representation is made as to the legal validity or adequacy of any provision in any specific transactions. It is not suitable for complex transactions. Texas Real Estate Commission, P.O. Box 12188, Austin, TX 78711-2188, 1-800-250-8732 or (512) 459-6544 (http://www.trec.state.tx.us) TREC No. 12-2. This form replaces TREC No. 12-1.

TREC No. 12-2

escrow accounts, if any. Buyers and Sellers should carefully read the notices on the addendum with Buyers taking seriously the advice to examine carefully any notes and deeds of trust to be assumed.

SELLER FINANCING

The final choice offered in paragraph 4 of the contract is for the Seller to accept part of the consideration in the form of a note secured by a deed of trust.

The TREC Form 26-5, Seller Financing Addendum, is added to the contract to address how the loan will be repaid, whether the note is assumable, and how payment of ad valorem taxes and insurance will be handled. (See Figure 5.7.) A prudent Seller should use an attorney any time **seller financing** is a part of the transaction. The attorney should be experienced in real estate law and understand the potential risks to the Seller's financial well-being when the Buyer defaults on the payments and decisive legal action against the borrower becomes necessary.

Once the financing is in place, the transaction will be a giant step closer to closing. An important part of the agreement between the parties addresses who will pay for what at or prior to the closing. Many of the expenses to be paid are loan related. Paragraph 12 reflects the most current practice and custom in Texas of who pays for what. Any of the items listed for the Seller may be paid for by the Buyer and many of the expenses listed for the Buyer may be paid by the Seller with the lender's knowledge and approval. To avoid any appearance of mortgage fraud, the parties should make certain that all loan-related charges are itemized in the HUD-1 at closing. Generally, who pays for what is negotiable between the parties; however, with certain loan programs the Buyers may be prohibited from paying certain expenses and may be required to pay certain things on their own behalf. It is best to check with a loan officer for current requirements.

To replace any definition of who pays for what in paragraph 12, the parties may define their agreement in the Special Provisions paragraph. (See Figure 5.8.) Who pays for something is a business detail that is appropriately addressed in the Special Provisions paragraph.

IT TAKES MORE THAN A DOWN PAYMENT TO CLOSE A TRANSACTION

The following two points need to be considered in paragraph 12:

1. **Loan Fees** are defined in paragraph 12A(2)(a). These are the same Loan Fees referenced in the TREC 40-3, Third Party Financing Condition Addendum. The fees include
   - loan origination fees,
   - discount points,

FIGURE 5.7

TREC 26-5

PROMULGATED BY THE TEXAS REAL ESTATE COMMISSION (TREC) 12-04-06

EQUAL HOUSING OPPORTUNITY

SELLER FINANCING ADDENDUM

TO CONTRACT CONCERNING THE PROPERTY AT

____

(Address of Property)

A. CREDIT DOCUMENTATION. To establish Buyer's creditworthiness, Buyer shall deliver to Seller within ____________ days after the effective date of this contract, ❑ credit report ❑ verification of employment, including salary ❑ verification of funds on deposit in financial institutions ❑ current financial statement and ❑ ____.
Buyer hereby authorizes any credit reporting agency to furnish copies of Buyer's credit reports to Seller at Buyer's sole expense.

B. CREDIT APPROVAL. If the credit documentation described in Paragraph A is not delivered within the specified time, Seller may terminate this contract by notice to Buyer within 7 days after expiration of the time for delivery, and the earnest money will be paid to Seller. If the credit documentation is timely delivered, and Seller determines in Seller's sole discretion that Buyer's credit is unacceptable, Seller may terminate this contract by notice to Buyer within 7 days after expiration of the time for delivery and the earnest money will be refunded to Buyer. If Seller does not terminate this contract, Seller will be deemed to have approved Buyer's creditworthiness.

C. PROMISSORY NOTE. The promissory note (Note) described in Paragraph 4 of this contract payable by Buyer to the order of Seller will bear interest at the rate of ______% per annum and be payable at the place designated by Seller. Buyer may prepay the Note in whole or in part at any time without penalty. Any prepayments are to be applied to the payment of the installments of principal last maturing and interest will immediately cease on the prepaid principal. The Note will contain a provision for payment of a late fee of 5% of any installment not paid within 10 days of the due date. Matured unpaid amounts will bear interest at the rate of 1½% per month or at the highest lawful rate, whichever is less. The Note will be payable as follows:

❑ (1) In one payment due ______________________________ after the date of the Note with interest payable ❑ at maturity ❑ monthly ❑ quarterly. (check one box only)

❑ (2) In monthly installments of $ _____________ ❑ including interest ❑ plus interest (check one box only) beginning ____________________ after the date of the Note and continuing monthly thereafter for ____________ months when the balance of the Note will be due and payable.

❑ (3) Interest only in monthly installments for the first ___________ month(s) and thereafter in installments of $_______________ ❑ including interest ❑ plus interest (check one box only) beginning ___________________ after the date of the Note and continuing monthly thereafter for _________ months when the balance of the Note will be due and payable.

D. DEED OF TRUST. The deed of trust securing the Note will provide for the following:

(1) PROPERTY TRANSFERS: (check one box only)

❑ (a) Consent Not Required: The Property may be sold, conveyed or leased without the consent of Seller, provided any subsequent buyer assumes the Note.

❑ (b) Consent Required: If all or any part of the Property is sold, conveyed, leased for a period longer than 3 years, leased with an option to purchase, or otherwise sold (including any contract for deed), without Seller's prior written consent, which consent may be withheld in Seller's sole discretion, Seller may declare the balance of the Note

FIGURE 5.7 (CONTINUED)

TREC 26-5

____
(Address of Property)

to be immediately due and payable. The creation of a subordinate lien, any conveyance under threat or order of condemnation, any deed solely between buyers, or the passage of title by reason of the death of a buyer or by operation of law will not entitle Seller to exercise the remedies provided in this paragraph.

NOTE: *Under (a) or (b), Buyer's liability to pay the Note will continue unless Buyer obtains a release of liability from Seller.*

(2) TAX AND INSURANCE ESCROW: (check one box only)

❑ (a) Escrow Not Required: Buyer shall furnish Seller, before each year's ad valorem taxes become delinquent, evidence that all ad valorem taxes on the Property have been paid. Buyer shall annually furnish Seller evidence of paid-up casualty insurance naming Seller as a mortgagee loss payee.

❑ (b) Escrow Required: With each installment Buyer shall deposit in escrow with Seller a pro rata part of the estimated annual ad valorem taxes and casualty insurance premiums for the Property. Buyer shall pay any deficiency within 30 days after notice from Seller. Buyer's failure to pay the deficiency will be a default under the deed of trust. Buyer is not required to deposit any escrow payments for taxes and insurance that are deposited with a superior lienholder. The casualty insurance must name Seller as a mortgagee loss payee.

(3) PRIOR LIENS: Any default under any lien superior to the lien securing the Note will be a default under the deed of trust securing the Note.

____________________ Buyer	____________________ Seller
____________________ Buyer	____________________ Seller

FIGURE 5.8

TREC 20-7 Paragraph 12

12. SETTLEMENT AND OTHER EXPENSES:
A. The following expenses must be paid at or prior to closing:
(1) Expenses payable by Seller (Seller's Expenses):
(a) Releases of existing liens, including prepayment penalties and recording fees; release of Seller's loan liability; tax statements or certificates; preparation of deed; one-half of escrow fee; and other expenses payable by Seller under this contract.
(b) Seller shall also pay an amount not to exceed $ ____________ to be applied in the following order: Buyer's Expenses which Buyer is prohibited from paying by FHA, VA, Texas Veterans Housing Assistance Program or other governmental loan programs, and then to other Buyer's Expenses as allowed by the lender.
(2) Expenses payable by Buyer (Buyer's Expenses):
(a) Loan origination, discount, buy-down, and commitment fees (Loan Fees).
(b) Appraisal fees; loan application fees; credit reports; preparation of loan documents; interest on the notes from date of disbursement to one month prior to dates of first monthly payments; recording fees; copies of easements and restrictions; mortgagee title policy with endorsements required by lender; loan-related inspection fees; photos; amortization schedules; one-half of escrow fee; all prepaid items, including required premiums for flood and hazard insurance, reserve deposits for insurance, ad valorem taxes and special governmental assessments; final compliance inspection; courier fee; repair inspection; underwriting fee; wire transfer fee; expenses incident to any loan; and other expenses payable by Buyer under this contract.
B. Buyer shall pay Private Mortgage Insurance Premium (PMI), VA Loan Funding Fee, or FHA Mortgage Insurance Premium (MIP) as required by the lender.
C. If any expense exceeds an amount expressly stated in this contract for such expense to be paid by a party, that party may terminate this contract unless the other party agrees to pay such excess. Buyer may not pay charges and fees expressly prohibited by FHA, VA, Texas Veterans Housing Assistance Program or other governmental loan program regulations.

- buydown, and
- commitment fees.

These Loan Fees are usually expressed as points. Remember that 1 point is equal to 1 percent of the loan amount. Interestingly, Loan Fees are not defined for VA financing.

2. The order of the application of what the Seller might agree to pay as additional expenses on the Buyer's behalf is clearly established in 12A(1)(b), as follows:
   - Buyer's expense which Buyer is prohibited by FHA or VA from paying
   - Texas Veterans Housing Assistance Program or other governmental loan programs
   - Other Buyer's expenses as allowed by the lender

The Buyer is required by the contract to pay private mortgage insurance. It can be paid in cash at closing or added to the amount of the loan. This is a point to be negotiated between a Buyer and the lender and does not involve the Sellers or license holders.

Finally, note that if any expense exceeds an amount set as an upper limit in the contract, a party may terminate the contract unless the other party agrees to pay the excess.

SUMMARY

A very large percentage of the blanks that must be completed in the purchase agreement address the financing. Because most Buyers will use some borrowed funds to complete the purchase, it is important for the professional real estate practitioner to be well informed about the available financing options and be able to guide the parties to a financing arrangement that best suits the needs of both parties. Be thoroughly familiar with the contract provisions and the content of each of the three addenda that are available to help the parties define their wishes.

Remember that there is a difference between financing approval and loan approval. Also, loan fees are a clearly defined term in the contract, and the order for the application of any money paid by the Seller to assist the Buyer with loan expenses is clearly defined in the contract.

Encourage parties to read and understand the documents before signing, and always be sure to advise someone who requires additional clarification to seek legal counsel before signing. Loans should never be assumed until the Buyer has carefully reviewed the note and deed of trust that is being assumed.

Real estate practitioners must carefully read and study the content of the promulgated forms before they attempt to act on behalf of a client or customer. Inexperienced real estate practitioners should consult more experienced individuals, such as the broker or the loan officer, for guidance.

CHAPTER 5 REVIEW QUESTIONS

1. Which option would *NEVER* require the use of a TREC-promulgated addendum to define the transaction's financial details?

   a. Seller financing
   b. Third party financing
   c. Cash
   d. Assumption of existing lien

2. If the Property does not satisfy the lender's underwriting requirements, the contract will terminate and the earnest money will be returned to the Buyer.

   a. True
   b. False

3. Which loan combination is *LEAST* likely to occur?

   a. Third party conventional first lien with Texas Veterans Housing Assistance Loan
   b. Third party conventional first lien with a third party conventional second lien
   c. Third party conventional second lien with assumption of an FHA-insured loan
   d. A new FHA-insured loan with a third party conventional second lien

4. The Seller is automatically released from liability when a loan is assumed with the lender's approval.

   a. True
   b. False

5. How many days does the contract give the Seller to terminate the contract after expiration of the time for the Buyer to deliver documentation for credit approval purposes?

   a. 5
   b. 7
   c. 10
   d. 15

6. What two documents are required to be executed when an assumption takes place without the release of liability being granted by the lender to the Seller?

   a. Vendor's lien and deed of trust to secure assumption
   b. A reaffirmation promissory note and deed of trust
   c. A release of original lien and deed of trust to secure assumption
   d. A special warranty deed and deed of trust to secure assumption

7. In paragraph 3 of the contract and the Third Party Financing Condition Addendum, each time the loan amount is recited it is with PMI, MIP, or VA-funding fee included in the amount.

   a. True
   b. False

8. Who establishes the interest rate for Texas Veterans Housing Assistance Program Loans?

   a. The Department of Veterans Affairs
   b. The local VA field office
   c. The individual lender
   d. The Texas Veterans Land Board

9. Conventional loan amounts in excess of what LTV ratio will generally require the purchaser to obtain PMI?

   a. 95%
   b. 90%
   c. 80%
   d. 75%

10. Financing approval and loan approval are the same thing.

    a. True
    b. False

HOMEWORK QUIZ

The following quiz does not have an answer key included with the answer keys in Appendix B. Students who are using this book as the basis for a correspondence course should record and submit their answers to their course provider as instructed by the provider. The student will submit his or her answers for the Homework Quiz at the end of each chapter and for each transaction in Chapter 11.

True or False?

1. The Seller Financing Addendum contains a blank for the interest rate to be charged on the loan carried back by the Seller.

2. With the exception of Section A on the Seller Financing Addendum, the parties are instructed to "check one box only."

3. The appraisal fee for a loan-related appraisal is included in the definition of Loan Fees.

4. When the Buyer assumes an existing conventional loan, the Buyer generally will be required to execute a deed of trust to secure assumption.

5. Only the Conventional Financing (A) section of the Third Party Financing Conditions Addendum provides a choice for the Buyer between a fixed-rate and an adjustable-rate loan.

CHAPTER SIX

6

Practice with the Money

Now familiar with the paragraphs of the contract and the addenda relating to financing, we will at this time practice filling in the applicable blanks for a variety of financing scenarios.

We will provide the relevant data needed to structure the financing. You will provide finance structuring solutions by filling in the appropriate contract paragraphs and addenda that are furnished following each scenario.

The scenarios will cover several of the more commonly encountered financing choices made by Buyers of Texas properties. These choices include the following:

Scenario 1: All Cash—No Financing
Scenario 2: Third Party 80% Conventional Financing
Scenario 3: Third Party 90% Conventional Financing
Scenario 4: Third Party 80/10/10 Conventional Financing
Scenario 5: FHA 203(B) Insured Financing
Scenario 6: VA-Guaranteed Financing
Scenario 7: Assumption with Seller Second Financing

After you have completed your work, check your work with the answer key in Appendix B.

■ SCENARIO 1: ALL CASH—NO FINANCING

The Thompsons want to purchase the Johnson's home and offer a purchase price of \$340,000. Mr. Thompson has recently inherited \$400,000. They decide to save money and to enjoy the benefits of having a home with no mortgage. They have studied the market carefully and know that they are paying a fair price.

Because there is no loan involved, they will not need to use any of the financing addenda.

Complete paragraphs 3, 4, and 12 of their purchase agreement. (See Figure 6.1, Figure 6.2, and Figure 6.3.)

May you enjoy a career with many transactions of this type.

Scenario 1

FIGURE 6.1

TREC 20-7 Paragraph 3

3. SALES PRICE:
A. Cash portion of Sales Price payable by Buyer at closing .... \$ 340,000
B. Sum of all financing described below (excluding any loan funding fee or mortgage insurance premium)... \$ -0-
C. Sales Price (Sum of A and B)... \$ 340,000

FIGURE 6.2

TREC 20-7 Paragraph 4

4. FINANCING: The portion of Sales Price not payable in cash will be paid as follows: (Check applicable boxes below)
❑ A. THIRD PARTY FINANCING: One or more third party mortgage loans in the total amount of \$ n/a (excluding any loan funding fee or mortgage insurance premium).
(1) Property Approval: If the Property does not satisfy the lenders' underwriting requirements for the loan(s), this contract will terminate and the earnest money will be refunded to Buyer.
(2) Financing Approval: (Check one box only)
❑ (a) This contract is subject to Buyer being approved for the financing described in the attached Third Party Financing Condition Addendum.
❑ (b) This contract is not subject to Buyer being approved for financing and does not involve FHA or VA financing.
❑ B. ASSUMPTION: The assumption of the unpaid principal balance of one or more promissory notes described in the attached TREC Loan Assumption Addendum.
❑ C. SELLER FINANCING: A promissory note from Buyer to Seller of \$ n/a, secured by vendor's and deed of trust liens, and containing the terms and conditions described in the attached TREC Seller Financing Addendum. If an owner policy of title insurance is furnished, Buyer shall furnish Seller with a mortgagee policy of title insurance.

FIGURE 6.3

TREC 20-7 Paragraph 12

12. SETTLEMENT AND OTHER EXPENSES:

A. The following expenses must be paid at or prior to closing:

(1) Expenses payable by Seller (Seller's Expenses):

(a) Releases of existing liens, including prepayment penalties and recording fees; release of Seller's loan liability; tax statements or certificates; preparation of deed; one-half of escrow fee; and other expenses payable by Seller under this contract.

(b) Seller shall also pay an amount not to exceed $ ____________ to be applied in the following order: Buyer's Expenses which Buyer is prohibited from paying by FHA, VA, Texas Veterans Housing Assistance Program or other governmental loan programs, and then to other Buyer's Expenses as allowed by the lender.

(2) Expenses payable by Buyer (Buyer's Expenses):

(a) Loan origination, discount, buy-down, and commitment fees (Loan Fees).

(b) Appraisal fees; loan application fees; credit reports; preparation of loan documents; interest on the notes from date of disbursement to one month prior to dates of first monthly payments; recording fees; copies of easements and restrictions; mortgagee title policy with endorsements required by lender; loan-related inspection fees; photos; amortization schedules; one-half of escrow fee; all prepaid items, including required premiums for flood and hazard insurance, reserve deposits for insurance, ad valorem taxes and special governmental assessments; final compliance inspection; courier fee; repair inspection; underwriting fee; wire transfer fee; expenses incident to any loan; and other expenses payable by Buyer under this contract.

B. Buyer shall pay Private Mortgage Insurance Premium (PMI), VA Loan Funding Fee, or FHA Mortgage Insurance Premium (MIP) as required by the lender.

C. If any expense exceeds an amount expressly stated in this contract for such expense to be paid by a party, that party may terminate this contract unless the other party agrees to pay such excess. Buyer may not pay charges and fees expressly prohibited by FHA, VA, Texas Veterans Housing Assistance Program or other governmental loan program regulations.

■ SCENARIO 2: THIRD PARTY 80% CONVENTIONAL FINANCING

Hilton Charles and his wife, Karen Charles, have been saving their money and investing it wisely to accumulate a significant down payment to purchase their dream home. They have about $110,000 to use as a down payment, pay closing costs and prepaids, and hope to have $15,000 to $20,000 remaining to spend on decorating.

They find a 4/2/2 in a wonderful neighborhood for $250,300. They offer $249,000, which the owners readily accept.

The contract is contingent upon the Buyers being approved for an 80 percent conventional loan and investing their extra savings to let the income help pay the note. They will not need to purchase PMI, pay discount, buydown, or commitment fees, nor will they ask the Seller to help them with any loan costs. They can obtain a 15-year fixed rate loan at 6.25 percent annual interest and anticipate that they can have financing approval within 20 days after the effective date of the contract. To provide a cushion for a possible upward adjustment in the market rate, they write the offer with a 6.5 percent maximum acceptable rate. They have not yet applied for financing approval. They do know that they will be charged a 1 percent loan origination fee. (See Figure 6.4, Figure 6.5, Figure 6.6, and Figure 6.7.)

Scenario 2

FIGURE 6.4

TREC 20-7 Paragraph 3

3. SALES PRICE:

A. Cash portion of Sales Price payable by Buyer at closing................. $________

B. Sum of all financing described below (excluding any loan funding fee or mortgage insurance premium).. $________

C. Sales Price (Sum of A and B).. $________

FIGURE 6.5

TREC 20-7 Paragraph 4

4. FINANCING: The portion of Sales Price not payable in cash will be paid as follows: (Check applicable boxes below)

☒ A. THIRD PARTY FINANCING: One or more third party mortgage loans in the total amount of $ 199,200 (excluding any loan funding fee or mortgage insurance premium).

(1) Property Approval: If the Property does not satisfy the lenders' underwriting requirements for the loan(s), this contract will terminate and the earnest money will be refunded to Buyer.

(2) Financing Approval: (Check one box only)

☒ (a) This contract is subject to Buyer being approved for the financing described in the attached Third Party Financing Condition Addendum.

☐ (b) This contract is not subject to Buyer being approved for financing and does not involve FHA or VA financing.

☐ B. ASSUMPTION: The assumption of the unpaid principal balance of one or more promissory notes described in the attached TREC Loan Assumption Addendum.

☐ C. SELLER FINANCING: A promissory note from Buyer to Seller of $ n/a, secured by vendor's and deed of trust liens, and containing the terms and conditions described in the attached TREC Seller Financing Addendum. If an owner policy of title insurance is furnished, Buyer shall furnish Seller with a mortgagee policy of title insurance.

FIGURE 6.6

TREC 20-7 Paragraph 12

12. SETTLEMENT AND OTHER EXPENSES:

A. The following expenses must be paid at or prior to closing:

(1) Expenses payable by Seller (Seller's Expenses):

(a) Releases of existing liens, including prepayment penalties and recording fees; release of Seller's loan liability; tax statements or certificates; preparation of deed; one-half of escrow fee; and other expenses payable by Seller under this contract.

(b) Seller shall also pay an amount not to exceed $ n/a to be applied in the following order: Buyer's Expenses which Buyer is prohibited from paying by FHA, VA, Texas Veterans Housing Assistance Program or other governmental loan programs, and then to other Buyer's Expenses as allowed by the lender.

(2) Expenses payable by Buyer (Buyer's Expenses):

(a) Loan origination, discount, buy-down, and commitment fees (Loan Fees).

(b) Appraisal fees; loan application fees; credit reports; preparation of loan documents; interest on the notes from date of disbursement to one month prior to dates of first monthly payments; recording fees; copies of easements and restrictions; mortgagee title policy with endorsements required by lender; loan-related inspection fees; photos; amortization schedules; one-half of escrow fee; all prepaid items, including required premiums for flood and hazard insurance, reserve deposits for insurance, ad valorem taxes and special governmental assessments; final compliance inspection; courier fee; repair inspection; underwriting fee; wire transfer fee; expenses incident to any loan; and other expenses payable by Buyer under this contract.

B. Buyer shall pay Private Mortgage Insurance Premium (PMI), VA Loan Funding Fee, or FHA Mortgage Insurance Premium (MIP) as required by the lender.

C. If any expense exceeds an amount expressly stated in this contract for such expense to be paid by a party, that party may terminate this contract unless the other party agrees to pay such excess. Buyer may not pay charges and fees expressly prohibited by FHA, VA, Texas Veterans Housing Assistance Program or other governmental loan program regulations.

FIGURE 6.7

TREC 40-3

12-10-07

EQUAL HOUSING OPPORTUNITY

PROMULGATED BY THE TEXAS REAL ESTATE COMMISSION (TREC)

THIRD PARTY FINANCING CONDITION ADDENDUM

TO CONTRACT CONCERNING THE PROPERTY AT

____

(Street Address and City)

Buyer shall apply promptly for all financing described below and make every reasonable effort to obtain approval for the financing (Financing Approval). Buyer shall furnish all information and documents required by lender for Financing Approval. Financing Approval will be deemed to have been obtained when (1) the terms of the loan(s) described below are available and (2) lender determines that Buyer has satisfied all of lender's financial requirements (those items relating to Buyer's assets, income and credit history). If Buyer cannot obtain Financing Approval, Buyer may give written notice to Seller within 20 days after the effective date of this contract and this contract will terminate and the earnest money will be refunded to Buyer. **If Buyer does not give such notice within the time required, this contract will no longer be subject to Financing Approval. Time is of the essence for this paragraph and strict compliance with the time for performance is required.**

NOTE: Financing Approval does not include approval of lender's underwriting requirements for the Property, as specified in Paragraph 4.A.(1) of the contract.

Each note must be secured by vendor's and deed of trust liens.

CHECK APPLICABLE BOXES:

☐ A. CONVENTIONAL FINANCING:

☒ (1) A first mortgage loan in the principal amount of $ 199,200 (excluding any financed PMI premium), due in full in 15 year(s), with interest not to exceed 6.5 % per annum for the first 15 year(s) of the loan with Loan Fees (loan origination, discount, buy-down, and commitment fees) not to exceed 1 % of the loan.

☐ (2) A second mortgage loan in the principal amount of $ n/a (excluding any financed PMI premium), due in full in n/a year(s), with interest not to exceed n/a % per annum for the first n/a year(s) of the loan with Loan Fees (loan origination, discount, buy-down, and commitment fees) not to exceed ________% of the loan.

☐ B. TEXAS VETERANS LOAN: A loan(s) from the Texas Veterans Land Board of $ n/a for a period in the total amount of n/a years at the interest rate established by the Texas Veterans Land Board.

☐ C. FHA INSURED FINANCING: A Section n/a FHA insured loan of not less than $ n/a (excluding any financed MIP), amortizable monthly for not less than n/a years, with interest not to exceed n/a % per annum for the first n/a year(s) of the loan with Loan Fees (loan origination, discount, buy-down, and commitment fees) not to exceed _________ % of the loan. As required by HUD-FHA, if FHA valuation is unknown, *"It is expressly agreed that, notwithstanding any other provision of this contract, the purchaser (Buyer) shall not be obligated to complete the purchase of the Property described herein or to incur any penalty by forfeiture of earnest money deposits or otherwise unless the purchaser (Buyer) has been given in accordance with HUD/FHA or VA requirements a written statement issued by the Federal Housing Commissioner, Department of Veterans Affairs, or a Direct Endorsement Lender setting forth the appraised value of the Property of not less than $ n/a . The purchaser (Buyer) shall have the privilege and option of proceeding with consummation of the contract without regard to the amount of the*

FIGURE 6.7 (CONTINUED)

TREC 40-3

Third Party Financing Condition Addendum Concerning Page 2 of 2 12-10-07

____

(Address of Property)

appraised valuation. The appraised valuation is arrived at to determine the maximum mortgage the Department of Housing and Urban Development will insure. HUD does not warrant the value or the condition of the Property. The purchaser (Buyer) should satisfy himself/herself that the price and the condition of the Property are acceptable."

NOTE: HUD 92564-CN "For Your Protection: Get a Home Inspection" must be attached to this Addendum.

❑ D. VA GUARANTEED FINANCING: A VA guaranteed loan of not less than $__n/a__ (excluding any financed Funding Fee), amortizable monthly for not less than __n/a__ years, with interest not to exceed __n/a__% per annum for the first __n/a__ year(s) of the loan with Loan Fees (loan origination, discount, buy-down, and commitment fees) not to exceed __n/a__% of the loan.

VA NOTICE TO BUYER: "*It is expressly agreed that, notwithstanding any other provisions of this contract, the Buyer shall not incur any penalty by forfeiture of earnest money or otherwise or be obligated to complete the purchase of the Property described herein, if the contract purchase price or cost exceeds the reasonable value of the Property established by the Department of Veterans Affairs. The Buyer shall, however, have the privilege and option of proceeding with the consummation of this contract without regard to the amount of the reasonable value established by the Department of Veterans Affairs.*"

If Buyer elects to complete the purchase at an amount in excess of the reasonable value established by VA, Buyer shall pay such excess amount in cash from a source which Buyer agrees to disclose to the VA and which Buyer represents will not be from borrowed funds except as approved by VA. If VA reasonable value of the Property is less than the Sales Price, Seller may reduce the Sales Price to an amount equal to the VA reasonable value and the sale will be closed at the lower Sales Price with proportionate adjustments to the down payment and the loan amount.

Buyer hereby authorizes any lender to furnish to the Seller or Buyer or their representatives information relating only to the status of Financing Approval of Buyer.

______________________ ______________________

Buyer Seller

______________________ ______________________

Buyer Seller

This form has been approved by the Texas Real Estate Commission for use with similarly approved or promulgated contract forms. Such approval relates to this form only. TREC forms are intended for use only by trained real estate licensees. No representation is made as to the legal validity or adequacy of any provision in any specific transactions. It is not intended for complex transactions. Texas Real Estate Commission, P.O. Box 12188, Austin, TX 78711-2188, 1-800-250-8732 or (512) 459-6544 (http://www.trec.state.tx.us) TREC No. 40-3. This form replaces TREC No. 40-2.

TREC NO. 40-3

■ SCENARIO 3: THIRD PARTY 90% CONVENTIONAL FINANCING

John Paul Gordon and his wife, Mary Ann Gordon, are offering Isabelle Gerhard $176,400 for her home. They have been preapproved for a loan not to exceed $160,400. The loan will be for 30 years and will have an interest rate of 6.75 percent for the first 3 years. After that it will be adjusted annually with adjustments being tied to the 11th Federal Reserve District Cost of Funds.

They will make a 10 percent down payment. They will be charged a 1 percent origination fee. The Gordons are asking Ms. Gerhard to assist the Buyers with their closing costs and related expenses in an amount of $1,500. The contract is not subject to borrower approval for financing. (See Figure 6.8, Figure 6.9, Figure 6.10, and Figure 6.11.) In practice, it is always best to encourage your Buyer to make the transaction subject to the borrower's being approved for financing.

Scenario 3

FIGURE 6.8

TREC 20-7 Paragraph 3

3. SALES PRICE:

A. Cash portion of Sales Price payable by Buyer at closing .... $ 17,640

B. Sum of all financing described below (excluding any loan funding fee or mortgage insurance premium).. $ 158,760

C. Sales Price (Sum of A and B).. $ 176,400

FIGURE 6.9

TREC 20-7 Paragraph 4

4. FINANCING: The portion of Sales Price not payable in cash will be paid as follows: (Check applicable boxes below)

☒ A. THIRD PARTY FINANCING: One or more third party mortgage loans in the total amount of $ 158,760 (excluding any loan funding fee or mortgage insurance premium).

(1) Property Approval: If the Property does not satisfy the lenders' underwriting requirements for the loan(s), this contract will terminate and the earnest money will be refunded to Buyer.

(2) Financing Approval: (Check one box only)

☐ (a) This contract is subject to Buyer being approved for the financing described in the attached Third Party Financing Condition Addendum.

☒ (b) This contract is not subject to Buyer being approved for financing and does not involve FHA or VA financing.

☐ B. ASSUMPTION: The assumption of the unpaid principal balance of one or more promissory notes described in the attached TREC Loan Assumption Addendum.

☐ C. SELLER FINANCING: A promissory note from Buyer to Seller of $ n/a , secured by vendor's and deed of trust liens, and containing the terms and conditions described in the attached TREC Seller Financing Addendum. If an owner policy of title insurance is furnished, Buyer shall furnish Seller with a mortgagee policy of title insurance.

FIGURE 6.10

TREC 20-7 Paragraph 12

12. SETTLEMENT AND OTHER EXPENSES:

A. The following expenses must be paid at or prior to closing:

(1) Expenses payable by Seller (Seller's Expenses):

(a) Releases of existing liens, including prepayment penalties and recording fees; release of Seller's loan liability; tax statements or certificates; preparation of deed; one-half of escrow fee; and other expenses payable by Seller under this contract.

(b) Seller shall also pay an amount not to exceed $ 1,500 to be applied in the following order: Buyer's Expenses which Buyer is prohibited from paying by FHA, VA, Texas Veterans Housing Assistance Program or other governmental loan programs, and then to other Buyer's Expenses as allowed by the lender.

(2) Expenses payable by Buyer (Buyer's Expenses):

(a) Loan origination, discount, buy-down, and commitment fees (Loan Fees).

(b) Appraisal fees; loan application fees; credit reports; preparation of loan documents; interest on the notes from date of disbursement to one month prior to dates of first monthly payments; recording fees; copies of easements and restrictions; mortgagee title policy with endorsements required by lender; loan-related inspection fees; photos; amortization schedules; one-half of escrow fee; all prepaid items, including required premiums for flood and hazard insurance, reserve deposits for insurance, ad valorem taxes and special governmental assessments; final compliance inspection; courier fee; repair inspection; underwriting fee; wire transfer fee; expenses incident to any loan; and other expenses payable by Buyer under this contract.

B. Buyer shall pay Private Mortgage Insurance Premium (PMI), VA Loan Funding Fee, or FHA Mortgage Insurance Premium (MIP) as required by the lender.

C. If any expense exceeds an amount expressly stated in this contract for such expense to be paid by a party, that party may terminate this contract unless the other party agrees to pay such excess. Buyer may not pay charges and fees expressly prohibited by FHA, VA, Texas Veterans Housing Assistance Program or other governmental loan program regulations.

FIGURE 6.11

TREC 40-3

12-10-07

EQUAL HOUSING OPPORTUNITY

PROMULGATED BY THE TEXAS REAL ESTATE COMMISSION (TREC)

THIRD PARTY FINANCING CONDITION ADDENDUM

TO CONTRACT CONCERNING THE PROPERTY AT

____

(Street Address and City)

Buyer shall apply promptly for all financing described below and make every reasonable effort to obtain approval for the financing (Financing Approval). Buyer shall furnish all information and documents required by lender for Financing Approval. Financing Approval will be deemed to have been obtained when (1) the terms of the loan(s) described below are available and (2) lender determines that Buyer has satisfied all of lender's financial requirements (those items relating to Buyer's assets, income and credit history). If Buyer cannot obtain Financing Approval, Buyer may give written notice to Seller within n/a days after the effective date of this contract and this contract will terminate and the earnest money will be refunded to Buyer. **If Buyer does not give such notice within the time required, this contract will no longer be subject to Financing Approval. Time is of the essence for this paragraph and strict compliance with the time for performance is required.**

NOTE: Financing Approval does not include approval of lender's underwriting requirements for the Property, as specified in Paragraph 4.A.(1) of the contract.

Each note must be secured by vendor's and deed of trust liens.

CHECK APPLICABLE BOXES:

☒ A. CONVENTIONAL FINANCING:

☒ (1) A first mortgage loan in the principal amount of $ 158,760 (excluding any financed PMI premium), due in full in 30 year(s), with interest not to exceed 6.75 % per annum for the first 3 year(s) of the loan with Loan Fees (loan origination, discount, buy-down, and commitment fees) not to exceed 1 % of the loan.

☐ (2) A second mortgage loan in the principal amount of $ n/a (excluding any financed PMI premium), due in full in n/a year(s), with interest not to exceed n/a % per annum for the first n/a year(s) of the loan with Loan Fees (loan origination, discount, buy-down, and commitment fees) not to exceed n/a % of the loan.

☐ B. TEXAS VETERANS LOAN: A loan(s) from the Texas Veterans Land Board of $ n/a for a period in the total amount of n/a years at the interest rate established by the Texas Veterans Land Board.

☐ C. FHA INSURED FINANCING: A Section n/a FHA insured loan of not less than $ n/a (excluding any financed MIP), amortizable monthly for not less than n/a years, with interest not to exceed n/a % per annum for the first n/a year(s) of the loan with Loan Fees (loan origination, discount, buy-down, and commitment fees) not to exceed n/a % of the loan. As required by HUD-FHA, if FHA valuation is unknown, *"It is expressly agreed that, notwithstanding any other provision of this contract, the purchaser (Buyer) shall not be obligated to complete the purchase of the Property described herein or to incur any penalty by forfeiture of earnest money deposits or otherwise unless the purchaser (Buyer) has been given in accordance with HUD/FHA or VA requirements a written statement issued by the Federal Housing Commissioner, Department of Veterans Affairs, or a Direct Endorsement Lender setting forth the appraised value of the Property of not less than $ n/a . The purchaser (Buyer) shall have the privilege and option of proceeding with consummation of the contract without regard to the amount of the*

Initialed for identification by Buyer____ _____ and Seller_____ _____

FIGURE 6.11 (CONTINUED)

TREC 40-3

____

(Address of Property)

appraised valuation. The appraised valuation is arrived at to determine the maximum mortgage the Department of Housing and Urban Development will insure. HUD does not warrant the value or the condition of the Property. The purchaser (Buyer) should satisfy himself/herself that the price and the condition of the Property are acceptable."

NOTE: HUD 92564-CN "For Your Protection: Get a Home Inspection" must be attached to this Addendum.

❑ D. VA GUARANTEED FINANCING: A VA guaranteed loan of not less than $__n/a__ (excluding any financed Funding Fee), amortizable monthly for not less than__n/a__years, with interest not to exceed__n/a__% per annum for the first __n/a__year(s) of the loan with Loan Fees (loan origination, discount, buy-down, and commitment fees) not to exceed __n/a__% of the loan.

VA NOTICE TO BUYER: "*It is expressly agreed that, notwithstanding any other provisions of this contract, the Buyer shall not incur any penalty by forfeiture of earnest money or otherwise or be obligated to complete the purchase of the Property described herein, if the contract purchase price or cost exceeds the reasonable value of the Property established by the Department of Veterans Affairs. The Buyer shall, however, have the privilege and option of proceeding with the consummation of this contract without regard to the amount of the reasonable value established by the Department of Veterans Affairs."*

If Buyer elects to complete the purchase at an amount in excess of the reasonable value established by VA, Buyer shall pay such excess amount in cash from a source which Buyer agrees to disclose to the VA and which Buyer represents will not be from borrowed funds except as approved by VA. If VA reasonable value of the Property is less than the Sales Price, Seller may reduce the Sales Price to an amount equal to the VA reasonable value and the sale will be closed at the lower Sales Price with proportionate adjustments to the down payment and the loan amount.

Buyer hereby authorizes any lender to furnish to the Seller or Buyer or their representatives information relating only to the status of Financing Approval of Buyer.

Buyer	Seller
Buyer	Seller

SCENARIO 4: THIRD PARTY 80/10/10 CONVENTIONAL FINANCING

The Buyers are under contract to buy their dream home for $435,000. They have been planning to make a 10 percent down payment and to finance the balance for 30 years, which would result in a loan of $391,500, a jumbo loan that would require PMI and would be available at 7.875 percent for 30 years. They can comfortably afford the resulting monthly payment.

Their buyer agent and loan officer recommend that they get a 30-year, fixed rate conforming loan of $348,000, currently available at 6.25 percent annual interest *and* simultaneously get a second mortgage loan of $43,500 at 7.5 percent annual interest for 15 years. After being shown the numbers, they decide that going for two loans is a wonderful idea. The second will not require any origination fee and will eliminate the need for them to carry PMI. As long as the conforming loan does not exceed an 80 percent loan-to-value ratio, Fannie Mae will not require PMI.

The Buyers do not ask the Sellers to contribute anything to the payment of their loan costs. The Buyers will pay the 1 point origination fee required on the first lien note.

They will apply immediately for the financing and have been assured by the loan officer that they will be able to obtain financing approval within 15 days after the effective date of the contract and the submission of their loan application. They decide to write the purchase agreement with 20 days for financing approval just to be on the safe side. The transaction is subject to financing approval. (See Figure 6.12, Figure 6.13, Figure 6.14, and Figure 6.15.)

Scenario 4

FIGURE 6.12

TREC 20-7 Paragraph 3

3. SALES PRICE:

A. Cash portion of Sales Price payable by Buyer at closing.................. $ 43,500

B. Sum of all financing described below (excluding any loan funding fee or mortgage insurance premium).. $ 391,500

C. Sales Price (Sum of A and B).. $ 435,000

FIGURE 6.13

TREC 20-7 Paragraph 4

4. FINANCING: The portion of Sales Price not payable in cash will be paid as follows: (Check applicable boxes below)

☐ A. THIRD PARTY FINANCING: One or more third party mortgage loans in the total amount of $ 391,500 (excluding any loan funding fee or mortgage insurance premium).

(1) Property Approval: If the Property does not satisfy the lenders' underwriting requirements for the loan(s), this contract will terminate and the earnest money will be refunded to Buyer.

(2) Financing Approval: (Check one box only)

☒ (a) This contract is subject to Buyer being approved for the financing described in the attached Third Party Financing Condition Addendum.

☐ (b) This contract is not subject to Buyer being approved for financing and does not involve FHA or VA financing.

☐ B. ASSUMPTION: The assumption of the unpaid principal balance of one or more promissory notes described in the attached TREC Loan Assumption Addendum.

☐ C. SELLER FINANCING: A promissory note from Buyer to Seller of $ n/a, secured by vendor's and deed of trust liens, and containing the terms and conditions described in the attached TREC Seller Financing Addendum. If an owner policy of title insurance is furnished, Buyer shall furnish Seller with a mortgagee policy of title insurance.

FIGURE 6.14

TREC 20-7 Paragraph 12

12. SETTLEMENT AND OTHER EXPENSES:

A. The following expenses must be paid at or prior to closing:

(1) Expenses payable by Seller (Seller's Expenses):

(a) Releases of existing liens, including prepayment penalties and recording fees; release of Seller's loan liability; tax statements or certificates; preparation of deed; one-half of escrow fee; and other expenses payable by Seller under this contract.

(b) Seller shall also pay an amount not to exceed $ n/a to be applied in the following order: Buyer's Expenses which Buyer is prohibited from paying by FHA, VA, Texas Veterans Housing Assistance Program or other governmental loan programs, and then to other Buyer's Expenses as allowed by the lender.

(2) Expenses payable by Buyer (Buyer's Expenses):

(a) Loan origination, discount, buy-down, and commitment fees (Loan Fees).

(b) Appraisal fees; loan application fees; credit reports; preparation of loan documents; interest on the notes from date of disbursement to one month prior to dates of first monthly payments; recording fees; copies of easements and restrictions; mortgagee title policy with endorsements required by lender; loan-related inspection fees; photos; amortization schedules; one-half of escrow fee; all prepaid items, including required premiums for flood and hazard insurance, reserve deposits for insurance, ad valorem taxes and special governmental assessments; final compliance inspection; courier fee; repair inspection; underwriting fee; wire transfer fee; expenses incident to any loan; and other expenses payable by Buyer under this contract.

B. Buyer shall pay Private Mortgage Insurance Premium (PMI), VA Loan Funding Fee, or FHA Mortgage Insurance Premium (MIP) as required by the lender.

C. If any expense exceeds an amount expressly stated in this contract for such expense to be paid by a party, that party may terminate this contract unless the other party agrees to pay such excess. Buyer may not pay charges and fees expressly prohibited by FHA, VA, Texas Veterans Housing Assistance Program or other governmental loan program regulations.

FIGURE 6.15

TREC 40-3

12-10-07

EQUAL HOUSING OPPORTUNITY

PROMULGATED BY THE TEXAS REAL ESTATE COMMISSION (TREC)

THIRD PARTY FINANCING CONDITION ADDENDUM

TO CONTRACT CONCERNING THE PROPERTY AT

____

(Street Address and City)

Buyer shall apply promptly for all financing described below and make every reasonable effort to obtain approval for the financing (Financing Approval). Buyer shall furnish all information and documents required by lender for Financing Approval. Financing Approval will be deemed to have been obtained when (1) the terms of the loan(s) described below are available and (2) lender determines that Buyer has satisfied all of lender's financial requirements (those items relating to Buyer's assets, income and credit history). If Buyer cannot obtain Financing Approval, Buyer may give written notice to Seller within 15 days after the effective date of this contract and this contract will terminate and the earnest money will be refunded to Buyer. **If Buyer does not give such notice within the time required, this contract will no longer be subject to Financing Approval. Time is of the essence for this paragraph and strict compliance with the time for performance is required.**

NOTE: Financing Approval does not include approval of lender's underwriting requirements for the Property, as specified in Paragraph 4.A.(1) of the contract.

Each note must be secured by vendor's and deed of trust liens.

CHECK APPLICABLE BOXES:

☐ A. CONVENTIONAL FINANCING:

☒ (1) A first mortgage loan in the principal amount of $ 348,000 (excluding any financed PMI premium), due in full in 30 year(s), with interest not to exceed 6.25 % per annum for the first 30 year(s) of the loan with Loan Fees (loan origination, discount, buy-down, and commitment fees) not to exceed 1 % of the loan.

☒ (2) A second mortgage loan in the principal amount of $ 43,500 (excluding any financed PMI premium), due in full in 15 year(s), with interest not to exceed 7.5 % per annum for the first 15 year(s) of the loan with Loan Fees (loan origination, discount, buy-down, and commitment fees) not to exceed 1 % of the loan.

☐ B. TEXAS VETERANS LOAN: A loan(s) from the Texas Veterans Land Board of $ n/a for a period in the total amount of n/a years at the interest rate established by the Texas Veterans Land Board.

☐ C. FHA INSURED FINANCING: A Section n/a FHA insured loan of not less than $ n/a (excluding any financed MIP), amortizable monthly for not less than n/a years, with interest not to exceed n/a % per annum for the first n/a year(s) of the loan with Loan Fees (loan origination, discount, buy-down, and commitment fees) not to exceed n/a % of the loan. As required by HUD-FHA, if FHA valuation is unknown, "*It is expressly agreed that, notwithstanding any other provision of this contract, the purchaser (Buyer) shall not be obligated to complete the purchase of the Property described herein or to incur any penalty by forfeiture of earnest money deposits or otherwise unless the purchaser (Buyer) has been given in accordance with HUD/FHA or VA requirements a written statement issued by the Federal Housing Commissioner, Department of Veterans Affairs, or a Direct Endorsement Lender setting forth the appraised value of the Property of not less than $ n/a . The purchaser (Buyer) shall have the privilege and option of proceeding with consummation of the contract without regard to the amount of the*

Initialed for identification by Buyer____ ____ and Seller____ ____ TREC NO. 40-3

FIGURE 6.15 (CONTINUED)

TREC 40-3

Third Party Financing Condition Addendum Concerning   Page 2 of 2 12-10-07

____
(Address of Property)

appraised valuation. The appraised valuation is arrived at to determine the maximum mortgage the Department of Housing and Urban Development will insure. HUD does not warrant the value or the condition of the Property. The purchaser (Buyer) should satisfy himself/herself that the price and the condition of the Property are acceptable."
NOTE: HUD 92564-CN "For Your Protection: Get a Home Inspection" must be attached to this Addendum.

❑ D. VA GUARANTEED FINANCING: A VA guaranteed loan of not less than $__n/a__ (excluding any financed Funding Fee), amortizable monthly for not less than __n/a__ years, with interest not to exceed __n/a__% per annum for the first __n/a__ year(s) of the loan with Loan Fees (loan origination, discount, buy-down, and commitment fees) not to exceed __n/a__% of the loan.

VA NOTICE TO BUYER: "*It is expressly agreed that, notwithstanding any other provisions of this contract, the Buyer shall not incur any penalty by forfeiture of earnest money or otherwise or be obligated to complete the purchase of the Property described herein, if the contract purchase price or cost exceeds the reasonable value of the Property established by the Department of Veterans Affairs. The Buyer shall, however, have the privilege and option of proceeding with the consummation of this contract without regard to the amount of the reasonable value established by the Department of Veterans Affairs."*

If Buyer elects to complete the purchase at an amount in excess of the reasonable value established by VA, Buyer shall pay such excess amount in cash from a source which Buyer agrees to disclose to the VA and which Buyer represents will not be from borrowed funds except as approved by VA. If VA reasonable value of the Property is less than the Sales Price, Seller may reduce the Sales Price to an amount equal to the VA reasonable value and the sale will be closed at the lower Sales Price with proportionate adjustments to the down payment and the loan amount.

Buyer hereby authorizes any lender to furnish to the Seller or Buyer or their representatives information relating only to the status of Financing Approval of Buyer.

______________________ ______________________
Buyer   Seller

______________________ ______________________
Buyer   Seller

This form has been approved by the Texas Real Estate Commission for use with similarly approved or promulgated contract forms. Such approval relates to this form only. TREC forms are intended for use only by trained real estate licensees. No representation is made as to the legal validity or adequacy of any provision in any specific transactions. It is not intended for complex transactions. Texas Real Estate Commission, P.O. Box 12188, Austin, TX 78711-2188, 1-800-250-8732 or (512) 459-6544 (http://www.trec.state.tx.us) TREC No. 40-3. This form replaces TREC No. 40-2.

TREC NO. 40-3

SCENARIO 5: FHA 203(B) INSURED FINANCING

Manuel Moritz and his wife, Estella Moritz, are first-time Buyers with limited funds who want to obtain an FHA 203(b) loan. They want to buy the Property owned by Barbara Johnson, who owns it as her separate Property.

Ms. Johnson is asking $118,500, but the Moritzes offer $115,000, which is accepted. They will apply for the FHA-insured loan within 5 days after the date of the contract and anticipate that they can get financing approval within 40 days after the effective date of the contract. Knowing that the Seller will get her money at closing, the Moritzes request possession at closing. They will pay the minimum down and ask the Seller to contribute $1,200 toward their closing expenses in addition to the $750 that FHA prohibits the borrower from paying.

By using an FHA 203(b) insured loan, the Moritzes will be able to move in with minimal cash up front. They can obtain a 30-year fixed rate loan at 5.75 percent annual interest.

The Buyers will pay the 1 point origination fee and 1 discount point. (See Figure 6.16, Figure 6.17, Figure 6.18, and Figure 6.19.)

Scenario 5

FIGURE 6.16

TREC 20-7 Paragraph 3

3. SALES PRICE:

A. Cash portion of Sales Price payable by Buyer at closing.................. $ 2,600

B. Sum of all financing described below (excluding any loan funding fee or mortgage insurance premium).. $ 112,400

C. Sales Price (Sum of A and B).. $ 115,000

1200
\+ 750
1950

FIGURE 6.17

TREC 20-7 Paragraph 4

4. FINANCING: The portion of Sales Price not payable in cash will be paid as follows: (Check applicable boxes below)

☒ A. THIRD PARTY FINANCING: One or more third party mortgage loans in the total amount of $ 112,400 (excluding any loan funding fee or mortgage insurance premium).

(1) Property Approval: If the Property does not satisfy the lenders' underwriting requirements for the loan(s), this contract will terminate and the earnest money will be refunded to Buyer.

(2) Financing Approval: (Check one box only)

☒ (a) This contract is subject to Buyer being approved for the financing described in the attached Third Party Financing Condition Addendum.

☐ (b) This contract is not subject to Buyer being approved for financing and does not involve FHA or VA financing.

☐ B. ASSUMPTION: The assumption of the unpaid principal balance of one or more promissory notes described in the attached TREC Loan Assumption Addendum.

☐ C. SELLER FINANCING: A promissory note from Buyer to Seller of $ n/a, secured by vendor's and deed of trust liens, and containing the terms and conditions described in the attached TREC Seller Financing Addendum. If an owner policy of title insurance is furnished, Buyer shall furnish Seller with a mortgagee policy of title insurance.

FIGURE 6.18

TREC 20-7 Paragraph 12

12. SETTLEMENT AND OTHER EXPENSES:

A. The following expenses must be paid at or prior to closing:

(1) Expenses payable by Seller (Seller's Expenses):

(a) Releases of existing liens, including prepayment penalties and recording fees; release of Seller's loan liability; tax statements or certificates; preparation of deed; one-half of escrow fee; and other expenses payable by Seller under this contract.

(b) Seller shall also pay an amount not to exceed $ 1950 to be applied in the following order: Buyer's Expenses which Buyer is prohibited from paying by FHA, VA, Texas Veterans Housing Assistance Program or other governmental loan programs, and then to other Buyer's Expenses as allowed by the lender.

(2) Expenses payable by Buyer (Buyer's Expenses):

(a) Loan origination, discount, buy-down, and commitment fees (Loan Fees).

(b) Appraisal fees; loan application fees; credit reports; preparation of loan documents; interest on the notes from date of disbursement to one month prior to dates of first monthly payments; recording fees; copies of easements and restrictions; mortgagee title policy with endorsements required by lender; loan-related inspection fees; photos; amortization schedules; one-half of escrow fee; all prepaid items, including required premiums for flood and hazard insurance, reserve deposits for insurance, ad valorem taxes and special governmental assessments; final compliance inspection; courier fee; repair inspection; underwriting fee; wire transfer fee; expenses incident to any loan; and other expenses payable by Buyer under this contract.

B. Buyer shall pay Private Mortgage Insurance Premium (PMI), VA Loan Funding Fee, or FHA Mortgage Insurance Premium (MIP) as required by the lender.

C. If any expense exceeds an amount expressly stated in this contract for such expense to be paid by a party, that party may terminate this contract unless the other party agrees to pay such excess. Buyer may not pay charges and fees expressly prohibited by FHA, VA, Texas Veterans Housing Assistance Program or other governmental loan program regulations.

FIGURE 6.19

TREC 40-3

12-10-07

EQUAL HOUSING OPPORTUNITY

PROMULGATED BY THE TEXAS REAL ESTATE COMMISSION (TREC)

THIRD PARTY FINANCING CONDITION ADDENDUM

TO CONTRACT CONCERNING THE PROPERTY AT

____

(Street Address and City)

Buyer shall apply promptly for all financing described below and make every reasonable effort to obtain approval for the financing (Financing Approval). Buyer shall furnish all information and documents required by lender for Financing Approval. Financing Approval will be deemed to have been obtained when (1) the terms of the loan(s) described below are available and (2) lender determines that Buyer has satisfied all of lender's financial requirements (those items relating to Buyer's assets, income and credit history). If Buyer cannot obtain Financing Approval, Buyer may give written notice to Seller within 20 days after the effective date of this contract and this contract will terminate and the earnest money will be refunded to Buyer. **If Buyer does not give such notice within the time required, this contract will no longer be subject to Financing Approval. Time is of the essence for this paragraph and strict compliance with the time for performance is required.**

NOTE: Financing Approval does not include approval of lender's underwriting requirements for the Property, as specified in Paragraph 4.A.(1) of the contract.

Each note must be secured by vendor's and deed of trust liens.

CHECK APPLICABLE BOXES:

☐ A. CONVENTIONAL FINANCING:

☐ (1) A first mortgage loan in the principal amount of $ n/a (excluding any financed PMI premium), due in full in n/a year(s), with interest not to exceed n/a % per annum for the first n/a year(s) of the loan with Loan Fees (loan origination, discount, buy-down, and commitment fees) not to exceed n/a % of the loan.

☐ (2) A second mortgage loan in the principal amount of $ n/a (excluding any financed PMI premium), due in full in n/a year(s), with interest not to exceed n/a % per annum for the first n/a year(s) of the loan with Loan Fees (loan origination, discount, buy-down, and commitment fees) not to exceed n/a % of the loan.

☐ B. TEXAS VETERANS LOAN: A loan(s) from the Texas Veterans Land Board of $ n/a for a period in the total amount of n/a years at the interest rate established by the Texas Veterans Land Board.

☒ C. FHA INSURED FINANCING: A Section 203(b) FHA insured loan of not less than $ 112,400 (excluding any financed MIP), amortizable monthly for not less than 30 years, with interest not to exceed 5.75 % per annum for the first 30 year(s) of the loan with Loan Fees (loan origination, discount, buy-down, and commitment fees) not to exceed 2 % of the loan. As required by HUD-FHA, if FHA valuation is unknown, "*It is expressly agreed that, notwithstanding any other provision of this contract, the purchaser (Buyer) shall not be obligated to complete the purchase of the Property described herein or to incur any penalty by forfeiture of earnest money deposits or otherwise unless the purchaser (Buyer) has been given in accordance with HUD/FHA or VA requirements a written statement issued by the Federal Housing Commissioner, Department of Veterans Affairs, or a Direct Endorsement Lender setting forth the appraised value of the Property of not less than $ 115,000. The purchaser (Buyer) shall have the privilege and option of proceeding with consummation of the contract without regard to the amount of the*

FIGURE 6.19 (CONTINUED)

TREC 40-3

____
(Address of Property)

appraised valuation. The appraised valuation is arrived at to determine the maximum mortgage the Department of Housing and Urban Development will insure. HUD does not warrant the value or the condition of the Property. The purchaser (Buyer) should satisfy himself/herself that the price and the condition of the Property are acceptable."

NOTE: HUD 92564-CN "For Your Protection: Get a Home Inspection" must be attached to this Addendum.

☐ D. VA GUARANTEED FINANCING: A VA guaranteed loan of not less than $___n/a___ (excluding any financed Funding Fee), amortizable monthly for not less than__n/a__years, with interest not to exceed__n/a__% per annum for the first __n/a__year(s) of the loan with Loan Fees (loan origination, discount, buy-down, and commitment fees) not to exceed __n/a__% of the loan.

VA NOTICE TO BUYER: *"It is expressly agreed that, notwithstanding any other provisions of this contract, the Buyer shall not incur any penalty by forfeiture of earnest money or otherwise or be obligated to complete the purchase of the Property described herein, if the contract purchase price or cost exceeds the reasonable value of the Property established by the Department of Veterans Affairs. The Buyer shall, however, have the privilege and option of proceeding with the consummation of this contract without regard to the amount of the reasonable value established by the Department of Veterans Affairs."*

If Buyer elects to complete the purchase at an amount in excess of the reasonable value established by VA, Buyer shall pay such excess amount in cash from a source which Buyer agrees to disclose to the VA and which Buyer represents will not be from borrowed funds except as approved by VA. If VA reasonable value of the Property is less than the Sales Price, Seller may reduce the Sales Price to an amount equal to the VA reasonable value and the sale will be closed at the lower Sales Price with proportionate adjustments to the down payment and the loan amount.

Buyer hereby authorizes any lender to furnish to the Seller or Buyer or their representatives information relating only to the status of Financing Approval of Buyer.

____________________	____________________
Buyer	Seller
____________________	____________________
Buyer	Seller

This form has been approved by the Texas Real Estate Commission for use with similarly approved or promulgated contract forms. Such approval relates to this form only. TREC forms are intended for use only by trained real estate licensees. No representation is made as to the legal validity or adequacy of any provision in any specific transactions. It is not intended for complex transactions. Texas Real Estate Commission, P.O. Box 12188, Austin, TX 78711-2188, 1-800-250-8732 or (512) 459-6544 (http://www.trec.state.tx.us) TREC No. 40-3. This form replaces TREC No. 40-2.

SCENARIO 6: VA-GUARANTEED FINANCING

Freddie Finkle, an unmarried man, has listed his home at 2365 Veterans Boulevard for sale with Friendly Agent Company.

Because they plan to use VA-guaranteed financing, the Buyers anticipate that they will be required to pay a 1 point origination fee. The Sellers will pay an amount not to exceed $1,100 toward the Buyer's nonallowable costs.

The Buyers are willing to pay $78,000 for the Property The Buyers have full entitlement. The Buyers have decided to borrow only $62,400 in order to keep the payments at a comfortable level. The Buyers anticipate that they can get financing approval within 30 days. They can obtain a 30-year fixed-rate loan at 7.25 percent annual interest rate. (See Figure 6.20, Figure 6.21, Figure 6.22, and Figure 6.23.)

Scenario 6

FIGURE 6.20

TREC 20-7 Paragraph 3

3. SALES PRICE:

A. Cash portion of Sales Price payable by Buyer at closing .... $ 15,600

B. Sum of all financing described below (excluding any loan funding fee or mortgage insurance premium).. $ 62,400

C. Sales Price (Sum of A and B).. $ 78,000

FIGURE 6.21

TREC 20-7 Paragraph 4

4. FINANCING: The portion of Sales Price not payable in cash will be paid as follows: (Check applicable boxes below)

☐ A. THIRD PARTY FINANCING: One or more third party mortgage loans in the total amount of $ 62,400 (excluding any loan funding fee or mortgage insurance premium).

(1) Property Approval: If the Property does not satisfy the lenders' underwriting requirements for the loan(s), this contract will terminate and the earnest money will be refunded to Buyer.

(2) Financing Approval: (Check one box only)

☐ (a) This contract is subject to Buyer being approved for the financing described in the attached Third Party Financing Condition Addendum.

☐ (b) This contract is not subject to Buyer being approved for financing and does not involve FHA or VA financing.

☐ B. ASSUMPTION: The assumption of the unpaid principal balance of one or more promissory notes described in the attached TREC Loan Assumption Addendum.

☐ C. SELLER FINANCING: A promissory note from Buyer to Seller of $ n/a, secured by vendor's and deed of trust liens, and containing the terms and conditions described in the attached TREC Seller Financing Addendum. If an owner policy of title insurance is furnished, Buyer shall furnish Seller with a mortgagee policy of title insurance.

FIGURE 6.22

TREC 20-7 Paragraph 12

12. SETTLEMENT AND OTHER EXPENSES:

A. The following expenses must be paid at or prior to closing:

(1) Expenses payable by Seller (Seller's Expenses):

(a) Releases of existing liens, including prepayment penalties and recording fees; release of Seller's loan liability; tax statements or certificates; preparation of deed; one-half of escrow fee; and other expenses payable by Seller under this contract.

(b) Seller shall also pay an amount not to exceed $ ___n/a___ to be applied in the following order: Buyer's Expenses which Buyer is prohibited from paying by FHA, VA, Texas Veterans Housing Assistance Program or other governmental loan programs, and then to other Buyer's Expenses as allowed by the lender.

(2) Expenses payable by Buyer (Buyer's Expenses):

(a) Loan origination, discount, buy-down, and commitment fees (Loan Fees).

(b) Appraisal fees; loan application fees; credit reports; preparation of loan documents; interest on the notes from date of disbursement to one month prior to dates of first monthly payments; recording fees; copies of easements and restrictions; mortgagee title policy with endorsements required by lender; loan-related inspection fees; photos; amortization schedules; one-half of escrow fee; all prepaid items, including required premiums for flood and hazard insurance, reserve deposits for insurance, ad valorem taxes and special governmental assessments; final compliance inspection; courier fee; repair inspection; underwriting fee; wire transfer fee; expenses incident to any loan; and other expenses payable by Buyer under this contract.

B. Buyer shall pay Private Mortgage Insurance Premium (PMI), VA Loan Funding Fee, or FHA Mortgage Insurance Premium (MIP) as required by the lender.

C. If any expense exceeds an amount expressly stated in this contract for such expense to be paid by a party, that party may terminate this contract unless the other party agrees to pay such excess. Buyer may not pay charges and fees expressly prohibited by FHA, VA, Texas Veterans Housing Assistance Program or other governmental loan program regulations.

FIGURE 6.23

TREC 40-3

12-10-07

EQUAL HOUSING OPPORTUNITY

PROMULGATED BY THE TEXAS REAL ESTATE COMMISSION (TREC)

THIRD PARTY FINANCING CONDITION ADDENDUM

TO CONTRACT CONCERNING THE PROPERTY AT

____

(Street Address and City)

Buyer shall apply promptly for all financing described below and make every reasonable effort to obtain approval for the financing (Financing Approval). Buyer shall furnish all information and documents required by lender for Financing Approval. Financing Approval will be deemed to have been obtained when (1) the terms of the loan(s) described below are available and (2) lender determines that Buyer has satisfied all of lender's financial requirements (those items relating to Buyer's assets, income and credit history). If Buyer cannot obtain Financing Approval, Buyer may give written notice to Seller within 30 days after the effective date of this contract and this contract will terminate and the earnest money will be refunded to Buyer. **If Buyer does not give such notice within the time required, this contract will no longer be subject to Financing Approval. Time is of the essence for this paragraph and strict compliance with the time for performance is required.**

NOTE: Financing Approval does not include approval of lender's underwriting requirements for the Property, as specified in Paragraph 4.A.(1) of the contract.

Each note must be secured by vendor's and deed of trust liens.

CHECK APPLICABLE BOXES:

☐ A. CONVENTIONAL FINANCING:

☐ (1) A first mortgage loan in the principal amount of $ n/a (excluding any financed PMI premium), due in full in n/a year(s), with interest not to exceed n/a % per annum for the first n/a year(s) of the loan with Loan Fees (loan origination, discount, buy-down, and commitment fees) not to exceed n/a % of the loan.

☐ (2) A second mortgage loan in the principal amount of $ n/a (excluding any financed PMI premium), due in full in n/a year(s), with interest not to exceed n/a % per annum for the first n/a year(s) of the loan with Loan Fees (loan origination, discount, buy-down, and commitment fees) not to exceed n/a % of the loan.

☐ B. TEXAS VETERANS LOAN: A loan(s) from the Texas Veterans Land Board of $ n/a for a period in the total amount of n/a years at the interest rate established by the Texas Veterans Land Board.

☐ C. FHA INSURED FINANCING: A Section n/a FHA insured loan of not less than $ n/a (excluding any financed MIP), amortizable monthly for not less than n/a years, with interest not to exceed n/a % per annum for the first n/a year(s) of the loan with Loan Fees (loan origination, discount, buy-down, and commitment fees) not to exceed n/a % of the loan. As required by HUD-FHA, if FHA valuation is unknown, *"It is expressly agreed that, notwithstanding any other provision of this contract, the purchaser (Buyer) shall not be obligated to complete the purchase of the Property described herein or to incur any penalty by forfeiture of earnest money deposits or otherwise unless the purchaser (Buyer) has been given in accordance with HUD/FHA or VA requirements a written statement issued by the Federal Housing Commissioner, Department of Veterans Affairs, or a Direct Endorsement Lender setting forth the appraised value of the Property of not less than $ n/a . The purchaser (Buyer) shall have the privilege and option of proceeding with consummation of the contract without regard to the amount of the*

Initialed for identification by Buyer____ _____ and Seller_____ _____ TREC NO. 40-3

FIGURE 6.23 (CONTINUED)

TREC 40-3

Third Party Financing Condition Addendum Concerning   Page 2 of 2 12-10-07

____
(Address of Property)

appraised valuation. The appraised valuation is arrived at to determine the maximum mortgage the Department of Housing and Urban Development will insure. HUD does not warrant the value or the condition of the Property. The purchaser (Buyer) should satisfy himself/herself that the price and the condition of the Property are acceptable."
NOTE: HUD 92564-CN "For Your Protection: Get a Home Inspection" must be attached to this Addendum.

☒ D. VA GUARANTEED FINANCING: A VA guaranteed loan of not less than $102,400 (excluding any financed Funding Fee), amortizable monthly for not less than 30 years, with interest not to exceed 7.25 % per annum for the first 30 year(s) of the loan with Loan Fees (loan origination, discount, buy-down, and commitment fees) not to exceed 1 % of the loan.

VA NOTICE TO BUYER: "*It is expressly agreed that, notwithstanding any other provisions of this contract, the Buyer shall not incur any penalty by forfeiture of earnest money or otherwise or be obligated to complete the purchase of the Property described herein, if the contract purchase price or cost exceeds the reasonable value of the Property established by the Department of Veterans Affairs. The Buyer shall, however, have the privilege and option of proceeding with the consummation of this contract without regard to the amount of the reasonable value established by the Department of Veterans Affairs."*

If Buyer elects to complete the purchase at an amount in excess of the reasonable value established by VA, Buyer shall pay such excess amount in cash from a source which Buyer agrees to disclose to the VA and which Buyer represents will not be from borrowed funds except as approved by VA. If VA reasonable value of the Property is less than the Sales Price, Seller may reduce the Sales Price to an amount equal to the VA reasonable value and the sale will be closed at the lower Sales Price with proportionate adjustments to the down payment and the loan amount.

Buyer hereby authorizes any lender to furnish to the Seller or Buyer or their representatives information relating only to the status of Financing Approval of Buyer.

Buyer	Seller
Buyer	Seller

This form has been approved by the Texas Real Estate Commission for use with similarly approved or promulgated contract forms. Such approval relates to this form only. TREC forms are intended for use only by trained real estate licensees. No representation is made as to the legal validity or adequacy of any provision in any specific transactions. It is not intended for complex transactions. Texas Real Estate Commission, P.O. Box 12188, Austin, TX 78711-2188, 1-800-250-8732 or (512) 459-6544 (http://www.trec.state.tx.us) TREC No. 40-3. This form replaces TREC No. 40-2.

TREC NO. 40-3

■ SCENARIO 7: ASSUMPTION WITH SELLER SECOND FINANCING

The Sellers are offering their duplex for sale and asking $158,000. It is currently financed with a VA-guaranteed loan with an outstanding balance of $100,000. The loan is at 5.75 percent annual interest. The Sellers are willing to carry back a second mortgage for $30,000 at 7 percent annual interest with payments due and payable on the first day of each month during the period of indebtedness. They want a Buyer to pay principal payments of $500 per month plus interest to liquidate the loan in 60 months. An escrow account is required unless paid to a first lienholder.

The Sellers have no desire to purchase another Property using VA-guaranteed financing and will not seek a restoration of entitlement.

The Buyer finds this a very attractive opportunity and offers the Sellers the asking price. The Buyer will assume the existing note, ask the Sellers to carry back a second mortgage on the terms specified, and pay the difference in cash. Although the Buyer believes that the transfer fee will be one-half of a point, the Buyer writes the offer for a 1 point transfer fee just to be safe. The Seller does want to reserve the right to approve any assumptor for the lien being carried by the Seller.

The Buyer will provide a credit report, verification of employment, verification of the cash funds on deposit at the bank, and a personal financial statement within three days after the effective date of the contract.

The loan being assumed is owned by Ginnie Mae with current monthly payments of $786 being paid to Chase Manhattan Mortgage Company. Any difference in the unpaid principal balance at closing will cause an adjustment to be made to the cash payable at closing. (See Figure 6.24, Figure 6.25, Figure 6.26, Figure 6.27, and Figure 6.28.)

Scenario 7

FIGURE 6.24

TREC 20-7 Paragraph 3

3. SALES PRICE:

A. Cash portion of Sales Price payable by Buyer at closing .... $ 28,000

B. Sum of all financing described below (excluding any loan funding fee or mortgage insurance premium).. $ 130,000

C. Sales Price (Sum of A and B)... $ 158,000

FIGURE 6.25

TREC 20-7 Paragraph 4

4. FINANCING: The portion of Sales Price not payable in cash will be paid as follows: (Check applicable boxes below)

❑ A. THIRD PARTY FINANCING: One or more third party mortgage loans in the total amount of $ n/a (excluding any loan funding fee or mortgage insurance premium).

(1) Property Approval: If the Property does not satisfy the lenders' underwriting requirements for the loan(s), this contract will terminate and the earnest money will be refunded to Buyer.

(2) Financing Approval: (Check one box only)

❑ (a) This contract is subject to Buyer being approved for the financing described in the attached Third Party Financing Condition Addendum.

❑ (b) This contract is not subject to Buyer being approved for financing and does not involve FHA or VA financing.

☒ B. ASSUMPTION: The assumption of the unpaid principal balance of one or more promissory notes described in the attached TREC Loan Assumption Addendum.

☒ C. SELLER FINANCING: A promissory note from Buyer to Seller of $ 30,000, secured by vendor's and deed of trust liens, and containing the terms and conditions described in the attached TREC Seller Financing Addendum. If an owner policy of title insurance is furnished, Buyer shall furnish Seller with a mortgagee policy of title insurance.

FIGURE 6.26

TREC 20-7 Paragraph 12

12. SETTLEMENT AND OTHER EXPENSES:

A. The following expenses must be paid at or prior to closing:

(1) Expenses payable by Seller (Seller's Expenses):

(a) Releases of existing liens, including prepayment penalties and recording fees; release of Seller's loan liability; tax statements or certificates; preparation of deed; one-half of escrow fee; and other expenses payable by Seller under this contract.

(b) Seller shall also pay an amount not to exceed $ n/a to be applied in the following order: Buyer's Expenses which Buyer is prohibited from paying by FHA, VA, Texas Veterans Housing Assistance Program or other governmental loan programs, and then to other Buyer's Expenses as allowed by the lender.

(2) Expenses payable by Buyer (Buyer's Expenses):

(a) Loan origination, discount, buy-down, and commitment fees (Loan Fees).

(b) Appraisal fees; loan application fees; credit reports; preparation of loan documents; interest on the notes from date of disbursement to one month prior to dates of first monthly payments; recording fees; copies of easements and restrictions; mortgagee title policy with endorsements required by lender; loan-related inspection fees; photos; amortization schedules; one-half of escrow fee; all prepaid items, including required premiums for flood and hazard insurance, reserve deposits for insurance, ad valorem taxes and special governmental assessments; final compliance inspection; courier fee; repair inspection; underwriting fee; wire transfer fee; expenses incident to any loan; and other expenses payable by Buyer under this contract.

B. Buyer shall pay Private Mortgage Insurance Premium (PMI), VA Loan Funding Fee, or FHA Mortgage Insurance Premium (MIP) as required by the lender.

C. If any expense exceeds an amount expressly stated in this contract for such expense to be paid by a party, that party may terminate this contract unless the other party agrees to pay such excess. Buyer may not pay charges and fees expressly prohibited by FHA, VA, Texas Veterans Housing Assistance Program or other governmental loan program regulations.

FIGURE 6.27

TREC 26-5

PROMULGATED BY THE TEXAS REAL ESTATE COMMISSION (TREC) 12-04-06

EQUAL HOUSING OPPORTUNITY

SELLER FINANCING ADDENDUM

TO CONTRACT CONCERNING THE PROPERTY AT

____

(Address of Property)

A. CREDIT DOCUMENTATION. To establish Buyer's creditworthiness, Buyer shall deliver to Seller within__3__days after the effective date of this contract, ☒ credit report ☒ verification of employment, including salary ☒ verification of funds on deposit in financial institutions ☒ current financial statement and ☐ __n/a_______________________________________. Buyer hereby authorizes any credit reporting agency to furnish copies of Buyer's credit reports to Seller at Buyer's sole expense.

B. CREDIT APPROVAL. If the credit documentation described in Paragraph A is not delivered within the specified time, Seller may terminate this contract by notice to Buyer within 7 days after expiration of the time for delivery, and the earnest money will be paid to Seller. If the credit documentation is timely delivered, and Seller determines in Seller's sole discretion that Buyer's credit is unacceptable, Seller may terminate this contract by notice to Buyer within 7 days after expiration of the time for delivery and the earnest money will be refunded to Buyer. If Seller does not terminate this contract, Seller will be deemed to have approved Buyer's creditworthiness.

C. PROMISSORY NOTE. The promissory note (Note) described in Paragraph 4 of this contract payable by Buyer to the order of Seller will bear interest at the rate of __7__% per annum and be payable at the place designated by Seller. Buyer may prepay the Note in whole or in part at any time without penalty. Any prepayments are to be applied to the payment of the installments of principal last maturing and interest will immediately cease on the prepaid principal. The Note will contain a provision for payment of a late fee of 5% of any installment not paid within 10 days of the due date. Matured unpaid amounts will bear interest at the rate of 1½% per month or at the highest lawful rate, whichever is less. The Note will be payable as follows:

☐ (1) In one payment due __n/a____________________ after the date of the Note with interest payable ☐ at maturity ☐ monthly ☐ quarterly. (check one box only)

☒ (2) In monthly installments of $ __500______ ☐ including interest ☒ plus interest (check one box only) beginning __first of the month__ after the date of the Note and continuing monthly thereafter for__60_____ months when the balance of the Note will be due and payable.

☐ (3) Interest only in monthly installments for the first __n/a____ month(s) and thereafter in installments of $__n/a______ ☐ including interest ☐ plus interest (check one box only) beginning __n/a_______ after the date of the Note and continuing monthly thereafter for __n/a__ months when the balance of the Note will be due and payable.

D. DEED OF TRUST. The deed of trust securing the Note will provide for the following:

(1) PROPERTY TRANSFERS: (check one box only)

☐ (a) Consent Not Required: The Property may be sold, conveyed or leased without the consent of Seller, provided any subsequent buyer assumes the Note.

☒ (b) Consent Required: If all or any part of the Property is sold, conveyed, leased for a period longer than 3 years, leased with an option to purchase, or otherwise sold (including any contract for deed), without Seller's prior written consent, which consent may be withheld in Seller's sole discretion, Seller may declare the balance of the Note

FIGURE 6.27 (CONTINUED)

TREC 26-5

Seller Financing Addendum Concerning Page 2 of 2 12-04-06

____
(Address of Property)

to be immediately due and payable. The creation of a subordinate lien, any conveyance under threat or order of condemnation, any deed solely between buyers, or the passage of title by reason of the death of a buyer or by operation of law will not entitle Seller to exercise the remedies provided in this paragraph.

NOTE: *Under (a) or (b), Buyer's liability to pay the Note will continue unless Buyer obtains a release of liability from Seller.*

(2) TAX AND INSURANCE ESCROW: (check one box only)

☐ (a) Escrow Not Required: Buyer shall furnish Seller, before each year's ad valorem taxes become delinquent, evidence that all ad valorem taxes on the Property have been paid. Buyer shall annually furnish Seller evidence of paid-up casualty insurance naming Seller as a mortgagee loss payee.

☒ (b) Escrow Required: With each installment Buyer shall deposit in escrow with Seller a pro rata part of the estimated annual ad valorem taxes and casualty insurance premiums for the Property. Buyer shall pay any deficiency within 30 days after notice from Seller. Buyer's failure to pay the deficiency will be a default under the deed of trust. Buyer is not required to deposit any escrow payments for taxes and insurance that are deposited with a superior lienholder. The casualty insurance must name Seller as a mortgagee loss payee.

(3) PRIOR LIENS: Any default under any lien superior to the lien securing the Note will be a default under the deed of trust securing the Note.

____________________ Buyer	____________________ Seller
____________________ Buyer	____________________ Seller

The form of this contract has been approved by the Texas Real Estate Commission for use with similarly approved or promulgated contract forms. TREC forms are intended for use only by trained real estate licensees. No representation is made as to the legal validity or adequacy of any provision in any specific transactions. It is not intended for complex transactions. Texas Real Estate Commission, P.O. Box 12188, Austin, TX 78711-2188, 1-800-250-8732 or (512) 459-6544 (http://www.trec.state.tx.us) TREC No. 26-5. This form replaces TREC No. 26-4.

TREC NO. 26-5

FIGURE 6.28

TREC 41-1

PROMULGATED BY THE TEXAS REAL ESTATE COMMISSION (TREC) 04-23-07

EQUAL HOUSING OPPORTUNITY

LOAN ASSUMPTION ADDENDUM
TO CONTRACT CONCERNING THE PROPERTY AT

____
(Address of Property)

A. CREDIT DOCUMENTATION. To establish Buyer's creditworthiness, Buyer shall deliver to Seller within 3 days after the effective date of this contract ☒ credit report ☒ verification of employment, including salary ☒ verification of funds on deposit in financial institutions ☒ current financial statement and ☐ n/a.
Buyer hereby authorizes any credit reporting agency to furnish copies of Buyer's credit reports to Seller at Buyer's sole expense.

B. CREDIT APPROVAL. If the credit documentation described in Paragraph A is not delivered within the specified time, Seller may terminate this contract by notice to Buyer within 7 days after expiration of the time for delivery, and the earnest money will be paid to Seller. If the credit documentation is timely delivered, and Seller determines in Seller's sole discretion that Buyer's credit is unacceptable, Seller may terminate this contract by notice to Buyer within 7 days after expiration of the time for delivery and the earnest money will be refunded to Buyer. If Seller does not terminate this contract within the time specified, Seller will be deemed to have approved Buyer's creditworthiness.

C. ASSUMPTION. Buyer's assumption of an existing note includes all obligations imposed by the deed of trust securing the note.

☒ (1) The unpaid principal balance of a first lien promissory note payable to Chase Manhattan Mortgage Company which unpaid balance at closing will be $ 100,000. The total current monthly payment including principal, interest and any reserve deposits is $ 786. Buyer's initial payment will be the first payment due after closing.

☐ (2) The unpaid principal balance of a second lien promissory note payable to n/a n/a which unpaid balance at closing will be $ n/a. The total current monthly payment including principal, interest and any reserve deposits is $ n/a. Buyer's initial payment will be the first payment due after closing.

If the unpaid principal balance of any assumed loan as of the Closing Date varies from the loan balance stated above, the ☒ cash payable at closing ☐ Sales Price will be adjusted by the amount of any variance. If the total principal balance of all assumed loans varies in an amount greater than $500 at closing, either party may terminate this contract and the earnest money will be refunded to Buyer unless the other party elects to pay the excess of the variance.

D. LOAN ASSUMPTION TERMS. Buyer may terminate this contract and the earnest money will be refunded to Buyer if the noteholder requires:

(1) payment of an assumption fee in excess of $ n/a in C(1) or $ n/a in C(2) and Seller declines to pay such excess, or

(2) an increase in the interest rate to more than n/a % in C(1) or n/a % in C(2), or

(3) any other modification of the loan documents.

E. CONSENT BY NOTEHOLDER. If the noteholder fails to consent to the assumption of the loan, either Seller or Buyer may terminate this contract by notice to the other party and the earnest money will be refunded to the Buyer.

F. SELLER'S LIENS. Unless Seller is released from liability on any assumed note, a vendor's lien and deed of trust to secure assumption will be required. The vendor's lien will automatically be

FIGURE 6.28 (CONTINUED)

TREC 41-1

____
(Address of Property)

released on delivery of an executed release by noteholder.

G. TAX AND INSURANCE ESCROW. If noteholder maintains an escrow account for ad valorem taxes, casualty insurance premiums or mortgage insurance premiums, Seller shall transfer the escrow account to Buyer without any deficiency. Buyer shall reimburse Seller for the amount in the transferred accounts.

NOTICE TO BUYER: If you are concerned about the possibility of future adjustments, monthly payments, interest rates or other terms, do not sign the contract without examining the notes and deeds of trust.

NOTICE TO SELLER: Your liability to pay the notes assumed by Buyer will continue unless you obtain a release of liability from the noteholders. If you are concerned about future liability, you should use the TREC Release of Liability Addendum.

Buyer	Seller
Buyer	Seller

This form has been approved by the Texas Real Estate Commission for use with similarly approved or promulgated contract forms. Such approval relates to this form only. TREC forms are intended for use only by trained real estate licensees. No representation is made as to the legal validity or adequacy of any provision in any specific transactions. It is not suitable for complex transactions. Texas Real Estate Commission, P.O. Box 12188, Austin, TX 78711-2188, 1-800-250-8732 or (512) 459-6544 (http://www.trec.state.tx.us) TREC No. 41-1. This form replaces TREC No. 41-0.

HOMEWORK QUIZ

The following quiz does not have an answer key included with the answer keys in Appendix B. Students who are using this book as the basis for a correspondence course should record and submit their answers to their course provider as instructed by the provider. The student will submit his or her answers for the Homework Quiz at the end of each chapter and for each transaction in Chapter 11.

True or False?

1. In Scenario 1, you should enter the same amount in paragraph 3A, 3B, and 3C.

2. Scenario 7 requires that you check only one box in paragraph 4 and that you add two addenda to the contract.

3. For Scenario 3, you will enter $160,400 in the blank for 3B and $176,400 in the blank for 3A.

4. In Scenario 5, the correct amount to enter in 3A is $118,500.

5. In Scenario 7, the Buyer will execute both a deed of trust and a deed of trust to secure assumption at closing.

CHAPTER SEVEN

The Property

■ KEY TERMS

abstract	earnest money	survey
annexation	notices	title policy
commitment	residential service contracts	

The Property is defined and identified by its legal description in the second paragraph of the contract. In this chapter, we continue our exploration of the building blocks of purchase agreements by examining the following in the TREC Form 20-7, One to Four Family Residential Contract (Resale):

- 5. Earnest Money
- 6. Title Policy and Survey
- 7. Property Condition

Read and study the content of these contract paragraphs carefully because they account for more than 25 percent of the wording of the agreement and address issues that are the basis of the vast majority of the litigation that is brought by one of the parties against the other or against the agents. Proceed carefully!

■ EARNEST MONEY

The **earnest money** serves two purposes. *The first purpose is to show good faith and serious intent on the part of the purchaser.* Note that earnest money is not necessary to bind the contract. The promise of the purchaser to buy and the promise of the Seller to deliver title are adequate consideration to create a legally binding executory contract. A listing agent might want to suggest that the Seller ask the Buyer to show serious intent by requesting a significant earnest money deposit. Around 3 percent to 5 percent of the purchase price is ideal; however, the parties may determine that a smaller or larger amount is appropriate for their particular transaction. Remember that the final decision is in the hands of the Buyer and the Seller. (See Figure 7.1.) *The second purpose of the deposited money is to serve as liquidated damages in the event of default as addressed in the identified remedies listed in paragraph 15.*

FIGURE 7.1

TREC 20-7 Paragraph 5

5. EARNEST MONEY: Upon execution of this contract by both parties, Buyer shall deposit $______________ as earnest money with ____, as escrow agent, at ____ (address). Buyer shall deposit additional earnest money of $__________________ with escrow agent within ______ days after the effective date of this contract. If Buyer fails to deposit the earnest money as required by this contract, Buyer will be in default.

The blanks calling for additional earnest money can be used when the Buyer is unable to make the full desired deposit at the time of signing the agreement. This might occur when the Buyer is waiting for a certificate of deposit (CD) to mature and does not want to delay signing the agreement or to cash the CD in early and lose the interest on the instrument. It should be noted that failure to deposit the earnest money in a timely manner constitutes a default and gives the Seller the right to exercise the default remedies established by agreement of the parties in paragraph 15.

The Texas real estate license holder should note that the TREC rule 535.159 requires that earnest money be deposited with the escrow agent selected by the parties by the close of the second business day of the escrow agent following the signing of the agreement. When the Buyer has tendered the offer in writing, the Seller has accepted the offer by signing the contract, and the Buyer has been notified of the Seller's acceptance, an executory contract exists, and the agent or the Buyer needs to deliver the earnest money to the escrow agent named in paragraph 5 of the contract.

■ TITLE POLICY

The contract is an agreement between the Buyer and the Seller and should reflect their wishes. Usually the company selected in paragraph 6 to issue the owner's **title policy** is the same chosen in paragraph 5 to serve as escrow agent; however, it is not mandatory. It is possible to list a title agency, in paragraph 5 and a title company, in paragraph 6. (See Figure 7.2 A&B.)

Who should choose the title company? Many would argue that because the Seller usually pays for the title policy, the Seller should choose the company that will issue the policy.

FIGURE 7.2 A&B

TREC 20-7 Paragraph 6

6. TITLE POLICY AND SURVEY:

A. TITLE POLICY: Seller shall furnish to Buyer at ❑Seller's ❑Buyer's expense an owner policy of title insurance (Title Policy) issued by ______ (Title Company) in the amount of the Sales Price, dated at or after closing, insuring Buyer against loss under the provisions of the Title Policy, subject to the promulgated exclusions (including existing building and zoning ordinances) and the following exceptions:

(1) Restrictive covenants common to the platted subdivision in which the Property is located.
(2) The standard printed exception for standby fees, taxes and assessments.
(3) Liens created as part of the financing described in Paragraph 4.
(4) Utility easements created by the dedication deed or plat of the subdivision in which the Property is located.
(5) Reservations or exceptions otherwise permitted by this contract or as may be approved by Buyer in writing.
(6) The standard printed exception as to marital rights.
(7) The standard printed exception as to waters, tidelands, beaches, streams, and related matters.
(8) The standard printed exception as to discrepancies, conflicts, shortages in area or boundary lines, encroachments or protrusions, or overlapping improvements. Buyer, at Buyer's expense, may have the exception amended to read, "shortages in area".

B. COMMITMENT: Within 20 days after the Title Company receives a copy of this contract, Seller shall furnish to Buyer a commitment for title insurance (Commitment) and, at Buyer's expense, legible copies of restrictive covenants and documents evidencing exceptions in the Commitment (Exception Documents) other than the standard printed exceptions. Seller authorizes the Title Company to deliver the Commitment and Exception Documents to Buyer at Buyer's address shown in Paragraph 21. If the Commitment and Exception Documents are not delivered to Buyer within the specified time, the time for delivery will be automatically extended up to 15 days or the Closing Date, whichever is earlier.

Who pays does not and should not automatically dictate who chooses something in a real estate transaction. For example, the Buyer is usually required to pay for an appraisal when the Buyer is seeking a new loan, but it is the lender who selects the appraiser and is the client of the appraiser. When utilizing a loan guaranteed by the Department of Veterans Affairs, the government regulations require that the Seller pay the legal fees for the preparation of the note and mortgage instrument for the borrower's loan. Before a Seller or listing agent attempts to dictate the title company, it should be noted that the owner's title policy is a contract between the Buyer and the title company. Also, a review of the Real Estate Settlement Procedures Act (RESPA), covering one- to four-family residential transactions that have financing related to the federal government, reveals that federal regulation prohibits the Seller from requiring the Buyer to use the services of a particular title provider. Visit *www.HUD.gov* to locate the RESPA legislation or refer to the HUD guide, *Settlement Costs*, which is given to Buyers at the time of loan application. Why should the Seller really care? Providing the title policy is an economical way for the Seller to show evidence of clear title and indemnify the Buyer from financial loss in the event of title failure. The premium cost is the same at all title companies in the state to insure the title of the Property with the same Sales Price.

The majority of transactions closed in Texas involve the issuance of a title policy to the Buyer of the property. Local custom often calls for the owner's policy of title insurance to be furnished at the Seller's expense. This is a point to be negotiated by the parties. When the parties have come to an agreement on this matter, check the appropriate box.

License holders should let the parties choose the title company that will issue the title policy. On RESPA-covered transactions involving purchases of a one- to four-family residential property with a federally related loan, the following regulation applies.

> RESPA 2608
>
> (a) No seller of property that will be purchased with the assistance of a federally related mortgage loan shall require, directly or indirectly, as a condition to selling the property, that title insurance covering the property be purchased by the Buyer from any particular title company.
>
> (b) Any Seller who violates the provisions of subsection (a) shall be liable to the Buyer in an amount equal to three times all charges made for such title insurance.

The reader should further consider that it is the Buyer who must live with the coverage and deal with the insurance company when a title problem rears its ugly head. A Buyer who is asking the Seller to pay for the policy may be willing to permit the Seller to choose. License holders should not dictate in this area; they should always ask. The same rule should be followed in the selection of a residential service contract provider, when you get to paragraph 7H.

In addition to identifying who issues and who pays for the title policy, paragraph 6A establishes that the policy is subject to the exclusions promulgated by the state insurance board in Austin, Texas. The eight exclusions are listed on page 2 of the contract.

The standard printed exception relates to discrepancies, conflicts, and shortages in area or boundary lines. It may be amended to include only *shortages in area* by the payment of an additional 15 percent to the title insurance premium and by providing a survey acceptable to the title company. Check with the title company about the amount and identify who will pay it as an additional business detail in paragraph 11 of the contract. The additional cost is 5 percent of the title insurance premium for homestead properties and 15 percent for others.

The agreement calls for the Seller to furnish the Buyer a **commitment** for title insurance and, at the Buyer's expense, legible copies of deed restrictions and documentation of any exceptions in the commitment within 20 days after the title company receives a copy of the contract. The Seller requests that the title company mail or hand deliver the commitment to the Buyer's address shown in paragraph 21 of the contract form. The parties agree that if the title company is unable to deliver within 20 days, the time for delivery is automatically extended up to 15 days *or* the closing date, whichever is sooner. After the Buyer receives the commitment, the Buyer has some days to object in writing to any matters disclosed in the commitment. The number of days will be determined by agreement of the parties.

In 6D there is a space in which the Buyer can list anything the Buyer may want to do on the property that may be prohibited by deed restrictions, building codes, and zoning ordinances. Examples of what may be listed here include conducting a home-based business from the premises, parking a motor home or boat in the driveway, erecting a basketball net, installing a satellite dish, or erecting a ten-foot privacy fence.

SURVEY

Paragraph 6C of the contract calls for the Seller to provide an existing **survey** or for a survey to be performed by a registered professional land surveyor acceptable to the title company or any lender. The parties will select one of three choices and determine the number of days to furnish the survey or survey and Seller's affidavit. The three choices address the issues of who will provide and pay for the survey and when it will be delivered. (See Figure 7.2 C&D.)

FIGURE 7.2 C&D

TREC 20-7 Paragraph 6

C. SURVEY: The survey must be made by a registered professional land surveyor acceptable to the Title Company and any lender. (Check one box only)

❑ (1) Within ________ days after the effective date of this contract, Seller shall furnish to Buyer and Title Company Seller's existing survey of the Property and a Residential Real Property Affidavit promulgated by the Texas Department of Insurance (Affidavit). If the existing survey or Affidavit is not acceptable to Title Company or Buyer's lender, Buyer shall obtain a new survey at ❑ Seller's ❑ Buyer's expense no later than 3 days prior to Closing Date. If Seller fails to furnish the existing survey or Affidavit within the time prescribed, Buyer shall obtain a new survey at Seller's expense no later than 3 days prior to Closing Date.

❑ (2) Within _______ days after the effective date of this contract, Buyer shall obtain a new survey at Buyer's expense. Buyer is deemed to receive the survey on the date of actual receipt or the date specified in this paragraph, whichever is earlier.

❑ (3) Within _______ days after the effective date of this contract, Seller, at Seller's expense shall furnish a new survey to Buyer.

D. OBJECTIONS: Buyer may object in writing to defects, exceptions, or encumbrances to title: disclosed on the survey other than items 6A(1) through (7) above; disclosed in the Commitment other than items 6A(1) through (8) above; or which prohibit the following use or activity: ____

____.

Buyer must object not later than (i) the Closing Date or (ii) ____________ days after Buyer receives the Commitment, Exception Documents, and the survey, whichever is earlier. Buyer's failure to object within the time allowed will constitute a waiver of Buyer's right to object; except that the requirements in Schedule C of the Commitment are not waived. Provided Seller is not obligated to incur any expense, Seller shall cure the timely objections of Buyer or any third party lender within 15 days after Seller receives the objections and the Closing Date will be extended as necessary. If objections are not cured within such 15 day period, this contract will terminate and the earnest money will be refunded to Buyer unless Buyer waives the objections.

The following is the content of the affidavit promulgated by the Texas Department of Insurance as required if 6C(1) is chosen:

RESIDENTIAL REAL PROPERTY AFFIDAVIT T-47

(May be modified as Appropriate for Commercial Transactions)

Date: ________________________ GF No.________________________

Names of Affiant(s) ____

Address of Affiant: ____

Description of Property: ____

County ___________________________, Texas

Name of Title Company: ____

Before me, the undersigned notary for the state of _______________, personally appeared Affiant(s) who after by me being duly sworn, stated:

1. We are the owners of the Property. (Or state other basis for knowledge by Affiant(s) of the Property, such as lease, management, neighbor, etc. For example, "Affiant is the manager of the property for the record title owners.")
2. We are familiar with the property and the improvements located on the Property.
3. We are closing a transaction requiring title insurance and the proposed insured owner or lender has requested area and boundary coverage in the title insurance policy(ies) to be issued in this transaction. We understand that the Company may make exceptions to the coverage of the title insurance as Company may deem appropriate. We understand that the owner of the Property, if the current transaction is a sale, may request a similar amendment to the area and boundary coverage in the Owner Policy of Title Insurance upon payment of the promulgated premium.
4. To the best of our actual knowledge and belief, since ____________________, there have been no:
   a. construction projects such as new structures, additional buildings, rooms, garages, swimming pools or other permanent improvements or fixtures:
   b. changes in the location of boundary fences or boundary walls:
   c. construction projects on immediately adjoining property(ies) which encroach on the property:
   d. conveyances, replattings, easement grants and/or easement dedications (such as a utility line) by any party affecting the Property.

   EXCEPT for the following (If None, Insert "none" Below:
5. We understand that Title Company is relying on the truthfulness of the statements made in this affidavit to provide the area and boundary coverage and upon the evidence of the existing real property survey of the Property. This Affidavit is not made for the benefit of any other parties and this Affidavit does not constitute a warranty or guarantee of the location of improvements.
6. We understand that we have no liability to Title Company or the title insurance company that will Issue the policy(ies) should the information in this Affidavit be incorrect other than information that we personally know to be incorrect and which we do not disclose to the Title Company.

____

____

SWORN AND SUBSCRIBED this ________ day of_______________, 20_______

____

Notary Public

Form T-47: Residential Real Property Affidavit

SEVEN REQUIRED NOTICES

In 6E, the following seven required statutory **notices** are provided for the Buyer's careful consideration before moving ahead with the purchase of the subject Property (See Figure 7.2E):

1. The Buyer is advised to have the **abstract** examined by an attorney of the Buyer's choosing or to get title insurance. The license holder has responsibility under the provisions of the TRELA to provide this notice in writing prior to having the parties sign the purchase agreement. The TREC has made it very easy for the license holder when a promulgated form is being used. The notice must advise the Buyer to call for a title policy or obtain an abstract to be reviewed by an attorney of his choosing prior to closing the transaction and accepting title to the Property.

2. The Buyer is well advised to learn as much as possible about the restrictions, rules, assessments, and operations of any homeowners' association that may exercise control over the Property; have the power to collect mandatory assessments; or even bring a foreclosure action against the homeowner and the Property. The provisions of the Texas Property Code may be accessed at *www.capitol.state.tx.us* under Legislative Resources. Click on Texas Statutes and scroll down to and click on Property Code. The TREC Form 36-4, Addendum for Property Subject to Mandatory Membership in an Owners' Association, is reproduced in Figure 7.3 The parties contractually agree that the Property is or is not subject to mandatory membership in an owners' association.

3. Statutorily created utility districts have the power to assess and collect significant taxes. Buyers need to understand what they are facing. Failure to pay the taxes levied by a statutory taxing district will result in foreclosure of the Property.

4. Owners of Property located near or abutting tidewater of Texas take on special risks that need to be thoroughly understood before taking title. (See Figure 7.4 and Figure 7.5.)

5. People choose to live in unincorporated areas for a variety of reasons. When individuals acquire land outside of a municipality, they need to be aware of the possibility of **annexation** at a future time. Buyers are advised to research the annexation issue before making a final decision to move forward with the acquisition of the Property A license holder should never attempt to predict what may happen in the future with regard to annexation, zoning, ad valorem taxation, school districts, and related issues. Provide customers and clients with information about where they can find the answers to their questions but do not provide the information. As an attorney friend advises, *be the source of the source but don't become the source*.

6. Properties are often located in certificated water and/or sewer districts. People buying in these areas may encounter special costs or charges that must be paid before water or sewer service may be received. The costs can amount to significant amounts of money. Prudent Buyers need to know precisely what their financial

obligations will be before completing a transaction. Surprises after closing can result in financial hardship for the Buyers and unhappy customers for the real estate professional.

7. If the Property lies within a public improvement district, the Property may face periodic assessments to retire the debt created by the installation of the improvement for the neighborhood.

It is important to review the notices with the customer or your client and introduce them to the TREC-promulgated addenda that may be applicable to their transaction.

INSPECTION OF THE PROPERTY

At times license holders, in their enthusiasm and desire to earn a commission, create false expectations on the part of the Buyers with regard to the condition of the Property. You and the Buyers would be better served if you advised them that the physical aspects of the Property may be something less than perfect and that they should have it thoroughly inspected and evaluated by professionals. The list of inspection possibilities is long and may involve the use of a wide variety of professionals.

Paragraph 7A of the contract establishes the right of the Buyer to have access at reasonable times to bring professional, licensed inspectors to examine the Property. The Seller is obligated to have the utilities turned on for the Buyer's inspections and re-inspections. In Chapter 5, we reviewed the notice about inspections that must be given to Buyers and incorporated into the purchase agreement as an addendum when a Buyer is purchasing with a FHA insured loan. No such notice is required for other types of loans, but all Buyers should be encouraged to carefully evaluate the physical condition of the Property's structural and mechanical components. It is prudent for Buyers to exercise the right established by paragraph 7A. (See Figure 7.6.)

FIGURE 7.2 E

TREC 20-7, Paragraph 6

E. TITLE NOTICES:

(1) ABSTRACT OR TITLE POLICY: Broker advises Buyer to have an abstract of title covering the Property examined by an attorney of Buyer's selection, or Buyer should be furnished with or obtain a Title Policy. If a Title Policy is furnished, the Commitment should be promptly reviewed by an attorney of Buyer's choice due to the time limitations on Buyer's right to object.

(2) MANDATORY OWNERS' ASSOCIATION MEMBERSHIP: The Property ❑ is ❑ is not subject to mandatory membership in an owners' association. If the Property is subject to mandatory membership in an owners' association, Seller notifies Buyer under §5.012, Texas Property Code, that, as a purchaser of property in the residential community in which the Property is located, you are obligated to be a member of the owners' association. Restrictive covenants governing the use and occupancy of the Property and a dedicatory instrument governing the establishment, maintenance, and operation of this residential community have been or will be recorded in the Real Property Records of the county in which the Property is located. Copies of the restrictive covenants and dedicatory instrument may be obtained from the county clerk. You are obligated to pay assessments to the owners' association. The amount of the assessments is subject to change. Your failure to pay the assessments could result in a lien on and the foreclosure of the Property. If Buyer is concerned about these matters, the TREC promulgated Addendum for Property Subject to Mandatory Membership in an Owner's Association should be used.

(3) STATUTORY TAX DISTRICTS: If the Property is situated in a utility or other statutorily created district providing water, sewer, drainage, or flood control facilities and services, Chapter 49, Texas Water Code, requires Seller to deliver and Buyer to sign the statutory notice relating to the tax rate, bonded indebtedness, or standby fee of the district prior to final execution of this contract.

(4) TIDE WATERS: If the Property abuts the tidally influenced waters of the state, §33.135, Texas Natural Resources Code, requires a notice regarding coastal area property to be included in the contract. An addendum containing the notice promulgated by TREC or required by the parties must be used.

(5) ANNEXATION: If the Property is located outside the limits of a municipality, Seller notifies Buyer under §5.011, Texas Property Code, that the Property may now or later be included in the extraterritorial jurisdiction of a municipality and may now or later be subject to annexation by the municipality. Each municipality maintains a map that depicts its boundaries and extraterritorial jurisdiction. To determine if the Property is located within a municipality's extraterritorial jurisdiction or is likely to be located within a municipality's extraterritorial jurisdiction, contact all municipalities located in the general proximity of the Property for further information.

(6) PROPERTY LOCATED IN A CERTIFICATED SERVICE AREA OF A UTILITY SERVICE PROVIDER: Notice required by §13.257, Water Code: The real property, described in Paragraph 2, that you are about to purchase may be located in a certificated water or sewer service area, which is authorized by law to provide water or sewer service to the properties in the certificated area. If your property is located in a certificated area there may be special costs or charges that you will be required to pay before you can receive water or sewer service. There may be a period required to construct lines or other facilities necessary to provide water or sewer service to your property. You are advised to determine if the property is in a certificated area and contact the utility service provider to determine the cost that you will be required to pay and the period, if any, that is required to provide water or sewer service to your property. The undersigned Buyer hereby acknowledges receipt of the foregoing notice at or before the execution of a binding contract for the purchase of the real property described in Paragraph 2 or at closing of purchase of the real property.

(7) PUBLIC IMPROVEMENT DISTRICTS: If the Property is in a public improvement district, §5.014, Property Code, requires Seller to notify Buyer as follows: As a purchaser of this parcel of real property you are obligated to pay an assessment to a municipality or county for an improvement project undertaken by a public improvement district under Chapter 372, Local Government Code. The assessment may be due annually or in periodic installments. More information concerning the amount of the assessment and the due dates of that assessment may be obtained from the municipality or county levying the assessment. The amount of the assessments is subject to change. Your failure to pay the assessments could result in a lien on and the foreclosure of your property.

FIGURE 7.3

TREC 36-4

PROMULGATED BY THE TEXAS REAL ESTATE COMMISSION (TREC) 02-13-06

EQUAL HOUSING OPPORTUNITY

ADDENDUM FOR PROPERTY SUBJECT TO MANDATORY MEMBERSHIP IN AN OWNERS' ASSOCIATION

(NOT FOR USE WITH CONDOMINIUMS)

ADDENDUM TO CONTRACT CONCERNING THE PROPERTY AT

____

(Street Address and City)

____

(Name of Owners' Association)

A. SUBDIVISON INFORMATION: "Subdivision Information" means: (i) the restrictions applying to the subdivision, (ii) the bylaws and rules of the Owners' Association, and (iii) a resale certificate, all of which were provided by the Owners' Association in compliance with Section 207.003 of the Texas Property Code.

(Check only one box):

❑ 1. Within _____ days after the effective date of the contract, Seller shall at Seller's expense deliver the Subdivision Information to Buyer. If Buyer does not receive the Subdivision Information, Buyer may terminate the contract at any time prior to closing and the earnest money will be refunded to Buyer. If Seller delivers the Subdivision Information, Buyer may terminate the contract for any reason within 7 days after Buyer receives the Subdivision Information or prior to closing, whichever first occurs, and the earnest money will be refunded to Buyer.

❑ 2. Buyer has received and approved the Subdivision Information before signing the contract.

❑ 3. Buyer does not require delivery of the Subdivision Information.

If Seller becomes aware of any material changes in the Subdivision Information, Seller shall immediately give notice to Buyer. Buyer may terminate the contract prior to closing by giving written notice to Seller if: (i) any of the Subdivision Information provided was not true; or (ii) any material adverse change in the Subdivision Information occurs prior to closing, and the earnest money will be refunded to Buyer.

B. FEES: Buyer shall pay any Owners' Association fees resulting from the transfer of the Property not to exceed $__________ and Seller shall pay any excess.

NOTICE TO BUYER REGARDING REPAIRS BY THE OWNERS' ASSOCIATION: The Owners' Association may have the sole responsibility to make certain repairs to the Property. If you are concerned about the condition of any part of the Property which the Owners' Association is required to repair, you should not sign the contract unless you are satisfied that the Owners' Association will make the desired repairs.

____________________ Buyer	____________________ Seller
____________________ Buyer	____________________ Seller

The form of this addendum has been approved by the Texas Real Estate Commission for use only with similarly approved or promulgated forms of contracts. Such approval relates to this contract form only. TREC forms are intended for use only by trained real estate licensees. No representation is made as to the legal validity or adequacy of any provision in any specific transactions. It is not intended for complex transactions. Texas Real Estate Commission, P.O. Box 12188, Austin, TX 78711-2188, 1-800-250-8732 or (512) 459-6544 (http://www.trec.state.tx.us) TREC No. 36-4. This form replaces TREC No. 36-3.

TREC NO. 36-4

FIGURE 7.4

TREC 34-3

PROMULGATED BY THE TEXAS REAL ESTATE COMMISSION (TREC) 12-10-07

EQUAL HOUSING OPPORTUNITY

ADDENDUM FOR PROPERTY LOCATED SEAWARD OF THE GULF INTRACOASTAL WATERWAY

(SECTION 61.025, TEXAS NATURAL RESOURCES CODE)

TO CONTRACT CONCERNING THE PROPERTY AT

____

(Address of Property)

DISCLOSURE NOTICE CONCERNING LEGAL AND ECONOMIC RISKS OF PURCHASING COASTAL REAL PROPERTY NEAR A BEACH

WARNING: THE FOLLOWING NOTICE OF POTENTIAL RISKS OF ECONOMIC LOSS TO YOU AS THE PURCHASER OF COASTAL REAL PROPERTY IS REQUIRED BY STATE LAW.

- READ THIS NOTICE CAREFULLY. DO NOT SIGN THIS CONTRACT UNTIL YOU FULLY UNDERSTAND THE RISKS YOU ARE ASSUMING.
- BY PURCHASING THIS PROPERTY, YOU MAY BE ASSUMING ECONOMIC RISKS OVER AND ABOVE THE RISKS INVOLVED IN PURCHASING INLAND REAL PROPERTY.
- IF YOU OWN A STRUCTURE LOCATED ON COASTAL REAL PROPERTY NEAR A GULF COAST BEACH, IT MAY COME TO BE LOCATED ON THE PUBLIC BEACH BECAUSE OF COASTAL EROSION AND STORM EVENTS.
- AS THE OWNER OF A STRUCTURE LOCATED ON THE PUBLIC BEACH, YOU COULD BE SUED BY THE STATE OF TEXAS AND ORDERED TO REMOVE THE STRUCTURE.
- THE COSTS OF REMOVING A STRUCTURE FROM THE PUBLIC BEACH AND ANY OTHER ECONOMIC LOSS INCURRED BECAUSE OF A REMOVAL ORDER WOULD BE SOLELY YOUR RESPONSIBILITY.

The real property described in this contract is located seaward of the Gulf Intracoastal Waterway to its southernmost point and then seaward of the longitudinal line also known as 97 degrees, 12', 19" which runs southerly to the international boundary from the intersection of the centerline of the Gulf Intracoastal Waterway and the Brownsville Ship Channel. If the property is in close proximity to a beach fronting the Gulf of Mexico, the purchaser is hereby advised that the public has acquired a right of use or easement to or over the area of any public beach by prescription, dedication, or presumption, or has retained a right by virtue of continuous right in the public since time immemorial, as recognized in law and custom.

The extreme seaward boundary of natural vegetation that spreads continuously inland customarily marks the landward boundary of the public easement. If there is no clearly marked natural vegetation line, the landward boundary of the easement is as provided by Sections 61.016 and 61.017, Natural Resources Code.

Much of the Gulf of Mexico coastline is eroding at rates of more than five feet per year. Erosion rates for all Texas Gulf property subject to the open beaches act are available from the Texas General Land Office.

State law prohibits any obstruction, barrier, restraint, or interference with the use of the public easement, including the placement of structures seaward of the landward boundary of the easement. OWNERS OF STRUCTURES ERECTED SEAWARD OF THE VEGETATION LINE (OR OTHER APPLICABLE EASEMENT BOUNDARY) OR THAT BECOME SEAWARD OF THE VEGETATION LINE AS A RESULT OF PROCESSES ARE SUBJECT TO A LAWSUIT BY THE STATE OF TEXAS TO REMOVE THE STRUCTURES.

The purchaser is hereby notified that the purchaser should: (1) determine the rate of shoreline erosion in the vicinity of the real property; and (2) seek the advice of an attorney or other qualified person before executing this contract or instrument of conveyance as to the relevance of these statutes and facts to the value of the property the purchaser is hereby purchasing or contracting to purchase.

Buyer	Seller
Buyer	Seller

This form has been approved by the Texas Real Estate Commission for use with similarly approved or promulgated contract forms. Such approval relates to this form only. TREC forms are intended for use only by trained real estate licensees. No representation is made as to the legal validity or adequacy of any provision in any specific transactions. It is not suitable for complex transactions. Texas Real Estate Commission, P.O. Box 12188, Austin, TX 78711-2188, 1-800-250-8732 or (512) 459-6544 (http://www.trec.state.tx.us) TREC No. 34-3. This form replaces TREC No. 34-2.

TREC No. 34-3

FIGURE 7.5

TREC 33-1

EQUAL HOUSING OPPORTUNITY

PROMULGATED BY THE TEXAS REAL ESTATE COMMISSION (TREC) 04-23-07

ADDENDUM FOR COASTAL AREA PROPERTY

(SECTION 33.135, TEXAS NATURAL RESOURCES CODE)

TO CONTRACT CONCERNING THE PROPERTY AT

____

(Address of Property)

NOTICE REGARDING COASTAL AREA PROPERTY

1. The real property described in and subject to this contract adjoins and shares a common boundary with the tidally influenced submerged lands of the state. The boundary is subject to change and can be determined accurately only by a survey on the ground made by a licensed state land surveyor in accordance with the original grant from the sovereign. The owner of the property described in this contract may gain or lose portions of the tract because of changes in the boundary.

2. The seller, transferor, or grantor has no knowledge of any prior fill as it relates to the property described in and subject to this contract except:________________________ ____ ____.

3. State law prohibits the use, encumbrance, construction, or placing of any structure in, on, or over state-owned submerged lands below the applicable tide line, without proper permission.

4. The purchaser or grantee is hereby advised to seek the advice of an attorney or other qualified person as to the legal nature and effect of the facts set forth in this notice on the property described in and subject to this contract. Information regarding the location of the applicable tide line as to the property described in and subject to this contract may be obtained from the surveying division of the General Land Office in Austin.

______________________	______________________
Buyer	Seller
______________________	______________________
Buyer	Seller

This form has been approved by the Texas Real Estate Commission for use with similarly approved or promulgated contract forms. Such approval relates to this form only. TREC forms are intended for use only by trained real estate licensees. No representation is made as to the legal validity or adequacy of any provision in any specific transactions. It is not suitable for complex transactions. Texas Real Estate Commission, P.O. Box 12188, Austin, TX 78711-2188, 1-800-250-8732 or (512) 459-6544 (http://www.trec.state.tx.us) TREC No. 33-1. This form replaces TREC No. 33-0.

TREC No. 33-1

FIGURE 7.6

TREC 20-7 Paragraph 7

7. PROPERTY CONDITION:

A. ACCESS,INSPECTIONS AND UTILITIES: Seller shall permit Buyer and Buyer's agents access to the Property at reasonable times. Buyer may have the Property inspected by inspectors selected by Buyer and licensed by TREC or otherwise permitted by law to make inspections. Seller at Seller's expense shall turn on existing utilities for inspections.

B. SELLER'S DISCLOSURE NOTICE PURSUANT TO §5.008, TEXAS PROPERTY CODE (Notice): (Check one box only)

❑ (1) Buyer has received the Notice.

❑ (2) Buyer has not received the Notice. Within ______ days after the effective date of this contract, Seller shall deliver the Notice to Buyer. If Buyer does not receive the Notice, Buyer may terminate this contract at any time prior to the closing and the earnest money will be refunded to Buyer. If Seller delivers the Notice, Buyer may terminate this contract for any reason within 7 days after Buyer receives the Notice or prior to the closing, whichever first occurs, and the earnest money will be refunded to Buyer.

❑ (3) The Seller is not required to furnish the notice under the Texas Property Code.

C. SELLER'S DISCLOSURE OF LEAD-BASED PAINT AND LEAD-BASED PAINT HAZARDS is required by Federal law for a residential dwelling constructed prior to 1978.

D. ACCEPTANCE OF PROPERTY CONDITION: Buyer accepts the Property in its present condition; provided Seller, at Seller's expense, shall complete the following specific repairs and treatments:____

____

E. LENDER REQUIRED REPAIRS AND TREATMENTS: Unless otherwise agreed in writing, neither party is obligated to pay for lender required repairs, which includes treatment for wood destroying insects. If the parties do not agree to pay for the lender required repairs or treatments, this contract will terminate and the earnest money will be refunded to Buyer. If the cost of lender required repairs and treatments exceeds 5% of the Sales Price, Buyer may terminate this contract and the earnest money will be refunded to Buyer.

F. COMPLETION OF REPAIRS AND TREATMENTS: Unless otherwise agreed in writing, Seller shall complete all agreed repairs and treatments prior to the Closing Date. All required permits must be obtained, and repairs and treatments must be performed by persons who are licensed or otherwise authorized by law to provide such repairs or treatments. At Buyer's election, any transferable warranties received by Seller with respect to the repairs and treatments will be transferred to Buyer at Buyer's expense. If Seller fails to complete any agreed repairs and treatments prior to the Closing Date, Buyer may do so and receive reimbursement from Seller at closing. The Closing Date will be extended up to 15 days, if necessary, to complete repairs and treatments.

G. ENVIRONMENTAL MATTERS: Buyer is advised that the presence of wetlands, toxic substances, including asbestos and wastes or other environmental hazards, or the presence of a threatened or endangered species or its habitat may affect Buyer's intended use of the Property. If Buyer is concerned about these matters, an addendum promulgated by TREC or required by the parties should be used.

H. RESIDENTIAL SERVICE CONTRACTS: Buyer may purchase a residential service contract from a residential service company licensed by TREC. If Buyer purchases a residential service contract, Seller shall reimburse Buyer at closing for the cost of the residential service contract in an amount not exceeding $______________. Buyer should review any residential service contract for the scope of coverage, exclusions and limitations. **The purchase of a residential service contract is optional. Similar coverage may be purchased from various companies authorized to do business in Texas.**

The Buyer may or may not have the right to terminate as a result of the findings of various inspectors. If a Buyer wants the ability to cancel the agreement if something is revealed in the inspection process or for any other reason, the Buyer needs to purchase the unrestricted right to terminate by utilizing the provisions provided in paragraph 23 of the promulgated contract. (See Figure 7.7.)

FIGURE 7.7

TREC 20-7 Paragraph 23

23. TERMINATION OPTION: For nominal consideration, the receipt of which is hereby acknowledged by Seller, and Buyer's agreement to pay Seller $_______________ (Option Fee) within 2 days after the effective date of this contract, Seller grants Buyer the unrestricted right to terminate this contract by giving notice of termination to Seller within _______ days after the effective date of this contract. If no dollar amount is stated as the Option Fee or if Buyer fails to pay the Option Fee within the time prescribed, this paragraph will not be a part of this contract and Buyer shall not have the unrestricted right to terminate this contract. If Buyer gives notice of termination within the time prescribed, the Option Fee will not be refunded; however, any earnest money will be refunded to Buyer. The Option Fee ❑will ❑will not be credited to the Sales Price at closing. **Time is of the essence for this paragraph and strict compliance with the time for performance is required.**

Please note the following three things that apply when the option is purchased:

1. Valuable consideration (money) must be tendered to the owner
2. Time is of the essence with regard to the option to terminate
3. The right is unrestricted; it is not limited to the results of inspections

Buyers may elect to use any number of professionals to help them evaluate a particular Property, including the following:

- Texas Real Estate Commission licensed real estate inspectors
- Structural engineers
- Electricians
- Plumbers
- Pest control specialists
- Heating and air-conditioning contractors
- Lead inspectors
- Governmental agencies
- Environmental specialists

Paragraph 7A grants access at reasonable times for the appropriate inspections to be done. It further agrees that the Seller, at Seller's expense, shall have utilities turned on for inspections.

Effective January 1, 1994, section 5.008 of the Texas Property Code requires Sellers of previously occupied residential dwelling units to furnish Buyers with a Seller's disclosure notice with content and information required by statute. Failure to provide the notice prior to signing an executory contract to purchase creates a voidable contract that may be terminated at the sole discretion of the Buyer. If it is furnished after an executory contract of purchase is signed, the Buyer has a period of seven days to terminate the contract without penalty or forfeiture of earnest money.

Following are the 11 exceptions stated in subsection (e) of section 5.008 of the Texas Property Code:

> (e) This section does not apply to a transfer:
>
> (1) pursuant to a court order or foreclosure sale;
>
> (2) by a trustee in bankruptcy;
>
> (3) to a mortgagee by a mortgagor or successor in interest, or to a beneficiary of a deed of trust by a trustor or successor in interest;
>
> (4) by a mortgagee or a beneficiary under a deed of trust who has acquired the real property at a sale conducted pursuant to a power of sale under a deed of trust or a sale pursuant to a court ordered foreclosure or has acquired the real property by a deed in lieu of foreclosure;
>
> (5) by a fiduciary in the course of the administration of a decedent's estate, guardianship, conservatorship, or trust;
>
> (6) from one co-owner to one or more other co-owners;
>
> (7) made to a spouse or to a person or persons in the lineal line of consanguinity of one or more of the transferors;
>
> (8) between spouses resulting from a decree of dissolution of marriage or a decree of legal separation or from a property settlement agreement incidental to such a decree;
>
> (9) to or from any governmental entity;
>
> (10) transfers of new residences of not more than one dwelling unit which have not previously been occupied for residential purposes; or
>
> (11) transfers of real property where the value of any dwelling does not exceed five percent (5%) of the value of the property. (Note: This provision typically excludes a ranch or farm sale.)

By checking the appropriate box in 7B, the parties define whether the

- buyer has received the notice,
- seller has a defined number of days to furnish it, or
- property is exempt from the requirement pursuant to the Texas Property Code.

Remember also that according to this section of the code and section 1101.556 of the TRELA, there is no duty to disclose specific information. Subsection (c) of 5.008 states the following:

> Sec. 1101.556. DISCLOSURE OF CERTAIN INFORMATION RELATING TO OCCUPANTS. Notwithstanding other law, a license holder is not required to inquire about, disclose, or release information relating to whether:
>
> (1) a previous or current occupant of real property had, may have had, has, or may have AIDS, an HIV-related illness, or an HIV infection as defined by the Centers for Disease Control and Prevention of the United States Public Health Service; or
>
> (2) a death occurred on a property by natural causes, suicide, or accident unrelated to the condition of the property.

The form that follows in Figure 7.8, the TREC Form OP-H, Seller's Disclosure of Property Condition, is made available for voluntary use by the customers and clients of license holders. Some license holders prefer to use a format developed by the Texas Association of REALTORS® (TAR), and some use a form developed by an in-house attorney. As long as the disclosure includes the minimum content established by 5.008, it is acceptable. The widely used TAR form is included here in Figure 7.9 even though it may be used only by members of TAR. The version approved by the TREC for voluntary use meets the requirements of section 5.008 of the Texas Property Code and may be used by all real estate license holders and their clients and customers. The TAR Seller Disclosure form is more detailed and addresses more items and issues than the statutory minimum that is published by the TREC. The TAR form is provided here for informational and study purposes only. Please do not reproduce and use the TAR form unless you are a member of the TAR.

Some license holders have the mistaken idea that the disclosure form must be signed by the Seller, acknowledged by the Buyer, and attached as an addendum to the purchase contract. The statute requires only that the Seller complete the written disclosure and give it to the Buyer. Do not list it as an addendum in paragraph 22. It is a disclosure of what the Seller knows. It is not a representation or warranty and therefore is not a promise or covenant exchanged between the parties. Some lawyers we have questioned on this matter feel that to reference it as an addendum in some way converts it from being simply a disclosure to a representation and warranty of the Property condition. Courts in both San Antonio, Texas, and Houston, Texas, have ruled that the attached Seller's disclosure was a representation by the Sellers and ruled in favor of the Buyers. We suggest that you follow the lead of the TREC and simply check the appropriate box in paragraph 7B that provides adequate documentation as to what the parties have done with regard to the matter of disclosure.

Paragraph 7C addresses the possibility of the presence of lead-based paint or lead-based paint hazards. License holders and Sellers must be certain that they follow the HUD guidelines with regard to the Seller's disclosure of the presence of lead-based paint and/or lead hazards. If the building permits for the construction of the home were issued prior to January 1, 1978, the addendum must be used to comply with the federal regulation to furnish a lead warning statement. You may use the TREC

FIGURE 7.8

TREC OP-H

APPROVED BY THE TEXAS REAL ESTATE COMMISSION (TREC)

09-01-07

EQUAL HOUSING OPPORTUNITY

SELLER'S DISCLOSURE OF PROPERTY CONDITION

(SECTION 5.008, TEXAS PROPERTY CODE)

CONCERNING THE PROPERTY AT ____
(Street Address and City)

THIS NOTICE IS A DISCLOSURE OF SELLER'S KNOWLEDGE OF THE CONDITION OF THE PROPERTY AS OF THE DATE SIGNED BY SELLER AND IS NOT A SUBSTITUTE FOR ANY INSPECTIONS OR WARRANTIES THE PURCHASER MAY WISH TO OBTAIN. IT IS NOT A WARRANTY OF ANY KIND BY SELLER OR SELLER'S AGENTS.

Seller ☐ is ☐ is not occupying the Property. If unoccupied, how long since Seller has occupied the Property?

1. The Property has the items checked below [Write Yes (Y), No (N), or Unknown (U)]:

__ Range	__ Oven	__ Microwave
__ Dishwasher	__ Trash Compactor	__ Disposal
__ Washer/Dryer Hookups	__ Window Screens	__ Rain Gutters
__ Security System	__ Fire Detection Equipment	__ Intercom System
__ TV Antenna	__ Smoke Detector	__ Satellite Dish
__ Ceiling Fan(s)	__ Smoke Detector-Hearing Impaired	__ Exhaust Fan(s)
__ Central A/C	__ Carbon Monoxide Alarm	__ Wall/Window Air Conditioning
__ Plumbing System	__ Emergency Escape Ladder(s)	__ Public Sewer System
__ Patio/Decking	__ Cable TV Wiring	__ Fences
__ Pool	__ Attic Fan(s)	__ Spa __ Hot Tub
__ Pool Equipment	__ Central Heating	__ Automatic Lawn Sprinkler System
__ Fireplace(s) & Chimney (Woodburning)	__ Septic System	__ Fireplace(s) & Chimney (Mock)
__ Gas Lines (Nat./LP)	__ Outdoor Grill	__ Carport
__ Garage: __ Attached __ Not Attached	__ Sauna	__ Water Supply __ City __ Well __ MUD __ Co-op
	__ Pool Heater	
__ Garage Door Opener(s): __ Electronic __ Controls	__ Water Heater: __ Gas __ Electric	

Roof Type: ______________________ Age: __________ (approx)

Are you (Seller) aware of any of the above items that are not in working condition, that have known defects or that are in need of repair? ☐ Yes ☐ No ☐ Unknown If yes, then describe. (Attach additional sheets if necessary): ______________________

2. Does the property have working smoke detectors installed in accordance with the smoke detector requirements of Chapter 766, Health and Safety Code? ☐ Yes ☐ No ☐ Unknown

If the answer to the question above is no or unknown, explain. (Attach additional sheets if necessary):

____

____

____

TREC No. OP-H

FIGURE 7.8 (CONTINUED)

TREC OP-H

Seller's Disclosure Notice Concerning the Property at______________________________ Page 2 09-01-07
(Street Address and City)

3. Are you (Seller) aware of any known defects/malfunctions in any of the following?

Write Yes (Y) if you are aware, write No (N) if you are not aware.

__ Interior Walls	__ Ceilings	__ Floors
__ Exterior Walls	__ Doors	__ Windows
__ Roof	__ Foundation/Slab(s)	__ Basement
__ Walls/Fences	__ Driveways	__ Sidewalks
__ Plumbing Sewers/Septics	__ Electrical Systems	__ Lighting Fixtures

__ Other Structural Components (Describe) ______________________________

____

____

4. Are you (Seller) aware of any of the following conditions? Write Yes (Y) if you are aware, write No (N) if you are not aware.

__ Active Termites (includes wood destroying insects)	__ Termite or Wood Rot Damage Needing Repair	__ Previous Termite Damage
__ Previous Termite Treatment	__ Previous Flooding	__ Improper Drainage
__ Water Penetration	__ Located in 100-Year Floodplain	__ Present Flood Insurance Coverage
__ Previous Structural or Roof Repair	__ Hazardous or Toxic Waste	__ Asbestos Components
__ Urea-formaldehyde Insulation	__ Radon Gas	__ Lead Based Paint
__ Aluminum Wiring	__ Previous Fires	__ Unplatted Easements
__ Landfill, Settling, Soil Movement, Fault Lines		__ Subsurface Structure or Pits
__ Previous Use of Premises for Manufacture of Methamphetamine		

5. Are you (Seller) aware of any item, equipment, or system in or on the Property that is in need of repair? ☐ Yes (iIf you are aware) ☐ No (if you are not aware). If yes, then describe. (Attach additional sheets if necessary)

____

____

____

6. Are you (Seller) aware of any of the following? Write Yes (Y) if you are aware, write No (N) if you are not aware.

__ Room additions, structural modifications, or other alterations or repairs made without necessary permits or not in compliance with building codes in effect at that time.

__ Homeowners' Association or maintenance fees or assessments.

__ Any "common area" (facilities such as pools, tennis courts, walkways, or other areas) co-owned in undivided interest with others.

__ Any notices of violations of deed restrictions or governmental ordinances affecting the condition or use of the Property.

__ Any lawsuits directly or indirectly affecting the Property.

__ Any condition on the Property which materially affects the physical health or safety of an individual.

If the answer to any of the above is yes explain. (Attach additional sheets if necessary):

____

____

____

FIGURE 7.8 (CONTINUED)

TREC OP-H

Seller's Disclosure Notice Concerning the Property at______________________________ Page 3 09-01-07
(Street Address and City)

7. If the property is located in a coastal area that is seaward of the Gulf Intracoastal Waterway or within 1,000 feet of the mean high tide bordering the Gulf of Mexico, the property may be subject to the Open Beaches Act or the Dune Protection Act (Chapter 61 or 63, Natural Resources Code, respectively) and a beachfront construction certificate or dune protection permit may be required for repairs or improvements. Contact the local government with ordinance authority over construction adjacent to public beaches for more information.

Date	Signature of Seller	Date	Signature of Seller

The undersigned purchaser hereby acknowledges receipt of the foregoing notice and acknowledges the property complies with the smoke detector requirements of Chapter 766, Health and Safety Code, or, if the property does not comply with the smoke detector requirements of Chapter 766, the buyer waives the buyer's rights to have smoke detectors installed in compliance with Chapter 766.

Date	Signature of Purchaser	Date	Signature of Purchaser

TREC No. OP-H

FIGURE 7.9

TAR Disclosure Notice

TEXAS ASSOCIATION OF REALTORS®

SELLER'S DISCLOSURE NOTICE

Section 5.008, Property Code requires a seller of residential property of not more than one dwelling unit to deliver a Seller's Disclosure Notice to a buyer on or before the effective date of a contract. **This form complies with and contains additional disclosures which exceed the minimum disclosures required by the Code.**

CONCERNING THE PROPERTY AT ____

THIS NOTICE IS A DISCLOSURE OF SELLER'S KNOWLEDGE OF THE CONDITION OF THE PROPERTY AS OF THE DATE SIGNED BY SELLER AND IS NOT A SUBSTITUTE FOR ANY INSPECTIONS OR WARRANTIES THE BUYER MAY WISH TO OBTAIN. IT IS NOT A WARRANTY OF ANY KIND BY SELLER, SELLER'S AGENTS, OR ANY OTHER AGENT.

Seller ❑ is ❑ is not occupying the Property. If unoccupied (by Seller), how long since Seller has occupied the Property? ❑ ______________________________ or ❑ never occupied the Property

Section 1. The Property has the items marked below: (Mark Yes (Y), No (N), or Unknown (U).)

This notice does not establish the items to be conveyed. The contract will determine which items will & will not convey.

Item	Y	N	U	Item	Y	N	U	Item	Y	N	U
Cable TV Wiring				Gas Lines (Nat/LP)				Pump: ❑ sump ❑ grinder			
Carbon Monoxide Det.				Hot Tub				Rain Gutters			
Ceiling Fans				Intercom System				Range/Stove			
Cooktop				Microwave				Roof/Attic Vents			
Dishwasher				Outdoor Grill				Sauna			
Disposal				Patio/Decking				Smoke Detector			
Emergency Escape Ladder(s)				Plumbing System				Smoke Detector – Hearing Impaired			
Exhaust Fans				Pool				Spa			
Fences				Pool Equipment				Trash Compactor			
Fire Detection Equip.				Pool Maint. Accessories				TV Antenna			
French Drain				Pool Heater				Washer/Dryer Hookup			
Gas Fixtures				Public Sewer System				Window Screens			

Item	Y	N	U	Additional Information
Central A/C				❑ electric ❑ gas number of units: ______
Evaporative Coolers				number of units: ______
Wall/Window AC Units				number of units: ______
Attic Fan(s)				if yes, describe: ______
Central Heat				❑ electric ❑ gas number of units: ______
Other Heat				if yes describe: ______
Oven				number of ovens: _____ ❑ electric ❑ gas ❑ other: ______
Fireplace & Chimney				❑ wood ❑ gas logs ❑ mock ❑ other: ______
Carport				❑ attached ❑ not attached
Garage				❑ attached ❑ not attached
Garage Door Openers				number of units: _____ number of remotes: ______
Satellite Dish & Controls				❑ owned ❑ leased from ______
Security System				❑ owned ❑ leased from ______
Water Heater				❑ electric ❑ gas ❑ other: ______ number of units: ______
Water Softener				❑ owned ❑ leased from ______
Underground Lawn Sprinkler				❑ automatic ❑ manual areas covered: ______
Septic / On-Site Sewer Facility				if yes, attach Information About On-Site Sewer Facility (TAR-1407)

FIGURE 7.9 (CONTINUED)

TAR Disclosure Notice

Concerning the Property at ______________________________

Water supply provided by: ❑ city ❑ well ❑ MUD ❑ co-op ❑ unknown ❑ other:____________
Was the Property built before 1978? ❑ yes ❑ no ❑ unknown
(If yes, complete, sign, and attach TAR-1906 concerning lead-based paint hazards).
Roof Type: ____________________ Age: ____________________(approximate)
Is there an overlay roof covering on the Property (shingles or roof covering placed over existing shingles or roof covering)? ❑ yes ❑ no ❑ unknown

Are you (Seller) aware of any of the items listed in this Section 1 that are not in working condition, that have defects, or are need of repair? ❑ yes ❑ no If yes, describe (attach additional sheets if necessary): ________
____
____
____

Section 2. Are you (Seller) aware of any defects or malfunctions in any of the following?: (Mark Yes (Y) if you are aware and No (N) if you are not aware.)

Item	Y	N	Item	Y	N	Item	Y	N
Basement			Floors			Sidewalks		
Ceilings			Foundation / Slab(s)			Walls / Fences		
Doors			Interior Walls			Windows		
Driveways			Lighting Fixtures			Other Structural Components		
Electrical Systems			Plumbing Systems					
Exterior Walls			Roof					

If the answer to any of the items in Section 2 is yes, explain (attach additional sheets if necessary): __________
____
____
____
____

Section 3. Are you (Seller) aware of any of the following conditions: (Mark Yes (Y) if you are aware and No (N) if you are not aware.)

Condition	Y	N	Condition	Y	N
Aluminum Wiring			Previous Roof Repairs		
Asbestos Components			Other Structural Repairs		
Diseased Trees: ❑ oak wilt ❑ ____________			Radon Gas		
Endangered Species/Habitat on Property			Settling		
Fault Lines			Soil Movement		
Hazardous or Toxic Waste			Subsurface Structure or Pits		
Improper Drainage			Underground Storage Tanks		
Intermittent or Weather Springs			Unplatted Easements		
Landfill			Unrecorded Easements		
Lead-Based Paint or Lead-Based Pt. Hazards			Urea-formaldehyde Insulation		
Encroachments onto the Property			Water Penetration		
Improvements encroaching on others' property			Wetlands on Property		
Located in 100-year Floodplain			Wood Rot		
Present Flood Insurance Coverage (If yes, attach TAR-1414)			Active infestation of termites or other wood-destroying insects (WDI)		
Previous Flooding into the Structures			Previous treatment for termites or WDI		
Previous Flooding onto the Property			Previous termite or WDI damage repaired		
Previous Fires			Termite or WDI damage needing repair		
Previous Foundation Repairs			Previous Use of Premises for Manufacture of Methamphetamine		

(TAR-1406) 7-2-07 Initialed by: Seller: _______,_______ and Buyer: _______, _______ Page 2 of 5

FIGURE 7.9 (CONTINUED)

TAR Disclosure Notice

Concerning the Property at ______________________________

If the answer to any of the items in Section 3 is yes, explain (attach additional sheets if necessary): __________

____
____
____
____
____

Section 4. Are you (Seller) aware of any item, equipment, or system in or on the Property that is in need of repair, which has not been previously disclosed in this notice? ❑ yes ❑ no If yes, explain (attach additional sheets if necessary): ______________________________

____
____
____
____
____

Section 5. Are you (Seller) aware of any of the following (Mark Yes (Y) if you are aware. Mark No (N) if you are not aware.)

Y	N	
❑	❑	Room additions, structural modifications, or other alterations or repairs made without necessary permits or not in compliance with building codes in effect at the time.
❑	❑	Homeowners' associations or maintenance fees or assessments. If yes, complete the following: Name of association: ______________________________ Manager's name: ______________ Phone: ______________ Fees or assessments are: $__________ per ______________ and are: ❑ mandatory ❑ voluntary Any unpaid fees or assessment for the Property? ❑ yes ($__________) ❑ no If the Property is in more than one association, provide information about the other associations below or attach information to this notice.
❑	❑	Any common area (facilities such as pools, tennis courts, walkways, or other) co-owned in undivided interest with others. If yes, complete the following: Any optional user fees for common facilities charged? ❑ yes ❑ no If yes, describe: __________ ______________________________
❑	❑	Any notices of violations of deed restrictions or governmental ordinances affecting the condition or use of the Property.
❑	❑	Any lawsuits or other legal proceedings directly or indirectly affecting the Property.
❑	❑	Any death on the Property except for those deaths cause by: natural causes, suicide, or accident unrelated to the condition of the Property.
❑	❑	Any condition on the Property which materially affects the health or safety of an individual.
❑	❑	Any repairs or treatments, other than routine maintenance, made to the Property to remediate environmental hazards such as asbestos, radon, lead-based paint, urea-formaldehyde, or mold. If yes, attach any certificates or other documentation identifying the extent of the remediation (for example, certificate of mold remediation or other remediation).

If the answer to any of the items in Section 5 is yes, explain (attach additional sheets if necessary): __________

____
____
____
____
____

FIGURE 7.9 (CONTINUED)

TAR Disclosure Notice

Concerning the Property at ______________________________

Section 6. Seller ❑ has ❑ has not attached a survey of the Property.

Section 7. Within the last 4 years, have you (Seller) received any written inspection reports from persons who regularly provide inspections and who are either licensed as inspectors or otherwise permitted by law to perform inspections? ❑ yes ❑ no If yes, attach copies and complete the following:

Inspection Date	Type	Name of Inspector	No. of Pages

Note: A buyer should not rely on the above-cited reports as a reflection of the current condition of the Property. A buyer should obtain inspections from inspectors chosen by the buyer.

Section 8. Check any tax exemption(s) which you (Seller) currently claim for the Property:

❑ Homestead ❑ Senior Citizen ❑ Disabled
❑ Wildlife Management ❑ Agricultural ❑ Disabled Veteran
❑ Other:______________________________ ❑ Unknown

Section 9. Have you (Seller) ever received proceeds for a claim for damage to the Property (for example, an insurance claim or a settlement or award in a legal proceeding) and not used the proceeds to make the repairs for which the claim was made? ❑ yes ❑ no If yes, explain:____________________

____

____

____

Section 10. Does the property have working smoke detectors installed in accordance with the smoke detector requirements of Chapter 766 of the Health and Safety Code?* ❑ unknown ❑ no ❑ yes. If no or unknown, explain. (Attach additional sheets if necessary):____________________

____

____

**Chapter 766 of the Health and Safety Code requires one-family or two-family dwellings to have working smoke detectors installed in accordance with the requirements of the building code in effect in the area in which the dwelling is located, including performance, location, and power source requirements. If you do not know the building code requirements in effect in your area, you may check unknown above or contact your local building official for more information.*

Seller acknowledges that the statements in this notice are true to the best of Seller's belief and that no person, including the broker(s), has instructed or influenced Seller to provide inaccurate information or to omit any material information.

______________________________ ______________________________
Signature of Seller Date Signature of Seller Date
Printed Name: ____________________ Printed Name: ____________________

FIGURE 7.9 (CONTINUED)

TAR Disclosure Notice

Concerning the Property at ______________________________

ADDITIONAL NOTICES TO BUYER:

(1) The Texas Department of Public Safety maintains a database that the public may search, at no cost, to determine if registered sex offenders are located in certain zip code areas. To search the database, visit www.txdps.state.tx.us. For information concerning past criminal activity in certain areas or neighborhoods, contact the local police department.

(2) If the property is located in a coastal area that is seaward of the Gulf Intracoastal Waterway or within 1,000 feet of the mean high tide bordering the Gulf of Mexico, the property may be subject to the Open Beaches Act or the Dune Protection Act (Chapter 61 or 63, Natural Resources Code, respectively) and a beachfront construction certificate or dune protection permit may be required for repairs or improvements. Contact the local government with ordinance authority over construction adjacent to public beaches for more information.

(3) If you are basing your offers on square footage, measurements, or boundaries, you should have those items independently measured to verify any reported information.

(4) The following providers currently provide service to the property:

Electric:______________	Sewer:______________
Water:______________	Cable:______________
Trash:______________	Natural Gas:______________
Local Phone:______________	Propane:______________

(5) This Seller's Disclosure Notice was completed by Seller as of the date signed. The brokers have relied on this notice as true and correct and have no reason to believe it to be false or inaccurate. YOU ARE ENCOURAGED TO HAVE AN INSPECTOR OF YOUR CHOICE INSPECT THE PROPERTY.

The undersigned Buyer acknowledges receipt of the foregoing notice and acknowledges the property complies with the smoke detector requirements of Chapter 766, Health and Safety Code, or, if the property does not comply with the smoke detector requirements of Chapter 766, the buyer waives the buyer's rights to have smoke detectors installed in compliance with Chapter 766.

Signature of Buyer Date	Signature of Buyer Date
Printed Name:______________	Printed Name:______________

Form OP-L, Addendum for Seller's Disclosure of Information on Lead-Based Paint and Lead-Base Paint Hazards as Required by Federal Law, that follows in Figure 7.10 or the HUD version.

In 7D the Buyer agrees that the Property is accepted in its present condition but gives the parties the ability to list some specific repairs that are to be completed by the Seller and at the Seller's expense prior to closing. An example of something that the Buyer might request is that the missing gutter on the back of the home be replaced prior to closing or that the damaged kitchen floor covering be replaced with a specific material prior to closing. Listing agents should take special note of the fact that there is no cap on the Seller's financial liability. No Seller should agree to complete the repairs listed in this paragraph until they have obtained bids or at least some idea of what the requested repair will cost.

When a lender requires a repair, it is usually something that involves significant dollars. It is not prudent to commit to pay potentially large sums of money until one knows the amount. The agreement of the parties states that neither is committed to pay for any lender-required repair. This can be negotiated by using the TREC Form 39-6, Amendment, seen in Figure 7.11.

On the following lines, identify and list five or six other uses for the TREC-promulgated Form 39-6, Amendment (to Contract Concerning the Property at):

1. ______________________________

2. ______________________________

3. ______________________________

4. ______________________________

5. ______________________________

6. ______________________________

7F provides for an extension of 15 days, if necessary, for the Seller to complete repairs and treatments. It also provides, although not at all a practical solution, that the Buyer may do the repairs prior to closing and receive reimbursement from the Seller for them at closing.

Buyers should always be given the opportunity to have the Property inspected for environmental hazards. Whether their concern is about radon, asbestos, mold, or any other concern, the Buyer should be satisfied that the Property does not pose a health hazard to the Buyer or the Buyer's family. Always offer the opportunity to use the TREC Form 28-1, Environmental Assessment, Threatened or Endangered Species, and Wetlands Amendment, and be certain to structure the transaction with an adequate time frame to accomplish the desired evaluation and to get the report from the inspector to the Buyer prior to the agreed period in the form for the termination of the contract by the Buyer. (See Figure 7.12.)

FIGURE 7.10

TREC OP-L

APPROVED BY THE TEXAS REAL ESTATE COMMISSION 02-09-2004

EQUAL HOUSING OPPORTUNITY

ADDENDUM FOR SELLER'S DISCLOSURE OF INFORMATION ON LEAD-BASED PAINT AND LEAD-BASED PAINT HAZARDS AS REQUIRED BY FEDERAL LAW

CONCERNING THE PROPERTY AT ______________________________
(Street Address and City)

A. **LEAD WARNING STATEMENT:** "Every purchaser of any interest in residential real property on which a residential dwelling was built prior to 1978 is notified that such property may present exposure to lead from lead-based paint that may place young children at risk of developing lead poisoning. Lead poisoning in young children may produce permanent neurological damage, including learning disabilities, reduced intelligence quotient, behavioral problems, and impaired memory. Lead poisoning also poses a particular risk to pregnant women. The seller of any interest in residential real property is required to provide the buyer with any information on lead-based paint hazards from risk assessments or inspections in the seller's possession and notify the buyer of any known lead-based paint hazards. A risk assessment or inspection for possible lead-paint hazards is recommended prior to purchase."
NOTICE: Inspector must be properly certified as required by federal law.

B. SELLER'S DISCLOSURE:

1. PRESENCE OF LEAD-BASED PAINT AND/OR LEAD-BASED PAINT HAZARDS (check on box only):
   - ❑(a) Known lead-based paint and/or lead-based paint hazards are present in the Property (explain): ________________________________.
   - ❑(b) Seller has no actual knowledge of lead-based paint and/or lead-based paint hazards in the Property.
2. RECORDS AND REPORTS AVAILABLE TO SELLER (check one box only):
   - ❑(a) Seller has provided the purchaser with all available records and reports pertaining to lead-based paint and/or lead-based paint hazards in the Property (list documents): ________________________________.
   - ❑(b) Seller has no reports or records pertaining to lead-based paint and/or lead-based paint hazards in the Property.

C. BUYER'S RIGHTS (check one box only)**:**

- ❑1. Buyer waives the opportunity to conduct a risk assessment or inspection of the Property for the presence of lead-based paint or lead-based paint hazards.
- ❑2. Within ten days after the effective date of this contract, Buyer may have the Property inspected by inspectors selected by Buyer. If lead-based paint or lead-based paint hazards are present, Buyer may terminate this contract by giving Seller written notice within 14 days after the effective date of this contract, and the earnest money will be refunded to Buyer.

D. BUYER'S ACKNOWLEDGMENT (check applicable boxes)**:**

- ❑1. Buyer has received copies of all information listed above.
- ❑2. Buyer has received the pamphlet *Protect Your Family from Lead in Your Home*.

E. BROKERS' ACKNOWLEDGMENT: Brokers have informed Seller of Seller's obligations under 42 U.S.C. 4852d to: (a) provide Buyer with the federally approved pamphlet on lead poisoning prevention; (b) complete this addendum; (c) disclose any known lead-based paint and/or lead-based paint hazards in the Property; (d) deliver all records and reports to Buyer pertaining to lead-based paint and/or lead-based paint hazards in the Property; (e) provide Buyer a period of up to 10 days to have the Property inspected; and (f) retain a completed copy of this addendum for at least 3 years following the sale. Brokers are aware of their responsibility to ensure compliance.

F. CERTIFICATION OF ACCURACY: The following persons have reviewed the information above and certify, to the best of their knowledge, that the information they have provided is true and accurate.

Buyer	Date	Seller	Date
Buyer	Date	Seller	Date
Other Broker	Date	Listing Broker	Date

The form of this addendum has been approved by the Texas Real Estate Commission for use only with similarly approved or promulgated forms of contracts. Such approval relates to this contract form only. TREC forms are intended for use only by trained real estate licensees. No representation is made as to the legal validity or adequacy of any provision in any specific transactions. It is not suitable for complex transactions. Texas Real Estate Commission, P.O. Box 12188, Austin, TX 78711-2188, 1-800-250-8732 or (512) 459-6544 (http://www.trec.state.tx.us)

Form OP-L 01A

FIGURE 7.11

TREC 39-6

PROMULGATED BY THE TEXAS REAL ESTATE COMMISSION (TREC) 02-13-06

EQUAL HOUSING OPPORTUNITY

AMENDMENT

TO CONTRACT CONCERNING THE PROPERTY AT

____

(Street Address and City)

Seller and Buyer amend the contract as follows: (check each applicable box)

❑(1) The Sales Price in Paragraph 3 of the contract is:

A. Cash portion of Sales Price payable by Buyer at closing .... $__________

B. Sum of financing described in the contract.. $__________

C. Sales Price (Sum of A and B) .... $__________

❑(2) In addition to any repairs and treatments otherwise required by the contract, Seller, at Seller's expense, shall complete the following repairs and treatments:

❑(3) The date in Paragraph 9 of the contract is changed to ____________________, 20_____.

❑(4) The amount in Paragraph 12A(1)(b) of the contract is changed to $ ______________.

❑(5) The cost of lender required repairs and treatment, as itemized on the attached list, will be paid as follows: $ ________________ by Seller; $ ________________ by Buyer.

❑(6) Buyer has paid Seller an additional Option Fee of $ ____________ for an extension of the unrestricted right to terminate the contract on or before ______________________, 20_______. This additional Option Fee ❑ will ❑ will not be credited to the Sales Price.

❑(7) Buyer waives the unrestricted right to terminate the contract for which the Option Fee was paid.

❑(8) The date for Buyer to give written notice to Seller that Buyer cannot obtain Financing Approval as set forth in the Third Party Financing Condition Addendum is changed to ____________, 20______.

❑(9) **Other Modifications**: (Insert only factual statements and business details applicable to this sale.)

EXECUTED the _____day of ______________________, 20_____ . (BROKER: FILL IN THE DATE OF FINAL ACCEPTANCE.)

______________________	______________________
Buyer	Seller
______________________	______________________
Buyer	Seller

This form has been approved by the Texas Real Estate Commission for use with similarly approved or promulgated contract forms. Such approval relates to this form only. TREC forms are intended for use only by trained real estate licensees. No representation is made as to the legal validity or adequacy of any provision in any specific transactions. It is not intended for complex transactions. Texas Real Estate Commission, P.O. Box 12188, Austin, TX 78711-2188, 1-800-250-8732 or (512) 459-6544 (http://www.trec.state.tx.us) TREC No. 39-6. This form replaces TREC No. 39-5.

TREC NO. 39-6

FIGURE 7.12

TREC 28-1

PROMULGATED BY THE TEXAS REAL ESTATE COMMISSION (TREC) 04-23-07

EQUAL HOUSING OPPORTUNITY

ENVIRONMENTAL ASSESSMENT, THREATENED OR ENDANGERED SPECIES, AND WETLANDS ADDENDUM

TO CONTRACT CONCERNING THE PROPERTY AT

____

(Address of Property)

- ☐ A. ENVIRONMENTAL ASSESSMENT: Buyer, at Buyer's expense, may obtain an environmental assessment report prepared by an environmental specialist.
- ☐ B. THREATENED OR ENDANGERED SPECIES: Buyer, at Buyer's expense, may obtain a report from a natural resources professional to determine if there are any threatened or endangered species or their habitats as defined by the Texas Parks and Wildlife Department or the U.S. Fish and Wildlife Service.
- ☐ C. WETLANDS: Buyer, at Buyer's expense, may obtain a report from an environmental specialist to determine if there are wetlands, as defined by federal or state law or regulation.

Within ______days after the effective date of the contract, Buyer may terminate the contract by furnishing Seller a copy of any report noted above that adversely affects the use of the Property and a notice of termination of the contract. Upon termination, the earnest money will be refunded to Buyer.

Buyer	Seller
Buyer	Seller

This form has been approved by the Texas Real Estate Commission for use with similarly approved or promulgated contract forms. Such approval relates to this form only. TREC forms are intended for use only by trained real estate licensees. No representation is made as to the legal validity or adequacy of any provision in any specific transactions. It is not suitable for complex transactions. Texas Real Estate Commission, P.O. Box 12188, Austin, TX 78711-2188, 1-800-250-8732 or (512) 459-6544 (http://www.trec.state.tx.us) TREC No. 28-1. This form replaces TREC No. 28-0.

Residential service contracts, addressed in 7H, are optional and can be purchased by either the Seller or the Buyer. While the cost is minimal, $300 and up for one year; the risk reduction factor for the Seller and the agent is enormous. Some license holders have found it to be such a good thing for consumers that they buy it for them. It is best, regardless of who is paying, that the Buyers have the opportunity to review available coverage and to select the desired coverage. The Sellers' financial liability for the cost of coverage can be capped by agreement in the contract.

SUMMARY

Make certain that paragraphs 6 and 7 are carefully read by each of the parties to the contract As an agent of either or both parties, you must remember that your role is to identify alternatives, alert them to potential danger areas, and encourage them to read and understand the agreement. Your role is not to make decisions, dictate, or define. Remember that it is their transaction; it is not your transaction unless you are listed as Seller or Buyer in the first paragraph of the contract.

You are not expected to have all knowledge; however, you are expected and required to advise parties to thoroughly investigate title, survey, and physical condition issues.

CHAPTER 7 REVIEW QUESTIONS

1. If the dollar amount of lender-required repairs exceeds 5 percent of the purchase price, who may terminate the contract?

   a. Seller
   b. Listing broker
   c. Lender
   d. Buyer

2. According to the provisions of the contract, who will purchase a residential service contract if so desired?

   a. Lender
   b. Seller
   c. Listing agent
   d. Buyer

3. How many days does the selected title company have after the title company receives a copy of the contract for the Seller to furnish to the Buyer a copy of the title commitment?

   a. 7
   b. 10
   c. 20
   d. 30

4. The Seller always has the right to select the company that will provide escrow services and issue a title policy.

   a. True
   b. False

5. Which is included in the contract's definition of Exception Documents?

   a. Survey
   b. Restrictive covenants
   c. Commitment
   d. Abstract

6. All residential lots in a platted subdivision are subject to mandatory membership in an owners' association.

   a. True
   b. False

7. How many days after receipt of the commitment does the Buyer have to object to defects, exceptions, or encumbrances to title?

   a. A number of days determined by the parties
   b. The statutorily mandated 15
   c. 10
   d. 7

8. If a title policy is furnished as evidence of good title, who should be asked to promptly review the commitment upon Buyer's receipt of it?

   a. Lender
   b. Buyer's attorney
   c. Seller's attorney
   d. Broker's attorney

9. Federal law requires the attachment of a lead-based paint and lead-based paint hazards addendum to the purchase agreement for housing units built prior to what year?

   a. 1978
   b. 1977
   c. 1988
   d. 1866

10. Should the Seller's disclosure notice pursuant to section 5.008 of the Texas Property Code be listed as an addendum to the contract?

   a. Yes
   b. No
   c. Only if required by the lender
   d. Only when required by the Seller

HOMEWORK QUIZ

The following quiz does not have an answer key included with the answer keys in Appendix B. Students who are using this book as the basis for a correspondence course should record and submit their answers to their course provider as instructed by the provider. The student will submit his or her answers for the Homework Quiz at the end of each chapter and for each transaction in Chapter 11.

True or False?

1. Earnest money deposited by the Buyer is absolutely required to have a valid, enforceable contract.

2. It is the Seller who agrees to furnish a title policy.

3. To remove the standard printed exception relating to discrepancies, conflicts, and shortages in area and boundary lines, the title company will charge an additional premium established by the Texas Department of Insurance.

4. TREC OP-H, approved for voluntary use, or a version approved by HUD, should be an addendum to every contract of purchase of a property with dwelling units built after 1998.

5. It is the Buyer who purchases a residential service contract.

CHAPTER EIGHT

8

The Ticking Clock

KEY TERMS

after
day
5 days
prior
reasonable time
7 days
time is of the essence

CONTRACT TIME

In previous chapters we carefully read and considered the promises exchanged between the Buyer and the Seller. These promises included points such as the Seller promising to deliver title using a general warranty deed and the Buyer promising to deliver good funds to the title company in a form acceptable to the title company. A very important part of the exchanged promises relates to time frames within which various activities are to be performed.

Confusion can occur when the license holders representing the Buyer and Seller are not clear about the timeliness in relation to the promises exchanged between them. In Chapter 1 we learned that contracts are usually interpreted by the court applying the *reasonable rule.* That is, the court will favor holding the parties to fulfill the promises made as long as the parties have acted in good faith and demonstrated intent to live by the terms of the contract. Some of the time frames are even stated in subjective terms such as *immediately* and/or *as soon as is reasonably possible*.

REASONABLE TIME VERSUS TIME IS OF THE ESSENCE

An agent representing either the Buyer or the Seller would be well advised to refrain from making definitive statements about compliance or noncompliance of meeting the time frames established in the contract. What a party or an agent feels is a reasonable amount of time to perform an act or duty may not be in alignment with what a court will define as a **reasonable time.** It is always unwise to proclaim that the parties are or are not in compliance with the terms. It is important to remember the rule about not practicing law without a license.

Of course, it is a little easier to know if time frames are being met when the parties contractually agree that **time is of the essence** as long as they know what defines a *day* and they understand when a *new day begins*. When using the TREC-promulgated forms, it also helps to know the definition of the word *after*.

DEFINING *AFTER* AND *PRIOR*

Throughout the TREC forms, most of the time frames are stated as *so many days* **after** *the effective date* of the contract. The effective date of the contract is day 0 with the next day being day 1. You will also find so many days **prior** to Closing Date**.** The *Closing Date* is day zero and does not count. In one instance, you will find a time frame stated as *so many days **after** the Title Company receives a copy* of the contract.

A **day** is a 24-hour period of time that begins at midnight and goes to the beginning of the next day. There is no such thing as a statutorily defined *business* or *work* day. As a real estate license holder, you will quickly learn that there are **7 days** in each week, 365 days in a year, with the exception of leap year, which has 366 days, and that every one of those days can be a work day. It becomes more confusing when an agent decides to use the abbreviation *wk*. Does *wk* stand for week or work? Learn and remember that all days are created equal with 24 hours in each and with each beginning at midnight, unless the parties contractually agree to something else.

On occasion, you may encounter a client's attorney who will want to redefine when a day begins and ends by noting a specific time such as ". . . at 5:00 pm on . . ." When dealing with situations such as obtaining loans, having inspections or repairs done, dealing with attorneys, and dealing with Title Companies that are not typically open on Saturday or Sunday, the attorney may choose to insert language that states ". . . days excluding Saturday and Sunday . . ." The TREC rules call for license holders to simply fill in the blanks and to refrain from creating additional or replacement wordings. When a client or customer wants the offer written to exclude Saturday and Sunday, simply enter a number that is two days more.

Let's say that you have Buyers that want **5 days** to raise objections to title, but they do not think that Saturday and Sunday should be included because the Title Company will not be open to help them on those days. Rather than write 5 days in the contract blank, simply write 7 days.

IN-CLASS EXERCISE

In this exercise, focus on becoming thoroughly familiar with the various time frames set forth in a contractual agreement. It might be a good idea to return to Chapter 3 in order to highlight there every reference to *time* or *days*. But first, please read the following and search the TREC 20-7 contract for the numbers to fill in the blanks correctly as you review the contract one more time:

_____ 1. Days for the title company to deliver commitment. Found in paragraph ____

_____ 2. Number of days the Seller has to cure objections raised by the Buyer. Found in paragraph ____

_____ 3. Days for a new survey to be obtained prior to closing date if the title company refuses to accept a current survey. Found in paragraph ____

_____ 4. Number of days to deposit additional earnest money. Found in paragraph ____

_____ 5. Days for the Buyer to terminate when the TREC Form OP-H, Seller's Disclosure of Property Condition, is delivered after the effective date of the contract. Found in paragraph ____

_____ 6. Number of days for closing to occur after objections to title have been cured. Found in paragraph ____

_____ 7. Number of days the contract is extended for the Seller to complete repairs caused by a casualty loss after the effective date of the contract. Found in paragraph ____

_____ 8. Number of days for the Seller to furnish the Buyer with a new survey. Found in paragraph ____

_____ 9. Number of days for a Buyer to obtain a new survey. Found in paragraph ____

_____ 10. Number of days before a title company may release earnest money to a demanding party. Found in paragraph ____

_____ 11. Number of days to terminate the contract under the option clause. Found in paragraph ____

_____ 12. Number of days for the Buyer to raise objections to the title commitment or the survey. Found in paragraph ____

_____ 13. In the space below list any other time frames that you discovered in the contract.

____

____

It is imperative that Buyers and Sellers understand that it is important to consider all of the time references in the contractual agreement rather that looking at only one time reference, such as the closing date located in paragraph 9. It is important to relate each of the time references to all the other time references in the agreement.

In the following exercise, you will be able to see that the time references in paragraph 6 of the TREC contract can dramatically override what is entered in paragraph 9. Paragraph 6 addresses title and survey concerns and establishes time frames. Paragraph 9 states that the closing will occur on or before the closing date or within a number of days after title objections have been cured. The license holder's task when filling in the contract blanks is to determine just how far beyond the stated closing date that the actual closing may occur if every time frame recited in paragraphs 6 and 9 must be fully utilized to accomplish the various tasks, such as obtaining the title commitment, review of it by the Buyer, and the curing of title and survey items by the Seller.

■ EXERCISE: HELP FOR SARAH LIST-A-LOT

A contract is fully negotiated between the Sellers and Buyers with an effective date of May 5. It was delivered to and receipted by the title company on the same day. It is to close on or before June 1. The Buyers are to have five days to raise objections relating to the title commitment or the survey.

If every time frame stated in the contract must be fully utilized, what is the latest date on which this contract can close without the necessity of amending the contract? The calendar in Figure 8.1 is provided for your convenience. Help Sarah, the listing agent, figure this one out. Hint: It is a date much later than June 1.

FIGURE 8.1

Calendar

January

S	M	T	W	T	F	S
1	2	3	4	5	6	7
8	9	10	11	12	13	14
15	16	17	18	19	20	21
22	23	24	25	26	27	28
29	30	31				

February

S	M	T	W	T	F	S
			1	2	3	4
5	6	7	8	9	10	11
12	13	14	15	16	17	18
19	20	21	22	23	24	25
26	27	28				

March

S	M	T	W	T	F	S
			1	2	3	4
5	6	7	8	9	10	11
12	13	14	15	16	17	18
19	20	21	22	23	24	25
26	27	28	29	30	31	

April

S	M	T	W	T	F	S
						1
2	3	4	5	6	7	8
9	10	11	12	13	14	15
16	17	18	19	20	21	22
23	24	25	26	27	28	29
30						

May

S	M	T	W	T	F	S
	1	2	3	4	5	6
7	8	9	10	11	12	13
14	15	16	17	18	19	20
21	22	23	24	25	26	27
28	29	30	31			

June

S	M	T	W	T	F	S
				1	2	3
4	5	6	7	8	9	10
11	12	13	14	15	16	17
18	19	20	21	22	23	24
25	26	27	28	29	30	

July

S	M	T	W	T	F	S
						1
2	3	4	5	6	7	8
9	10	11	12	13	14	15
16	17	18	19	20	21	22
23	24	25	26	27	28	29
30	31					

August

S	M	T	W	T	F	S
		1	2	3	4	5
6	7	8	9	10	11	12
13	14	15	16	17	18	19
20	21	22	23	24	25	26
27	28	29	30	31		

September

S	M	T	W	T	F	S
					1	2
3	4	5	6	7	8	9
10	11	12	13	14	15	16
17	18	19	20	21	22	23
24	25	26	27	28	29	30

October

S	M	T	W	T	F	S
1	2	3	4	5	6	7
8	9	10	11	12	13	14
15	16	17	18	19	20	21
22	23	24	25	26	27	28
29	30	31				

November

S	M	T	W	T	F	S
			1	2	3	4
5	6	7	8	9	10	11
12	13	14	15	16	17	18
19	20	21	22	23	24	25
26	27	28	29	30		

December

S	M	T	W	T	F	S
					1	2
3	4	5	6	7	8	9
10	11	12	13	14	15	16
17	18	19	20	21	22	23
24	25	26	27	28	29	30
31						

HOMEWORK QUIZ

The following quiz does not have an answer key included with the answer keys in Appendix B. Students who are using this book as the basis for a correspondence course should record and submit their answers to their course provider as instructed by the provider. The student will submit his or her answers for the Homework Quiz at the end of each chapter and for each transaction in Chapter 11.

True or False?

1. When a contract contains the words *time is of the essence* for a particular provision, the parties agree that strict compliance with the time frame established by the contract is an essential element of the contract and shall be strictly enforced with interpreting the agreement.

2. The term *days* in the TREC-promulgated forms means business days rather than calendar days.

3. The promulgated contract calls for the title company to deliver a Title Commitment within 20 days after the title company receives a copy of the contract.

4. The date entered in paragraph 9 establishes an exact date on which the closing will occur.

5. For purposes of interpreting when contract time provisions begin and end, it is important to remember that days begin and end at 5:00 PM CST.

CHAPTER NINE

The Remaining Provisions

KEY TERMS

- assignment
- backup offers
- business details
- closing
- default
- escrow
- funding
- general warranty deed
- imputed notice
- liquidated damages
- Loan Fee
- mediation
- MIP
- PMI
- prevailing party
- temporary lease
- VA-funding fee
- wetland

BROKERS' FEES

License holders are particularly fond of the paragraph that instructs the officer handling **escrow** to pay them. (See Figure 9.1.)

FIGURE 9.1

TREC 20-7 Paragraph 8

8. BROKERS' FEES: All obligations of the parties for payment of brokers' fees are contained in separate written agreements.

Brokerage fees are not a part of the agreement between the Seller and the Buyer but rather are an issue between the Seller and the listing broker and the Buyer and the Buyer's broker. With regard to a subagent who brings to the transaction a customer, specifically a Buyer who has chosen not to be represented, how the cooperating broker is to be compensated is a matter between the listing broker and the selling broker. Commission splits between salespersons and the brokers who sponsor them are to be defined by their employment or independent contractor working agreement.

A clear understanding of who is being represented by whom is required by the TRELA. A box addressing this important issue is found on page 8 of the contract forms and is identified as Broker Information and Ratification of Fee. (See Figure 9.2.) **This box is not a part of the contract between the Seller and the Buyer.** It is set apart from the contract by being printed on a separate page and placed in a separate border. Brokers who represent Sellers and Buyers in the same transaction are reminded that section 1101.559 of the TRELA requires that the broker have written permission from each of the parties to function as an intermediary. Effective with the revisions made to the TRELA in 2005, a broker and the broker's associates who do not precisely follow the statutory requirements when attempting to represent both the Buyer and the Seller in the same transaction may face disciplinary action by the TREC. Dual representation without first obtaining the written authority to do so from each of the parties is a violation of the act.

FIGURE 9.2

TREC 20-7, Broker Information and Ratification of Fee

Contract Concerning ______________________________ Page 8 of 8 02-13-06
(Address of Property)

BROKER INFORMATION AND RATIFICATION OF FEE

Listing Broker has agreed to pay Other Broker ____________________ of the total sales price when Listing Broker's fee is received. Escrow Agent is authorized and directed to pay Other Broker from Listing Broker's fee at closing.

Other Broker — License No.	Listing Broker — License No.
represents ☐ Buyer only as Buyer's agent ☐ Seller as Listing Broker's subagent	represents ☐ Seller and Buyer as an intermediary ☐ Seller only as Seller's agent
Associate — Telephone	Listing Associate — Telephone
Broker's Address	Listing Associate's Office Address — Facsimile
City — State — Zip	City — State — Zip
Facsimile	Email Address
Email Address	Selling Associate — Telephone
	Selling Associate's Office Address — Facsimile
	City — State — Zip
	Email Address

When entering the information in the Broker Information box on page 8 of the TREC Form 20-7, remember that there is no other broker involved in an in-house transaction. Be clear as to who is being represented; be clear as to who represents whom.

CLOSING AND POSSESSION

Closing and the Buyer's possession of the Property are important issues addressed in paragraphs 9 and 10. (See Figure 9.3.) Closing needs to occur on or before a specific date, while possession should generally be granted at the happening of a defined event, such as closing or **funding** From time to time you may have a transaction in which the Buyer takes possession prior to closing or a Seller remains in the Property for some period after closing.

If a Buyer moves in before closing and funding or a Seller remains after closing and funding, a landlord/tenant relationship exists. The relationship must be clearly defined by a Seller's or Buyer's **temporary lease.** Please examine the TREC-promulgated forms that follow. Failure to use the appropriate temporary lease will create a tenancy at sufferance. Pay particular attention to the provisions relating to insurance coverage on the Property during the tenancy period. A temporary lease may not be used to address any tenancy that exceeds 90 days. If the tenancy exceeds 90 days, the owner will need to regard the Property as a residential rental Property and bring it into compliance with Chapter 92 of the Texas Property Code, the chapter that defines security devices, smoke detectors, and other features that must be provided in a residential rental unit.

FIGURE 9.3

TREC 20-7 Paragraphs 9 and 10

9. CLOSING:

A. The closing of the sale will be on or before ______________________, 20_____, or within 7 days after objections made under Paragraph 6D have been cured or waived, whichever date is later (Closing Date). If either party fails to close the sale by the Closing Date, the non-defaulting party may exercise the remedies contained in Paragraph 15.

B. At closing:

(1) Seller shall execute and deliver a general warranty deed conveying title to the Property to Buyer and showing no additional exceptions to those permitted in Paragraph 6 and furnish tax statements or certificates showing no delinquent taxes on the Property.

(2) Buyer shall pay the Sales Price in good funds acceptable to the escrow agent.

(3) Seller and Buyer shall execute and deliver any notices, statements, certificates, affidavits, releases, loan documents and other documents required of them by this contract, the Commitment or law necessary for the closing of the sale and the issuance of the Title Policy.

C. Unless expressly prohibited by written agreement, Seller may continue to show the Property and receive, negotiate and accept back up offers.

D. All covenants, representations and warranties in this contract survive closing.

10. POSSESSION: Seller shall deliver to Buyer possession of the Property in its present or required condition, ordinary wear and tear excepted: ❑ upon closing and funding ❑ according to a temporary residential lease form promulgated by TREC or other written lease required by the parties. Any possession by Buyer prior to closing or by Seller after closing which is not authorized by a written lease will establish a tenancy at sufferance relationship between the parties. **Consult your insurance agent prior to change of ownership and possession because insurance coverage may be limited or terminated. The absence of a written lease or appropriate insurance coverage may expose the parties to economic loss.**

What if the owner is willing to permit the occupancy prior to or after closing as a courtesy and does not demand or expect any rental payments? The possession by anyone who is not the current owner creates a landlord and tenant relationship. If no rent is to be charged, indicate none or zero in the appropriate blank on the temporary lease. Remember from Chapter 1 that it does not require money to create a valid bilateral contract.

A good business practice is to take digital photographs at the beginning of any tenancy to record the condition of the Property at the beginning of the tenancy. Draw the attention of the parties to the Repairs and Maintenance part of the agreement at paragraph 13 of both the temporary leases, namely the TREC Form 15-4, Seller's Temporary Residential Lease, and the TREC Form 16-4, Buyer's Temporary Residential Lease. Also, be very specific and detailed about utilities, pets, and any *holding over*. It is usually prudent to have the tenant pay a large per diem rental for each day of hold over. (See Figure 9.4 and Figure 9.5.)

■ SPECIAL PROVISIONS

When the parties need to add factual statements or **business details** to their agreement, they may use paragraph 11. (See Figure 9.6.) When the parties want to define legal rights and remedies, they should seek competent legal advice. When the parties ask the agents to write language that defines legal rights and remedies, agents should advise them to seek competent legal advice.

A *factual statement* states what someone will or will not do. A *legal right* or *remedy* states what will happen if someone does or does not do a particular act.

Things that can be added in paragraph 11 include:

- An inventory list
- A preclosing walk-through inspection
- Documents available for review prior to closing
- Who will pay for specific costs that may be incurred
- Notice that a license holder acting on his and her own behalf holds a real estate license

Do not write a statement that the Buyer's offer is automatically withdrawn at a particular point in time if the Seller has not made a response to the offer.

The agent should always make certain that an offer is properly withdrawn before assisting a Buyer to make an offer on another property.

FIGURE 9.4

TREC 15-4

PROMULGATED BY THE TEXAS REAL ESTATE COMMISSION (TREC) 12-04-06

(NOTICE: For use only when SELLER occupies the property for no more than 90 days AFTER the closing)

EQUAL HOUSING OPPORTUNITY

SELLER'S TEMPORARY RESIDENTIAL LEASE

1. **PARTIES:** The parties to this Lease are____ (Landlord) and ____(Tenant).
2. **LEASE:** Landlord leases to Tenant the Property described in the Contract between Landlord as Buyer and Tenant as Seller known as ____(address).
3. **TERM:** The term of this Lease commences on the date the sale covered by the Contract is closed and funded and terminates __________________, unless terminated earlier by reason of other provisions.
4. **RENTAL:** Tenant shall pay to Landlord as rental $__________ per day (excluding the day of closing and funding) with the full amount of rental for the term of the Lease to be paid at the time of funding of the sale. Tenant will not be entitled to a refund of rental if this Lease terminates early due to Tenant's default or voluntary surrender of the Property.
5. **DEPOSIT:** Tenant shall pay to Landlord at the time of funding of the sale $____________as a deposit to secure performance of this Lease by Tenant. Landlord may use the deposit to satisfy Tenant's obligations under this Lease. Landlord shall refund any unused portion of the deposit to Tenant with an itemized list of all deductions from the deposit within 30 days after Tenant (a) surrenders possession of the Property and (b) provides Landlord written notice of Tenant's forwarding address.
6. **UTILITIES:** Tenant shall pay all utility charges except ______________________________________ which Landlord shall pay.
7. **USE OF PROPERTY:** Tenant may use the Property only for residential purposes. Tenant may not assign this Lease or sublet any part of the Property.
8. **PETS:** Tenant may not keep pets on the Property except ____________________________________.
9. **CONDITION OF PROPERTY:** Tenant accepts the Property in its present condition and state of repair at the commencement of the Lease. Upon termination, Tenant shall surrender the Property to Landlord in the condition required under the Contract, except normal wear and tear and any casualty loss.
10. **ALTERATIONS:** Tenant may not alter the Property or install improvements or fixtures without the prior written consent of the Landlord. Any improvements or fixtures placed on the Property during the Lease become the Property of Landlord.
11. **SPECIAL PROVISIONS:**

12. **INSPECTIONS:** Landlord may enter at reasonable times to inspect the Property. Tenant shall provide Landlord door keys and access codes to allow access to the Property during the term of Lease.
13. **LAWS:** Tenant shall comply with all applicable laws, restrictions, ordinances, rules and regulations with respect to the Property.
14. **REPAIRS AND MAINTENANCE:** <u>Except as otherwise provided in this Lease, Tenant shall bear all expense of repairing and maintaining the Property, including but not limited to the yard, trees and shrubs, unless otherwise required by the Texas Property Code. Tenant shall promptly repair at Tenant's expense any damage to the Property caused directly or indirectly by any act or omission of the Tenant or any person other than the Landlord, Landlord's agents or invitees.</u>

Initialed for identification by Landlord _______ and Tenant___________ TREC NO. 15-4

FIGURE 9.4 (CONTINUED)

TREC 15-4

Seller's Temporary Residential Lease ______________________ Page 2 of 2 12-04-06
(Address of Property)

15. INDEMNITY: Tenant indemnifies Landlord from the claims of all third parties for injury or damage to the person or property of such third party arising from the use or occupancy of the Property by Tenant. This indemnification includes attorney's fees, costs and expenses incurred by Landlord.

16. INSURANCE: Landlord and Tenant shall each maintain such insurance on the contents and Property as each party may deem appropriate during the term of this Lease. NOTE: CONSULT YOUR INSURANCE AGENT; POSSESSION OF THE PROPERTY BY SELLER AS TENANT MAY CHANGE INSURANCE POLICY COVERAGE.

17. DEFAULT: If Tenant fails to perform or observe any provision of this Lease and fails, within 24 hours after notice by Landlord, to commence and diligently pursue to remedy such failure, Tenant will be in default.

18. TERMINATION: This Lease terminates upon expiration of the term specified in Paragraph 3 or upon Tenant's default under this Lease.

19. HOLDING OVER: Tenant shall surrender possession of the Property upon termination of this Lease. Any possession by Tenant after termination creates a tenancy at sufferance and will not operate to renew or extend this Lease. Tenant shall pay $______ per day during the period of any possession after termination as damages, in addition to any other remedies to which Landlord is entitled.

20. ATTORNEY'S FEES: The prevailing party in any legal proceeding brought under or with respect to this Lease is entitled to recover from the non-prevailing party all costs of such proceeding and reasonable attorney's fees.

21. SMOKE DETECTORS: The Texas Property Code requires Landlord to install smoke detectors in certain locations within the Property at Landlord's expense. Tenant expressly waives Landlord's duty to inspect and repair smoke detectors.

22. SECURITY DEVICES: The requirements of the Texas Property Code relating to security devices do not apply to a residential lease for a term of 90 days or less.

23. CONSULT YOUR ATTORNEY: Real estate licensees cannot give legal advice. This Lease is intended to be legally binding. READ IT CAREFULLY. If you do not understand the effect of this Lease, consult your attorney BEFORE signing.

24. NOTICES: All notices from one party to the other must be in writing and are effective when mailed to, hand-delivered at, or transmitted by facsimile or electronic transmission as follows:

To Landlord: ______________________	**To Tenant:** ______________________
______________________	______________________
______________________	______________________
______________________	______________________
Telephone: ( ) ______________	Telephone: ( ) ______________
Facsimile: ( ) ______________	Facsimile: ( ) ______________
E-mail: ______________	E-mail: ______________

______________________ Landlord ______________________ Tenant

______________________ Landlord ______________________ Tenant

The form of this contract has been approved by the Texas Real Estate Commission. TREC forms are intended for use only by trained real estate licensees. No representation is made as to the legal validity or adequacy of any provision in any specific transactions. It is not intended for complex transactions. Texas Real Estate Commission, P.O. Box 12188, Austin, TX 78711-2188, 1-800-250-8732 or (512) 459-6544 (http://www.trec.state.tx.us) TREC NO. 15-4. This form replaces TREC NO. 15-3.

FIGURE 9.5

TREC 16-4

PROMULGATED BY THE TEXAS REAL ESTATE COMMISSION (TREC) 12-04-06

(NOTICE: For use only when BUYER occupies the property for no more than 90 days PRIOR the closing)

EQUAL HOUSING OPPORTUNITY

BUYER'S TEMPORARY RESIDENTIAL LEASE

1. **PARTIES:** The parties to this Lease are____ (Landlord) and ____(Tenant).

2. **LEASE:** Landlord leases to Tenant the Property described in the Contract between Landlord as Seller and Tenant as Buyer known as ____(address).

3. **TERM:** The term of this Lease commences ____________________________ and terminates as specified in Paragraph 18.

4. **RENTAL:** Rental will be $______________ per day. Upon commencement of this Lease, Tenant shall pay to Landlord the full amount of rental of $ ______________ for the anticipated term of the Lease (commencement date to the Closing Date specified in Paragraph 9 of the Contract). If the actual term of this Lease differs from the anticipated term, any additional rent or reimbursement will be paid at closing. No portion of the rental will be applied to payment of any items covered by the Contract.

5. **DEPOSIT:** Tenant has paid to Landlord $____________________ as a deposit to secure performance of this Lease by Tenant. If this Lease is terminated before the Closing Date, Landlord may use the deposit to satisfy Tenant's obligations under this Lease. Landlord shall refund to Tenant any unused portion of the deposit together with an itemized list of all deductions from the deposit within 30 days after Tenant (a) surrenders possession of the Property and (b) provides Landlord written notice of Tenant's forwarding address. If this Lease is terminated by the closing and funding of the sale of the Property, the deposit will be refunded to Tenant at closing and funding.
   <u>NOTICE:</u> The deposit must be in addition to the earnest money under the Contract.

6. **UTILITIES:** Tenant shall pay all utility connections, deposits and charges except ____, which Landlord shall pay.

7. **USE OF PROPERTY:** Tenant may use the Property only for residential purposes. Tenant may not assign this Lease or sublet any part of the Property.

8. **PETS:** Tenant may not keep pets on the Property except ___________________________________.

9. **CONDITION OF PROPERTY:** Tenant accepts the Property in its present condition and state of repair, but Landlord shall make all repairs and improvements required by the Contract. If this Lease is terminated prior to closing, Tenant shall surrender possession of the Property to Landlord in its present condition, as improved by Landlord, except normal wear and tear and any casualty loss.

10. **ALTERATIONS:** Tenant may not: (a) make any holes or drive nails into the woodwork, floors, walls or ceilings (b) alter, paint or decorate the Property or (c) install improvements or fixtures without the prior written consent of Landlord. Any improvements or fixtures placed on the Property during the Lease become a part of the Property.

11. **SPECIAL PROVISIONS:**

12. **INSPECTIONS:** Landlord may enter at reasonable times to inspect, replace, repair or complete the improvements. Tenant shall provide Landlord door keys and access codes to allow access to the Property during the term of the Lease.

13. **LAWS:** Tenant shall comply with all applicable laws, restrictions, ordinances, rules and regulations with respect to the Property.

14. **REPAIRS AND MAINTENANCE:** <u>Except as otherwise provided in this Lease, Tenant shall bear all expense of repairing, replacing and maintaining the Property, including but not limited to the yard, trees, shrubs, and all equipment and appliances, unless otherwise required by the Texas Property Code. Tenant shall promptly repair at Tenant's expense any damage to the Property caused directly or indirectly by any act or omission of the Tenant or any person other than the Landlord, Landlord's agents or invitees.</u>

Initialed for identification by Landlord _______ and Tenant___________ TREC NO. 16-4

FIGURE 9.5 (CONTINUED)

TREC 16-4

15. INDEMNITY: Tenant indemnifies Landlord from the claims of all third parties for injury or damage to the person or property of such third party arising from the use or occupancy of the Property by Tenant. This indemnification includes attorney's fees, costs and expenses incurred by Landlord.

16. INSURANCE: Landlord and Tenant shall each maintain such insurance on the contents and Property as each party may deem appropriate during the term of this Lease. NOTE: CONSULT YOUR INSURANCE AGENT; POSSESSION OF THE PROPERTY BY BUYER AS TENANT MAY CHANGE INSURANCE POLICY COVERAGE.

17. DEFAULT: If Tenant fails to perform or observe any provision of this Lease and fails, within 24 hours after notice by Landlord, to commence and diligently pursue to remedy such failure, Tenant will be in default.

18. TERMINATION: This Lease terminates upon (a) closing and funding of the sale under the Contract, (b) termination of the Contract prior to closing, (c) Tenant's default under this Lease, or (d) Tenant's default under the Contract, whichever occurs first. Upon termination other than by closing and funding of the sale, Tenant shall surrender possession of the property.

19. HOLDING OVER: Any possession by Tenant after termination creates a tenancy at sufferance and will not operate to renew or extend this Lease. Tenant shall pay $_______ per day during the period of any possession after termination as damages, in addition to any other remedies to which Landlord is entitled.

20. ATTORNEY'S FEES: The prevailing party in any legal proceeding brought under or with respect to this Lease is entitled to recover from the non-prevailing party all costs of such proceeding and reasonable attorney's fees.

21. SMOKE DETECTORS: The Texas Property Code requires Landlord to install smoke detectors in certain locations within the Property at Landlord's expense. Tenant expressly waives Landlord's duty to inspect and repair smoke detectors.

22. SECURITY DEVICES: The requirements of the Texas Property Code relating to security devices do not apply to a residential lease for a term of 90 days or less.

23. CONSULT YOUR ATTORNEY: Real estate licensees cannot give legal advice. This Lease is intended to be legally binding. READ IT CAREFULLY. If you do not understand the effect of this Lease, consult your attorney BEFORE signing.

24. NOTICES: All notices from one party to the other must be in writing and are effective when mailed to, hand-delivered at, or transmitted by facsimile or electronic transmission as follows:

To Landlord: ______________________	**To Tenant:** ______________________
______________________	______________________
______________________	______________________
______________________	______________________
Telephone: ( ) ______________	Telephone: ( ) ______________
Facsimile: ( ) ______________	Facsimile: ( ) ______________
E-mail: ______________________	E-mail: ______________________

______________________	______________________
Landlord	Tenant
______________________	______________________
Landlord	Tenant

The form of this contract has been approved by the Texas Real Estate Commission. TREC forms are intended for use only by trained real estate licensees. No representation is made as to the legal validity or adequacy of any provision in any specific transactions. It is not intended for complex transactions. Texas Real Estate Commission, P.O. Box 12188, Austin, TX 78711-2188, 1-800-250-8732 or (512) 459-6544 (http://www.trec.state.tx.us) TREC NO. 16-4. This form replaces TREC NO. 16-3.

FIGURE 9.6

TREC 20-7 Paragraph 11

11. SPECIAL PROVISIONS: (Insert only factual statements and business details applicable to the sale. TREC rules prohibit licensees from adding factual statements or business details for which a contract addendum, lease or other form has been promulgated by TREC for mandatory use.)

When the provisions are extensive and require more than the space provided, the parties may need to seek the assistance of a competent attorney. The TREC has kept the space small for good reason.

The following are examples of things that *may not* be addressed in Special Provisions paragraph 11:

The transaction is contingent upon the sale of another Property (see the TREC Form 10-5, Addendum for Sale of Other Property by Buyer).

- The contract is in a second or backup position (see the TREC Form 11-6, Addendum for "Back-Up" Contract).
- The assumption transaction is contingent upon the Seller's release of liability or, in the case of a VA-guaranteed loan, restoration of VA entitlement (see the TREC Form 12-2, Addendum for Release of Liability on Assumption of FHA, VA or Conventional Loan/Restoration of Seller's Entitlement).
- Arrangements for the Seller to stay after closing or the Buyer to possess before closing (see the TREC Form 15-4, Seller's Temporary Residential Lease, and the TREC Form 16-4, Buyer's Temporary Residential Lease).
- The contract is contingent upon satisfactory inspections to the Buyer.
- The parties agree that in the event of a dispute they will try *mediation* before bringing a lawsuit.
- Any wording that defines legal rights and remedies, such as *contingent upon, terminate, refund earnest money on demand, cancel,* and so forth.
- Parties should contact an attorney before using the words *time is of the essence.*

SETTLEMENT AND OTHER EXPENSES

Paragraph 12 defines who will pay for what and reflects current custom in Texas at the time of adoption of the form. The paragraph is uncomplicated and can easily be understood with a reasonably careful reading. Although we examined it in Chapter 3, paragraph 12 bears rereading. (See Figure 9.7.)

FIGURE 9.7

TREC 20-7 Paragraph 12

12. SETTLEMENT AND OTHER EXPENSES:

A. The following expenses must be paid at or prior to closing:

(1) Expenses payable by Seller (Seller's Expenses):

(a) Releases of existing liens, including prepayment penalties and recording fees; release of Seller's loan liability; tax statements or certificates; preparation of deed; one-half of escrow fee; and other expenses payable by Seller under this contract.

(b) Seller shall also pay an amount not to exceed $ ____________ to be applied in the following order: Buyer's Expenses which Buyer is prohibited from paying by FHA, VA, Texas Veterans Housing Assistance Program or other governmental loan programs, and then to other Buyer's Expenses as allowed by the lender.

(2) Expenses payable by Buyer (Buyer's Expenses):

(a) Loan origination, discount, buy-down, and commitment fees (Loan Fees).

(b) Appraisal fees; loan application fees; credit reports; preparation of loan documents; interest on the notes from date of disbursement to one month prior to dates of first monthly payments; recording fees; copies of easements and restrictions; mortgagee title policy with endorsements required by lender; loan-related inspection fees; photos; amortization schedules; one-half of escrow fee; all prepaid items, including required premiums for flood and hazard insurance, reserve deposits for insurance, ad valorem taxes and special governmental assessments; final compliance inspection; courier fee; repair inspection; underwriting fee; wire transfer fee; expenses incident to any loan; and other expenses payable by Buyer under this contract.

B. Buyer shall pay Private Mortgage Insurance Premium (PMI), VA Loan Funding Fee, or FHA Mortgage Insurance Premium (MIP) as required by the lender.

C. If any expense exceeds an amount expressly stated in this contract for such expense to be paid by a party, that party may terminate this contract unless the other party agrees to pay such excess. Buyer may not pay charges and fees expressly prohibited by FHA, VA, Texas Veterans Housing Assistance Program or other governmental loan program regulations.

The Seller's typical expenses are listed in 12A(1) and the Buyer's in 12A(2). The parties can agree to shift any of these expenses by going to paragraph 11 and setting down their agreement. If the Seller is to contribute funds to pay a portion of the Buyer's Expenses, please note that the blank in 12A(b) calls for a specific dollar amount. A competent listing agent would never recommend that a Seller accept an offer that uses vague things as *TBD*, or *as permitted by lender*, or *as needed*. The Seller should understand that any dollar amount that is entered in this blank will move to the Buyer's side of the closing statement.

The paragraphs in Figure 9.8 are self-explanatory; however, do take note that items subject to proration in paragraph 13 will be prorated *through* the day of closing. The Seller will be charged the expense for closing day whether the parties close early in the morning or just before the title company closes.

It is important to note that if a party accepts the earnest money as **liquidated damages** under the provisions of paragraph 15, both parties are released from the contract and have no further recourse against each other. A license holder should never give legal advice by directing a customer or client to choose one of the three specific remedies set down in paragraph 15. Help parties to read and to understand that there are possibilities open to them. Let an attorney advise them as to which is their best choice given a particular set of circumstances.

FIGURE 9.8

TREC 20-7 Paragraphs 13, 14, and 15

13. PRORATIONS: Taxes for the current year, interest, maintenance fees, assessments, dues and rents will be prorated through the Closing Date. The tax proration may be calculated taking into consideration any change in exemptions that will affect the current year's taxes. If taxes for the current year vary from the amount prorated at closing, the parties shall adjust the prorations when tax statements for the current year are available. If taxes are not paid at or prior to closing, Buyer shall pay taxes for the current year.

14. CASUALTY LOSS: If any part of the Property is damaged or destroyed by fire or other casualty after the effective date of this contract, Seller shall restore the Property to its previous condition as soon as reasonably possible, but in any event by the Closing Date. If Seller fails to do so due to factors beyond Seller's control, Buyer may (a) terminate this contract and the earnest money will be refunded to Buyer (b) extend the time for performance up to 15 days and the Closing Date will be extended as necessary or (c) accept the Property in its damaged condition with an assignment of insurance proceeds and receive credit from Seller at closing in the amount of the deductible under the insurance policy. Seller's obligations under this paragraph are independent of any other obligations of Seller under this contract.

15. DEFAULT: If Buyer fails to comply with this contract, Buyer will be in default, and Seller may (a) enforce specific performance, seek such other relief as may be provided by law, or both, or (b) terminate this contract and receive the earnest money as liquidated damages, thereby releasing both parties from this contract. If, due to factors beyond Seller's control, Seller fails within the time allowed to make any non-casualty repairs or deliver the Commitment, or survey, if required of Seller, Buyer may (a) extend the time for performance up to 15 days and the Closing Date will be extended as necessary or (b) terminate this contract as the sole remedy and receive the earnest money. If Seller fails to comply with this contract for any other reason, Seller will be in default and Buyer may (a) enforce specific performance, seek such other relief as may be provided by law, or both, or (b) terminate this contract and receive the earnest money, thereby releasing both parties from this contract.

■ MEDIATION

Please carefully read paragraph 16 that follows relating to dispute resolution. (See Figure 9.9.) A license holder should have a general understanding of the benefits and limitations of litigation, arbitration, and meditation. In litigation a judge or a jury will decide the outcome, an outcome that can be appealed to a higher court for consideration. In arbitration, the parties present their positions to a third, disinterested party who listens and then renders a decision that may or may not be binding. The decision reached in arbitration is binding on the parties only if they have contractually agreed that it will be so prior to the arbitration hearing.

Mediation has become the preferred alternative dispute-resolution approach in Texas and has enjoyed a very high success rate. In *mediation*, a third, disinterested party facilitates communication between the disputing parties to enable them to move toward a point of agreement. The mediator does not need to be a subject area expert. The mediator does not make decisions as to who is right or wrong. A skilled mediator will set the ground rules for the discussions, keep the parties focused by asking probing questions, and help each of the parties listen to what the other party has to say. If the parties reach agreement, they will reduce the agreement to writing and will be legally bound to the new contract that they have created between themselves. If they do not reach agreement, they will usually move on to either binding arbitration or litigation.

FIGURE 9.9

TREC 20-7 Paragraph 16

16. MEDIATION: It is the policy of the State of Texas to encourage resolution of disputes through alternative dispute resolution procedures such as mediation. Any dispute between Seller and Buyer related to this contract which is not resolved through informal discussion ❑will ❑will not be submitted to a mutually acceptable mediation service or provider. The parties to the mediation shall bear the mediation costs equally. This paragraph does not preclude a party from seeking equitable relief from a court of competent jurisdiction.

Why Choose Mediation?

The parties are advised and encouraged to submit to mediation disputes that cannot be resolved through informal discussion. When you encourage parties to agree to mediation, be sure to point out that a contractual agreement is being made to bear the mediation costs equally. The cost can range from zero dollars (or a small number), if the services of a county-operated alternative dispute resolution center is used, to hundreds or even thousands of dollars if a private mediator is hired.

Under the provisions of the Texas statute relating to alternative dispute resolution, only a judge has been given authority to compel parties to mediation. License holders can encourage parties to submit disputes to mediation by pointing out the benefits, but they cannot compel the parties to do so. License holders should be familiar with the process and should be able to explain what it is, and is not, to Buyer and Seller customers and clients.

In 1987, by the passage of Senate Bill 1436, the Texas legislature enacted the following Dispute Resolution Act:

> THE STATUTORY PROVISIONS
> SUBCHAPTER B.
> ALTERNATIVE DISPUTE RESOLUTION PROCEDURES
>
> Sec. 154.021. REFERRAL OF PENDING DISPUTES FOR ALTERNATIVE DISPUTE RESOLUTION PROCEDURE. (a) A court may, on its own motion or the motion of a party, refer a pending dispute for resolution by an alternative dispute resolution procedure including:
>
>> (1) an alternative dispute resolution system established under Chapter 26, Acts of the 68th Legislature, Regular Session, 1983 (Article 2372aa, Vernon's Texas Civil Statutes);
>>
>> (2) a dispute resolution organization; or

(3) a nonjudicial and informally conducted forum for the voluntary settlement of citizens' disputes through the intervention of an impartial third party, including those alternative dispute resolution procedures described under this subchapter.

(b) The court shall confer with the parties in the determination of the most appropriate alternative dispute resolution procedure.

Sec. 154.022. NOTIFICATION AND OBJECTION. (a) If a court determines that a pending dispute is appropriate for referral under Section 154.021, the court shall notify the parties of its determination.

(b) Any party may, within 10 days after receiving the notice under Subsection (a), file a written objection to the referral.

(c) If the court finds that there is a reasonable basis for an objection filed under Subsection (b), the court may not refer the dispute under Section 154.021.

Sec. 154.023. MEDIATION

(a) Mediation is a forum in which an impartial person, the mediator, facilitates communication between parties to promote reconciliation, settlement, or understanding among them.

(b) A mediator may not impose his own judgment on the issues for that of the parties.

The Mediation Process

Mediation might be defined as a process through which two or more parties to a dispute voluntarily meet and attempt to find a mutually agreeable settlement with the assistance of a neutral third party, a mediator. The mediator *does not*

- render decisions,
- offer advice,
- pass judgment, or
- resolve the dispute.

The mediator *does*

- facilitate communication between the parties,
- remain impartial, and
- establish the ground rules for the mediation.

On the day of mediation, the parties may bring any information that will help explain their respective positions. However, it is important to remember that mediation is an informal process with no formal rules of evidence, disposition, or witnesses. The mediation meeting is privileged and confidential. Under Texas statute the mediator or any party to the mediation is prohibited from telling the court anything said during the mediation. The most a mediator may report to the court is that the case did or did not settle.

The four most frequently cited advantages of mediation are the following:

1. Low cost
2. Fast—much quicker than litigation
3. Private—whereas everything that happens or is said in court is public
4. Win-Win—Offering an opportunity for *both parties to win*

The cost of mediation is shared equally by the parties and can range from a few hundred dollars to $1,500 or more. The fee will be determined by the mediator and will vary, depending on the complexity of the issues, the experience of the mediator, the complexity of the case, and the time involved.

In real estate what type of disputes can be mediated? Almost any dispute between Buyers and Sellers, landlords and tenants, and brokers and clients can and, in the interest of all parties concerned, should be mediated. The only disputes that cannot and should not be mediated are those that include a possible charge or allegation of criminal misconduct.

When the parties reach a point of agreement, the mediation moves to the final stage of the process, in which the parties set down, or memorialize, the essential terms of their agreement. When signed by each party, the parties are bound to fulfill the terms of their agreement just as they would be bound by any other contract into which they might enter.

OTHER CONTRACT PROVISIONS

Attorney's Fees

The wording concerning the attorney's fee is straightforward and common to most real estate related agreements. (See Figure 9.10.) It appears that the Broker-Lawyer Committee and the TREC intended for the wording to include license holders who might become a party in a legal proceeding brought under or with respect to the subject transaction.

FIGURE 9.10

TREC 20-7 Paragraph 17

17. ATTORNEY'S FEES: The prevailing party in any legal proceeding related to this contract is entitled to recover reasonable attorney's fees and all costs of such proceeding incurred by the prevailing party.

The TREC-promulgated contracts have an interesting provision in paragraph 18C. (See Figure 9.11.) The parties give the escrow agent the ability to, after due notice, release the earnest money to a party making a written demand for it. The title company may, after a 15-day period, release the money to the demanding party; however, the title company is not required to do so. If the title company chooses to release the money to the demanding party, the parties agree to release the escrow agent from all adverse claims related to the disbursal of the earnest money when the detailed procedure is followed by the title company.

FIGURE 9.11

TREC 20-7 Paragraph 18

18. ESCROW:

A. ESCROW: The escrow agent is not (i) a party to this contract and does not have liability for the performance or nonperformance of any party to this contract, (ii) liable for interest on the earnest money and (iii) liable for the loss of any earnest money caused by the failure of any financial institution in which the earnest money has been deposited unless the financial institution is acting as escrow agent.

B. EXPENSES: At closing, the earnest money must be applied first to any cash down payment, then to Buyer's Expenses and any excess refunded to Buyer. If no closing occurs, escrow agent may require payment of unpaid expenses incurred on behalf of the parties and a written release of liability of escrow agent from all parties.

C. DEMAND: Upon termination of this contract, either party or the escrow agent may send a release of earnest money to each party and the parties shall execute counterparts of the release and deliver same to the escrow agent. If either party fails to execute the release, either party may make a written demand to the escrow agent for the earnest money. If only one party makes written demand for the earnest money, escrow agent shall promptly provide a copy of the demand to the other party. If escrow agent does not receive written objection to the demand from the other party within 15 days, escrow agent may disburse the earnest money to the party making demand reduced by the amount of unpaid expenses incurred on behalf of the party receiving the earnest money and escrow agent may pay the same to the creditors. If escrow agent complies with the provisions of this paragraph, each party hereby releases escrow agent from all adverse claims related to the disbursal of the earnest money.

D. DAMAGES: Any party who wrongfully fails or refuses to sign a release acceptable to the escrow agent within 7 days of receipt of the request will be liable to the other party for liquidated damages of three times the amount of the earnest money.

E. NOTICES: Escrow agent's notices will be effective when sent in compliance with Paragraph 21. Notice of objection to the demand will be deemed effective upon receipt by escrow agent.

Sellers should note that all representations made in the agreement transfer to the warranty deed and survive closing. (See Figure 9.12.) This is a good reason to keep the Seller's disclosure notice addressed by section 5.008 of the Texas Property Code separate from the contract.

FIGURE 9.12

TREC 20-7 Paragraph 19

19. REPRESENTATIONS: Seller represents that as of the Closing Date (a) there will be no liens, assessments, or security interests against the Property which will not be satisfied out of the sales proceeds unless securing payment of any loans assumed by Buyer and (b) assumed loans will not be in default. If any representation of Seller in this contract is untrue on the Closing Date, Seller will be in default.

When closing takes place at a title company, the escrow agent makes certain that Internal Revenue Service (IRS) regulations are followed. (See Figure 9.13.) The parties should read the paragraph and seek answers to their questions from qualified sources.

FIGURE 9.13

TREC 20-7 Paragraph 20

20. FEDERAL TAX REQUIREMENTS: If Seller is a "foreign person," as defined by applicable law, or if Seller fails to deliver an affidavit to Buyer that Seller is not a "foreign person," then Buyer shall withhold from the sales proceeds an amount sufficient to comply with applicable tax law and deliver the same to the Internal Revenue Service together with appropriate tax forms. Internal Revenue Service regulations require filing written reports if currency in excess of specified amounts is received in the transaction.

Notices

Ask the Buyer and Seller where notices are to be mailed, e-mailed, or transmitted by facsimile machine. (See Figure 9.14.) Texas courts will require validation of a contract evidenced by facsimile signatures. It is best to obtain the original signature of each of the parties at the signature lines.

FIGURE 9.14

TREC 20-7 Paragraph 21

21. NOTICES: All notices from one party to the other must be in writing and are effective when mailed to, hand-delivered at, or transmitted by facsimile or electronic transmission as follows:

To Buyer at: ______________________	**To Seller at:** ______________________
______________________	______________________
______________________	______________________
______________________	______________________
Telephone: ( ) ______________________	Telephone: ( ) ______________________
Facsimile: ( ) ______________________	Facsimile: ( ) ______________________
E-mail: ______________________	E-mail: ______________________

Please be aware that the contract specifies that notices are effective when delivered to the Buyer or the Seller. Common law has generally held that a notice given to a principal's agent *may* constitute an effective delivery to the Buyer or Seller. This is known as **imputed notice.** It is presumed that tendering money or notifying one's agent is the same as notifying the person directly. *Be careful here!* The language of the contract form is very specific in paragraph 21. Deliver notices as stated.

If the Buyer is a customer rather than a client, the Buyer does not have an agent. Delivery of the notice to a co-op agent, acting as a subagent, does not constitute delivery of the notice to the Buyer. Remember that the subagent works for and represents the Seller. When a transaction involves both a Seller's agent and a Buyer's agent, notifying a client's agent will generally be construed as giving constructive or imputed notice to the client.

The following list identifies some of the notices and documents identified in the contract that may need to be delivered:

- Notice of termination during the option period
- Homeowners' association resale certificate
- Financial documentation of Buyer as identified in paragraph 4E
- Title commitment
- Survey
- Lender required repairs
- Demand for release of earnest money deposit

Agreement of Parties

Any addenda that are to be a part of the agreement must be identified in the agreement. The TREC has made it very easy for the parties and the agents to make certain that all addenda are listed. (See Figure 9.15.) Failure to list or reference an addendum in the agreement can cause serious problems. If it is not referenced in the contract, a court is not likely to accept the addendum in question as a part of the agreement.

Do *not* list the following:

- Seller's disclosure notice
- Information about brokerage services
- The TAR Notification of Intermediary Relationship form

FIGURE 9.15

TREC 20-7 Paragraph 22

22. AGREEMENT OF PARTIES: This contract contains the entire agreement of the parties and cannot be changed except by their written agreement. Addenda which are a part of this contract are (Check all applicable boxes):

- ❑ Third Party Financing Condition Addendum
- ❑ Seller Financing Addendum
- ❑ Loan Assumption Addendum
- ❑ Buyer's Temporary Residential Lease
- ❑ Seller's Temporary Residential Lease
- ❑ Addendum for Sale of Other Property by Buyer
- ❑ Addendum for Seller's Disclosure of Information on Lead-based Paint and Lead-based Paint Hazards as Required by Federal Law
- ❑ Addendum for Property Subject to Mandatory Membership in an Owners' Association
- ❑ Environmental Assessment, Threatened or Endangered Species and Wetlands Addendum
- ❑ Addendum for "Back-Up" Contract
- ❑ Addendum for Coastal Area Property
- ❑ Addendum for Property Located Seaward of the Gulf Intracoastal Waterway
- ❑ Addendum for Release of Liability on Assumption of FHA, VA, or Conventional Loan Restoration of Seller's Entitlement for VA Guaranteed Loan
- ❑ Other (list): ____________________________

Termination Option

Paragraph 23 is perhaps the most misunderstood paragraph of the contract. (See Figure 9.16.) Please note the following five points:

1. There is no termination option if the Buyer fails to pay the money to the Seller. The agreement is for the Buyer to pay the Seller within two days of the effective date of the contract. When the Seller accepts the terms and the Option Fee, the Seller should execute the agreement and the Seller's receipt that follows on page 8. (See Figure 9.17.) The Seller's agent may accept the Option Fee on behalf of the Seller client and sign the receipt. The agent will sign the agent's name. To sign the Seller's name would be an act of forgery.

FIGURE 9.16

TREC 20-7 Paragraph 23

23. TERMINATION OPTION: For nominal consideration, the receipt of which is hereby acknowledged by Seller, and Buyer's agreement to pay Seller $________________ (Option Fee) within 2 days after the effective date of this contract, Seller grants Buyer the unrestricted right to terminate this contract by giving notice of termination to Seller within _______ days after the effective date of this contract. If no dollar amount is stated as the Option Fee or if Buyer fails to pay the Option Fee within the time prescribed, this paragraph will not be a part of this contract and Buyer shall not have the unrestricted right to terminate this contract. If Buyer gives notice of termination within the time prescribed, the Option Fee will not be refunded; however, any earnest money will be refunded to Buyer. The Option Fee ❑will ❑will not be credited to the Sales Price at closing. **Time is of the essence for this paragraph and strict compliance with the time for performance is required.**

FIGURE 9.17

TREC 20-7 Option Fee Receipt

OPTION FEE RECEIPT

Receipt of $______________ (Option Fee) in the form of __________________ is acknowledged.

____________________________ ____________________________

Seller or Listing Broker Date

2. Time is of the essence; therefore, a specific number of days must be defined and the right will end at midnight on the last day of the option period. The first day of the option is the day *after* the effective date of the contract.
3. The right to terminate is an unrestricted right. The Buyer may terminate for any reason and has no obligation to give a reason.
4. At the agreement of the parties, the Option Fee may be credited against the Sales Price if so indicated by the parties. Failure to make an election by checking one of the boxes creates confusion.
5. To exercise the unrestricted right to terminate, the Buyer must deliver the promulgated notice, the TREC Form 38-1, Notice of Termination of Contract, to the Seller prior to expiration of the option period. (See Figure 9.18.) Failure to deliver the notice means that the Buyer is obligated to close the transaction according to the terms of the contract.

Finalizing the Agreement

When in doubt, parties to the contract should consult an expert *before* signing. (See Figure 9.19.)

Please note that it is the broker's duty to fill in the effective date when the last party has signed *and* the other party has been notified of the acceptance. When the contract form states "Executed the _____ day of ______ 20___," it is identifying the date there has been an offer, acceptance, and notification of the acceptance of the offer. In legal terminology, a fully executed contract is one that has been completed and gone to closing.

FIGURE 9.18

TREC 38-1

10-29-01

PROMULGATED BY THE TEXAS REAL ESTATE COMMISSION (TREC)

NOTICE OF TERMINATION OF CONTRACT

To: Seller(s)

In accordance with the unrestricted right of Buyer to terminate the contract between

____

as Seller and ____

as Buyer dated ____________________, 20_____ for the Property located at ____________

____,

Buyer notifies Seller that the contract is terminated.

________________________________	________________________________
Buyer Date	Buyer Date

This form has been approved by the Texas Real Estate Commission for use with similarly approved or promulgated contract forms. Such approval relates to this form only. TREC forms are intended for use only by trained real estate licensees. No representation is made as to the legal validity or adequacy of any provision in any specific transactions. It is not suitable for complex transactions. Texas Real Estate Commission, P.O. Box 12188, Austin, TX 78711-2188, 1-800-250-8732 or (512) 459-6544 (http://www.trec.state.tx.us) TREC No. 38-1. This form replaces TREC No. 38-0.

01A

FIGURE 9.19

TREC 20-7 Paragraph 24

24. CONSULT AN ATTORNEY: Real estate licensees cannot give legal advice. READ THIS CONTRACT CAREFULLY. If you do not understand the effect of this contract, consult an attorney BEFORE signing.

Buyer's Attorney is: ______________________ ______________________

Telephone: ( ) ______________________

Facsimile: ( ) ______________________

E-mail: ______________________

Seller's Attorney is: ______________________ ______________________

Telephone: ( ) ______________________

Facsimile: ( ) ______________________

E-mail: ______________________

EXECUTED the ______day of ______________________, 20____ (EFFECTIVE DATE).
(BROKER: FILL IN THE DATE OF FINAL ACCEPTANCE.)

______________________ Buyer

______________________ Seller

______________________ Buyer

______________________ Seller

FIGURE 9.20

TREC 20-7 Seller's Receipt

CONTRACT AND EARNEST MONEY RECEIPT

Receipt of ❑Contract and ❑$__________________ Earnest Money in the form of __________________ is acknowledged.

Escrow Agent: ______________________ Date: ______________________

By: ______________________

____
Email Address

____
Address

Telephone (______) ______________________

____
City State Zip

Facsimile: (______) ______________________

The agent should deposit the contract and earnest money, if any, to the escrow agent immediately and obtain a receipted copy of the contract for all affected parties. (See Figure 9.20.)

Note that the receipt is issued by the escrow agent, not the listing or selling license holder. Some escrow agents may choose to use their own receipt form for the contract and the earnest money instead of the form at the end of the contract form.

Brokers and salespersons are reminded that the TREC rules require that the license holder deposit the earnest money with the escrow agent by the close of business on the second business day of the escrow company after the execution of the contract by the principals. The only exception occurs when the principals agree that a deposit may be delayed and a different time is expressly defined in paragraph 11 of the contract [Rule 535.159 (I)].

Once the contract has been finalized, it can only be altered by the written agreement of all parties. To accomplish a desired change, the parties may use the TREC Form 39-6, Amendment, seen in Figure 9.21, or consult an attorney. To remove any confusion on what the agreement is, carry forward all past provisions to subsequent amendments when the contract is amended multiple times between the effective date of the contract and closing.

Over the period of time between the execution of the contract, as identified by the effective date entered by the broker, and the closing of the transaction, the contract may be amended any number of times by the mutual agreement of the parties. Please note that, once the agreement has been created, neither party is under any obligation to renegotiate any provision of it. A party can always ask to renegotiate, but that does not obligate the other party to say yes to a renegotiation.

The following two addenda do not really fit with the discussion of any particular paragraph or provision of the basic contract; they are not frequently used in current markets. They were created at the time when the Texas real estate markets were very different than they are today. In a *seller's market,* when demand for available properties exceeded available supply, the TREC Form 10-5, Addendum for Sale of Other Property by Buyer, was created to enter into a contract of purchase but to give the Buyer an out if the Buyer's current property did not sell. From the Seller's perspective, it is not a particularly good idea to take the Property off the market while waiting for the Buyer's property to sell. While the addendum permits the Seller to continue to offer the Property and to consider other offers, the reality of the marketplace is that license holders working with Buyers show available properties first and only show pending properties with contingencies as a last resort. If you do use the addendum, be sure to give careful attention to the time frames. The wording in the addendum states that *time is of the essence* and demands strict compliance with the times set down. Do not confuse this addendum with the statement in paragraph 9 that addresses the Seller's right to continue to show the Property for possible consideration of **backup offers.**

The TREC Form 11-6, Addendum for "Back-Up" Contract, is designed to be used when a desired property is under contract with another Buyer. (See Figure 9.23.) The second Buyer can create an agreement of purchase in which the Buyer is entitled to purchase the Property only if the existing contract does not close. It creates a contingency for the Seller in which it is agreed that "I'll sell you my Property, if the existing contract does not close." Again, one must give careful attention to the time frames established by the addendum. For the purpose of the addendum, *time is of the essence*. Upon execution of a backup contract, earnest money is deposited with the named title company and the option fee is paid to the Seller.

FIGURE 9.21

TREC 39-6

PROMULGATED BY THE TEXAS REAL ESTATE COMMISSION (TREC) 02-13-06

EQUAL HOUSING OPPORTUNITY

AMENDMENT

TO CONTRACT CONCERNING THE PROPERTY AT

____

(Street Address and City)

Seller and Buyer amend the contract as follows: (check each applicable box)

❑(1) The Sales Price in Paragraph 3 of the contract is:
A. Cash portion of Sales Price payable by Buyer at closing .... $______________
B. Sum of financing described in the contract .... $______________
C. Sales Price (Sum of A and B) .... $______________

❑(2) In addition to any repairs and treatments otherwise required by the contract, Seller, at Seller's expense, shall complete the following repairs and treatments:

❑(3) The date in Paragraph 9 of the contract is changed to _________________________, 20_______.

❑(4) The amount in Paragraph 12A(1)(b) of the contract is changed to $ ____________________.

❑(5) The cost of lender required repairs and treatment, as itemized on the attached list, will be paid as follows: $ _______________________ by Seller; $ ________________________ by Buyer.

❑(6) Buyer has paid Seller an additional Option Fee of $ __________________ for an extension of the unrestricted right to terminate the contract on or before _____________________________, 20________. This additional Option Fee ❑ will ❑ will not be credited to the Sales Price.

❑(7) Buyer waives the unrestricted right to terminate the contract for which the Option Fee was paid.

❑(8) The date for Buyer to give written notice to Seller that Buyer cannot obtain Financing Approval as set forth in the Third Party Financing Condition Addendum is changed to ________________, 20_______.

❑(9) **Other Modifications**: (Insert only factual statements and business details applicable to this sale.)

EXECUTED the ______day of ____________________________, 20_____ . (BROKER: FILL IN THE DATE OF FINAL ACCEPTANCE.)

______________________ Buyer	______________________ Seller
______________________ Buyer	______________________ Seller

This form has been approved by the Texas Real Estate Commission for use with similarly approved or promulgated contract forms. Such approval relates to this form only. TREC forms are intended for use only by trained real estate licensees. No representation is made as to the legal validity or adequacy of any provision in any specific transactions. It is not intended for complex transactions. Texas Real Estate Commission, P.O. Box 12188, Austin, TX 78711-2188, 1-800-250-8732 or (512) 459-6544 (http://www.trec.state.tx.us) TREC No. 39-6. This form replaces TREC No. 39-5.

TREC NO. 39-6

FIGURE 9.22

TREC 10-5

04-23-07

EQUAL HOUSING OPPORTUNITY

PROMULGATED BY THE TEXAS REAL ESTATE COMMISSION (TREC)

ADDENDUM FOR SALE OF OTHER PROPERTY BY BUYER

TO CONTRACT CONCERNING THE PROPERTY AT

____
(Address of Property)

A. The contract is contingent upon Buyer's **receipt of the proceeds** from the sale of Buyer's property at____ (Address) on or before ____________________, 20______ (the Contingency). If the Contingency is not satisfied or waived by Buyer by the above date, the contract will terminate automatically and the earnest money will be refunded to Buyer.

NOTICE: The date inserted in this Paragraph should be no later than the Closing Date specified in Paragraph 9 of the contract.

B. If Seller accepts a written offer to sell the Property, Seller shall notify Buyer (1) of such acceptance **AND** (2) that Seller requires Buyer to waive the Contingency. Buyer must waive the Contingency on or before the ______________ day after Seller's notice to Buyer; otherwise the contract will terminate automatically and the earnest money will be refunded to Buyer.

C. Buyer may waive the Contingency only by notifying Seller of the waiver and depositing $__________ with escrow agent as additional earnest money. All notices and waivers must be in writing and are effective when delivered in accordance with the contract.

D. If Buyer waives the Contingency and fails to close and fund solely due to Buyer's non-receipt of proceeds from Buyer's sale of the Property described in Paragraph A, Buyer will be in default. If such default occurs, Seller may exercise the remedies specified in Paragraph 15 of the contract.

E. For purposes of this Addendum time is of the essence; strict compliance with the times for performance stated herein is required.

______________________________	______________________________
Buyer	Seller
______________________________	______________________________
Buyer	Seller

This form has been approved by the Texas Real Estate Commission for use with similarly approved or promulgated contract forms. Such approval relates to this form only. TREC forms are intended for use only by trained real estate licensees. No representation is made as to the legal validity or adequacy of any provision in any specific transactions. It is not suitable for complex transactions. Texas Real Estate Commission, P.O. Box 12188, Austin, TX 78711-2188, 1-800-250-8732 or (512) 459-6544 (http://www.trec.state.tx.us) TREC No. 10-5. This form replaces TREC No. 10-4.

FIGURE 9.23

TREC 11-6

PROMULGATED BY THE TEXAS REAL ESTATE COMMISSION (TREC) 04-23-07

EQUAL HOUSING OPPORTUNITY

ADDENDUM FOR "BACK-UP" CONTRACT

TO CONTRACT CONCERNING THE PROPERTY AT

____

(Address of Property)

A. The contract to which this Addendum is attached (the Back-Up Contract) is binding upon execution by the parties, and the earnest money and any Option Fee must be paid as provided in the Back-Up Contract. The Back-Up Contract is contingent upon the termination of a previous contract (the First Contract) dated ____________________________, 20_______, for the sale of Property. Except as provided by this Addendum, neither party is required to perform under the Back-Up Contract while it is contingent upon the termination of the First Contract.

B. If the First Contract does not terminate on or before ____________________________, 20_____, the Back-Up Contract terminates and the earnest money will be refunded to Buyer. Seller must notify Buyer immediately of the termination of the First Contract. For purposes of performance, the effective date of the Back-Up Contract changes to the date Buyer receives notice of termination of the First Contract (Amended Effective Date).

C. An amendment or modification of the First Contract will not terminate the First Contract.

D. If Buyer has the unrestricted right to terminate the Back-Up Contract, the time for giving notice of termination begins on the effective date of the Back-Up Contract, continues after the Amended Effective Date and ends upon the expiration of Buyer's unrestricted right to terminate the Back-Up Contract.

E. For purposes of this Addendum, time is of the essence. Strict compliance with the times for performance stated herein is required.

______________________	______________________
Buyer	Seller
______________________	______________________
Buyer	Seller

This form has been approved by the Texas Real Estate Commission for use with similarly approved or promulgated contract forms. Such approval relates to this form only. TREC forms are intended for use only by trained real estate licensees. No representation is made as to the legal validity or adequacy of any provision in any specific transactions. It is not suitable for complex transactions. Texas Real Estate Commission, P.O. Box 12188, Austin, TX 78711-2188, 1-800-250-8732 or (512) 459-6544 (http://www.trec.state.tx.us) TREC No. 11-6. This form replaces TREC No. 11-5.

TREC No. 11-6

The form is designed to create only one backup contract. For multiple backup contracts, the parties will need to consult legal counsel.

■ SUMMARY

When completing contract forms, make certain to correctly complete all required blanks. In a blank in the main body of the contract form that is not applicable, insert N/A. Remember, some blanks need the word *none*. There is a different meaning interpreted between "none" and "not applicable." For blanks that follow a box you have not checked, do nothing.

If the agreement went through a counteroffer process, have all changes been properly initialed by each of the parties? Did you date the contract when the Buyer was notified of the Seller's written acceptance of the Buyer's written offer or, if a counteroffer occurred, when the Seller was notified of the Buyer's written (initialed the changes) acceptance of the Seller's written counteroffer? Remember that it is not a counteroffer if the Seller has not responded with a signature and initials to any changes or modifications to the Buyer's original offer.

CHAPTER 9 REVIEW QUESTIONS

1. Who determines the amount of liquidated damages?

   a. Court
   b. Parties
   c. Title company
   d. Agent

2. Who is responsible for deciding when and to whom earnest money is released?

   a. Escrow officer
   b. Seller
   c. Buyer
   d. Parties

3. What type of deed is to be delivered by the Seller to the Buyer at closing?

   a. Quitclaim
   b. Special warranty
   c. Deed of trust
   d. General warranty

4. Loan fees include all of the following *EXCEPT*

   a. commitment.
   b. buydown.
   c. funding fee.
   d. discount.

5. If the parties agree to mediation, they are precluded from seeking equitable relief from the court.

   a. True
   b. False

6. Which is a proper way to deliver a notice from one party to another according to the provisions of the promulgated contract form?

   a. U.S. mail
   b. Facsimile
   c. Hand delivered
   d. All are acceptable

7. The agent should always write in the TREC Form OP-H, Seller's Disclosure of Property Condition, as a listed addendum after checking the boxes for the various TREC-promulgated addenda that have been used to create the agreement.

   a. True
   b. False

8. How will the taxes for the current year be prorated at closing?

   a. To the day of closing
   b. Through the day of closing
   c. Up to the day of closing
   d. Through the day after closing

9. The Seller's obligations in the Casualty Loss paragraph (14) are included in the obligations of the Seller in the Property Condition paragraph (7).

   a. True
   b. False

10. According to the printed TREC-promulgated form, who is to pay for the copies of easements and restrictions?

   a. Buyer
   b. Seller
   c. Agent
   d. Lender

HOMEWORK QUIZ

The following quiz does not have an answer key included with the answer keys in Appendix B. Students who are using this book as the basis for a correspondence course should record and submit their answers to their course provider as instructed by the provider. The student will submit his or her answers for the Homework Quiz at the end of each chapter and for each transaction in Chapter 11.

True or False?

1. Parties who agree to mediate also agree to split the cost of mediation services equally.

2. Between the effective date of the contract and closing, the parties agree that the Seller may not continue to show the Property and receive, negotiate, and accept backup offers.

3. A legal right or remedy states what will happen if a party to a contract does or does not do a particular act.

4. To keep the parties on track, a salesperson or broker should add the words *time is of the essence* in paragraph 11.

5. If the Seller accepts the earnest money as liquidated damages when the Buyer defaults, the Seller can file suit to seek additional money damages.

CHAPTER TEN

10

The Other Promulgated Contracts and Additional Forms

KEY TERMS

completed construction
condominium documents
construction documents
incomplete construction
mineral interests
R-factors
rollback tax
royalty
surface leases
timber interests
water rights

Now thoroughly familiar with the provisions of the most frequently used promulgated form and the promulgated addenda that may be attached to that form, we will focus attention on the other promulgated forms.

NEW HOME CONTRACTS

In Chapter 1, we learned that Property owners can instruct the license holders to use a form preferred by the owner rather than a TREC-promulgated form. Most builders will require you to use the contract form that they provide. New homes may be sold using one of two TREC forms when the builder does not specify. The TREC Forms that address two types of new homes are as follows:

1. **Completed construction** (usually *spec* homes) (the TREC Form 24-7)
2. **Incomplete construction** (the TREC Form 23-7)

Each of the two forms will have different considerations and issues to be addressed, particularly in paragraph 2, Property, and paragraph 7, Property Condition. The reader is advised to check the TREC Web site at *www.trec.state.tx.us* for current versions before using a new home contract form to structure a transaction.

Federal law requires that builders reveal to the Buyer the **R-factors** of the insulation installed in the new home. They may be included in the contract or in an addendum attached to the contract. The TREC-promulgated contracts address the R-factors in the Property condition paragraph. Other topics that should be addressed include:

- Construction documents
- Cost adjustments
- Buyer selections
- Completion dates
- Possible delays
- Warranties

It is always prudent for a Buyer to seek legal counsel before signing a builder's contract or before agreeing to the provisions of a contract that addresses **incomplete construction.** An already completed home in the builder's inventory should be treated in the same manner as a previously occupied resale home with regard to inspections and evaluations by competent professionals. A Buyer should never assume that everything in a new home is properly installed and working properly. A license holder who fails to advise the client to seek the counsel of other professionals is not demonstrating minimum standards of care required by the TREC rules and the fiduciary duties owed to clients.

Find the differences between the TREC Form 20-7 and the two contract forms, the TREC Form 23-7, New Home Contract (Incomplete Construction), seen in Figure 10.1, and the TREC Form 24-7, New Home Contract (Completed Construction), seen in Figure 10.2.

The Texas legislature added a provision to the Property Code in 2007 requiring that all contracts of sale for new construction include an addendum that addresses certain warranties and building and performance standards. It also provides valuable information to the Buyer about the Texas Residential Construction Commission, including a toll-free number to contact the Texas Residential Construction Commission to find out whether the builder has a valid certificate of registration. (See Figure 10.3.)

FARM AND RANCH

The TREC Form 25-5, Farm and Ranch Contract, calls for a metes-and-bounds legal description rather than reference to a recorded plat. (See Figure 10.4.) When selling a farm or ranch Property, the parties must address issues and items that are not considerations in the other types of properties addressed by TREC-promulgated forms. These elements include:

- Crops
- Equipment
- **Mineral interests**
- **Royalties**
- **Timber interests**
- Mineral leases
- **Surface leases**
- Other restrictions and exceptions already existing or to be created
- **Water rights**
- Rights and obligations of applicable government programs and cooperative or association memberships

A unique feature of the contract is the provision in paragraph 3 that allows for an adjustment to the Sales Price based on the results of the survey that may be done after the effective date of the contract. The contract caps the adjustment at 10 percent of the Sales Price and gives either party the ability to terminate the agreement if the needed adjustment exceeds that amount.

Paragraph 13 discusses rollback taxes. A **rollback tax** is an additional tax that is collected when an agriculture-use Property is no longer used for agricultural purposes and no longer qualifies for a reduced tax rate. When the use of the Property is changed to a nonagricultural use, the difference between the reduced agricultural rate and the higher non-agricultural rate must be paid for a statutory number of years prior to the year of the change in use. On an expensive parcel of land, the difference in tax can amount to a very significant amount of money. The Buyer and Seller must come to an agreement about who will pay the rollback taxes. The obligations imposed by their agreement in the contract will survive closing.

CONDOMINIUM

The current version of the TREC 30-6, Residential Condominium Contract (Resale), was adopted at the same time as the TREC Form 20-7. The TREC Form 30-6 is very similar to the TREC Form 20-7 with the exception of the unique provisions relating solely to condominium transactions and the statutory requirements of the Texas Uniform Condominium Act, chapters 81 and 82 of the Texas Property Code.

A study of paragraph 2 will reveal the primary differences between the condominium form and the single-family form that you have studied so thoroughly. Another significant difference will be found in paragraph 6 where the survey provisions have been deleted. Calling for a survey in a condominium transaction is uncommon.

The TREC Form 30-6, Residential Condominium Contract (Resale), is seen in Figure 10.5 on page 216, and the TREC Form 32-1, Condominium Resale Certificate, is seen in Figure 10.9 on page 234.

UNIMPROVED PROPERTY

Due to the lack of fixtures and accessories found in an unimproved property, paragraph 2 of the unimproved property form is considerably less involved and complicated than some paragraphs found in the other forms. A Buyer of an unimproved building lot must carefully research zoning ordinances, restrictive covenants, availability of utilities, access, and other matters that will affect the suitability of the building lot for the Buyer's intended use of it. An adequate termination option should be purchased to provide a suitable amount of time to make absolutely certain that the Property is suitable. For a copy of the TREC 9-6, Unimproved Property Contract, see Figure 10.6.

NONCONTRACT FORMS

The forms that follow are published by the TREC to address important issues and concerns, but they are not a part of any contractual agreement between Buyer and Seller.

The promulgated TREC Form 1-1, Consumer Information Form, is to be prominently displayed in the office of every licensed inspector and broker in Texas. (See Figure 10.7.) Residential brokers must also display the HUD fair housing poster with the equal housing opportunity logo.

The optional Notice Concerning Recognized Hazards warns the consumer that injury or property loss can result from a variety of improperly installed or malfunctioning mechanical equipment. The Notice Concerning Recognized Hazards is not promulgated as a mandatory use form, but rather it is a convenient tool that the license holder may use to assist the parties in making informed decisions.

Sections 1101.557, 1101.558, 1101.559, 1101.560, and 1101.561 of the license law addresses agency relationships between license holders and the public. One provision requires that a license holder, at the first substantive discussion, provide the prospect with the Information About Brokerage Services. A *substantive discussion* is defined as the first discussion at which substantive information about a particular Property or a prospect's ability to buy or lease occurs. The notice must be printed in a font no smaller than 10-point type.

The TREC Form OP-C, Notice to Prospective Buyer, is published by the TREC for voluntary use by license holders. (See Figure 10.8.) It is not a TREC or a statutory requirement that the person receiving it must also sign it. It is not an addendum to the contract.

The Texas licensing law requires that a license holder notify every Buyer in writing that the Buyer should obtain an owners' title policy or an abstract of title that should then be reviewed by the Buyer's attorney. When the agreement of purchase between the Seller and the Buyer has been reduced to writing by using one of the TREC-promulgated contract forms, this title notice requirement has been fulfilled by the wording of the first in the group of notices in paragraph 6 of the contract. A TREC rule requires that the license holder give the notice no later than the time at which a purchase agreement is signed by the Buyer.

When the contract is drawn by a party's attorney, the TREC Form OP-C may be used to give the notice. The form is not promulgated. It is published for voluntary use by the license holder to make it easier to comply with the law. Failure to deliver this notice when required can lead to loss of the broker's ability to seek the aid of a Texas court to attempt to collect a brokerage fee to which the broker might feel entitled.

Remember that before attempting to use any of the TREC-promulgated contracts and addendums or any voluntary-use forms, carefully read them and understand their content. Help the parties identify the business details that need to be addressed and then carefully fill in the appropriate blanks, check the appropriate boxes, and enter N/A where necessary.

Encourage each party to carefully read the agreement and advise that competent legal counsel should be consulted if unusual matters are present. It is a good practice to always read paragraph 24 to a party before the contract is signed. Encouraging people to seek legal advice is an effective way to reduce your risk of being sued. Stick to defining the business details. Let attorneys address the legal rights and remedies.

Although license holders do not complete the promulgated resale certificates, they should be thoroughly familiar with the content of both the TREC Form 32-1, Condominium Resale Certificate, seen in Figure 10.9 on page 234, and the TREC Form 37-1, Subdivision Information, Including Resale Certificate for Property Subject to Mandatory Membership in an Owners' Association, seen in Figure 10.10 on page 236.

FIGURE 10.1

TREC 23-7

PROMULGATED BY THE TEXAS REAL ESTATE COMMISSION (TREC) 12-10-07

NEW HOME CONTRACT

(Incomplete Construction)

NOTICE: Not For Use For Condominium Transactions or Closings Prior to Completion of Construction

1. **PARTIES:** ______________________________ (Seller) agrees to sell and convey to ______________________________ (Buyer) and Buyer agrees to buy from Seller the Property described below.

2. **PROPERTY:** Lot __________, Block ________, ______________________________ Addition, City of ______________________, County of ____________________, Texas, known as ______________________________ (address/zip code), or as described on attached exhibit, together with: (i) improvements, fixtures and all other property described in the Construction Documents; and (ii) all rights, privileges and appurtenances thereto, including but not limited to: permits, easements, and cooperative and association memberships. All property sold by this contract is called the "Property".

3. **SALES PRICE:**
   A. Cash portion of Sales Price payable by Buyer at closing................. $__________
   B. Sum of all financing described below (excluding any loan funding fee or mortgage insurance premium) .... $__________
   C. Sales Price (Sum of A and B) .... $__________

4. **FINANCING:** The portion of Sales Price not payable in cash will be paid as follows: (Check applicable boxes below)
   ☐ A. THIRD PARTY FINANCING: One or more third party mortgage loans in the total amount of $____________ (excluding any loan funding fee or mortgage insurance premium).
   (1) Property Approval: If the Property does not satisfy the lenders' underwriting requirements for the loan(s), this contract will terminate and the earnest money will be refunded to Buyer.
   (2) Financing Approval: (Check one box only)
   ☐ (a) This contract is subject to Buyer being approved for the financing described in the attached Third Party Financing Condition Addendum.
   ☐ (b) This contract is not subject to Buyer being approved for financing and does not involve FHA or VA financing.
   ☐ B. ASSUMPTION: The assumption of the unpaid principal balance of one or more promissory notes described in the attached TREC Loan Assumption Addendum.
   ☐ C. SELLER FINANCING: A promissory note from Buyer to Seller of $____________, secured by vendor's and deed of trust liens, and containing the terms and conditions described in the attached TREC Seller Financing Addendum. If an owner policy of title insurance is furnished, Buyer shall furnish Seller with a mortgagee policy of title insurance.

5. **EARNEST MONEY:** Upon execution of this contract by both parties, Buyer shall deposit $__________ as earnest money with ______________________________, as escrow agent, at ______________________________ (address). Buyer shall deposit additional earnest money of $______________ with escrow agent within ______ days after the effective date of this contract. If Buyer fails to deposit the earnest money as required by this contract, Buyer will be in default.

6. **TITLE POLICY AND SURVEY:**
   A. TITLE POLICY: Seller shall furnish to Buyer at ☐Seller's ☐Buyer's expense an owner policy of title insurance (Title Policy) issued by ______________________________ (Title Company) in the amount of the Sales Price, dated at or after closing, insuring Buyer against loss under the provisions of the Title Policy, subject to the promulgated exclusions (including existing building and zoning ordinances) and the following exceptions:
   (1) Restrictive covenants common to the platted subdivision in which the Property is located.
   (2) The standard printed exception for standby fees, taxes and assessments.
   (3) Liens created as part of the financing described in Paragraph 4.
   (4) Utility easements created by the dedication deed or plat of the subdivision in which the Property is located.
   (5) Reservations or exceptions otherwise permitted by this contract or as may be approved by Buyer in writing.
   (6) The standard printed exception as to marital rights.
   (7) The standard printed exception as to waters, tidelands, beaches, streams, and related matters.
   (8) The standard printed exception as to discrepancies, conflicts, shortages in area or boundary lines, encroachments or protrusions, or overlapping improvements. Buyer, at Buyer's expense, may have the exception amended to read, "shortages in area".

FIGURE 10.1 (CONTINUED)

TREC 23-7

Contract Concerning ____ Page 2 of 9 12-10-07
(Address of Property)

B. COMMITMENT: Within 20 days after the Title Company receives a copy of this contract, Seller shall furnish to Buyer a commitment for title insurance (Commitment) and, at Buyer's expense, legible copies of restrictive covenants and documents evidencing exceptions in the Commitment (Exception Documents) other than the standard printed exceptions. Seller authorizes the Title Company to deliver the Commitment and Exception Documents to Buyer at Buyer's address shown in Paragraph 21. If the Commitment and Exception Documents are not delivered to Buyer within the specified time, the time for delivery will be automatically extended up to 15 days or the Closing Date, whichever is earlier.

C. SURVEY: The survey must be made after the Substantial Completion Date by a registered professional land surveyor acceptable to the Title Company and any lender.
(Check one box only)
❑ (1) At least ______ days prior to the Closing Date, Seller, at Seller's expense, shall provide a new survey to Buyer.
❑ (2) At least ________ days prior to the Closing Date, Buyer, at Buyer's expense, shall obtain a new survey. Buyer is deemed to receive the survey on the date of actual receipt or the date specified in this paragraph, whichever is earlier.

D. OBJECTIONS: Buyer may object in writing to defects, exceptions, or encumbrances to title: disclosed on the survey other than items 6A(1) through (7) above; disclosed in the Commitment other than items 6A(1) through (8) above; or which prohibit the following use or activity: ____.
Buyer must object not later than (i) the Closing Date or (ii) _____ days after Buyer receives the Commitment, Exception Documents, and the survey, whichever is earlier. Buyer's failure to object within the time allowed will constitute a waiver of Buyer's right to object; except that the requirements in Schedule C of the Commitment are not waived. Provided Seller is not obligated to incur any expense, Seller shall cure the timely objections of Buyer or any third party lender within 15 days after Seller receives the objections and the Closing Date will be extended as necessary. If objections are not cured within such 15 day period, this contract will terminate and the earnest money will be refunded to Buyer unless Buyer waives the objections.

E. TITLE NOTICES:
(1) ABSTRACT OR TITLE POLICY: Broker advises Buyer to have an abstract of title covering the Property examined by an attorney of Buyer's selection, or Buyer should be furnished with or obtain a Title Policy. If a Title Policy is furnished, the Commitment should be promptly reviewed by an attorney of Buyer's choice due to the time limitations on Buyer's right to object.
(2) MANDATORY OWNERS' ASSOCIATION MEMBERSHIP: The Property ❑ is ❑ is not subject to mandatory membership in an owners' association. If the Property is subject to mandatory membership in an owners' association, Seller notifies Buyer under §5.012, Texas Property Code, that, as a purchaser of property in the residential community in which the Property is located, you are obligated to be a member of the owners' association. Restrictive covenants governing the use and occupancy of the Property and a dedicatory instrument governing the establishment, maintenance, and operation of this residential community have been or will be recorded in the Real Property Records of the county in which the Property is located. Copies of the restrictive covenants and dedicatory instrument may be obtained from the county clerk. You are obligated to pay assessments to the owners' association. The amount of the assessments is subject to change. Your failure to pay the assessments could result in a lien on and the foreclosure of the Property. If Buyer is concerned about these matters, the TREC promulgated Addendum for Property Subject to Mandatory Membership in an Owner's Association should be used.
(3) STATUTORY TAX DISTRICTS: If the Property is situated in a utility or other statutorily created district providing water, sewer, drainage, or flood control facilities and services, Chapter 49, Texas Water Code, requires Seller to deliver and Buyer to sign the statutory notice relating to the tax rate, bonded indebtedness, or standby fee of the district prior to final execution of this contract.
(4) TIDE WATERS: If the Property abuts the tidally influenced waters of the state, §33.135, Texas Natural Resources Code, requires a notice regarding coastal area property to be included in the contract. An addendum containing the notice promulgated by TREC or required by the parties must be used.
(5) ANNEXATION: If the Property is located outside the limits of a municipality, Seller notifies Buyer under §5.011, Texas Property Code, that the Property may now or later be included in the extraterritorial jurisdiction of a municipality and may now or later be subject to annexation by the municipality. Each municipality maintains a map that depicts its boundaries and extraterritorial jurisdiction. To determine if the Property is located within a municipality's extraterritorial jurisdiction or is likely to be located within a municipality's extraterritorial jurisdiction, contact all municipalities located in the general proximity of the Property for further information.

Initialed for identification by Buyer______ ______ and Seller _______ ______ TREC NO. 23-7

FIGURE 10.1 (CONTINUED)

TREC 23-7

(6) PROPERTY LOCATED IN A CERTIFICATED SERVICE AREA OF A UTILITY SERVICE PROVIDER: Notice required by §13.257, Water Code: The real property, described in Paragraph 2, that you are about to purchase may be located in a certificated water or sewer service area, which is authorized by law to provide water or sewer service to the properties in the certificated area. If your property is located in a certificated area there may be special costs or charges that you will be required to pay before you can receive water or sewer service. There may be a period required to construct lines or other facilities necessary to provide water or sewer service to your property. You are advised to determine if the property is in a certificated area and contact the utility service provider to determine the cost that you will be required to pay and the period, if any, that is required to provide water or sewer service to your property. The undersigned Buyer hereby acknowledges receipt of the foregoing notice at or before the execution of a binding contract for the purchase of the real property described in Paragraph 2 or at closing of purchase of the real property.

(7) PUBLIC IMPROVEMENT DISTRICTS: If the Property is in a public improvement district, §5.014, Property Code, requires Seller to notify Buyer as follows: As a purchaser of this parcel of real property you are obligated to pay an assessment to a municipality or county for an improvement project undertaken by a public improvement district under Chapter 372, Local Government Code. The assessment may be due annually or in periodic installments. More information concerning the amount of the assessment and the due dates of that assessment may be obtained from the municipality or county levying the assessment. The amount of the assessments is subject to change. Your failure to pay the assessments could result in a lien on and the foreclosure of your property.

7. PROPERTY CONDITION:

A. ACCESS AND INSPECTIONS: Seller shall permit Buyer and Buyer's agents access to the Property at reasonable times. Buyer may have the Property inspected by inspectors selected by Buyer and licensed by TREC or otherwise permitted by law to make inspections.

B. CONSTRUCTION DOCUMENTS: Seller shall complete all improvements to the Property with due diligence in accordance with the Construction Documents. "Construction Documents" means the plans and specifications, the finish out schedules, any change orders, and any allowances related to the plans and specifications, finish out schedules, and change orders. The Construction Documents have been signed by the parties and are incorporated into this contract by reference.

C. COST ADJUSTMENTS: All change orders must be in writing. Increase in costs resulting from change orders or items selected by Buyer which exceed the allowances specified in the Construction Documents will be paid by Buyer as follows:______________________________
____.
A decrease in costs resulting from change orders and unused allowances will reduce the Sales Price, with proportionate adjustments to the amounts in Paragraphs 3A and 3B as required by lender.

D. BUYER'S SELECTIONS: If the Construction Documents permit selections by Buyer, Buyer's selections will conform to Seller's normal standards as set out in the Construction Documents or will not, in Seller's judgment, adversely affect the marketability of the Property. Buyer will make required selections within ______ days after notice from Seller.

E. COMPLETION: Seller must commence construction no later than ________ days after the effective date of this contract. The improvements will be substantially completed in accordance with the Construction Documents and ready for occupancy not later than __________________________, 20____ . The improvements will be deemed to be substantially completed in accordance with the Construction Documents upon the final inspection and approval by all applicable governmental authorities and any lender (Substantial Completion Date). Construction delays caused by acts of God, fire or other casualty, strikes, boycotts or nonavailability of materials for which no substitute of comparable quality and price is available will be added to the time allowed for substantial completion of the construction. However, in no event may the time for substantial completion extend beyond the Closing Date. Seller may substitute materials, equipment and appliances of comparable quality for those specified in the Construction Documents.

F. WARRANTIES: Except as expressly set forth in this contract, a separate writing, or provided by law, Seller makes no other express warranties. Seller shall assign to Buyer at closing all assignable manufacturer warranties.

G. INSULATION: As required by Federal Trade Commission Regulations, the information relating to the insulation installed or to be installed in the Improvements at the Property is: (check only one box below)

❑ (1) as shown in the attached specifications.

❑ (2) as follows:

a) Exterior walls of improved living areas: insulated with ______________________ insulation to a thickness of ______________ inches which yields an R-Value of ____.

b) Walls in other areas of the home: insulated with ____________________________

FIGURE 10.1 (CONTINUED)

TREC 23-7

Contract Concerning ____ Page 4 of 9 12-10-07
(Address of Property)

insulation to a thickness of _______ inches which yields an R-Value of ___________.

c) Ceilings in improved living areas: insulated with___________________________ insulation to a thickness of _________ inches which yields an R-Value of _________.

d) Floors of improved living areas not applied to a slab foundation: insulated with insulation to a thickness of ___ inches which yields an R-Value of ____.

e) Other insulated areas: insulated with ___________________________insulation to a thickness of _________ inches which yields an R-Value of ___________.

All stated R-Values are based on information provided by the manufacturer of the insulation.

H. ENVIRONMENTAL MATTERS: Buyer is advised that the presence of wetlands, toxic substances, including asbestos and wastes or other environmental hazards, or the presence of a threatened or endangered species or its habitat may affect Buyer's intended use of the Property. If Buyer is concerned about these matters, an addendum promulgated by TREC or required by the parties should be used.

I. SELLER'S DISCLOSURE: Except as otherwise disclosed in this contract, Seller has no knowledge of the following:

(1) any flooding of the Property which has had a material adverse effect on the use of the Property;
(2) any pending or threatened litigation, condemnation, or special assessment affecting the Property;
(3) any environmental hazards or conditions materially affecting the Property;
(4) any dumpsite, landfill, or underground tanks or containers now or previously located on the Property;
(5) any wetlands, as defined by federal or state law or regulation, affecting the Property; or
(6) any threatened or endangered species or their habitat affecting the Property.

8. BROKERS' FEES: All obligations of the parties for payment of brokers' fees are contained in separate written agreements.

9. CLOSING:

A. The closing of the sale will be on or before ______________________, 20_____, or within 7 days after objections made under Paragraph 6D have been cured or waived, whichever date is later (Closing Date). If either party fails to close the sale by the Closing Date, the non-defaulting party may exercise the remedies contained in Paragraph 15.

B. At closing:

(1) Seller shall execute and deliver a general warranty deed conveying title to the Property to Buyer and showing no additional exceptions to those permitted in Paragraph 6 and furnish tax statements or certificates showing no delinquent taxes on the Property.
(2) Buyer shall pay the Sales Price in good funds acceptable to the escrow agent.
(3) Seller and Buyer shall execute and deliver any notices, statements, certificates, affidavits, releases, loan documents and other documents required of them by this contract, the Commitment or law necessary for the closing of the sale and the issuance of the Title Policy.

C. Unless expressly prohibited by written agreement, Seller may continue to show the Property and receive, negotiate and accept back up offers.

D. All covenants, representations and warranties in this contract survive closing.

10. POSSESSION: Seller shall deliver to Buyer possession of the Property: ❑ upon closing and funding ❑ according to a temporary residential lease form promulgated by TREC or other written lease required by the parties. Any possession by Buyer prior to closing or by Seller after closing which is not authorized by a written lease will establish a tenancy at sufferance relationship between the parties. **Consult your insurance agent prior to change of ownership and possession because insurance coverage may be limited or terminated. The absence of a written lease or appropriate insurance coverage may expose the parties to economic loss.**

11. SPECIAL PROVISIONS: (Insert only factual statements and business details applicable to the sale. TREC rules prohibit licensees from adding factual statements or business details for which a contract addendum, lease or other form has been promulgated by TREC for mandatory use.)

Initialed for identification by Buyer_____ _____ and Seller ______ _____ TREC NO. 23-7

FIGURE 10.1 (CONTINUED)

TREC 23-7

12. SETTLEMENT AND OTHER EXPENSES:

A. The following expenses must be paid at or prior to closing:

(1) Expenses payable by Seller (Seller's Expenses):

(a) Releases of existing liens, including prepayment penalties and recording fees; release of Seller's loan liability; tax statements or certificates; preparation of deed; one-half of escrow fee; and other expenses payable by Seller under this contract.

(b) Seller shall also pay an amount not to exceed $ ____________ to be applied in the following order: Buyer's Expenses which Buyer is prohibited from paying by FHA, VA, Texas Veterans Housing Assistance Program or other governmental loan programs, and then to other Buyer's Expenses as allowed by the lender.

(2) Expenses payable by Buyer (Buyer's Expenses):

(a) Loan origination, discount, buy-down, and commitment fees (Loan Fees).

(b) Appraisal fees; loan application fees; credit reports; preparation of loan documents; interest on the notes from date of disbursement to one month prior to dates of first monthly payments; recording fees; copies of easements and restrictions; mortgagee title policy with endorsements required by lender; loan-related inspection fees; photos; amortization schedules; one-half of escrow fee; all prepaid items, including required premiums for flood and hazard insurance, reserve deposits for insurance, ad valorem taxes and special governmental assessments; final compliance inspection; courier fee; repair inspection; underwriting fee; wire transfer fee; expenses incident to any loan; and other expenses payable by Buyer under this contract.

B. Buyer shall pay Private Mortgage Insurance Premium (PMI), VA Loan Funding Fee, or FHA Mortgage Insurance Premium (MIP) as required by the lender.

C. If any expense exceeds an amount expressly stated in this contract for such expense to be paid by a party, that party may terminate this contract unless the other party agrees to pay such excess. Buyer may not pay charges and fees expressly prohibited by FHA, VA, Texas Veterans Housing Assistance Program or other governmental loan program regulations.

13. PRORATIONS AND ROLLBACK TAXES:

A. PRORATIONS: Taxes for the current year, maintenance fees, assessments, dues and rents will be prorated through the Closing Date. The tax proration may be calculated taking into consideration any change in exemptions that will affect the current year's taxes. If taxes for the current year vary from the amount prorated at closing, the parties shall adjust the prorations when tax statements for the current year are available. If taxes are not paid at or prior to closing, Buyer will be obligated to pay taxes for the current year.

B. ROLLBACK TAXES: If Seller's change in use of the Property prior to closing or denial of a special use valuation on the Property results in additional taxes, penalties or interest (Assessments) for periods prior to closing, the Assessments will be the obligation of Seller. Obligations imposed by this paragraph will survive closing.

14. CASUALTY LOSS: If any part of the Property is damaged or destroyed by fire or other casualty after the effective date of this contract, Seller shall restore the Property to its previous condition as soon as reasonably possible, but in any event by the Closing Date. If Seller fails to do so due to factors beyond Seller's control, Buyer may (a) terminate this contract and the earnest money will be refunded to Buyer (b) extend the time for performance up to 45 days and the Closing Date will be extended as necessary or (c) accept the Property in its damaged condition with an assignment of insurance proceeds and receive credit from Seller at closing in the amount of the deductible under the insurance policy. Seller's obligations under this paragraph are independent of any other obligations of Seller under this contract.

15. DEFAULT: If Buyer fails to comply with this contract, Buyer will be in default, and Seller may (a) enforce specific performance, seek such other relief as may be provided by law, or both, or (b) terminate this contract and receive the earnest money as liquidated damages, thereby releasing both parties from this contract. If, due to factors beyond Seller's control, Seller fails to substantially complete the improvements by the Closing Date or fails within the time allowed to make any non casualty repairs or deliver the Commitment, or survey, if required of Seller, Buyer may (a) extend the time for performance up to 45 days and the Closing Date will be extended as necessary or (b) terminate this contract as the sole remedy and receive the earnest money. If Seller fails to comply with this contract for any other reason, Seller will be in default and Buyer may (a) enforce specific performance, seek such other relief as may be provided by law, or both, or (b) terminate this contract and receive the earnest money, thereby releasing both parties from this contract.

16. MEDIATION: It is the policy of the State of Texas to encourage resolution of disputes through alternative dispute resolution procedures such as mediation. Subject to applicable law, any dispute between Seller and Buyer related to this contract which is not resolved through informal discussion ☐will ☐will not be submitted to a mutually acceptable mediation service or provider. The parties to the mediation shall bear the mediation costs equally. This paragraph does not preclude a party from seeking equitable relief from a court of competent jurisdiction.

FIGURE 10.1 (CONTINUED)

TREC 23-7

Contract Concerning ______________________________ Page 6 of 9 12-10-07
(Address of Property)

17. ATTORNEY'S FEES: The prevailing party in any legal proceeding related to this contract is entitled to recover reasonable attorney's fees and all costs of such proceeding incurred by the prevailing party.

18. ESCROW:

A. ESCROW: The escrow agent is not (i) a party to this contract and does not have liability for the performance or nonperformance of any party to this contract, (ii) liable for interest on the earnest money and (iii) liable for the loss of any earnest money caused by the failure of any financial institution in which the earnest money has been deposited unless the financial institution is acting as escrow agent.

B. EXPENSES: At closing, the earnest money must be applied first to any cash down payment, then to Buyer's Expenses and any excess refunded to Buyer. If no closing occurs, escrow agent may require payment of unpaid expenses incurred on behalf of the parties and a written release of liability of escrow agent from all parties.

C. DEMAND: Upon termination of this contract, either party or the escrow agent may send a release of earnest money to each party and the parties shall execute counterparts of the release and deliver same to the escrow agent. If either party fails to execute the release, either party may make a written demand to the escrow agent for the earnest money. If only one party makes written demand for the earnest money, escrow agent shall promptly provide a copy of the demand to the other party. If escrow agent does not receive written objection to the demand from the other party within 15 days, escrow agent may disburse the earnest money to the party making demand reduced by the amount of unpaid expenses incurred on behalf of the party receiving the earnest money and escrow agent may pay the same to the creditors. If escrow agent complies with the provisions of this paragraph, each party hereby releases escrow agent from all adverse claims related to the disbursal of the earnest money.

D. DAMAGES: Any party who wrongfully fails or refuses to sign a release acceptable to the escrow agent within 7 days of receipt of the request will be liable to the other party for liquidated damages of three times the amount of the earnest money.

E. NOTICES: Escrow agent's notices will be effective when sent in compliance with Paragraph 21. Notice of objection to the demand will be deemed effective upon receipt by escrow agent.

19. REPRESENTATIONS: Seller represents that as of the Closing Date there will be no liens, assessments, or security interests against the Property which will not be satisfied out of the sales proceeds. If any representation of Seller in this contract is untrue on the Closing Date, Seller will be in default.

20. FEDERAL TAX REQUIREMENTS: If Seller is a "foreign person," as defined by applicable law, or if Seller fails to deliver an affidavit to Buyer that Seller is not a "foreign person," then Buyer shall withhold from the sales proceeds an amount sufficient to comply with applicable tax law and deliver the same to the Internal Revenue Service together with appropriate tax forms. Internal Revenue Service regulations require filing written reports if currency in excess of specified amounts is received in the transaction.

21. NOTICES: All notices from one party to the other must be in writing and are effective when mailed to, hand-delivered at, or transmitted by facsimile or electronic transmission as follows:

To Buyer at: ____________	**To Seller at:** ____________
____________	____________
____________	____________
Telephone: ( ) ____________	Telephone: ( ) ____________
Facsimile: ( ) ____________	Facsimile: ( ) ____________
E-mail: ____________	E-mail: ____________

FIGURE 10.1 (CONTINUED)

TREC 23-7

22. AGREEMENT OF PARTIES: This contract contains the entire agreement of the parties and cannot be changed except by their written agreement. Addenda which are a part of this contract are (check all applicable boxes):

- ❑ Third Party Financing Condition Addendum
- ❑ Seller Financing Addendum
- ❑ Addendum for Property Subject to Mandatory Membership in an Owners' Association
- ❑ Buyer's Temporary Residential Lease
- ❑ Addendum for Sale of Other Property by Buyer
- ❑ Addendum Containing Required Notices Under §420.01 and §420.002, Texas Property Code
- ❑ Addendum for "Back-Up" Contract
- ❑ Addendum for Coastal Area Property
- ❑ Environmental Assessment, Threatened or Endangered Species and Wetlands Addendum
- ❑ Addendum for Property Located Seaward of the Gulf Intracoastal Waterway
- ❑ Other (list): ______________________
____
____
____

23. TERMINATION OPTION: For nominal consideration, the receipt of which is hereby acknowledged by Seller, and Buyer's agreement to pay Seller $______________ (Option Fee) within 2 days after the effective date of this contract, Seller grants Buyer the unrestricted right to terminate this contract by giving notice of termination to Seller within ________ days after the effective date of this contract. If no dollar amount is stated as the Option Fee or if Buyer fails to pay the Option Fee within the time prescribed, this paragraph will not be a part of this contract and Buyer shall not have the unrestricted right to terminate this contract. If Buyer gives notice of termination within the time prescribed, the Option Fee will not be refunded; however, any earnest money will be refunded to Buyer. The Option Fee ❑will ❑will not be credited to the Sales Price at closing. **Time is of the essence for this paragraph and strict compliance with the time for performance is required.**

24. CONSULT AN ATTORNEY: Real estate licensees cannot give legal advice. READ THIS CONTRACT CAREFULLY. If you do not understand the effect of this contract, consult an attorney BEFORE signing.

Buyer's	Seller's
Attorney is: ______________________	Attorney is: ______________________
______________________	______________________
Telephone: ( ) ______________	Telephone: ( ) ______________
Facsimile: ( ) ______________	Facsimile: ( ) ______________
E-mail: ______________________	E-mail: ______________________

FIGURE 10.1 (CONTINUED)

TREC 23-7

Contract Concerning ____ Page 8 of 9 12-10-07
(Address of Property)

EXECUTED the ______day of ________________________, 20_____ (EFFECTIVE DATE). (BROKER: FILL IN THE DATE OF FINAL ACCEPTANCE.)

This contract is subject to Chapter 27 of the Texas Property Code. The provisions of that chapter may affect your right to recover damages arising from a construction defect. If you have a complaint concerning a construction defect and that defect has not been corrected as may be required by law or by contract, you must provide the notice required by Chapter 27 of the Texas Property Code to the contractor by certified mail, return receipt requested, not later than the 60th day before the date you file suit to recover damages in a court of law or initiate arbitration. The notice must refer to Chapter 27 of the Texas Property Code and must describe the construction defect. If requested by the contractor, you must provide the contractor an opportunity to inspect and cure the defect as provided by Section 27.004 of the Texas Property Code.

____
Buyer

____
Buyer

____
Seller

____
Seller

The form of this contract has been approved by the Texas Real Estate Commission. TREC forms are intended for use only by trained real estate licensees. No representation is made as to the legal validity or adequacy of any provision in any specific transactions. It is not intended for complex transactions. Texas Real Estate Commission, P.O. Box 12188, Austin, TX 78711-2188, 1-800-250-8732 or (512) 459-6544 (http://www.trec.state.tx.us) TREC NO. 23-7. This form replaces TREC NO. 23-6.

FIGURE 10.1 (CONTINUED)

TREC 23-7

Contract Concerning ____ Page 9 of 9 12-10-07
(Address of Property)

BROKER INFORMATION AND RATIFICATION OF FEE

Listing Broker has agreed to pay Other Broker ____________________ of the total sales price when Listing Broker's fee is received. Escrow Agent is authorized and directed to pay Other Broker from Listing Broker's fee at closing.

______________________________ Other Broker License No.	______________________________ Listing Broker License No.
represents ❑ Buyer only as Buyer's agent ❑ Seller as Listing Broker's subagent	represents ❑ Seller and Buyer as an intermediary ❑ Seller only as Seller's agent
______________________________ Associate Telephone	______________________________ Listing Associate Telephone
______________________________ Broker's Address	______________________________ Listing Associate's Office Address Facsimile
______________________________ City State Zip	______________________________ City State Zip
______________________________ Facsimile	______________________________ Email Address
______________________________ Email Address	______________________________ Selling Associate Telephone
	______________________________ Selling Associate's Office Address Facsimile
	______________________________ City State Zip
	______________________________ Email Address

OPTION FEE RECEIPT

Receipt of $______________ (Option Fee) in the form of ________________ is acknowledged.

______________________ ______________________
Seller or Listing Broker Date

CONTRACT AND EARNEST MONEY RECEIPT

Receipt of ❑Contract and ❑$______________ Earnest Money in the form of ______________ is acknowledged.
Escrow Agent: ______________________________ Date: ______________

By: ______________________________ ______________________
Email Address

______________________________ Telephone (_____) ______________
Address

______________________________ Facsimile: (_____) ______________
City State Zip

TREC NO. 23-7

FIGURE 10.2

TREC 24-7

PROMULGATED BY THE TEXAS REAL ESTATE COMMISSION (TREC) 12-10-07

EQUAL HOUSING OPPORTUNITY

NEW HOME CONTRACT

(Completed Construction)

NOTICE: Not For Use For Condominium Transactions or Closings Prior to Completion of Construction

1. **PARTIES:** ______________________________ (Seller) agrees to sell and convey to ______________________________ (Buyer) and Buyer agrees to buy from Seller the Property described below.

2. **PROPERTY:** Lot __________, Block ________, ______________________________ Addition, City of ______________________, County of ______________________, Texas, known as ______________________________ (address/zip code), or as described on attached exhibit, together with: (i) improvements, fixtures and all other property located thereon; and (ii) all rights, privileges and appurtenances thereto, including but not limited to: permits, easements, and cooperative and association memberships. All property sold by this contract is called the "Property".

3. **SALES PRICE:**
   A. Cash portion of Sales Price payable by Buyer at closing .... $__________
   B. Sum of all financing described below (excluding any loan funding fee or mortgage insurance premium) .... $__________
   C. Sales Price (Sum of A and B) .... $__________

4. **FINANCING:** The portion of Sales Price not payable in cash will be paid as follows: (Check applicable boxes below)
   ❑ A. THIRD PARTY FINANCING: One or more third party mortgage loans in the total amount of $______________ (excluding any loan funding fee or mortgage insurance premium).
   (1) Property Approval: If the Property does not satisfy the lenders' underwriting requirements for the loan(s), this contract will terminate and the earnest money will be refunded to Buyer.
   (2) Financing Approval: (Check one box only)
   ❑ (a) This contract is subject to Buyer being approved for the financing described in the attached Third Party Financing Condition Addendum.
   ❑ (b) This contract is not subject to Buyer being approved for financing and does not involve FHA or VA financing.
   ❑ B. ASSUMPTION: The assumption of the unpaid principal balance of one or more promissory notes described in the attached TREC Loan Assumption Addendum.
   ❑ C. SELLER FINANCING: A promissory note from Buyer to Seller of $______________, secured by vendor's and deed of trust liens, and containing the terms and conditions described in the attached TREC Seller Financing Addendum. If an owner policy of title insurance is furnished, Buyer shall furnish Seller with a mortgagee policy of title insurance.

5. **EARNEST MONEY:** Upon execution of this contract by both parties, Buyer shall deposit $__________ as earnest money with ______________________________, as escrow agent, at ______________________________ (address). Buyer shall deposit additional earnest money of $______________ with escrow agent within _______ days after the effective date of this contract. If Buyer fails to deposit the earnest money as required by this contract, Buyer will be in default.

6. **TITLE POLICY AND SURVEY:**
   A. TITLE POLICY: Seller shall furnish to Buyer at ❑Seller's ❑Buyer's expense an owner policy of title insurance (Title Policy) issued by ______________________________ (Title Company) in the amount of the Sales Price, dated at or after closing, insuring Buyer against loss under the provisions of the Title Policy, subject to the promulgated exclusions (including existing building and zoning ordinances) and the following exceptions:
   (1) Restrictive covenants common to the platted subdivision in which the Property is located.
   (2) The standard printed exception for standby fees, taxes and assessments.
   (3) Liens created as part of the financing described in Paragraph 4.
   (4) Utility easements created by the dedication deed or plat of the subdivision in which the Property is located.
   (5) Reservations or exceptions otherwise permitted by this contract or as may be approved by Buyer in writing.
   (6) The standard printed exception as to marital rights.
   (7) The standard printed exception as to waters, tidelands, beaches, streams, and related matters.
   (8) The standard printed exception as to discrepancies, conflicts, shortages in area or boundary lines, encroachments or protrusions, or overlapping improvements. Buyer, at Buyer's expense, may have the exception amended to read, "shortages in area".
   B. COMMITMENT: Within 20 days after the Title Company receives a copy of this contract, Seller shall furnish to Buyer a commitment for title insurance (Commitment) and, at Buyer's expense, legible copies of restrictive covenants and documents evidencing exceptions in the Commitment (Exception Documents) other than the standard printed exceptions. Seller

FIGURE 10.2 (CONTINUED)

TREC 24-7

authorizes the Title Company to deliver the Commitment and Exception Documents to Buyer at Buyer's address shown in Paragraph 21. If the Commitment and Exception Documents are not delivered to Buyer within the specified time, the time for delivery will be automatically extended up to 15 days or the Closing Date, whichever is earlier.

C. SURVEY: The survey must be made by a registered professional land surveyor acceptable to the Title Company and any lender. (Check one box only)

❑ (1) Within ________ days after the effective date of this contract, Seller shall furnish to Buyer and Title Company Seller's existing survey of the Property and a Residential Real Property Affidavit promulgated by the Texas Department of Insurance (Affidavit). If the existing survey or Affidavit is not acceptable to Title Company or Buyer's lender, Buyer shall obtain a new survey at ❑ Seller's ❑ Buyer's expense no later than 3 days prior to Closing Date. If Seller fails to furnish the existing survey or Affidavit within the time prescribed, Buyer shall obtain a new survey at Seller's expense no later than 3 days prior to Closing Date.

❑ (2) Within _______ days after the effective date of this contract, Buyer shall obtain a new survey at Buyer's expense. Buyer is deemed to receive the survey on the date of actual receipt or the date specified in this paragraph, whichever is earlier.

❑ (3) Within ______ days after the effective date of this contract, Seller, at Seller's expense shall furnish a new survey to Buyer.

D. OBJECTIONS: Buyer may object in writing to defects, exceptions, or encumbrances to title: disclosed on the survey other than items 6A(1) through (7) above; disclosed in the Commitment other than items 6A(1) through (8) above; or which prohibit the following use or activity: ______________________________.
Buyer must object not later than (i) the Closing Date or (ii) _____ days after Buyer receives the Commitment, Exception Documents, and the survey, whichever is earlier. Buyer's failure to object within the time allowed will constitute a waiver of Buyer's right to object; except that the requirements in Schedule C of the Commitment are not waived. Provided Seller is not obligated to incur any expense, Seller shall cure the timely objections of Buyer or any third party lender within 15 days after Seller receives the objections and the Closing Date will be extended as necessary. If objections are not cured within such 15 day period, this contract will terminate and the earnest money will be refunded to Buyer unless Buyer waives the objections.

E. TITLE NOTICES:

(1) ABSTRACT OR TITLE POLICY: Broker advises Buyer to have an abstract of title covering the Property examined by an attorney of Buyer's selection, or Buyer should be furnished with or obtain a Title Policy. If a Title Policy is furnished, the Commitment should be promptly reviewed by an attorney of Buyer's choice due to the time limitations on Buyer's right to object.

(2) MANDATORY OWNERS' ASSOCIATION MEMBERSHIP: The Property ❑ is ❑ is not subject to mandatory membership in an owners' association. If the Property is subject to mandatory membership in an owners' association, Seller notifies Buyer under §5.012, Texas Property Code, that, as a purchaser of property in the residential community in which the Property is located, you are obligated to be a member of the owners' association. Restrictive covenants governing the use and occupancy of the Property and a dedicatory instrument governing the establishment, maintenance, and operation of this residential community have been or will be recorded in the Real Property Records of the county in which the Property is located. Copies of the restrictive covenants and dedicatory instrument may be obtained from the county clerk. You are obligated to pay assessments to the owners' association. The amount of the assessments is subject to change. Your failure to pay the assessments could result in a lien on and the foreclosure of the Property. If Buyer is concerned about these matters, the TREC promulgated Addendum for Property Subject to Mandatory Membership in an Owner's Association should be used.

(3) STATUTORY TAX DISTRICTS: If the Property is situated in a utility or other statutorily created district providing water, sewer, drainage, or flood control facilities and services, Chapter 49, Texas Water Code, requires Seller to deliver and Buyer to sign the statutory notice relating to the tax rate, bonded indebtedness, or standby fee of the district prior to final execution of this contract.

(4) TIDE WATERS: If the Property abuts the tidally influenced waters of the state, §33.135, Texas Natural Resources Code, requires a notice regarding coastal area property to be included in the contract. An addendum containing the notice promulgated by TREC or required by the parties must be used.

(5) ANNEXATION: If the Property is located outside the limits of a municipality, Seller notifies Buyer under §5.011, Texas Property Code, that the Property may now or later be included in the extraterritorial jurisdiction of a municipality and may now or later be subject to annexation by the municipality. Each municipality maintains a map that depicts its boundaries and extraterritorial jurisdiction. To determine if the Property is located within a municipality's extraterritorial jurisdiction or is likely to be located within a municipality's extraterritorial jurisdiction, contact all municipalities located in the general proximity of the

FIGURE 10.2 (CONTINUED)

TREC 24-7

Contract Concerning ______________________________ Page 3 of 9 12-10-07
(Address of Property)

Property for further information.

(6) PROPERTY LOCATED IN A CERTIFICATED SERVICE AREA OF A UTILITY SERVICE PROVIDER: Notice required by §13.257, Water Code: The real property, described in Paragraph 2, that you are about to purchase may be located in a certificated water or sewer service area, which is authorized by law to provide water or sewer service to the properties in the certificated area. If your property is located in a certificated area there may be special costs or charges that you will be required to pay before you can receive water or sewer service. There may be a period required to construct lines or other facilities necessary to provide water or sewer service to your property. You are advised to determine if the property is in a certificated area and contact the utility service provider to determine the cost that you will be required to pay and the period, if any, that is required to provide water or sewer service to your property. The undersigned Buyer hereby acknowledges receipt of the foregoing notice at or before the execution of a binding contract for the purchase of the real property described in Paragraph 2 or at closing of purchase of the real property.

(7) PUBLIC IMPROVEMENT DISTRICTS: If the Property is in a public improvement district, §5.014, Property Code, requires Seller to notify Buyer as follows: As a purchaser of this parcel of real property you are obligated to pay an assessment to a municipality or county for an improvement project undertaken by a public improvement district under Chapter 372, Local Government Code. The assessment may be due annually or in periodic installments. More information concerning the amount of the assessment and the due dates of that assessment may be obtained from the municipality or county levying the assessment. The amount of the assessments is subject to change. Your failure to pay the assessments could result in a lien on and the foreclosure of your property.

7. PROPERTY CONDITION:

A. ACCESS,INSPECTIONS AND UTILITIES: Seller shall permit Buyer and Buyer's agents access to the Property at reasonable times. Buyer may have the Property inspected by inspectors selected by Buyer and licensed by TREC or otherwise permitted by law to make inspections. Seller shall pay for turning on existing utilities for inspections.

B. ACCEPTANCE OF PROPERTY CONDITION: Buyer accepts the Property in its present condition; provided Seller, at Seller's expense, shall complete the following specific repairs and treatments; and make the following improvements: ______________________________

____

C. WARRANTIES: Except as expressly set forth in this contract, a separate writing, or provided by law, Seller makes no other express warranties. Seller shall assign to Buyer at closing all assignable manufacturer warranties.

D. INSULATION: As required by Federal Trade Commission Regulations, the information relating to the insulation installed or to be installed in the Improvements at the Property is: (check only one box below)

☐ (1) as shown in the attached specifications.

☐ (2) as follows:

a) Exterior walls of improved living areas: insulated with ____________________ insulation to a thickness of ________ inches which yields an R-Value of ________.

b) Walls in other areas of the home: insulated with____________________ insulation to a thickness of _______ inches which yields an R-Value of __________.

c) Ceilings in improved living areas: insulated with____________________ insulation to a thickness of ________ inches which yields an R-Value of ________.

d) Floors of improved living areas not applied to a slab foundation: insulated with insulation to a thickness of ___ inches which yields an R-Value of ____.

e) Other insulated areas:insulated with ____________________insulation to a thickness of ________ inches which yields an R-Value of __________.

All stated R-Values are based on information provided by the manufacturer of the insulation.

E. LENDER REQUIRED REPAIRS AND TREATMENTS: Unless otherwise agreed in writing, neither party is obligated to pay for lender required repairs, which includes treatment for wood destroying insects. If the parties do not agree to pay for the lender required repairs or treatments, this contract will terminate and the earnest money will be refunded to Buyer. If the cost of lender required repairs and treatments exceeds 5% of the Sales Price, Buyer may terminate this contract and the earnest money will be refunded to Buyer.

F. COMPLETION OF REPAIRS, TREATMENTS, AND IMPROVEMENTS: Unless otherwise agreed in writing, Seller shall complete all agreed repairs, treatments, and improvements (Work) prior to the Closing Date. All required permits must be obtained, and Work must be performed by persons who are licensed or otherwise authorized by law to provide such Work. At Buyer's election, any transferable warranties received by Seller with respect to the Work will be transferred to Buyer at Buyer's expense. If Seller fails to complete any agreed Work prior to the Closing Date, Buyer may do so and receive reimbursement from Seller at closing. The Closing Date will be extended up to 15 days, if necessary, to complete Work.

Initialed for identification by Buyer______ ______ and Seller _______ ______ TREC NO. 24-7

FIGURE 10.2 (CONTINUED)

TREC 24-7

Contract Concerning ____ Page 4 of 9 12-10-07
(Address of Property)

G. ENVIRONMENTAL MATTERS: Buyer is advised that the presence of wetlands, toxic substances, including asbestos and wastes or other environmental hazards or the presence of a threatened or endangered species or its habitat may affect Buyer's intended use of the Property. If Buyer is concerned about these matters, an addendum promulgated by TREC or required by the parties should be used.

H. SELLER'S DISCLOSURE: Except as otherwise disclosed in this contract, Seller has no knowledge of the following:
(1) any flooding of the Property which has had a material adverse effect on the use of the Property;
(2) any pending or threatened litigation, condemnation, or special assessment affecting the Property;
(3) any environmental hazards or conditions materially affecting the Property;
(4) any dumpsite, landfill, or underground tanks or containers now or previously located on the Property;
(5) any wetlands, as defined by federal or state law or regulation, affecting the Property; or
(6) any threatened or endangered species or their habitat affecting the Property.

I. RESIDENTIAL SERVICE CONTRACTS: Buyer may purchase a residential service contract from a residential service company licensed by TREC. If Buyer purchases a residential service contract, Seller shall reimburse Buyer at closing for the cost of the residential service contract in an amount not exceeding $_______________ . Buyer should review any residential service contract for the scope of coverage, exclusions and limitations. **The purchase of a residential service contract is optional. Similar coverage may be purchased from various companies authorized to do business in Texas.**

8. BROKERS' FEES: All obligations of the parties for payment of brokers' fees are contained in separate written agreements.

9. CLOSING:

A. The closing of the sale will be on or before ____________________, 20_____, or within 7 days after objections made under Paragraph 6D have been cured or waived, whichever date is later (Closing Date). If either party fails to close the sale by the Closing Date, the non-defaulting party may exercise the remedies contained in Paragraph 15.

B. At closing:
(1)Seller shall execute and deliver a general warranty deed conveying title to the Property to Buyer and showing no additional exceptions to those permitted in Paragraph 6 and furnish tax statements or certificates showing no delinquent taxes on the Property.
(2)Buyer shall pay the Sales Price in good funds acceptable to the escrow agent.
(3)Seller and Buyer shall execute and deliver any notices, statements, certificates, affidavits, releases, loan documents and other documents required of them by this contract, the Commitment or law necessary for the closing of the sale and the issuance of the Title Policy.

C. Unless expressly prohibited by written agreement, Seller may continue to show the Property and receive, negotiate and accept back up offers.

D. All covenants, representations and warranties in this contract survive closing.

10. POSSESSION: Seller shall deliver to Buyer possession of the Property in its present or required condition, ordinary wear and tear excepted: ❑ upon closing and funding ❑ according to a temporary residential lease form promulgated by TREC or other written lease required by the parties. Any possession by Buyer prior to closing or by Seller after closing which is not authorized by a written lease will establish a tenancy at sufferance relationship between the parties. **Consult your insurance agent prior to change of ownership and possession because insurance coverage may be limited or terminated. The absence of a written lease or appropriate insurance coverage may expose the parties to economic loss.**

11. SPECIAL PROVISIONS: (Insert only factual statements and business details applicable to the sale. TREC rules prohibit licensees from adding factual statements or business details for which a contract addendum, lease or other form has been promulgated by TREC for mandatory use.)

Initialed for identification by Buyer______ ______ and Seller _______ ______ TREC NO. 24-7

FIGURE 10.2 (CONTINUED)

TREC 24-7

Contract Concerning ____ Page 5 of 9 12-10-07
(Address of Property)

12. SETTLEMENT AND OTHER EXPENSES:

A. The following expenses must be paid at or prior to closing:

(1) Expenses payable by Seller (Seller's Expenses):

(a)Releases of existing liens, including prepayment penalties and recording fees; release of Seller's loan liability; tax statements or certificates; preparation of deed; one-half of escrow fee; and other expenses payable by Seller under this contract.

(b)Seller shall also pay an amount not to exceed $ ____________ to be applied in the following order: Buyer's Expenses which Buyer is prohibited from paying by FHA, VA, Texas Veterans Housing Assistance Program or other governmental loan programs, and then to other Buyer's Expenses as allowed by the lender.

(2) Expenses payable by Buyer (Buyer's Expenses):

(a) Loan origination, discount, buy-down, and commitment fees (Loan Fees).

(b) Appraisal fees; loan application fees; credit reports; preparation of loan documents; interest on the notes from date of disbursement to one month prior to dates of first monthly payments; recording fees; copies of easements and restrictions; mortgagee title policy with endorsements required by lender; loan-related inspection fees; photos; amortization schedules; one-half of escrow fee; all prepaid items, including required premiums for flood and hazard insurance, reserve deposits for insurance, ad valorem taxes and special governmental assessments; final compliance inspection; courier fee; repair inspection; underwriting fee; wire transfer fee; expenses incident to any loan; and other expenses payable by Buyer under this contract.

B. Buyer shall pay Private Mortgage Insurance Premium (PMI), VA Loan Funding Fee, or FHA Mortgage Insurance Premium (MIP) as required by the lender.

C. If any expense exceeds an amount expressly stated in this contract for such expense to be paid by a party, that party may terminate this contract unless the other party agrees to pay such excess. Buyer may not pay charges and fees expressly prohibited by FHA, VA, Texas Veterans Housing Assistance Program or other governmental loan program regulations.

13. PRORATIONS AND ROLLBACK TAXES:

A. PRORATIONS: Taxes for the current year, maintenance fees, assessments, dues and rents will be prorated through the Closing Date. The tax proration may be calculated taking into consideration any change in exemptions that will affect the current year's taxes. If taxes for the current year vary from the amount prorated at closing, the parties shall adjust the prorations when tax statements for the current year are available. If taxes are not paid at or prior to closing, Buyer will be obligated to pay taxes for the current year.

B. ROLLBACK TAXES: If Seller's change in use of the Property prior to closing or denial of a special use valuation on the Property results in additional taxes, penalties or interest (Assessments) for periods prior to closing, the Assessments will be the obligation of Seller. Obligations imposed by this paragraph will survive closing.

14. CASUALTY LOSS: If any part of the Property is damaged or destroyed by fire or other casualty after the effective date of this contract, Seller shall restore the Property to its previous condition as soon as reasonably possible, but in any event by the Closing Date. If Seller fails to do so due to factors beyond Seller's control, Buyer may (a) terminate this contract and the earnest money will be refunded to Buyer (b) extend the time for performance up to 15 days and the Closing Date will be extended as necessary or (c) accept the Property in its damaged condition with an assignment of insurance proceeds and receive credit from Seller at closing in the amount of the deductible under the insurance policy. Seller's obligations under this paragraph are independent of any other obligations of Seller under this contract.

15. DEFAULT: If Buyer fails to comply with this contract, Buyer will be in default, and Seller may (a) enforce specific performance, seek such other relief as may be provided by law, or both, or (b) terminate this contract and receive the earnest money as liquidated damages, thereby releasing both parties from this contract. If, due to factors beyond Seller's control, Seller fails within the time allowed to make any non-casualty repairs or deliver the Commitment, or survey, if required of Seller, Buyer may (a) extend the time for performance up to 15 days and the Closing Date will be extended as necessary or (b) terminate this contract as the sole remedy and receive the earnest money. If Seller fails to comply with this contract for any other reason, Seller will be in default and Buyer may (a) enforce specific performance, seek such other relief as may be provided by law, or both, or (b) terminate this contract and receive the earnest money, thereby releasing both parties from this contract.

16. MEDIATION: It is the policy of the State of Texas to encourage resolution of disputes through alternative dispute resolution procedures such as mediation. Subject to applicable law, any dispute between Seller and Buyer related to this contract which is not resolved through informal discussion ☐will ☐will not be submitted to a mutually acceptable mediation service or provider. The parties to the mediation shall bear the mediation costs equally. This paragraph does not preclude a party from seeking equitable relief from a court of competent jurisdiction.

Initialed for identification by Buyer_____ _____ and Seller _____ _____ TREC NO. 24-7

FIGURE 10.2 (CONTINUED)

TREC 24-7

17. ATTORNEY'S FEES: The prevailing party in any legal proceeding related to this contract is entitled to recover reasonable attorney's fees and all costs of such proceeding incurred by the prevailing party.

18. ESCROW:

A. ESCROW: The escrow agent is not (i) a party to this contract and does not have liability for the performance or nonperformance of any party to this contract, (ii) liable for interest on the earnest money and (iii) liable for the loss of any earnest money caused by the failure of any financial institution in which the earnest money has been deposited unless the financial institution is acting as escrow agent.

B. EXPENSES: At closing, the earnest money must be applied first to any cash down payment, then to Buyer's Expenses and any excess refunded to Buyer. If no closing occurs, escrow agent may require payment of unpaid expenses incurred on behalf of the parties and a written release of liability of escrow agent from all parties.

C. DEMAND: Upon termination of this contract, either party or the escrow agent may send a release of earnest money to each party and the parties shall execute counterparts of the release and deliver same to the escrow agent. If either party fails to execute the release, either party may make a written demand to the escrow agent for the earnest money. If only one party makes written demand for the earnest money, escrow agent shall promptly provide a copy of the demand to the other party. If escrow agent does not receive written objection to the demand from the other party within 15 days, escrow agent may disburse the earnest money to the party making demand reduced by the amount of unpaid expenses incurred on behalf of the party receiving the earnest money and escrow agent may pay the same to the creditors. If escrow agent complies with the provisions of this paragraph, each party hereby releases escrow agent from all adverse claims related to the disbursal of the earnest money.

D. DAMAGES: Any party who wrongfully fails or refuses to sign a release acceptable to the escrow agent within 7 days of receipt of the request will be liable to the other party for liquidated damages of three times the amount of the earnest money.

E. NOTICES: Escrow agent's notices will be effective when sent in compliance with Paragraph 21. Notice of objection to the demand will be deemed effective upon receipt by escrow agent.

19. REPRESENTATIONS: Seller represents that as of the Closing Date there will be no liens, assessments, or security interests against the Property which will not be satisfied out of the sales proceeds. If any representation of Seller in this contract is untrue on the Closing Date, Seller will be in default.

20. FEDERAL TAX REQUIREMENTS: If Seller is a "foreign person," as defined by applicable law, or if Seller fails to deliver an affidavit to Buyer that Seller is not a "foreign person," then Buyer shall withhold from the sales proceeds an amount sufficient to comply with applicable tax law and deliver the same to the Internal Revenue Service together with appropriate tax forms. Internal Revenue Service regulations require filing written reports if currency in excess of specified amounts is received in the transaction.

21. NOTICES: All notices from one party to the other must be in writing and are effective when mailed to, hand-delivered at, or transmitted by facsimile or electronic transmission as follows:

To Buyer at:	**To Seller at:**
______________________	______________________
______________________	______________________
______________________	______________________
Telephone: ( ) ____________	Telephone: ( ) ____________
Facsimile: ( ) ____________	Facsimile: ( ) ____________
E-mail: ____________	E-mail: ____________

FIGURE 10.2 (CONTINUED)

TREC 24-7

Contract Concerning ____ Page 7 of 9 12-10-07
(Address of Property)

22. AGREEMENT OF PARTIES: This contract contains the entire agreement of the parties and cannot be changed except by their written agreement. Addenda which are a part of this contract are (check all applicable boxes):

- ❑ Third Party Financing Condition Addendum
- ❑ Seller Financing Addendum
- ❑ Addendum for Property Subject to Mandatory Membership in an Owners' Association
- ❑ Buyer's Temporary Residential Lease
- ❑ Addendum for Sale of Other Property by Buyer
- ❑ Addendum Containing Required Notices Under §420.01 and §420.002, Texas Property Code
- ❑ Addendum for "Back-Up" Contract
- ❑ Addendum for Coastal Area Property
- ❑ Environmental Assessment, Threatened or Endangered Species and Wetlands Addendum
- ❑ Addendum for Property Located Seaward of the Gulf Intracoastal Waterway
- ❑ Other (list): ______________________

23. TERMINATION OPTION: For nominal consideration, the receipt of which is hereby acknowledged by Seller, and Buyer's agreement to pay Seller $_______________ (Option Fee) within 2 days after the effective date of this contract, Seller grants Buyer the unrestricted right to terminate this contract by giving notice of termination to Seller within _______ days after the effective date of this contract. If no dollar amount is stated as the Option Fee or if Buyer fails to pay the Option Fee within the time prescribed, this paragraph will not be a part of this contract and Buyer shall not have the unrestricted right to terminate this contract. If Buyer gives notice of termination within the time prescribed, the Option Fee will not be refunded; however, any earnest money will be refunded to Buyer. The Option Fee ❑will ❑will not be credited to the Sales Price at closing. **Time is of the essence for this paragraph and strict compliance with the time for performance is required.**

24. CONSULT AN ATTORNEY: Real estate licensees cannot give legal advice. READ THIS CONTRACT CAREFULLY. If you do not understand the effect of this contract, consult an attorney BEFORE signing.

Buyer's Attorney is: ______________________	Seller's Attorney is: ______________________
______________________	______________________
Telephone: ( ) ______________	Telephone: ( ) ______________
Facsimile: ( ) ______________	Facsimile: ( ) ______________
E-mail: ______________________	E-mail: ______________________

Initialed for identification by Buyer______ ______ and Seller _______ ______ TREC NO. 24-7

FIGURE 10.2 (CONTINUED)

TREC 24-7

Contract Concerning ____ Page 8 of 9 12-10-07
(Address of Property)

EXECUTED the ______day of ________________________, 20___ (EFFECTIVE DATE).
(BROKER: FILL IN THE DATE OF FINAL ACCEPTANCE.)

This contract is subject to Chapter 27 of the Texas Property Code. The provisions of that chapter may affect your right to recover damages arising from a construction defect. If you have a complaint concerning a construction defect and that defect has not been corrected as may be required by law or by contract, you must provide the notice required by Chapter 27 of the Texas Property Code to the contractor by certified mail, return receipt requested, not later than the 60th day before the date you file suit to recover damages in a court of law or initiate arbitration. The notice must refer to Chapter 27 of the Texas Property Code and must describe the construction defect. If requested by the contractor, you must provide the contractor an opportunity to inspect and cure the defect as provided by Section 27.004 of the Texas Property Code.

____
Buyer

____
Buyer

____
Seller

____
Seller

The form of this contract has been approved by the Texas Real Estate Commission. TREC forms are intended for use only by trained real estate licensees. No representation is made as to the legal validity or adequacy of any provision in any specific transactions. It is not intended for complex transactions. Texas Real Estate Commission, P.O. Box 12188, Austin, TX 78711-2188, 1-800-250-8732 or (512) 459-6544 (http://www.trec.state.tx.us) TREC NO. 24-7. This form replaces TREC NO. 24-6.

FIGURE 10.2 (CONTINUED)

TREC 24-7

Contract Concerning ______________________________ Page 9 of 9 12-10-07
(Address of Property)

BROKER INFORMATION AND RATIFICATION OF FEE

Listing Broker has agreed to pay Other Broker ______________ of the total sales price when Listing Broker's fee is received. Escrow Agent is authorized and directed to pay Other Broker from Listing Broker's fee at closing.

Other Broker — License No.	Listing Broker — License No.
represents ❑ Buyer only as Buyer's agent ❑ Seller as Listing Broker's subagent	represents ❑ Seller and Buyer as an intermediary ❑ Seller only as Seller's agent
Associate — Telephone	Listing Associate — Telephone
Broker's Address	Listing Associate's Office Address — Facsimile
City — State — Zip	City — State — Zip
Facsimile	Email Address
Email Address	Selling Associate — Telephone
	Selling Associate's Office Address — Facsimile
	City — State — Zip
	Email Address

OPTION FEE RECEIPT

Receipt of $______________ (Option Fee) in the form of ______________ is acknowledged.

Seller or Listing Broker ______________ Date ______________

CONTRACT AND EARNEST MONEY RECEIPT

Receipt of ❑Contract and ❑$______________ Earnest Money in the form of ______________ is acknowledged.
Escrow Agent: ______________ Date: ______________

By: ______________ Email Address

Address ______________ Telephone (____) ______________

City State Zip ______________ Facsimile: (____) ______________

TREC NO. 24-7

FIGURE 10.3

TREC 43-0

PROMULGATED BY THE TEXAS REAL ESTATE COMMISSION (TREC) 12-10-2007

ADDENDUM CONTAINING REQUIRED NOTICES UNDER §5.016, §420.001 AND §420.002, TEXAS PROPERTY CODE

TO CONTRACT CONCERNING THE PROPERTY AT

____

(Address of Property)

❑ A. **NOTICE OF NONAPPLICABILITY OF CERTAIN WARRANTIES AND BUILDING AND PERFORMANCE STANDARDS.**

The property that is subject to this contract is exempt from Title 16, Property Code, including the provisions of that title that provide statutory warranties and building and performance standards.

B. **NOTICE TO BUYER REQUIRED BY SECTION 420.001, TEXAS PROPERTY CODE.**

STATE LAW REQUIRES THAT A PERSON HOLD A CERTIFICATE OF REGISTRATION FROM THE TEXAS RESIDENTIAL CONSTRUCTION COMMISSION IF THE PERSON CONTRACTS TO CONSTRUCT A NEW HOME OR IF THE PERSON CONTRACTS TO CONSTRUCT A MATERIAL IMPROVEMENT TO AN EXISTING HOME OR CERTAIN IMPROVEMENTS TO THE INTERIOR OF AN EXISTING HOME AND THE TOTAL COST OF THE IMPROVEMENTS IS $10,000 OR MORE (INCLUDING LABOR AND MATERIALS).

YOU MAY CONTACT THE TEXAS RESIDENTIAL CONSTRUCTION COMMISSION AT 1-877-651-8722 TO FIND OUT WHETHER THE BUILDER HAS A VALID CERTIFICATE OF REGISTRATION. THE COMMISSION HAS INFORMATION AVAILABLE ON THE HISTORY OF BUILDERS, INCLUDING SUSPENSIONS, REVOCATIONS, COMPLAINTS, AND RESOLUTION OF COMPLAINTS.

THIS CONTRACT IS SUBJECT TO CHAPTER 426, TEXAS PROPERTY CODE. THE PROVISIONS OF THAT CHAPTER GOVERN THE PROCESS THAT MUST BE FOLLOWED IN THE EVENT A DISPUTE ARISES OUT OF AN ALLEGED CONSTRUCTION DEFECT. IF YOU HAVE A COMPLAINT CONCERNING A CONSTRUCTION DEFECT YOU MAY CONTACT THE TEXAS RESIDENTIAL CONSTRUCTION COMMISSION AT THE TOLL-FREE TELEPHONE NUMBER TO LEARN HOW TO PROCEED UNDER THE STATE-SPONSORED INSPECTION AND DISPUTE RESOLUTION PROCESS.

C. **INFORMATION REQUIRED BY SECTION 420.002, TEXAS PROPERTY CODE.**

Name of Builder: ____

Certificate of Registration Number: ____

______________________	______________________
Buyer	Seller
______________________	______________________
Buyer	Seller

This form has been approved by the Texas Real Estate Commission for use with similarly approved or promulgated contract forms. Such approval relates to this form only. TREC forms are intended for use only by trained real estate licensees. No representation is made as to the legal validity or adequacy of any provision in any specific transaction. It is not suitable for complex transactions. Texas Real Estate Commission, P.O. Box 12188, Austin, TX 78711-2188, 1-800-250-8732 or (512) 459-6544 (http://www.trec.state.tx.us) TREC No. 43-0.

TREC No. 43-0

FIGURE 10.4

TREC 25-5

PROMULGATED BY THE TEXAS REAL ESTATE COMMISSION (TREC) 02-13-06

EQUAL HOUSING OPPORTUNITY

FARM AND RANCH CONTRACT

1. **PARTIES:** ______________________ (Seller) agrees to sell and convey to ______________________ (Buyer) and Buyer agrees to buy from Seller the Property described below.

2. **PROPERTY:** The land, improvements, accessories and crops are collectively referred to as the "Property".
   A. LAND: The land situated in the County of ______________________, Texas, described as follows:

   or as described on attached exhibit, also known as ______________________ (address/zip code), together with all rights, privileges, and appurtenances pertaining thereto, including but not limited to: water rights, claims, permits, strips and gores, easements, and cooperative or association memberships.

   B. IMPROVEMENTS:
   (1) FARM and RANCH IMPROVEMENTS: The following **permanently installed and built-in items**, if any: windmills, tanks, barns, pens, fences, gates, sheds, outbuildings, and corrals.
   (2) RESIDENTIAL IMPROVEMENTS: The house, garage, and all other fixtures and improvements attached to the above-described real property, including without limitation, the following **permanently installed and built-in items,** if any: all equipment and appliances, valances, screens, shutters, awnings, wall-to-wall carpeting, mirrors, ceiling fans, attic fans, mail boxes, television antennas and satellite dish system and equipment, heating and air-conditioning units, security and fire detection equipment, wiring, plumbing and lighting fixtures, chandeliers, water softener system, kitchen equipment, garage door openers, cleaning equipment, shrubbery, landscaping, outdoor cooking equipment, and all other property owned by Seller and attached to the above described real property.

   C. ACCESSORIES:
   (1) FARM AND RANCH ACCESSORIES: The following described related accessories: (check boxes of conveyed accessories) ❑ portable buildings ❑ hunting blinds ❑ game feeders ❑ livestock feeders and troughs ❑ irrigation equipment ❑ fuel tanks ❑ submersible pumps ❑ pressure tanks ❑ corrals ❑ gates ❑ chutes ❑ other:______________________
   (2) RESIDENTIAL ACCESSORIES: The following described related accessories, if any: window air conditioning units, stove, fireplace screens, curtains and rods, blinds, window shades, draperies and rods, controls for satellite dish system, controls for garage door openers, entry gate controls, door keys, mailbox keys, above ground pool, swimming pool equipment and maintenance accessories, and artificial fireplace logs.

   D. CROPS: Unless otherwise agreed in writing, Seller has the right to harvest all growing crops until delivery of possession of the Property.

   E. EXCLUSIONS: The following improvements, accessories, and crops will be retained by Seller and excluded: ______________________

   F. RESERVATIONS: Seller reserves the following mineral, water, royalty, timber, or other interests:______________________

3. **SALES PRICE:**
   A. Cash portion of Sales Price payable by Buyer at closing .... $__________
   B. Sum of all financing described below (excluding any loan funding fee or mortgage insurance premium) .... $__________
   C. Sales Price (Sum of A and B) .... $__________
   D. The Sales Price ❑ will ❑ will not be adjusted based on the survey required by Paragraph 6C. If the Sales Price is adjusted, the Sales Price will be calculated on the basis of $ __________ per acre. If the Sales Price is adjusted by more than 10%, either party may terminate this contract by providing written notice to the other party within ______ days after the terminating party receives the survey. If neither party terminates this contract or if the variance is 10% or less, the adjustment will be made to the amount in ❑ 3A ❑ 3B ❑ proportionately to 3A and 3B.

Initialed for identification by Buyer______ ______ and Seller _______ ______ TREC NO. 25-5

FIGURE 10.4 (CONTINUED)

TREC 25-5

4. FINANCING: The portion of Sales Price not payable in cash will be paid as follows: (Check applicable boxes below)

❑ A. THIRD PARTY FINANCING: One or more third party mortgage loans in the total amount of $______________ (excluding any loan funding fee or mortgage insurance premium).

(1) Property Approval: If the Property does not satisfy the lenders' underwriting requirements for the loan(s), this contract will terminate and the earnest money will be refunded to Buyer.

(2) Financing Approval: (Check one box only)

❑ (a) This contract is subject to Buyer being approved for the financing described in the attached Third Party Financing Condition Addendum.

❑ (b) This contract is not subject to Buyer being approved for financing and does not involve FHA or VA financing.

❑ B. ASSUMPTION: The assumption of the unpaid principal balance of one or more promissory notes described in the attached TREC Loan Assumption Addendum.

❑ C. SELLER FINANCING: A promissory note from Buyer to Seller of $______________, secured by vendor's and deed of trust liens, and containing the terms and conditions described in the attached TREC Seller Financing Addendum. If an owner policy of title insurance is furnished, Buyer shall furnish Seller with a mortgagee policy of title insurance.

5. EARNEST MONEY: Upon execution of this contract by both parties, Buyer shall deposit $__________ as earnest money with ____, as escrow agent, at ____ (address). Buyer shall deposit additional earnest money of $________________ with escrow agent within ______ days after the effective date of this contract. If Buyer fails to deposit the earnest money as required by this contract, Buyer will be in default.

6. TITLE POLICY AND SURVEY:

A. TITLE POLICY: Seller shall furnish to Buyer at ❑Seller's ❑Buyer's expense an owner policy of title insurance (Title Policy) issued by: ____ (Title Company) in the amount of the Sales Price, dated at or after closing, insuring Buyer against loss under the provisions of the Title Policy, subject to the promulgated exclusions (including existing building and zoning ordinances) and the following exceptions:

(1) The standard printed exception for standby fees, taxes and assessments.

(2) Liens created as part of the financing described in Paragraph 4.

(3) Reservations or exceptions otherwise permitted by this contract or as may be approved by Buyer in writing.

(4) The standard printed exception as to marital rights.

(5) The standard printed exception as to waters, tidelands, beaches, streams, and related matters.

(6) The standard printed exception as to discrepancies, conflicts, shortages in area or boundary lines, encroachments or protrusions, or overlapping improvements. Buyer, at Buyer's expense, may have the exception amended to read, "shortages in area".

B. COMMITMENT: Within 20 days after the Title Company receives a copy of this contract, Seller shall furnish to Buyer a commitment for title insurance (Commitment) and, at Buyer's expense, legible copies of restrictive covenants and documents evidencing exceptions in the Commitment (Exception Documents) other than the standard printed exceptions. Seller authorizes the Title Company to deliver the Commitment and Exception Documents to Buyer at Buyer's address shown in Paragraph 21. If the Commitment and Exception Documents are not delivered to Buyer within the specified time, the time for delivery will be automatically extended up to 15 days or the Closing Date, whichever is earlier.

C. SURVEY: The survey must be made by a registered professional land surveyor acceptable to the Title Company and any lender. (Check one box only):

❑ (1) Within _______ days after the effective date of this contract, Seller shall furnish to Buyer and Title Company Seller's existing survey of the Property and a Residential Real Property Affidavit promulgated by the Texas Department of Insurance (Affidavit). The existing survey ❑ will ❑ will not be recertified to a date subsequent to the effective date of this contract at the expense of ❑ Buyer ❑ Seller. If the existing survey is not approved by the Title Company or Buyer's Lender, a new survey will be obtained at the expense of ❑ Buyer ❑ Seller no later than 3 days prior to Closing Date. If Seller fails to furnish the existing survey or Affidavit within the time prescribed, Buyer shall obtain a new survey at Seller's expense no later than 3 days prior to Closing Date.

❑ (2) Within ______ days after the effective date of this contract, Buyer shall obtain a new survey at Buyer's expense. Buyer is deemed to receive the survey on the date of actual receipt or the date specified in this paragraph, whichever is earlier.

❑ (3) Within ______ days after the effective date of this contract, Seller, at Seller's expense shall furnish a new survey to Buyer.

❑ (4) No survey is required.

FIGURE 10.4 (CONTINUED)

TREC 25-5

Contract Concerning ____ Page 3 of 9 02-13-06
(Address of Property)

D. OBJECTIONS: Buyer may object in writing to (i) defects, exceptions, or encumbrances to title disclosed on the survey other than items 6A(1) through (5) above; or disclosed in the Commitment other than items 6A(1) through (6) above; (ii) any portion of the Property lying in a special flood hazard area (Zone V or A) as shown on the current Federal Emergency Management Agency map; or (iii) any exceptions which prohibit the following use or activity:
____
____

Buyer must object not later than (i) the Closing Date or (ii) _____ days after Buyer receives the Commitment, Exception Documents, and the survey, whichever is earlier. Buyer's failure to object within the time allowed will constitute a waiver of Buyer's right to object; except that the requirements in Schedule C of the Commitment are not waived. Provided Seller is not obligated to incur any expense, Seller shall cure the timely objections of Buyer or any third party lender within 15 days after Seller receives the objections and the Closing Date will be extended as necessary. If objections are not cured within such 15 day period, this contract will terminate and the earnest money will be refunded to Buyer unless Buyer waives the objections.

E. EXCEPTION DOCUMENTS: Prior to the execution of the contract, Seller has provided Buyer with copies of the Exception Documents listed below or on the attached exhibit. Matters reflected in the Exception Documents listed below or on the attached exhibit will be permitted exceptions in the Title Policy and will not be a basis for objection to title:

Document	Date	Recording Reference
____________	________	________
____________	________	________
____________	________	________
____________	________	________
____________	________	________
____________	________	________

F. SURFACE LEASES: Prior to the execution of the contract, Seller has provided Buyer with copies of written leases and given notice of oral leases (Leases) listed below or on the attached exhibit. The following Leases will be permitted exceptions in the Title Policy and will not be a basis for objection to title:______________________________
____
____

G. TITLE NOTICES:

(1) ABSTRACT OR TITLE POLICY: Broker advises Buyer to have an abstract of title covering the Property examined by an attorney of Buyer's selection, or Buyer should be furnished with or obtain a Title Policy. If a Title Policy is furnished, the Commitment should be promptly reviewed by an attorney of Buyer's choice due to the time limitations on Buyer's right to object.

(2) STATUTORY TAX DISTRICTS: If the Property is situated in a utility or other statutorily created district providing water, sewer, drainage, or flood control facilities and services, Chapter 49, Texas Water Code, requires Seller to deliver and Buyer to sign the statutory notice relating to the tax rate, bonded indebtedness, or standby fee of the district prior to final execution of this contract.

(3) TIDE WATERS: If the Property abuts the tidally influenced waters of the state, §33.135, Texas Natural Resources Code, requires a notice regarding coastal area property to be included in the contract. An addendum containing the notice promulgated by TREC or required by the parties must be used.

(4) ANNEXATION: If the Property is located outside the limits of a municipality, Seller notifies Buyer under §5.011, Texas Property Code, that the Property may now or later be included in the extraterritorial jurisdiction of a municipality and may now or later be subject to annexation by the municipality. Each municipality maintains a map that depicts its boundaries and extraterritorial jurisdiction. To determine if the Property is located within a municipality's extraterritorial jurisdiction or is likely to be located within a municipality's extraterritorial jurisdiction, contact all municipalities located in the general proximity of the Property for further information.

(5) PROPERTY LOCATED IN A CERTIFICATED SERVICE AREA OF A UTILITY SERVICE PROVIDER: Notice required by §13.257, Water Code: The real property, described in

Initialed for identification by Buyer______ ______ and Seller _______ ______ TREC NO. 25-5

FIGURE 10.4 (CONTINUED)

TREC 25-5

Paragraph 2, that you are about to purchase may be located in a certificated water or sewer service area, which is authorized by law to provide water or sewer service to the properties in the certificated area. If your property is located in a certificated area there may be special costs or charges that you will be required to pay before you can receive water or sewer service. There may be a period required to construct lines or other facilities necessary to provide water or sewer service to your property. You are advised to determine if the property is in a certificated area and contact the utility service provider to determine the cost that you will be required to pay and the period, if any, that is required to provide water or sewer service to your property. The undersigned Buyer hereby acknowledges receipt of the foregoing notice at or before the execution of a binding contract for the purchase of the real property described in Paragraph 2 or at closing of purchase of the real property.

(6) PUBLIC IMPROVEMENT DISTRICTS: If the Property is in a public improvement district, §5.014, Property Code, requires Seller to notify Buyer as follows: As a purchaser of this parcel of real property you are obligated to pay an assessment to a municipality or county for an improvement project undertaken by a public improvement district under Chapter 372, Local Government Code. The assessment may be due annually or in periodic installments. More information concerning the amount of the assessment and the due dates of that assessment may be obtained from the municipality or county levying the assessment. The amount of the assessments is subject to change. Your failure to pay the assessments could result in a lien on and the foreclosure of your property.

(7) TEXAS AGRICULTURAL DEVELOPMENT DISTRICT: The Property ☐ is ☐ is not located in a Texas Agricultural Development District. For additional information contact the Texas Department of Agriculture.

7. PROPERTY CONDITION:

A. ACCESS,INSPECTIONS AND UTILITIES: Seller shall permit Buyer and Buyer's agents access to the Property at reasonable times. Buyer may have the Property inspected by inspectors selected by Buyer and licensed by TREC or otherwise permitted by law to make inspections. Seller at Seller's expense shall turn on existing utilities for inspections.

NOTICE: Buyer should determine the availability of utilities to the Property suitable to satisfy Buyer's needs.

B. SELLER'S DISCLOSURE NOTICE PURSUANT TO §5.008, TEXAS PROPERTY CODE (Notice): (Check one box only)

☐ (1) Buyer has received the Notice

☐ (2) Buyer has not received the Notice. Within _______ days after the effective date of this contract, Seller shall deliver the Notice to Buyer. If Buyer does not receive the Notice, Buyer may terminate this contract at any time prior to the closing and the earnest money will be refunded to Buyer. If Seller delivers the Notice, Buyer may terminate this contract for any reason within 7 days after Buyer receives the Notice or prior to the closing, whichever first occurs, and the earnest money will be refunded to Buyer.

☐ (3) The Texas Property Code does not require this Seller to furnish the Notice.

C. SELLER'S DISCLOSURE OF LEAD-BASED PAINT AND LEAD-BASED PAINT HAZARDS is required by Federal law for a residential dwelling constructed prior to 1978.

D. ACCEPTANCE OF PROPERTY CONDITION: Buyer accepts the Property in its present condition; provided Seller, at Seller's expense, shall complete the following specific repairs and treatments: _______________.

E. COMPLETION OF REPAIRS: Unless otherwise agreed in writing, Seller shall complete all agreed repairs prior to the Closing Date. All required permits must be obtained, and repairs must be performed by persons who are licensed or otherwise permitted by law to provide such repairs. At Buyer's election, any transferable warranties received by Seller with respect to the repairs will be transferred to Buyer at Buyer's expense. If Seller fails to complete any agreed repairs prior to the Closing Date, Buyer may do so and receive reimbursement from Seller at closing. The Closing Date will be extended up to 15 days, if necessary, to complete repairs.

F. LENDER REQUIRED REPAIRS AND TREATMENTS: Unless otherwise agreed in writing, neither party is obligated to pay for lender required repairs, which includes treatment for wood destroying insects. If the parties do not agree to pay for the lender required repairs or treatments, this contract will terminate and the earnest money will be refunded to Buyer. If the cost of lender required repairs and treatments exceeds 5% of the Sales Price, Buyer may terminate this contract and the earnest money will be refunded to Buyer.

G. ENVIRONMENTAL MATTERS: Buyer is advised that the presence of wetlands, toxic substances, including asbestos and wastes or other environmental hazards, or the presence of a threatened or endangered species or its habitat may affect Buyer's intended use of the Property. If Buyer is concerned about these matters, an addendum promulgated by TREC or required by the parties should be used.

H. SELLER'S DISCLOSURES: Except as otherwise disclosed in this contract, Seller has no knowledge of the following:

(1) any flooding of the Property which has had a material adverse effect on the use of the Property;

(2) any pending or threatened litigation, condemnation, or special assessment affecting the Property;

FIGURE 10.4 (CONTINUED)

TREC 25-5

Contract Concerning ____ Page 5 of 9 12-10-07
(Address of Property)

12. SETTLEMENT AND OTHER EXPENSES:

A. The following expenses must be paid at or prior to closing:

(1) Expenses payable by Seller (Seller's Expenses):

(a)Releases of existing liens, including prepayment penalties and recording fees; release of Seller's loan liability; tax statements or certificates; preparation of deed; one-half of escrow fee; and other expenses payable by Seller under this contract.

(b)Seller shall also pay an amount not to exceed $ ____________ to be applied in the following order: Buyer's Expenses which Buyer is prohibited from paying by FHA, VA, Texas Veterans Housing Assistance Program or other governmental loan programs, and then to other Buyer's Expenses as allowed by the lender.

(2) Expenses payable by Buyer (Buyer's Expenses):

(a) Loan origination, discount, buy-down, and commitment fees (Loan Fees).

(b) Appraisal fees; loan application fees; credit reports; preparation of loan documents; interest on the notes from date of disbursement to one month prior to dates of first monthly payments; recording fees; copies of easements and restrictions; mortgagee title policy with endorsements required by lender; loan-related inspection fees; photos; amortization schedules; one-half of escrow fee; all prepaid items, including required premiums for flood and hazard insurance, reserve deposits for insurance, ad valorem taxes and special governmental assessments; final compliance inspection; courier fee; repair inspection; underwriting fee; wire transfer fee; expenses incident to any loan; and other expenses payable by Buyer under this contract.

B. Buyer shall pay Private Mortgage Insurance Premium (PMI), VA Loan Funding Fee, or FHA Mortgage Insurance Premium (MIP) as required by the lender.

C. If any expense exceeds an amount expressly stated in this contract for such expense to be paid by a party, that party may terminate this contract unless the other party agrees to pay such excess. Buyer may not pay charges and fees expressly prohibited by FHA, VA, Texas Veterans Housing Assistance Program or other governmental loan program regulations.

13. PRORATIONS AND ROLLBACK TAXES:

A. PRORATIONS: Taxes for the current year, maintenance fees, assessments, dues and rents will be prorated through the Closing Date. The tax proration may be calculated taking into consideration any change in exemptions that will affect the current year's taxes. If taxes for the current year vary from the amount prorated at closing, the parties shall adjust the prorations when tax statements for the current year are available. If taxes are not paid at or prior to closing, Buyer will be obligated to pay taxes for the current year.

B. ROLLBACK TAXES: If Seller's change in use of the Property prior to closing or denial of a special use valuation on the Property results in additional taxes, penalties or interest (Assessments) for periods prior to closing, the Assessments will be the obligation of Seller. Obligations imposed by this paragraph will survive closing.

14. CASUALTY LOSS: If any part of the Property is damaged or destroyed by fire or other casualty after the effective date of this contract, Seller shall restore the Property to its previous condition as soon as reasonably possible, but in any event by the Closing Date. If Seller fails to do so due to factors beyond Seller's control, Buyer may (a) terminate this contract and the earnest money will be refunded to Buyer (b) extend the time for performance up to 15 days and the Closing Date will be extended as necessary or (c) accept the Property in its damaged condition with an assignment of insurance proceeds and receive credit from Seller at closing in the amount of the deductible under the insurance policy. Seller's obligations under this paragraph are independent of any other obligations of Seller under this contract.

15. DEFAULT: If Buyer fails to comply with this contract, Buyer will be in default, and Seller may (a) enforce specific performance, seek such other relief as may be provided by law, or both, or (b) terminate this contract and receive the earnest money as liquidated damages, thereby releasing both parties from this contract. If, due to factors beyond Seller's control, Seller fails within the time allowed to make any non-casualty repairs or deliver the Commitment, or survey, if required of Seller, Buyer may (a) extend the time for performance up to 15 days and the Closing Date will be extended as necessary or (b) terminate this contract as the sole remedy and receive the earnest money. If Seller fails to comply with this contract for any other reason, Seller will be in default and Buyer may (a) enforce specific performance, seek such other relief as may be provided by law, or both, or (b) terminate this contract and receive the earnest money, thereby releasing both parties from this contract.

16. MEDIATION: It is the policy of the State of Texas to encourage resolution of disputes through alternative dispute resolution procedures such as mediation. Subject to applicable law, any dispute between Seller and Buyer related to this contract which is not resolved through informal discussion ☐will ☐will not be submitted to a mutually acceptable mediation service or provider. The parties to the mediation shall bear the mediation costs equally. This paragraph does not preclude a party from seeking equitable relief from a court of competent jurisdiction.

Initialed for identification by Buyer______ ______ and Seller ______ ______ TREC NO. 24-7

FIGURE 10.4 (CONTINUED)

TREC 25-5

12. SETTLEMENT AND OTHER EXPENSES:

A. The following expenses must be paid at or prior to closing:

(1) Expenses payable by Seller (Seller's Expenses):

(a) Releases of existing liens, including prepayment penalties and recording fees; release of Seller's loan liability; tax statements or certificates; preparation of deed; one-half of escrow fee; and other expenses payable by Seller under this contract.

(b) Seller shall also pay an amount not to exceed $ ____________ to be applied in the following order: Buyer's Expenses which Buyer is prohibited from paying by FHA, VA, Texas Veterans Housing Assistance Program or other governmental loan programs, and then to other Buyer's Expenses as allowed by the lender.

(2) Expenses payable by Buyer (Buyer's Expenses):

(a) Loan origination, discount, buy-down, and commitment fees (Loan Fees).

(b) Appraisal fees; loan application fees; credit reports; preparation of loan documents; interest on the notes from date of disbursement to one month prior to dates of first monthly payments; recording fees; copies of easements and restrictions; mortgagee title policy with endorsements required by lender; loan-related inspection fees; photos; amortization schedules; one-half of escrow fee; all prepaid items, including required premiums for flood and hazard insurance, reserve deposits for insurance, ad valorem taxes and special governmental assessments; final compliance inspection; courier fee; repair inspection; underwriting fee; wire transfer fee; expenses incident to any loan; and other expenses payable by Buyer under this contract.

B. Buyer shall pay Private Mortgage Insurance Premium (PMI), VA Loan Funding Fee, or FHA Mortgage Insurance Premium (MIP) as required by the lender.

C. If any expense exceeds an amount expressly stated in this contract for such expense to be paid by a party, that party may terminate this contract unless the other party agrees to pay such excess. Buyer may not pay charges and fees expressly prohibited by FHA, VA, Texas Veterans Housing Assistance Program or other governmental loan program regulations.

13. PRORATIONS AND ROLLBACK TAXES:

A. PRORATIONS: Taxes for the current year, interest, maintenance fees, assessments, dues and rents will be prorated through the Closing Date. The tax proration may be calculated taking into consideration any change in exemptions that will affect the current year's taxes. If taxes for the current year vary from the amount prorated at closing, the parties shall adjust the prorations when tax statements for the current year are available. If taxes are not paid at or prior to closing, Buyer shall pay taxes for the current year. Rentals which are unknown at time of closing will be prorated between Buyer and Seller when they become known.

B. ROLLBACK TAXES: If this sale or Buyer's use of the Property after closing results in the assessment of additional taxes, penalties or interest (Assessments) for periods prior to closing, the Assessments will be the obligation of Buyer. If Seller's change in use of the Property prior to closing or denial of a special use valuation on the Property claimed by Seller results in Assessments for periods prior to closing, the Assessments will be the obligation of Seller. Obligations imposed by this paragraph will survive closing.

14. CASUALTY LOSS: If any part of the Property is damaged or destroyed by fire or other casualty after the effective date of this contract, Seller shall restore the Property to its previous condition as soon as reasonably possible, but in any event by the Closing Date. If Seller fails to do so due to factors beyond Seller's control, Buyer may (a) terminate this contract and the earnest money will be refunded to Buyer, (b) extend the time for performance up to 15 days and the Closing Date will be extended as necessary or (c) accept the Property in its damaged condition with an assignment of insurance proceeds and receive credit from Seller at closing in the amount of the deductible under the insurance policy. Seller's obligations under this paragraph are independent of any other obligations of Seller under this contract.

15. DEFAULT: If Buyer fails to comply with this contract, Buyer will be in default, and Seller may (a) enforce specific performance, seek such other relief as may be provided by law, or both, or (b) terminate this contract and receive the earnest money as liquidated damages, thereby releasing both parties from this contract. If, due to factors beyond Seller's control, Seller fails within the time allowed to make any non-casualty repairs or deliver the Commitment, or survey, if required of Seller, Buyer may (a) extend the time for performance up to 15 days and the Closing Date will be extended as necessary or (b) terminate this contract as the sole remedy and receive the earnest money. If Seller fails to comply with this contract for any other reason, Seller will be in default and Buyer may (a) enforce specific performance, seek such other relief as may be provided by law, or both, or (b) terminate this contract and receive the earnest money, thereby releasing both parties from this contract.

16. MEDIATION: It is the policy of the State of Texas to encourage resolution of disputes through alternative dispute resolution procedures such as mediation. Any dispute between Seller and Buyer related to this contract which is not resolved through informal discussion ❑will ❑will not be submitted to a mutually acceptable mediation service or provider. The parties to the mediation shall bear the mediation costs equally. This paragraph does not preclude a party from seeking

FIGURE 10.4 (CONTINUED)

TREC 25-5

equitable relief from a court of competent jurisdiction.

17. ATTORNEY'S FEES: The prevailing party in any legal proceeding related to this contract is entitled to recover reasonable attorney's fees and all costs of such proceeding incurred by the prevailing party.

18. ESCROW:

A. ESCROW: The escrow agent is not (i) a party to this contract and does not have liability for the performance or nonperformance of any party to this contract, (ii) liable for interest on the earnest money and (iii) liable for the loss of any earnest money caused by the failure of any financial institution in which the earnest money has been deposited unless the financial institution is acting as escrow agent.

B. EXPENSES: At closing, the earnest money must be applied first to any cash down payment, then to Buyer's Expenses and any excess refunded to Buyer. If no closing occurs, escrow agent may require payment of unpaid expenses incurred on behalf of the parties and a written release of liability of escrow agent from all parties.

C. DEMAND: Upon termination of this contract, either party or the escrow agent may send a release of earnest money to each party and the parties shall execute counterparts of the release and deliver same to the escrow agent. If either party fails to execute the release, either party may make a written demand to the escrow agent for the earnest money. If only one party makes written demand for the earnest money, escrow agent shall promptly provide a copy of the demand to the other party. If escrow agent does not receive written objection to the demand from the other party within 15 days, escrow agent may disburse the earnest money to the party making demand reduced by the amount of unpaid expenses incurred on behalf of the party receiving the earnest money and escrow agent may pay the same to the creditors. If escrow agent complies with the provisions of this paragraph, each party hereby releases escrow agent from all adverse claims related to the disbursal of the earnest money.

D. DAMAGES: Any party who wrongfully fails or refuses to sign a release acceptable to the escrow agent within 7 days of receipt of the request will be liable to the other party for liquidated damages of three times the amount of the earnest money.

E. NOTICES: Escrow agent's notices will be effective when sent in compliance with Paragraph 21. Notice of objection to the demand will be deemed effective upon receipt by escrow agent.

19. REPRESENTATIONS: Seller represents that as of the Closing Date (a) there will be no liens, assessments, or security interests against the Property which will not be satisfied out of the sales proceeds unless securing payment of any loans assumed by Buyer and (b) assumed loans will not be in default. If any representation of Seller in this contract is untrue on the Closing Date, Seller will be in default.

20. FEDERAL TAX REQUIREMENTS: If Seller is a "foreign person," as defined by applicable law, or if Seller fails to deliver an affidavit to Buyer that Seller is not a "foreign person," then Buyer shall withhold from the sales proceeds an amount sufficient to comply with applicable tax law and deliver the same to the Internal Revenue Service together with appropriate tax forms. Internal Revenue Service regulations require filing written reports if currency in excess of specified amounts is received in the transaction.

21. NOTICES: All notices from one party to the other must be in writing and are effective when mailed to, hand-delivered at, or transmitted by facsimile or electronic transmission as follows:

To Buyer at:	**To Seller at:**
______________________	______________________
______________________	______________________
______________________	______________________
Telephone: ( ) ______________	Telephone: ( ) ______________
Facsimile: ( ) ______________	Facsimile: ( ) ______________
E-mail: ______________	E-mail: ______________

FIGURE 10.4 (CONTINUED)

TREC 25-5

22. **AGREEMENT OF PARTIES:** This contract contains the entire agreement of the parties and cannot be changed except by their written agreement. Addenda which are a part of this contract are (check all applicable boxes):

- ❑ Third Party Financing Condition Addendum
- ❑ Seller Financing Addendum
- ❑ Loan Assumption Addendum
- ❑ Buyer's Temporary Residential Lease
- ❑ Seller's Temporary Residential Lease
- ❑ Addendum for Sale of Other Property by Buyer
- ❑ Addendum for Seller's Disclosure of Information on Lead-based Paint and Lead-based Paint Hazards as Required by Federal Law
- ❑ Environmental Assessment, Threatened or Endangered Species and Wetlands Addendum
- ❑ Addendum for Coastal Area Property
- ❑ Addendum for Property Located Seaward of the Gulf Intracoastal Waterway
- ❑ Addendum for "Back-Up" Contract
- ❑ Other (list): ______________________ ______________________

23. **TERMINATION OPTION:** For nominal consideration, the receipt of which is hereby acknowledged by Seller, and Buyer's agreement to pay Seller $____________ (Option Fee) within 2 days after the effective date of this contract, Seller grants Buyer the unrestricted right to terminate this contract by giving notice of termination to Seller within _______ days after the effective date of this contract. If no dollar amount is stated as the Option Fee or if Buyer fails to pay the Option Fee within the time prescribed, this paragraph will not be a part of this contract and Buyer shall not have the unrestricted right to terminate this contract. If Buyer gives notice of termination within the time prescribed, the Option Fee will not be refunded; however, any earnest money will be refunded to Buyer. The Option Fee ❑will ❑will not be credited to the Sales Price at closing. **Time is of the essence for this paragraph and strict compliance with the time for performance is required.**

24. **CONSULT AN ATTORNEY:** Real estate licensees cannot give legal advice. READ THIS CONTRACT CAREFULLY. If you do not understand the effect of this contract, consult an attorney BEFORE signing.

Buyer's	Seller's
Attorney is: ______________________	Attorney is: ______________________
______________________	______________________
Telephone: ( ) ______________	Telephone: ( ) ______________
Facsimile: ( ) ______________	Facsimile: ( ) ______________
E-mail: ______________________	E-mail: ______________________

EXECUTED the _______day of _______________________, 20_____ (EFFECTIVE DATE).
(BROKER: FILL IN THE DATE OF FINAL ACCEPTANCE.)

______________________	______________________
Buyer	Seller
______________________	______________________
Buyer	Seller

The form of this contract has been approved by the Texas Real Estate Commission. TREC forms are intended for use only by trained real estate licensees. No representation is made as to the legal validity or adequacy of any provision in any specific transactions. It is not intended for complex transactions. Texas Real Estate Commission, P.O. Box 12188, Austin, TX 78711-2188, 1-800-250-8732 or (512) 459-6544 (http://www.trec.state.tx.us) TREC NO. 25-5. This form replaces TREC NO. 25-4.

FIGURE 10.4 (CONTINUED)

TREC 25-5

Contract Concerning ____ Page 9 of 9 02-13-06
(Address of Property)

RATIFICATION OF FEE

Listing Broker has agreed to pay Other Broker______________ of the total Sales Price when Listing Broker's fee is received. Escrow Agent is authorized and directed to pay Other Broker from Listing Broker's fee at closing.

Other Broker: Listing Broker:

By: ______________________________ By: ______________________________

BROKER INFORMATION AND AGREEMENT FOR PAYMENT OF BROKERS' FEES

Other Broker License No.	Listing or Principal Broker License No.
Associate	Associate
Address	Address
City State Zip	City State Zip
Telephone Facsimile	Telephone Facsimile
E-mail	E-mail
represents ❑ Buyer only as Buyer's agent ❑ Seller as Listing Broker's subagent	represents ❑ Seller only ❑ Buyer only ❑ Seller and Buyer as an intermediary

Upon closing of the sale by Seller to Buyer of the Property described in the contract to which this fee agreement is attached: (a) ❑Seller ❑ Buyer will pay Listing/Principal Broker ❑a cash fee of $ ____________________ or ❑ _____% of the total Sales Price; and (b) ❑Seller ❑ Buyer will pay Other Broker ❑a cash fee of $__________or ❑ _______% of the total Sales Price. Seller/Buyer authorizes and directs Escrow Agent to pay the brokers from the proceeds at closing.

Brokers' fees are negotiable. Brokers' fees or the sharing of fees between brokers are not fixed, controlled, recommended, suggested or maintained by the Texas Real Estate Commission.

Seller	Buyer
Seller	Buyer

Do not sign if there is a separate written agreement for payment of Brokers' fees.

OPTION FEE RECEIPT

Receipt of $________________ (Option Fee) in the form of ______________________ is acknowledged.

Seller or Listing Broker Date

CONTRACT AND EARNEST MONEY RECEIPT

Receipt of ❑Contract and ❑$_________________ Earnest Money in the form of _________________ is acknowledged.

Escrow Agent: ______________________________________ Date: ________________

By: ______________________________________ Email Address

Telephone (______) ________________

Address

Facsimile: (______) ________________

City State Zip

TREC NO. 25-5

FIGURE 10.5

TREC 30-6

EQUAL HOUSING OPPORTUNITY

PROMULGATED BY THE TEXAS REAL ESTATE COMMISSION (TREC) 12-04-06

NOTICE: Not For Use Where Seller Owns Fee Simple Title To Land Beneath Unit

RESIDENTIAL CONDOMINIUM CONTRACT (RESALE)

1. PARTIES: ______________________________ (Seller) agrees to sell and convey to ______________________________(Buyer) and Buyer agrees to buy from Seller the Property described below.

2. PROPERTY AND CONDOMINIUM DOCUMENTS:

A. The Condominium Unit, improvements and accessories described below are collectively referred to as the "Property".

(1) CONDOMINIUM UNIT: Unit ___________, in Building ______________, of ______________________________, a condominium project, located at ______________________________(address/zip code), City of ______________________,County of ______________________, Texas, described in the Condominium Declaration and Plat and any amendments thereto of record in said County; together with such Unit's undivided interest in the Common Elements designated by the Declaration, including those areas reserved as Limited Common Elements appurtenant to the Unit and such other rights to use the Common Elements which have been specifically assigned to the Unit in any other manner. Parking areas assigned to the Unit are:______________________________.

(2) IMPROVEMENTS: All fixtures and improvements attached to the above described real property including without limitation, the following **permanently installed and built-in items**, if any: all equipment and appliances, valances, screens, shutters, awnings, wall-to-wall carpeting, mirrors, ceiling fans, attic fans, mail boxes, television antennas and satellite dish system and equipment, heating and air conditioning units, security and fire detection equipment, wiring, plumbing and lighting fixtures, chandeliers, shrubbery, landscaping, outdoor cooking equipment, and all other property owned by Seller and attached to the above described Condominium Unit.

(3) ACCESSORIES: The following described related accessories, if any: window air conditioning units, stove, fireplace screens, curtains and rods, blinds, window shades, draperies and rods, controls for satellite dish system, controls for garage door openers, entry gate controls, door keys, mailbox keys, and artificial fireplace logs.

(4) EXCLUSIONS: The following improvements and accessories will be retained by Seller and removed prior to delivery of possession: ______________________________ ______________________________.

B. The Declaration, Bylaws and any Rules of the Association are called "Documents". (Check one box only):

❑ (1) Buyer has received a copy of the Documents. Buyer is advised to read the Documents before signing the contract.

❑ (2) Buyer has not received a copy of the Documents. Seller shall deliver the Documents to Buyer within _________ days after the effective date of the contract. Buyer may cancel the contract before the sixth day after Buyer receives the Documents by hand-delivering or mailing written notice of cancellation to Seller by certified United States mail, return receipt requested.

C. The Resale Certificate from the condominium owners association (the Association) is called the "Certificate". The Certificate must be in a form promulgated by TREC or required by the parties. The Certificate must have been prepared no more than 3 months before the date it is delivered to Buyer and must contain at a minimum the information required by Section 82.157, Texas Property Code.

(Check one box only):

❑ (1) Buyer has received the Certificate.

❑ (2) Buyer has not received the Certificate. Seller shall deliver the Certificate to Buyer within ________days after the effective date of the contract. Buyer may cancel the contract before the sixth day after the date Buyer receives the Certificate by hand-delivering or mailing written notice of cancellation to Seller by certified United States mail, return receipt requested.

❑ (3) Buyer has received Seller's affidavit that Seller requested information from the Association concerning its financial condition as required by the Texas Property Code, and that the Association did not provide a Certificate or information required in the Certificate. Buyer and Seller agree to waive the requirement to furnish the Certificate.

3. SALES PRICE:

A. Cash portion of Sales Price payable by Buyer at closing .... $__________________

B Sum of all financing described below (excluding any loan funding fee or mortgage insurance premium).. $__________________

C. Sales Price (Sum of A and B).. $__________________

FIGURE 10.5 (CONTINUED)

TREC 30-6

Contract Concerning____ Page 2 of 8 12-04-06
(Address of Property)

4. FINANCING: The portion of Sales Price not payable in cash will be paid as follows: (Check applicable boxes below)

❑ A. THIRD PARTY FINANCING: One or more third party mortgage loans in the total amount of $_______________ (excluding any loan funding fee or mortgage insurance premium).

(1) Property Approval: If the Property does not satisfy the lenders' underwriting requirements for the loan(s), this contract will terminate and the earnest money will be refunded to Buyer.

(2) Financing Approval: (Check one box only)

❑ (a) This contract is subject to Buyer being approved for the financing described in the attached Third Party Financing Condition Addendum.

❑ (b) This contract is not subject to Buyer being approved for financing and does not involve FHA or VA financing.

❑ B. ASSUMPTION: The assumption of the unpaid principal balance of one or more promissory notes described in the attached TREC Loan Assumption Addendum.

❑ C. SELLER FINANCING: A promissory note from Buyer to Seller of $__________________, secured by vendor's and deed of trust liens, and containing the terms and conditions described in the attached TREC Seller Financing Addendum. If an owner policy of title insurance is furnished, Buyer shall furnish Seller with a mortgagee policy of title insurance.

5. EARNEST MONEY: Upon execution of this contract by both parties, Buyer shall deposit $____________ as earnest money with ____________________________________, as escrow agent, at ____ (address). Buyer shall deposit additional earnest money of $__________________ with escrow agent within _______ days after the effective date of this contract. If Buyer fails to deposit the earnest money as required by this contract, Buyer will be in default.

6. TITLE POLICY:

A. TITLE POLICY: Seller shall furnish to Buyer at ❑Seller's ❑Buyer's expense an owner policy of title insurance (Title Policy) issued by ____ (Title Company) in the amount of the Sales Price, dated at or after closing, insuring Buyer against loss under the provisions of the Title Policy, subject to the promulgated exclusions (including existing building and zoning ordinances) and the following exceptions:

(1) Restrictive covenants common to the platted subdivision in which the Property is located.
(2) The standard printed exception for standby fees, taxes and assessments.
(3) Liens created as part of the financing described in Paragraph 4.
(4) Terms and provisions of the Documents including the assessments and platted easements.
(5) Reservations or exceptions otherwise permitted by this contract or as may be approved by Buyer in writing.
(6) The standard printed exception as to marital rights.
(7) The standard printed exception as to waters, tidelands, beaches, streams, and related matters.
(8) The standard printed exception as to discrepancies, conflicts, shortages in area or boundary lines, encroachments or protrusions, or overlapping improvements.

B. COMMITMENT: Within 20 days after the Title Company receives a copy of this contract, Seller shall furnish to Buyer a commitment for title insurance (Commitment) and, at Buyer's expense, legible copies of restrictive covenants and documents evidencing exceptions in the Commitment (Exception Documents) other than the standard printed exceptions. Seller authorizes the Title Company to deliver the Commitment and Exception Documents to Buyer at Buyer's address shown in Paragraph 21. If the Commitment and Exception Documents are not delivered to Buyer within the specified time, the time for delivery will be automatically extended up to 15 days or the Closing Date, whichever is earlier.

C. OBJECTIONS: Buyer may object in writing to defects, exceptions, or encumbrances to title: disclosed in the Commitment other than items 6A(1) through (8) above; or which prohibit the following use or activity: ____.
Buyer must object not later than (i) the Closing Date or (ii) _____ days after Buyer receives the Commitment and Exception Documents, whichever is earlier. Buyer's failure to object within the time allowed will constitute a waiver of Buyer's right to object; except that the requirements in Schedule C of the Commitment are not waived. Provided Seller is not obligated to incur any expense, Seller shall cure the timely objections of Buyer or any third party lender within 15 days after Seller receives the objections and the Closing Date will be extended as necessary. If objections are not cured within such 15 day period, this contract will terminate and the earnest money will be refunded to Buyer unless Buyer waives the objections.

D. TITLE NOTICES:

(1) ABSTRACT OR TITLE POLICY: Broker advises Buyer to have an abstract of title covering the Property examined by an attorney of Buyer's selection, or Buyer should be furnished with or obtain a Title Policy. If a Title Policy is furnished, the Commitment should be promptly reviewed by an attorney of Buyer's choice due to the time limitations on Buyer's right to object.

Initialed for identification by Buyer______ ______ and Seller _______ ______ TREC NO. 30-6

FIGURE 10.5 (CONTINUED)

TREC 30-6

(2) STATUTORY TAX DISTRICTS: If the Property is situated in a utility or other statutorily created district providing water, sewer, drainage, or flood control facilities and services, Chapter 49, Texas Water Code, requires Seller to deliver and Buyer to sign the statutory notice relating to the tax rate, bonded indebtedness, or standby fee of the district prior to final execution of this contract.

(3) TIDE WATERS: If the Property abuts the tidally influenced waters of the state, §33.135, Texas Natural Resources Code, requires a notice regarding coastal area property to be included in the contract. An addendum containing the notice promulgated by TREC or required by the parties must be used.

(4) ANNEXATION: If the Property is located outside the limits of a municipality, Seller notifies Buyer under §5.011, Texas Property Code, that the Property may now or later be included in the extraterritorial jurisdiction of a municipality and may now or later be subject to annexation by the municipality. Each municipality maintains a map that depicts its boundaries and extraterritorial jurisdiction. To determine if the Property is located within a municipality's extraterritorial jurisdiction or is likely to be located within a municipality's extraterritorial jurisdiction, contact all municipalities located in the general proximity of the Property for further information.

(5) PROPERTY LOCATED IN A CERTIFICATED SERVICE AREA OF A UTILITY SERVICE PROVIDER: Notice required by §13.257, Water Code: The real property, described in Paragraph 2, that you are about to purchase may be located in a certificated water or sewer service area, which is authorized by law to provide water or sewer service to the properties in the certificated area. If your property is located in a certificated area there may be special costs or charges that you will be required to pay before you can receive water or sewer service. There may be a period required to construct lines or other facilities necessary to provide water or sewer service to your property. You are advised to determine if the property is in a certificated area and contact the utility service provider to determine the cost that you will be required to pay and the period, if any, that is required to provide water or sewer service to your property. The undersigned Buyer hereby acknowledges receipt of the foregoing notice at or before the execution of a binding contract for the purchase of the real property described in Paragraph 2 or at closing of purchase of the real property.

7. PROPERTY CONDITION:

A. ACCESS,INSPECTIONS AND UTILITIES: Seller shall permit Buyer and Buyer's agents access to the Property at reasonable times. Buyer may have the Property inspected by inspectors selected by Buyer and licensed by TREC or otherwise permitted by law to make inspections. Seller at Seller's expense shall turn on existing utilities for inspections.

B. SELLER'S DISCLOSURE NOTICE PURSUANT TO §5.008, TEXAS PROPERTY CODE (Notice): (Check one box only)

☐ (1) Buyer has received the Notice.

☐ (2) Buyer has not received the Notice. Within _______ days after the effective date of this contract, Seller shall deliver the Notice to Buyer. If Buyer does not receive the Notice, Buyer may terminate this contract at any time prior to the closing and the earnest money will be refunded to Buyer. If Seller delivers the Notice, Buyer may terminate this contract for any reason within 7 days after Buyer receives the Notice or prior to the closing, whichever first occurs, and the earnest money will be refunded to Buyer.

☐ (3) The Texas Property Code does not require this Seller to furnish the Notice.

C. SELLER'S DISCLOSURE OF LEAD-BASED PAINT AND LEAD-BASED PAINT HAZARDS is required by Federal law for a residential dwelling constructed prior to 1978.

D. ACCEPTANCE OF PROPERTY CONDITION: Buyer accepts the Property in its present condition; provided Seller, at Seller's expense, shall complete the following specific repairs and treatments:____
____.

E. LENDER REQUIRED REPAIRS AND TREATMENTS: Unless otherwise agreed in writing, neither party is obligated to pay for lender required repairs, which includes treatment for wood destroying insects. If the parties do not agree to pay for the lender required repairs or treatments, this contract will terminate and the earnest money will be refunded to Buyer. If the cost of lender required repairs and treatments exceeds 5% of the Sales Price, Buyer may terminate this contract and the earnest money will be refunded to Buyer.

F. COMPLETION OF REPAIRS AND TREATMENTS: Unless otherwise agreed in writing, Seller shall complete all agreed repairs and treatments prior to the Closing Date. All required permits must be obtained, and repairs and treatments must be performed by persons who are licensed or otherwise authorized by law to provide such repairs or treatments. At Buyer's election, any transferable warranties received by Seller with respect to the repairs and treatments will be transferred to Buyer at Buyer's expense. If Seller fails to complete any agreed repairs and treatments prior to the Closing Date, Buyer may do so and receive reimbursement from Seller at closing. The Closing Date will be extended up to 15 days, if necessary, to complete repairs and treatments.

FIGURE 10.5 (CONTINUED)

TREC 30-6

Contract Concerning____Page 4 of 8 12-04-06
(Address of Property)

G. ENVIRONMENTAL MATTERS: Buyer is advised that the presence of wetlands, toxic substances, including asbestos and wastes or other environmental hazards or the presence of a threatened or endangered species or its habitat may affect Buyer's intended use of the Property. If Buyer is concerned about these matters, an addendum promulgated by TREC or required by the parties should be used.

H. RESIDENTIAL SERVICE CONTRACTS: Buyer may purchase a residential service contract from a residential service company licensed by TREC. If Buyer purchases a residential service contract, Seller shall reimburse Buyer at closing for the cost of the residential service contract in an amount not exceeding $_______________. Buyer should review any residential service contract for the scope of coverage, exclusions and limitations. **The purchase of a residential service contract is optional. Similar coverage may be purchased from various companies authorized to do business in Texas.**

8.BROKERS' FEES: All obligations of the parties for payment of brokers' fees are contained in separate written agreements.

9. CLOSING:

A. The closing of the sale will be on or before ____________________, 20____, or within 7 days after objections to matters disclosed in the Commitment have been cured, whichever date is later (Closing Date). If either party fails to close the sale by the Closing Date, the non-defaulting party may exercise the remedies contained in Paragraph 15.

B. At closing:

(1) Seller shall execute and deliver a general warranty deed conveying title to the Property to Buyer and showing no additional exceptions to those permitted in Paragraph 6 and furnish tax statements or certificates showing no delinquent taxes on the Property.

(2) Buyer shall pay the Sales Price in good funds acceptable to the escrow agent.

(3) Seller and Buyer shall execute and deliver any notices, statements, certificates, affidavits, releases, loan documents and other documents required of them by this contract, the Commitment or law necessary for the closing of the sale and the issuance of the Title Policy.

C. Unless expressly prohibited by written agreement, Seller may continue to show the Property and receive, negotiate and accept back up offers.

D. All covenants, representations and warranties in this contract survive closing.

10. POSSESSION: Seller shall deliver to Buyer possession of the Property in its present or required condition, ordinary wear and tear excepted: ❑ upon closing and funding ❑ according to a temporary residential lease form promulgated by TREC or other written lease required by the parties. Any possession by Buyer prior to closing or by Seller after closing which is not authorized by a written lease will establish a tenancy at sufferance relationship between the parties. **Consult your insurance agent prior to change of ownership and possession because insurance coverage may be limited or terminated. The absence of a written lease or appropriate insurance coverage may expose the parties to economic loss.**

11. SPECIAL PROVISIONS: (Insert only factual statements and business details applicable to the sale. TREC rules prohibit licensees from adding factual statements or business details for which a contract addendum, lease or other form has been promulgated by TREC for mandatory use.)

12. SETTLEMENT AND OTHER EXPENSES:

A. The following expenses must be paid at or prior to closing:

(1)Expenses payable by Seller (Seller's Expenses):

(a) Releases of existing liens, including prepayment penalties and recording fees; lender, FHA, or VA completion requirements; tax statements or certificates; preparation of deed; one-half of escrow fee; and other expenses payable by Seller under this contract.

(b) Seller shall also pay an amount not to exceed $ _____________ to be applied in the following order: Buyer's Expenses which Buyer is prohibited from paying by FHA, VA, Texas Veterans Housing Assistance Program or other governmental loan programs, and then to other Buyer's Expenses as allowed by the lender.

Initialed for identification by Buyer______ ______ and Seller _______ ______ TREC NO. 30-6

FIGURE 10.5 (CONTINUED)

TREC 30-6

(2) Expenses payable by Buyer (Buyer's Expenses):
(a) Loan origination, discount, buy-down, and commitment fees (Loan Fees).
(b) Appraisal fees; loan application fees; credit reports; preparation of loan documents; interest on the notes from date of disbursement to one month prior to dates of first monthly payments; recording fees; copies of easements and restrictions; mortgagee title policy with endorsements required by lender; loan-related inspection fees; photos; amortization schedules; one-half of escrow fee; all prepaid items, including required premiums for flood and hazard insurance, reserve deposits for insurance, ad valorem taxes and special governmental assessments; final compliance inspection; courier fee; repair inspection; underwriting fee; wire transfer fee; expenses incident to any loan; and other expenses payable by Buyer under this contract.
(3) Any Association fees resulting from the transfer of the property will be paid by ❑ Seller ❑ Buyer.

B. Buyer shall pay Private Mortgage Insurance Premium (PMI), VA Loan Funding Fee, or FHA Mortgage Insurance Premium (MIP) as required by the lender.

C. If any expense exceeds an amount expressly stated in this contract for such expense to be paid by a party, that party may terminate this contract unless the other party agrees to pay such excess. Buyer may not pay charges and fees expressly prohibited by FHA, VA, Texas Veteran's Housing Assistance Program or other governmental loan program regulations.

13. **PRORATIONS:** Taxes for the current year, interest, maintenance fees, regular condominium assessments, dues and rents will be prorated through the Closing Date. The tax proration may be calculated taking into consideration any change in exemptions that will affect the current year's taxes. If taxes for the current year vary from the amount prorated at closing, the parties shall adjust the prorations when tax statements for the current year are available. If taxes are not paid at or prior to closing, Buyer shall pay taxes for the current year. Cash reserves from regular condominium assessments for deferred maintenance or capital improvements established by the Association will not be credited to Seller. Any special condominium assessment due and unpaid at closing will be the obligation of Seller.

14. **CASUALTY LOSS:** If any part of the Unit which Seller is solely obligated to maintain and repair under the terms of the Declaration is damaged or destroyed by fire or other casualty, Seller shall restore the same to its previous condition as soon as reasonably possible, but in any event by the Closing Date. If Seller fails to do so due to factors beyond Seller's control, Buyer may (a) terminate this contract and the earnest money will be refunded to Buyer, (b) extend the time for performance up to 15 days and the Closing Date will be extended as necessary or (c) accept the Property in its damaged condition with an assignment of insurance proceeds and receive credit from Seller at closing in the amount of the deductible under the insurance policy. If any part of the Common Elements or Limited Common Elements appurtenant to the Unit is damaged or destroyed by fire or other casualty loss, Buyer will have 7 days from receipt of notice of such casualty loss within which to notify Seller in writing that the contract will be terminated unless Buyer receives written confirmation from the Association that the damaged condition will be restored to its previous condition within a reasonable time at no cost to Buyer. Unless Buyer gives such notice within such time, Buyer will be deemed to have accepted the Property without confirmation of such restoration. Seller will have 7 days from the date of receipt of Buyer's notice within which to cause to be delivered to Buyer such confirmation. If written confirmation is not delivered to Buyer as required above, Buyer may terminate this contract and the earnest money will be refunded to Buyer. Seller's obligations under this paragraph are independent of any other obligations of Seller under this contract.

15. **DEFAULT:** If Buyer fails to comply with this contract, Buyer will be in default, and Seller may (a) enforce specific performance, seek such other relief as may be provided by law, or both, or (b) terminate this contract and receive the earnest money as liquidated damages, thereby releasing both parties from this contract. If, due to factors beyond Seller's control, Seller fails within the time allowed to make any non-casualty repairs or deliver the Commitment, if required of Seller, Buyer may (a) extend the time for performance up to 15 days and the Closing Date will be extended as necessary or (b) terminate this contract as the sole remedy and receive the earnest money. If Seller fails to comply with this contract for any other reason, Seller will be in default and Buyer may (a) enforce specific performance, seek such other relief as may be provided by law, or both, or (b) terminate this contract and receive the earnest money, thereby releasing both parties from this contract.

16. **MEDIATION:** It is the policy of the State of Texas to encourage resolution of disputes through alternative dispute resolution procedures such as mediation. Any dispute between Seller and Buyer related to this contract which is not resolved through informal discussion ❑will ❑will not be submitted to a mutually acceptable mediation service or provider. The parties to the mediation shall bear the mediation costs equally. This paragraph does not preclude a party from seeking equitable relief from a court of competent jurisdiction.

FIGURE 10.5 (CONTINUED)

TREC 30-6

Contract Concerning____ Page 6 of 8 12-04-06
(Address of Property)

17. ATTORNEY'S FEES: The prevailing party in any legal proceeding related to this contract is entitled to recover reasonable attorney's fees and all costs of such proceeding incurred by the prevailing party.

18. ESCROW:

A. ESCROW: The escrow agent is not (i) a party to this contract and does not have liability for the performance or nonperformance of any party to this contract, (ii) liable for interest on the earnest money and (iii) liable for the loss of any earnest money caused by the failure of any financial institution in which the earnest money has been deposited unless the financial institution is acting as escrow agent.

B. EXPENSES: At closing, the earnest money must be applied first to any cash down payment, then to Buyer's Expenses and any excess refunded to Buyer. If no closing occurs, escrow agent may require payment of unpaid expenses incurred on behalf of the parties and a written release of liability of escrow agent from all parties.

C. DEMAND: Upon termination of this contract, either party or the escrow agent may send a release of earnest money to each party and the parties shall execute counterparts of the release and deliver same to the escrow agent. If either party fails to execute the release, either party may make a written demand to the escrow agent for the earnest money. If only one party makes written demand for the earnest money, escrow agent shall promptly provide a copy of the demand to the other party. If escrow agent does not receive written objection to the demand from the other party within 15 days, escrow agent may disburse the earnest money to the party making demand reduced by the amount of unpaid expenses incurred on behalf of the party receiving the earnest money and escrow agent may pay the same to the creditors. If escrow agent complies with the provisions of this paragraph, each party hereby releases escrow agent from all adverse claims related to the disbursal of the earnest money.

D. DAMAGES: Any party who wrongfully fails or refuses to sign a release acceptable to the escrow agent within 7 days of receipt of the request will be liable to the other party for liquidated damages of three times the amount of the earnest money.

E. NOTICES: Escrow agent's notices will be effective when sent in compliance with Paragraph 21. Notice of objection to the demand will be deemed effective upon receipt by escrow agent.

19. REPRESENTATIONS: Seller represents that as of the Closing Date (a) there will be no liens, assessments, or security interests against the Property which will not be satisfied out of the sales proceeds unless securing payment of any loans assumed by Buyer, (b) assumed loans will not be in default, and (c) Seller has no knowledge of any misrepresentation or errors in the Certificate or any material changes in the information contained therein. If any representation of Seller in this contract or the Certificate is untrue on the Closing Date, Seller will be in default.

20. FEDERAL TAX REQUIREMENTS: If Seller is a "foreign person," as defined by applicable law, or if Seller fails to deliver an affidavit to Buyer that Seller is not a "foreign person," then Buyer shall withhold from the sales proceeds an amount sufficient to comply with applicable tax law and deliver the same to the Internal Revenue Service together with appropriate tax forms. Internal Revenue Service regulations require filing written reports if currency in excess of specified amounts is received in the transaction.

21. NOTICES: All notices from one party to the other must be in writing and are effective when mailed to, hand-delivered at, or transmitted by facsimile or electronic transmission as follows:

To Buyer at:	**To Seller at:**
____________________	____________________
____________________	____________________
____________________	____________________
Telephone: ( ) ________	Telephone: ( ) ________
Facsimile: ( ) ________	Facsimile: ( ) ________
E-mail: ____________	E-mail: ____________

Initialed for identification by Buyer______ ______ and Seller ______ ______ TREC NO. 30-6

FIGURE 10.5 (CONTINUED)

TREC 30-6

22. **AGREEMENT OF PARTIES:** This contract contains the entire agreement of the parties and cannot be changed except by their written agreement. Addenda which are a part of this contract are (check all applicable boxes):

- ❑ Third Party Financing Condition Addendum
- ❑ Loan Assumption Addendum
- ❑ Buyer's Temporary Residential Lease
- ❑ Seller's Temporary Residential Lease
- ❑ Addendum for Sale of Other Property by Buyer
- ❑ Addendum for "Back-Up" Contract
- ❑ Seller Financing Addendum
- ❑ Addendum for Property Located Seaward of the Gulf Intracoastal Waterway
- ❑ Addendum for Seller's Disclosure of Information on Lead-based Paint and Lead-based Paint Hazards as Required by Federal Law
- ❑ Environmental Assessment, Threatened or Endangered Species and Wetlands Addendum
- ❑ Addendum for Coastal Area Property
- ❑ Addendum for Release of Liability on Assumption of FHA, VA, or Conventional Loan Restoration of Seller's Entitlement for VA Guaranteed Loan
- ❑ Other (list): ______________________
  ____

23. **TERMINATION OPTION:** For nominal consideration, the receipt of which is hereby acknowledged by Seller, and Buyer's agreement to pay Seller $______________ (Option Fee) within 2 days after the effective date of this contract, Seller grants Buyer the unrestricted right to terminate this contract by giving notice of termination to Seller within _______ days after the effective date of this contract. If no dollar amount is stated as the Option Fee or if Buyer fails to pay the Option Fee within the time prescribed, this paragraph will not be a part of this contract and Buyer shall not have the unrestricted right to terminate this contract. If Buyer gives notice of termination within the time prescribed, the Option Fee will not be refunded; however, any earnest money will be refunded to Buyer. The Option Fee ❑will ❑will not be credited to the Sales Price at closing. **Time is of the essence for this paragraph and strict compliance with the time for performance is required.**

24. **CONSULT AN ATTORNEY:** Real estate licensees cannot give legal advice. READ THIS CONTRACT CAREFULLY. If you do not understand the effect of this contract, consult an attorney BEFORE signing.

Buyer's Attorney is: ______________________	Seller's Attorney is: ______________________
______________________	______________________
Telephone: ( ) ______________	Telephone: ( ) ______________
Facsimile: ( ) ______________	Facsimile: ( ) ______________
E-mail: ______________________	E-mail: ______________________

EXECUTED the _____day of ________________________, 20____ (EFFECTIVE DATE).
(BROKER: FILL IN THE DATE OF FINAL ACCEPTANCE.)

______________________	______________________
Buyer	Seller
______________________	______________________
Buyer	Seller

The form of this contract has been approved by the Texas Real Estate Commission. TREC forms are intended for use only by trained real estate licensees. No representation is made as to the legal validity or adequacy of any provision in any specific transactions. It is not intended for complex transactions. Texas Real Estate Commission, P.O. Box 12188, Austin, TX 78711-2188, 1-800-250-8732 or (512) 459-6544 (http://www.trec.state.tx.us) TREC NO. 30-6. This form replaces TREC NO. 30-5.

FIGURE 10.5 (CONTINUED)

TREC 30-6

Contract Concerning______________________________Page 8 of 8 12-04-06
(Address of Property)

BROKER INFORMATION AND RATIFICATION OF FEE

Listing Broker has agreed to pay Other Broker ______________________ of the total sales price when Listing Broker's fee is received. Escrow Agent is authorized and directed to pay Other Broker from Listing Broker's fee at closing.

Other Broker License No.	Listing Broker License No.
represents ❑ Buyer only as Buyer's agent ❑ Seller as Listing Broker's subagent	represents ❑ Seller and Buyer as an intermediary ❑ Seller only as Seller's agent
Associate Telephone	Listing Associate Telephone
Broker's Address	Listing Associate's Office Address Facsimile
City State Zip	City State Zip
Facsimile	Email Address
Email Address	Selling Associate Telephone
	Selling Associate's Office Address Facsimile
	City State Zip
	Email Address

OPTION FEE RECEIPT

Receipt of $______________ (Option Fee) in the form of ______________ is acknowledged.

______________________ ______________________
Seller or Listing Broker Date

CONTRACT AND EARNEST MONEY RECEIPT

Receipt of ❑Contract and ❑$______________ Earnest Money in the form of ______________ is acknowledged.
Escrow Agent: ______________________ Date: ______________

By: ______________________ ______________________
Email Address

______________________ Telephone (____) ______________
Address

______________________ Facsimile: (____) ______________
City State Zip

TREC NO. 30-6

FIGURE 10.6

TREC 9-6

PROMULGATED BY THE TEXAS REAL ESTATE COMMISSION (TREC) 02-13-06

EQUAL HOUSING OPPORTUNITY

UNIMPROVED PROPERTY CONTRACT

NOTICE: Not For Use For Condominium Transactions

1. **PARTIES:** ______________________________ (Seller) agrees to sell and convey to ______________________________ (Buyer) and Buyer agrees to buy from Seller the Property described below.

2. **PROPERTY:** Lot ______, Block ______, ______________________________ Addition, City of ______________________________, County of ______________________________, Texas, known as ______________________________ (address/zip code), or as described on attached exhibit together with all rights, privileges and appurtenances pertaining thereto, including but not limited to: water rights, claims, permits, strips and gores, easements, and cooperative or association memberships (the Property).

3. **SALES PRICE:**
   A. Cash portion of Sales Price payable by Buyer at closing................. $__________________
   B. Sum of all financing described below (excluding any loan funding fee or mortgage insurance premium) .... $__________________
   C. Sales Price (Sum of A and B) .... $__________________

4. **FINANCING:** The portion of Sales Price not payable in cash will be paid as follows: (Check applicable boxes below)
   ❑ A. THIRD PARTY FINANCING: One or more third party mortgage loans in the total amount of $______________ (excluding any loan funding fee or mortgage insurance premium).
   (1) Property Approval: If the Property does not satisfy the lenders' underwriting requirements for the loan(s), this contract will terminate and the earnest money will be refunded to Buyer.
   (2) Financing Approval: (Check one box only)
   ❑(a) This contract is subject to Buyer being approved for the financing described in the attached Third Party Financing Condition Addendum.
   ❑(b) This contract is not subject to Buyer being approved for financing and does not involve FHA or VA financing.
   ❑ B. ASSUMPTION: The assumption of the unpaid principal balance of one or more promissory notes described in the attached TREC Loan Assumption Addendum.
   ❑ C. SELLER FINANCING: A promissory note from Buyer to Seller of $______________, secured by vendor's and deed of trust liens, and containing the terms and conditions described in the attached TREC Seller Financing Addendum. If an owner policy of title insurance is furnished, Buyer shall furnish Seller with a mortgagee policy of title insurance.

5. **EARNEST MONEY:** Upon execution of this contract by both parties, Buyer shall deposit $__________ as earnest money with ______________________________, as escrow agent, at ______________________________ (address). Buyer shall deposit additional earnest money of $______________ with escrow agent within _____ days after the effective date of this contract. If Buyer fails to deposit the earnest money as required by this contract, Buyer will be in default.

6. **TITLE POLICY AND SURVEY:**
   A. TITLE POLICY: Seller shall furnish to Buyer at ❑Seller's ❑Buyer's expense an owner policy of title insurance (Title Policy) issued by ______________________________ (Title Company) in the amount of the Sales Price, dated at or after closing, insuring Buyer against loss under the provisions of the Title Policy, subject to the promulgated exclusions (including existing building and zoning ordinances) and the following exceptions:
   (1) Restrictive covenants common to the platted subdivision in which the Property is located.
   (2) The standard printed exception for standby fees, taxes and assessments.
   (3) Liens created as part of the financing described in Paragraph 4.
   (4) Utility easements created by the dedication deed or plat of the subdivision in which the Property is located.
   (5) Reservations or exceptions otherwise permitted by this contract or as may be approved by Buyer in writing.
   (6) The standard printed exception as to marital rights.
   (7) The standard printed exception as to waters, tidelands, beaches, streams, and related matters.
   (8) The standard printed exception as to discrepancies, conflicts, shortages in area or boundary lines, encroachments or protrusions, or overlapping improvements. Buyer, at Buyer's expense, may have the exception amended to read, "shortages in area".
   B. COMMITMENT: Within 20 days after the Title Company receives a copy of this contract, Seller shall furnish to Buyer a commitment for title insurance (Commitment) and, at Buyer's

Initialed for identification by Buyer______ ______ and Seller _______ ______ TREC NO. 9-6

FIGURE 10.6 (CONTINUED)

TREC 9-6

expense, legible copies of restrictive covenants and documents evidencing exceptions in the Commitment (Exception Documents) other than the standard printed exceptions. Seller authorizes the Title Company to deliver the Commitment and Exception Documents to Buyer at Buyer's address shown in Paragraph 21. If the Commitment and Exception Documents are not delivered to Buyer within the specified time, the time for delivery will be automatically extended up to 15 days or the Closing Date, whichever is earlier.

C. SURVEY: The survey must be made by a registered professional land surveyor acceptable to the Title Company and any lender. (Check one box only)

❑ (1) Within ______ days after the effective date of this contract, Seller shall furnish to Buyer and Title Company Seller's existing survey of the Property and a Residential Real Property Affidavit promulgated by the Texas Department of Insurance (Affidavit). If the existing survey or Affidavit is not acceptable to Title Company or Buyer's lender, Buyer shall obtain a new survey at ❑ Seller's ❑ Buyer's expense no later than 3 days prior to Closing Date. If Seller fails to furnish the existing survey or Affidavit within the time prescribed, Buyer shall obtain a new survey at Seller's expense no later than 3 days prior to Closing Date.

❑ (2) Within _______ days after the effective date of this contract, Buyer shall obtain a new survey at Buyer's expense. Buyer is deemed to receive the survey on the date of actual receipt or the date specified in this paragraph, whichever is earlier.

❑ (3) Within _______ days after the effective date of this contract, Seller, at Seller's expense shall furnish a new survey to Buyer.

D. OBJECTIONS: Buyer may object in writing to (i) defects, exceptions, or encumbrances to title: disclosed on the survey other than items 6A(1) through (7) above; or disclosed in the Commitment other than items 6A(1) through (8) above; (ii) any portion of the Property lying in a special flood hazard area (Zone V or A) as shown on the current Federal Emergency Management Agency map; or (iii) any exceptions which prohibit the following use or activity:

____

____.

Buyer must object not later than (i) the Closing Date or (ii) _____ days after Buyer receives the Commitment, Exception Documents, and the survey, whichever is earlier. Buyer's failure to object within the time allowed will constitute a waiver of Buyer's right to object; except that the requirements in Schedule C of the Commitment are not waived. Provided Seller is not obligated to incur any expense, Seller shall cure the timely objections of Buyer or any third party lender within 15 days after Seller receives the objections and the Closing Date will be extended as necessary. If objections are not cured within such 15 day period, this contract will terminate and the earnest money will be refunded to Buyer unless Buyer waives the objections.

E. TITLE NOTICES:

(1) ABSTRACT OR TITLE POLICY: Broker advises Buyer to have an abstract of title covering the Property examined by an attorney of Buyer's selection, or Buyer should be furnished with or obtain a Title Policy. If a Title Policy is furnished, the Commitment should be promptly reviewed by an attorney of Buyer's choice due to the time limitations on Buyer's right to object.

(2) MANDATORY OWNERS' ASSOCIATION MEMBERSHIP: The Property ❑ is ❑ is not subject to mandatory membership in an owners' association. If the Property is subject to mandatory membership in an owners' association, Seller notifies Buyer under §5.012, Texas Property Code, that, as a purchaser of property in the residential community in which the Property is located, you are obligated to be a member of the owners' association. Restrictive covenants governing the use and occupancy of the Property and a dedicatory instrument governing the establishment, maintenance, and operation of this residential community have been or will be recorded in the Real Property Records of the county in which the Property is located. Copies of the restrictive covenants and dedicatory instrument may be obtained from the county clerk. You are obligated to pay assessments to the owners' association. The amount of the assessments is subject to change. Your failure to pay the assessments could result in a lien on and the foreclosure of the Property. If Buyer is concerned about these matters, the TREC promulgated Addendum for Property Subject to Mandatory Membership in an Owner's Association should be used.

(3) STATUTORY TAX DISTRICTS: If the Property is situated in a utility or other statutorily created district providing water, sewer, drainage, or flood control facilities and services, Chapter 49, Texas Water Code, requires Seller to deliver and Buyer to sign the statutory notice relating to the tax rate, bonded indebtedness, or standby fee of the district prior to final execution of this contract.

(4) TIDE WATERS: If the Property abuts the tidally influenced waters of the state, §33.135, Texas Natural Resources Code, requires a notice regarding coastal area property to be included in the contract. An addendum containing the notice promulgated by TREC or required by the parties must be used.

(5) ANNEXATION: If the Property is located outside the limits of a municipality, Seller notifies Buyer under §5.011, Texas Property Code, that the Property may now or later be included in the extraterritorial jurisdiction of a municipality and may now or later be subject to

FIGURE 10.6 (CONTINUED)

TREC 9-6

annexation by the municipality. Each municipality maintains a map that depicts its boundaries and extraterritorial jurisdiction. To determine if the Property is located within a municipality's extraterritorial jurisdiction or is likely to be located within a municipality's extraterritorial jurisdiction, contact all municipalities located in the general proximity of the Property for further information.

(6) PROPERTY LOCATED IN A CERTIFICATED SERVICE AREA OF A UTILITY SERVICE PROVIDER: Notice required by §13.257, Water Code: The real property, described in Paragraph 2, that you are about to purchase may be located in a certificated water or sewer service area, which is authorized by law to provide water or sewer service to the properties in the certificated area. If your property is located in a certificated area there may be special costs or charges that you will be required to pay before you can receive water or sewer service. There may be a period required to construct lines or other facilities necessary to provide water or sewer service to your property. You are advised to determine if the property is in a certificated area and contact the utility service provider to determine the cost that you will be required to pay and the period, if any, that is required to provide water or sewer service to your property. The undersigned Buyer hereby acknowledges receipt of the foregoing notice at or before the execution of a binding contract for the purchase of the real property described in Paragraph 2 or at closing of purchase of the real property.

(7) PUBLIC IMPROVEMENT DISTRICTS: If the Property is in a public improvement district, §5.014, Property Code, requires Seller to notify Buyer as follows: As a purchaser of this parcel of real property you are obligated to pay an assessment to a municipality or county for an improvement project undertaken by a public improvement district under Chapter 372, Local Government Code. The assessment may be due annually or in periodic installments. More information concerning the amount of the assessment and the due dates of that assessment may be obtained from the municipality or county levying the assessment. The amount of the assessments is subject to change. Your failure to pay the assessments could result in a lien on and the foreclosure of your property.

(8) TEXAS AGRICULTURAL DEVELOPMENT DISTRICT: The Property ☐ is ☐ is not located in a Texas Agricultural Development District. For additional information, contact the Texas Department of Agriculture.

7. PROPERTY CONDITION:

A. ACCESS,INSPECTIONS AND UTILITIES: Seller shall permit Buyer and Buyer's agents access to the Property at reasonable times. Buyer may have the Property inspected by inspectors selected by Buyer and licensed by TREC or otherwise permitted by law to make inspections. Seller at Seller's expense shall turn on existing utilities for inspections.
NOTICE: Buyer should determine the availability of utilities to the Property suitable to satisfy Buyer's needs.

B. ACCEPTANCE OF PROPERTY CONDITION: Buyer accepts the Property in its present condition; provided Seller, at Seller's expense, shall complete the following:______________________
____.

C. COMPLETION OF REPAIRS: Unless otherwise agreed in writing, Seller shall complete all agreed repairs prior to the Closing Date. All required permits must be obtained, and repairs must be performed by persons who are licensed or otherwise permitted by law to provide such repairs. At Buyer's election, any transferable warranties received by Seller with respect to the repairs will be transferred to Buyer at Buyer's expense. If Seller fails to complete any agreed repairs prior to the Closing Date, Buyer may do so and receive reimbursement from Seller at closing. The Closing Date will be extended up to 15 days, if necessary, to complete repairs.

D. ENVIRONMENTAL MATTERS: Buyer is advised that the presence of wetlands, toxic substances, including asbestos and wastes or other environmental hazards, or the presence of a threatened or endangered species or its habitat may affect Buyer's intended use of the Property. If Buyer is concerned about these matters, an addendum promulgated by TREC or required by the parties should be used.

E. SELLER'S DISCLOSURES: Except as otherwise disclosed in this contract, Seller has no knowledge of the following:
(1) any flooding of the Property;
(2) any pending or threatened litigation, condemnation, or special assessment affecting the Property;
(3) any environmental hazards or conditions affecting the Property;
(4) any dumpsite, landfill, or underground tanks or containers now or previously located on the Property;
(5) any wetlands, as defined by federal or state law or regulation, affecting the Property; or
(6) any threatened or endangered species or their habitat affecting the Property.

8. BROKERS' FEES: All obligations of the parties for payment of brokers' fees are contained in separate written agreements.

9. CLOSING:

A. The closing of the sale will be on or before ____________________, 20_____, or within 7 days after objections made under Paragraph 6D have been cured or waived, whichever date is later

FIGURE 10.6 (CONTINUED)

TREC 9-6

Contract Concerning ____ Page 4 of 8 02-13-06
(Address of Property)

(Closing Date). If either party fails to close the sale by the Closing Date, the non-defaulting party may exercise the remedies contained in Paragraph 15.

B. At closing:
  (1)Seller shall execute and deliver a general warranty deed conveying title to the Property to Buyer and showing no additional exceptions to those permitted in Paragraph 6 and furnish tax statements or certificates showing no delinquent taxes on the Property.
  (2)Buyer shall pay the Sales Price in good funds acceptable to the escrow agent.
  (3)Seller and Buyer shall execute and deliver any notices, statements, certificates, affidavits, releases, loan documents and other documents required of them by this contract, the Commitment or law necessary for the closing of the sale and the issuance of the Title Policy.

C. Unless expressly prohibited by written agreement, Seller may continue to show the Property and receive, negotiate and accept back up offers.

D. All covenants, representations and warranties in this contract survive closing.

10. POSSESSION: Seller shall deliver to Buyer possession of the Property in its present or required condition upon closing and funding.

11. SPECIAL PROVISIONS: (Insert only factual statements and business details applicable to the sale. TREC rules prohibit licensees from adding factual statements or business details for which a contract addendum or other form has been promulgated by TREC for mandatory use.)

12. SETTLEMENT AND OTHER EXPENSES:

A. The following expenses must be paid at or prior to closing:
  (1)Expenses payable by Seller (Seller's Expenses):
    (a)Releases of existing liens, including prepayment penalties and recording fees; release of Seller's loan liability; tax statements or certificates; preparation of deed; one-half of escrow fee; and other expenses payable by Seller under this contract.
    (b)Seller shall also pay an amount not to exceed $ ______________ to be applied in the following order: Buyer's Expenses which Buyer is prohibited from paying by FHA, VA, Texas Veterans Housing Assistance Program or other governmental loan programs, and then to other Buyer's Expenses as allowed by the lender.
  (2) Expenses payable by Buyer (Buyer's Expenses):
    (a)Loan origination, discount, buy-down, and commitment fees (Loan Fees).
    (b)Appraisal fees; loan application fees; credit reports; preparation of loan documents; interest on the notes from date of disbursement to one month prior to dates of first monthly payments; recording fees; copies of easements and restrictions; mortgagee title policy with endorsements required by lender; loan-related inspection fees; photos; amortization schedules; one-half of escrow fee; all prepaid items, including required premiums for flood and hazard insurance, reserve deposits for insurance, ad valorem taxes and special governmental assessments; final compliance inspection; courier fee; repair inspection; underwriting fee; wire transfer fee; expenses incident to any loan; and other expenses payable by Buyer under this contract.

B. Buyer shall pay Private Mortgage Insurance Premium (PMI), VA Loan Funding Fee, or FHA Mortgage Insurance Premium (MIP) as required by the lender.

C. If any expense exceeds an amount expressly stated in this contract for such expense to be paid by a party, that party may terminate this contract unless the other party agrees to pay such excess. Buyer may not pay charges and fees expressly prohibited by FHA, VA, Texas Veterans Housing Assistance Program or other governmental loan program regulations.

Initialed for identification by Buyer______ ______ and Seller ______ ______ TREC NO. 9-6

FIGURE 10.6 (CONTINUED)

TREC 9-6

13. PRORATIONS AND ROLLBACK TAXES:

A. PRORATIONS: Taxes for the current year, interest, maintenance fees, assessments, dues and rents will be prorated through the Closing Date. The tax proration may be calculated taking into consideration any change in exemptions that will affect the current year's taxes. If taxes for the current year vary from the amount prorated at closing, the parties shall adjust the prorations when tax statements for the current year are available. If taxes are not paid at or prior to closing, Buyer shall pay taxes for the current year.

B. ROLLBACK TAXES: If this sale or Buyer's use of the Property after closing results in the assessment of additional taxes, penalties or interest (Assessments) for periods prior to closing, the Assessments will be the obligation of Buyer. If Seller's change in use of the Property prior to closing or denial of a special use valuation on the Property claimed by Seller results in Assessments for periods prior to closing, the Assessments will be the obligation of Seller. Obligations imposed by this paragraph will survive closing.

14. CASUALTY LOSS: If any part of the Property is damaged or destroyed by fire or other casualty after the effective date of this contract, Seller shall restore the Property to its previous condition as soon as reasonably possible, but in any event by the Closing Date. If Seller fails to do so due to factors beyond Seller's control, Buyer may (a) terminate this contract and the earnest money will be refunded to Buyer (b) extend the time for performance up to 15 days and the Closing Date will be extended as necessary or (c) accept the Property in its damaged condition with an assignment of insurance proceeds and receive credit from Seller at closing in the amount of the deductible under the insurance policy. Seller's obligations under this paragraph are independent of any other obligations of Seller under this contract.

15. DEFAULT: If Buyer fails to comply with this contract, Buyer will be in default, and Seller may (a) enforce specific performance, seek such other relief as may be provided by law, or both, or (b) terminate this contract and receive the earnest money as liquidated damages, thereby releasing both parties from this contract. If, due to factors beyond Seller's control, Seller fails within the time allowed to make any non-casualty repairs or deliver the Commitment, or survey, if required of Seller, Buyer may (a) extend the time for performance up to 15 days and the Closing Date will be extended as necessary or (b) terminate this contract as the sole remedy and receive the earnest money. If Seller fails to comply with this contract for any other reason, Seller will be in default and Buyer may (a) enforce specific performance, seek such other relief as may be provided by law, or both, or (b) terminate this contract and receive the earnest money, thereby releasing both parties from this contract.

16. MEDIATION: It is the policy of the State of Texas to encourage resolution of disputes through alternative dispute resolution procedures such as mediation. Any dispute between Seller and Buyer related to this contract which is not resolved through informal discussion ☐will ☐will not be submitted to a mutually acceptable mediation service or provider. The parties to the mediation shall bear the mediation costs equally. This paragraph does not preclude a party from seeking equitable relief from a court of competent jurisdiction.

17. ATTORNEY'S FEES: The prevailing party in any legal proceeding related to this contract is entitled to recover reasonable attorney's fees and all costs of such proceeding incurred by the prevailing party.

18. ESCROW:

A. ESCROW: The escrow agent is not (i) a party to this contract and does not have liability for the performance or nonperformance of any party to this contract, (ii) liable for interest on the earnest money and (iii) liable for the loss of any earnest money caused by the failure of any financial institution in which the earnest money has been deposited unless the financial institution is acting as escrow agent.

B. EXPENSES: At closing, the earnest money must be applied first to any cash down payment, then to Buyer's Expenses and any excess refunded to Buyer. If no closing occurs, escrow agent may require payment of unpaid expenses incurred on behalf of the parties and a written release of liability of escrow agent from all parties.

C. DEMAND: Upon termination of this contract, either party or the escrow agent may send a release of earnest money to each party and the parties shall execute counterparts of the release and deliver same to the escrow agent. If either party fails to execute the release, either party may make a written demand to the escrow agent for the earnest money. If only one party makes written demand for the earnest money, escrow agent shall promptly provide a copy of the demand to the other party. If escrow agent does not receive written objection to the demand from the other party within 15 days, escrow agent may disburse the earnest money to the party making demand reduced by the amount of unpaid expenses incurred on behalf of the party receiving the earnest money and escrow agent may pay the same to the creditors. If escrow agent complies with the provisions of this paragraph, each party hereby releases escrow agent from all adverse claims related to the disbursal of the earnest money.

FIGURE 10.6 (CONTINUED)

TREC 9-6

Contract Concerning ______________________________ Page 6 of 8 02-13-06
(Address of Property)

D. DAMAGES: Any party who wrongfully fails or refuses to sign a release acceptable to the escrow agent within 7 days of receipt of the request will be liable to the other party for liquidated damages of three times the amount of the earnest money.

E. NOTICES: Escrow agent's notices will be effective when sent in compliance with Paragraph 21. Notice of objection to the demand will be deemed effective upon receipt by escrow agent.

19. REPRESENTATIONS: Seller represents that as of the Closing Date (a) there will be no liens, assessments, or security interests against the Property which will not be satisfied out of the sales proceeds unless securing payment of any loans assumed by Buyer and (b) assumed loans will not be in default. If any representation of Seller in this contract is untrue on the Closing Date, Seller will be in default.

20. FEDERAL TAX REQUIREMENTS: If Seller is a "foreign person," as defined by applicable law, or if Seller fails to deliver an affidavit to Buyer that Seller is not a "foreign person," then Buyer shall withhold from the sales proceeds an amount sufficient to comply with applicable tax law and deliver the same to the Internal Revenue Service together with appropriate tax forms. Internal Revenue Service regulations require filing written reports if currency in excess of specified amounts is received in the transaction.

21. NOTICES: All notices from one party to the other must be in writing and are effective when mailed to, hand-delivered at, or transmitted by facsimile or electronic transmission as follows:

To Buyer at:	**To Seller at:**
______________________	______________________
______________________	______________________
______________________	______________________
Telephone: ( ) ____________	Telephone: ( ) ____________
Facsimile: ( ) ____________	Facsimile: ( ) ____________
E-mail: ____________	E-mail: ____________

22. AGREEMENT OF PARTIES: This contract contains the entire agreement of the parties and cannot be changed except by their written agreement. Addenda which are a part of this contract are (check all applicable boxes):

- ☐ Third Party Financing Condition Addendum
- ☐ Environmental Assessment, Threatened or Endangered Species and Wetlands Addendum
- ☐ Seller Financing Addendum
- ☐ Addendum for Coastal Area Property
- ☐ Loan Assumption Addendum
- ☐ Addendum for Property Located Seaward of the Gulf Intracoastal Waterway
- ☐ Addendum for Property Subject to Mandatory Membership in an Owners' Association
- ☐ Addendum for Release of Liability on Assumption of FHA, VA, or Conventional Loan Restoration of Seller's Entitlement for VA Guaranteed Loan
- ☐ Addendum for Sale of Other Property by Buyer
- ☐ Addendum for "Back-Up" Contract

☐ Other (list): ____

____

____

____

Initialed for identification by Buyer______ ______ and Seller ______ ______ TREC NO. 9-6

FIGURE 10.6 (CONTINUED)

TREC 9-6

23. **TERMINATION OPTION:** For nominal consideration, the receipt of which is hereby acknowledged by Seller, and Buyer's agreement to pay Seller $________________ (Option Fee) within 2 days after the effective date of this contract, Seller grants Buyer the unrestricted right to terminate this contract by giving notice of termination to Seller within ________ days after the effective date of this contract. If no dollar amount is stated as the Option Fee or if Buyer fails to pay the Option Fee within the time prescribed, this paragraph will not be a part of this contract and Buyer shall not have the unrestricted right to terminate this contract. If Buyer gives notice of termination within the time prescribed, the Option Fee will not be refunded; however, any earnest money will be refunded to Buyer. The Option Fee ❑will ❑will not be credited to the Sales Price at closing. **Time is of the essence for this paragraph and strict compliance with the time for performance is required.**

24. **CONSULT AN ATTORNEY:** Real estate licensees cannot give legal advice. READ THIS CONTRACT CAREFULLY. If you do not understand the effect of this contract, consult an attorney BEFORE signing.

Buyer's Attorney is: ______________________	Seller's Attorney is: ______________________
______________________	______________________
Telephone: ( ) ______________	Telephone: ( ) ______________
Facsimile: ( ) ______________	Facsimile: ( ) ______________
E-mail: ______________________	E-mail: ______________________

EXECUTED the ______day of ___________________________, 20_____ (EFFECTIVE DATE). (BROKER: FILL IN THE DATE OF FINAL ACCEPTANCE.)

______________________	______________________
Buyer	Seller
______________________	______________________
Buyer	Seller

The form of this contract has been approved by the Texas Real Estate Commission. TREC forms are intended for use only by trained real estate licensees. No representation is made as to the legal validity or adequacy of any provision in any specific transactions. It is not intended for complex transactions. Texas Real Estate Commission, P.O. Box 12188, Austin, TX 78711-2188, 1-800-250-8732 or (512) 459-6544 (http://www.trec.state.tx.us) TREC NO. 9-6. This form replaces TREC NO. 9-5.

FIGURE 10.6 (CONTINUED)

TREC 9-6

Contract Concerning ______________________________ Page 8 of 8 02-13-06
(Address of Property)

BROKER INFORMATION AND RATIFICATION OF FEE

Listing Broker has agreed to pay Other Broker ______________ of the total sales price when Listing Broker's fee is received. Escrow Agent is authorized and directed to pay Other Broker from Listing Broker's fee at closing.

Other Broker — License No.	Listing Broker — License No.
represents ❑ Buyer only as Buyer's agent ❑ Seller as Listing Broker's subagent	represents ❑ Seller and Buyer as an intermediary ❑ Seller only as Seller's agent
Associate — Telephone	Listing Associate — Telephone
Broker's Address	Listing Associate's Office Address — Facsimile
City — State — Zip	City — State — Zip
Facsimile	Email Address
Email Address	Selling Associate — Telephone
	Selling Associate's Office Address — Facsimile
	City — State — Zip
	Email Address

OPTION FEE RECEIPT

Receipt of $______________ (Option Fee) in the form of ______________ is acknowledged.

Seller or Listing Broker ______________ Date ______________

CONTRACT AND EARNEST MONEY RECEIPT

Receipt of ❑Contract and ❑$______________ Earnest Money in the form of ______________ is acknowledged.

Escrow Agent: ______________ Date: ______________

By: ______________ Email Address ______________

Address ______________ Telephone (____) ______________

City State Zip ______________ Facsimile: (____) ______________

TREC NO. 9-6

FIGURE 10.7

Consumer Information Form 1-1

THIS FIRM IS

LICENSED AND REGULATED

BY THE

TEXAS REAL ESTATE

COMMISSION (TREC)

TREC ADMINISTERS TWO RECOVERY FUNDS

WHICH MAY BE USED TO SATISFY JUDGMENTS

AGAINST INSPECTORS AND REAL ESTATE

LICENSEES INVOLVING A VIOLATION OF THE LAW.

COMPLAINTS OR INQUIRIES SHOULD

BE DIRECTED TO

TEXAS REAL ESTATE COMMISSION
P.O. BOX 12188
AUSTIN, TEXAS 78711-2188

(512) 465-3960

Consumer Information Form 1-1 (8-91)

FIGURE 10.8

TREC OP-C

APPROVED BY THE TEXAS REAL ESTATE COMMISSION

NOTICE TO PROSPECTIVE BUYER

As required by law, I advise you to have the abstract covering the property known as ____ (Address) examined by an attorney of your own selection OR you should be furnished with or obtain a policy of title insurance.

If the property is situated in a Utility District, Chapter 49 of the Texas Water Code requires you to sign and acknowledge the statutory notice from the seller of the property relating to the tax rate, bonded indebtedness or standby fee of the District.

DATED: ______________________ , __________ .

____
Brokerage Company Name

____
Broker or Sales Associate

I have received a copy of this **NOTICE TO PROSPECTIVE BUYER.**

____
Prospective Buyer

____
Prospective Buyer

This form has been approved by the Texas Real Estate Commission (TREC) for use when a contract of sale has not been promulgated by TREC. The form should be presented before an offer to purchase is signed by the prospective buyer. Texas Real Estate Commission, P.O. Box 12188, Austin, Texas 78711-2188, 1-800-250-8732 or (512) 459-6544 (http://www.trec.state.tx.us). TREC Notice to Prospective Buyer.(12/99) OP-C replaces MA-C.

01A TREC NO. OP-C

FIGURE 10.9

TREC 32-1

EQUAL HOUSING OPPORTUNITY

PROMULGATED BY THE TEXAS REAL ESTATE COMMISSION (TREC) 04-23-07

CONDOMINIUM RESALE CERTIFICATE

(Section 82.157 Texas Property Code)

Condominium Certificate concerning Condominium Unit _____, in Building _______, of _______________ ________________________________,a condominium project, located at _____________________ ________________________________(Address), City of _________________________, County of _________________________, Texas, on behalf of the condominium owners association (the Association) by the Association's governing body (the Board).

A. The Declaration ❑does ❑does not contain a right of first refusal or other restraint that restricts the right to transfer the Unit. If a right of first refusal or other restraint exists, see Section _______of the Declaration.

B. The periodic common expense assessment for the Unit is $____________ per ________________.

C. There ❑ is ❑is not a common expense or special assessment due and unpaid by the Seller to the Association. The total unpaid amount is $_____________ and is for __________________________.

D. Other amounts ❑are ❑are not payable by Seller to the Association. The total unpaid amount is $________________and is for ____.

E. Capital expenditures approved by the Association for the next 12 months are $______________.

F. Reserves for capital expenditures are $______________;of this amount $___________________ has been designated for____.

G. The current operating budget of the Association is attached.

H. The amount of unsatisfied judgments against the Association is $ __________________________.

I. There ❑are ❑are not any suits pending against the Association. The nature of the suits is ____.

J. The Association ❑does ❑does not provide insurance coverage for the benefit of unit owners as per the attached summary from the Association's insurance agent.

K. The Board ❑has ❑has no knowledge of alterations or improvements to the Unit or to the limited common elements assigned to the Unit or any portion of the project that violate any provision of the Declaration, by-laws or rules of the Association. Known violations are:_______________________ ____.

L. The Board ❑has ❑has not received notice from a governmental authority concerning violations of health or building codes with respect to the Unit, the limited common elements assigned to the Unit, or any other portion of the condominium project. Notices received are: _____ ____.

M. The remaining term of any leasehold estate that affects the condominium is _________________ and the provisions governing an extension or a renewal of the lease are: ___________________ ____ ____.

N. The name, mailing address and telephone number of the Association's managing agent are:

____

(Name) (Telephone Number)

____

(Mailing Address)

FIGURE 10.9 (CONTINUED)

TREC 32-1

Condominium Resale Certificate Concerning Page 2 of 2 04-23-07

____

(Address of Property)

O. Association fees resulting from the transfer of the unit described above $ ________________.

P. Required contribution, if any, to the capital reserves account $ ________________________.

REQUIRED ATTACHMENTS:

1. Operating Budget
2. Insurance Summary

NOTICE: The Certificate must be prepared no more than three months before the date it is delivered to Buyer.

____

(Name of Condominium Owners Association)

By: ______________________________ ______________________________
Title

______________________________ ______________________________
Mailing Address E-mail

______________________________ ______________________________
Telephone Number Date

Received: ______________________________, 20 _______

______________________________ ______________________________
Buyer Buyer

This form has been approved by the Texas Real Estate Commission for use with similarly approved or promulgated contract forms. Such approval relates to this form only. TREC forms are intended for use only by trained real estate licensees. No representation is made as to the legal validity or adequacy of any provision in any specific transactions. It is not suitable for complex transactions. Texas Real Estate Commission, P.O. Box 12188, Austin, TX 78711-2188, 1-800-250-8732 or (512) 459-6544 (http://www.trec.state.tx.us) TREC No. 32-1. This form replaces TREC No. 32-0.

FIGURE 10.10

TREC 37-2

PROMULGATED BY THE TEXAS REAL ESTATE COMMISSION (TREC) 02-13-06

EQUAL HOUSING OPPORTUNITY

SUBDIVISION INFORMATION, INCLUDING RESALE CERTIFICATE FOR PROPERTY SUBJECT TO MANDATORY MEMBERSHIP IN AN OWNERS' ASSOCIATION

(Section 207.003, Texas Property Code)

(NOT FOR USE WITH CONDOMINIUMS)

Resale Certificate concerning the Property (including any common areas assigned to the Property) located at ______________________________ (Street Address), City of ______________________________, County of ____________________, Texas, prepared by the property owners' association (the Owners' Association).

A. The Property ❑ is ❑ is not subject to a right of first refusal or other restraint contained in the restrictions or restrictive covenants that restricts the owner's right to transfer the owner's property.

B. The current regular assessment for the Property is $____________________ per ____________________.

C. A special assessment for the Property due after the date the resale certificate was prepared is $______________ payable as follows ______________________________.

D. The total of all amounts due and unpaid to the Owners' Association that are attributable to the Property is $ ________________ .

E. The capital expenditures approved by the Owners' Association for its current fiscal year are $ ____________________.

F. The amount of reserves for capital expenditures is $____________________.

G. Unsatisfied judgments against the Owners' Association total $____________________.

H. There ❑ are ❑ are not any suits pending against the Owners' Association. The style and cause number of each pending suit is: ______________________________
____
______________________________.

I. The Owners' Association's board ❑ has actual knowledge ❑ has no actual knowledge of conditions on the Property in violation of the restrictions applying to the subdivision or the bylaws or rules of the Owners' Association. Known violations are: ______________________________
____
______________________________.

J. The Owners' Association ❑ has ❑ has not received notice from any governmental authority regarding health or building code violations with respect to the Property or any common areas or common facilities owned or leased by the Owners' Association. A summary or copy of each notice is attached.

K. The Owners' Association fees resulting from the transfer of the Property are $____________________, payable to ______________________________.

Initialed for identification by Buyer____ ____ and Seller____ ____ TREC NO. 37-2

FIGURE 10.10 (CONTINUED)

TREC 37-2

Subdivision Information Concerning ______________________________ Page 2 of 2 02-13-06
(Address of Property)

L. The Owners' Association's managing agent is ______________________________
(Name of Agent)

____
(Mailing Address)

______________________ ______________________
(Telephone Number) (Fax Number)

M. The restrictions ☐ do ☐ do not allow foreclosure of the Owners' Association's lien on the Property for failure to pay assessments.

REQUIRED ATTACHMENTS:

1. Restrictions
2. Rules
3. Bylaws
4. Current Balance Sheet
5. Current Operating Budget
6. Certificate of Insurance concerning Property and Liability Insurance for Common Areas and Facilities
7. Any Governmental Notices of Health or Housing Code Violations

NOTICE: This Subdivision Information may change at any time.

____
Name of Owners' Association

By: ______________________________

Title: ______________________________

Mailing Address: ______________________________

E-mail: ______________________________

Date: ______________________________

This form has been approved by the Texas Real Estate commission for use only with similarly approved or promulgated contract forms. No representation is made as to the legal validity or adequacy of any provision in any specific transaction. Texas Real Estate Commission, P.O. Box 12188, Austin, TX 78711-2188, 1-800-250-8732 or (512) 459-6544 (http://www.trec.state.tx.us) TREC No. 37-2. This form replaces TREC No. 37-1.

TREC NO. 37-2

CHAPTER 10 REVIEW QUESTIONS

1. Rollback taxes are an issue addressed in the condominium contract promulgated by the TREC.

   a. True
   b. False

2. Who will complete the promulgated resale certificate?

   a. Seller
   b. Buyer
   c. Homeowners' association
   d. Listing agent

3. The TREC Form OP-C, Notice to Prospective Buyer, *MUST* be used with every transaction and be included with every contract as an addendum.

   a. True
   b. False

4. Who need *NOT* prominently display the TREC Form 1-1, Consumer Information Form?

   a. Real estate brokers
   b. Real estate inspectors
   c. Residential service contract companies
   d. Residential real estate brokerage firms

5. How many recovery funds are administered by the TREC according to the TREC Form 1-1, Consumer Information Form?

   a. Two
   b. Three
   c. One
   d. Five

HOMEWORK QUIZ

The following quiz does not have an answer key included with the answer keys in Appendix B. Students who are using this book as the basis for a correspondence course should record and submit their answers to their course provider as instructed by the provider. The student will submit his or her answers for the Homework Quiz at the end of each chapter and for each transaction in Chapter 11.

True or False?

1. Federal law requires that the R-factors of the insulation installed in new homes be included in the purchase contract between the Buyer and the builder.

2. New construction contracts must have a statutory addendum attached as required by sections 420.01 and 420.002 of the Texas Property Code.

3. The Farm and Ranch Contract, TREC 25-5, has the same accessories list as the TREC 20-7.

4. Paragraph 6 of the Farm and Ranch Contract, TREC 25-5, has an additional paragraph to address surface leases.

5. The Resale Certificate addressed in paragraph 2 of the Residential Condominium Contract, TREC 30-6, must have been prepared no less than 90 days prior to the date of delivery to the Buyer.

6. The Residential Condominium Contract, TREC 30-6, can be used for newly constructed condominiums.

7. In the TREC 30-6 form, the Declaration, Bylaws, and Rules of the Association are defined as Documents.

8. The Unimproved Property Contract is for use when the property has no improvements.

9. Consumer Information Form 1-1 is strictly for voluntary use by Texas-licensed brokers.

10. Rollback taxes are addressed in all of the TREC-promulgated contract forms except the Unimproved Property Contract, TREC 9-6/r.

CHAPTER ELEVEN

Practice Makes Perfect

Now that we have learned the basics of contract law in Texas, the details of the content of the TREC-promulgated forms, the provisions of the license act, and the rules of the TREC that relate to permitted and prohibited activity on the part of license holders, we will now enhance what we have learned by completing the following case studies. Your instructor will choose which of the following will be completed as part of the classroom study; the other cases can be completed on your own in your leisure.

Every transaction is unique because it may have special considerations that may be addressed by promulgated addenda or it may require the services of a real estate attorney. In the case studies that follow, you have the opportunity to complete promulgated contracts for some of the more commonly encountered situations. Addenda have been completed for you so that you might focus on correctly completing the contract forms. Arrows in the left margins indicate where specific information has been inserted in the form. Your instructor may provide additional information for some of the cases. Because relatively few addresses are provided for you other than the Property address, you will need to provide missing addresses. Be creative!

Please note the following:

- Read the case information carefully
- Make notes in the margin as you read the case study
- Complete the forms using a pencil. When your instructor walks through the transaction with you or you check your work against the answer key on the Web site referenced above, you can easily make any necessary corrections.
- Be sure to put **N/A** in blanks that are not needed for the particular transaction. Do not leave open holes in the agreement

- Be sure to identify all attached addenda in paragraph 22 that are a part of the agreement
- Have fun! Ask questions. Read carefully

TRANSACTION 1: 80% CONVENTIONAL FIXED-RATE LOAN (USING: TREC 20-7, 40-3, 36-4, 28-1, AND 39-6. SEE FIGURE 11.1 THROUGH FIGURE 11.5.)

John Paul Gordon and his wife, Mary Anne Gordon, want to purchase a home owned by Isabelle Gertrude Gerhard, an unmarried resident of Houston, Texas.

The Property is identified as Lot 6, Block 10 in Section 1 of the Windswept Addition of Harris County, Texas. It is more commonly known as 2615 Pleasure Point Drive, Houston, Texas 77084. The Property is subject to the rules and assessments of a mandatory owners' association.

The Buyers have received and approved a copy of the owners' association resale certificate prior to signing the purchase agreement. The Buyers are willing to pay $50 of the $100 transfer fee charged by the owners' association. The Buyers want to be certain that parking an RV in the driveway is permitted.

Ms. Gerhard will remove the draperies from the master bedroom prior to closing. She will leave all other items listed in paragraph 2 of the standard purchase agreement.

Although Ms. Gerhard is asking $106,000 for the Property, the Buyers have decided to offer $96,000. They have made loan application and expect that they can have financing approval within 25 days after the effective date of the contract. The contract is to be subject to the Gordon's financing approval. They agree to apply for an 80 percent conventional loan at 6 percent with a 15-year amortization and with no private mortgage insurance required.

To show how serious their intent is, the Buyers deposit $10,000 earnest money with No Cloud Title Company at 1700 South Main, Houston, Texas 77001. They feel that it would be unreasonable for the Seller to require that any additional earnest money be deposited.

The Buyers are willing to pay for a new survey to be delivered within 20 days after the effective date of the contract and ask that the Seller pay for the owners' title policy to demonstrate that the title is free of encumbrances as of the date of closing. The Buyers want 5 days to review the title commitment and deed restrictions.

Prior to signing the offer to purchase, the Buyers receive and review the Seller's Property disclosure form required by section 5.008 of the Texas Property Code.

The Gordons are willing to pay Ms. Gerhard $300 for a 7-day option to terminate period. The $300 will be credited to the sale price if they complete the transaction.

By attaching the appropriate addendum, the parties agree that the Buyers will have 20 days to have environmental assessments performed. Because the home was built in 1985, they have not attached the lead-based paint/hazard addendum. They do not feel that lead is an issue.

They want to close on or before the 30th day after the date of the contract and want possession to be granted at closing or the funding of their loan, whichever is later. The Buyers will pay for all typical loan costs required by the lender. They will pay a 1 percent loan origination fee and do not anticipate that the lender will charge any discount points. No commitment fee or buydown will be applicable.

The Property has been listed by Smooth Sales Realty Company (The TREC #7657321) and is being sold by a company that represents only Buyers, Buyer's Broker Realty (The TREC #1234567). The agents obtain the correct addresses and numbers to be entered in paragraph 21 of the purchase contract. The listing broker, through the local multiple listing service (MLS), has agreed to pay the selling broker a fee equal to 3 percent of the sale price. Both agents inform their clients of the advantages of mediation, but the parties do not want to make the financial commitment to split the cost of mediation.

Five days into the option period the Buyer decides to approach the Seller and ask the Seller to replace the defective flooring in the kitchen. The Seller agrees to credit the Buyers $1,400 at closing to replace the floor covering rather than become involved in choosing and installing new flooring.

FIGURE 11.1

TREC 20-7

EQUAL HOUSING OPPORTUNITY

02-13-06

PROMULGATED BY THE TEXAS REAL ESTATE COMMISSION (TREC)

ONE TO FOUR FAMILY RESIDENTIAL CONTRACT (RESALE)

NOTICE: Not For Use For Condominium Transactions

1. PARTIES: Isabelle Gertrude Gerhard, an unmarried person (Seller) agrees to sell and convey to John Paul Gordon and wife Mary Anne Gordon (Buyer) and Buyer agrees to buy from Seller the Property described below.

2. PROPERTY:

A. LAND: Lot 6 Block 2, Section 1 of Windswept Addition, City of Houston, County of Harris, Texas, known as 2615 Pleasure Point Drive 77024 (address/zip code), or as described on attached exhibit.

B. IMPROVEMENTS: The house, garage and all other fixtures and improvements attached to the above-described real property, including without limitation, the following **permanently installed and built-in items,** if any: all equipment and appliances, valances, screens, shutters, awnings, wall-to-wall carpeting, mirrors, ceiling fans, attic fans, mail boxes, television antennas and satellite dish system and equipment, heating and air-conditioning units, security and fire detection equipment, wiring, plumbing and lighting fixtures, chandeliers, water softener system, kitchen equipment, garage door openers, cleaning equipment, shrubbery, landscaping, outdoor cooking equipment, and all other property owned by Seller and attached to the above described real property.

C. ACCESSORIES: The following described related accessories, if any: window air conditioning units, stove, fireplace screens, curtains and rods, blinds, window shades, draperies and rods, controls for satellite dish system, controls for garage door openers, entry gate controls, door keys, mailbox keys, above ground pool, swimming pool equipment and maintenance accessories, and artificial fireplace logs.

D. EXCLUSIONS: The following improvements and accessories will be retained by Seller and removed prior to delivery of possession: draperies in master bedroom.

The land, improvements and accessories are collectively referred to as the "Property".

3. SALES PRICE:

A. Cash portion of Sales Price payable by Buyer at closing $19,200

B. Sum of all financing described below (excluding any loan funding fee or mortgage insurance premium) $76,800

C. Sales Price (Sum of A and B) $96,000

4. FINANCING: The portion of Sales Price not payable in cash will be paid as follows: (Check applicable boxes below)

☒ A. THIRD PARTY FINANCING: One or more third party mortgage loans in the total amount of $76,800 (excluding any loan funding fee or mortgage insurance premium).

(1) Property Approval: If the Property does not satisfy the lenders' underwriting requirements for the loan(s), this contract will terminate and the earnest money will be refunded to Buyer.

(2) Financing Approval: (Check one box only)

☒ (a) This contract is subject to Buyer being approved for the financing described in the attached Third Party Financing Condition Addendum.

☐ (b) This contract is not subject to Buyer being approved for financing and does not involve FHA or VA financing.

☐ B. ASSUMPTION: The assumption of the unpaid principal balance of one or more promissory notes described in the attached TREC Loan Assumption Addendum.

☐ C. SELLER FINANCING: A promissory note from Buyer to Seller of $ n/a, secured by vendor's and deed of trust liens, and containing the terms and conditions described in the attached TREC Seller Financing Addendum. If an owner policy of title insurance is furnished, Buyer shall furnish Seller with a mortgagee policy of title insurance.

5. EARNEST MONEY: Upon execution of this contract by both parties, Buyer shall deposit $10,000 as earnest money with No Cloud Title Company, as escrow agent, at 1700 South Main, Houston, TX 77001 (address). Buyer shall deposit additional earnest money of $ n/a with escrow agent within n/a days after the effective date of this contract. If Buyer fails to deposit the earnest money as required by this contract, Buyer will be in default.

6. TITLE POLICY AND SURVEY:

A. TITLE POLICY: Seller shall furnish to Buyer at ☒ Seller's ☐ Buyer's expense an owner policy of title insurance (Title Policy) issued by No Cloud Title Company (Title Company) in the amount of the Sales Price, dated at or after closing, insuring Buyer

Initialed for identification by Buyer______ ______ and Seller ______ ______ TREC NO. 20-7

FIGURE 11.1 (CONTINUED)

TREC 20-7

Contract Concerning [illegible] Page 2 of 8 02-13-06
(Address of Property)

against loss under the provisions of the Title Policy, subject to the promulgated exclusions (including existing building and zoning ordinances) and the following exceptions:

(1) Restrictive covenants common to the platted subdivision in which the Property is located.
(2) The standard printed exception for standby fees, taxes and assessments.
(3) Liens created as part of the financing described in Paragraph 4.
(4) Utility easements created by the dedication deed or plat of the subdivision in which the Property is located.
(5) Reservations or exceptions otherwise permitted by this contract or as may be approved by Buyer in writing.
(6) The standard printed exception as to marital rights.
(7) The standard printed exception as to waters, tidelands, beaches, streams, and related matters.
(8) The standard printed exception as to discrepancies, conflicts, shortages in area or boundary lines, encroachments or protrusions, or overlapping improvements. Buyer, at Buyer's expense, may have the exception amended to read, "shortages in area".

B. COMMITMENT: Within 20 days after the Title Company receives a copy of this contract, Seller shall furnish to Buyer a commitment for title insurance (Commitment) and, at Buyer's expense, legible copies of restrictive covenants and documents evidencing exceptions in the Commitment (Exception Documents) other than the standard printed exceptions. Seller authorizes the Title Company to deliver the Commitment and Exception Documents to Buyer at Buyer's address shown in Paragraph 21. If the Commitment and Exception Documents are not delivered to Buyer within the specified time, the time for delivery will be automatically extended up to 15 days or the Closing Date, whichever is earlier.

C. SURVEY: The survey must be made by a registered professional land surveyor acceptable to the Title Company and any lender. (Check one box only)

☐ (1) Within n/a days after the effective date of this contract, Seller shall furnish to Buyer and Title Company Seller's existing survey of the Property and a Residential Real Property Affidavit promulgated by the Texas Department of Insurance (Affidavit). If the existing survey or Affidavit is not acceptable to Title Company or Buyer's lender, Buyer shall obtain a new survey at ☐ Seller's ☐ Buyer's expense no later than 3 days prior to Closing Date. If Seller fails to furnish the existing survey or Affidavit within the time prescribed, Buyer shall obtain a new survey at Seller's expense no later than 3 days prior to Closing Date.

☒ (2) Within 20 days after the effective date of this contract, Buyer shall obtain a new survey at Buyer's expense. Buyer is deemed to receive the survey on the date of actual receipt or the date specified in this paragraph, whichever is earlier.

☐ (3) Within n/a days after the effective date of this contract, Seller, at Seller's expense shall furnish a new survey to Buyer.

D. OBJECTIONS: Buyer may object in writing to defects, exceptions, or encumbrances to title: disclosed on the survey other than items 6A(1) through (7) above; disclosed in the Commitment other than items 6A(1) through (8) above; or which prohibit the following use or activity: none
______________________________.

Buyer must object not later than (i) the Closing Date or (ii) 95 days after Buyer receives the Commitment, Exception Documents, and the survey, whichever is earlier. Buyer's failure to object within the time allowed will constitute a waiver of Buyer's right to object; except that the requirements in Schedule C of the Commitment are not waived. Provided Seller is not obligated to incur any expense, Seller shall cure the timely objections of Buyer or any third party lender within 15 days after Seller receives the objections and the Closing Date will be extended as necessary. If objections are not cured within such 15 day period, this contract will terminate and the earnest money will be refunded to Buyer unless Buyer waives the objections.

E. TITLE NOTICES:

(1) ABSTRACT OR TITLE POLICY: Broker advises Buyer to have an abstract of title covering the Property examined by an attorney of Buyer's selection, or Buyer should be furnished with or obtain a Title Policy. If a Title Policy is furnished, the Commitment should be promptly reviewed by an attorney of Buyer's choice due to the time limitations on Buyer's right to object.

(2) MANDATORY OWNERS' ASSOCIATION MEMBERSHIP: The Property ☒ is ☐ is not subject to mandatory membership in an owners' association. If the Property is subject to mandatory membership in an owners' association, Seller notifies Buyer under §5.012, Texas Property Code, that, as a purchaser of property in the residential community in which the Property is located, you are obligated to be a member of the owners' association. Restrictive covenants governing the use and occupancy of the Property and a dedicatory instrument governing the establishment, maintenance, and operation of this residential community have been or will be recorded in the Real Property Records of the county in which the Property is located. Copies of the restrictive covenants and dedicatory instrument may be obtained from the county clerk. You are obligated to pay

Initialed for identification by Buyer______ ______ and Seller _______ ______ TREC NO. 20-7

FIGURE 11.1 (CONTINUED)

TREC 20-7

Contract Concerning ______________________ Page 3 of 8 02-13-06
(Address of Property)

assessments to the owners' association. The amount of the assessments is subject to change. Your failure to pay the assessments could result in a lien on and the foreclosure of the Property. If Buyer is concerned about these matters, the TREC promulgated Addendum for Property Subject to Mandatory Membership in an Owner's Association should be used.

(3) STATUTORY TAX DISTRICTS: If the Property is situated in a utility or other statutorily created district providing water, sewer, drainage, or flood control facilities and services, Chapter 49, Texas Water Code, requires Seller to deliver and Buyer to sign the statutory notice relating to the tax rate, bonded indebtedness, or standby fee of the district prior to final execution of this contract.

(4) TIDE WATERS: If the Property abuts the tidally influenced waters of the state, §33.135, Texas Natural Resources Code, requires a notice regarding coastal area property to be included in the contract. An addendum containing the notice promulgated by TREC or required by the parties must be used.

(5) ANNEXATION: If the Property is located outside the limits of a municipality, Seller notifies Buyer under §5.011, Texas Property Code, that the Property may now or later be included in the extraterritorial jurisdiction of a municipality and may now or later be subject to annexation by the municipality. Each municipality maintains a map that depicts its boundaries and extraterritorial jurisdiction. To determine if the Property is located within a municipality's extraterritorial jurisdiction or is likely to be located within a municipality's extraterritorial jurisdiction, contact all municipalities located in the general proximity of the Property for further information.

(6) PROPERTY LOCATED IN A CERTIFICATED SERVICE AREA OF A UTILITY SERVICE PROVIDER: Notice required by §13.257, Water Code: The real property, described in Paragraph 2, that you are about to purchase may be located in a certificated water or sewer service area, which is authorized by law to provide water or sewer service to the properties in the certificated area. If your property is located in a certificated area there may be special costs or charges that you will be required to pay before you can receive water or sewer service. There may be a period required to construct lines or other facilities necessary to provide water or sewer service to your property. You are advised to determine if the property is in a certificated area and contact the utility service provider to determine the cost that you will be required to pay and the period, if any, that is required to provide water or sewer service to your property. The undersigned Buyer hereby acknowledges receipt of the foregoing notice at or before the execution of a binding contract for the purchase of the real property described in Paragraph 2 or at closing of purchase of the real property.

(7) PUBLIC IMPROVEMENT DISTRICTS: If the Property is in a public improvement district, §5.014, Property Code, requires Seller to notify Buyer as follows: As a purchaser of this parcel of real property you are obligated to pay an assessment to a municipality or county for an improvement project undertaken by a public improvement district under Chapter 372, Local Government Code. The assessment may be due annually or in periodic installments. More information concerning the amount of the assessment and the due dates of that assessment may be obtained from the municipality or county levying the assessment. The amount of the assessments is subject to change. Your failure to pay the assessments could result in a lien on and the foreclosure of your property.

7. PROPERTY CONDITION:

A. ACCESS,INSPECTIONS AND UTILITIES: Seller shall permit Buyer and Buyer's agents access to the Property at reasonable times. Buyer may have the Property inspected by inspectors selected by Buyer and licensed by TREC or otherwise permitted by law to make inspections. Seller at Seller's expense shall turn on existing utilities for inspections.

B. SELLER'S DISCLOSURE NOTICE PURSUANT TO §5.008, TEXAS PROPERTY CODE (Notice): (Check one box only)

☒ (1) Buyer has received the Notice.

☐ (2) Buyer has not received the Notice. Within n/a days after the effective date of this contract, Seller shall deliver the Notice to Buyer. If Buyer does not receive the Notice, Buyer may terminate this contract at any time prior to the closing and the earnest money will be refunded to Buyer. If Seller delivers the Notice, Buyer may terminate this contract for any reason within 7 days after Buyer receives the Notice or prior to the closing, whichever first occurs, and the earnest money will be refunded to Buyer.

☐ (3) The Seller is not required to furnish the notice under the Texas Property Code.

C. SELLER'S DISCLOSURE OF LEAD-BASED PAINT AND LEAD-BASED PAINT HAZARDS is required by Federal law for a residential dwelling constructed prior to 1978.

D. ACCEPTANCE OF PROPERTY CONDITION: Buyer accepts the Property in its present condition; provided Seller, at Seller's expense, shall complete the following specific repairs and treatments: none

E. LENDER REQUIRED REPAIRS AND TREATMENTS: Unless otherwise agreed in writing, neither party is obligated to pay for lender required repairs, which includes treatment for wood

Initialed for identification by Buyer______ ______ and Seller _______ ______ TREC NO. 20-7

FIGURE 11.1 (CONTINUED)

TREC 20-7

Contract Concerning 2615 Pleasure Point Drive, Houston, TX 77084 Page 4 of 8 02-13-06
(Address of Property)

destroying insects. If the parties do not agree to pay for the lender required repairs or treatments, this contract will terminate and the earnest money will be refunded to Buyer. If the cost of lender required repairs and treatments exceeds 5% of the Sales Price, Buyer may terminate this contract and the earnest money will be refunded to Buyer.

F. COMPLETION OF REPAIRS AND TREATMENTS: Unless otherwise agreed in writing, Seller shall complete all agreed repairs and treatments prior to the Closing Date. All required permits must be obtained, and repairs and treatments must be performed by persons who are licensed or otherwise authorized by law to provide such repairs or treatments. At Buyer's election, any transferable warranties received by Seller with respect to the repairs and treatments will be transferred to Buyer at Buyer's expense. If Seller fails to complete any agreed repairs and treatments prior to the Closing Date, Buyer may do so and receive reimbursement from Seller at closing. The Closing Date will be extended up to 15 days, if necessary, to complete repairs and treatments.

G. ENVIRONMENTAL MATTERS: Buyer is advised that the presence of wetlands, toxic substances, including asbestos and wastes or other environmental hazards, or the presence of a threatened or endangered species or its habitat may affect Buyer's intended use of the Property. If Buyer is concerned about these matters, an addendum promulgated by TREC or required by the parties should be used.

H. RESIDENTIAL SERVICE CONTRACTS: Buyer may purchase a residential service contract from a residential service company licensed by TREC. If Buyer purchases a residential service contract, Seller shall reimburse Buyer at closing for the cost of the residential service contract in an amount not exceeding $ n/a . Buyer should review any residential service contract for the scope of coverage, exclusions and limitations. **The purchase of a residential service contract is optional. Similar coverage may be purchased from various companies authorized to do business in Texas.**

8. **BROKERS' FEES:** All obligations of the parties for payment of brokers' fees are contained in separate written agreements.

9. **CLOSING:**

A. The closing of the sale will be on or before December 4, 20 08, or within 7 days after objections made under Paragraph 6D have been cured or waived, whichever date is later (Closing Date). If either party fails to close the sale by the Closing Date, the non-defaulting party may exercise the remedies contained in Paragraph 15.

B. At closing:

(1) Seller shall execute and deliver a general warranty deed conveying title to the Property to Buyer and showing no additional exceptions to those permitted in Paragraph 6 and furnish tax statements or certificates showing no delinquent taxes on the Property.

(2) Buyer shall pay the Sales Price in good funds acceptable to the escrow agent.

(3) Seller and Buyer shall execute and deliver any notices, statements, certificates, affidavits, releases, loan documents and other documents required of them by this contract, the Commitment or law necessary for the closing of the sale and the issuance of the Title Policy.

C. Unless expressly prohibited by written agreement, Seller may continue to show the Property and receive, negotiate and accept back up offers.

D. All covenants, representations and warranties in this contract survive closing.

10. **POSSESSION:** Seller shall deliver to Buyer possession of the Property in its present or required condition, ordinary wear and tear excepted: ☒ upon closing and funding ☐ according to a temporary residential lease form promulgated by TREC or other written lease required by the parties. Any possession by Buyer prior to closing or by Seller after closing which is not authorized by a written lease will establish a tenancy at sufferance relationship between the parties. **Consult your insurance agent prior to change of ownership and possession because insurance coverage may be limited or terminated. The absence of a written lease or appropriate insurance coverage may expose the parties to economic loss.**

11. **SPECIAL PROVISIONS:** (Insert only factual statements and business details applicable to the sale. TREC rules prohibit licensees from adding factual statements or business details for which a contract addendum, lease or other form has been promulgated by TREC for mandatory use.) none

Initialed for identification by Buyer_____ _____ and Seller _____ _____ TREC NO. 20-7

FIGURE 11.1 (CONTINUED)

TREC 20-7

12. SETTLEMENT AND OTHER EXPENSES:

A. The following expenses must be paid at or prior to closing:

(1) Expenses payable by Seller (Seller's Expenses):

(a) Releases of existing liens, including prepayment penalties and recording fees; release of Seller's loan liability; tax statements or certificates; preparation of deed; one-half of escrow fee; and other expenses payable by Seller under this contract.

(b) Seller shall also pay an amount not to exceed $ none to be applied in the following order: Buyer's Expenses which Buyer is prohibited from paying by FHA, VA, Texas Veterans Housing Assistance Program or other governmental loan programs, and then to other Buyer's Expenses as allowed by the lender.

(2) Expenses payable by Buyer (Buyer's Expenses):

(a) Loan origination, discount, buy-down, and commitment fees (Loan Fees).

(b) Appraisal fees; loan application fees; credit reports; preparation of loan documents; interest on the notes from date of disbursement to one month prior to dates of first monthly payments; recording fees; copies of easements and restrictions; mortgagee title policy with endorsements required by lender; loan-related inspection fees; photos; amortization schedules; one-half of escrow fee; all prepaid items, including required premiums for flood and hazard insurance, reserve deposits for insurance, ad valorem taxes and special governmental assessments; final compliance inspection; courier fee; repair inspection; underwriting fee; wire transfer fee; expenses incident to any loan; and other expenses payable by Buyer under this contract.

B. Buyer shall pay Private Mortgage Insurance Premium (PMI), VA Loan Funding Fee, or FHA Mortgage Insurance Premium (MIP) as required by the lender.

C. If any expense exceeds an amount expressly stated in this contract for such expense to be paid by a party, that party may terminate this contract unless the other party agrees to pay such excess. Buyer may not pay charges and fees expressly prohibited by FHA, VA, Texas Veterans Housing Assistance Program or other governmental loan program regulations.

13. PRORATIONS: Taxes for the current year, interest, maintenance fees, assessments, dues and rents will be prorated through the Closing Date. The tax proration may be calculated taking into consideration any change in exemptions that will affect the current year's taxes. If taxes for the current year vary from the amount prorated at closing, the parties shall adjust the prorations when tax statements for the current year are available. If taxes are not paid at or prior to closing, Buyer shall pay taxes for the current year.

14. CASUALTY LOSS: If any part of the Property is damaged or destroyed by fire or other casualty after the effective date of this contract, Seller shall restore the Property to its previous condition as soon as reasonably possible, but in any event by the Closing Date. If Seller fails to do so due to factors beyond Seller's control, Buyer may (a) terminate this contract and the earnest money will be refunded to Buyer (b) extend the time for performance up to 15 days and the Closing Date will be extended as necessary or (c) accept the Property in its damaged condition with an assignment of insurance proceeds and receive credit from Seller at closing in the amount of the deductible under the insurance policy. Seller's obligations under this paragraph are independent of any other obligations of Seller under this contract.

15. DEFAULT: If Buyer fails to comply with this contract, Buyer will be in default, and Seller may (a) enforce specific performance, seek such other relief as may be provided by law, or both, or (b) terminate this contract and receive the earnest money as liquidated damages, thereby releasing both parties from this contract. If, due to factors beyond Seller's control, Seller fails within the time allowed to make any non-casualty repairs or deliver the Commitment, or survey, if required of Seller, Buyer may (a) extend the time for performance up to 15 days and the Closing Date will be extended as necessary or (b) terminate this contract as the sole remedy and receive the earnest money. If Seller fails to comply with this contract for any other reason, Seller will be in default and Buyer may (a) enforce specific performance, seek such other relief as may be provided by law, or both, or (b) terminate this contract and receive the earnest money, thereby releasing both parties from this contract.

16. MEDIATION: It is the policy of the State of Texas to encourage resolution of disputes through alternative dispute resolution procedures such as mediation. Any dispute between Seller and Buyer related to this contract which is not resolved through informal discussion ☐will ☒will not be submitted to a mutually acceptable mediation service or provider. The parties to the mediation shall bear the mediation costs equally. This paragraph does not preclude a party from seeking equitable relief from a court of competent jurisdiction.

17. ATTORNEY'S FEES: The prevailing party in any legal proceeding related to this contract is entitled to recover reasonable attorney's fees and all costs of such proceeding incurred by the prevailing party.

FIGURE 11.1 (CONTINUED)

TREC 20-7

Contract Concerning 2615 Pleasure Point Drive, Houston, TX 77084 Page 6 of 8 02-13-06
(Address of Property)

18. ESCROW:

A. ESCROW: The escrow agent is not (i) a party to this contract and does not have liability for the performance or nonperformance of any party to this contract, (ii) liable for interest on the earnest money and (iii) liable for the loss of any earnest money caused by the failure of any financial institution in which the earnest money has been deposited unless the financial institution is acting as escrow agent.

B. EXPENSES: At closing, the earnest money must be applied first to any cash down payment, then to Buyer's Expenses and any excess refunded to Buyer. If no closing occurs, escrow agent may require payment of unpaid expenses incurred on behalf of the parties and a written release of liability of escrow agent from all parties.

C. DEMAND: Upon termination of this contract, either party or the escrow agent may send a release of earnest money to each party and the parties shall execute counterparts of the release and deliver same to the escrow agent. If either party fails to execute the release, either party may make a written demand to the escrow agent for the earnest money. If only one party makes written demand for the earnest money, escrow agent shall promptly provide a copy of the demand to the other party. If escrow agent does not receive written objection to the demand from the other party within 15 days, escrow agent may disburse the earnest money to the party making demand reduced by the amount of unpaid expenses incurred on behalf of the party receiving the earnest money and escrow agent may pay the same to the creditors. If escrow agent complies with the provisions of this paragraph, each party hereby releases escrow agent from all adverse claims related to the disbursal of the earnest money.

D. DAMAGES: Any party who wrongfully fails or refuses to sign a release acceptable to the escrow agent within 7 days of receipt of the request will be liable to the other party for liquidated damages of three times the amount of the earnest money.

E. NOTICES: Escrow agent's notices will be effective when sent in compliance with Paragraph 21. Notice of objection to the demand will be deemed effective upon receipt by escrow agent.

19. REPRESENTATIONS: Seller represents that as of the Closing Date (a) there will be no liens, assessments, or security interests against the Property which will not be satisfied out of the sales proceeds unless securing payment of any loans assumed by Buyer and (b) assumed loans will not be in default. If any representation of Seller in this contract is untrue on the Closing Date, Seller will be in default.

20. FEDERAL TAX REQUIREMENTS: If Seller is a "foreign person," as defined by applicable law, or if Seller fails to deliver an affidavit to Buyer that Seller is not a "foreign person," then Buyer shall withhold from the sales proceeds an amount sufficient to comply with applicable tax law and deliver the same to the Internal Revenue Service together with appropriate tax forms. Internal Revenue Service regulations require filing written reports if currency in excess of specified amounts is received in the transaction.

21. NOTICES: All notices from one party to the other must be in writing and are effective when mailed to, hand-delivered at, or transmitted by facsimile or electronic transmission as follows:

To Buyer at:	**To Seller at:**
[illegible] Bear Creek Drive	2615 Pleasure Point
Houston TX 77[illegible]	Houston TX 77084
n/a	n/a
n/a	n/a
Telephone: (123) 456-7890	Telephone: (123) 345-[illegible]
Facsimile: (123) 445-6789	Facsimile: (123) 234-[illegible]
E-mail: [illegible]	E-mail: [illegible]@sellers.com

Initialed for identification by Buyer______ ______ and Seller ______ ______ TREC NO. 20-7

FIGURE 11.1 (CONTINUED)

TREC 20-7

Contract Concerning 2614 Pleasure Point Drive, Houston, TX 77084 (Address of Property) Page 7 of 8 02-13-06

22. AGREEMENT OF PARTIES: This contract contains the entire agreement of the parties and cannot be changed except by their written agreement. Addenda which are a part of this contract are (Check all applicable boxes):

- ☒ Third Party Financing Condition Addendum
- ☐ Seller Financing Addendum
- ☐ Loan Assumption Addendum
- ☐ Buyer's Temporary Residential Lease
- ☐ Seller's Temporary Residential Lease
- ☐ Addendum for Sale of Other Property by Buyer
- ☐ Addendum for Seller's Disclosure of Information on Lead-based Paint and Lead-based Paint Hazards as Required by Federal Law
- ☒ Addendum for Property Subject to Mandatory Membership in an Owners' Association
- ☒ Environmental Assessment, Threatened or Endangered Species and Wetlands Addendum
- ☐ Addendum for "Back-Up" Contract
- ☐ Addendum for Coastal Area Property
- ☐ Addendum for Property Located Seaward of the Gulf Intracoastal Waterway
- ☐ Addendum for Release of Liability on Assumption of FHA, VA, or Conventional Loan Restoration of Seller's Entitlement for VA Guaranteed Loan
- ☐ Other (list): n/a

23. TERMINATION OPTION: For nominal consideration, the receipt of which is hereby acknowledged by Seller, and Buyer's agreement to pay Seller $ 300 (Option Fee) within 2 days after the effective date of this contract, Seller grants Buyer the unrestricted right to terminate this contract by giving notice of termination to Seller within 7 days after the effective date of this contract. If no dollar amount is stated as the Option Fee or if Buyer fails to pay the Option Fee within the time prescribed, this paragraph will not be a part of this contract and Buyer shall not have the unrestricted right to terminate this contract. If Buyer gives notice of termination within the time prescribed, the Option Fee will not be refunded; however, any earnest money will be refunded to Buyer. The Option Fee ☒will ☐will not be credited to the Sales Price at closing. **Time is of the essence for this paragraph and strict compliance with the time for performance is required.**

24. CONSULT AN ATTORNEY: Real estate licensees cannot give legal advice. READ THIS CONTRACT CAREFULLY. If you do not understand the effect of this contract, consult an attorney BEFORE signing.

Buyer's	Seller's
Attorney is: none chosen at this time	Attorney is: none chosen at this time
Telephone: ( ) n/a	Telephone: ( ) n/a
Facsimile: ( ) n/a	Facsimile: ( ) n/a
E-mail: n/a	E-mail: n/a

EXECUTED the 4 day of November, 20 08 (EFFECTIVE DATE). (BROKER: FILL IN THE DATE OF FINAL ACCEPTANCE.)

John Paul Gordon	Isabelle Gertrude [illegible]
Buyer	Seller
Mary Anne Gordon	n/a
Buyer	Seller

The form of this contract has been approved by the Texas Real Estate Commission. TREC forms are intended for use only by trained real estate licensees. No representation is made as to the legal validity or adequacy of any provision in any specific transactions. It is not intended for complex transactions. Texas Real Estate Commission, P.O. Box 12188, Austin, TX 78711-2188, 1-800-250-8732 or (512) 459-6544 (http://www.trec.state.tx.us) TREC NO. 20-7. This form replaces TREC NO. 20-6.

TREC NO. 20-7

FIGURE 11.1 (CONTINUED)

TREC 20-7

Contract Concerning ______________________________ Page 8 of 8 02-13-06
(Address of Property)

BROKER INFORMATION AND RATIFICATION OF FEE

Listing Broker has agreed to pay Other Broker ______________ of the total sales price when Listing Broker's fee is received. Escrow Agent is authorized and directed to pay Other Broker from Listing Broker's fee at closing.

____
Other Broker License No.

represents
☒ Buyer only as Buyer's agent
☐ Seller as Listing Broker's subagent

____
Associate Telephone

____
Broker's Address

____
City State Zip

____
Facsimile

____
Email Address

____
Listing Broker License No.

represents
☐ Seller and Buyer as an intermediary
☒ Seller only as Seller's agent

____
Listing Associate Telephone

____
Listing Associate's Office Address Facsimile

____
City State Zip

____
Email Address

____
Selling Associate Telephone

____
Selling Associate's Office Address Facsimile

____
City State Zip

____
Email Address

OPTION FEE RECEIPT

Receipt of $__________ (Option Fee) in the form of __________ is acknowledged.

____
Seller or Listing Broker

____
Date

CONTRACT AND EARNEST MONEY RECEIPT

Receipt of ☒Contract and ☐$__________ Earnest Money in the form of __________ is acknowledged.

Escrow Agent: ______________________ Date: ______________

By: ______________________

____
Email Address

____
Address

Telephone (____) ____________

____
City State Zip

Facsimile: (____) ____________

TREC NO. 20-7

FIGURE 11.2

TREC 40-3

12-10-07

EQUAL HOUSING OPPORTUNITY

PROMULGATED BY THE TEXAS REAL ESTATE COMMISSION (TREC)

THIRD PARTY FINANCING CONDITION ADDENDUM

TO CONTRACT CONCERNING THE PROPERTY AT

→ 2615 Pleasure Point Drive Houston, TX

(Street Address and City)

Buyer shall apply promptly for all financing described below and make every reasonable effort to obtain approval for the financing (Financing Approval). Buyer shall furnish all information and documents required by lender for Financing Approval. Financing Approval will be deemed to have been obtained when (1) the terms of the loan(s) described below are available and (2) lender determines that Buyer has satisfied all of lender's financial requirements (those items relating to Buyer's assets, income and credit history). If Buyer cannot obtain Financing Approval, Buyer may give written notice to Seller within 25 days after the effective date of this contract and this contract will terminate and the earnest money will be refunded to Buyer. **If Buyer does not give such notice within the time required, this contract will no longer be subject to Financing Approval. Time is of the essence for this paragraph and strict compliance with the time for performance is required.**

NOTE: Financing Approval does not include approval of lender's underwriting requirements for the Property, as specified in Paragraph 4.A.(1) of the contract.

Each note must be secured by vendor's and deed of trust liens.

CHECK APPLICABLE BOXES:

→ ☒ A. CONVENTIONAL FINANCING:

☒ (1) A first mortgage loan in the principal amount of $ 76,800 (excluding any financed PMI premium), due in full in 15 year(s), with interest not to exceed 6 % per annum for the first 15 year(s) of the loan with Loan Fees (loan origination, discount, buy-down, and commitment fees) not to exceed 1 % of the loan.

☐ (2) A second mortgage loan in the principal amount of $ n/a (excluding any financed PMI premium), due in full in n/a year(s), with interest not to exceed n/a % per annum for the first n/a year(s) of the loan with Loan Fees (loan origination, discount, buy-down, and commitment fees) not to exceed n/a % of the loan.

☐ B. TEXAS VETERANS LOAN: A loan(s) from the Texas Veterans Land Board of $ n/a for a period in the total amount of n/a years at the interest rate established by the Texas Veterans Land Board.

☐ C. FHA INSURED FINANCING: A Section n/a FHA insured loan of not less than $ n/a (excluding any financed MIP), amortizable monthly for not less than n/a years, with interest not to exceed n/a % per annum for the first n/a year(s) of the loan with Loan Fees (loan origination, discount, buy-down, and commitment fees) not to exceed n/a % of the loan. As required by HUD-FHA, if FHA valuation is unknown, *"It is expressly agreed that, notwithstanding any other provision of this contract, the purchaser (Buyer) shall not be obligated to complete the purchase of the Property described herein or to incur any penalty by forfeiture of earnest money deposits or otherwise unless the purchaser (Buyer) has been given in accordance with HUD/FHA or VA requirements a written statement issued by the Federal Housing Commissioner, Department of Veterans Affairs, or a Direct Endorsement Lender setting forth the appraised value of the Property of not less than $* n/a*. The purchaser (Buyer) shall have the privilege and option of proceeding with consummation of the contract without regard to the amount of the*

Initialed for identification by Buyer____ ____ and Seller____ ____ TREC NO. 40-3

FIGURE 11.2 (CONTINUED)

TREC 40-3

→

Third Party Financing Condition Addendum Concerning Page 2 of 2 12-10-07

2615 Pleasure Point Drive Houston, TX

(Address of Property)

appraised valuation. The appraised valuation is arrived at to determine the maximum mortgage the Department of Housing and Urban Development will insure. HUD does not warrant the value or the condition of the Property. The purchaser (Buyer) should satisfy himself/herself that the price and the condition of the Property are acceptable."
NOTE: HUD 92564-CN "For Your Protection: Get a Home Inspection" must be attached to this Addendum.

❑ D. VA GUARANTEED FINANCING: A VA guaranteed loan of not less than $ n/a (excluding any financed Funding Fee), amortizable monthly for not less than n/a years, with interest not to exceed n/a % per annum for the first n/a year(s) of the loan with Loan Fees (loan origination, discount, buy-down, and commitment fees) not to exceed n/a % of the loan.

VA NOTICE TO BUYER: "*It is expressly agreed that, notwithstanding any other provisions of this contract, the Buyer shall not incur any penalty by forfeiture of earnest money or otherwise or be obligated to complete the purchase of the Property described herein, if the contract purchase price or cost exceeds the reasonable value of the Property established by the Department of Veterans Affairs. The Buyer shall, however, have the privilege and option of proceeding with the consummation of this contract without regard to the amount of the reasonable value established by the Department of Veterans Affairs."*

If Buyer elects to complete the purchase at an amount in excess of the reasonable value established by VA, Buyer shall pay such excess amount in cash from a source which Buyer agrees to disclose to the VA and which Buyer represents will not be from borrowed funds except as approved by VA. If VA reasonable value of the Property is less than the Sales Price, Seller may reduce the Sales Price to an amount equal to the VA reasonable value and the sale will be closed at the lower Sales Price with proportionate adjustments to the down payment and the loan amount.

Buyer hereby authorizes any lender to furnish to the Seller or Buyer or their representatives information relating only to the status of Financing Approval of Buyer.

John Paul Gordon	Isabelle Gertrude Bernard
Buyer	Seller
Mary Lane Gordon	n/a
Buyer	Seller

FIGURE 11.3

TREC 36-4

PROMULGATED BY THE TEXAS REAL ESTATE COMMISSION (TREC) 02-13-06

EQUAL HOUSING OPPORTUNITY

ADDENDUM FOR PROPERTY SUBJECT TO MANDATORY MEMBERSHIP IN AN OWNERS' ASSOCIATION

(NOT FOR USE WITH CONDOMINIUMS)

ADDENDUM TO CONTRACT CONCERNING THE PROPERTY AT

→ 2615 Pleasure Point Drive Houston, TX

(Street Address and City)

→ Windswept Homeowners' Association

(Name of Owners' Association)

A. SUBDIVISON INFORMATION: "Subdivision Information" means: (i) the restrictions applying to the subdivision, (ii) the bylaws and rules of the Owners' Association, and (iii) a resale certificate, all of which were provided by the Owners' Association in compliance with Section 207.003 of the Texas Property Code.

(Check only one box):

☐ 1. Within n/a days after the effective date of the contract, Seller shall at Seller's expense deliver the Subdivision Information to Buyer. If Buyer does not receive the Subdivision Information, Buyer may terminate the contract at any time prior to closing and the earnest money will be refunded to Buyer. If Seller delivers the Subdivision Information, Buyer may terminate the contract for any reason within 7 days after Buyer receives the Subdivision Information or prior to closing, whichever first occurs, and the earnest money will be refunded to Buyer.

→ ☒ 2. Buyer has received and approved the Subdivision Information before signing the contract.

☐ 3. Buyer does not require delivery of the Subdivision Information.

If Seller becomes aware of any material changes in the Subdivision Information, Seller shall immediately give notice to Buyer. Buyer may terminate the contract prior to closing by giving written notice to Seller if: (i) any of the Subdivision Information provided was not true; or (ii) any material adverse change in the Subdivision Information occurs prior to closing, and the earnest money will be refunded to Buyer.

→ **B. FEES:** Buyer shall pay any Owners' Association fees resulting from the transfer of the Property not to exceed $ 50 and Seller shall pay any excess.

NOTICE TO BUYER REGARDING REPAIRS BY THE OWNERS' ASSOCIATION: The Owners' Association may have the sole responsibility to make certain repairs to the Property. If you are concerned about the condition of any part of the Property which the Owners' Association is required to repair, you should not sign the contract unless you are satisfied that the Owners' Association will make the desired repairs.

John Paul Gordon	Isabelle [illegible]
Buyer	Seller
Mary Anne Gordon	n/a
Buyer	Seller

The form of this addendum has been approved by the Texas Real Estate Commission for use only with similarly approved or promulgated forms of contracts. Such approval relates to this contract form only. TREC forms are intended for use only by trained real estate licensees. No representation is made as to the legal validity or adequacy of any provision in any specific transactions. It is not intended for complex transactions. Texas Real Estate Commission, P.O. Box 12188, Austin, TX 78711-2188, 1-800-250-8732 or (512) 459-6544 (http://www.trec.state.tx.us) TREC No. 36-4. This form replaces TREC No. 36-3.

TREC NO. 36-4

FIGURE 11.4

TREC 28-1

PROMULGATED BY THE TEXAS REAL ESTATE COMMISSION (TREC) 04-23-07

EQUAL HOUSING OPPORTUNITY

ENVIRONMENTAL ASSESSMENT, THREATENED OR ENDANGERED SPECIES, AND WETLANDS ADDENDUM

TO CONTRACT CONCERNING THE PROPERTY AT

→ 2615 Pleasure Point Drive Houston, TX
(Address of Property)

→ ☒ A. ENVIRONMENTAL ASSESSMENT: Buyer, at Buyer's expense, may obtain an environmental assessment report prepared by an environmental specialist.

☐ B. THREATENED OR ENDANGERED SPECIES: Buyer, at Buyer's expense, may obtain a report from a natural resources professional to determine if there are any threatened or endangered species or their habitats as defined by the Texas Parks and Wildlife Department or the U.S. Fish and Wildlife Service.

☐ C. WETLANDS: Buyer, at Buyer's expense, may obtain a report from an environmental specialist to determine if there are wetlands, as defined by federal or state law or regulation.

→ Within 20 days after the effective date of the contract, Buyer may terminate the contract by furnishing Seller a copy of any report noted above that adversely affects the use of the Property and a notice of termination of the contract. Upon termination, the earnest money will be refunded to Buyer.

Buyer	Seller
Buyer	Seller

This form has been approved by the Texas Real Estate Commission for use with similarly approved or promulgated contract forms. Such approval relates to this form only. TREC forms are intended for use only by trained real estate licensees. No representation is made as to the legal validity or adequacy of any provision in any specific transactions. It is not suitable for complex transactions. Texas Real Estate Commission, P.O. Box 12188, Austin, TX 78711-2188, 1-800-250-8732 or (512) 459-6544 (http://www.trec.state.tx.us) TREC No. 28-1. This form replaces TREC No. 28-0.

TREC No. 28-1

FIGURE 11.5

TREC 39-6

PROMULGATED BY THE TEXAS REAL ESTATE COMMISSION (TREC) 02-13-06

EQUAL HOUSING OPPORTUNITY

AMENDMENT

TO CONTRACT CONCERNING THE PROPERTY AT

→ 2615 Pleasure Point Drive Houston, TX

(Street Address and City)

Seller and Buyer amend the contract as follows: (check each applicable box)

☐(1) The Sales Price in Paragraph 3 of the contract is:
A. Cash portion of Sales Price payable by Buyer at closing .... $ n/a
B. Sum of financing described in the contract .... $ n/a
C. Sales Price (Sum of A and B) .... $ n/a

☐(2) In addition to any repairs and treatments otherwise required by the contract, Seller, at Seller's expense, shall complete the following repairs and treatments:

☐(3) The date in Paragraph 9 of the contract is changed to n/a, 20 n/a.

☐(4) The amount in Paragraph 12A(1)(b) of the contract is changed to $ n/a.

☐(5) The cost of lender required repairs and treatment, as itemized on the attached list, will be paid as follows: $ n/a by Seller; $ n/a by Buyer.

☐(6) Buyer has paid Seller an additional Option Fee of $ n/a for an extension of the unrestricted right to terminate the contract on or before n/a, 20______. This additional Option Fee ☐ will ☐ will not be credited to the Sales Price.

☐(7) Buyer waives the unrestricted right to terminate the contract for which the Option Fee was paid.

☐(8) The date for Buyer to give written notice to Seller that Buyer cannot obtain Financing Approval as set forth in the Third Party Financing Condition Addendum is changed to n/a, 20 n/a.

→ ☒(9) **Other Modifications:** (Insert only factual statements and business details applicable to this sale.)

Seller will credit Buyer $ 1,400 at closing to replace defective flooring in the kitchen.

EXECUTED the 11 day of November, 20 08. (BROKER: FILL IN THE DATE OF FINAL ACCEPTANCE.)

John Paul Gordon	Isabelle Gertrude Gerhard
Buyer	Seller
Mary Anne Gordon	n/a
Buyer	Seller

This form has been approved by the Texas Real Estate Commission for use with similarly approved or promulgated contract forms. Such approval relates to this form only. TREC forms are intended for use only by trained real estate licensees. No representation is made as to the legal validity or adequacy of any provision in any specific transactions. It is not intended for complex transactions. Texas Real Estate Commission, P.O. Box 12188, Austin, TX 78711-2188, 1-800-250-8732 or (512) 459-6544 (http://www.trec.state.tx.us) TREC No. 39-6. This form replaces TREC No. 39-5.

TREC NO. 39-6

TRANSACTION 2: 90% CONVENTIONAL FIXED-RATE LOAN WITH PMI *(USING: TREC 20-7, 40-3, AND OP-L LEAD-BASED PAINT ADDENDUM SEE FIGURE 11.6 THROUGH FIGURE 11.8.)*

John Charles Wayne and his spouse, Sharon Sidekick Wayne, want to buy the home owned by Thomas A. Smith and his wife, Molly Bea Smith. Although the Property is subject to mandatory membership in an owners' association, the Waynes do not attach the addendum regarding association membership. There are no excluded fixtures at 3510 Mimosa Lane in Bellaire, Harris County, Texas 77404. On the plat of Shadyacres Addition, the Property is identified as Lot 7, Block 7.

The Waynes are willing to pay $180,000 for the Property and will promptly apply for a 90 percent, 30-year fixed-rate loan at 7.5 percent annual interest They anticipate that all lender requirements can be met, approval can be received within 30 days of the effective date of the contract, and that they can close within 40 days. They anticipate that they may have to pay up to one discount point to obtain the desired interest rate, and request that the Seller be liable for one-half of any discount required by the lender. The lender is charging a 1 percent loan origination fee.

To show good faith, they deposit $4,000 earnest money with Protective Title Company and will deposit another $4,000 within 30 days after the effective date of this contract. As previously agreed at the time of listing, the Sellers will pay for the owners' title policy. The Buyers are requesting the Smiths to furnish their existing survey within 3 days after the effective dates and are willing to pay for a new survey if the existing one is not acceptable to the lender. They want 7 days to review the survey and title documents.

Prior to making their offer, the Buyers received the Sellers' disclosure form. Their purchase agreement contains the lead-based paint addendum because the house was built in 1965. They wish to purchase a 10-day option to terminate period and have given the agent a check for $400 to compensate the Sellers for giving the option. The option fee will be credited to the sale price at closing. They plan to have a variety of structural and mechanical evaluations done. They are asking the Seller to provide a residential service contract from Home Warranty Inc. in an amount not to exceed $325.

The Buyers reserve the opportunity to do a walk-through during the 4 hours prior to closing and want to be granted possession at funding, which they anticipate will be at the closing table. The parties have agreed to mediate any dispute they cannot resolve by informal negotiation.

The Buyers are customers who are purchasing the Property at an open house being held by the Sellers' agent, Sarah Listalot, Broker (The TREC #0234567).

With regard to the lead-based paint addendum, Seller has no knowledge of lead-based paint or hazards and the Buyers have no current plans to conduct a risk assessment. The Buyers have been furnished the HUD lead pamphlet.

FIGURE 11.6

TREC 20-7

02-13-06

EQUAL HOUSING OPPORTUNITY

PROMULGATED BY THE TEXAS REAL ESTATE COMMISSION (TREC)

ONE TO FOUR FAMILY RESIDENTIAL CONTRACT (RESALE)

NOTICE: Not For Use For Condominium Transactions

1. PARTIES: Thomas Arnold Smith and wife Molly Bea Smith (Seller) agrees to sell and convey to John Charles Wayne and wife Sharon Sidekick Wayne (Buyer) and Buyer agrees to buy from Seller the Property described below.

2. PROPERTY:

A. LAND: Lot 7 Block 7, Shady Acres Addition, City of Bellaire, County of Harris, Texas, known as 3510 Mimosa Lane 77404 (address/zip code), or as described on attached exhibit.

B. IMPROVEMENTS: The house, garage and all other fixtures and improvements attached to the above-described real property, including without limitation, the following **permanently installed and built-in items,** if any: all equipment and appliances, valances, screens, shutters, awnings, wall-to-wall carpeting, mirrors, ceiling fans, attic fans, mail boxes, television antennas and satellite dish system and equipment, heating and air-conditioning units, security and fire detection equipment, wiring, plumbing and lighting fixtures, chandeliers, water softener system, kitchen equipment, garage door openers, cleaning equipment, shrubbery, landscaping, outdoor cooking equipment, and all other property owned by Seller and attached to the above described real property.

C. ACCESSORIES: The following described related accessories, if any: window air conditioning units, stove, fireplace screens, curtains and rods, blinds, window shades, draperies and rods, controls for satellite dish system, controls for garage door openers, entry gate controls, door keys, mailbox keys, above ground pool, swimming pool equipment and maintenance accessories, and artificial fireplace logs.

D. EXCLUSIONS: The following improvements and accessories will be retained by Seller and removed prior to delivery of possession: none.

The land, improvements and accessories are collectively referred to as the "Property".

3. SALES PRICE:

A. Cash portion of Sales Price payable by Buyer at closing................. $ 18,000

B. Sum of all financing described below (excluding any loan funding fee or mortgage insurance premium)... $ 162,000

C. Sales Price (Sum of A and B).. $ 180,000

4. FINANCING: The portion of Sales Price not payable in cash will be paid as follows: (Check applicable boxes below)

☒ A. THIRD PARTY FINANCING: One or more third party mortgage loans in the total amount of $ 162,000 (excluding any loan funding fee or mortgage insurance premium).

(1) Property Approval: If the Property does not satisfy the lenders' underwriting requirements for the loan(s), this contract will terminate and the earnest money will be refunded to Buyer.

(2) Financing Approval: (Check one box only)

☒ (a) This contract is subject to Buyer being approved for the financing described in the attached Third Party Financing Condition Addendum.

☐ (b) This contract is not subject to Buyer being approved for financing and does not involve FHA or VA financing.

☐ B. ASSUMPTION: The assumption of the unpaid principal balance of one or more promissory notes described in the attached TREC Loan Assumption Addendum.

☐ C. SELLER FINANCING: A promissory note from Buyer to Seller of $ n/a, secured by vendor's and deed of trust liens, and containing the terms and conditions described in the attached TREC Seller Financing Addendum. If an owner policy of title insurance is furnished, Buyer shall furnish Seller with a mortgagee policy of title insurance.

5. EARNEST MONEY: Upon execution of this contract by both parties, Buyer shall deposit $ 4,000 as earnest money with Protective Title Company, as escrow agent, at 123 Title Street, Bellaire, TX 77404 (address). Buyer shall deposit additional earnest money of $ 4000 with escrow agent within 30 days after the effective date of this contract. If Buyer fails to deposit the earnest money as required by this contract, Buyer will be in default.

6. TITLE POLICY AND SURVEY:

A. TITLE POLICY: Seller shall furnish to Buyer at ☒ Seller's ☐ Buyer's expense an owner policy of title insurance (Title Policy) issued by Protective Title Company (Title Company) in the amount of the Sales Price, dated at or after closing, insuring Buyer

Initialed for identification by Buyer______ ______ and Seller _______ ______ TREC NO. 20-7

FIGURE 11.6 (CONTINUED)

TREC 20-7

Contract Concerning 3510 Mimosa Lane, Bellaire, TX 77404 Page 2 of 8 02-13-06
(Address of Property)

against loss under the provisions of the Title Policy, subject to the promulgated exclusions (including existing building and zoning ordinances) and the following exceptions:

(1) Restrictive covenants common to the platted subdivision in which the Property is located.
(2) The standard printed exception for standby fees, taxes and assessments.
(3) Liens created as part of the financing described in Paragraph 4.
(4) Utility easements created by the dedication deed or plat of the subdivision in which the Property is located.
(5) Reservations or exceptions otherwise permitted by this contract or as may be approved by Buyer in writing.
(6) The standard printed exception as to marital rights.
(7) The standard printed exception as to waters, tidelands, beaches, streams, and related matters.
(8) The standard printed exception as to discrepancies, conflicts, shortages in area or boundary lines, encroachments or protrusions, or overlapping improvements. Buyer, at Buyer's expense, may have the exception amended to read, "shortages in area".

B. COMMITMENT: Within 20 days after the Title Company receives a copy of this contract, Seller shall furnish to Buyer a commitment for title insurance (Commitment) and, at Buyer's expense, legible copies of restrictive covenants and documents evidencing exceptions in the Commitment (Exception Documents) other than the standard printed exceptions. Seller authorizes the Title Company to deliver the Commitment and Exception Documents to Buyer at Buyer's address shown in Paragraph 21. If the Commitment and Exception Documents are not delivered to Buyer within the specified time, the time for delivery will be automatically extended up to 15 days or the Closing Date, whichever is earlier.

C. SURVEY: The survey must be made by a registered professional land surveyor acceptable to the Title Company and any lender. (Check one box only)

☒ (1) Within 3 days after the effective date of this contract, Seller shall furnish to Buyer and Title Company Seller's existing survey of the Property and a Residential Real Property Affidavit promulgated by the Texas Department of Insurance (Affidavit). If the existing survey or Affidavit is not acceptable to Title Company or Buyer's lender, Buyer shall obtain a new survey at ☐ Seller's ☒ Buyer's expense no later than 3 days prior to Closing Date. If Seller fails to furnish the existing survey or Affidavit within the time prescribed, Buyer shall obtain a new survey at Seller's expense no later than 3 days prior to Closing Date.

☐ (2) Within n/a days after the effective date of this contract, Buyer shall obtain a new survey at Buyer's expense. Buyer is deemed to receive the survey on the date of actual receipt or the date specified in this paragraph, whichever is earlier.

☐ (3) Within n/a days after the effective date of this contract, Seller, at Seller's expense shall furnish a new survey to Buyer.

D. OBJECTIONS: Buyer may object in writing to defects, exceptions, or encumbrances to title: disclosed on the survey other than items 6A(1) through (7) above; disclosed in the Commitment other than items 6A(1) through (8) above; or which prohibit the following use or activity: n/a
____.

Buyer must object not later than (i) the Closing Date or (ii) 7 days after Buyer receives the Commitment, Exception Documents, and the survey, whichever is earlier. Buyer's failure to object within the time allowed will constitute a waiver of Buyer's right to object; except that the requirements in Schedule C of the Commitment are not waived. Provided Seller is not obligated to incur any expense, Seller shall cure the timely objections of Buyer or any third party lender within 15 days after Seller receives the objections and the Closing Date will be extended as necessary. If objections are not cured within such 15 day period, this contract will terminate and the earnest money will be refunded to Buyer unless Buyer waives the objections.

E. TITLE NOTICES:

(1) ABSTRACT OR TITLE POLICY: Broker advises Buyer to have an abstract of title covering the Property examined by an attorney of Buyer's selection, or Buyer should be furnished with or obtain a Title Policy. If a Title Policy is furnished, the Commitment should be promptly reviewed by an attorney of Buyer's choice due to the time limitations on Buyer's right to object.

(2) MANDATORY OWNERS' ASSOCIATION MEMBERSHIP: The Property ☒ is ☐ is not subject to mandatory membership in an owners' association. If the Property is subject to mandatory membership in an owners' association, Seller notifies Buyer under §5.012, Texas Property Code, that, as a purchaser of property in the residential community in which the Property is located, you are obligated to be a member of the owners' association. Restrictive covenants governing the use and occupancy of the Property and a dedicatory instrument governing the establishment, maintenance, and operation of this residential community have been or will be recorded in the Real Property Records of the county in which the Property is located. Copies of the restrictive covenants and dedicatory instrument may be obtained from the county clerk. You are obligated to pay

Initialed for identification by Buyer_____ _____ and Seller _____ _____ TREC NO. 20-7

FIGURE 11.6 (CONTINUED)

TREC 20-7

Contract Concerning 3510 Mimosa Lane, Bellaire, TX 77404 Page 3 of 8 02-13-06
(Address of Property)

assessments to the owners' association. The amount of the assessments is subject to change. Your failure to pay the assessments could result in a lien on and the foreclosure of the Property. If Buyer is concerned about these matters, the TREC promulgated Addendum for Property Subject to Mandatory Membership in an Owner's Association should be used.

(3) STATUTORY TAX DISTRICTS: If the Property is situated in a utility or other statutorily created district providing water, sewer, drainage, or flood control facilities and services, Chapter 49, Texas Water Code, requires Seller to deliver and Buyer to sign the statutory notice relating to the tax rate, bonded indebtedness, or standby fee of the district prior to final execution of this contract.

(4) TIDE WATERS: If the Property abuts the tidally influenced waters of the state, §33.135, Texas Natural Resources Code, requires a notice regarding coastal area property to be included in the contract. An addendum containing the notice promulgated by TREC or required by the parties must be used.

(5) ANNEXATION: If the Property is located outside the limits of a municipality, Seller notifies Buyer under §5.011, Texas Property Code, that the Property may now or later be included in the extraterritorial jurisdiction of a municipality and may now or later be subject to annexation by the municipality. Each municipality maintains a map that depicts its boundaries and extraterritorial jurisdiction. To determine if the Property is located within a municipality's extraterritorial jurisdiction or is likely to be located within a municipality's extraterritorial jurisdiction, contact all municipalities located in the general proximity of the Property for further information.

(6) PROPERTY LOCATED IN A CERTIFICATED SERVICE AREA OF A UTILITY SERVICE PROVIDER: Notice required by §13.257, Water Code: The real property, described in Paragraph 2, that you are about to purchase may be located in a certificated water or sewer service area, which is authorized by law to provide water or sewer service to the properties in the certificated area. If your property is located in a certificated area there may be special costs or charges that you will be required to pay before you can receive water or sewer service. There may be a period required to construct lines or other facilities necessary to provide water or sewer service to your property. You are advised to determine if the property is in a certificated area and contact the utility service provider to determine the cost that you will be required to pay and the period, if any, that is required to provide water or sewer service to your property. The undersigned Buyer hereby acknowledges receipt of the foregoing notice at or before the execution of a binding contract for the purchase of the real property described in Paragraph 2 or at closing of purchase of the real property.

(7) PUBLIC IMPROVEMENT DISTRICTS: If the Property is in a public improvement district, §5.014, Property Code, requires Seller to notify Buyer as follows: As a purchaser of this parcel of real property you are obligated to pay an assessment to a municipality or county for an improvement project undertaken by a public improvement district under Chapter 372, Local Government Code. The assessment may be due annually or in periodic installments. More information concerning the amount of the assessment and the due dates of that assessment may be obtained from the municipality or county levying the assessment. The amount of the assessments is subject to change. Your failure to pay the assessments could result in a lien on and the foreclosure of your property.

7. PROPERTY CONDITION:

A. ACCESS,INSPECTIONS AND UTILITIES: Seller shall permit Buyer and Buyer's agents access to the Property at reasonable times. Buyer may have the Property inspected by inspectors selected by Buyer and licensed by TREC or otherwise permitted by law to make inspections. Seller at Seller's expense shall turn on existing utilities for inspections.

B. SELLER'S DISCLOSURE NOTICE PURSUANT TO §5.008, TEXAS PROPERTY CODE (Notice): (Check one box only)

☒ (1) Buyer has received the Notice.

☐ (2) Buyer has not received the Notice. Within n/a days after the effective date of this contract, Seller shall deliver the Notice to Buyer. If Buyer does not receive the Notice, Buyer may terminate this contract at any time prior to the closing and the earnest money will be refunded to Buyer. If Seller delivers the Notice, Buyer may terminate this contract for any reason within 7 days after Buyer receives the Notice or prior to the closing, whichever first occurs, and the earnest money will be refunded to Buyer.

☐ (3) The Seller is not required to furnish the notice under the Texas Property Code.

C. SELLER'S DISCLOSURE OF LEAD-BASED PAINT AND LEAD-BASED PAINT HAZARDS is required by Federal law for a residential dwelling constructed prior to 1978.

D. ACCEPTANCE OF PROPERTY CONDITION: Buyer accepts the Property in its present condition; provided Seller, at Seller's expense, shall complete the following specific repairs and treatments: none

E. LENDER REQUIRED REPAIRS AND TREATMENTS: Unless otherwise agreed in writing, neither party is obligated to pay for lender required repairs, which includes treatment for wood

Initialed for identification by Buyer_____ _____ and Seller _____ _____ TREC NO. 20-7

FIGURE 11.6 (CONTINUED)

TREC 20-7

Contract Concerning 3510 Mimosa Lane, Bellaire, TX 77404 Page 4 of 8 02-13-06
(Address of Property)

destroying insects. If the parties do not agree to pay for the lender required repairs or treatments, this contract will terminate and the earnest money will be refunded to Buyer. If the cost of lender required repairs and treatments exceeds 5% of the Sales Price, Buyer may terminate this contract and the earnest money will be refunded to Buyer.

F. COMPLETION OF REPAIRS AND TREATMENTS: Unless otherwise agreed in writing, Seller shall complete all agreed repairs and treatments prior to the Closing Date. All required permits must be obtained, and repairs and treatments must be performed by persons who are licensed or otherwise authorized by law to provide such repairs or treatments. At Buyer's election, any transferable warranties received by Seller with respect to the repairs and treatments will be transferred to Buyer at Buyer's expense. If Seller fails to complete any agreed repairs and treatments prior to the Closing Date, Buyer may do so and receive reimbursement from Seller at closing. The Closing Date will be extended up to 15 days, if necessary, to complete repairs and treatments.

G. ENVIRONMENTAL MATTERS: Buyer is advised that the presence of wetlands, toxic substances, including asbestos and wastes or other environmental hazards, or the presence of a threatened or endangered species or its habitat may affect Buyer's intended use of the Property. If Buyer is concerned about these matters, an addendum promulgated by TREC or required by the parties should be used.

H. RESIDENTIAL SERVICE CONTRACTS: Buyer may purchase a residential service contract from a residential service company licensed by TREC. If Buyer purchases a residential service contract, Seller shall reimburse Buyer at closing for the cost of the residential service contract in an amount not exceeding $ 325. Buyer should review any residential service contract for the scope of coverage, exclusions and limitations. **The purchase of a residential service contract is optional. Similar coverage may be purchased from various companies authorized to do business in Texas.**

8. BROKERS' FEES: All obligations of the parties for payment of brokers' fees are contained in separate written agreements.

9. CLOSING:

A. The closing of the sale will be on or before December 16, 20 08, or within 7 days after objections made under Paragraph 6D have been cured or waived, whichever date is later (Closing Date). If either party fails to close the sale by the Closing Date, the non-defaulting party may exercise the remedies contained in Paragraph 15.

B. At closing:

(1) Seller shall execute and deliver a general warranty deed conveying title to the Property to Buyer and showing no additional exceptions to those permitted in Paragraph 6 and furnish tax statements or certificates showing no delinquent taxes on the Property.

(2) Buyer shall pay the Sales Price in good funds acceptable to the escrow agent.

(3) Seller and Buyer shall execute and deliver any notices, statements, certificates, affidavits, releases, loan documents and other documents required of them by this contract, the Commitment or law necessary for the closing of the sale and the issuance of the Title Policy.

C. Unless expressly prohibited by written agreement, Seller may continue to show the Property and receive, negotiate and accept back up offers.

D. All covenants, representations and warranties in this contract survive closing.

10. POSSESSION: Seller shall deliver to Buyer possession of the Property in its present or required condition, ordinary wear and tear excepted: ☒ upon closing and funding ☐ according to a temporary residential lease form promulgated by TREC or other written lease required by the parties. Any possession by Buyer prior to closing or by Seller after closing which is not authorized by a written lease will establish a tenancy at sufferance relationship between the parties. **Consult your insurance agent prior to change of ownership and possession because insurance coverage may be limited or terminated. The absence of a written lease or appropriate insurance coverage may expose the parties to economic loss.**

11. SPECIAL PROVISIONS: (Insert only factual statements and business details applicable to the sale. TREC rules prohibit licensees from adding factual statements or business details for which a contract addendum, lease or other form has been promulgated by TREC for mandatory use.)

Buyers may to a [illegible]

Initialed for identification by Buyer_____ _____ and Seller _____ _____ TREC NO. 20-7

FIGURE 11.6 (CONTINUED)

TREC 20-7

Contract Concerning 3510 Mimosa Lane, Houston, TX 77404 Page 5 of 8 02-13-06
(Address of Property)

12. SETTLEMENT AND OTHER EXPENSES:

A. The following expenses must be paid at or prior to closing:

(1) Expenses payable by Seller (Seller's Expenses):

(a) Releases of existing liens, including prepayment penalties and recording fees; release of Seller's loan liability; tax statements or certificates; preparation of deed; one-half of escrow fee; and other expenses payable by Seller under this contract.

(b) Seller shall also pay an amount not to exceed $ 810 to be applied in the following order: Buyer's Expenses which Buyer is prohibited from paying by FHA, VA, Texas Veterans Housing Assistance Program or other governmental loan programs, and then to other Buyer's Expenses as allowed by the lender.

(2) Expenses payable by Buyer (Buyer's Expenses):

(a) Loan origination, discount, buy-down, and commitment fees (Loan Fees).

(b) Appraisal fees; loan application fees; credit reports; preparation of loan documents; interest on the notes from date of disbursement to one month prior to dates of first monthly payments; recording fees; copies of easements and restrictions; mortgagee title policy with endorsements required by lender; loan-related inspection fees; photos; amortization schedules; one-half of escrow fee; all prepaid items, including required premiums for flood and hazard insurance, reserve deposits for insurance, ad valorem taxes and special governmental assessments; final compliance inspection; courier fee; repair inspection; underwriting fee; wire transfer fee; expenses incident to any loan; and other expenses payable by Buyer under this contract.

B. Buyer shall pay Private Mortgage Insurance Premium (PMI), VA Loan Funding Fee, or FHA Mortgage Insurance Premium (MIP) as required by the lender.

C. If any expense exceeds an amount expressly stated in this contract for such expense to be paid by a party, that party may terminate this contract unless the other party agrees to pay such excess. Buyer may not pay charges and fees expressly prohibited by FHA, VA, Texas Veterans Housing Assistance Program or other governmental loan program regulations.

13. PRORATIONS: Taxes for the current year, interest, maintenance fees, assessments, dues and rents will be prorated through the Closing Date. The tax proration may be calculated taking into consideration any change in exemptions that will affect the current year's taxes. If taxes for the current year vary from the amount prorated at closing, the parties shall adjust the prorations when tax statements for the current year are available. If taxes are not paid at or prior to closing, Buyer shall pay taxes for the current year.

14. CASUALTY LOSS: If any part of the Property is damaged or destroyed by fire or other casualty after the effective date of this contract, Seller shall restore the Property to its previous condition as soon as reasonably possible, but in any event by the Closing Date. If Seller fails to do so due to factors beyond Seller's control, Buyer may (a) terminate this contract and the earnest money will be refunded to Buyer (b) extend the time for performance up to 15 days and the Closing Date will be extended as necessary or (c) accept the Property in its damaged condition with an assignment of insurance proceeds and receive credit from Seller at closing in the amount of the deductible under the insurance policy. Seller's obligations under this paragraph are independent of any other obligations of Seller under this contract.

15. DEFAULT: If Buyer fails to comply with this contract, Buyer will be in default, and Seller may (a) enforce specific performance, seek such other relief as may be provided by law, or both, or (b) terminate this contract and receive the earnest money as liquidated damages, thereby releasing both parties from this contract. If, due to factors beyond Seller's control, Seller fails within the time allowed to make any non-casualty repairs or deliver the Commitment, or survey, if required of Seller, Buyer may (a) extend the time for performance up to 15 days and the Closing Date will be extended as necessary or (b) terminate this contract as the sole remedy and receive the earnest money. If Seller fails to comply with this contract for any other reason, Seller will be in default and Buyer may (a) enforce specific performance, seek such other relief as may be provided by law, or both, or (b) terminate this contract and receive the earnest money, thereby releasing both parties from this contract.

16. MEDIATION: It is the policy of the State of Texas to encourage resolution of disputes through alternative dispute resolution procedures such as mediation. Any dispute between Seller and Buyer related to this contract which is not resolved through informal discussion ☒will ☐will not be submitted to a mutually acceptable mediation service or provider. The parties to the mediation shall bear the mediation costs equally. This paragraph does not preclude a party from seeking equitable relief from a court of competent jurisdiction.

17. ATTORNEY'S FEES: The prevailing party in any legal proceeding related to this contract is entitled to recover reasonable attorney's fees and all costs of such proceeding incurred by the prevailing party.

Initialed for identification by Buyer_____ _____ and Seller _____ _____ TREC NO. 20-7

FIGURE 11.6 (CONTINUED)

TREC 20-7

Contract Concerning 5510 Mimosa Lane, Bellaire, TX 77404 Page 6 of 8 02-13-06
(Address of Property)

18. ESCROW:

A. ESCROW: The escrow agent is not (i) a party to this contract and does not have liability for the performance or nonperformance of any party to this contract, (ii) liable for interest on the earnest money and (iii) liable for the loss of any earnest money caused by the failure of any financial institution in which the earnest money has been deposited unless the financial institution is acting as escrow agent.

B. EXPENSES: At closing, the earnest money must be applied first to any cash down payment, then to Buyer's Expenses and any excess refunded to Buyer. If no closing occurs, escrow agent may require payment of unpaid expenses incurred on behalf of the parties and a written release of liability of escrow agent from all parties.

C. DEMAND: Upon termination of this contract, either party or the escrow agent may send a release of earnest money to each party and the parties shall execute counterparts of the release and deliver same to the escrow agent. If either party fails to execute the release, either party may make a written demand to the escrow agent for the earnest money. If only one party makes written demand for the earnest money, escrow agent shall promptly provide a copy of the demand to the other party. If escrow agent does not receive written objection to the demand from the other party within 15 days, escrow agent may disburse the earnest money to the party making demand reduced by the amount of unpaid expenses incurred on behalf of the party receiving the earnest money and escrow agent may pay the same to the creditors. If escrow agent complies with the provisions of this paragraph, each party hereby releases escrow agent from all adverse claims related to the disbursal of the earnest money.

D. DAMAGES: Any party who wrongfully fails or refuses to sign a release acceptable to the escrow agent within 7 days of receipt of the request will be liable to the other party for liquidated damages of three times the amount of the earnest money.

E. NOTICES: Escrow agent's notices will be effective when sent in compliance with Paragraph 21. Notice of objection to the demand will be deemed effective upon receipt by escrow agent.

19. REPRESENTATIONS: Seller represents that as of the Closing Date (a) there will be no liens, assessments, or security interests against the Property which will not be satisfied out of the sales proceeds unless securing payment of any loans assumed by Buyer and (b) assumed loans will not be in default. If any representation of Seller in this contract is untrue on the Closing Date, Seller will be in default.

20. FEDERAL TAX REQUIREMENTS: If Seller is a "foreign person," as defined by applicable law, or if Seller fails to deliver an affidavit to Buyer that Seller is not a "foreign person," then Buyer shall withhold from the sales proceeds an amount sufficient to comply with applicable tax law and deliver the same to the Internal Revenue Service together with appropriate tax forms. Internal Revenue Service regulations require filing written reports if currency in excess of specified amounts is received in the transaction.

21. NOTICES: All notices from one party to the other must be in writing and are effective when mailed to, hand-delivered at, or transmitted by facsimile or electronic transmission as follows:

To Buyer at:	**To Seller at:**
123 Address Lane	5510 Mimosa Lane
Bellaire, TX 77404	Bellaire, TX 77404
n/a	n/a
n/a	n/a
Telephone: (123) 456-7890	Telephone: (123) 445-6789
Facsimile: (123) 455	Facsimile: (123) 456-7891
E-mail: buyer@buyers.com	E-mail: seller@sellers.com

FIGURE 11.6 (CONTINUED)

TREC 20-7

Contract Concerning 3510 Mimosa Lane, Bellaire TX 77404 Page 7 of 8 02-13-06
(Address of Property)

22. AGREEMENT OF PARTIES: This contract contains the entire agreement of the parties and cannot be changed except by their written agreement. Addenda which are a part of this contract are (Check all applicable boxes):

- ☒ Third Party Financing Condition Addendum
- ☐ Seller Financing Addendum
- ☐ Loan Assumption Addendum
- ☐ Buyer's Temporary Residential Lease
- ☐ Seller's Temporary Residential Lease
- ☐ Addendum for Sale of Other Property by Buyer
- ☒ Addendum for Seller's Disclosure of Information on Lead-based Paint and Lead-based Paint Hazards as Required by Federal Law
- ☐ Addendum for Property Subject to Mandatory Membership in an Owners' Association
- ☐ Environmental Assessment, Threatened or Endangered Species and Wetlands Addendum
- ☐ Addendum for "Back-Up" Contract
- ☐ Addendum for Coastal Area Property
- ☐ Addendum for Property Located Seaward of the Gulf Intracoastal Waterway
- ☐ Addendum for Release of Liability on Assumption of FHA, VA, or Conventional Loan Restoration of Seller's Entitlement for VA Guaranteed Loan
- ☐ Other (list): n/a

23. TERMINATION OPTION: For nominal consideration, the receipt of which is hereby acknowledged by Seller, and Buyer's agreement to pay Seller $400 (Option Fee) within 2 days after the effective date of this contract, Seller grants Buyer the unrestricted right to terminate this contract by giving notice of termination to Seller within 10 days after the effective date of this contract. If no dollar amount is stated as the Option Fee or if Buyer fails to pay the Option Fee within the time prescribed, this paragraph will not be a part of this contract and Buyer shall not have the unrestricted right to terminate this contract. If Buyer gives notice of termination within the time prescribed, the Option Fee will not be refunded; however, any earnest money will be refunded to Buyer. The Option Fee ☒will ☐will not be credited to the Sales Price at closing. **Time is of the essence for this paragraph and strict compliance with the time for performance is required.**

24. CONSULT AN ATTORNEY: Real estate licensees cannot give legal advice. READ THIS CONTRACT CAREFULLY. If you do not understand the effect of this contract, consult an attorney BEFORE signing.

Buyer's	Seller's
Attorney is: none chosen at this time	Attorney is:
Telephone: ( ) n/a	Telephone: ( )
Facsimile: ( ) n/a	Facsimile: ( )
E-mail: n/a	E-mail:

EXECUTED the 06 day of November, 2008 (EFFECTIVE DATE).
(BROKER: FILL IN THE DATE OF FINAL ACCEPTANCE.)

John Charles Wayne	Thomas A. Smith
Buyer	Seller
Sharon Sidekick Wayne	Molly Bea Smith
Buyer	Seller

The form of this contract has been approved by the Texas Real Estate Commission. TREC forms are intended for use only by trained real estate licensees. No representation is made as to the legal validity or adequacy of any provision in any specific transactions. It is not intended for complex transactions. Texas Real Estate Commission, P.O. Box 12188, Austin, TX 78711-2188, 1-800-250-8732 or (512) 459-6544 (http://www.trec.state.tx.us) TREC NO. 20-7. This form replaces TREC NO. 20-6.

FIGURE 11.6 (CONTINUED)

TREC 20-7

Contract Concerning 3510 Mimosa Lane, Bellaire, TX 77404 Page 8 of 8 02-13-06
(Address of Property)

BROKER INFORMATION AND RATIFICATION OF FEE

Listing Broker has agreed to pay Other Broker n/a of the total sales price when Listing Broker's fee is received. Escrow Agent is authorized and directed to pay Other Broker from Listing Broker's fee at closing.

n/a — n/a Other Broker — License No.	Sarah Listalot — 1234567 Listing Broker — License No.
represents ☐ Buyer only as Buyer's agent ☐ Seller as Listing Broker's subagent	represents ☐ Seller and Buyer as an intermediary ☒ Seller only as Seller's agent
n/a Associate — Telephone	n/a Listing Associate — Telephone
n/a Broker's Address	n/a Listing Associate's Office Address — Facsimile
n/a City — State — Zip	n/a City — State — Zip
n/a Facsimile	n/a Email Address
n/a Email Address	n/a Selling Associate — Telephone
	n/a Selling Associate's Office Address — Facsimile
	n/a City — State — Zip
	n/a Email Address

OPTION FEE RECEIPT

Receipt of $ 400 (Option Fee) in the form of personal check #987 is acknowledged.

Sarah Listalot — Seller or Listing Broker

11-08-08 — Date

CONTRACT AND EARNEST MONEY RECEIPT

Receipt of ☒ Contract and ☐ $ 4000 Earnest Money in the form of personal check #... is acknowledged.

Escrow Agent: John Doe Date: 11-08-08

By: Protective Title Company

email@email.com — Email Address

123 Title Street — Address

Telephone (123)

Bellaire — City; TX — State; 77404 — Zip

Facsimile: (123) 222-2222

TREC NO. 20-7

FIGURE 11.7

TREC 40-3

12-10-07

EQUAL HOUSING OPPORTUNITY

PROMULGATED BY THE TEXAS REAL ESTATE COMMISSION (TREC)

THIRD PARTY FINANCING CONDITION ADDENDUM

TO CONTRACT CONCERNING THE PROPERTY AT

→ 3510 Mimosa Lane Bellaire, TX

(Street Address and City)

Buyer shall apply promptly for all financing described below and make every reasonable effort to obtain approval for the financing (Financing Approval). Buyer shall furnish all information and documents required by lender for Financing Approval. Financing Approval will be deemed to have been obtained when (1) the terms of the loan(s) described below are available and (2) lender determines that Buyer has satisfied all of lender's financial requirements (those items relating to Buyer's assets, income and credit history). If Buyer cannot obtain Financing Approval, Buyer may give written notice to Seller within 30 days after the effective date of this contract and this contract will terminate and the earnest money will be refunded to Buyer. **If Buyer does not give such notice within the time required, this contract will no longer be subject to Financing Approval. Time is of the essence for this paragraph and strict compliance with the time for performance is required.**

NOTE: Financing Approval does not include approval of lender's underwriting requirements for the Property, as specified in Paragraph 4.A.(1) of the contract.

Each note must be secured by vendor's and deed of trust liens.

CHECK APPLICABLE BOXES:

→ ☒ A. CONVENTIONAL FINANCING:

☒ (1) A first mortgage loan in the principal amount of $ 162,000 (excluding any financed PMI premium), due in full in 30 year(s), with interest not to exceed 7.5 % per annum for the first 30 year(s) of the loan with Loan Fees (loan origination, discount, buy-down, and commitment fees) not to exceed 2 % of the loan.

☐ (2) A second mortgage loan in the principal amount of $ n/a (excluding any financed PMI premium), due in full in n/a year(s), with interest not to exceed n/a % per annum for the first n/a year(s) of the loan with Loan Fees (loan origination, discount, buy-down, and commitment fees) not to exceed n/a % of the loan.

☐ B. TEXAS VETERANS LOAN: A loan(s) from the Texas Veterans Land Board of $ n/a for a period in the total amount of n/a years at the interest rate established by the Texas Veterans Land Board.

☐ C. FHA INSURED FINANCING: A Section n/a FHA insured loan of not less than $ n/a (excluding any financed MIP), amortizable monthly for not less than n/a years, with interest not to exceed n/a % per annum for the first n/a year(s) of the loan with Loan Fees (loan origination, discount, buy-down, and commitment fees) not to exceed n/a % of the loan. As required by HUD-FHA, if FHA valuation is unknown, *"It is expressly agreed that, notwithstanding any other provision of this contract, the purchaser (Buyer) shall not be obligated to complete the purchase of the Property described herein or to incur any penalty by forfeiture of earnest money deposits or otherwise unless the purchaser (Buyer) has been given in accordance with HUD/FHA or VA requirements a written statement issued by the Federal Housing Commissioner, Department of Veterans Affairs, or a Direct Endorsement Lender setting forth the appraised value of the Property of not less than $ n/a . The purchaser (Buyer) shall have the privilege and option of proceeding with consummation of the contract without regard to the amount of the*

Initialed for identification by Buyer____ _____ and Seller_____ _____ TREC NO. 40-3

FIGURE 11.7 (CONTINUED)

TREC 40-3

Third Party Financing Condition Addendum Concerning — Page 2 of 2 12-10-07

3510 Mimosa Lane Bellaire, TX

(Address of Property)

appraised valuation. The appraised valuation is arrived at to determine the maximum mortgage the Department of Housing and Urban Development will insure. HUD does not warrant the value or the condition of the Property. The purchaser (Buyer) should satisfy himself/herself that the price and the condition of the Property are acceptable."

NOTE: HUD 92564-CN "For Your Protection: Get a Home Inspection" must be attached to this Addendum.

☐ D. VA GUARANTEED FINANCING: A VA guaranteed loan of not less than $__________ (excluding any financed Funding Fee), amortizable monthly for not less than______years, with interest not to exceed______% per annum for the first ______year(s) of the loan with Loan Fees (loan origination, discount, buy-down, and commitment fees) not to exceed ______% of the loan.

VA NOTICE TO BUYER: "*It is expressly agreed that, notwithstanding any other provisions of this contract, the Buyer shall not incur any penalty by forfeiture of earnest money or otherwise or be obligated to complete the purchase of the Property described herein, if the contract purchase price or cost exceeds the reasonable value of the Property established by the Department of Veterans Affairs. The Buyer shall, however, have the privilege and option of proceeding with the consummation of this contract without regard to the amount of the reasonable value established by the Department of Veterans Affairs."*

If Buyer elects to complete the purchase at an amount in excess of the reasonable value established by VA, Buyer shall pay such excess amount in cash from a source which Buyer agrees to disclose to the VA and which Buyer represents will not be from borrowed funds except as approved by VA. If VA reasonable value of the Property is less than the Sales Price, Seller may reduce the Sales Price to an amount equal to the VA reasonable value and the sale will be closed at the lower Sales Price with proportionate adjustments to the down payment and the loan amount.

Buyer hereby authorizes any lender to furnish to the Seller or Buyer or their representatives information relating only to the status of Financing Approval of Buyer.

John Charles Wayne	Thomas A. Smith
Buyer	Seller
Sharon Sidekick Wayne	Betty Bea Smith
Buyer	Seller

This form has been approved by the Texas Real Estate Commission for use with similarly approved or promulgated contract forms. Such approval relates to this form only. TREC forms are intended for use only by trained real estate licensees. No representation is made as to the legal validity or adequacy of any provision in any specific transactions. It is not intended for complex transactions. Texas Real Estate Commission, P.O. Box 12188, Austin, TX 78711-2188, 1-800-250-8732 or (512) 459-6544 (http://www.trec.state.tx.us) TREC No. 40-3. This form replaces TREC No. 40-2.

TREC NO. 40-3

FIGURE 11.8

TREC OP-L

APPROVED BY THE TEXAS REAL ESTATE COMMISSION 02-09-2004

EQUAL HOUSING OPPORTUNITY

ADDENDUM FOR SELLER'S DISCLOSURE OF INFORMATION ON LEAD-BASED PAINT AND LEAD-BASED PAINT HAZARDS AS REQUIRED BY FEDERAL LAW

CONCERNING THE PROPERTY AT 3510 Mimosa Lane Bellaire, TX
(Street Address and City)

A. **LEAD WARNING STATEMENT:** "Every purchaser of any interest in residential real property on which a residential dwelling was built prior to 1978 is notified that such property may present exposure to lead from lead-based paint that may place young children at risk of developing lead poisoning. Lead poisoning in young children may produce permanent neurological damage, including learning disabilities, reduced intelligence quotient, behavioral problems, and impaired memory. Lead poisoning also poses a particular risk to pregnant women. The seller of any interest in residential real property is required to provide the buyer with any information on lead-based paint hazards from risk assessments or inspections in the seller's possession and notify the buyer of any known lead-based paint hazards. A risk assessment or inspection for possible lead-paint hazards is recommended prior to purchase."
NOTICE: Inspector must be properly certified as required by federal law.

B. SELLER'S DISCLOSURE:

1. PRESENCE OF LEAD-BASED PAINT AND/OR LEAD-BASED PAINT HAZARDS (check on box only):
   ☐ (a) Known lead-based paint and/or lead-based paint hazards are present in the Property (explain): n/a
   ☒ (b) Seller has no actual knowledge of lead-based paint and/or lead-based paint hazards in the Property.
2. RECORDS AND REPORTS AVAILABLE TO SELLER (check one box only):
   ☐ (a) Seller has provided the purchaser with all available records and reports pertaining to lead-based paint and/or lead-based paint hazards in the Property (list documents): n/a
   ☐ (b) Seller has no reports or records pertaining to lead-based paint and/or lead-based paint hazards in the Property.

C. BUYER'S RIGHTS (check one box only):

☒ 1. Buyer waives the opportunity to conduct a risk assessment or inspection of the Property for the presence of lead-based paint or lead-based paint hazards.
☒ 2. Within ten days after the effective date of this contract, Buyer may have the Property inspected by inspectors selected by Buyer. If lead-based paint or lead-based paint hazards are present, Buyer may terminate this contract by giving Seller written notice within 14 days after the effective date of this contract, and the earnest money will be refunded to Buyer.

D. BUYER'S ACKNOWLEDGMENT (check applicable boxes):

☐ 1. Buyer has received copies of all information listed above.
☒ 2. Buyer has received the pamphlet *Protect Your Family from Lead in Your Home.*

E. BROKERS' ACKNOWLEDGMENT: Brokers have informed Seller of Seller's obligations under 42 U.S.C. 4852d to: (a) provide Buyer with the federally approved pamphlet on lead poisoning prevention; (b) complete this addendum; (c) disclose any known lead-based paint and/or lead-based paint hazards in the Property; (d) deliver all records and reports to Buyer pertaining to lead-based paint and/or lead-based paint hazards in the Property; (e) provide Buyer a period of up to 10 days to have the Property inspected; and (f) retain a completed copy of this addendum for at least 3 years following the sale. Brokers are aware of their responsibility to ensure compliance.

F. CERTIFICATION OF ACCURACY: The following persons have reviewed the information above and certify, to the best of their knowledge, that the information they have provided is true and accurate.

John Charles Wayne	11-06-08	Thomas A. Smith	11-06-08
Buyer	Date	Seller	Date
Sharon Sidekick	11-06-08	Molly Bea Smith	11-06-08
Buyer	Date	Seller	Date
n/a		Sarah Listalot	11-06-08
Other Broker	Date	Listing Broker	Date

The form of this addendum has been approved by the Texas Real Estate Commission for use only with similarly approved or promulgated forms of contracts. Such approval relates to this contract form only. TREC forms are intended for use only by trained real estate licensees. No representation is made as to the legal validity or adequacy of any provision in any specific transactions. It is not suitable for complex transactions. Texas Real Estate Commission, P.O. Box 12188, Austin, TX 78711-2188, 1-800-250-8732 or (512) 459-6544 (http://www.trec.state.tx.us)

Form OP-L 01A

TRANSACTION 3: 80% CONVENTIONAL ARM (USING: TREC 20-7 AND 40-3. SEE FIGURE 11.9 AND FIGURE 11.10.)

Susan Helen Seller, an unmarried woman, will sell her lake home to Henry A. Homebuyer and his spouse, Hanna S. Homebuyer. Not being located in a city, town, or village, the Property is identified by a metes-and-bounds description as evidenced in the purchase agreement by attached Exhibit A. The Property is not in a plated subdivision. It is located in Harrison County and has a mailing address of 42 Pleasure Lake Drive, Podunk, Texas 77072. Ms. Seller will have the leased security system and the water softener removed prior to closing.

The Buyers will pay $126,000 for the Property and have already applied for an 80 percent ARM loan. They have not yet been approved for this financing. They feel they can get approval within 20 days and close within 30 days after the effective date of the contract. They have researched the market and know they can get a 15-year ARM loan with an interest rate of 6 percent or less for the first three years of the loan.

The Homebuyers have written a check for $1,500 made payable to Buyer's Choice Title Company. They will pay for the owners' title policy as well as the survey that is to be delivered within 15 days after the date of the contract. They want 3 days to review the survey that will be furnished to their lender.

Because the house was built in 1979, the lead addendum is not attached. The Buyers have received the Seller's disclosure notice. The Buyers accept the Property in its present condition, provided the Seller will repair the septic system and bring it up to current county code as evidenced by a county inspection certificate.

The Buyers want possession at closing and funding and will pay for the appraisal required by the lender. The Buyers want all of their notices delivered to their attorney's office at 2225 High Street, Podunk, Texas 77071. Attorney Michael Phelps will review the offer prior to signing by the Buyers.

The Seller will receive her notices through the listing agent.

The Buyers are customers who were shown the Property by salesperson Sam Smith, from Happy Buyer Realty. Seller's Choice Realty Services promoted the Property through the MLS. Lester Listor is the listing associate. The selling commission is 3.5 percent of the Sales Price.

The parties feel that it is a good idea to agree to try mediation before resorting to litigation. They agree to split the cost of mediation should it become necessary.

FIGURE 11.9

TREC 20-7

02-13-06

EQUAL HOUSING OPPORTUNITY

PROMULGATED BY THE TEXAS REAL ESTATE COMMISSION (TREC)

ONE TO FOUR FAMILY RESIDENTIAL CONTRACT (RESALE)

NOTICE: Not For Use For Condominium Transactions

1. **PARTIES:** ______________________________ (Seller) agrees to sell and convey to ______________________________ (Buyer) and Buyer agrees to buy from Seller the Property described below.

2. **PROPERTY:**
   A. LAND: Lot ______ Block ________, ______________________ Addition, City of ______________________, County of ________________, Texas, known as ______________________________ (address/zip code), or as described on attached exhibit.
   B. IMPROVEMENTS: The house, garage and all other fixtures and improvements attached to the above-described real property, including without limitation, the following **permanently installed and built-in items,** if any: all equipment and appliances, valances, screens, shutters, awnings, wall-to-wall carpeting, mirrors, ceiling fans, attic fans, mail boxes, television antennas and satellite dish system and equipment, heating and air-conditioning units, security and fire detection equipment, wiring, plumbing and lighting fixtures, chandeliers, water softener system, kitchen equipment, garage door openers, cleaning equipment, shrubbery, landscaping, outdoor cooking equipment, and all other property owned by Seller and attached to the above described real property.
   C. ACCESSORIES: The following described related accessories, if any: window air conditioning units, stove, fireplace screens, curtains and rods, blinds, window shades, draperies and rods, controls for satellite dish system, controls for garage door openers, entry gate controls, door keys, mailbox keys, above ground pool, swimming pool equipment and maintenance accessories, and artificial fireplace logs.
   D. EXCLUSIONS: The following improvements and accessories will be retained by Seller and removed prior to delivery of possession: ______________________________ ______________________________.

   The land, improvements and accessories are collectively referred to as the "Property".

3. **SALES PRICE:**
   A. Cash portion of Sales Price payable by Buyer at closing .... $________________
   B. Sum of all financing described below (excluding any loan funding fee or mortgage insurance premium) .... $________________
   C. Sales Price (Sum of A and B) .... $________________

4. **FINANCING:** The portion of Sales Price not payable in cash will be paid as follows: (Check applicable boxes below)
   ❑ A. THIRD PARTY FINANCING: One or more third party mortgage loans in the total amount of $______________ (excluding any loan funding fee or mortgage insurance premium).
   (1) Property Approval: If the Property does not satisfy the lenders' underwriting requirements for the loan(s), this contract will terminate and the earnest money will be refunded to Buyer.
   (2) Financing Approval: (Check one box only)
   ❑ (a) This contract is subject to Buyer being approved for the financing described in the attached Third Party Financing Condition Addendum.
   ❑ (b) This contract is not subject to Buyer being approved for financing and does not involve FHA or VA financing.
   ❑ B. ASSUMPTION: The assumption of the unpaid principal balance of one or more promissory notes described in the attached TREC Loan Assumption Addendum.
   ❑ C. SELLER FINANCING: A promissory note from Buyer to Seller of $________________, secured by vendor's and deed of trust liens, and containing the terms and conditions described in the attached TREC Seller Financing Addendum. If an owner policy of title insurance is furnished, Buyer shall furnish Seller with a mortgagee policy of title insurance.

5. **EARNEST MONEY:** Upon execution of this contract by both parties, Buyer shall deposit $______________ as earnest money with ______________________________, as escrow agent, at ______________________________ (address). Buyer shall deposit additional earnest money of $__________________ with escrow agent within ______ days after the effective date of this contract. If Buyer fails to deposit the earnest money as required by this contract, Buyer will be in default.

6. **TITLE POLICY AND SURVEY:**
   A. TITLE POLICY: Seller shall furnish to Buyer at ❑Seller's ❑Buyer's expense an owner policy of title insurance (Title Policy) issued by ______________________________ (Title Company) in the amount of the Sales Price, dated at or after closing, insuring Buyer

Initialed for identification by Buyer______ ______ and Seller _______ ______ TREC NO. 20-7

FIGURE 11.9 (CONTINUED)

TREC 20-7

Contract Concerning ______________________________ Page 2 of 8 02-13-06
(Address of Property)

against loss under the provisions of the Title Policy, subject to the promulgated exclusions (including existing building and zoning ordinances) and the following exceptions:

(1) Restrictive covenants common to the platted subdivision in which the Property is located.
(2) The standard printed exception for standby fees, taxes and assessments.
(3) Liens created as part of the financing described in Paragraph 4.
(4) Utility easements created by the dedication deed or plat of the subdivision in which the Property is located.
(5) Reservations or exceptions otherwise permitted by this contract or as may be approved by Buyer in writing.
(6) The standard printed exception as to marital rights.
(7) The standard printed exception as to waters, tidelands, beaches, streams, and related matters.
(8) The standard printed exception as to discrepancies, conflicts, shortages in area or boundary lines, encroachments or protrusions, or overlapping improvements. Buyer, at Buyer's expense, may have the exception amended to read, "shortages in area".

B. COMMITMENT: Within 20 days after the Title Company receives a copy of this contract, Seller shall furnish to Buyer a commitment for title insurance (Commitment) and, at Buyer's expense, legible copies of restrictive covenants and documents evidencing exceptions in the Commitment (Exception Documents) other than the standard printed exceptions. Seller authorizes the Title Company to deliver the Commitment and Exception Documents to Buyer at Buyer's address shown in Paragraph 21. If the Commitment and Exception Documents are not delivered to Buyer within the specified time, the time for delivery will be automatically extended up to 15 days or the Closing Date, whichever is earlier.

C. SURVEY: The survey must be made by a registered professional land surveyor acceptable to the Title Company and any lender. (Check one box only)

❑ (1) Within ________ days after the effective date of this contract, Seller shall furnish to Buyer and Title Company Seller's existing survey of the Property and a Residential Real Property Affidavit promulgated by the Texas Department of Insurance (Affidavit). If the existing survey or Affidavit is not acceptable to Title Company or Buyer's lender, Buyer shall obtain a new survey at ❑ Seller's ❑ Buyer's expense no later than 3 days prior to Closing Date. If Seller fails to furnish the existing survey or Affidavit within the time prescribed, Buyer shall obtain a new survey at Seller's expense no later than 3 days prior to Closing Date.

❑ (2) Within _______ days after the effective date of this contract, Buyer shall obtain a new survey at Buyer's expense. Buyer is deemed to receive the survey on the date of actual receipt or the date specified in this paragraph, whichever is earlier.

❑ (3) Within ______ days after the effective date of this contract, Seller, at Seller's expense shall furnish a new survey to Buyer.

D. OBJECTIONS: Buyer may object in writing to defects, exceptions, or encumbrances to title: disclosed on the survey other than items 6A(1) through (7) above; disclosed in the Commitment other than items 6A(1) through (8) above; or which prohibit the following use or activity: ____

____.

Buyer must object not later than (i) the Closing Date or (ii) ____________ days after Buyer receives the Commitment, Exception Documents, and the survey, whichever is earlier. Buyer's failure to object within the time allowed will constitute a waiver of Buyer's right to object; except that the requirements in Schedule C of the Commitment are not waived. Provided Seller is not obligated to incur any expense, Seller shall cure the timely objections of Buyer or any third party lender within 15 days after Seller receives the objections and the Closing Date will be extended as necessary. If objections are not cured within such 15 day period, this contract will terminate and the earnest money will be refunded to Buyer unless Buyer waives the objections.

E. TITLE NOTICES:

(1) ABSTRACT OR TITLE POLICY: Broker advises Buyer to have an abstract of title covering the Property examined by an attorney of Buyer's selection, or Buyer should be furnished with or obtain a Title Policy. If a Title Policy is furnished, the Commitment should be promptly reviewed by an attorney of Buyer's choice due to the time limitations on Buyer's right to object.

(2) MANDATORY OWNERS' ASSOCIATION MEMBERSHIP: The Property ❑ is ❑ is not subject to mandatory membership in an owners' association. If the Property is subject to mandatory membership in an owners' association, Seller notifies Buyer under §5.012, Texas Property Code, that, as a purchaser of property in the residential community in which the Property is located, you are obligated to be a member of the owners' association. Restrictive covenants governing the use and occupancy of the Property and a dedicatory instrument governing the establishment, maintenance, and operation of this residential community have been or will be recorded in the Real Property Records of the county in which the Property is located. Copies of the restrictive covenants and dedicatory instrument may be obtained from the county clerk. You are obligated to pay

Initialed for identification by Buyer______ ______ and Seller _______ ______ TREC NO. 20-7

FIGURE 11.9 (CONTINUED)

TREC 20-7

assessments to the owners' association. The amount of the assessments is subject to change. Your failure to pay the assessments could result in a lien on and the foreclosure of the Property. If Buyer is concerned about these matters, the TREC promulgated Addendum for Property Subject to Mandatory Membership in an Owner's Association should be used.

(3) STATUTORY TAX DISTRICTS: If the Property is situated in a utility or other statutorily created district providing water, sewer, drainage, or flood control facilities and services, Chapter 49, Texas Water Code, requires Seller to deliver and Buyer to sign the statutory notice relating to the tax rate, bonded indebtedness, or standby fee of the district prior to final execution of this contract.

(4) TIDE WATERS: If the Property abuts the tidally influenced waters of the state, §33.135, Texas Natural Resources Code, requires a notice regarding coastal area property to be included in the contract. An addendum containing the notice promulgated by TREC or required by the parties must be used.

(5) ANNEXATION: If the Property is located outside the limits of a municipality, Seller notifies Buyer under §5.011, Texas Property Code, that the Property may now or later be included in the extraterritorial jurisdiction of a municipality and may now or later be subject to annexation by the municipality. Each municipality maintains a map that depicts its boundaries and extraterritorial jurisdiction. To determine if the Property is located within a municipality's extraterritorial jurisdiction or is likely to be located within a municipality's extraterritorial jurisdiction, contact all municipalities located in the general proximity of the Property for further information.

(6) PROPERTY LOCATED IN A CERTIFICATED SERVICE AREA OF A UTILITY SERVICE PROVIDER: Notice required by §13.257, Water Code: The real property, described in Paragraph 2, that you are about to purchase may be located in a certificated water or sewer service area, which is authorized by law to provide water or sewer service to the properties in the certificated area. If your property is located in a certificated area there may be special costs or charges that you will be required to pay before you can receive water or sewer service. There may be a period required to construct lines or other facilities necessary to provide water or sewer service to your property. You are advised to determine if the property is in a certificated area and contact the utility service provider to determine the cost that you will be required to pay and the period, if any, that is required to provide water or sewer service to your property. The undersigned Buyer hereby acknowledges receipt of the foregoing notice at or before the execution of a binding contract for the purchase of the real property described in Paragraph 2 or at closing of purchase of the real property.

(7) PUBLIC IMPROVEMENT DISTRICTS: If the Property is in a public improvement district, §5.014, Property Code, requires Seller to notify Buyer as follows: As a purchaser of this parcel of real property you are obligated to pay an assessment to a municipality or county for an improvement project undertaken by a public improvement district under Chapter 372, Local Government Code. The assessment may be due annually or in periodic installments. More information concerning the amount of the assessment and the due dates of that assessment may be obtained from the municipality or county levying the assessment. The amount of the assessments is subject to change. Your failure to pay the assessments could result in a lien on and the foreclosure of your property.

7. PROPERTY CONDITION:

A. ACCESS,INSPECTIONS AND UTILITIES: Seller shall permit Buyer and Buyer's agents access to the Property at reasonable times. Buyer may have the Property inspected by inspectors selected by Buyer and licensed by TREC or otherwise permitted by law to make inspections. Seller at Seller's expense shall turn on existing utilities for inspections.

B. SELLER'S DISCLOSURE NOTICE PURSUANT TO §5.008, TEXAS PROPERTY CODE (Notice): (Check one box only)

☐ (1) Buyer has received the Notice.

☐ (2) Buyer has not received the Notice. Within ______ days after the effective date of this contract, Seller shall deliver the Notice to Buyer. If Buyer does not receive the Notice, Buyer may terminate this contract at any time prior to the closing and the earnest money will be refunded to Buyer. If Seller delivers the Notice, Buyer may terminate this contract for any reason within 7 days after Buyer receives the Notice or prior to the closing, whichever first occurs, and the earnest money will be refunded to Buyer.

☐ (3) The Seller is not required to furnish the notice under the Texas Property Code.

C. SELLER'S DISCLOSURE OF LEAD-BASED PAINT AND LEAD-BASED PAINT HAZARDS is required by Federal law for a residential dwelling constructed prior to 1978.

D. ACCEPTANCE OF PROPERTY CONDITION: Buyer accepts the Property in its present condition; provided Seller, at Seller's expense, shall complete the following specific repairs and treatments:____

____

E. LENDER REQUIRED REPAIRS AND TREATMENTS: Unless otherwise agreed in writing, neither party is obligated to pay for lender required repairs, which includes treatment for wood

FIGURE 11.9 (CONTINUED)

TREC 20-7

Contract Concerning ____ Page 4 of 8 02-13-06
(Address of Property)

destroying insects. If the parties do not agree to pay for the lender required repairs or treatments, this contract will terminate and the earnest money will be refunded to Buyer. If the cost of lender required repairs and treatments exceeds 5% of the Sales Price, Buyer may terminate this contract and the earnest money will be refunded to Buyer.

F. COMPLETION OF REPAIRS AND TREATMENTS: Unless otherwise agreed in writing, Seller shall complete all agreed repairs and treatments prior to the Closing Date. All required permits must be obtained, and repairs and treatments must be performed by persons who are licensed or otherwise authorized by law to provide such repairs or treatments. At Buyer's election, any transferable warranties received by Seller with respect to the repairs and treatments will be transferred to Buyer at Buyer's expense. If Seller fails to complete any agreed repairs and treatments prior to the Closing Date, Buyer may do so and receive reimbursement from Seller at closing. The Closing Date will be extended up to 15 days, if necessary, to complete repairs and treatments.

G. ENVIRONMENTAL MATTERS: Buyer is advised that the presence of wetlands, toxic substances, including asbestos and wastes or other environmental hazards, or the presence of a threatened or endangered species or its habitat may affect Buyer's intended use of the Property. If Buyer is concerned about these matters, an addendum promulgated by TREC or required by the parties should be used.

H. RESIDENTIAL SERVICE CONTRACTS: Buyer may purchase a residential service contract from a residential service company licensed by TREC. If Buyer purchases a residential service contract, Seller shall reimburse Buyer at closing for the cost of the residential service contract in an amount not exceeding $______________. Buyer should review any residential service contract for the scope of coverage, exclusions and limitations. **The purchase of a residential service contract is optional. Similar coverage may be purchased from various companies authorized to do business in Texas.**

8. **BROKERS' FEES:** All obligations of the parties for payment of brokers' fees are contained in separate written agreements.

9. **CLOSING:**

A. The closing of the sale will be on or before ____________________, 20____, or within 7 days after objections made under Paragraph 6D have been cured or waived, whichever date is later (Closing Date). If either party fails to close the sale by the Closing Date, the non-defaulting party may exercise the remedies contained in Paragraph 15.

B. At closing:

(1) Seller shall execute and deliver a general warranty deed conveying title to the Property to Buyer and showing no additional exceptions to those permitted in Paragraph 6 and furnish tax statements or certificates showing no delinquent taxes on the Property.

(2) Buyer shall pay the Sales Price in good funds acceptable to the escrow agent.

(3) Seller and Buyer shall execute and deliver any notices, statements, certificates, affidavits, releases, loan documents and other documents required of them by this contract, the Commitment or law necessary for the closing of the sale and the issuance of the Title Policy.

C. Unless expressly prohibited by written agreement, Seller may continue to show the Property and receive, negotiate and accept back up offers.

D. All covenants, representations and warranties in this contract survive closing.

10. **POSSESSION:** Seller shall deliver to Buyer possession of the Property in its present or required condition, ordinary wear and tear excepted: ☐ upon closing and funding ☐ according to a temporary residential lease form promulgated by TREC or other written lease required by the parties. Any possession by Buyer prior to closing or by Seller after closing which is not authorized by a written lease will establish a tenancy at sufferance relationship between the parties. **Consult your insurance agent prior to change of ownership and possession because insurance coverage may be limited or terminated. The absence of a written lease or appropriate insurance coverage may expose the parties to economic loss.**

11. **SPECIAL PROVISIONS:** (Insert only factual statements and business details applicable to the sale. TREC rules prohibit licensees from adding factual statements or business details for which a contract addendum, lease or other form has been promulgated by TREC for mandatory use.)

Initialed for identification by Buyer______ ______ and Seller _______ ______ TREC NO. 20-7

FIGURE 11.9 (CONTINUED)

TREC 20-7

12. SETTLEMENT AND OTHER EXPENSES:

A. The following expenses must be paid at or prior to closing:

(1) Expenses payable by Seller (Seller's Expenses):

(a) Releases of existing liens, including prepayment penalties and recording fees; release of Seller's loan liability; tax statements or certificates; preparation of deed; one-half of escrow fee; and other expenses payable by Seller under this contract.

(b) Seller shall also pay an amount not to exceed $ ____________ to be applied in the following order: Buyer's Expenses which Buyer is prohibited from paying by FHA, VA, Texas Veterans Housing Assistance Program or other governmental loan programs, and then to other Buyer's Expenses as allowed by the lender.

(2) Expenses payable by Buyer (Buyer's Expenses):

(a) Loan origination, discount, buy-down, and commitment fees (Loan Fees).

(b) Appraisal fees; loan application fees; credit reports; preparation of loan documents; interest on the notes from date of disbursement to one month prior to dates of first monthly payments; recording fees; copies of easements and restrictions; mortgagee title policy with endorsements required by lender; loan-related inspection fees; photos; amortization schedules; one-half of escrow fee; all prepaid items, including required premiums for flood and hazard insurance, reserve deposits for insurance, ad valorem taxes and special governmental assessments; final compliance inspection; courier fee; repair inspection; underwriting fee; wire transfer fee; expenses incident to any loan; and other expenses payable by Buyer under this contract.

B. Buyer shall pay Private Mortgage Insurance Premium (PMI), VA Loan Funding Fee, or FHA Mortgage Insurance Premium (MIP) as required by the lender.

C. If any expense exceeds an amount expressly stated in this contract for such expense to be paid by a party, that party may terminate this contract unless the other party agrees to pay such excess. Buyer may not pay charges and fees expressly prohibited by FHA, VA, Texas Veterans Housing Assistance Program or other governmental loan program regulations.

13. PRORATIONS: Taxes for the current year, interest, maintenance fees, assessments, dues and rents will be prorated through the Closing Date. The tax proration may be calculated taking into consideration any change in exemptions that will affect the current year's taxes. If taxes for the current year vary from the amount prorated at closing, the parties shall adjust the prorations when tax statements for the current year are available. If taxes are not paid at or prior to closing, Buyer shall pay taxes for the current year.

14. CASUALTY LOSS: If any part of the Property is damaged or destroyed by fire or other casualty after the effective date of this contract, Seller shall restore the Property to its previous condition as soon as reasonably possible, but in any event by the Closing Date. If Seller fails to do so due to factors beyond Seller's control, Buyer may (a) terminate this contract and the earnest money will be refunded to Buyer (b) extend the time for performance up to 15 days and the Closing Date will be extended as necessary or (c) accept the Property in its damaged condition with an assignment of insurance proceeds and receive credit from Seller at closing in the amount of the deductible under the insurance policy. Seller's obligations under this paragraph are independent of any other obligations of Seller under this contract.

15. DEFAULT: If Buyer fails to comply with this contract, Buyer will be in default, and Seller may (a) enforce specific performance, seek such other relief as may be provided by law, or both, or (b) terminate this contract and receive the earnest money as liquidated damages, thereby releasing both parties from this contract. If, due to factors beyond Seller's control, Seller fails within the time allowed to make any non-casualty repairs or deliver the Commitment, or survey, if required of Seller, Buyer may (a) extend the time for performance up to 15 days and the Closing Date will be extended as necessary or (b) terminate this contract as the sole remedy and receive the earnest money. If Seller fails to comply with this contract for any other reason, Seller will be in default and Buyer may (a) enforce specific performance, seek such other relief as may be provided by law, or both, or (b) terminate this contract and receive the earnest money, thereby releasing both parties from this contract.

16. MEDIATION: It is the policy of the State of Texas to encourage resolution of disputes through alternative dispute resolution procedures such as mediation. Any dispute between Seller and Buyer related to this contract which is not resolved through informal discussion ☐will ☐will not be submitted to a mutually acceptable mediation service or provider. The parties to the mediation shall bear the mediation costs equally. This paragraph does not preclude a party from seeking equitable relief from a court of competent jurisdiction.

17. ATTORNEY'S FEES: The prevailing party in any legal proceeding related to this contract is entitled to recover reasonable attorney's fees and all costs of such proceeding incurred by the prevailing party.

FIGURE 11.9 (CONTINUED)

TREC 20-7

Contract Concerning ______________________________ Page 6 of 8 02-13-06
(Address of Property)

18. ESCROW:

A. ESCROW: The escrow agent is not (i) a party to this contract and does not have liability for the performance or nonperformance of any party to this contract, (ii) liable for interest on the earnest money and (iii) liable for the loss of any earnest money caused by the failure of any financial institution in which the earnest money has been deposited unless the financial institution is acting as escrow agent.

B. EXPENSES: At closing, the earnest money must be applied first to any cash down payment, then to Buyer's Expenses and any excess refunded to Buyer. If no closing occurs, escrow agent may require payment of unpaid expenses incurred on behalf of the parties and a written release of liability of escrow agent from all parties.

C. DEMAND: Upon termination of this contract, either party or the escrow agent may send a release of earnest money to each party and the parties shall execute counterparts of the release and deliver same to the escrow agent. If either party fails to execute the release, either party may make a written demand to the escrow agent for the earnest money. If only one party makes written demand for the earnest money, escrow agent shall promptly provide a copy of the demand to the other party. If escrow agent does not receive written objection to the demand from the other party within 15 days, escrow agent may disburse the earnest money to the party making demand reduced by the amount of unpaid expenses incurred on behalf of the party receiving the earnest money and escrow agent may pay the same to the creditors. If escrow agent complies with the provisions of this paragraph, each party hereby releases escrow agent from all adverse claims related to the disbursal of the earnest money.

D. DAMAGES: Any party who wrongfully fails or refuses to sign a release acceptable to the escrow agent within 7 days of receipt of the request will be liable to the other party for liquidated damages of three times the amount of the earnest money.

E. NOTICES: Escrow agent's notices will be effective when sent in compliance with Paragraph 21. Notice of objection to the demand will be deemed effective upon receipt by escrow agent.

19. REPRESENTATIONS: Seller represents that as of the Closing Date (a) there will be no liens, assessments, or security interests against the Property which will not be satisfied out of the sales proceeds unless securing payment of any loans assumed by Buyer and (b) assumed loans will not be in default. If any representation of Seller in this contract is untrue on the Closing Date, Seller will be in default.

20. FEDERAL TAX REQUIREMENTS: If Seller is a "foreign person," as defined by applicable law, or if Seller fails to deliver an affidavit to Buyer that Seller is not a "foreign person," then Buyer shall withhold from the sales proceeds an amount sufficient to comply with applicable tax law and deliver the same to the Internal Revenue Service together with appropriate tax forms. Internal Revenue Service regulations require filing written reports if currency in excess of specified amounts is received in the transaction.

21. NOTICES: All notices from one party to the other must be in writing and are effective when mailed to, hand-delivered at, or transmitted by facsimile or electronic transmission as follows:

To Buyer at: ______________________	**To Seller at:** ______________________
______________________	______________________
______________________	______________________
______________________	______________________
Telephone: ( ) ______________________	Telephone: ( ) ______________________
Facsimile: ( ) ______________________	Facsimile: ( ) ______________________
E-mail: ______________________	E-mail: ______________________

Initialed for identification by Buyer______ ______ and Seller ______ ______ TREC NO. 20-7

FIGURE 11.9 (CONTINUED)

TREC 20-7

Contract Concerning ____ Page 7 of 8 02-13-06
(Address of Property)

22. AGREEMENT OF PARTIES: This contract contains the entire agreement of the parties and cannot be changed except by their written agreement. Addenda which are a part of this contract are (Check all applicable boxes):

- ❑ Third Party Financing Condition Addendum
- ❑ Seller Financing Addendum
- ❑ Loan Assumption Addendum
- ❑ Buyer's Temporary Residential Lease
- ❑ Seller's Temporary Residential Lease
- ❑ Addendum for Sale of Other Property by Buyer
- ❑ Addendum for Seller's Disclosure of Information on Lead-based Paint and Lead-based Paint Hazards as Required by Federal Law
- ❑ Addendum for Property Subject to Mandatory Membership in an Owners' Association
- ❑ Environmental Assessment, Threatened or Endangered Species and Wetlands Addendum
- ❑ Addendum for "Back-Up" Contract
- ❑ Addendum for Coastal Area Property
- ❑ Addendum for Property Located Seaward of the Gulf Intracoastal Waterway
- ❑ Addendum for Release of Liability on Assumption of FHA, VA, or Conventional Loan Restoration of Seller's Entitlement for VA Guaranteed Loan
- ❑ Other (list): ______________________
  ____

23. TERMINATION OPTION: For nominal consideration, the receipt of which is hereby acknowledged by Seller, and Buyer's agreement to pay Seller $__________ (Option Fee) within 2 days after the effective date of this contract, Seller grants Buyer the unrestricted right to terminate this contract by giving notice of termination to Seller within _______ days after the effective date of this contract. If no dollar amount is stated as the Option Fee or if Buyer fails to pay the Option Fee within the time prescribed, this paragraph will not be a part of this contract and Buyer shall not have the unrestricted right to terminate this contract. If Buyer gives notice of termination within the time prescribed, the Option Fee will not be refunded; however, any earnest money will be refunded to Buyer. The Option Fee ❑will ❑will not be credited to the Sales Price at closing. **Time is of the essence for this paragraph and strict compliance with the time for performance is required.**

24. CONSULT AN ATTORNEY: Real estate licensees cannot give legal advice. READ THIS CONTRACT CAREFULLY. If you do not understand the effect of this contract, consult an attorney BEFORE signing.

Buyer's Attorney is: ______________________	Seller's Attorney is: ______________________
______________________	______________________
Telephone: ( ) ______________________	Telephone: ( ) ______________________
Facsimile: ( ) ______________________	Facsimile: ( ) ______________________
E-mail: ______________________	E-mail: ______________________

EXECUTED the ______day of ____________________, 20____ (EFFECTIVE DATE).
(BROKER: FILL IN THE DATE OF FINAL ACCEPTANCE.)

______________________	______________________
Buyer	Seller
______________________	______________________
Buyer	Seller

The form of this contract has been approved by the Texas Real Estate Commission. TREC forms are intended for use only by trained real estate licensees. No representation is made as to the legal validity or adequacy of any provision in any specific transactions. It is not intended for complex transactions. Texas Real Estate Commission, P.O. Box 12188, Austin, TX 78711-2188, 1-800-250-8732 or (512) 459-6544 (http://www.trec.state.tx.us) TREC NO. 20-7. This form replaces TREC NO. 20-6.

FIGURE 11.9 (CONTINUED)

TREC 20-7

Contract Concerning ______________________________ Page 8 of 8 02-13-06
(Address of Property)

BROKER INFORMATION AND RATIFICATION OF FEE

Listing Broker has agreed to pay Other Broker ____________________ of the total sales price when Listing Broker's fee is received. Escrow Agent is authorized and directed to pay Other Broker from Listing Broker's fee at closing.

Other Broker ____________ License No.

represents ❑ Buyer only as Buyer's agent
❑ Seller as Listing Broker's subagent

Associate ____________ Telephone

Broker's Address

City ____ State ____ Zip

Facsimile

Email Address

Listing Broker ____________ License No.

represents ❑ Seller and Buyer as an intermediary
❑ Seller only as Seller's agent

Listing Associate ____________ Telephone

Listing Associate's Office Address ____ Facsimile

City ____ State ____ Zip

Email Address

Selling Associate ____________ Telephone

Selling Associate's Office Address ____ Facsimile

City ____ State ____ Zip

Email Address

OPTION FEE RECEIPT

Receipt of $____________ (Option Fee) in the form of ________________ is acknowledged.

Seller or Listing Broker ____________ Date

CONTRACT AND EARNEST MONEY RECEIPT

Receipt of ❑Contract and ❑$______________ Earnest Money in the form of ______________ is acknowledged.

Escrow Agent: ______________________ Date: ______________

By: ______________________ Email Address

Address ______________________ Telephone (____) ______________

City ____ State ____ Zip ____ Facsimile: (____) ______________

TREC NO. 20-7

FIGURE 11.10

TREC 40-3

12-10-07

EQUAL HOUSING OPPORTUNITY

PROMULGATED BY THE TEXAS REAL ESTATE COMMISSION (TREC)

THIRD PARTY FINANCING CONDITION ADDENDUM

TO CONTRACT CONCERNING THE PROPERTY AT

→ 42 Pleasure Lake Drive Podunk, TX

(Street Address and City)

Buyer shall apply promptly for all financing described below and make every reasonable effort to obtain approval for the financing (Financing Approval). Buyer shall furnish all information and documents required by lender for Financing Approval. Financing Approval will be deemed to have been obtained when (1) the terms of the loan(s) described below are available and (2) lender determines that Buyer has satisfied all of lender's financial requirements (those items relating to Buyer's assets, income and credit history). If Buyer cannot obtain Financing Approval, Buyer may give written notice to Seller within 20 days after the effective date of this contract and this contract will terminate and the earnest money will be refunded to Buyer. **If Buyer does not give such notice within the time required, this contract will no longer be subject to Financing Approval. Time is of the essence for this paragraph and strict compliance with the time for performance is required.**

NOTE: Financing Approval does not include approval of lender's underwriting requirements for the Property, as specified in Paragraph 4.A.(1) of the contract.

Each note must be secured by vendor's and deed of trust liens.

CHECK APPLICABLE BOXES:

→ ☒ A. CONVENTIONAL FINANCING:

☒ (1) A first mortgage loan in the principal amount of $ 100,800 (excluding any financed PMI premium), due in full in 15 year(s), with interest not to exceed 6 % per annum for the first 3 year(s) of the loan with Loan Fees (loan origination, discount, buy-down, and commitment fees) not to exceed 1 % of the loan.

☐ (2) A second mortgage loan in the principal amount of $________(excluding any financed PMI premium), due in full in ______year(s), with interest not to exceed _____% per annum for the first ______year(s) of the loan with Loan Fees (loan origination, discount, buy-down, and commitment fees) not to exceed _____% of the loan.

☐ B. TEXAS VETERANS LOAN: A loan(s) from the Texas Veterans Land Board of $_______ for a period in the total amount of _____years at the interest rate established by the Texas Veterans Land Board.

☐ C. FHA INSURED FINANCING: A Section ________ FHA insured loan of not less than $________ (excluding any financed MIP), amortizable monthly for not less than _____years, with interest not to exceed _____% per annum for the first _____year(s) of the loan with Loan Fees (loan origination, discount, buy-down, and commitment fees) not to exceed _____ % of the loan. As required by HUD-FHA, if FHA valuation is unknown, *"It is expressly agreed that, notwithstanding any other provision of this contract, the purchaser (Buyer) shall not be obligated to complete the purchase of the Property described herein or to incur any penalty by forfeiture of earnest money deposits or otherwise unless the purchaser (Buyer) has been given in accordance with HUD/FHA or VA requirements a written statement issued by the Federal Housing Commissioner, Department of Veterans Affairs, or a Direct Endorsement Lender setting forth the appraised value of the Property of not less than $________. The purchaser (Buyer) shall have the privilege and option of proceeding with consummation of the contract without regard to the amount of the*

FIGURE 11.10 (CONTINUED)

TREC 40-3

Third Party Financing Condition Addendum Concerning Page 2 of 2 12-10-07

42 Pleasure Lake Drive Podunk, TX

(Address of Property)

appraised valuation. The appraised valuation is arrived at to determine the maximum mortgage the Department of Housing and Urban Development will insure. HUD does not warrant the value or the condition of the Property. The purchaser (Buyer) should satisfy himself/herself that the price and the condition of the Property are acceptable."

NOTE: HUD 92564-CN "For Your Protection: Get a Home Inspection" must be attached to this Addendum.

❑ D. VA GUARANTEED FINANCING: A VA guaranteed loan of not less than $__________________ (excluding any financed Funding Fee), amortizable monthly for not less than________years, with interest not to exceed_________% per annum for the first ________year(s) of the loan with Loan Fees (loan origination, discount, buy down, and commitment fees) not to exceed _________% of the loan.

VA NOTICE TO BUYER: "*It is expressly agreed that, notwithstanding any other provisions of this contract, the Buyer shall not incur any penalty by forfeiture of earnest money or otherwise or be obligated to complete the purchase of the Property described herein, if the contract purchase price or cost exceeds the reasonable value of the Property established by the Department of Veterans Affairs. The Buyer shall, however, have the privilege and option of proceeding with the consummation of this contract without regard to the amount of the reasonable value established by the Department of Veterans Affairs.*"

If Buyer elects to complete the purchase at an amount in excess of the reasonable value established by VA, Buyer shall pay such excess amount in cash from a source which Buyer agrees to disclose to the VA and which Buyer represents will not be from borrowed funds except as approved by VA. If VA reasonable value of the Property is less than the Sales Price, Seller may reduce the Sales Price to an amount equal to the VA reasonable value and the sale will be closed at the lower Sales Price with proportionate adjustments to the down payment and the loan amount.

Buyer hereby authorizes any lender to furnish to the Seller or Buyer or their representatives information relating only to the status of Financing Approval of Buyer.

Buyer	Seller
Buyer	Seller

This form has been approved by the Texas Real Estate Commission for use with similarly approved or promulgated contract forms. Such approval relates to this form only. TREC forms are intended for use only by trained real estate licensees. No representation is made as to the legal validity or adequacy of any provision in any specific transactions. It is not intended for complex transactions. Texas Real Estate Commission, P.O. Box 12188, Austin, TX 78711-2188, 1-800-250-8732 or (512) 459-6544 (http://www.trec.state.tx.us) TREC No. 40-3. This form replaces TREC No. 40-2.

TREC NO. 40-3

TRANSACTION 4: VA-GUARANTEED LOAN *(USING: TREC 20-7, 40-3, 15-4, 10-5, AND OP-L LEAD-BASED PAINT ADDENDUM. SEE FIGURE 11.11 THROUGH FIGURE 11.15.)*

Freddie Mac, an unmarried man, has listed his home at 2365 Veterans Boulevard for sale with Friendly Agent Company. He gives the agent permission to put it in the local MLS and offer other companies the opportunity to function as subagents. Sam Smith, an associate at Peter Finch Realty, shows the Property to Victor and Victoria Vet who make an offer of purchase Although Sam has offered them the opportunity for representation, they choose to be customers and understand that anything they say to Sam may be repeated to the listing agent and the Seller. Sam will be paid 2.75 percent of the Sales Price as the selling commission.

The Property is legally identified as Lot 64, Block 83 in Section 2 of the Friendly Hills Addition of Austin, Travis County, Texas. Although it is subject to mandatory membership in the homeowners' association, the Buyers elect not to use the HOA addendum to call for the Seller to provide information. They have spoken to an officer of the association and feel that they have learned everything they need to know. The Property receives mail at zip code 78711.

The Buyers write a check for $1,000 to Buyer's Choice Title Company as earnest money and $200 to the Seller as an Option Fee to have 8 days to have the Property inspected and back out if they find any significant problems. The Option Fee will be credited to the Sales Price at closing.

The Seller will pay for the owners' title policy, as well as the survey, which is to be done within 10 days of the effective date of the contract. The Vets have not asked the Seller to pay any additional Buyer closing costs other than the $1,100 Buyer nonallowable fees the Seller is required to pay by VA. The Buyers will pay for the 1 percent VA-funding fee and the 1 point loan origination fee. They want 3 days to examine the lender-required survey.

The lead-based paint addendum is made a part of the contract. Mr. Smith has provided them with the EPA lead paint pamphlet. The Seller has no knowledge or records concerning lead-based paint. The Buyers will have an inspection for lead paint just to be safe. The Buyer has not yet received the Seller's disclosure notice but asks the Seller to furnish it within 3 days after the effective date of the contract.

The Buyers are willing to pay $78,000 for the Property. Although Mrs. Vet has full entitlement, the Vets have decided to borrow only $62,400 in order to keep their payments at a comfortable level. They can get loan approval within 30 days and close on or before October 20. They can obtain a 30-year fixed-rate loan at 7.25 percent annual interest rate.

They would like possession at closing and table funding. They compromise and agree to permit the Seller to remain 4 days after funding because they are making the transaction contingent upon selling their present home at 1565 Travis Lane. It is under contract and should close on or before October 1. The Buyers agree to permit the Seller to continue to show the Property. If the Seller receives and accepts a satisfactory offer from another Buyer, the Seller shall waive the contingency by 5:00 PM on the 3rd day after the Buyers receive the Seller's notice. To waive the contingency, the Buyers agree that $5,000 additional earnest money will be deposited with the escrow agent.

For the Seller's temporary leasehold, Mr. Mac will pay $50 per day and $100 per day for any holdover. The Buyers waive any requirement for a security deposit. They all agree to mediate any dispute should it become necessary.

FIGURE 11.11

TREC 20-7

EQUAL HOUSING OPPORTUNITY

02-13-06

PROMULGATED BY THE TEXAS REAL ESTATE COMMISSION (TREC)

ONE TO FOUR FAMILY RESIDENTIAL CONTRACT (RESALE)

NOTICE: Not For Use For Condominium Transactions

1. **PARTIES:** ______________________________ (Seller) agrees to sell and convey to ______________________________ (Buyer) and Buyer agrees to buy from Seller the Property described below.

2. **PROPERTY:**
   A. LAND: Lot ______ Block ________, ______________________ Addition, City of ______________________, County of ________________, Texas, known as ______________________ (address/zip code), or as described on attached exhibit.
   B. IMPROVEMENTS: The house, garage and all other fixtures and improvements attached to the above-described real property, including without limitation, the following **permanently installed and built-in items,** if any: all equipment and appliances, valances, screens, shutters, awnings, wall-to-wall carpeting, mirrors, ceiling fans, attic fans, mail boxes, television antennas and satellite dish system and equipment, heating and air-conditioning units, security and fire detection equipment, wiring, plumbing and lighting fixtures, chandeliers, water softener system, kitchen equipment, garage door openers, cleaning equipment, shrubbery, landscaping, outdoor cooking equipment, and all other property owned by Seller and attached to the above described real property.
   C. ACCESSORIES: The following described related accessories, if any: window air conditioning units, stove, fireplace screens, curtains and rods, blinds, window shades, draperies and rods, controls for satellite dish system, controls for garage door openers, entry gate controls, door keys, mailbox keys, above ground pool, swimming pool equipment and maintenance accessories, and artificial fireplace logs.
   D. EXCLUSIONS: The following improvements and accessories will be retained by Seller and removed prior to delivery of possession: ______________________________ ______________________________.

   The land, improvements and accessories are collectively referred to as the "Property".

3. **SALES PRICE:**
   A. Cash portion of Sales Price payable by Buyer at closing .... $________________
   B. Sum of all financing described below (excluding any loan funding fee or mortgage insurance premium).. $________________
   C. Sales Price (Sum of A and B)... $________________

4. **FINANCING:** The portion of Sales Price not payable in cash will be paid as follows: (Check applicable boxes below)
   ❑ A. THIRD PARTY FINANCING: One or more third party mortgage loans in the total amount of $______________ (excluding any loan funding fee or mortgage insurance premium).
   (1) Property Approval: If the Property does not satisfy the lenders' underwriting requirements for the loan(s), this contract will terminate and the earnest money will be refunded to Buyer.
   (2) Financing Approval: (Check one box only)
   ❑ (a) This contract is subject to Buyer being approved for the financing described in the attached Third Party Financing Condition Addendum.
   ❑ (b) This contract is not subject to Buyer being approved for financing and does not involve FHA or VA financing.
   ❑ B. ASSUMPTION: The assumption of the unpaid principal balance of one or more promissory notes described in the attached TREC Loan Assumption Addendum.
   ❑ C. SELLER FINANCING: A promissory note from Buyer to Seller of $________________, secured by vendor's and deed of trust liens, and containing the terms and conditions described in the attached TREC Seller Financing Addendum. If an owner policy of title insurance is furnished, Buyer shall furnish Seller with a mortgagee policy of title insurance.

5. **EARNEST MONEY:** Upon execution of this contract by both parties, Buyer shall deposit $______________ as earnest money with ______________________________, as escrow agent, at ______________________________ (address). Buyer shall deposit additional earnest money of $________________ with escrow agent within ______ days after the effective date of this contract. If Buyer fails to deposit the earnest money as required by this contract, Buyer will be in default.

6. **TITLE POLICY AND SURVEY:**
   A. TITLE POLICY: Seller shall furnish to Buyer at ❑Seller's ❑Buyer's expense an owner policy of title insurance (Title Policy) issued by ______________________________ (Title Company) in the amount of the Sales Price, dated at or after closing, insuring Buyer

Initialed for identification by Buyer______ ______ and Seller _______ ______ TREC NO. 20-7

FIGURE 11.11 (CONTINUED)

TREC 20-7

against loss under the provisions of the Title Policy, subject to the promulgated exclusions (including existing building and zoning ordinances) and the following exceptions:

(1) Restrictive covenants common to the platted subdivision in which the Property is located.
(2) The standard printed exception for standby fees, taxes and assessments.
(3) Liens created as part of the financing described in Paragraph 4.
(4) Utility easements created by the dedication deed or plat of the subdivision in which the Property is located.
(5) Reservations or exceptions otherwise permitted by this contract or as may be approved by Buyer in writing.
(6) The standard printed exception as to marital rights.
(7) The standard printed exception as to waters, tidelands, beaches, streams, and related matters.
(8) The standard printed exception as to discrepancies, conflicts, shortages in area or boundary lines, encroachments or protrusions, or overlapping improvements. Buyer, at Buyer's expense, may have the exception amended to read, "shortages in area".

B. COMMITMENT: Within 20 days after the Title Company receives a copy of this contract, Seller shall furnish to Buyer a commitment for title insurance (Commitment) and, at Buyer's expense, legible copies of restrictive covenants and documents evidencing exceptions in the Commitment (Exception Documents) other than the standard printed exceptions. Seller authorizes the Title Company to deliver the Commitment and Exception Documents to Buyer at Buyer's address shown in Paragraph 21. If the Commitment and Exception Documents are not delivered to Buyer within the specified time, the time for delivery will be automatically extended up to 15 days or the Closing Date, whichever is earlier.

C. SURVEY: The survey must be made by a registered professional land surveyor acceptable to the Title Company and any lender. (Check one box only)

❑ (1) Within ________ days after the effective date of this contract, Seller shall furnish to Buyer and Title Company Seller's existing survey of the Property and a Residential Real Property Affidavit promulgated by the Texas Department of Insurance (Affidavit). If the existing survey or Affidavit is not acceptable to Title Company or Buyer's lender, Buyer shall obtain a new survey at ❑ Seller's ❑ Buyer's expense no later than 3 days prior to Closing Date. If Seller fails to furnish the existing survey or Affidavit within the time prescribed, Buyer shall obtain a new survey at Seller's expense no later than 3 days prior to Closing Date.

❑ (2) Within _______ days after the effective date of this contract, Buyer shall obtain a new survey at Buyer's expense. Buyer is deemed to receive the survey on the date of actual receipt or the date specified in this paragraph, whichever is earlier.

❑ (3) Within ______ days after the effective date of this contract, Seller, at Seller's expense shall furnish a new survey to Buyer.

D. OBJECTIONS: Buyer may object in writing to defects, exceptions, or encumbrances to title: disclosed on the survey other than items 6A(1) through (7) above; disclosed in the Commitment other than items 6A(1) through (8) above; or which prohibit the following use or activity: ____
____.

Buyer must object not later than (i) the Closing Date or (ii) ____________ days after Buyer receives the Commitment, Exception Documents, and the survey, whichever is earlier. Buyer's failure to object within the time allowed will constitute a waiver of Buyer's right to object; except that the requirements in Schedule C of the Commitment are not waived. Provided Seller is not obligated to incur any expense, Seller shall cure the timely objections of Buyer or any third party lender within 15 days after Seller receives the objections and the Closing Date will be extended as necessary. If objections are not cured within such 15 day period, this contract will terminate and the earnest money will be refunded to Buyer unless Buyer waives the objections.

E. TITLE NOTICES:

(1) ABSTRACT OR TITLE POLICY: Broker advises Buyer to have an abstract of title covering the Property examined by an attorney of Buyer's selection, or Buyer should be furnished with or obtain a Title Policy. If a Title Policy is furnished, the Commitment should be promptly reviewed by an attorney of Buyer's choice due to the time limitations on Buyer's right to object.

(2) MANDATORY OWNERS' ASSOCIATION MEMBERSHIP: The Property ❑ is ❑ is not subject to mandatory membership in an owners' association. If the Property is subject to mandatory membership in an owners' association, Seller notifies Buyer under §5.012, Texas Property Code, that, as a purchaser of property in the residential community in which the Property is located, you are obligated to be a member of the owners' association. Restrictive covenants governing the use and occupancy of the Property and a dedicatory instrument governing the establishment, maintenance, and operation of this residential community have been or will be recorded in the Real Property Records of the county in which the Property is located. Copies of the restrictive covenants and dedicatory instrument may be obtained from the county clerk. You are obligated to pay

FIGURE 11.11 (CONTINUED)

TREC 20-7

assessments to the owners' association. The amount of the assessments is subject to change. Your failure to pay the assessments could result in a lien on and the foreclosure of the Property. If Buyer is concerned about these matters, the TREC promulgated Addendum for Property Subject to Mandatory Membership in an Owner's Association should be used.

(3) STATUTORY TAX DISTRICTS: If the Property is situated in a utility or other statutorily created district providing water, sewer, drainage, or flood control facilities and services, Chapter 49, Texas Water Code, requires Seller to deliver and Buyer to sign the statutory notice relating to the tax rate, bonded indebtedness, or standby fee of the district prior to final execution of this contract.

(4) TIDE WATERS: If the Property abuts the tidally influenced waters of the state, §33.135, Texas Natural Resources Code, requires a notice regarding coastal area property to be included in the contract. An addendum containing the notice promulgated by TREC or required by the parties must be used.

(5) ANNEXATION: If the Property is located outside the limits of a municipality, Seller notifies Buyer under §5.011, Texas Property Code, that the Property may now or later be included in the extraterritorial jurisdiction of a municipality and may now or later be subject to annexation by the municipality. Each municipality maintains a map that depicts its boundaries and extraterritorial jurisdiction. To determine if the Property is located within a municipality's extraterritorial jurisdiction or is likely to be located within a municipality's extraterritorial jurisdiction, contact all municipalities located in the general proximity of the Property for further information.

(6) PROPERTY LOCATED IN A CERTIFICATED SERVICE AREA OF A UTILITY SERVICE PROVIDER: Notice required by §13.257, Water Code: The real property, described in Paragraph 2, that you are about to purchase may be located in a certificated water or sewer service area, which is authorized by law to provide water or sewer service to the properties in the certificated area. If your property is located in a certificated area there may be special costs or charges that you will be required to pay before you can receive water or sewer service. There may be a period required to construct lines or other facilities necessary to provide water or sewer service to your property. You are advised to determine if the property is in a certificated area and contact the utility service provider to determine the cost that you will be required to pay and the period, if any, that is required to provide water or sewer service to your property. The undersigned Buyer hereby acknowledges receipt of the foregoing notice at or before the execution of a binding contract for the purchase of the real property described in Paragraph 2 or at closing of purchase of the real property.

(7) PUBLIC IMPROVEMENT DISTRICTS: If the Property is in a public improvement district, §5.014, Property Code, requires Seller to notify Buyer as follows: As a purchaser of this parcel of real property you are obligated to pay an assessment to a municipality or county for an improvement project undertaken by a public improvement district under Chapter 372, Local Government Code. The assessment may be due annually or in periodic installments. More information concerning the amount of the assessment and the due dates of that assessment may be obtained from the municipality or county levying the assessment. The amount of the assessments is subject to change. Your failure to pay the assessments could result in a lien on and the foreclosure of your property.

7. PROPERTY CONDITION:

A. ACCESS,INSPECTIONS AND UTILITIES: Seller shall permit Buyer and Buyer's agents access to the Property at reasonable times. Buyer may have the Property inspected by inspectors selected by Buyer and licensed by TREC or otherwise permitted by law to make inspections. Seller at Seller's expense shall turn on existing utilities for inspections.

B. SELLER'S DISCLOSURE NOTICE PURSUANT TO §5.008, TEXAS PROPERTY CODE (Notice): (Check one box only)

❑ (1) Buyer has received the Notice.

❑ (2) Buyer has not received the Notice. Within ______ days after the effective date of this contract, Seller shall deliver the Notice to Buyer. If Buyer does not receive the Notice, Buyer may terminate this contract at any time prior to the closing and the earnest money will be refunded to Buyer. If Seller delivers the Notice, Buyer may terminate this contract for any reason within 7 days after Buyer receives the Notice or prior to the closing, whichever first occurs, and the earnest money will be refunded to Buyer.

❑ (3) The Seller is not required to furnish the notice under the Texas Property Code.

C. SELLER'S DISCLOSURE OF LEAD-BASED PAINT AND LEAD-BASED PAINT HAZARDS is required by Federal law for a residential dwelling constructed prior to 1978.

D. ACCEPTANCE OF PROPERTY CONDITION: Buyer accepts the Property in its present condition; provided Seller, at Seller's expense, shall complete the following specific repairs and treatments:____

____

E. LENDER REQUIRED REPAIRS AND TREATMENTS: Unless otherwise agreed in writing, neither party is obligated to pay for lender required repairs, which includes treatment for wood

FIGURE 11.11 (CONTINUED)

TREC 20-7

Contract Concerning ____ Page 4 of 8 02-13-06
(Address of Property)

destroying insects. If the parties do not agree to pay for the lender required repairs or treatments, this contract will terminate and the earnest money will be refunded to Buyer. If the cost of lender required repairs and treatments exceeds 5% of the Sales Price, Buyer may terminate this contract and the earnest money will be refunded to Buyer.

F. COMPLETION OF REPAIRS AND TREATMENTS: Unless otherwise agreed in writing, Seller shall complete all agreed repairs and treatments prior to the Closing Date. All required permits must be obtained, and repairs and treatments must be performed by persons who are licensed or otherwise authorized by law to provide such repairs or treatments. At Buyer's election, any transferable warranties received by Seller with respect to the repairs and treatments will be transferred to Buyer at Buyer's expense. If Seller fails to complete any agreed repairs and treatments prior to the Closing Date, Buyer may do so and receive reimbursement from Seller at closing. The Closing Date will be extended up to 15 days, if necessary, to complete repairs and treatments.

G. ENVIRONMENTAL MATTERS: Buyer is advised that the presence of wetlands, toxic substances, including asbestos and wastes or other environmental hazards, or the presence of a threatened or endangered species or its habitat may affect Buyer's intended use of the Property. If Buyer is concerned about these matters, an addendum promulgated by TREC or required by the parties should be used.

H. RESIDENTIAL SERVICE CONTRACTS: Buyer may purchase a residential service contract from a residential service company licensed by TREC. If Buyer purchases a residential service contract, Seller shall reimburse Buyer at closing for the cost of the residential service contract in an amount not exceeding $______________. Buyer should review any residential service contract for the scope of coverage, exclusions and limitations. **The purchase of a residential service contract is optional. Similar coverage may be purchased from various companies authorized to do business in Texas.**

8. BROKERS' FEES: All obligations of the parties for payment of brokers' fees are contained in separate written agreements.

9. CLOSING:

A. The closing of the sale will be on or before ____________________, 20____, or within 7 days after objections made under Paragraph 6D have been cured or waived, whichever date is later (Closing Date). If either party fails to close the sale by the Closing Date, the non-defaulting party may exercise the remedies contained in Paragraph 15.

B. At closing:

(1) Seller shall execute and deliver a general warranty deed conveying title to the Property to Buyer and showing no additional exceptions to those permitted in Paragraph 6 and furnish tax statements or certificates showing no delinquent taxes on the Property.

(2) Buyer shall pay the Sales Price in good funds acceptable to the escrow agent.

(3) Seller and Buyer shall execute and deliver any notices, statements, certificates, affidavits, releases, loan documents and other documents required of them by this contract, the Commitment or law necessary for the closing of the sale and the issuance of the Title Policy.

C. Unless expressly prohibited by written agreement, Seller may continue to show the Property and receive, negotiate and accept back up offers.

D. All covenants, representations and warranties in this contract survive closing.

10. POSSESSION: Seller shall deliver to Buyer possession of the Property in its present or required condition, ordinary wear and tear excepted: ❑ upon closing and funding ❑ according to a temporary residential lease form promulgated by TREC or other written lease required by the parties. Any possession by Buyer prior to closing or by Seller after closing which is not authorized by a written lease will establish a tenancy at sufferance relationship between the parties. **Consult your insurance agent prior to change of ownership and possession because insurance coverage may be limited or terminated. The absence of a written lease or appropriate insurance coverage may expose the parties to economic loss.**

11. SPECIAL PROVISIONS: (Insert only factual statements and business details applicable to the sale. TREC rules prohibit licensees from adding factual statements or business details for which a contract addendum, lease or other form has been promulgated by TREC for mandatory use.)

Initialed for identification by Buyer______ ______ and Seller _______ ______ TREC NO. 20-7

FIGURE 11.11 (CONTINUED)

TREC 20-7

Contract Concerning ____ Page 5 of 8 02-13-06
(Address of Property)

12. SETTLEMENT AND OTHER EXPENSES:

A. The following expenses must be paid at or prior to closing:

(1) Expenses payable by Seller (Seller's Expenses):

(a) Releases of existing liens, including prepayment penalties and recording fees; release of Seller's loan liability; tax statements or certificates; preparation of deed; one-half of escrow fee; and other expenses payable by Seller under this contract.

(b) Seller shall also pay an amount not to exceed $ ___________ to be applied in the following order: Buyer's Expenses which Buyer is prohibited from paying by FHA, VA, Texas Veterans Housing Assistance Program or other governmental loan programs, and then to other Buyer's Expenses as allowed by the lender.

(2) Expenses payable by Buyer (Buyer's Expenses):

(a) Loan origination, discount, buy-down, and commitment fees (Loan Fees).

(b) Appraisal fees; loan application fees; credit reports; preparation of loan documents; interest on the notes from date of disbursement to one month prior to dates of first monthly payments; recording fees; copies of easements and restrictions; mortgagee title policy with endorsements required by lender; loan-related inspection fees; photos; amortization schedules; one-half of escrow fee; all prepaid items, including required premiums for flood and hazard insurance, reserve deposits for insurance, ad valorem taxes and special governmental assessments; final compliance inspection; courier fee; repair inspection; underwriting fee; wire transfer fee; expenses incident to any loan; and other expenses payable by Buyer under this contract.

B. Buyer shall pay Private Mortgage Insurance Premium (PMI), VA Loan Funding Fee, or FHA Mortgage Insurance Premium (MIP) as required by the lender.

C. If any expense exceeds an amount expressly stated in this contract for such expense to be paid by a party, that party may terminate this contract unless the other party agrees to pay such excess. Buyer may not pay charges and fees expressly prohibited by FHA, VA, Texas Veterans Housing Assistance Program or other governmental loan program regulations.

13. PRORATIONS: Taxes for the current year, interest, maintenance fees, assessments, dues and rents will be prorated through the Closing Date. The tax proration may be calculated taking into consideration any change in exemptions that will affect the current year's taxes. If taxes for the current year vary from the amount prorated at closing, the parties shall adjust the prorations when tax statements for the current year are available. If taxes are not paid at or prior to closing, Buyer shall pay taxes for the current year.

14. CASUALTY LOSS: If any part of the Property is damaged or destroyed by fire or other casualty after the effective date of this contract, Seller shall restore the Property to its previous condition as soon as reasonably possible, but in any event by the Closing Date. If Seller fails to do so due to factors beyond Seller's control, Buyer may (a) terminate this contract and the earnest money will be refunded to Buyer (b) extend the time for performance up to 15 days and the Closing Date will be extended as necessary or (c) accept the Property in its damaged condition with an assignment of insurance proceeds and receive credit from Seller at closing in the amount of the deductible under the insurance policy. Seller's obligations under this paragraph are independent of any other obligations of Seller under this contract.

15. DEFAULT: If Buyer fails to comply with this contract, Buyer will be in default, and Seller may (a) enforce specific performance, seek such other relief as may be provided by law, or both, or (b) terminate this contract and receive the earnest money as liquidated damages, thereby releasing both parties from this contract. If, due to factors beyond Seller's control, Seller fails within the time allowed to make any non-casualty repairs or deliver the Commitment, or survey, if required of Seller, Buyer may (a) extend the time for performance up to 15 days and the Closing Date will be extended as necessary or (b) terminate this contract as the sole remedy and receive the earnest money. If Seller fails to comply with this contract for any other reason, Seller will be in default and Buyer may (a) enforce specific performance, seek such other relief as may be provided by law, or both, or (b) terminate this contract and receive the earnest money, thereby releasing both parties from this contract.

16. MEDIATION: It is the policy of the State of Texas to encourage resolution of disputes through alternative dispute resolution procedures such as mediation. Any dispute between Seller and Buyer related to this contract which is not resolved through informal discussion ☐will ☐will not be submitted to a mutually acceptable mediation service or provider. The parties to the mediation shall bear the mediation costs equally. This paragraph does not preclude a party from seeking equitable relief from a court of competent jurisdiction.

17. ATTORNEY'S FEES: The prevailing party in any legal proceeding related to this contract is entitled to recover reasonable attorney's fees and all costs of such proceeding incurred by the prevailing party.

Initialed for identification by Buyer______ ______ and Seller _______ ______ TREC NO. 20-7

FIGURE 11.11 (CONTINUED)

TREC 20-7

Contract Concerning ____ Page 6 of 8 02-13-06
(Address of Property)

18. ESCROW:

A. ESCROW: The escrow agent is not (i) a party to this contract and does not have liability for the performance or nonperformance of any party to this contract, (ii) liable for interest on the earnest money and (iii) liable for the loss of any earnest money caused by the failure of any financial institution in which the earnest money has been deposited unless the financial institution is acting as escrow agent.

B. EXPENSES: At closing, the earnest money must be applied first to any cash down payment, then to Buyer's Expenses and any excess refunded to Buyer. If no closing occurs, escrow agent may require payment of unpaid expenses incurred on behalf of the parties and a written release of liability of escrow agent from all parties.

C. DEMAND: Upon termination of this contract, either party or the escrow agent may send a release of earnest money to each party and the parties shall execute counterparts of the release and deliver same to the escrow agent. If either party fails to execute the release, either party may make a written demand to the escrow agent for the earnest money. If only one party makes written demand for the earnest money, escrow agent shall promptly provide a copy of the demand to the other party. If escrow agent does not receive written objection to the demand from the other party within 15 days, escrow agent may disburse the earnest money to the party making demand reduced by the amount of unpaid expenses incurred on behalf of the party receiving the earnest money and escrow agent may pay the same to the creditors. If escrow agent complies with the provisions of this paragraph, each party hereby releases escrow agent from all adverse claims related to the disbursal of the earnest money.

D. DAMAGES: Any party who wrongfully fails or refuses to sign a release acceptable to the escrow agent within 7 days of receipt of the request will be liable to the other party for liquidated damages of three times the amount of the earnest money.

E. NOTICES: Escrow agent's notices will be effective when sent in compliance with Paragraph 21. Notice of objection to the demand will be deemed effective upon receipt by escrow agent.

19. REPRESENTATIONS: Seller represents that as of the Closing Date (a) there will be no liens, assessments, or security interests against the Property which will not be satisfied out of the sales proceeds unless securing payment of any loans assumed by Buyer and (b) assumed loans will not be in default. If any representation of Seller in this contract is untrue on the Closing Date, Seller will be in default.

20. FEDERAL TAX REQUIREMENTS: If Seller is a "foreign person," as defined by applicable law, or if Seller fails to deliver an affidavit to Buyer that Seller is not a "foreign person," then Buyer shall withhold from the sales proceeds an amount sufficient to comply with applicable tax law and deliver the same to the Internal Revenue Service together with appropriate tax forms. Internal Revenue Service regulations require filing written reports if currency in excess of specified amounts is received in the transaction.

21. NOTICES: All notices from one party to the other must be in writing and are effective when mailed to, hand-delivered at, or transmitted by facsimile or electronic transmission as follows:

To Buyer at: ______________________	**To Seller at:** ______________________
______________________	______________________
______________________	______________________
______________________	______________________
Telephone: ( ) ______________	Telephone: ( ) ______________
Facsimile: ( ) ______________	Facsimile: ( ) ______________
E-mail: ______________________	E-mail: ______________________

Initialed for identification by Buyer______ ______ and Seller ______ ______ TREC NO. 20-7

FIGURE 11.11 (CONTINUED)

TREC 20-7

Contract Concerning ____ Page 7 of 8 02-13-06
(Address of Property)

22. AGREEMENT OF PARTIES: This contract contains the entire agreement of the parties and cannot be changed except by their written agreement. Addenda which are a part of this contract are (Check all applicable boxes):

- ❑ Third Party Financing Condition Addendum
- ❑ Seller Financing Addendum
- ❑ Loan Assumption Addendum
- ❑ Buyer's Temporary Residential Lease
- ❑ Seller's Temporary Residential Lease
- ❑ Addendum for Sale of Other Property by Buyer
- ❑ Addendum for Seller's Disclosure of Information on Lead-based Paint and Lead-based Paint Hazards as Required by Federal Law
- ❑ Addendum for Property Subject to Mandatory Membership in an Owners' Association
- ❑ Environmental Assessment, Threatened or Endangered Species and Wetlands Addendum
- ❑ Addendum for "Back-Up" Contract
- ❑ Addendum for Coastal Area Property
- ❑ Addendum for Property Located Seaward of the Gulf Intracoastal Waterway
- ❑ Addendum for Release of Liability on Assumption of FHA, VA, or Conventional Loan Restoration of Seller's Entitlement for VA Guaranteed Loan
- ❑ Other (list): ______________________________
____

23. TERMINATION OPTION: For nominal consideration, the receipt of which is hereby acknowledged by Seller, and Buyer's agreement to pay Seller $______________ (Option Fee) within 2 days after the effective date of this contract, Seller grants Buyer the unrestricted right to terminate this contract by giving notice of termination to Seller within _______ days after the effective date of this contract. If no dollar amount is stated as the Option Fee or if Buyer fails to pay the Option Fee within the time prescribed, this paragraph will not be a part of this contract and Buyer shall not have the unrestricted right to terminate this contract. If Buyer gives notice of termination within the time prescribed, the Option Fee will not be refunded; however, any earnest money will be refunded to Buyer. The Option Fee ❑will ❑will not be credited to the Sales Price at closing. **Time is of the essence for this paragraph and strict compliance with the time for performance is required.**

24. CONSULT AN ATTORNEY: Real estate licensees cannot give legal advice. READ THIS CONTRACT CAREFULLY. If you do not understand the effect of this contract, consult an attorney BEFORE signing.

Buyer's	Seller's
Attorney is: ______________________	Attorney is: ______________________
______________________	______________________
Telephone: ( ) ______________	Telephone: ( ) ______________
Facsimile: ( ) ______________	Facsimile: ( ) ______________
E-mail: ______________________	E-mail: ______________________

EXECUTED the ______day of ____________________, 20____ (EFFECTIVE DATE).
(BROKER: FILL IN THE DATE OF FINAL ACCEPTANCE.)

______________________	______________________
Buyer	Seller
______________________	______________________
Buyer	Seller

The form of this contract has been approved by the Texas Real Estate Commission. TREC forms are intended for use only by trained real estate licensees. No representation is made as to the legal validity or adequacy of any provision in any specific transactions. It is not intended for complex transactions. Texas Real Estate Commission, P.O. Box 12188, Austin, TX 78711-2188, 1-800-250-8732 or (512) 459-6544 (http://www.trec.state.tx.us) TREC NO. 20-7. This form replaces TREC NO. 20-6.

TREC NO. 20-7

FIGURE 11.11 (CONTINUED)

TREC 20-7

Contract Concerning ______________________________ Page 8 of 8 02-13-06
(Address of Property)

BROKER INFORMATION AND RATIFICATION OF FEE

Listing Broker has agreed to pay Other Broker ______________ of the total sales price when Listing Broker's fee is received. Escrow Agent is authorized and directed to pay Other Broker from Listing Broker's fee at closing.

Other Broker — License No.	Listing Broker — License No.
represents ❑ Buyer only as Buyer's agent ❑ Seller as Listing Broker's subagent	represents ❑ Seller and Buyer as an intermediary ❑ Seller only as Seller's agent
Associate — Telephone	Listing Associate — Telephone
Broker's Address	Listing Associate's Office Address — Facsimile
City — State — Zip	City — State — Zip
Facsimile	Email Address
Email Address	Selling Associate — Telephone
	Selling Associate's Office Address — Facsimile
	City — State — Zip
	Email Address

OPTION FEE RECEIPT

Receipt of $__________ (Option Fee) in the form of ______________ is acknowledged.

Seller or Listing Broker ______________ Date ______________

CONTRACT AND EARNEST MONEY RECEIPT

Receipt of ❑Contract and ❑$__________ Earnest Money in the form of ______________ is acknowledged.

Escrow Agent: ______________ Date: ______________

By: ______________ Email Address

Address ______________ Telephone (____) ______________

City State Zip ______________ Facsimile: (____) ______________

TREC NO. 20-7

FIGURE 11.12

TREC 40-3

12-10-07

EQUAL HOUSING OPPORTUNITY

PROMULGATED BY THE TEXAS REAL ESTATE COMMISSION (TREC)

THIRD PARTY FINANCING CONDITION ADDENDUM

TO CONTRACT CONCERNING THE PROPERTY AT

→ 2365 Veterans Blvd. Austin, TX

(Street Address and City)

Buyer shall apply promptly for all financing described below and make every reasonable effort to obtain approval for the financing (Financing Approval). Buyer shall furnish all information and documents required by lender for Financing Approval. Financing Approval will be deemed to have been obtained when (1) the terms of the loan(s) described below are available and (2) lender determines that Buyer has satisfied all of lender's financial requirements (those items relating to Buyer's assets, income and credit history). If Buyer cannot obtain Financing Approval, Buyer may give written notice to Seller within 30 days after the effective date of this contract and this contract will terminate and the earnest money will be refunded to Buyer. **If Buyer does not give such notice within the time required, this contract will no longer be subject to Financing Approval. Time is of the essence for this paragraph and strict compliance with the time for performance is required.**

NOTE: Financing Approval does not include approval of lender's underwriting requirements for the Property, as specified in Paragraph 4.A.(1) of the contract.

Each note must be secured by vendor's and deed of trust liens.

CHECK APPLICABLE BOXES:

❑ A. CONVENTIONAL FINANCING:

❑ (1) A first mortgage loan in the principal amount of $ ____________ (excluding any financed PMI premium), due in full in ________ year(s), with interest not to exceed ______% per annum for the first _______year(s) of the loan with Loan Fees (loan origination, discount, buy-down, and commitment fees) not to exceed ________% of the loan.

❑ (2) A second mortgage loan in the principal amount of $____________(excluding any financed PMI premium), due in full in __________year(s), with interest not to exceed ______% per annum for the first ____________year(s) of the loan with Loan Fees (loan origination, discount, buy-down, and commitment fees) not to exceed ________% of the loan.

❑ B. TEXAS VETERANS LOAN: A loan(s) from the Texas Veterans Land Board of $____________ for a period in the total amount of _____years at the interest rate established by the Texas Veterans Land Board.

❑ C. FHA INSURED FINANCING: A Section ______________ FHA insured loan of not less than $________________ (excluding any financed MIP), amortizable monthly for not less than ________years, with interest not to exceed _______% per annum for the first ______year(s) of the loan with Loan Fees (loan origination, discount, buy-down, and commitment fees) not to exceed __________ % of the loan. As required by HUD-FHA, if FHA valuation is unknown, "*It is expressly agreed that, notwithstanding any other provision of this contract, the purchaser (Buyer) shall not be obligated to complete the purchase of the Property described herein or to incur any penalty by forfeiture of earnest money deposits or otherwise unless the purchaser (Buyer) has been given in accordance with HUD/FHA or VA requirements a written statement issued by the Federal Housing Commissioner, Department of Veterans Affairs, or a Direct Endorsement Lender setting forth the appraised value of the Property of not less than $________________. The purchaser (Buyer) shall have the privilege and option of proceeding with consummation of the contract without regard to the amount of the*

FIGURE 11.12 (CONTINUED)

TREC 40-3

Third Party Financing Condition Addendum Concerning

Page 2 of 2 12-10-07

2365 Veterans Blvd. Austin, TX

(Address of Property)

appraised valuation. The appraised valuation is arrived at to determine the maximum mortgage the Department of Housing and Urban Development will insure. HUD does not warrant the value or the condition of the Property. The purchaser (Buyer) should satisfy himself/herself that the price and the condition of the Property are acceptable."

NOTE: HUD 92564-CN "For Your Protection: Get a Home Inspection" must be attached to this Addendum.

☒ D. VA GUARANTEED FINANCING: A VA guaranteed loan of not less than $ 62,400 (excluding any financed Funding Fee), amortizable monthly for not less than 30 years, with interest not to exceed 7.25 % per annum for the first 30 year(s) of the loan with Loan Fees (loan origination, discount, buy-down, and commitment fees) not to exceed 1 % of the loan.

VA NOTICE TO BUYER: "*It is expressly agreed that, notwithstanding any other provisions of this contract, the Buyer shall not incur any penalty by forfeiture of earnest money or otherwise or be obligated to complete the purchase of the Property described herein, if the contract purchase price or cost exceeds the reasonable value of the Property established by the Department of Veterans Affairs. The Buyer shall, however, have the privilege and option of proceeding with the consummation of this contract without regard to the amount of the reasonable value established by the Department of Veterans Affairs."*

If Buyer elects to complete the purchase at an amount in excess of the reasonable value established by VA, Buyer shall pay such excess amount in cash from a source which Buyer agrees to disclose to the VA and which Buyer represents will not be from borrowed funds except as approved by VA. If VA reasonable value of the Property is less than the Sales Price, Seller may reduce the Sales Price to an amount equal to the VA reasonable value and the sale will be closed at the lower Sales Price with proportionate adjustments to the down payment and the loan amount.

Buyer hereby authorizes any lender to furnish to the Seller or Buyer or their representatives information relating only to the status of Financing Approval of Buyer.

Buyer	Seller
Buyer	Seller

This form has been approved by the Texas Real Estate Commission for use with similarly approved or promulgated contract forms. Such approval relates to this form only. TREC forms are intended for use only by trained real estate licensees. No representation is made as to the legal validity or adequacy of any provision in any specific transactions. It is not intended for complex transactions. Texas Real Estate Commission, P.O. Box 12188, Austin, TX 78711-2188, 1-800-250-8732 or (512) 459-6544 (http://www.trec.state.tx.us) TREC No. 40-3. This form replaces TREC No. 40-2.

TREC NO. 40-3

FIGURE 11.13

TREC 15-4

PROMULGATED BY THE TEXAS REAL ESTATE COMMISSION (TREC) 12-04-06

(NOTICE: For use only when SELLER occupies the property for no more than 90 days AFTER the closing)

EQUAL HOUSING OPPORTUNITY

SELLER'S TEMPORARY RESIDENTIAL LEASE

→ 1. **PARTIES:** The parties to this Lease are Victor Vet and wife Victoria Vet (Landlord) and Freddie Mac, a single person (Tenant).

→ 2. **LEASE:** Landlord leases to Tenant the Property described in the Contract between Landlord as Buyer and Tenant as Seller known as 2365 Veterans Blvd. Austin, TX 78711 (address).

3. **TERM:** The term of this Lease commences on the date the sale covered by the Contract is closed and funded and terminates four days after funding, unless terminated earlier by reason of other provisions.

4. **RENTAL:** Tenant shall pay to Landlord as rental $ 50 per day (excluding the day of closing and funding) with the full amount of rental for the term of the Lease to be paid at the time of funding of the sale. Tenant will not be entitled to a refund of rental if this Lease terminates early due to Tenant's default or voluntary surrender of the Property.

→ 5. **DEPOSIT:** Tenant shall pay to Landlord at the time of funding of the sale $ N/A as a deposit to secure performance of this Lease by Tenant. Landlord may use the deposit to satisfy Tenant's obligations under this Lease. Landlord shall refund any unused portion of the deposit to Tenant with an itemized list of all deductions from the deposit within 30 days after Tenant (a) surrenders possession of the Property and (b) provides Landlord written notice of Tenant's forwarding address.

→ 6. **UTILITIES:** Tenant shall pay all utility charges except None which Landlord shall pay.

7. **USE OF PROPERTY:** Tenant may use the Property only for residential purposes. Tenant may not assign this Lease or sublet any part of the Property.

→ 8. **PETS:** Tenant may not keep pets on the Property except N/A.

9. **CONDITION OF PROPERTY:** Tenant accepts the Property in its present condition and state of repair at the commencement of the Lease. Upon termination, Tenant shall surrender the Property to Landlord in the condition required under the Contract, except normal wear and tear and any casualty loss.

10. **ALTERATIONS:** Tenant may not alter the Property or install improvements or fixtures without the prior written consent of the Landlord. Any improvements or fixtures placed on the Property during the Lease become the Property of Landlord.

→ 11. **SPECIAL PROVISIONS:**

None

12. **INSPECTIONS:** Landlord may enter at reasonable times to inspect the Property. Tenant shall provide Landlord door keys and access codes to allow access to the Property during the term of Lease.

13. **LAWS:** Tenant shall comply with all applicable laws, restrictions, ordinances, rules and regulations with respect to the Property.

14. **REPAIRS AND MAINTENANCE:** Except as otherwise provided in this Lease, Tenant shall bear all expense of repairing and maintaining the Property, including but not limited to the yard, trees and shrubs, unless otherwise required by the Texas Property Code. Tenant shall promptly repair at Tenant's expense any damage to the Property caused directly or indirectly by any act or omission of the Tenant or any person other than the Landlord, Landlord's agents or invitees.

Initialed for identification by Landlord _______ and Tenant ___________ TREC NO. 15-4

FIGURE 11.13 (CONTINUED)

TREC 15-4

Seller's Temporary Residential Lease ______________________________ Page 2 of 2 12-04-06
(Address of Property)

15. INDEMNITY: Tenant indemnifies Landlord from the claims of all third parties for injury or damage to the person or property of such third party arising from the use or occupancy of the Property by Tenant. This indemnification includes attorney's fees, costs and expenses incurred by Landlord.

16. INSURANCE: Landlord and Tenant shall each maintain such insurance on the contents and Property as each party may deem appropriate during the term of this Lease. NOTE: CONSULT YOUR INSURANCE AGENT; POSSESSION OF THE PROPERTY BY SELLER AS TENANT MAY CHANGE INSURANCE POLICY COVERAGE.

17. DEFAULT: If Tenant fails to perform or observe any provision of this Lease and fails, within 24 hours after notice by Landlord, to commence and diligently pursue to remedy such failure, Tenant will be in default.

18. TERMINATION: This Lease terminates upon expiration of the term specified in Paragraph 3 or upon Tenant's default under this Lease.

19. HOLDING OVER: Tenant shall surrender possession of the Property upon termination of this Lease. Any possession by Tenant after termination creates a tenancy at sufferance and will not operate to renew or extend this Lease. Tenant shall pay $ 100 per day during the period of any possession after termination as damages, in addition to any other remedies to which Landlord is entitled.

20. ATTORNEY'S FEES: The prevailing party in any legal proceeding brought under or with respect to this Lease is entitled to recover from the non-prevailing party all costs of such proceeding and reasonable attorney's fees.

21. SMOKE DETECTORS: The Texas Property Code requires Landlord to install smoke detectors in certain locations within the Property at Landlord's expense. Tenant expressly waives Landlord's duty to inspect and repair smoke detectors.

22. SECURITY DEVICES: The requirements of the Texas Property Code relating to security devices do not apply to a residential lease for a term of 90 days or less.

23. CONSULT YOUR ATTORNEY: Real estate licensees cannot give legal advice. This Lease is intended to be legally binding. READ IT CAREFULLY. If you do not understand the effect of this Lease, consult your attorney BEFORE signing.

24. NOTICES: All notices from one party to the other must be in writing and are effective when mailed to, hand-delivered at, or transmitted by facsimile or electronic transmission as follows:

→ **To Landlord:** ______________________	**To Tenant:** ______________________
______________________	______________________
______________________	______________________
______________________	______________________
→ Telephone: ( ) ______________	Telephone: ( ) ______________
→ Facsimile: ( ) ______________	Facsimile: ( ) ______________
→ E-mail: ______________________	E-mail: ______________________

______________________	______________________
Landlord	Tenant
______________________	______________________
Landlord	Tenant

TREC NO. 15-4

FIGURE 11.14

TREC 10-5

04-23-07

PROMULGATED BY THE TEXAS REAL ESTATE COMMISSION (TREC)

EQUAL HOUSING OPPORTUNITY

ADDENDUM FOR SALE OF OTHER PROPERTY BY BUYER

TO CONTRACT CONCERNING THE PROPERTY AT

→ 2365 Veterans Blvd. Austin, TX
(Address of Property)

→ **A.** The contract is contingent upon Buyer's **receipt of the proceeds** from the sale of Buyer's property at 1565 Travis Lane Houston, TX 77085 (Address) on or before October 3, 20 08 (the Contingency). If the Contingency is not satisfied or waived by Buyer by the above date, the contract will terminate automatically and the earnest money will be refunded to Buyer.

NOTICE: The date inserted in this Paragraph should be no later than the Closing Date specified in Paragraph 9 of the contract.

→ **B.** If Seller accepts a written offer to sell the Property, Seller shall notify Buyer (1) of such acceptance **AND** (2) that Seller requires Buyer to waive the Contingency. Buyer must waive the Contingency on or before the 3rd day after Seller's notice to Buyer; otherwise the contract will terminate automatically and the earnest money will be refunded to Buyer.

→ **C.** Buyer may waive the Contingency only by notifying Seller of the waiver and depositing $ 5,000 with escrow agent as additional earnest money. All notices and waivers must be in writing and are effective when delivered in accordance with the contract.

D. If Buyer waives the Contingency and fails to close and fund solely due to Buyer's non-receipt of proceeds from Buyer's sale of the Property described in Paragraph A, Buyer will be in default. If such default occurs, Seller may exercise the remedies specified in Paragraph 15 of the contract.

E. For purposes of this Addendum time is of the essence; strict compliance with the times for performance stated herein is required.

Buyer	Seller
Buyer	Seller

This form has been approved by the Texas Real Estate Commission for use with similarly approved or promulgated contract forms. Such approval relates to this form only. TREC forms are intended for use only by trained real estate licensees. No representation is made as to the legal validity or adequacy of any provision in any specific transactions. It is not suitable for complex transactions. Texas Real Estate Commission, P.O. Box 12188, Austin, TX 78711-2188, 1-800-250-8732 or (512) 459-6544 (http://www.trec.state.tx.us) TREC No. 10-5. This form replaces TREC No. 10-4.

TREC No. 10-5

FIGURE 11.15

TREC OP-L

APPROVED BY THE TEXAS REAL ESTATE COMMISSION 02-09-2004

EQUAL HOUSING OPPORTUNITY

ADDENDUM FOR SELLER'S DISCLOSURE OF INFORMATION ON LEAD-BASED PAINT AND LEAD-BASED PAINT HAZARDS AS REQUIRED BY FEDERAL LAW

➔ CONCERNING THE PROPERTY AT 2365 Veterans Blvd. Austin, TX
(Street Address and City)

A. **LEAD WARNING STATEMENT:** "Every purchaser of any interest in residential real property on which a residential dwelling was built prior to 1978 is notified that such property may present exposure to lead from lead-based paint that may place young children at risk of developing lead poisoning. Lead poisoning in young children may produce permanent neurological damage, including learning disabilities, reduced intelligence quotient, behavioral problems, and impaired memory. Lead poisoning also poses a particular risk to pregnant women. The seller of any interest in residential real property is required to provide the buyer with any information on lead-based paint hazards from risk assessments or inspections in the seller's possession and notify the buyer of any known lead-based paint hazards. A risk assessment or inspection for possible lead-paint hazards is recommended prior to purchase."
NOTICE: Inspector must be properly certified as required by federal law.

B. SELLER'S DISCLOSURE:

1. PRESENCE OF LEAD-BASED PAINT AND/OR LEAD-BASED PAINT HAZARDS (check on box only):
   ☐ (a) Known lead-based paint and/or lead-based paint hazards are present in the Property (explain): ________
   ➔ ☒ (b) Seller has no actual knowledge of lead-based paint and/or lead-based paint hazards in the Property.
2. RECORDS AND REPORTS AVAILABLE TO SELLER (check one box only):
   ☐ (a) Seller has provided the purchaser with all available records and reports pertaining to lead-based paint and/or lead-based paint hazards in the Property (list documents): ________
   ☐ (b) Seller has no reports or records pertaining to lead-based paint and/or lead-based paint hazards in the Property.

C. BUYER'S RIGHTS (check one box only):

☐ 1. Buyer waives the opportunity to conduct a risk assessment or inspection of the Property for the presence of lead-based paint or lead-based paint hazards.
➔ ☒ 2. Within ten days after the effective date of this contract, Buyer may have the Property inspected by inspectors selected by Buyer. If lead-based paint or lead-based paint hazards are present, Buyer may terminate this contract by giving Seller written notice within 14 days after the effective date of this contract, and the earnest money will be refunded to Buyer.

D. BUYER'S ACKNOWLEDGMENT (check applicable boxes):

☐ 1. Buyer has received copies of all information listed above.
➔ ☒ 2. Buyer has received the pamphlet *Protect Your Family from Lead in Your Home*.

E. BROKERS' ACKNOWLEDGMENT: Brokers have informed Seller of Seller's obligations under 42 U.S.C. 4852d to: (a) provide Buyer with the federally approved pamphlet on lead poisoning prevention; (b) complete this addendum; (c) disclose any known lead-based paint and/or lead-based paint hazards in the Property; (d) deliver all records and reports to Buyer pertaining to lead-based paint and/or lead-based paint hazards in the Property; (e) provide Buyer a period of up to 10 days to have the Property inspected; and (f) retain a completed copy of this addendum for at least 3 years following the sale. Brokers are aware of their responsibility to ensure compliance.

F. CERTIFICATION OF ACCURACY: The following persons have reviewed the information above and certify, to the best of their knowledge, that the information they have provided is true and accurate.

Buyer	Date	Seller	Date
Buyer	Date	Seller	Date
Other Broker	Date	Listing Broker	Date

The form of this addendum has been approved by the Texas Real Estate Commission for use only with similarly approved or promulgated forms of contracts. Such approval relates to this contract form only. TREC forms are intended for use only by trained real estate licensees. No representation is made as to the legal validity or adequacy of any provision in any specific transactions. It is not suitable for complex transactions. Texas Real Estate Commission, P.O. Box 12188, Austin, TX 78711-2188, 1-800-250-8732 or (512) 459-6544 (http://www.trec.state.tx.us)

Form OP-L 01A

TRANSACTION 5: SELLER FINANCE *(USING: TREC 20-7, 26-5, AND 28-1. SEE FIGURE 11.16 THROUGH FIGURE 11.18.)*

Thomas J. Swanson and his wife, Sarah J. Swanson, will purchase a second home. It is known as Lot 6, Block 8 of the Happily-Ever-After Addition of Waco, McLennan County, Texas, 76710. They are willing to pay $73,500 for it if the owner, Samuel Jay Johnson, a bachelor, will owner finance $25,000 for 5 years at 7 percent annual interest. The Buyers will pay monthly interest only until maturity when the principal balance is due. They agree to a due-on-sale clause in the deed of trust and will provide paid tax receipts by February 1 of each year the loan is outstanding.

The Swansons request a title policy issued by Secure Title Company and a new survey showing no encroachments or easements other than the 10-foot utility easement at the rear of the lot. The Buyers want 10 days for objections to survey and title commitment. The Seller will pay for the title policy. The Swansons want to make certain that cable TV services are available. They have received the Seller's Disclosure Notice and buy a 10-day option to terminate for $150 to have the opportunity to thoroughly evaluate the Property. The Option Fee will not be credited to the Sales Price at closing. Possession will be granted at closing and funding.

The Property is not subject to a mandatory owners' association assessment. It is listed with Smooth Sails Realty through whom the Buyers purchase it without representation. They will close on or before May 27, which is within 15 days of the effective date of the contract. The Seller requests that the Buyer furnish a current credit report within 5 days after the effective date of the contract as evidence of good credit.

The Property is located at 15630 Paradise Avenue in Waco, Texas 76710. The Buyer wants deletion of the common title policy exclusion relating to discrepancies, conflicts and shortages in area or boundary, and is willing to pay the additional 5 percent policy premium required by the title company. Earnest money in the amount of $2,000 has been tendered. The Sellers will provide a new survey within 10 days at the Seller's expense. The survey will be acceptable to the title company. The purchasers want to have an environmental assessment performed to make certain that there is no contamination and that no toxic materials are present. This they will do within 10 days after the effective date of the contract. The parties also agree to mediate any disputes that may arise.

FIGURE 11.16

TREC 20-7

02-13-06

EQUAL HOUSING OPPORTUNITY

PROMULGATED BY THE TEXAS REAL ESTATE COMMISSION (TREC)

ONE TO FOUR FAMILY RESIDENTIAL CONTRACT (RESALE)

NOTICE: Not For Use For Condominium Transactions

1. **PARTIES:** Samuel Jay Johnson, a single person (Seller) agrees to sell and convey to Thomas J. Swanson and wife Sarah J. Swanson (Buyer) and Buyer agrees to buy from Seller the Property described below.

2. **PROPERTY:**
   A. LAND: Lot 6 Block 8, Happily-Ever-After Addition, City of Waco, County of McLennan, Texas, known as ______ (address/zip code), or as described on attached exhibit.
   B. IMPROVEMENTS: The house, garage and all other fixtures and improvements attached to the above-described real property, including without limitation, the following **permanently installed and built-in items,** if any: all equipment and appliances, valances, screens, shutters, awnings, wall-to-wall carpeting, mirrors, ceiling fans, attic fans, mail boxes, television antennas and satellite dish system and equipment, heating and air-conditioning units, security and fire detection equipment, wiring, plumbing and lighting fixtures, chandeliers, water softener system, kitchen equipment, garage door openers, cleaning equipment, shrubbery, landscaping, outdoor cooking equipment, and all other property owned by Seller and attached to the above described real property.
   C. ACCESSORIES: The following described related accessories, if any: window air conditioning units, stove, fireplace screens, curtains and rods, blinds, window shades, draperies and rods, controls for satellite dish system, controls for garage door openers, entry gate controls, door keys, mailbox keys, above ground pool, swimming pool equipment and maintenance accessories, and artificial fireplace logs.
   D. EXCLUSIONS: The following improvements and accessories will be retained by Seller and removed prior to delivery of possession: ______.

   The land, improvements and accessories are collectively referred to as the "Property".

3. **SALES PRICE:**
   A. Cash portion of Sales Price payable by Buyer at closing .... $______
   B. Sum of all financing described below (excluding any loan funding fee or mortgage insurance premium)... $______
   C. Sales Price (Sum of A and B).. $______

4. **FINANCING:** The portion of Sales Price not payable in cash will be paid as follows: (Check applicable boxes below)
   ☐ A. THIRD PARTY FINANCING: One or more third party mortgage loans in the total amount of $ n/a (excluding any loan funding fee or mortgage insurance premium).
   (1) Property Approval: If the Property does not satisfy the lenders' underwriting requirements for the loan(s), this contract will terminate and the earnest money will be refunded to Buyer.
   (2) Financing Approval: (Check one box only)
   ☐ (a) This contract is subject to Buyer being approved for the financing described in the attached Third Party Financing Condition Addendum.
   ☐ (b) This contract is not subject to Buyer being approved for financing and does not involve FHA or VA financing.
   ☐ B. ASSUMPTION: The assumption of the unpaid principal balance of one or more promissory notes described in the attached TREC Loan Assumption Addendum.
   ☒ C. SELLER FINANCING: A promissory note from Buyer to Seller of $______, secured by vendor's and deed of trust liens, and containing the terms and conditions described in the attached TREC Seller Financing Addendum. If an owner policy of title insurance is furnished, Buyer shall furnish Seller with a mortgagee policy of title insurance.

5. **EARNEST MONEY:** Upon execution of this contract by both parties, Buyer shall deposit $2000 as earnest money with ______, as escrow agent, at ______ (address). Buyer shall deposit additional earnest money of $______ with escrow agent within n/a days after the effective date of this contract. If Buyer fails to deposit the earnest money as required by this contract, Buyer will be in default.

6. **TITLE POLICY AND SURVEY:**
   A. TITLE POLICY: Seller shall furnish to Buyer at ☒Seller's ☐Buyer's expense an owner policy of title insurance (Title Policy) issued by ______ (Title Company) in the amount of the Sales Price, dated at or after closing, insuring Buyer

Initialed for identification by Buyer______ ______ and Seller ______ ______ TREC NO. 20-7

FIGURE 11.16 (CONTINUED)

TREC 20-7

Contract Concerning 15630 Paradise Avenue, Waco, TX 76710 Page 2 of 8 02-13-06
(Address of Property)

against loss under the provisions of the Title Policy, subject to the promulgated exclusions (including existing building and zoning ordinances) and the following exceptions:

(1) Restrictive covenants common to the platted subdivision in which the Property is located.
(2) The standard printed exception for standby fees, taxes and assessments.
(3) Liens created as part of the financing described in Paragraph 4.
(4) Utility easements created by the dedication deed or plat of the subdivision in which the Property is located.
(5) Reservations or exceptions otherwise permitted by this contract or as may be approved by Buyer in writing.
(6) The standard printed exception as to marital rights.
(7) The standard printed exception as to waters, tidelands, beaches, streams, and related matters.
(8) The standard printed exception as to discrepancies, conflicts, shortages in area or boundary lines, encroachments or protrusions, or overlapping improvements. Buyer, at Buyer's expense, may have the exception amended to read, "shortages in area".

B. COMMITMENT: Within 20 days after the Title Company receives a copy of this contract, Seller shall furnish to Buyer a commitment for title insurance (Commitment) and, at Buyer's expense, legible copies of restrictive covenants and documents evidencing exceptions in the Commitment (Exception Documents) other than the standard printed exceptions. Seller authorizes the Title Company to deliver the Commitment and Exception Documents to Buyer at Buyer's address shown in Paragraph 21. If the Commitment and Exception Documents are not delivered to Buyer within the specified time, the time for delivery will be automatically extended up to 15 days or the Closing Date, whichever is earlier.

C. SURVEY: The survey must be made by a registered professional land surveyor acceptable to the Title Company and any lender. (Check one box only)

☐ (1) Within n/a days after the effective date of this contract, Seller shall furnish to Buyer and Title Company Seller's existing survey of the Property and a Residential Real Property Affidavit promulgated by the Texas Department of Insurance (Affidavit). If the existing survey or Affidavit is not acceptable to Title Company or Buyer's lender, Buyer shall obtain a new survey at ☐ Seller's ☐ Buyer's expense no later than 3 days prior to Closing Date. If Seller fails to furnish the existing survey or Affidavit within the time prescribed, Buyer shall obtain a new survey at Seller's expense no later than 3 days prior to Closing Date.

☐ (2) Within n/a days after the effective date of this contract, Buyer shall obtain a new survey at Buyer's expense. Buyer is deemed to receive the survey on the date of actual receipt or the date specified in this paragraph, whichever is earlier.

☒ (3) Within 10 days after the effective date of this contract, Seller, at Seller's expense shall furnish a new survey to Buyer.

D. OBJECTIONS: Buyer may object in writing to defects, exceptions, or encumbrances to title: disclosed on the survey other than items 6A(1) through (7) above; disclosed in the Commitment other than items 6A(1) through (8) above; or which prohibit the following use or activity: n/a
________________________________.

Buyer must object not later than (i) the Closing Date or (ii) 10 days after Buyer receives the Commitment, Exception Documents, and the survey, whichever is earlier. Buyer's failure to object within the time allowed will constitute a waiver of Buyer's right to object; except that the requirements in Schedule C of the Commitment are not waived. Provided Seller is not obligated to incur any expense, Seller shall cure the timely objections of Buyer or any third party lender within 15 days after Seller receives the objections and the Closing Date will be extended as necessary. If objections are not cured within such 15 day period, this contract will terminate and the earnest money will be refunded to Buyer unless Buyer waives the objections.

E. TITLE NOTICES:

(1) ABSTRACT OR TITLE POLICY: Broker advises Buyer to have an abstract of title covering the Property examined by an attorney of Buyer's selection, or Buyer should be furnished with or obtain a Title Policy. If a Title Policy is furnished, the Commitment should be promptly reviewed by an attorney of Buyer's choice due to the time limitations on Buyer's right to object.

(2) MANDATORY OWNERS' ASSOCIATION MEMBERSHIP: The Property ☐ is ☒ is not subject to mandatory membership in an owners' association. If the Property is subject to mandatory membership in an owners' association, Seller notifies Buyer under §5.012, Texas Property Code, that, as a purchaser of property in the residential community in which the Property is located, you are obligated to be a member of the owners' association. Restrictive covenants governing the use and occupancy of the Property and a dedicatory instrument governing the establishment, maintenance, and operation of this residential community have been or will be recorded in the Real Property Records of the county in which the Property is located. Copies of the restrictive covenants and dedicatory instrument may be obtained from the county clerk. You are obligated to pay

Initialed for identification by Buyer______ ______ and Seller _______ ______ TREC NO. 20-7

FIGURE 11.16 (CONTINUED)

TREC 20-7

assessments to the owners' association. The amount of the assessments is subject to change. Your failure to pay the assessments could result in a lien on and the foreclosure of the Property. If Buyer is concerned about these matters, the TREC promulgated Addendum for Property Subject to Mandatory Membership in an Owner's Association should be used.

(3) STATUTORY TAX DISTRICTS: If the Property is situated in a utility or other statutorily created district providing water, sewer, drainage, or flood control facilities and services, Chapter 49, Texas Water Code, requires Seller to deliver and Buyer to sign the statutory notice relating to the tax rate, bonded indebtedness, or standby fee of the district prior to final execution of this contract.

(4) TIDE WATERS: If the Property abuts the tidally influenced waters of the state, §33.135, Texas Natural Resources Code, requires a notice regarding coastal area property to be included in the contract. An addendum containing the notice promulgated by TREC or required by the parties must be used.

(5) ANNEXATION: If the Property is located outside the limits of a municipality, Seller notifies Buyer under §5.011, Texas Property Code, that the Property may now or later be included in the extraterritorial jurisdiction of a municipality and may now or later be subject to annexation by the municipality. Each municipality maintains a map that depicts its boundaries and extraterritorial jurisdiction. To determine if the Property is located within a municipality's extraterritorial jurisdiction or is likely to be located within a municipality's extraterritorial jurisdiction, contact all municipalities located in the general proximity of the Property for further information.

(6) PROPERTY LOCATED IN A CERTIFICATED SERVICE AREA OF A UTILITY SERVICE PROVIDER: Notice required by §13.257, Water Code: The real property, described in Paragraph 2, that you are about to purchase may be located in a certificated water or sewer service area, which is authorized by law to provide water or sewer service to the properties in the certificated area. If your property is located in a certificated area there may be special costs or charges that you will be required to pay before you can receive water or sewer service. There may be a period required to construct lines or other facilities necessary to provide water or sewer service to your property. You are advised to determine if the property is in a certificated area and contact the utility service provider to determine the cost that you will be required to pay and the period, if any, that is required to provide water or sewer service to your property. The undersigned Buyer hereby acknowledges receipt of the foregoing notice at or before the execution of a binding contract for the purchase of the real property described in Paragraph 2 or at closing of purchase of the real property.

(7) PUBLIC IMPROVEMENT DISTRICTS: If the Property is in a public improvement district, §5.014, Property Code, requires Seller to notify Buyer as follows: As a purchaser of this parcel of real property you are obligated to pay an assessment to a municipality or county for an improvement project undertaken by a public improvement district under Chapter 372, Local Government Code. The assessment may be due annually or in periodic installments. More information concerning the amount of the assessment and the due dates of that assessment may be obtained from the municipality or county levying the assessment. The amount of the assessments is subject to change. Your failure to pay the assessments could result in a lien on and the foreclosure of your property.

7. PROPERTY CONDITION:

A. ACCESS,INSPECTIONS AND UTILITIES: Seller shall permit Buyer and Buyer's agents access to the Property at reasonable times. Buyer may have the Property inspected by inspectors selected by Buyer and licensed by TREC or otherwise permitted by law to make inspections. Seller at Seller's expense shall turn on existing utilities for inspections.

B. SELLER'S DISCLOSURE NOTICE PURSUANT TO §5.008, TEXAS PROPERTY CODE (Notice): (Check one box only)

☒ (1) Buyer has received the Notice.

☐ (2) Buyer has not received the Notice. Within n/a days after the effective date of this contract, Seller shall deliver the Notice to Buyer. If Buyer does not receive the Notice, Buyer may terminate this contract at any time prior to the closing and the earnest money will be refunded to Buyer. If Seller delivers the Notice, Buyer may terminate this contract for any reason within 7 days after Buyer receives the Notice or prior to the closing, whichever first occurs, and the earnest money will be refunded to Buyer.

☐ (3) The Seller is not required to furnish the notice under the Texas Property Code.

C. SELLER'S DISCLOSURE OF LEAD-BASED PAINT AND LEAD-BASED PAINT HAZARDS is required by Federal law for a residential dwelling constructed prior to 1978.

D. ACCEPTANCE OF PROPERTY CONDITION: Buyer accepts the Property in its present condition; provided Seller, at Seller's expense, shall complete the following specific repairs and treatments: none

E. LENDER REQUIRED REPAIRS AND TREATMENTS: Unless otherwise agreed in writing, neither party is obligated to pay for lender required repairs, which includes treatment for wood

FIGURE 11.16 (CONTINUED)

TREC 20-7

destroying insects. If the parties do not agree to pay for the lender required repairs or treatments, this contract will terminate and the earnest money will be refunded to Buyer. If the cost of lender required repairs and treatments exceeds 5% of the Sales Price, Buyer may terminate this contract and the earnest money will be refunded to Buyer.

F. COMPLETION OF REPAIRS AND TREATMENTS: Unless otherwise agreed in writing, Seller shall complete all agreed repairs and treatments prior to the Closing Date. All required permits must be obtained, and repairs and treatments must be performed by persons who are licensed or otherwise authorized by law to provide such repairs or treatments. At Buyer's election, any transferable warranties received by Seller with respect to the repairs and treatments will be transferred to Buyer at Buyer's expense. If Seller fails to complete any agreed repairs and treatments prior to the Closing Date, Buyer may do so and receive reimbursement from Seller at closing. The Closing Date will be extended up to 15 days, if necessary, to complete repairs and treatments.

G. ENVIRONMENTAL MATTERS: Buyer is advised that the presence of wetlands, toxic substances, including asbestos and wastes or other environmental hazards, or the presence of a threatened or endangered species or its habitat may affect Buyer's intended use of the Property. If Buyer is concerned about these matters, an addendum promulgated by TREC or required by the parties should be used.

H. RESIDENTIAL SERVICE CONTRACTS: Buyer may purchase a residential service contract from a residential service company licensed by TREC. If Buyer purchases a residential service contract, Seller shall reimburse Buyer at closing for the cost of the residential service contract in an amount not exceeding $ n/a . Buyer should review any residential service contract for the scope of coverage, exclusions and limitations. **The purchase of a residential service contract is optional. Similar coverage may be purchased from various companies authorized to do business in Texas.**

8. **BROKERS' FEES:** All obligations of the parties for payment of brokers' fees are contained in separate written agreements.

9. **CLOSING:**

A. The closing of the sale will be on or before May 27, 2008, or within 7 days after objections made under Paragraph 6D have been cured or waived, whichever date is later (Closing Date). If either party fails to close the sale by the Closing Date, the non-defaulting party may exercise the remedies contained in Paragraph 15.

B. At closing:

(1) Seller shall execute and deliver a general warranty deed conveying title to the Property to Buyer and showing no additional exceptions to those permitted in Paragraph 6 and furnish tax statements or certificates showing no delinquent taxes on the Property.

(2) Buyer shall pay the Sales Price in good funds acceptable to the escrow agent.

(3) Seller and Buyer shall execute and deliver any notices, statements, certificates, affidavits, releases, loan documents and other documents required of them by this contract, the Commitment or law necessary for the closing of the sale and the issuance of the Title Policy.

C. Unless expressly prohibited by written agreement, Seller may continue to show the Property and receive, negotiate and accept back up offers.

D. All covenants, representations and warranties in this contract survive closing.

10. **POSSESSION:** Seller shall deliver to Buyer possession of the Property in its present or required condition, ordinary wear and tear excepted: ☒ upon closing and funding ☐ according to a temporary residential lease form promulgated by TREC or other written lease required by the parties. Any possession by Buyer prior to closing or by Seller after closing which is not authorized by a written lease will establish a tenancy at sufferance relationship between the parties. **Consult your insurance agent prior to change of ownership and possession because insurance coverage may be limited or terminated. The absence of a written lease or appropriate insurance coverage may expose the parties to economic loss.**

11. **SPECIAL PROVISIONS:** (Insert only factual statements and business details applicable to the sale. TREC rules prohibit licensees from adding factual statements or business details for which a contract addendum, lease or other form has been promulgated by TREC for mandatory use.)

Buyer to pay additional premium for deletion of exceptions [illegible] in paragraph 6A.

FIGURE 11.16 (CONTINUED)

TREC 20-7

Contract Concerning ______________________ Page 5 of 8 02-13-06
(Address of Property)

12. SETTLEMENT AND OTHER EXPENSES:

A. The following expenses must be paid at or prior to closing:

(1) Expenses payable by Seller (Seller's Expenses):

(a) Releases of existing liens, including prepayment penalties and recording fees; release of Seller's loan liability; tax statements or certificates; preparation of deed; one-half of escrow fee; and other expenses payable by Seller under this contract.

(b) Seller shall also pay an amount not to exceed $ ________ to be applied in the following order: Buyer's Expenses which Buyer is prohibited from paying by FHA, VA, Texas Veterans Housing Assistance Program or other governmental loan programs, and then to other Buyer's Expenses as allowed by the lender.

(2) Expenses payable by Buyer (Buyer's Expenses):

(a) Loan origination, discount, buy-down, and commitment fees (Loan Fees).

(b) Appraisal fees; loan application fees; credit reports; preparation of loan documents; interest on the notes from date of disbursement to one month prior to dates of first monthly payments; recording fees; copies of easements and restrictions; mortgagee title policy with endorsements required by lender; loan-related inspection fees; photos; amortization schedules; one-half of escrow fee; all prepaid items, including required premiums for flood and hazard insurance, reserve deposits for insurance, ad valorem taxes and special governmental assessments; final compliance inspection; courier fee; repair inspection; underwriting fee; wire transfer fee; expenses incident to any loan; and other expenses payable by Buyer under this contract.

B. Buyer shall pay Private Mortgage Insurance Premium (PMI), VA Loan Funding Fee, or FHA Mortgage Insurance Premium (MIP) as required by the lender.

C. If any expense exceeds an amount expressly stated in this contract for such expense to be paid by a party, that party may terminate this contract unless the other party agrees to pay such excess. Buyer may not pay charges and fees expressly prohibited by FHA, VA, Texas Veterans Housing Assistance Program or other governmental loan program regulations.

13. PRORATIONS: Taxes for the current year, interest, maintenance fees, assessments, dues and rents will be prorated through the Closing Date. The tax proration may be calculated taking into consideration any change in exemptions that will affect the current year's taxes. If taxes for the current year vary from the amount prorated at closing, the parties shall adjust the prorations when tax statements for the current year are available. If taxes are not paid at or prior to closing, Buyer shall pay taxes for the current year.

14. CASUALTY LOSS: If any part of the Property is damaged or destroyed by fire or other casualty after the effective date of this contract, Seller shall restore the Property to its previous condition as soon as reasonably possible, but in any event by the Closing Date. If Seller fails to do so due to factors beyond Seller's control, Buyer may (a) terminate this contract and the earnest money will be refunded to Buyer (b) extend the time for performance up to 15 days and the Closing Date will be extended as necessary or (c) accept the Property in its damaged condition with an assignment of insurance proceeds and receive credit from Seller at closing in the amount of the deductible under the insurance policy. Seller's obligations under this paragraph are independent of any other obligations of Seller under this contract.

15. DEFAULT: If Buyer fails to comply with this contract, Buyer will be in default, and Seller may (a) enforce specific performance, seek such other relief as may be provided by law, or both, or (b) terminate this contract and receive the earnest money as liquidated damages, thereby releasing both parties from this contract. If, due to factors beyond Seller's control, Seller fails within the time allowed to make any non-casualty repairs or deliver the Commitment, or survey, if required of Seller, Buyer may (a) extend the time for performance up to 15 days and the Closing Date will be extended as necessary or (b) terminate this contract as the sole remedy and receive the earnest money. If Seller fails to comply with this contract for any other reason, Seller will be in default and Buyer may (a) enforce specific performance, seek such other relief as may be provided by law, or both, or (b) terminate this contract and receive the earnest money, thereby releasing both parties from this contract.

16. MEDIATION: It is the policy of the State of Texas to encourage resolution of disputes through alternative dispute resolution procedures such as mediation. Any dispute between Seller and Buyer related to this contract which is not resolved through informal discussion ☒will ☐will not be submitted to a mutually acceptable mediation service or provider. The parties to the mediation shall bear the mediation costs equally. This paragraph does not preclude a party from seeking equitable relief from a court of competent jurisdiction.

17. ATTORNEY'S FEES: The prevailing party in any legal proceeding related to this contract is entitled to recover reasonable attorney's fees and all costs of such proceeding incurred by the prevailing party.

Initialed for identification by Buyer_____ _____ and Seller _____ _____ TREC NO. 20-7

FIGURE 11.16 (CONTINUED)

TREC 20-7

18. ESCROW:

A. ESCROW: The escrow agent is not (i) a party to this contract and does not have liability for the performance or nonperformance of any party to this contract, (ii) liable for interest on the earnest money and (iii) liable for the loss of any earnest money caused by the failure of any financial institution in which the earnest money has been deposited unless the financial institution is acting as escrow agent.

B. EXPENSES: At closing, the earnest money must be applied first to any cash down payment, then to Buyer's Expenses and any excess refunded to Buyer. If no closing occurs, escrow agent may require payment of unpaid expenses incurred on behalf of the parties and a written release of liability of escrow agent from all parties.

C. DEMAND: Upon termination of this contract, either party or the escrow agent may send a release of earnest money to each party and the parties shall execute counterparts of the release and deliver same to the escrow agent. If either party fails to execute the release, either party may make a written demand to the escrow agent for the earnest money. If only one party makes written demand for the earnest money, escrow agent shall promptly provide a copy of the demand to the other party. If escrow agent does not receive written objection to the demand from the other party within 15 days, escrow agent may disburse the earnest money to the party making demand reduced by the amount of unpaid expenses incurred on behalf of the party receiving the earnest money and escrow agent may pay the same to the creditors. If escrow agent complies with the provisions of this paragraph, each party hereby releases escrow agent from all adverse claims related to the disbursal of the earnest money.

D. DAMAGES: Any party who wrongfully fails or refuses to sign a release acceptable to the escrow agent within 7 days of receipt of the request will be liable to the other party for liquidated damages of three times the amount of the earnest money.

E. NOTICES: Escrow agent's notices will be effective when sent in compliance with Paragraph 21. Notice of objection to the demand will be deemed effective upon receipt by escrow agent.

19. REPRESENTATIONS: Seller represents that as of the Closing Date (a) there will be no liens, assessments, or security interests against the Property which will not be satisfied out of the sales proceeds unless securing payment of any loans assumed by Buyer and (b) assumed loans will not be in default. If any representation of Seller in this contract is untrue on the Closing Date, Seller will be in default.

20. FEDERAL TAX REQUIREMENTS: If Seller is a "foreign person," as defined by applicable law, or if Seller fails to deliver an affidavit to Buyer that Seller is not a "foreign person," then Buyer shall withhold from the sales proceeds an amount sufficient to comply with applicable tax law and deliver the same to the Internal Revenue Service together with appropriate tax forms. Internal Revenue Service regulations require filing written reports if currency in excess of specified amounts is received in the transaction.

21. NOTICES: All notices from one party to the other must be in writing and are effective when mailed to, hand-delivered at, or transmitted by facsimile or electronic transmission as follows:

To Buyer at:		**To Seller at:**	
	1408 Swan Drive		15630 Paradise avenue
	Waco, TX 76710		Waco, TX 76710
	n/a		n/a
	n/a		n/a
Telephone:	(555) 555-0000	Telephone:	(555) 555-0001
Facsimile:	(555) 555-0002	Facsimile:	(555) 555-0003
E-mail:	buyer@buyers.com	E-mail:	seller@sellers.com

FIGURE 11.16 (CONTINUED)

TREC 20-7

Contract Concerning 3520 Practice Avenue, Waco, TX 76710 Page 7 of 8 02-13-06
(Address of Property)

22. AGREEMENT OF PARTIES: This contract contains the entire agreement of the parties and cannot be changed except by their written agreement. Addenda which are a part of this contract are (Check all applicable boxes):

- ☐ Third Party Financing Condition Addendum
- ☒ Seller Financing Addendum
- ☐ Loan Assumption Addendum
- ☐ Buyer's Temporary Residential Lease
- ☐ Seller's Temporary Residential Lease
- ☐ Addendum for Sale of Other Property by Buyer
- ☐ Addendum for Seller's Disclosure of Information on Lead-based Paint and Lead-based Paint Hazards as Required by Federal Law
- ☐ Addendum for Property Subject to Mandatory Membership in an Owners' Association
- ☒ Environmental Assessment, Threatened or Endangered Species and Wetlands Addendum
- ☐ Addendum for "Back-Up" Contract
- ☐ Addendum for Coastal Area Property
- ☐ Addendum for Property Located Seaward of the Gulf Intracoastal Waterway
- ☐ Addendum for Release of Liability on Assumption of FHA, VA, or Conventional Loan Restoration of Seller's Entitlement for VA Guaranteed Loan
- ☐ Other (list): n/a

23. TERMINATION OPTION: For nominal consideration, the receipt of which is hereby acknowledged by Seller, and Buyer's agreement to pay Seller $150 (Option Fee) within 2 days after the effective date of this contract, Seller grants Buyer the unrestricted right to terminate this contract by giving notice of termination to Seller within 10 days after the effective date of this contract. If no dollar amount is stated as the Option Fee or if Buyer fails to pay the Option Fee within the time prescribed, this paragraph will not be a part of this contract and Buyer shall not have the unrestricted right to terminate this contract. If Buyer gives notice of termination within the time prescribed, the Option Fee will not be refunded; however, any earnest money will be refunded to Buyer. The Option Fee ☐will ☒will not be credited to the Sales Price at closing. **Time is of the essence for this paragraph and strict compliance with the time for performance is required.**

24. CONSULT AN ATTORNEY: Real estate licensees cannot give legal advice. READ THIS CONTRACT CAREFULLY. If you do not understand the effect of this contract, consult an attorney BEFORE signing.

Buyer's	Seller's
Attorney is: none chosen at this time	Attorney is:
n/a	
Telephone: ( ) n/a	Telephone: ( )
Facsimile: ( ) n/a	Facsimile: ( )
E-mail: n/a	E-mail:

EXECUTED the 12 day of May, 2008 (EFFECTIVE DATE).
(BROKER: FILL IN THE DATE OF FINAL ACCEPTANCE.)

Thomas J. Swanson	Samuel Jay Johnson
Buyer	Seller
Sarah J. Swanson	n/a
Buyer	Seller

The form of this contract has been approved by the Texas Real Estate Commission. TREC forms are intended for use only by trained real estate licensees. No representation is made as to the legal validity or adequacy of any provision in any specific transactions. It is not intended for complex transactions. Texas Real Estate Commission, P.O. Box 12188, Austin, TX 78711-2188, 1-800-250-8732 or (512) 459-6544 (http://www.trec.state.tx.us) TREC NO. 20-7. This form replaces TREC NO. 20-6.

TREC NO. 20-7

FIGURE 11.16 (CONTINUED)

TREC 20-7

Contract Concerning 15630 Paradise Avenue, Waco, TX 76710 Page 8 of 8 02-13-06
(Address of Property)

BROKER INFORMATION AND RATIFICATION OF FEE

Listing Broker has agreed to pay Other Broker n/a of the total sales price when Listing Broker's fee is received. Escrow Agent is authorized and directed to pay Other Broker from Listing Broker's fee at closing.

n/a n/a
Other Broker License No.

represents ☐ Buyer only as Buyer's agent
☐ Seller as Listing Broker's subagent

n/a n/a
Associate Telephone

n/a
Broker's Address

n/a n/a n/a
City State Zip

n/a
Facsimile

n/a
Email Address

Smooth Sails Realty Company 0234567
Listing Broker License No.

represents ☐ Seller and Buyer as an intermediary
☒ Seller only as Seller's agent

Jane Doe (555)555-2222
Listing Associate Telephone

1010 Listing Street (555)555-3333
Listing Associate's Office Address Facsimile

Waco TX 76710
City State Zip

listing@associates.com
Email Address

William Williams (555)555-4444
Selling Associate Telephone

1011 Selling Street (555)555-5555
Selling Associate's Office Address Facsimile

Waco TX 76710
City State Zip

selling@associates.com
Email Address

OPTION FEE RECEIPT

Receipt of $ 150 (Option Fee) in the form of personal check #122 is acknowledged.

Smooth Sails Realty Company
Seller or Listing Broker

5-14-08
Date

CONTRACT AND EARNEST MONEY RECEIPT

Receipt of ☒Contract and ☐$ 2000 Earnest Money in the form of personal check #122 is acknowledged.

Escrow Agent: John Doe Date: 5-14-08

By: Secure Title Company

email@email.com
Email Address

3214 Title Drive
Address

Telephone (555) 555-7777

Waco TX 76710
City State Zip

Facsimile: (555) 555-7778

FIGURE 11.17

TREC 26-5

PROMULGATED BY THE TEXAS REAL ESTATE COMMISSION (TREC) 12-04-06

EQUAL HOUSING OPPORTUNITY

SELLER FINANCING ADDENDUM

TO CONTRACT CONCERNING THE PROPERTY AT

15630 Paradise Avenue Waco, TX

(Address of Property)

→ **A. CREDIT DOCUMENTATION.** To establish Buyer's creditworthiness, Buyer shall deliver to Seller within 5 days after the effective date of this contract, ☒ credit report ☐ verification of employment, including salary ☐ verification of funds on deposit in financial institutions ☐ current financial statement and ☐ n/a.

Buyer hereby authorizes any credit reporting agency to furnish copies of Buyer's credit reports to Seller at Buyer's sole expense.

B. CREDIT APPROVAL. If the credit documentation described in Paragraph A is not delivered within the specified time, Seller may terminate this contract by notice to Buyer within 7 days after expiration of the time for delivery, and the earnest money will be paid to Seller. If the credit documentation is timely delivered, and Seller determines in Seller's sole discretion that Buyer's credit is unacceptable, Seller may terminate this contract by notice to Buyer within 7 days after expiration of the time for delivery and the earnest money will be refunded to Buyer. If Seller does not terminate this contract, Seller will be deemed to have approved Buyer's creditworthiness.

C. PROMISSORY NOTE. The promissory note (Note) described in Paragraph 4 of this contract payable by Buyer to the order of Seller will bear interest at the rate of 7 % per annum and be payable at the place designated by Seller. Buyer may prepay the Note in whole or in part at any time without penalty. Any prepayments are to be applied to the payment of the installments of principal last maturing and interest will immediately cease on the prepaid principal. The Note will contain a provision for payment of a late fee of 5% of any installment not paid within 10 days of the due date. Matured unpaid amounts will bear interest at the rate of 1½% per month or at the highest lawful rate, whichever is less. The Note will be payable as follows:

→ ☒ (1) In one payment due 5 years after the date of the Note with interest payable ☐ at maturity ☒ monthly ☐ quarterly. (check one box only)

☐ (2) In monthly installments of $ n/a ☐ including interest ☐ plus interest (check one box only) beginning n/a after the date of the Note and continuing monthly thereafter for n/a months when the balance of the Note will be due and payable.

☐ (3) Interest only in monthly installments for the first n/a month(s) and thereafter in installments of $ n/a ☐ including interest ☐ plus interest (check one box only) beginning n/a after the date of the Note and continuing monthly thereafter for n/a months when the balance of the Note will be due and payable.

D. DEED OF TRUST. The deed of trust securing the Note will provide for the following:

(1) PROPERTY TRANSFERS: (check one box only)

☐ (a) Consent Not Required: The Property may be sold, conveyed or leased without the consent of Seller, provided any subsequent buyer assumes the Note.

→ ☒ (b) Consent Required: If all or any part of the Property is sold, conveyed, leased for a period longer than 3 years, leased with an option to purchase, or otherwise sold (including any contract for deed), without Seller's prior written consent, which consent may be withheld in Seller's sole discretion, Seller may declare the balance of the Note

FIGURE 11.17 (CONTINUED)

TREC 26-5

Seller Financing Addendum Concerning Page 2 of 2 12-04-06

→ 15630 Paradise Avenue Waco, TX

(Address of Property)

to be immediately due and payable. The creation of a subordinate lien, any conveyance under threat or order of condemnation, any deed solely between buyers, or the passage of title by reason of the death of a buyer or by operation of law will not entitle Seller to exercise the remedies provided in this paragraph.

NOTE: *Under (a) or (b), Buyer's liability to pay the Note will continue unless Buyer obtains a release of liability from Seller.*

(2) TAX AND INSURANCE ESCROW: (check one box only)

☒ (a) Escrow Not Required: Buyer shall furnish Seller, before each year's ad valorem taxes become delinquent, evidence that all ad valorem taxes on the Property have been paid. Buyer shall annually furnish Seller evidence of paid-up casualty insurance naming Seller as a mortgagee loss payee.

☐ (b) Escrow Required: With each installment Buyer shall deposit in escrow with Seller a pro rata part of the estimated annual ad valorem taxes and casualty insurance premiums for the Property. Buyer shall pay any deficiency within 30 days after notice from Seller. Buyer's failure to pay the deficiency will be a default under the deed of trust. Buyer is not required to deposit any escrow payments for taxes and insurance that are deposited with a superior lienholder. The casualty insurance must name Seller as a mortgagee loss payee.

(3) PRIOR LIENS: Any default under any lien superior to the lien securing the Note will be a default under the deed of trust securing the Note.

Thomas J. Swanson	Samuel Jay Johnson
Buyer	Seller
Sarah J. Swanson	n/a
Buyer	Seller

The form of this contract has been approved by the Texas Real Estate Commission for use with similarly approved or promulgated contract forms. TREC forms are intended for use only by trained real estate licensees. No representation is made as to the legal validity or adequacy of any provision in any specific transactions. It is not intended for complex transactions. Texas Real Estate Commission, P.O. Box 12188, Austin, TX 78711-2188, 1-800-250-8732 or (512) 459-6544 (http://www.trec.state.tx.us) TREC No. 26-5. This form replaces TREC No. 26-4.

TREC NO. 26-5

FIGURE 11.18

TREC 28-1

PROMULGATED BY THE TEXAS REAL ESTATE COMMISSION (TREC) 04-23-07

EQUAL HOUSING OPPORTUNITY

ENVIRONMENTAL ASSESSMENT, THREATENED OR ENDANGERED SPECIES, AND WETLANDS ADDENDUM

TO CONTRACT CONCERNING THE PROPERTY AT

→ 15630 Paradise Avenue Waco, TX

(Address of Property)

☒ A. ENVIRONMENTAL ASSESSMENT: Buyer, at Buyer's expense, may obtain an environmental assessment report prepared by an environmental specialist.

☐ B. THREATENED OR ENDANGERED SPECIES: Buyer, at Buyer's expense, may obtain a report from a natural resources professional to determine if there are any threatened or endangered species or their habitats as defined by the Texas Parks and Wildlife Department or the U.S. Fish and Wildlife Service.

☐ C. WETLANDS: Buyer, at Buyer's expense, may obtain a report from an environmental specialist to determine if there are wetlands, as defined by federal or state law or regulation.

→ Within 10 days after the effective date of the contract, Buyer may terminate the contract by furnishing Seller a copy of any report noted above that adversely affects the use of the Property and a notice of termination of the contract. Upon termination, the earnest money will be refunded to Buyer.

Thomas J. Swanson	Samuel Jay Johnson
Buyer	Seller
Sarah T. Swanson	n/a
Buyer	Seller

This form has been approved by the Texas Real Estate Commission for use with similarly approved or promulgated contract forms. Such approval relates to this form only. TREC forms are intended for use only by trained real estate licensees. No representation is made as to the legal validity or adequacy of any provision in any specific transactions. It is not suitable for complex transactions. Texas Real Estate Commission, P.O. Box 12188, Austin, TX 78711-2188, 1-800-250-8732 or (512) 459-6544 (http://www.trec.state.tx.us) TREC No. 28-1. This form replaces TREC No. 28-0.

TREC No. 28-1

TRANSACTION 6: ALL CASH (*USING: TREC 25-5, OP-L LEAD-BASED PAINT ADDENDUM, AND 28-1. SEE FIGURE 11.19 THROUGH FIGURE 11.21.*)

Fannie Phyllis Farmer, a widow, will sell her Pecos County ranch to William Robert (Billy Bob) Richman and his wife, Mae Bea (Sissy) Richman. The Property is described by a rather lengthy metes-and-bounds description that is attached to the purchase agreement and identified as Exhibit A. It is known as 2520 Farmer Road, Pecos, Texas 78789. It is not located in a Texas Agricultural Development District.

There are no crops or equipment included in the sale. There are no outstanding mineral or timber interests; however, Phyllis will retain 50 percent of the gas and oil interests at closing. The Buyers request that the Seller furnishes, at her own expense, a new survey of the Property within 20 days after the effective date of the contract and are asking for 7 days to review the survey and title documents. They call for an abstract to be furnished within 30 days after the effective date of the contract, and they will have it reviewed by their real estate attorney, Ronald Hawkeye Redundant.

The Buyers will pay $895,000 cash for the Property. According to the Seller, the farm is 350 acres. If, after reviewing the survey, it is found to be more or less than 350 acres, the sale price will be adjusted $2,500 per acre over or under. If any price adjustment exceeds 10 percent of the Sales Price, either party may terminate the contract within 10 days after receipt of the survey. They tender $100,000 earnest money with Pecos County Abstract Company who will close the transaction in about 30 days on December 23.

The Buyers choose not to have any inspections done and accept the Property in its present condition. They have received the Seller's disclosure of Property condition form. They have also waived their right to have the farmhouse inspected for lead-based paint hazards; however, they request 20 days to have environmental assessments done. They will have all of the present ramshackle buildings demolished to make way for the new 12,000-square-foot house. Rollback taxes will not be an issue because the Buyers plan no change in the use of the Property.

The listing broker is Hilton Charles, the owner of Country Properties. Richard Hutchinson, an independent broker, represents the Buyers. The Buyer's broker will be paid a selling fee of $10,000, which will be paid from the listing broker's fee at closing.

FIGURE 11.19

TREC 25-5

PROMULGATED BY THE TEXAS REAL ESTATE COMMISSION (TREC) 02-13-06

EQUAL HOUSING OPPORTUNITY

FARM AND RANCH CONTRACT

1. **PARTIES:** Fannie Phyllis Farmer, a widow (Seller) agrees to sell and convey to William Robert Richman and wife Mae Bea Richman (Buyer) and Buyer agrees to buy from Seller the Property described below.

2. **PROPERTY:** The land, improvements, accessories and crops are collectively referred to as the "Property".
   A. LAND: The land situated in the County of Pecos, Texas, described as follows: see attached metes-and-bounds property description Exhibit A

   or as described on attached exhibit, also known as 2520 Farmer Road Pecos, TX 79789 (address/zip code), together with all rights, privileges, and appurtenances pertaining thereto, including but not limited to: water rights, claims, permits, strips and gores, easements, and cooperative or association memberships.

   B. IMPROVEMENTS:
   (1) FARM and RANCH IMPROVEMENTS: The following **permanently installed and built-in items**, if any: windmills, tanks, barns, pens, fences, gates, sheds, outbuildings, and corrals.
   (2) RESIDENTIAL IMPROVEMENTS: The house, garage, and all other fixtures and improvements attached to the above-described real property, including without limitation, the following **permanently installed and built-in items,** if any: all equipment and appliances, valances, screens, shutters, awnings, wall-to-wall carpeting, mirrors, ceiling fans, attic fans, mail boxes, television antennas and satellite dish system and equipment, heating and air-conditioning units, security and fire detection equipment, wiring, plumbing and lighting fixtures, chandeliers, water softener system, kitchen equipment, garage door openers, cleaning equipment, shrubbery, landscaping, outdoor cooking equipment, and all other property owned by Seller and attached to the above described real property.

   C. ACCESSORIES:
   (1) FARM AND RANCH ACCESSORIES: The following described related accessories: (check boxes of conveyed accessories) ☐ portable buildings ☐ hunting blinds ☐ game feeders ☐ livestock feeders and troughs ☐ irrigation equipment ☐ fuel tanks ☐ submersible pumps ☐ pressure tanks ☐ corrals ☐ gates ☐ chutes ☐ other: n/a
   (2) RESIDENTIAL ACCESSORIES: The following described related accessories, if any: window air conditioning units, stove, fireplace screens, curtains and rods, blinds, window shades, draperies and rods, controls for satellite dish system, controls for garage door openers, entry gate controls, door keys, mailbox keys, above ground pool, swimming pool equipment and maintenance accessories, and artificial fireplace logs.

   D. CROPS: Unless otherwise agreed in writing, Seller has the right to harvest all growing crops until delivery of possession of the Property.

   E. EXCLUSIONS: The following improvements, accessories, and crops will be retained by Seller and excluded: n/a

   F. RESERVATIONS: Seller reserves the following mineral, water, royalty, timber, or other interests: 50% of gas and oil interests

3. **SALES PRICE:**
   A. Cash portion of Sales Price payable by Buyer at closing .... $ 895,000
   B. Sum of all financing described below (excluding any loan funding fee or mortgage insurance premium) .... $ -0-
   C. Sales Price (Sum of A and B) .... $ 895,000
   D. The Sales Price ☒ will ☐ will not be adjusted based on the survey required by Paragraph 6C. If the Sales Price is adjusted, the Sales Price will be calculated on the basis of $ 2,500 per acre. If the Sales Price is adjusted by more than 10%, either party may terminate this contract by providing written notice to the other party within 10 days after the terminating party receives the survey. If neither party terminates this contract or if the variance is 10% or less, the adjustment will be made to the amount in ☒ 3A ☐ 3B ☐ proportionately to 3A and 3B.

Initialed for identification by Buyer______ ______ and Seller ______ ______ TREC NO. 25-5

FIGURE 11.19 (CONTINUED)

TREC 25-5

Contract Concerning 2520 Farmer Road, Pecos, TX 78789 Page 2 of 9 02-13-06
(Address of Property)

4. FINANCING: The portion of Sales Price not payable in cash will be paid as follows: (Check applicable boxes below)

❑ A. THIRD PARTY FINANCING: One or more third party mortgage loans in the total amount of $ n/a (excluding any loan funding fee or mortgage insurance premium).

(1) Property Approval: If the Property does not satisfy the lenders' underwriting requirements for the loan(s), this contract will terminate and the earnest money will be refunded to Buyer.

(2) Financing Approval: (Check one box only)

❑ (a) This contract is subject to Buyer being approved for the financing described in the attached Third Party Financing Condition Addendum.

❑ (b) This contract is not subject to Buyer being approved for financing and does not involve FHA or VA financing.

❑ B. ASSUMPTION: The assumption of the unpaid principal balance of one or more promissory notes described in the attached TREC Loan Assumption Addendum.

❑ C. SELLER FINANCING: A promissory note from Buyer to Seller of $ n/a, secured by vendor's and deed of trust liens, and containing the terms and conditions described in the attached TREC Seller Financing Addendum. If an owner policy of title insurance is furnished, Buyer shall furnish Seller with a mortgagee policy of title insurance.

5. EARNEST MONEY: Upon execution of this contract by both parties, Buyer shall deposit $ 100,000 as earnest money with Pecos County Abstract Company, as escrow agent, at 123 Abstract Road, Pecos, TX 78789 (address). Buyer shall deposit additional earnest money of $ n/a with escrow agent within n/a days after the effective date of this contract. If Buyer fails to deposit the earnest money as required by this contract, Buyer will be in default.

6. TITLE POLICY AND SURVEY:

A. TITLE POLICY: Seller shall furnish to Buyer at ❑ Seller's ❑ Buyer's expense an owner policy of title insurance (Title Policy) issued by: n/a (Title Company) in the amount of the Sales Price, dated at or after closing, insuring Buyer against loss under the provisions of the Title Policy, subject to the promulgated exclusions (including existing building and zoning ordinances) and the following exceptions:

(1) The standard printed exception for standby fees, taxes and assessments.

(2) Liens created as part of the financing described in Paragraph 4.

(3) Reservations or exceptions otherwise permitted by this contract or as may be approved by Buyer in writing.

(4) The standard printed exception as to marital rights.

(5) The standard printed exception as to waters, tidelands, beaches, streams, and related matters.

(6) The standard printed exception as to discrepancies, conflicts, shortages in area or boundary lines, encroachments or protrusions, or overlapping improvements. Buyer, at Buyer's expense, may have the exception amended to read, "shortages in area".

B. COMMITMENT: Within 20 days after the Title Company receives a copy of this contract, Seller shall furnish to Buyer a commitment for title insurance (Commitment) and, at Buyer's expense, legible copies of restrictive covenants and documents evidencing exceptions in the Commitment (Exception Documents) other than the standard printed exceptions. Seller authorizes the Title Company to deliver the Commitment and Exception Documents to Buyer at Buyer's address shown in Paragraph 21. If the Commitment and Exception Documents are not delivered to Buyer within the specified time, the time for delivery will be automatically extended up to 15 days or the Closing Date, whichever is earlier.

C. SURVEY: The survey must be made by a registered professional land surveyor acceptable to the Title Company and any lender. (Check one box only):

❑ (1) Within n/a days after the effective date of this contract, Seller shall furnish to Buyer and Title Company Seller's existing survey of the Property and a Residential Real Property Affidavit promulgated by the Texas Department of Insurance (Affidavit). The existing survey ❑ will ❑ will not be recertified to a date subsequent to the effective date of this contract at the expense of ❑ Buyer ❑ Seller. If the existing survey is not approved by the Title Company or Buyer's Lender, a new survey will be obtained at the expense of ❑ Buyer ❑ Seller no later than 3 days prior to Closing Date. If Seller fails to furnish the existing survey or Affidavit within the time prescribed, Buyer shall obtain a new survey at Seller's expense no later than 3 days prior to Closing Date.

❑ (2) Within n/a days after the effective date of this contract, Buyer shall obtain a new survey at Buyer's expense. Buyer is deemed to receive the survey on the date of actual receipt or the date specified in this paragraph, whichever is earlier.

☒ (3) Within 20 days after the effective date of this contract, Seller, at Seller's expense shall furnish a new survey to Buyer.

❑ (4) No survey is required.

Initialed for identification by Buyer_____ _____ and Seller _____ _____ TREC NO. 25-5

FIGURE 11.19 (CONTINUED)

TREC 25-5

Contract Concerning 2520 Farmer Road, Pecos, TX 78789 Page 3 of 9 02-13-06
(Address of Property)

D. OBJECTIONS: Buyer may object in writing to (i) defects, exceptions, or encumbrances to title disclosed on the survey other than items 6A(1) through (5) above; or disclosed in the Commitment other than items 6A(1) through (6) above; (ii) any portion of the Property lying in a special flood hazard area (Zone V or A) as shown on the current Federal Emergency Management Agency map; or (iii) any exceptions which prohibit the following use or activity: n/a

Buyer must object not later than (i) the Closing Date or (ii) 7 days after Buyer receives the Commitment, Exception Documents, and the survey, whichever is earlier. Buyer's failure to object within the time allowed will constitute a waiver of Buyer's right to object; except that the requirements in Schedule C of the Commitment are not waived. Provided Seller is not obligated to incur any expense, Seller shall cure the timely objections of Buyer or any third party lender within 15 days after Seller receives the objections and the Closing Date will be extended as necessary. If objections are not cured within such 15 day period, this contract will terminate and the earnest money will be refunded to Buyer unless Buyer waives the objections.

E. EXCEPTION DOCUMENTS: Prior to the execution of the contract, Seller has provided Buyer with copies of the Exception Documents listed below or on the attached exhibit. Matters reflected in the Exception Documents listed below or on the attached exhibit will be permitted exceptions in the Title Policy and will not be a basis for objection to title:

Document	Date	Recording Reference
n/a	n/a	n/a
n/a	n/a	n/a
n/a	n/a	n/a
n/a	n/a	n/a
n/a	n/a	n/a
n/a	n/a	n/a

F. SURFACE LEASES: Prior to the execution of the contract, Seller has provided Buyer with copies of written leases and given notice of oral leases (Leases) listed below or on the attached exhibit. The following Leases will be permitted exceptions in the Title Policy and will not be a basis for objection to title: n/a

G. TITLE NOTICES:

(1) ABSTRACT OR TITLE POLICY: Broker advises Buyer to have an abstract of title covering the Property examined by an attorney of Buyer's selection, or Buyer should be furnished with or obtain a Title Policy. If a Title Policy is furnished, the Commitment should be promptly reviewed by an attorney of Buyer's choice due to the time limitations on Buyer's right to object.

(2) STATUTORY TAX DISTRICTS: If the Property is situated in a utility or other statutorily created district providing water, sewer, drainage, or flood control facilities and services, Chapter 49, Texas Water Code, requires Seller to deliver and Buyer to sign the statutory notice relating to the tax rate, bonded indebtedness, or standby fee of the district prior to final execution of this contract.

(3) TIDE WATERS: If the Property abuts the tidally influenced waters of the state, §33.135, Texas Natural Resources Code, requires a notice regarding coastal area property to be included in the contract. An addendum containing the notice promulgated by TREC or required by the parties must be used.

(4) ANNEXATION: If the Property is located outside the limits of a municipality, Seller notifies Buyer under §5.011, Texas Property Code, that the Property may now or later be included in the extraterritorial jurisdiction of a municipality and may now or later be subject to annexation by the municipality. Each municipality maintains a map that depicts its boundaries and extraterritorial jurisdiction. To determine if the Property is located within a municipality's extraterritorial jurisdiction or is likely to be located within a municipality's extraterritorial jurisdiction, contact all municipalities located in the general proximity of the Property for further information.

(5) PROPERTY LOCATED IN A CERTIFICATED SERVICE AREA OF A UTILITY SERVICE PROVIDER: Notice required by §13.257, Water Code: The real property, described in

FIGURE 11.19 (CONTINUED)

TREC 25-5

Contract Concerning 2520 Farmer Road, Pecos, TX 78789 Page 4 of 9 02-13-06
(Address of Property)

Paragraph 2, that you are about to purchase may be located in a certificated water or sewer service area, which is authorized by law to provide water or sewer service to the properties in the certificated area. If your property is located in a certificated area there may be special costs or charges that you will be required to pay before you can receive water or sewer service. There may be a period required to construct lines or other facilities necessary to provide water or sewer service to your property. You are advised to determine if the property is in a certificated area and contact the utility service provider to determine the cost that you will be required to pay and the period, if any, that is required to provide water or sewer service to your property. The undersigned Buyer hereby acknowledges receipt of the foregoing notice at or before the execution of a binding contract for the purchase of the real property described in Paragraph 2 or at closing of purchase of the real property.

(6) PUBLIC IMPROVEMENT DISTRICTS: If the Property is in a public improvement district, §5.014, Property Code, requires Seller to notify Buyer as follows: As a purchaser of this parcel of real property you are obligated to pay an assessment to a municipality or county for an improvement project undertaken by a public improvement district under Chapter 372, Local Government Code. The assessment may be due annually or in periodic installments. More information concerning the amount of the assessment and the due dates of that assessment may be obtained from the municipality or county levying the assessment. The amount of the assessments is subject to change. Your failure to pay the assessments could result in a lien on and the foreclosure of your property.

(7) TEXAS AGRICULTURAL DEVELOPMENT DISTRICT: The Property ☐ is ☒ is not located in a Texas Agricultural Development District. For additional information contact the Texas Department of Agriculture.

7. PROPERTY CONDITION:

A. ACCESS,INSPECTIONS AND UTILITIES: Seller shall permit Buyer and Buyer's agents access to the Property at reasonable times. Buyer may have the Property inspected by inspectors selected by Buyer and licensed by TREC or otherwise permitted by law to make inspections. Seller at Seller's expense shall turn on existing utilities for inspections.
NOTICE: Buyer should determine the availability of utilities to the Property suitable to satisfy Buyer's needs.

B. SELLER'S DISCLOSURE NOTICE PURSUANT TO §5.008, TEXAS PROPERTY CODE (Notice): (Check one box only)
☒ (1) Buyer has received the Notice
☐ (2) Buyer has not received the Notice. Within n/a days after the effective date of this contract, Seller shall deliver the Notice to Buyer. If Buyer does not receive the Notice, Buyer may terminate this contract at any time prior to the closing and the earnest money will be refunded to Buyer. If Seller delivers the Notice, Buyer may terminate this contract for any reason within 7 days after Buyer receives the Notice or prior to the closing, whichever first occurs, and the earnest money will be refunded to Buyer.
☐ (3) The Texas Property Code does not require this Seller to furnish the Notice.

C. SELLER'S DISCLOSURE OF LEAD-BASED PAINT AND LEAD-BASED PAINT HAZARDS is required by Federal law for a residential dwelling constructed prior to 1978.

D. ACCEPTANCE OF PROPERTY CONDITION: Buyer accepts the Property in its present condition; provided Seller, at Seller's expense, shall complete the following specific repairs and treatments: n/a.

E. COMPLETION OF REPAIRS: Unless otherwise agreed in writing, Seller shall complete all agreed repairs prior to the Closing Date. All required permits must be obtained, and repairs must be performed by persons who are licensed or otherwise permitted by law to provide such repairs. At Buyer's election, any transferable warranties received by Seller with respect to the repairs will be transferred to Buyer at Buyer's expense. If Seller fails to complete any agreed repairs prior to the Closing Date, Buyer may do so and receive reimbursement from Seller at closing. The Closing Date will be extended up to 15 days, if necessary, to complete repairs.

F. LENDER REQUIRED REPAIRS AND TREATMENTS: Unless otherwise agreed in writing, neither party is obligated to pay for lender required repairs, which includes treatment for wood destroying insects. If the parties do not agree to pay for the lender required repairs or treatments, this contract will terminate and the earnest money will be refunded to Buyer. If the cost of lender required repairs and treatments exceeds 5% of the Sales Price, Buyer may terminate this contract and the earnest money will be refunded to Buyer.

G.ENVIRONMENTAL MATTERS: Buyer is advised that the presence of wetlands, toxic substances, including asbestos and wastes or other environmental hazards, or the presence of a threatened or endangered species or its habitat may affect Buyer's intended use of the Property. If Buyer is concerned about these matters, an addendum promulgated by TREC or required by the parties should be used.

H. SELLER'S DISCLOSURES: Except as otherwise disclosed in this contract, Seller has no knowledge of the following:
(1) any flooding of the Property which has had a material adverse effect on the use of the Property;
(2) any pending or threatened litigation, condemnation, or special assessment affecting the Property;

Initialed for identification by Buyer_____ _____ and Seller _____ _____ TREC NO. 25-5

FIGURE 11.19 (CONTINUED)

TREC 25-5

Contract Concerning 2520 Farmer Road, Pecos, TX 78789 Page 5 of 9 02-13-06
(Address of Property)

(3) any environmental hazards or conditions materially affecting the Property;
(4) any dumpsite, landfill, or underground tanks or containers now or previously located on the Property;
(5) any wetlands, as defined by federal or state law or regulation, affecting the Property; or
(6) any threatened or endangered species or their habitat affecting the Property.

I. RESIDENTIAL SERVICE CONTRACTS: Buyer may purchase a residential service contract from a residential service company licensed by TREC. If Buyer purchases a residential service contract, Seller shall reimburse Buyer at closing for the cost of the residential service contract in an amount not exceeding $ n/a . Buyer should review any residential service contract for the scope of coverage, exclusions and limitations. **The purchase of a residential service contract is optional. Similar coverage may be purchased from various companies authorized to do business in Texas.**

J. GOVERNMENT PROGRAMS: The Property is subject to the government programs listed below or on the attached exhibit: n/a
Seller shall provide Buyer with copies of all governmental program agreements. Any allocation or proration of payment under governmental programs is made by separate agreement between the parties which will survive closing.

8. BROKERS' FEES: All obligations of the parties for payment of brokers' fees are contained in separate written agreements.

9. CLOSING:

A. The closing of the sale will be on or before December 23 , 20 08 , or within 7 days after objections made under Paragraph 6D have been cured or waived, whichever date is later (Closing Date). If either party fails to close the sale by the Closing Date, the non-defaulting party may exercise the remedies contained in Paragraph 15.

B. At closing:
(1) Seller shall execute and deliver a general warranty deed conveying title to the Property to Buyer and showing no additional exceptions to those permitted in Paragraph 6, an assignment of Leases, and furnish tax statements or certificates showing no delinquent taxes on the Property.
(2) Buyer shall pay the Sales Price in good funds acceptable to the escrow agent.
(3) Seller and Buyer shall execute and deliver any notices, statements, certificates, affidavits, releases, loan documents and other documents required of them by this contract, the Commitment or law necessary for the closing of the sale and the issuance of the Title Policy.

C. Unless expressly prohibited by written agreement, Seller may continue to show the Property and receive, negotiate and accept back up offers.

D. All covenants, representations and warranties in this contract survive closing.

10. POSSESSION: Seller shall deliver to Buyer possession of the Property in its present or required condition, ordinary wear and tear excepted: ☒ upon closing and funding ☐ according to a temporary residential lease form promulgated by TREC or other written lease required by the parties. Any possession by Buyer prior to closing or by Seller after closing which is not authorized by a written lease will establish a tenancy at sufferance relationship between the parties. **Consult your insurance agent prior to change of ownership and possession because insurance coverage may be limited or terminated. The absence of a written lease or appropriate insurance coverage may expose the parties to economic loss.**

11. SPECIAL PROVISIONS: (Insert only factual statements and business details applicable to the sale. TREC rules prohibit licensees from adding factual statements or business details for which a contract addendum or other form has been promulgated by TREC for mandatory use.)

Seller is to provide buyer with an abstract within 30 days after the effective date of this contract to be reviewed by buyer's attorney.

Initialed for identification by Buyer______ ______ and Seller _______ ______ TREC NO. 25-5

FIGURE 11.19 (CONTINUED)

TREC 25-5

12. SETTLEMENT AND OTHER EXPENSES:

A. The following expenses must be paid at or prior to closing:

(1)Expenses payable by Seller (Seller's Expenses):

(a) Releases of existing liens, including prepayment penalties and recording fees; release of Seller's loan liability; tax statements or certificates; preparation of deed; one-half of escrow fee; and other expenses payable by Seller under this contract.

(b) Seller shall also pay an amount not to exceed $ n/a to be applied in the following order: Buyer's Expenses which Buyer is prohibited from paying by FHA, VA, Texas Veterans Housing Assistance Program or other governmental loan programs, and then to other Buyer's Expenses as allowed by the lender.

(2) Expenses payable by Buyer (Buyer's Expenses):

(a) Loan origination, discount, buy-down, and commitment fees (Loan Fees).

(b) Appraisal fees; loan application fees; credit reports; preparation of loan documents; interest on the notes from date of disbursement to one month prior to dates of first monthly payments; recording fees; copies of easements and restrictions; mortgagee title policy with endorsements required by lender; loan-related inspection fees; photos; amortization schedules; one-half of escrow fee; all prepaid items, including required premiums for flood and hazard insurance, reserve deposits for insurance, ad valorem taxes and special governmental assessments; final compliance inspection; courier fee; repair inspection; underwriting fee; wire transfer fee; expenses incident to any loan; and other expenses payable by Buyer under this contract.

B. Buyer shall pay Private Mortgage Insurance Premium (PMI), VA Loan Funding Fee, or FHA Mortgage Insurance Premium (MIP) as required by the lender.

C. If any expense exceeds an amount expressly stated in this contract for such expense to be paid by a party, that party may terminate this contract unless the other party agrees to pay such excess. Buyer may not pay charges and fees expressly prohibited by FHA, VA, Texas Veterans Housing Assistance Program or other governmental loan program regulations.

13. PRORATIONS AND ROLLBACK TAXES:

A. PRORATIONS: Taxes for the current year, interest, maintenance fees, assessments, dues and rents will be prorated through the Closing Date. The tax proration may be calculated taking into consideration any change in exemptions that will affect the current year's taxes. If taxes for the current year vary from the amount prorated at closing, the parties shall adjust the prorations when tax statements for the current year are available. If taxes are not paid at or prior to closing, Buyer shall pay taxes for the current year. Rentals which are unknown at time of closing will be prorated between Buyer and Seller when they become known.

B. ROLLBACK TAXES: If this sale or Buyer's use of the Property after closing results in the assessment of additional taxes, penalties or interest (Assessments) for periods prior to closing, the Assessments will be the obligation of Buyer. If Seller's change in use of the Property prior to closing or denial of a special use valuation on the Property claimed by Seller results in Assessments for periods prior to closing, the Assessments will be the obligation of Seller. Obligations imposed by this paragraph will survive closing.

14. CASUALTY LOSS: If any part of the Property is damaged or destroyed by fire or other casualty after the effective date of this contract, Seller shall restore the Property to its previous condition as soon as reasonably possible, but in any event by the Closing Date. If Seller fails to do so due to factors beyond Seller's control, Buyer may (a) terminate this contract and the earnest money will be refunded to Buyer, (b) extend the time for performance up to 15 days and the Closing Date will be extended as necessary or (c) accept the Property in its damaged condition with an assignment of insurance proceeds and receive credit from Seller at closing in the amount of the deductible under the insurance policy. Seller's obligations under this paragraph are independent of any other obligations of Seller under this contract.

15. DEFAULT: If Buyer fails to comply with this contract, Buyer will be in default, and Seller may (a) enforce specific performance, seek such other relief as may be provided by law, or both, or (b) terminate this contract and receive the earnest money as liquidated damages, thereby releasing both parties from this contract. If, due to factors beyond Seller's control, Seller fails within the time allowed to make any non-casualty repairs or deliver the Commitment, or survey, if required of Seller, Buyer may (a) extend the time for performance up to 15 days and the Closing Date will be extended as necessary or (b) terminate this contract as the sole remedy and receive the earnest money. If Seller fails to comply with this contract for any other reason, Seller will be in default and Buyer may (a) enforce specific performance, seek such other relief as may be provided by law, or both, or (b) terminate this contract and receive the earnest money, thereby releasing both parties from this contract.

16. MEDIATION: It is the policy of the State of Texas to encourage resolution of disputes through alternative dispute resolution procedures such as mediation. Any dispute between Seller and Buyer related to this contract which is not resolved through informal discussion ☐will ☒will not be submitted to a mutually acceptable mediation service or provider. The parties to the mediation shall bear the mediation costs equally. This paragraph does not preclude a party from seeking

FIGURE 11.19 (CONTINUED)

TREC 25-5

Contract Concerning 2520 Farmer Road, Pecos, TX 78789 Page 7 of 9 02-13-06
(Address of Property)

equitable relief from a court of competent jurisdiction.

17. ATTORNEY'S FEES: The prevailing party in any legal proceeding related to this contract is entitled to recover reasonable attorney's fees and all costs of such proceeding incurred by the prevailing party.

18. ESCROW:

A. ESCROW: The escrow agent is not (i) a party to this contract and does not have liability for the performance or nonperformance of any party to this contract, (ii) liable for interest on the earnest money and (iii) liable for the loss of any earnest money caused by the failure of any financial institution in which the earnest money has been deposited unless the financial institution is acting as escrow agent.

B. EXPENSES: At closing, the earnest money must be applied first to any cash down payment, then to Buyer's Expenses and any excess refunded to Buyer. If no closing occurs, escrow agent may require payment of unpaid expenses incurred on behalf of the parties and a written release of liability of escrow agent from all parties.

C. DEMAND: Upon termination of this contract, either party or the escrow agent may send a release of earnest money to each party and the parties shall execute counterparts of the release and deliver same to the escrow agent. If either party fails to execute the release, either party may make a written demand to the escrow agent for the earnest money. If only one party makes written demand for the earnest money, escrow agent shall promptly provide a copy of the demand to the other party. If escrow agent does not receive written objection to the demand from the other party within 15 days, escrow agent may disburse the earnest money to the party making demand reduced by the amount of unpaid expenses incurred on behalf of the party receiving the earnest money and escrow agent may pay the same to the creditors. If escrow agent complies with the provisions of this paragraph, each party hereby releases escrow agent from all adverse claims related to the disbursal of the earnest money.

D. DAMAGES: Any party who wrongfully fails or refuses to sign a release acceptable to the escrow agent within 7 days of receipt of the request will be liable to the other party for liquidated damages of three times the amount of the earnest money.

E. NOTICES: Escrow agent's notices will be effective when sent in compliance with Paragraph 21. Notice of objection to the demand will be deemed effective upon receipt by escrow agent.

19. REPRESENTATIONS: Seller represents that as of the Closing Date (a) there will be no liens, assessments, or security interests against the Property which will not be satisfied out of the sales proceeds unless securing payment of any loans assumed by Buyer and (b) assumed loans will not be in default. If any representation of Seller in this contract is untrue on the Closing Date, Seller will be in default.

20. FEDERAL TAX REQUIREMENTS: If Seller is a "foreign person," as defined by applicable law, or if Seller fails to deliver an affidavit to Buyer that Seller is not a "foreign person," then Buyer shall withhold from the sales proceeds an amount sufficient to comply with applicable tax law and deliver the same to the Internal Revenue Service together with appropriate tax forms. Internal Revenue Service regulations require filing written reports if currency in excess of specified amounts is received in the transaction.

21. NOTICES: All notices from one party to the other must be in writing and are effective when mailed to, hand-delivered at, or transmitted by facsimile or electronic transmission as follows:

To Buyer at:	**To Seller at:**
5555 Buyer Road	2520 Farmer Road
Pecos, TX 78789	Pecos, TX 78789
n/a	n/a
Telephone: (555) 555-0001	Telephone: (555) 555-0003
Facsimile: (555) 555-0002	Facsimile: (555) 555-0004
E-mail: buyer@buyers.com	E-mail: seller@sellers.com

Initialed for identification by Buyer______ ______ and Seller ______ ______ TREC NO. 25-5

FIGURE 11.19 (CONTINUED)

TREC 25-5

Contract Concerning 2520 Farmer Road, Pecos, TX 76789 Page 8 of 9 02-13-06
(Address of Property)

22. AGREEMENT OF PARTIES: This contract contains the entire agreement of the parties and cannot be changed except by their written agreement. Addenda which are a part of this contract are (check all applicable boxes):

- ☐ Third Party Financing Condition Addendum
- ☒ Addendum for Seller's Disclosure of Information on Lead-based Paint and Lead-based Paint Hazards as Required by Federal Law
- ☐ Seller Financing Addendum
- ☒ Environmental Assessment, Threatened or Endangered Species and Wetlands Addendum
- ☐ Loan Assumption Addendum
- ☐ Addendum for Coastal Area Property
- ☐ Buyer's Temporary Residential Lease
- ☐ Addendum for Property Located Seaward of the Gulf Intracoastal Waterway
- ☐ Seller's Temporary Residential Lease
- ☐ Addendum for "Back-Up" Contract
- ☐ Addendum for Sale of Other Property by Buyer
- ☐ Other (list): n/a

23. TERMINATION OPTION: For nominal consideration, the receipt of which is hereby acknowledged by Seller, and Buyer's agreement to pay Seller $ n/a (Option Fee) within 2 days after the effective date of this contract, Seller grants Buyer the unrestricted right to terminate this contract by giving notice of termination to Seller within n/a days after the effective date of this contract. If no dollar amount is stated as the Option Fee or if Buyer fails to pay the Option Fee within the time prescribed, this paragraph will not be a part of this contract and Buyer shall not have the unrestricted right to terminate this contract. If Buyer gives notice of termination within the time prescribed, the Option Fee will not be refunded; however, any earnest money will be refunded to Buyer. The Option Fee ☐will ☐will not be credited to the Sales Price at closing. **Time is of the essence for this paragraph and strict compliance with the time for performance is required.**

24. CONSULT AN ATTORNEY: Real estate licensees cannot give legal advice. READ THIS CONTRACT CAREFULLY. If you do not understand the effect of this contract, consult an attorney BEFORE signing.

Buyer's	Seller's
Attorney is: Ronald Hawkeye Redundant	Attorney is:
n/a	
Telephone: (555) 555-0000	Telephone: ( )
Facsimile: (555) 555-0010	Facsimile: ( )
E-mail: attorney@attorney.com	E-mail:

EXECUTED the 23 day of November, 20 08 (EFFECTIVE DATE). (BROKER: FILL IN THE DATE OF FINAL ACCEPTANCE.)

William Robert Richman	Fannie Phyllis Farmer
Buyer	Seller
Mae Bea Richman	n/a
Buyer	Seller

The form of this contract has been approved by the Texas Real Estate Commission. TREC forms are intended for use only by trained real estate licensees. No representation is made as to the legal validity or adequacy of any provision in any specific transactions. It is not intended for complex transactions. Texas Real Estate Commission, P.O. Box 12188, Austin, TX 78711-2188, 1-800-250-8732 or (512) 459-6544 (http://www.trec.state.tx.us) TREC NO. 25-5. This form replaces TREC NO. 25-4.

TREC NO. 25-5

FIGURE 11.19 (CONTINUED)

TREC 25-5

Contract Concerning 2520 Farmer Road, Pecos, TX 78789 Page 9 of 9 02-13-06
(Address of Property)

RATIFICATION OF FEE

Listing Broker has agreed to pay Other Broker $10,000 of the total Sales Price when Listing Broker's fee is received. Escrow Agent is authorized and directed to pay Other Broker from Listing Broker's fee at closing.

Other Broker: By: Richard Hutchinson

Listing Broker: By: Hilton Charles

BROKER INFORMATION AND AGREEMENT FOR PAYMENT OF BROKERS' FEES

Richard Hutchinson 0234567 Other Broker License No.	Hilton Charles 0127643 Listing or Principal Broker License No.
Associate	Associate
123 Estate Road Address	321 Broker Road Address
Pecos TX 78789 City State Zip	Pecos TX 78789 City State Zip
Telephone Facsimile	Telephone Facsimile
E-mail	E-mail
represents ☒ Buyer only as Buyer's agent ☐ Seller as Listing Broker's subagent	represents ☒ Seller only ☐ Buyer only ☐ Seller and Buyer as an intermediary

Upon closing of the sale by Seller to Buyer of the Property described in the contract to which this fee agreement is attached: (a) ☒Seller ☐ Buyer will pay Listing/Principal Broker ☒a cash fee of $ 25,000 or ☐ n/a % of the total Sales Price; and (b) ☐Seller ☐ Buyer will pay Other Broker ☐a cash fee of $ n/a or ☐ n/a % of the total Sales Price. Seller/Buyer authorizes and directs Escrow Agent to pay the brokers from the proceeds at closing.

Brokers' fees are negotiable. Brokers' fees or the sharing of fees between brokers are not fixed, controlled, recommended, suggested or maintained by the Texas Real Estate Commission.

Fannie Phyllis Farmer Seller	William Robert Richman Buyer
n/a Seller	Mae Bea Richman Buyer

Do not sign if there is a separate written agreement for payment of Brokers' fees.

OPTION FEE RECEIPT

Receipt of $ n/a (Option Fee) in the form of n/a is acknowledged.

Hilton Charles
Seller or Listing Broker

Date

CONTRACT AND EARNEST MONEY RECEIPT

Receipt of ☒Contract and ☐$ 100,000 Earnest Money in the form of check # 1234 is acknowledged.

Escrow Agent: John Doe Date:

By: Pecos County Abstract Company

Email Address

123 Abstract Road
Address

Telephone (555) 555-5555

Pecos TX 78789
City State Zip

Facsimile: (555) 555-5556

TREC NO. 25-5

FIGURE 11.20

TREC OP-L

APPROVED BY THE TEXAS REAL ESTATE COMMISSION 02-09-2004

EQUAL HOUSING OPPORTUNITY

ADDENDUM FOR SELLER'S DISCLOSURE OF INFORMATION ON LEAD-BASED PAINT AND LEAD-BASED PAINT HAZARDS AS REQUIRED BY FEDERAL LAW

→ CONCERNING THE PROPERTY AT 2520 Farmer Road Pecos, TX
(Street Address and City)

A. **LEAD WARNING STATEMENT:** "Every purchaser of any interest in residential real property on which a residential dwelling was built prior to 1978 is notified that such property may present exposure to lead from lead-based paint that may place young children at risk of developing lead poisoning. Lead poisoning in young children may produce permanent neurological damage, including learning disabilities, reduced intelligence quotient, behavioral problems, and impaired memory. Lead poisoning also poses a particular risk to pregnant women. The seller of any interest in residential real property is required to provide the buyer with any information on lead-based paint hazards from risk assessments or inspections in the seller's possession and notify the buyer of any known lead-based paint hazards. A risk assessment or inspection for possible lead-paint hazards is recommended prior to purchase."
NOTICE: Inspector must be properly certified as required by federal law.

B. SELLER'S DISCLOSURE:

1. PRESENCE OF LEAD-BASED PAINT AND/OR LEAD-BASED PAINT HAZARDS (check on box only):
   ☐ (a) Known lead-based paint and/or lead-based paint hazards are present in the Property (explain): n/a
   → ☒ (b) Seller has no actual knowledge of lead-based paint and/or lead-based paint hazards in the Property.
2. RECORDS AND REPORTS AVAILABLE TO SELLER (check one box only):
   ☐ (a) Seller has provided the purchaser with all available records and reports pertaining to lead-based paint and/or lead-based paint hazards in the Property (list documents): n/a
   → ☒ (b) Seller has no reports or records pertaining to lead-based paint and/or lead-based paint hazards in the Property.

C. BUYER'S RIGHTS (check one box only)**:**

→ ☒ 1. Buyer waives the opportunity to conduct a risk assessment or inspection of the Property for the presence of lead-based paint or lead-based paint hazards.
☐ 2. Within ten days after the effective date of this contract, Buyer may have the Property inspected by inspectors selected by Buyer. If lead-based paint or lead-based paint hazards are present, Buyer may terminate this contract by giving Seller written notice within 14 days after the effective date of this contract, and the earnest money will be refunded to Buyer.

D. BUYER'S ACKNOWLEDGMENT (check applicable boxes)**:**

☐ 1. Buyer has received copies of all information listed above.
→ ☒ 2. Buyer has received the pamphlet *Protect Your Family from Lead in Your Home.*

E. BROKERS' ACKNOWLEDGMENT: Brokers have informed Seller of Seller's obligations under 42 U.S.C. 4852d to: (a) provide Buyer with the federally approved pamphlet on lead poisoning prevention; (b) complete this addendum; (c) disclose any known lead-based paint and/or lead-based paint hazards in the Property; (d) deliver all records and reports to Buyer pertaining to lead-based paint and/or lead-based paint hazards in the Property; (e) provide Buyer a period of up to 10 days to have the Property inspected; and (f) retain a completed copy of this addendum for at least 3 years following the sale. Brokers are aware of their responsibility to ensure compliance.

F. CERTIFICATION OF ACCURACY: The following persons have reviewed the information above and certify, to the best of their knowledge, that the information they have provided is true and accurate.

William Robert Richman		Fannie Phyllis Farmer	
Buyer	Date	Seller	Date
Mae Bea Richman		n/a	
Buyer	Date	Seller	Date
Richard Hutchinson		Hilton Charles	
Other Broker	Date	Listing Broker	Date

The form of this addendum has been approved by the Texas Real Estate Commission for use only with similarly approved or promulgated forms of contracts. Such approval relates to this contract form only. TREC forms are intended for use only by trained real estate licensees. No representation is made as to the legal validity or adequacy of any provision in any specific transactions. It is not suitable for complex transactions. Texas Real Estate Commission, P.O. Box 12188, Austin, TX 78711-2188, 1-800-250-8732 or (512) 459-6544 (http://www.trec.state.tx.us)

Form OP-L 01A

FIGURE 11.21

TREC 28-1

PROMULGATED BY THE TEXAS REAL ESTATE COMMISSION (TREC) 04-23-07

EQUAL HOUSING OPPORTUNITY

ENVIRONMENTAL ASSESSMENT, THREATENED OR ENDANGERED SPECIES, AND WETLANDS ADDENDUM

TO CONTRACT CONCERNING THE PROPERTY AT

→ 2520 Farmer Road Pecos, TX

(Address of Property)

→ ☒ A. ENVIRONMENTAL ASSESSMENT: Buyer, at Buyer's expense, may obtain an environmental assessment report prepared by an environmental specialist.

☐ B. THREATENED OR ENDANGERED SPECIES: Buyer, at Buyer's expense, may obtain a report from a natural resources professional to determine if there are any threatened or endangered species or their habitats as defined by the Texas Parks and Wildlife Department or the U.S. Fish and Wildlife Service.

☐ C. WETLANDS: Buyer, at Buyer's expense, may obtain a report from an environmental specialist to determine if there are wetlands, as defined by federal or state law or regulation.

→ Within 10 days after the effective date of the contract, Buyer may terminate the contract by furnishing Seller a copy of any report noted above that adversely affects the use of the Property and a notice of termination of the contract. Upon termination, the earnest money will be refunded to Buyer.

William Robert Richman	Fannie Phyllis Farmer
Buyer	Seller
Mae Bea Richman	n/a
Buyer	Seller

This form has been approved by the Texas Real Estate Commission for use with similarly approved or promulgated contract forms. Such approval relates to this form only. TREC forms are intended for use only by trained real estate licensees. No representation is made as to the legal validity or adequacy of any provision in any specific transactions. It is not suitable for complex transactions. Texas Real Estate Commission, P.O. Box 12188, Austin, TX 78711-2188, 1-800-250-8732 or (512) 459-6544 (http://www.trec.state.tx.us) TREC No. 28-1. This form replaces TREC No. 28-0.

TREC No. 28-1

TRANSACTION 7: ASSUMPTION WITH RELEASE OF LIABILITY (*USING: TREC 30-6, 41-1, 11-6, 33-1, 34-3, AND 12-2. SEE FIGURE 11.22 THROUGH FIGURE 11.27.*)

Unit 623 of Building B of the condominium project known as Freedom Flats, Phase II, in Corpus Christi, Nueces County, Texas, is being sold to Bernie Bryan Buyer and spouse, Beverly Barbara Buyer, by Peter Paul Pastor and his wife, Sarah Sue Pastor. The Property is more commonly known as 1215 Market Street, Apartment 623. Ownership of the unit includes two parking spaces identified as numbers 1654 and 1658 in the adjoining parking garage. The zip code is 78411.

Prior to signing the agreement of purchase, the Buyers received, reviewed, and accepted all of the condominium documents, as well as the Condominium Resale Certificate (TREC Form 32-1) that was prepared and signed by the secretary of the owners' association 20 days ago.

The Buyers will pay $368,200 for the unit and assume the Seller's existing conventional loan with an outstanding balance of $265,008. The loan is a portfolio loan held by Deep Pocket Mortgage Company, Inc. The Buyers will apply for assumption approval within 3 days after the effective date of the contract. They will close within 30 days of the effective date of this contract, which will allow for closing on June 16. The current loan is at 6.75 percent and may be escalated to 7.25 percent upon assumption. If the loan balance is a few dollars more or less at closing, the cash payable at closing will be adjusted to compensate for any variance. The lender will charge a 1-point transfer fee, which will be paid by the Buyer.

The Buyers will pay for the owners' title policy. The Buyer received the Seller's disclosure notice and accepts the Property in its present condition provided the Seller, at Seller's expense, shall replace the nonfunctioning garbage disposal and the broken faucet in the bathroom. Because the project was built in 1979, it is not subject to the HUD lead-based paint disclosure requirement. No repairs to any of the common elements are required.

The Seller has informed the Buyers that the monthly principal, interest, taxes, and insurance (PITI) payment is $2,885 and the monthly maintenance fee is $236 The resale certificate furnished by the secretary of the owners' association confirmed the amount of the maintenance fee. The Buyer will pay any transfer or processing fee charged by the owners' association.

The Seller will have the purchase agreement reviewed by attorney Michael Holmes prior to signing the agreement.

The unit has been listed with Skyline Realty. The listing company will pay the subagent, Downhome Realty, a selling fee equal to 3.25 percent of the selling price of the Property.

A sum of $2,000 in earnest money is delivered to Buyer's Choice Title Company, who will issue an owners' policy at closing.

The Seller will deliver a copy of the note and deed of trust to the Buyer for review within 3 days after the effective date of the purchase agreement. The Buyers also request that copies of every document they will be asked to sign at closing be delivered to them for review a minimum of 48 hours prior to closing.

The Sellers will permit the loan to be assumed only if they are released from liability and will not close if the lender refuses to release them. The Buyers and the Sellers will apply for the release within 3 days after the effective date of the contract. The Seller has agreed to pay a release fee not to exceed $200.

There is already an existing contract in place, dated May 5, between the Sellers and a bachelor by the name of Gordon Robinson. If the Seller notifies the Buyers on or before 5 pm on May 20 that the contract with Mr. Robinson is terminated, this agreement is no longer subject to the contingency, and the effective date of this contract will be amended to be the date of termination of the previous contract.

The Seller has no knowledge of any prior fill as it relates to the Property.

FIGURE 11.22

TREC 30-6

EQUAL HOUSING OPPORTUNITY

PROMULGATED BY THE TEXAS REAL ESTATE COMMISSION (TREC) 12-04-06
NOTICE: Not For Use Where Seller Owns Fee Simple Title To Land Beneath Unit

RESIDENTIAL CONDOMINIUM CONTRACT (RESALE)

1. PARTIES: ______________________________ (Seller) agrees to sell and convey to ______________________________ (Buyer) and Buyer agrees to buy from Seller the Property described below.

2. PROPERTY AND CONDOMINIUM DOCUMENTS:

A. The Condominium Unit, improvements and accessories described below are collectively referred to as the "Property".

(1) CONDOMINIUM UNIT: Unit __________, in Building ____________________, of ______________________________, a condominium project, located at ______________________________ (address/zip code), City of ____________________, County of ____________________, Texas, described in the Condominium Declaration and Plat and any amendments thereto of record in said County; together with such Unit's undivided interest in the Common Elements designated by the Declaration, including those areas reserved as Limited Common Elements appurtenant to the Unit and such other rights to use the Common Elements which have been specifically assigned to the Unit in any other manner. Parking areas assigned to the Unit are: ______________________________.

(2) IMPROVEMENTS: All fixtures and improvements attached to the above described real property including without limitation, the following **permanently installed and built-in items**, if any: all equipment and appliances, valances, screens, shutters, awnings, wall-to-wall carpeting, mirrors, ceiling fans, attic fans, mail boxes, television antennas and satellite dish system and equipment, heating and air conditioning units, security and fire detection equipment, wiring, plumbing and lighting fixtures, chandeliers, shrubbery, landscaping, outdoor cooking equipment, and all other property owned by Seller and attached to the above described Condominium Unit.

(3) ACCESSORIES: The following described related accessories, if any: window air conditioning units, stove, fireplace screens, curtains and rods, blinds, window shades, draperies and rods, controls for satellite dish system, controls for garage door openers, entry gate controls, door keys, mailbox keys, and artificial fireplace logs.

(4) EXCLUSIONS: The following improvements and accessories will be retained by Seller and removed prior to delivery of possession: ______________________________
______________________________.

B. The Declaration, Bylaws and any Rules of the Association are called "Documents". (Check one box only):

❑ (1) Buyer has received a copy of the Documents. Buyer is advised to read the Documents before signing the contract.

❑ (2) Buyer has not received a copy of the Documents. Seller shall deliver the Documents to Buyer within ________ days after the effective date of the contract. Buyer may cancel the contract before the sixth day after Buyer receives the Documents by hand-delivering or mailing written notice of cancellation to Seller by certified United States mail, return receipt requested.

C. The Resale Certificate from the condominium owners association (the Association) is called the "Certificate". The Certificate must be in a form promulgated by TREC or required by the parties. The Certificate must have been prepared no more than 3 months before the date it is delivered to Buyer and must contain at a minimum the information required by Section 82.157, Texas Property Code.
(Check one box only):

❑ (1) Buyer has received the Certificate.

❑ (2) Buyer has not received the Certificate. Seller shall deliver the Certificate to Buyer within ________days after the effective date of the contract. Buyer may cancel the contract before the sixth day after the date Buyer receives the Certificate by hand-delivering or mailing written notice of cancellation to Seller by certified United States mail, return receipt requested.

❑ (3) Buyer has received Seller's affidavit that Seller requested information from the Association concerning its financial condition as required by the Texas Property Code, and that the Association did not provide a Certificate or information required in the Certificate. Buyer and Seller agree to waive the requirement to furnish the Certificate.

3. SALES PRICE:

A. Cash portion of Sales Price payable by Buyer at closing .... $____________________

B Sum of all financing described below (excluding any loan funding fee or mortgage insurance premium).. $____________________

C. Sales Price (Sum of A and B).. $____________________

Initialed for identification by Buyer______ ______ and Seller ______ ______ TREC NO. 30-6

FIGURE 11.22 (CONTINUED)

TREC 30-6

Contract Concerning____Page 2 of 8 12-04-06
(Address of Property)

4. FINANCING: The portion of Sales Price not payable in cash will be paid as follows: (Check applicable boxes below)

❑ A. THIRD PARTY FINANCING: One or more third party mortgage loans in the total amount of $______________ (excluding any loan funding fee or mortgage insurance premium).

(1) Property Approval: If the Property does not satisfy the lenders' underwriting requirements for the loan(s), this contract will terminate and the earnest money will be refunded to Buyer.

(2) Financing Approval: (Check one box only)

❑ (a) This contract is subject to Buyer being approved for the financing described in the attached Third Party Financing Condition Addendum.

❑ (b) This contract is not subject to Buyer being approved for financing and does not involve FHA or VA financing.

❑ B. ASSUMPTION: The assumption of the unpaid principal balance of one or more promissory notes described in the attached TREC Loan Assumption Addendum.

❑ C. SELLER FINANCING: A promissory note from Buyer to Seller of $________________, secured by vendor's and deed of trust liens, and containing the terms and conditions described in the attached TREC Seller Financing Addendum. If an owner policy of title insurance is furnished, Buyer shall furnish Seller with a mortgagee policy of title insurance.

5. EARNEST MONEY: Upon execution of this contract by both parties, Buyer shall deposit $__________ as earnest money with ____, as escrow agent, at ____ (address). Buyer shall deposit additional earnest money of $________________ with escrow agent within _______ days after the effective date of this contract. If Buyer fails to deposit the earnest money as required by this contract, Buyer will be in default.

6. TITLE POLICY:

A. TITLE POLICY: Seller shall furnish to Buyer at ❑Seller's ❑Buyer's expense an owner policy of title insurance (Title Policy) issued by ____ (Title Company) in the amount of the Sales Price, dated at or after closing, insuring Buyer against loss under the provisions of the Title Policy, subject to the promulgated exclusions (including existing building and zoning ordinances) and the following exceptions:

(1) Restrictive covenants common to the platted subdivision in which the Property is located.
(2) The standard printed exception for standby fees, taxes and assessments.
(3) Liens created as part of the financing described in Paragraph 4.
(4) Terms and provisions of the Documents including the assessments and platted easements.
(5) Reservations or exceptions otherwise permitted by this contract or as may be approved by Buyer in writing.
(6) The standard printed exception as to marital rights.
(7) The standard printed exception as to waters, tidelands, beaches, streams, and related matters.
(8) The standard printed exception as to discrepancies, conflicts, shortages in area or boundary lines, encroachments or protrusions, or overlapping improvements.

B. COMMITMENT: Within 20 days after the Title Company receives a copy of this contract, Seller shall furnish to Buyer a commitment for title insurance (Commitment) and, at Buyer's expense, legible copies of restrictive covenants and documents evidencing exceptions in the Commitment (Exception Documents) other than the standard printed exceptions. Seller authorizes the Title Company to deliver the Commitment and Exception Documents to Buyer at Buyer's address shown in Paragraph 21. If the Commitment and Exception Documents are not delivered to Buyer within the specified time, the time for delivery will be automatically extended up to 15 days or the Closing Date, whichever is earlier.

C. OBJECTIONS: Buyer may object in writing to defects, exceptions, or encumbrances to title: disclosed in the Commitment other than items 6A(1) through (8) above; or which prohibit the following use or activity: ____.
Buyer must object not later than (i) the Closing Date or (ii) _____ days after Buyer receives the Commitment and Exception Documents, whichever is earlier. Buyer's failure to object within the time allowed will constitute a waiver of Buyer's right to object; except that the requirements in Schedule C of the Commitment are not waived. Provided Seller is not obligated to incur any expense, Seller shall cure the timely objections of Buyer or any third party lender within 15 days after Seller receives the objections and the Closing Date will be extended as necessary. If objections are not cured within such 15 day period, this contract will terminate and the earnest money will be refunded to Buyer unless Buyer waives the objections.

D. TITLE NOTICES:

(1) ABSTRACT OR TITLE POLICY: Broker advises Buyer to have an abstract of title covering the Property examined by an attorney of Buyer's selection, or Buyer should be furnished with or obtain a Title Policy. If a Title Policy is furnished, the Commitment should be promptly reviewed by an attorney of Buyer's choice due to the time limitations on Buyer's right to object.

Initialed for identification by Buyer______ ______ and Seller _______ ______ TREC NO. 30-6

FIGURE 11.22 (CONTINUED)

TREC 30-6

(2) STATUTORY TAX DISTRICTS: If the Property is situated in a utility or other statutorily created district providing water, sewer, drainage, or flood control facilities and services, Chapter 49, Texas Water Code, requires Seller to deliver and Buyer to sign the statutory notice relating to the tax rate, bonded indebtedness, or standby fee of the district prior to final execution of this contract.

(3) TIDE WATERS: If the Property abuts the tidally influenced waters of the state, §33.135, Texas Natural Resources Code, requires a notice regarding coastal area property to be included in the contract. An addendum containing the notice promulgated by TREC or required by the parties must be used.

(4) ANNEXATION: If the Property is located outside the limits of a municipality, Seller notifies Buyer under §5.011, Texas Property Code, that the Property may now or later be included in the extraterritorial jurisdiction of a municipality and may now or later be subject to annexation by the municipality. Each municipality maintains a map that depicts its boundaries and extraterritorial jurisdiction. To determine if the Property is located within a municipality's extraterritorial jurisdiction or is likely to be located within a municipality's extraterritorial jurisdiction, contact all municipalities located in the general proximity of the Property for further information.

(5) PROPERTY LOCATED IN A CERTIFICATED SERVICE AREA OF A UTILITY SERVICE PROVIDER: Notice required by §13.257, Water Code: The real property, described in Paragraph 2, that you are about to purchase may be located in a certificated water or sewer service area, which is authorized by law to provide water or sewer service to the properties in the certificated area. If your property is located in a certificated area there may be special costs or charges that you will be required to pay before you can receive water or sewer service. There may be a period required to construct lines or other facilities necessary to provide water or sewer service to your property. You are advised to determine if the property is in a certificated area and contact the utility service provider to determine the cost that you will be required to pay and the period, if any, that is required to provide water or sewer service to your property. The undersigned Buyer hereby acknowledges receipt of the foregoing notice at or before the execution of a binding contract for the purchase of the real property described in Paragraph 2 or at closing of purchase of the real property.

7. PROPERTY CONDITION:

A. ACCESS,INSPECTIONS AND UTILITIES: Seller shall permit Buyer and Buyer's agents access to the Property at reasonable times. Buyer may have the Property inspected by inspectors selected by Buyer and licensed by TREC or otherwise permitted by law to make inspections. Seller at Seller's expense shall turn on existing utilities for inspections.

B. SELLER'S DISCLOSURE NOTICE PURSUANT TO §5.008, TEXAS PROPERTY CODE (Notice): (Check one box only)

❑ (1) Buyer has received the Notice.

❑ (2) Buyer has not received the Notice. Within _______ days after the effective date of this contract, Seller shall deliver the Notice to Buyer. If Buyer does not receive the Notice, Buyer may terminate this contract at any time prior to the closing and the earnest money will be refunded to Buyer. If Seller delivers the Notice, Buyer may terminate this contract for any reason within 7 days after Buyer receives the Notice or prior to the closing, whichever first occurs, and the earnest money will be refunded to Buyer.

❑ (3) The Texas Property Code does not require this Seller to furnish the Notice.

C. SELLER'S DISCLOSURE OF LEAD-BASED PAINT AND LEAD-BASED PAINT HAZARDS is required by Federal law for a residential dwelling constructed prior to 1978.

D. ACCEPTANCE OF PROPERTY CONDITION: Buyer accepts the Property in its present condition; provided Seller, at Seller's expense, shall complete the following specific repairs and treatments:____
____.

E. LENDER REQUIRED REPAIRS AND TREATMENTS: Unless otherwise agreed in writing, neither party is obligated to pay for lender required repairs, which includes treatment for wood destroying insects. If the parties do not agree to pay for the lender required repairs or treatments, this contract will terminate and the earnest money will be refunded to Buyer. If the cost of lender required repairs and treatments exceeds 5% of the Sales Price, Buyer may terminate this contract and the earnest money will be refunded to Buyer.

F. COMPLETION OF REPAIRS AND TREATMENTS: Unless otherwise agreed in writing, Seller shall complete all agreed repairs and treatments prior to the Closing Date. All required permits must be obtained, and repairs and treatments must be performed by persons who are licensed or otherwise authorized by law to provide such repairs or treatments. At Buyer's election, any transferable warranties received by Seller with respect to the repairs and treatments will be transferred to Buyer at Buyer's expense. If Seller fails to complete any agreed repairs and treatments prior to the Closing Date, Buyer may do so and receive reimbursement from Seller at closing. The Closing Date will be extended up to 15 days, if necessary, to complete repairs and treatments.

FIGURE 11.22 (CONTINUED)

TREC 30-6

G. ENVIRONMENTAL MATTERS: Buyer is advised that the presence of wetlands, toxic substances, including asbestos and wastes or other environmental hazards or the presence of a threatened or endangered species or its habitat may affect Buyer's intended use of the Property. If Buyer is concerned about these matters, an addendum promulgated by TREC or required by the parties should be used.

H. RESIDENTIAL SERVICE CONTRACTS: Buyer may purchase a residential service contract from a residential service company licensed by TREC. If Buyer purchases a residential service contract, Seller shall reimburse Buyer at closing for the cost of the residential service contract in an amount not exceeding $_______________. Buyer should review any residential service contract for the scope of coverage, exclusions and limitations. **The purchase of a residential service contract is optional. Similar coverage may be purchased from various companies authorized to do business in Texas.**

8. BROKERS' FEES: All obligations of the parties for payment of brokers' fees are contained in separate written agreements.

9. CLOSING:

A. The closing of the sale will be on or before ____________________, 20____, or within 7 days after objections to matters disclosed in the Commitment have been cured, whichever date is later (Closing Date). If either party fails to close the sale by the Closing Date, the non-defaulting party may exercise the remedies contained in Paragraph 15.

B. At closing:

(1) Seller shall execute and deliver a general warranty deed conveying title to the Property to Buyer and showing no additional exceptions to those permitted in Paragraph 6 and furnish tax statements or certificates showing no delinquent taxes on the Property.

(2) Buyer shall pay the Sales Price in good funds acceptable to the escrow agent.

(3) Seller and Buyer shall execute and deliver any notices, statements, certificates, affidavits, releases, loan documents and other documents required of them by this contract, the Commitment or law necessary for the closing of the sale and the issuance of the Title Policy.

C. Unless expressly prohibited by written agreement, Seller may continue to show the Property and receive, negotiate and accept back up offers.

D. All covenants, representations and warranties in this contract survive closing.

10. POSSESSION: Seller shall deliver to Buyer possession of the Property in its present or required condition, ordinary wear and tear excepted: ❑ upon closing and funding ❑ according to a temporary residential lease form promulgated by TREC or other written lease required by the parties. Any possession by Buyer prior to closing or by Seller after closing which is not authorized by a written lease will establish a tenancy at sufferance relationship between the parties. **Consult your insurance agent prior to change of ownership and possession because insurance coverage may be limited or terminated. The absence of a written lease or appropriate insurance coverage may expose the parties to economic loss.**

11. SPECIAL PROVISIONS: (Insert only factual statements and business details applicable to the sale. TREC rules prohibit licensees from adding factual statements or business details for which a contract addendum, lease or other form has been promulgated by TREC for mandatory use.)

12. SETTLEMENT AND OTHER EXPENSES:

A. The following expenses must be paid at or prior to closing:

(1) Expenses payable by Seller (Seller's Expenses):

(a) Releases of existing liens, including prepayment penalties and recording fees; lender, FHA, or VA completion requirements; tax statements or certificates; preparation of deed; one-half of escrow fee; and other expenses payable by Seller under this contract.

(b) Seller shall also pay an amount not to exceed $ ____________ to be applied in the following order: Buyer's Expenses which Buyer is prohibited from paying by FHA, VA, Texas Veterans Housing Assistance Program or other governmental loan programs, and then to other Buyer's Expenses as allowed by the lender.

FIGURE 11.22 (CONTINUED)

TREC 30-6

(2) Expenses payable by Buyer (Buyer's Expenses):
  (a) Loan origination, discount, buy-down, and commitment fees (Loan Fees).
  (b) Appraisal fees; loan application fees; credit reports; preparation of loan documents; interest on the notes from date of disbursement to one month prior to dates of first monthly payments; recording fees; copies of easements and restrictions; mortgagee title policy with endorsements required by lender; loan-related inspection fees; photos; amortization schedules; one-half of escrow fee; all prepaid items, including required premiums for flood and hazard insurance, reserve deposits for insurance, ad valorem taxes and special governmental assessments; final compliance inspection; courier fee; repair inspection; underwriting fee; wire transfer fee; expenses incident to any loan; and other expenses payable by Buyer under this contract.

(3) Any Association fees resulting from the transfer of the property will be paid by ❑ Seller ❑ Buyer.

B. Buyer shall pay Private Mortgage Insurance Premium (PMI), VA Loan Funding Fee, or FHA Mortgage Insurance Premium (MIP) as required by the lender.

C. If any expense exceeds an amount expressly stated in this contract for such expense to be paid by a party, that party may terminate this contract unless the other party agrees to pay such excess. Buyer may not pay charges and fees expressly prohibited by FHA, VA, Texas Veteran's Housing Assistance Program or other governmental loan program regulations.

13. **PRORATIONS:** Taxes for the current year, interest, maintenance fees, regular condominium assessments, dues and rents will be prorated through the Closing Date. The tax proration may be calculated taking into consideration any change in exemptions that will affect the current year's taxes. If taxes for the current year vary from the amount prorated at closing, the parties shall adjust the prorations when tax statements for the current year are available. If taxes are not paid at or prior to closing, Buyer shall pay taxes for the current year. Cash reserves from regular condominium assessments for deferred maintenance or capital improvements established by the Association will not be credited to Seller. Any special condominium assessment due and unpaid at closing will be the obligation of Seller.

14. **CASUALTY LOSS:** If any part of the Unit which Seller is solely obligated to maintain and repair under the terms of the Declaration is damaged or destroyed by fire or other casualty, Seller shall restore the same to its previous condition as soon as reasonably possible, but in any event by the Closing Date. If Seller fails to do so due to factors beyond Seller's control, Buyer may (a) terminate this contract and the earnest money will be refunded to Buyer, (b) extend the time for performance up to 15 days and the Closing Date will be extended as necessary or (c) accept the Property in its damaged condition with an assignment of insurance proceeds and receive credit from Seller at closing in the amount of the deductible under the insurance policy. If any part of the Common Elements or Limited Common Elements appurtenant to the Unit is damaged or destroyed by fire or other casualty loss, Buyer will have 7 days from receipt of notice of such casualty loss within which to notify Seller in writing that the contract will be terminated unless Buyer receives written confirmation from the Association that the damaged condition will be restored to its previous condition within a reasonable time at no cost to Buyer. Unless Buyer gives such notice within such time, Buyer will be deemed to have accepted the Property without confirmation of such restoration. Seller will have 7 days from the date of receipt of Buyer's notice within which to cause to be delivered to Buyer such confirmation. If written confirmation is not delivered to Buyer as required above, Buyer may terminate this contract and the earnest money will be refunded to Buyer. Seller's obligations under this paragraph are independent of any other obligations of Seller under this contract.

15. **DEFAULT:** If Buyer fails to comply with this contract, Buyer will be in default, and Seller may (a) enforce specific performance, seek such other relief as may be provided by law, or both, or (b) terminate this contract and receive the earnest money as liquidated damages, thereby releasing both parties from this contract. If, due to factors beyond Seller's control, Seller fails within the time allowed to make any non-casualty repairs or deliver the Commitment, if required of Seller, Buyer may (a) extend the time for performance up to 15 days and the Closing Date will be extended as necessary or (b) terminate this contract as the sole remedy and receive the earnest money. If Seller fails to comply with this contract for any other reason, Seller will be in default and Buyer may (a) enforce specific performance, seek such other relief as may be provided by law, or both, or (b) terminate this contract and receive the earnest money, thereby releasing both parties from this contract.

16. **MEDIATION:** It is the policy of the State of Texas to encourage resolution of disputes through alternative dispute resolution procedures such as mediation. Any dispute between Seller and Buyer related to this contract which is not resolved through informal discussion ❑will ❑will not be submitted to a mutually acceptable mediation service or provider. The parties to the mediation shall bear the mediation costs equally. This paragraph does not preclude a party from seeking equitable relief from a court of competent jurisdiction.

FIGURE 11.22 (CONTINUED)

TREC 30-6

Contract Concerning____ Page 6 of 8 12-04-06
(Address of Property)

17. ATTORNEY'S FEES: The prevailing party in any legal proceeding related to this contract is entitled to recover reasonable attorney's fees and all costs of such proceeding incurred by the prevailing party.

18. ESCROW:

A. ESCROW: The escrow agent is not (i) a party to this contract and does not have liability for the performance or nonperformance of any party to this contract, (ii) liable for interest on the earnest money and (iii) liable for the loss of any earnest money caused by the failure of any financial institution in which the earnest money has been deposited unless the financial institution is acting as escrow agent.

B. EXPENSES: At closing, the earnest money must be applied first to any cash down payment, then to Buyer's Expenses and any excess refunded to Buyer. If no closing occurs, escrow agent may require payment of unpaid expenses incurred on behalf of the parties and a written release of liability of escrow agent from all parties.

C. DEMAND: Upon termination of this contract, either party or the escrow agent may send a release of earnest money to each party and the parties shall execute counterparts of the release and deliver same to the escrow agent. If either party fails to execute the release, either party may make a written demand to the escrow agent for the earnest money. If only one party makes written demand for the earnest money, escrow agent shall promptly provide a copy of the demand to the other party. If escrow agent does not receive written objection to the demand from the other party within 15 days, escrow agent may disburse the earnest money to the party making demand reduced by the amount of unpaid expenses incurred on behalf of the party receiving the earnest money and escrow agent may pay the same to the creditors. If escrow agent complies with the provisions of this paragraph, each party hereby releases escrow agent from all adverse claims related to the disbursal of the earnest money.

D. DAMAGES: Any party who wrongfully fails or refuses to sign a release acceptable to the escrow agent within 7 days of receipt of the request will be liable to the other party for liquidated damages of three times the amount of the earnest money.

E. NOTICES: Escrow agent's notices will be effective when sent in compliance with Paragraph 21. Notice of objection to the demand will be deemed effective upon receipt by escrow agent.

19. REPRESENTATIONS: Seller represents that as of the Closing Date (a) there will be no liens, assessments, or security interests against the Property which will not be satisfied out of the sales proceeds unless securing payment of any loans assumed by Buyer, (b) assumed loans will not be in default, and (c) Seller has no knowledge of any misrepresentation or errors in the Certificate or any material changes in the information contained therein. If any representation of Seller in this contract or the Certificate is untrue on the Closing Date, Seller will be in default.

20. FEDERAL TAX REQUIREMENTS: If Seller is a "foreign person," as defined by applicable law, or if Seller fails to deliver an affidavit to Buyer that Seller is not a "foreign person," then Buyer shall withhold from the sales proceeds an amount sufficient to comply with applicable tax law and deliver the same to the Internal Revenue Service together with appropriate tax forms. Internal Revenue Service regulations require filing written reports if currency in excess of specified amounts is received in the transaction.

21. NOTICES: All notices from one party to the other must be in writing and are effective when mailed to, hand-delivered at, or transmitted by facsimile or electronic transmission as follows:

To Buyer at:	**To Seller at:**
____________________	____________________
____________________	____________________
____________________	____________________
Telephone: ( ) __________	Telephone: ( ) __________
Facsimile: ( ) __________	Facsimile: ( ) __________
E-mail: ______________	E-mail: ______________

Initialed for identification by Buyer______ ______ and Seller ______ ______ TREC NO. 30-6

FIGURE 11.22 (CONTINUED)

TREC 30-6

22. AGREEMENT OF PARTIES: This contract contains the entire agreement of the parties and cannot be changed except by their written agreement. Addenda which are a part of this contract are (check all applicable boxes):

- ❑ Third Party Financing Condition Addendum
- ❑ Loan Assumption Addendum
- ❑ Buyer's Temporary Residential Lease
- ❑ Seller's Temporary Residential Lease
- ❑ Addendum for Sale of Other Property by Buyer
- ❑ Addendum for "Back-Up" Contract
- ❑ Seller Financing Addendum
- ❑ Addendum for Property Located Seaward of the Gulf Intracoastal Waterway
- ❑ Addendum for Seller's Disclosure of Information on Lead-based Paint and Lead-based Paint Hazards as Required by Federal Law
- ❑ Environmental Assessment, Threatened or Endangered Species and Wetlands Addendum
- ❑ Addendum for Coastal Area Property
- ❑ Addendum for Release of Liability on Assumption of FHA, VA, or Conventional Loan Restoration of Seller's Entitlement for VA Guaranteed Loan
- ❑ Other (list): ______________________
  ____

23. TERMINATION OPTION: For nominal consideration, the receipt of which is hereby acknowledged by Seller, and Buyer's agreement to pay Seller $________________ (Option Fee) within 2 days after the effective date of this contract, Seller grants Buyer the unrestricted right to terminate this contract by giving notice of termination to Seller within _______ days after the effective date of this contract. If no dollar amount is stated as the Option Fee or if Buyer fails to pay the Option Fee within the time prescribed, this paragraph will not be a part of this contract and Buyer shall not have the unrestricted right to terminate this contract. If Buyer gives notice of termination within the time prescribed, the Option Fee will not be refunded; however, any earnest money will be refunded to Buyer. The Option Fee ❑will ❑will not be credited to the Sales Price at closing. **Time is of the essence for this paragraph and strict compliance with the time for performance is required.**

24. CONSULT AN ATTORNEY: Real estate licensees cannot give legal advice. READ THIS CONTRACT CAREFULLY. If you do not understand the effect of this contract, consult an attorney BEFORE signing.

Buyer's Attorney is: ______________________	Seller's Attorney is: ______________________
______________________	______________________
Telephone: (___) ______________	Telephone: (___) ______________
Facsimile: (___) ______________	Facsimile: (___) ______________
E-mail: ______________________	E-mail: ______________________

EXECUTED the _____day of __________________________, 20____ (EFFECTIVE DATE). (BROKER: FILL IN THE DATE OF FINAL ACCEPTANCE.)

______________________	______________________
Buyer	Seller
______________________	______________________
Buyer	Seller

The form of this contract has been approved by the Texas Real Estate Commission. TREC forms are intended for use only by trained real estate licensees. No representation is made as to the legal validity or adequacy of any provision in any specific transactions. It is not intended for complex transactions. Texas Real Estate Commission, P.O. Box 12188, Austin, TX 78711-2188, 1-800-250-8732 or (512) 459-6544 (http://www.trec.state.tx.us) TREC NO. 30-6. This form replaces TREC NO. 30-5.

FIGURE 11.22 (CONTINUED)

TREC 30-6

Contract Concerning____ Page 8 of 8 12-04-06
(Address of Property)

BROKER INFORMATION AND RATIFICATION OF FEE

Listing Broker has agreed to pay Other Broker ______________________ of the total sales price when Listing Broker's fee is received. Escrow Agent is authorized and directed to pay Other Broker from Listing Broker's fee at closing.

______________________________ Other Broker License No.	______________________________ Listing Broker License No.
represents ❑ Buyer only as Buyer's agent ❑ Seller as Listing Broker's subagent	represents ❑ Seller and Buyer as an intermediary ❑ Seller only as Seller's agent
______________________________ Associate Telephone	______________________________ Listing Associate Telephone
______________________________ Broker's Address	______________________________ Listing Associate's Office Address Facsimile
______________________________ City State Zip	______________________________ City State Zip
______________________________ Facsimile	______________________________ Email Address
______________________________ Email Address	______________________________ Selling Associate Telephone
	______________________________ Selling Associate's Office Address Facsimile
	______________________________ City State Zip
	______________________________ Email Address

OPTION FEE RECEIPT

Receipt of $______________ (Option Fee) in the form of ____________________ is acknowledged.

______________________________ ______________________________
Seller or Listing Broker Date

CONTRACT AND EARNEST MONEY RECEIPT

Receipt of ❑Contract and ❑$________________ Earnest Money in the form of ________________ is acknowledged.

Escrow Agent: ______________________________ Date: ____________________

By: ______________________________ ____________________
Email Address

______________________________ Telephone (_____) ______________
Address

______________________________ Facsimile: (_____) ______________
City State Zip

TREC NO. 30-6

FIGURE 11.23

TREC 41-1

PROMULGATED BY THE TEXAS REAL ESTATE COMMISSION (TREC) 04-23-07

EQUAL HOUSING OPPORTUNITY

LOAN ASSUMPTION ADDENDUM
TO CONTRACT CONCERNING THE PROPERTY AT

→ 1215 Market Street, Apt. 623 Corpus Christi, TX
(Address of Property)

→ A. **CREDIT DOCUMENTATION.** To establish Buyer's creditworthiness, Buyer shall deliver to Seller within 5 days after the effective date of this contract ☒ credit report ☐ verification of employment, including salary ☐ verification of funds on deposit in financial institutions ☐ current financial statement and ☐ ____________________.
Buyer hereby authorizes any credit reporting agency to furnish copies of Buyer's credit reports to Seller at Buyer's sole expense.

B. **CREDIT APPROVAL.** If the credit documentation described in Paragraph A is not delivered within the specified time, Seller may terminate this contract by notice to Buyer within 7 days after expiration of the time for delivery, and the earnest money will be paid to Seller. If the credit documentation is timely delivered, and Seller determines in Seller's sole discretion that Buyer's credit is unacceptable, Seller may terminate this contract by notice to Buyer within 7 days after expiration of the time for delivery and the earnest money will be refunded to Buyer. If Seller does not terminate this contract within the time specified, Seller will be deemed to have approved Buyer's creditworthiness.

→ C. **ASSUMPTION.** Buyer's assumption of an existing note includes all obligations imposed by the deed of trust securing the note.

☒ (1) The unpaid principal balance of a first lien promissory note payable to Deep Pocket Mortgage Co. which unpaid balance at closing will be $ 265,800. The total current monthly payment including principal, interest and any reserve deposits is $ 2,885. Buyer's initial payment will be the first payment due after closing.

☐ (2) The unpaid principal balance of a second lien promissory note payable to ____________ ____________ which unpaid balance at closing will be $ ____________. The total current monthly payment including principal, interest and any reserve deposits is $ ____________. Buyer's initial payment will be the first payment due after closing.

If the unpaid principal balance of any assumed loan as of the Closing Date varies from the loan balance stated above, the ☒ cash payable at closing ☐ Sales Price will be adjusted by the amount of any variance. If the total principal balance of all assumed loans varies in an amount greater than $500 at closing, either party may terminate this contract and the earnest money will be refunded to Buyer unless the other party elects to pay the excess of the variance.

D. **LOAN ASSUMPTION TERMS.** Buyer may terminate this contract and the earnest money will be refunded to Buyer if the noteholder requires:

(1) payment of an assumption fee in excess of $ ________ in C(1) or $ __________ in C(2) and Seller declines to pay such excess, or

(2) an increase in the interest rate to more than _____% in C(1) or _____% in C(2), or

(3) any other modification of the loan documents.

E. **CONSENT BY NOTEHOLDER.** If the noteholder fails to consent to the assumption of the loan, either Seller or Buyer may terminate this contract by notice to the other party and the earnest money will be refunded to the Buyer.

F. **SELLER'S LIENS.** Unless Seller is released from liability on any assumed note, a vendor's lien and deed of trust to secure assumption will be required. The vendor's lien will automatically be

FIGURE 11.23 (CONTINUED)

TREC 41-1

Loan Assumption Addendum Concerning — Page 2 of 2 04-23-07

1215 Market Street, Apt. 623 Corpus Christi, TX
(Address of Property)

released on delivery of an executed release by noteholder.

G. TAX AND INSURANCE ESCROW. If noteholder maintains an escrow account for ad valorem taxes, casualty insurance premiums or mortgage insurance premiums, Seller shall transfer the escrow account to Buyer without any deficiency. Buyer shall reimburse Seller for the amount in the transferred accounts.

NOTICE TO BUYER: If you are concerned about the possibility of future adjustments, monthly payments, interest rates or other terms, do not sign the contract without examining the notes and deeds of trust.

NOTICE TO SELLER: Your liability to pay the notes assumed by Buyer will continue unless you obtain a release of liability from the noteholders. If you are concerned about future liability, you should use the TREC Release of Liability Addendum.

______________________	______________________
Buyer	Seller
______________________	______________________
Buyer	Seller

This form has been approved by the Texas Real Estate Commission for use with similarly approved or promulgated contract forms. Such approval relates to this form only. TREC forms are intended for use only by trained real estate licensees. No representation is made as to the legal validity or adequacy of any provision in any specific transactions. It is not suitable for complex transactions. Texas Real Estate Commission, P.O. Box 12188, Austin, TX 78711-2188, 1-800-250-8732 or (512) 459-6544 (http://www.trec.state.tx.us) TREC No. 41-1. This form replaces TREC No. 41-0.

FIGURE 11.24

TREC 11-6

PROMULGATED BY THE TEXAS REAL ESTATE COMMISSION (TREC) 04-23-07

EQUAL HOUSING OPPORTUNITY

ADDENDUM FOR "BACK-UP" CONTRACT

TO CONTRACT CONCERNING THE PROPERTY AT

→ 1215 Market Street, Apt. 623 Corpus Christi, TX
(Address of Property)

→ A. The contract to which this Addendum is attached (the Back-Up Contract) is binding upon execution by the parties, and the earnest money and any Option Fee must be paid as provided in the Back-Up Contract. The Back-Up Contract is contingent upon the termination of a previous contract (the First Contract) dated May 5, 20 08, for the sale of Property. Except as provided by this Addendum, neither party is required to perform under the Back-Up Contract while it is contingent upon the termination of the First Contract.

B. If the First Contract does not terminate on or before May 20, 20 08, the Back-Up Contract terminates and the earnest money will be refunded to Buyer. Seller must notify Buyer immediately of the termination of the First Contract. For purposes of performance, the effective date of the Back-Up Contract changes to the date Buyer receives notice of termination of the First Contract (Amended Effective Date).

C. An amendment or modification of the First Contract will not terminate the First Contract.

D. If Buyer has the unrestricted right to terminate the Back-Up Contract, the time for giving notice of termination begins on the effective date of the Back-Up Contract, continues after the Amended Effective Date and ends upon the expiration of Buyer's unrestricted right to terminate the Back-Up Contract.

E. For purposes of this Addendum, time is of the essence. Strict compliance with the times for performance stated herein is required.

Buyer	Seller
Buyer	Seller

This form has been approved by the Texas Real Estate Commission for use with similarly approved or promulgated contract forms. Such approval relates to this form only. TREC forms are intended for use only by trained real estate licensees. No representation is made as to the legal validity or adequacy of any provision in any specific transactions. It is not suitable for complex transactions. Texas Real Estate Commission, P.O. Box 12188, Austin, TX 78711-2188, 1-800-250-8732 or (512) 459-6544 (http://www.trec.state.tx.us) TREC No. 11-6. This form replaces TREC No. 11-5.

TREC No. 11-6

FIGURE 11.25

TREC 33-1

PROMULGATED BY THE TEXAS REAL ESTATE COMMISSION (TREC) 04-23-07

EQUAL HOUSING OPPORTUNITY

ADDENDUM FOR COASTAL AREA PROPERTY

(SECTION 33.135, TEXAS NATURAL RESOURCES CODE)

TO CONTRACT CONCERNING THE PROPERTY AT

➔ 1215 Market Street, Apt. 623 Corpus Christi, TX
(Address of Property)

NOTICE REGARDING COASTAL AREA PROPERTY

1. The real property described in and subject to this contract adjoins and shares a common boundary with the tidally influenced submerged lands of the state. The boundary is subject to change and can be determined accurately only by a survey on the ground made by a licensed state land surveyor in accordance with the original grant from the sovereign. The owner of the property described in this contract may gain or lose portions of the tract because of changes in the boundary.

➔

2. The seller, transferor, or grantor has no knowledge of any prior fill as it relates to the property described in and subject to this contract except: None ______________________________.

3. State law prohibits the use, encumbrance, construction, or placing of any structure in, on, or over state-owned submerged lands below the applicable tide line, without proper permission.

4. The purchaser or grantee is hereby advised to seek the advice of an attorney or other qualified person as to the legal nature and effect of the facts set forth in this notice on the property described in and subject to this contract. Information regarding the location of the applicable tide line as to the property described in and subject to this contract may be obtained from the surveying division of the General Land Office in Austin.

Buyer	Seller
Buyer	Seller

This form has been approved by the Texas Real Estate Commission for use with similarly approved or promulgated contract forms. Such approval relates to this form only. TREC forms are intended for use only by trained real estate licensees. No representation is made as to the legal validity or adequacy of any provision in any specific transactions. It is not suitable for complex transactions. Texas Real Estate Commission, P.O. Box 12188, Austin, TX 78711-2188, 1-800-250-8732 or (512) 459-6544 (http://www.trec.state.tx.us) TREC No. 33-1. This form replaces TREC No. 33-0.

TREC No. 33-1

FIGURE 11.26

TREC-34-3

PROMULGATED BY THE TEXAS REAL ESTATE COMMISSION (TREC) 12-10-07

EQUAL HOUSING OPPORTUNITY

ADDENDUM FOR PROPERTY LOCATED SEAWARD OF THE GULF INTRACOASTAL WATERWAY

(SECTION 61.025, TEXAS NATURAL RESOURCES CODE)

TO CONTRACT CONCERNING THE PROPERTY AT

→ 1215 Market Street, Apt. 623 Corpus Christi, TX

(Address of Property)

DISCLOSURE NOTICE CONCERNING LEGAL AND ECONOMIC RISKS OF PURCHASING COASTAL REAL PROPERTY NEAR A BEACH

WARNING: THE FOLLOWING NOTICE OF POTENTIAL RISKS OF ECONOMIC LOSS TO YOU AS THE PURCHASER OF COASTAL REAL PROPERTY IS REQUIRED BY STATE LAW.

- READ THIS NOTICE CAREFULLY. DO NOT SIGN THIS CONTRACT UNTIL YOU FULLY UNDERSTAND THE RISKS YOU ARE ASSUMING.
- BY PURCHASING THIS PROPERTY, YOU MAY BE ASSUMING ECONOMIC RISKS OVER AND ABOVE THE RISKS INVOLVED IN PURCHASING INLAND REAL PROPERTY.
- IF YOU OWN A STRUCTURE LOCATED ON COASTAL REAL PROPERTY NEAR A GULF COAST BEACH, IT MAY COME TO BE LOCATED ON THE PUBLIC BEACH BECAUSE OF COASTAL EROSION AND STORM EVENTS.
- AS THE OWNER OF A STRUCTURE LOCATED ON THE PUBLIC BEACH, YOU COULD BE SUED BY THE STATE OF TEXAS AND ORDERED TO REMOVE THE STRUCTURE.
- THE COSTS OF REMOVING A STRUCTURE FROM THE PUBLIC BEACH AND ANY OTHER ECONOMIC LOSS INCURRED BECAUSE OF A REMOVAL ORDER WOULD BE SOLELY YOUR RESPONSIBILITY.

The real property described in this contract is located seaward of the Gulf Intracoastal Waterway to its southernmost point and then seaward of the longitudinal line also known as 97 degrees, 12', 19" which runs southerly to the international boundary from the intersection of the centerline of the Gulf Intracoastal Waterway and the Brownsville Ship Channel. If the property is in close proximity to a beach fronting the Gulf of Mexico, the purchaser is hereby advised that the public has acquired a right of use or easement to or over the area of any public beach by prescription, dedication, or presumption, or has retained a right by virtue of continuous right in the public since time immemorial, as recognized in law and custom.

The extreme seaward boundary of natural vegetation that spreads continuously inland customarily marks the landward boundary of the public easement. If there is no clearly marked natural vegetation line, the landward boundary of the easement is as provided by Sections 61.016 and 61.017, Natural Resources Code.

Much of the Gulf of Mexico coastline is eroding at rates of more than five feet per year. Erosion rates for all Texas Gulf property subject to the open beaches act are available from the Texas General Land Office.

State law prohibits any obstruction, barrier, restraint, or interference with the use of the public easement, including the placement of structures seaward of the landward boundary of the easement. OWNERS OF STRUCTURES ERECTED SEAWARD OF THE VEGETATION LINE (OR OTHER APPLICABLE EASEMENT BOUNDARY) OR THAT BECOME SEAWARD OF THE VEGETATION LINE AS A RESULT OF PROCESSES ARE SUBJECT TO A LAWSUIT BY THE STATE OF TEXAS TO REMOVE THE STRUCTURES.

The purchaser is hereby notified that the purchaser should: (1) determine the rate of shoreline erosion in the vicinity of the real property; and (2) seek the advice of an attorney or other qualified person before executing this contract or instrument of conveyance as to the relevance of these statutes and facts to the value of the property the purchaser is hereby purchasing or contracting to purchase.

Buyer	Seller
Buyer	Seller

This form has been approved by the Texas Real Estate Commission for use with similarly approved or promulgated contract forms. Such approval relates to this form only. TREC forms are intended for use only by trained real estate licensees. No representation is made as to the legal validity or adequacy of any provision in any specific transactions. It is not suitable for complex transactions. Texas Real Estate Commission, P.O. Box 12188, Austin, TX 78711-2188, 1-800-250-8732 or (512) 459-6544 (http://www.trec.state.tx.us) TREC No. 34-3. This form replaces TREC No. 34-2.

TREC No. 34-3

FIGURE 11.27

TREC 12-2

EQUAL HOUSING OPPORTUNITY

PROMULGATED BY THE TEXAS REAL ESTATE COMMISSION (TREC) 04-23-07

ADDENDUM FOR RELEASE OF LIABILITY ON ASSUMED LOAN AND/OR RESTORATION OF SELLER'S VA ENTITLEMENT

TO CONTRACT CONCERNING THE PROPERTY AT

1215 Market Street, Apt. 623 Corpus Christi, TX
(Address of Property)

→ ☒ **A. RELEASE OF SELLER'S LIABILITY ON LOAN TO BE ASSUMED:**

Within 3 days after the effective date of this contract Seller and Buyer shall apply for release of Seller's liability from (a) any conventional lender, (b) VA and any lender whose loan has been guaranteed by VA, or (c) FHA and any lender whose loan has been insured by FHA. Seller and Buyer shall furnish all required information and documents. If any release of liability has not been approved by the Closing Date: (check one box only)

→ ☒ (1) This contract will terminate and the earnest money will be refunded to Buyer.

☐ (2) Failure to obtain release approval will not delay closing.

☐ **B. RESTORATION OF SELLER'S ENTITLEMENT FOR VA LOAN:**

Within ____________ days after the effective date of this contract Seller and Buyer shall apply for restoration of Seller's VA entitlement and shall furnish all information and documents required by VA. If restoration has not been approved by the Closing Date: (check one box only)

☐ (1) This contract will terminate and the earnest money will be refunded to Buyer.

☐ (2) Failure to obtain restoration approval will not delay closing.

NOTICE: VA will not restore Seller's VA entitlement unless Buyer: (a) is a veteran, (b) has sufficient unused VA entitlement and (c) is otherwise qualified. If Seller desires restoration of VA entitlement, paragraphs A and B should be used.

Seller shall pay the cost of securing the release and restoration.

Seller's deed will contain any loan assumption clause required by FHA, VA or any lender.

Buyer	Seller
Buyer	Seller

This form has been approved by the Texas Real Estate Commission for use with similarly approved or promulgated contract forms. Such approval relates to this form only. TREC forms are intended for use only by trained real estate licensees. No representation is made as to the legal validity or adequacy of any provision in any specific transactions. It is not suitable for complex transactions. Texas Real Estate Commission, P.O. Box 12188, Austin, TX 78711-2188, 1-800-250-8732 or (512) 459-6544 (http://www.trec.state.tx.us) TREC No. 12-2. This form replaces TREC No. 12-1.

TREC No. 12-2

TRANSACTION 8: 90% CONVENTIONAL FIXED-RATE LOAN WITH PMI *(USING: TREC 20-7, 40-3, 36-4, 28-1, 33-1, AND 34-3. SEE FIGURE 11.28 THROUGH FIGURE 11.33.)*

Russell A. Janes and his spouse, Anna M. Janes, have agreed to sell their gulf-front home to Peter Paul Prospect and his spouse, Priscilla B. Prospect, for $387,800. The Prospects will obtain a 90 percent conventional loan. It will require one discount point as well as one point for origination, which will be paid by the Buyers. The loan will be a 30-year fixed rate at 7 percent. The contract is subject to financing approval.

The Property is located at 12656 Rolling Waves Lane in Galveston County, Texas. It is more fully described as Lot 6, Block 6, Sandy Dunes Addition, Section 2 of Galveston County, Texas. Although it is located outside the city limits, it has a Galveston, Texas, mailing address. The zip code is 77573. The house was built in 1981.

Because the Property is subject to membership in and the assessments of a very active owners' association, the Prospects want the Sellers to furnish the resale certificate from the association. This will be obtained within 15 days after the effective date of the contract. The Buyer will pay the HOA transfer fee of $100.

The Sellers will remove the leased security system from the Property prior to closing and have agreed to leave the bedspread that matches the draperies in the master bedroom.

The Buyers have selected Buyer's Choice Title Company to hold their $25,000 earnest money deposit and want them to issue the owners' title policy at closing. They request 10 days to get the survey and 2 days to make objections. The Buyers will pay for the new survey. They anticipate they can get financing approval in 20 days and close in 30 days. The Sellers will pay for owners' title policy. Possession will be granted at funding.

The Prospects do not like the looks of some of the plants on the Property and want to have the soil tested for toxic materials. They feel that they can have the tests performed and get the results within 20 days after the effective date of the contract.

In exchange for the payment of $500 to the Seller, the Buyers want an unrestricted 5-day right to inspect the Property If they find anything that they consider unusual, they want to be able to terminate the purchase agreement without forfeiture of their earnest money. If they proceed to closing, the $500 will be credited to the purchase price.

Smooth Sales Realty, Inc., who also has a Buyer representation agreement with the Prospects, has listed the Property. Both parties have signed a written authorization to permit the broker to function as an intermediary and to allow the broker to appoint Susan Smart, salesperson, to work with the Sellers and Sammy Sharp, broker associate, to work with and advise the Buyers. The broker has given the parties the proper written notification of who has been appointed to whom to give advice.

The Seller furnished the Seller's disclosure form prior to the offer being made. The parties are all very reasonable people and will probably get to the closing table without a hitch; however, to be on the safe side, they agree to select a mutually acceptable mediator when and if the need arises and to split the mediator's fee equally.

The Buyers will take the prepared offer to their attorney, Rachel Review, prior to signing.

At the advice of the attorney, the Buyers require that all documents be prepared and made available to them 48 hours prior to closing for review. They will close on or before April 4.

FIGURE 11.28

TREC 20-7

EQUAL HOUSING OPPORTUNITY

02-13-06

PROMULGATED BY THE TEXAS REAL ESTATE COMMISSION (TREC)

ONE TO FOUR FAMILY RESIDENTIAL CONTRACT (RESALE)

NOTICE: Not For Use For Condominium Transactions

1. **PARTIES:** ______________________________ (Seller) agrees to sell and convey to ______________________________ (Buyer) and Buyer agrees to buy from Seller the Property described below.

2. **PROPERTY:**
   A. LAND: Lot ______ Block ________, ______________________ Addition, City of ________________, County of ______________, Texas, known as ______________________________ (address/zip code), or as described on attached exhibit.
   B. IMPROVEMENTS: The house, garage and all other fixtures and improvements attached to the above-described real property, including without limitation, the following **permanently installed and built-in items,** if any: all equipment and appliances, valances, screens, shutters, awnings, wall-to-wall carpeting, mirrors, ceiling fans, attic fans, mail boxes, television antennas and satellite dish system and equipment, heating and air-conditioning units, security and fire detection equipment, wiring, plumbing and lighting fixtures, chandeliers, water softener system, kitchen equipment, garage door openers, cleaning equipment, shrubbery, landscaping, outdoor cooking equipment, and all other property owned by Seller and attached to the above described real property.
   C. ACCESSORIES: The following described related accessories, if any: window air conditioning units, stove, fireplace screens, curtains and rods, blinds, window shades, draperies and rods, controls for satellite dish system, controls for garage door openers, entry gate controls, door keys, mailbox keys, above ground pool, swimming pool equipment and maintenance accessories, and artificial fireplace logs.
   D. EXCLUSIONS: The following improvements and accessories will be retained by Seller and removed prior to delivery of possession: ______________________________ ______________________________.

   The land, improvements and accessories are collectively referred to as the "Property".

3. **SALES PRICE:**
   A. Cash portion of Sales Price payable by Buyer at closing................. $______________
   B. Sum of all financing described below (excluding any loan funding fee or mortgage insurance premium)... $______________
   C. Sales Price (Sum of A and B).. $______________

4. **FINANCING:** The portion of Sales Price not payable in cash will be paid as follows: (Check applicable boxes below)
   ☐ A. THIRD PARTY FINANCING: One or more third party mortgage loans in the total amount of $______________ (excluding any loan funding fee or mortgage insurance premium).
   (1) Property Approval: If the Property does not satisfy the lenders' underwriting requirements for the loan(s), this contract will terminate and the earnest money will be refunded to Buyer.
   (2) Financing Approval: (Check one box only)
   ☐ (a) This contract is subject to Buyer being approved for the financing described in the attached Third Party Financing Condition Addendum.
   ☐ (b) This contract is not subject to Buyer being approved for financing and does not involve FHA or VA financing.
   ☐ B. ASSUMPTION: The assumption of the unpaid principal balance of one or more promissory notes described in the attached TREC Loan Assumption Addendum.
   ☐ C. SELLER FINANCING: A promissory note from Buyer to Seller of $______________, secured by vendor's and deed of trust liens, and containing the terms and conditions described in the attached TREC Seller Financing Addendum. If an owner policy of title insurance is furnished, Buyer shall furnish Seller with a mortgagee policy of title insurance.

5. **EARNEST MONEY:** Upon execution of this contract by both parties, Buyer shall deposit $______________ as earnest money with ______________________________, as escrow agent, at ______________________________ (address). Buyer shall deposit additional earnest money of $______________ with escrow agent within ______ days after the effective date of this contract. If Buyer fails to deposit the earnest money as required by this contract, Buyer will be in default.

6. **TITLE POLICY AND SURVEY:**
   A. TITLE POLICY: Seller shall furnish to Buyer at ☐Seller's ☐Buyer's expense an owner policy of title insurance (Title Policy) issued by ______________________________ (Title Company) in the amount of the Sales Price, dated at or after closing, insuring Buyer

Initialed for identification by Buyer______ ______ and Seller ______ ______ TREC NO. 20-7

FIGURE 11.28 (CONTINUED)

TREC 20-7

Contract Concerning ____ Page 2 of 8 02-13-06
(Address of Property)

against loss under the provisions of the Title Policy, subject to the promulgated exclusions (including existing building and zoning ordinances) and the following exceptions:
(1) Restrictive covenants common to the platted subdivision in which the Property is located.
(2) The standard printed exception for standby fees, taxes and assessments.
(3) Liens created as part of the financing described in Paragraph 4.
(4) Utility easements created by the dedication deed or plat of the subdivision in which the Property is located.
(5) Reservations or exceptions otherwise permitted by this contract or as may be approved by Buyer in writing.
(6) The standard printed exception as to marital rights.
(7) The standard printed exception as to waters, tidelands, beaches, streams, and related matters.
(8) The standard printed exception as to discrepancies, conflicts, shortages in area or boundary lines, encroachments or protrusions, or overlapping improvements. Buyer, at Buyer's expense, may have the exception amended to read, "shortages in area".

B. COMMITMENT: Within 20 days after the Title Company receives a copy of this contract, Seller shall furnish to Buyer a commitment for title insurance (Commitment) and, at Buyer's expense, legible copies of restrictive covenants and documents evidencing exceptions in the Commitment (Exception Documents) other than the standard printed exceptions. Seller authorizes the Title Company to deliver the Commitment and Exception Documents to Buyer at Buyer's address shown in Paragraph 21. If the Commitment and Exception Documents are not delivered to Buyer within the specified time, the time for delivery will be automatically extended up to 15 days or the Closing Date, whichever is earlier.

C. SURVEY: The survey must be made by a registered professional land surveyor acceptable to the Title Company and any lender. (Check one box only)

❑ (1) Within ________ days after the effective date of this contract, Seller shall furnish to Buyer and Title Company Seller's existing survey of the Property and a Residential Real Property Affidavit promulgated by the Texas Department of Insurance (Affidavit). If the existing survey or Affidavit is not acceptable to Title Company or Buyer's lender, Buyer shall obtain a new survey at ❑ Seller's ❑ Buyer's expense no later than 3 days prior to Closing Date. If Seller fails to furnish the existing survey or Affidavit within the time prescribed, Buyer shall obtain a new survey at Seller's expense no later than 3 days prior to Closing Date.

❑ (2) Within _______ days after the effective date of this contract, Buyer shall obtain a new survey at Buyer's expense. Buyer is deemed to receive the survey on the date of actual receipt or the date specified in this paragraph, whichever is earlier.

❑ (3) Within ______ days after the effective date of this contract, Seller, at Seller's expense shall furnish a new survey to Buyer.

D. OBJECTIONS: Buyer may object in writing to defects, exceptions, or encumbrances to title: disclosed on the survey other than items 6A(1) through (7) above; disclosed in the Commitment other than items 6A(1) through (8) above; or which prohibit the following use or activity: ____
____.
Buyer must object not later than (i) the Closing Date or (ii) ____________ days after Buyer receives the Commitment, Exception Documents, and the survey, whichever is earlier. Buyer's failure to object within the time allowed will constitute a waiver of Buyer's right to object; except that the requirements in Schedule C of the Commitment are not waived. Provided Seller is not obligated to incur any expense, Seller shall cure the timely objections of Buyer or any third party lender within 15 days after Seller receives the objections and the Closing Date will be extended as necessary. If objections are not cured within such 15 day period, this contract will terminate and the earnest money will be refunded to Buyer unless Buyer waives the objections.

E. TITLE NOTICES:
(1) ABSTRACT OR TITLE POLICY: Broker advises Buyer to have an abstract of title covering the Property examined by an attorney of Buyer's selection, or Buyer should be furnished with or obtain a Title Policy. If a Title Policy is furnished, the Commitment should be promptly reviewed by an attorney of Buyer's choice due to the time limitations on Buyer's right to object.
(2) MANDATORY OWNERS' ASSOCIATION MEMBERSHIP: The Property ❑ is ❑ is not subject to mandatory membership in an owners' association. If the Property is subject to mandatory membership in an owners' association, Seller notifies Buyer under §5.012, Texas Property Code, that, as a purchaser of property in the residential community in which the Property is located, you are obligated to be a member of the owners' association. Restrictive covenants governing the use and occupancy of the Property and a dedicatory instrument governing the establishment, maintenance, and operation of this residential community have been or will be recorded in the Real Property Records of the county in which the Property is located. Copies of the restrictive covenants and dedicatory instrument may be obtained from the county clerk. You are obligated to pay

Initialed for identification by Buyer______ ______ and Seller _______ ______ TREC NO. 20-7

FIGURE 11.28 (CONTINUED)

TREC 20-7

assessments to the owners' association. The amount of the assessments is subject to change. Your failure to pay the assessments could result in a lien on and the foreclosure of the Property. If Buyer is concerned about these matters, the TREC promulgated Addendum for Property Subject to Mandatory Membership in an Owner's Association should be used.

(3) STATUTORY TAX DISTRICTS: If the Property is situated in a utility or other statutorily created district providing water, sewer, drainage, or flood control facilities and services, Chapter 49, Texas Water Code, requires Seller to deliver and Buyer to sign the statutory notice relating to the tax rate, bonded indebtedness, or standby fee of the district prior to final execution of this contract.

(4) TIDE WATERS: If the Property abuts the tidally influenced waters of the state, §33.135, Texas Natural Resources Code, requires a notice regarding coastal area property to be included in the contract. An addendum containing the notice promulgated by TREC or required by the parties must be used.

(5) ANNEXATION: If the Property is located outside the limits of a municipality, Seller notifies Buyer under §5.011, Texas Property Code, that the Property may now or later be included in the extraterritorial jurisdiction of a municipality and may now or later be subject to annexation by the municipality. Each municipality maintains a map that depicts its boundaries and extraterritorial jurisdiction. To determine if the Property is located within a municipality's extraterritorial jurisdiction or is likely to be located within a municipality's extraterritorial jurisdiction, contact all municipalities located in the general proximity of the Property for further information.

(6) PROPERTY LOCATED IN A CERTIFICATED SERVICE AREA OF A UTILITY SERVICE PROVIDER: Notice required by §13.257, Water Code: The real property, described in Paragraph 2, that you are about to purchase may be located in a certificated water or sewer service area, which is authorized by law to provide water or sewer service to the properties in the certificated area. If your property is located in a certificated area there may be special costs or charges that you will be required to pay before you can receive water or sewer service. There may be a period required to construct lines or other facilities necessary to provide water or sewer service to your property. You are advised to determine if the property is in a certificated area and contact the utility service provider to determine the cost that you will be required to pay and the period, if any, that is required to provide water or sewer service to your property. The undersigned Buyer hereby acknowledges receipt of the foregoing notice at or before the execution of a binding contract for the purchase of the real property described in Paragraph 2 or at closing of purchase of the real property.

(7) PUBLIC IMPROVEMENT DISTRICTS: If the Property is in a public improvement district, §5.014, Property Code, requires Seller to notify Buyer as follows: As a purchaser of this parcel of real property you are obligated to pay an assessment to a municipality or county for an improvement project undertaken by a public improvement district under Chapter 372, Local Government Code. The assessment may be due annually or in periodic installments. More information concerning the amount of the assessment and the due dates of that assessment may be obtained from the municipality or county levying the assessment. The amount of the assessments is subject to change. Your failure to pay the assessments could result in a lien on and the foreclosure of your property.

7. PROPERTY CONDITION:

A. ACCESS,INSPECTIONS AND UTILITIES: Seller shall permit Buyer and Buyer's agents access to the Property at reasonable times. Buyer may have the Property inspected by inspectors selected by Buyer and licensed by TREC or otherwise permitted by law to make inspections. Seller at Seller's expense shall turn on existing utilities for inspections.

B. SELLER'S DISCLOSURE NOTICE PURSUANT TO §5.008, TEXAS PROPERTY CODE (Notice): (Check one box only)

☐ (1) Buyer has received the Notice.

☐ (2) Buyer has not received the Notice. Within ______ days after the effective date of this contract, Seller shall deliver the Notice to Buyer. If Buyer does not receive the Notice, Buyer may terminate this contract at any time prior to the closing and the earnest money will be refunded to Buyer. If Seller delivers the Notice, Buyer may terminate this contract for any reason within 7 days after Buyer receives the Notice or prior to the closing, whichever first occurs, and the earnest money will be refunded to Buyer.

☐ (3) The Seller is not required to furnish the notice under the Texas Property Code.

C. SELLER'S DISCLOSURE OF LEAD-BASED PAINT AND LEAD-BASED PAINT HAZARDS is required by Federal law for a residential dwelling constructed prior to 1978.

D. ACCEPTANCE OF PROPERTY CONDITION: Buyer accepts the Property in its present condition; provided Seller, at Seller's expense, shall complete the following specific repairs and treatments: ____

____

E. LENDER REQUIRED REPAIRS AND TREATMENTS: Unless otherwise agreed in writing, neither party is obligated to pay for lender required repairs, which includes treatment for wood

FIGURE 11.28 (CONTINUED)

TREC 20-7

destroying insects. If the parties do not agree to pay for the lender required repairs or treatments, this contract will terminate and the earnest money will be refunded to Buyer. If the cost of lender required repairs and treatments exceeds 5% of the Sales Price, Buyer may terminate this contract and the earnest money will be refunded to Buyer.

F. COMPLETION OF REPAIRS AND TREATMENTS: Unless otherwise agreed in writing, Seller shall complete all agreed repairs and treatments prior to the Closing Date. All required permits must be obtained, and repairs and treatments must be performed by persons who are licensed or otherwise authorized by law to provide such repairs or treatments. At Buyer's election, any transferable warranties received by Seller with respect to the repairs and treatments will be transferred to Buyer at Buyer's expense. If Seller fails to complete any agreed repairs and treatments prior to the Closing Date, Buyer may do so and receive reimbursement from Seller at closing. The Closing Date will be extended up to 15 days, if necessary, to complete repairs and treatments.

G. ENVIRONMENTAL MATTERS: Buyer is advised that the presence of wetlands, toxic substances, including asbestos and wastes or other environmental hazards, or the presence of a threatened or endangered species or its habitat may affect Buyer's intended use of the Property. If Buyer is concerned about these matters, an addendum promulgated by TREC or required by the parties should be used.

H. RESIDENTIAL SERVICE CONTRACTS: Buyer may purchase a residential service contract from a residential service company licensed by TREC. If Buyer purchases a residential service contract, Seller shall reimburse Buyer at closing for the cost of the residential service contract in an amount not exceeding $______________. Buyer should review any residential service contract for the scope of coverage, exclusions and limitations. **The purchase of a residential service contract is optional. Similar coverage may be purchased from various companies authorized to do business in Texas.**

8. **BROKERS' FEES:** All obligations of the parties for payment of brokers' fees are contained in separate written agreements.

9. **CLOSING:**

A. The closing of the sale will be on or before ____________________, 20____, or within 7 days after objections made under Paragraph 6D have been cured or waived, whichever date is later (Closing Date). If either party fails to close the sale by the Closing Date, the non-defaulting party may exercise the remedies contained in Paragraph 15.

B. At closing:

(1) Seller shall execute and deliver a general warranty deed conveying title to the Property to Buyer and showing no additional exceptions to those permitted in Paragraph 6 and furnish tax statements or certificates showing no delinquent taxes on the Property.

(2) Buyer shall pay the Sales Price in good funds acceptable to the escrow agent.

(3) Seller and Buyer shall execute and deliver any notices, statements, certificates, affidavits, releases, loan documents and other documents required of them by this contract, the Commitment or law necessary for the closing of the sale and the issuance of the Title Policy.

C. Unless expressly prohibited by written agreement, Seller may continue to show the Property and receive, negotiate and accept back up offers.

D. All covenants, representations and warranties in this contract survive closing.

10. **POSSESSION:** Seller shall deliver to Buyer possession of the Property in its present or required condition, ordinary wear and tear excepted: ❑ upon closing and funding ❑ according to a temporary residential lease form promulgated by TREC or other written lease required by the parties. Any possession by Buyer prior to closing or by Seller after closing which is not authorized by a written lease will establish a tenancy at sufferance relationship between the parties. **Consult your insurance agent prior to change of ownership and possession because insurance coverage may be limited or terminated. The absence of a written lease or appropriate insurance coverage may expose the parties to economic loss.**

11. **SPECIAL PROVISIONS:** (Insert only factual statements and business details applicable to the sale. TREC rules prohibit licensees from adding factual statements or business details for which a contract addendum, lease or other form has been promulgated by TREC for mandatory use.)

FIGURE 11.28 (CONTINUED)

TREC 20-7

12. SETTLEMENT AND OTHER EXPENSES:

A. The following expenses must be paid at or prior to closing:

(1) Expenses payable by Seller (Seller's Expenses):

(a) Releases of existing liens, including prepayment penalties and recording fees; release of Seller's loan liability; tax statements or certificates; preparation of deed; one-half of escrow fee; and other expenses payable by Seller under this contract.

(b) Seller shall also pay an amount not to exceed $ ____________ to be applied in the following order: Buyer's Expenses which Buyer is prohibited from paying by FHA, VA, Texas Veterans Housing Assistance Program or other governmental loan programs, and then to other Buyer's Expenses as allowed by the lender.

(2) Expenses payable by Buyer (Buyer's Expenses):

(a) Loan origination, discount, buy-down, and commitment fees (Loan Fees).

(b) Appraisal fees; loan application fees; credit reports; preparation of loan documents; interest on the notes from date of disbursement to one month prior to dates of first monthly payments; recording fees; copies of easements and restrictions; mortgagee title policy with endorsements required by lender; loan-related inspection fees; photos; amortization schedules; one-half of escrow fee; all prepaid items, including required premiums for flood and hazard insurance, reserve deposits for insurance, ad valorem taxes and special governmental assessments; final compliance inspection; courier fee; repair inspection; underwriting fee; wire transfer fee; expenses incident to any loan; and other expenses payable by Buyer under this contract.

B. Buyer shall pay Private Mortgage Insurance Premium (PMI), VA Loan Funding Fee, or FHA Mortgage Insurance Premium (MIP) as required by the lender.

C. If any expense exceeds an amount expressly stated in this contract for such expense to be paid by a party, that party may terminate this contract unless the other party agrees to pay such excess. Buyer may not pay charges and fees expressly prohibited by FHA, VA, Texas Veterans Housing Assistance Program or other governmental loan program regulations.

13. PRORATIONS: Taxes for the current year, interest, maintenance fees, assessments, dues and rents will be prorated through the Closing Date. The tax proration may be calculated taking into consideration any change in exemptions that will affect the current year's taxes. If taxes for the current year vary from the amount prorated at closing, the parties shall adjust the prorations when tax statements for the current year are available. If taxes are not paid at or prior to closing, Buyer shall pay taxes for the current year.

14. CASUALTY LOSS: If any part of the Property is damaged or destroyed by fire or other casualty after the effective date of this contract, Seller shall restore the Property to its previous condition as soon as reasonably possible, but in any event by the Closing Date. If Seller fails to do so due to factors beyond Seller's control, Buyer may (a) terminate this contract and the earnest money will be refunded to Buyer (b) extend the time for performance up to 15 days and the Closing Date will be extended as necessary or (c) accept the Property in its damaged condition with an assignment of insurance proceeds and receive credit from Seller at closing in the amount of the deductible under the insurance policy. Seller's obligations under this paragraph are independent of any other obligations of Seller under this contract.

15. DEFAULT: If Buyer fails to comply with this contract, Buyer will be in default, and Seller may (a) enforce specific performance, seek such other relief as may be provided by law, or both, or (b) terminate this contract and receive the earnest money as liquidated damages, thereby releasing both parties from this contract. If, due to factors beyond Seller's control, Seller fails within the time allowed to make any non-casualty repairs or deliver the Commitment, or survey, if required of Seller, Buyer may (a) extend the time for performance up to 15 days and the Closing Date will be extended as necessary or (b) terminate this contract as the sole remedy and receive the earnest money. If Seller fails to comply with this contract for any other reason, Seller will be in default and Buyer may (a) enforce specific performance, seek such other relief as may be provided by law, or both, or (b) terminate this contract and receive the earnest money, thereby releasing both parties from this contract.

16. MEDIATION: It is the policy of the State of Texas to encourage resolution of disputes through alternative dispute resolution procedures such as mediation. Any dispute between Seller and Buyer related to this contract which is not resolved through informal discussion ❑will ❑will not be submitted to a mutually acceptable mediation service or provider. The parties to the mediation shall bear the mediation costs equally. This paragraph does not preclude a party from seeking equitable relief from a court of competent jurisdiction.

17. ATTORNEY'S FEES: The prevailing party in any legal proceeding related to this contract is entitled to recover reasonable attorney's fees and all costs of such proceeding incurred by the prevailing party.

FIGURE 11.28 (CONTINUED)

TREC 20-7

Contract Concerning ____ Page 6 of 8 02-13-06
(Address of Property)

18. ESCROW:

A. ESCROW: The escrow agent is not (i) a party to this contract and does not have liability for the performance or nonperformance of any party to this contract, (ii) liable for interest on the earnest money and (iii) liable for the loss of any earnest money caused by the failure of any financial institution in which the earnest money has been deposited unless the financial institution is acting as escrow agent.

B. EXPENSES: At closing, the earnest money must be applied first to any cash down payment, then to Buyer's Expenses and any excess refunded to Buyer. If no closing occurs, escrow agent may require payment of unpaid expenses incurred on behalf of the parties and a written release of liability of escrow agent from all parties.

C. DEMAND: Upon termination of this contract, either party or the escrow agent may send a release of earnest money to each party and the parties shall execute counterparts of the release and deliver same to the escrow agent. If either party fails to execute the release, either party may make a written demand to the escrow agent for the earnest money. If only one party makes written demand for the earnest money, escrow agent shall promptly provide a copy of the demand to the other party. If escrow agent does not receive written objection to the demand from the other party within 15 days, escrow agent may disburse the earnest money to the party making demand reduced by the amount of unpaid expenses incurred on behalf of the party receiving the earnest money and escrow agent may pay the same to the creditors. If escrow agent complies with the provisions of this paragraph, each party hereby releases escrow agent from all adverse claims related to the disbursal of the earnest money.

D. DAMAGES: Any party who wrongfully fails or refuses to sign a release acceptable to the escrow agent within 7 days of receipt of the request will be liable to the other party for liquidated damages of three times the amount of the earnest money.

E. NOTICES: Escrow agent's notices will be effective when sent in compliance with Paragraph 21. Notice of objection to the demand will be deemed effective upon receipt by escrow agent.

19. REPRESENTATIONS: Seller represents that as of the Closing Date (a) there will be no liens, assessments, or security interests against the Property which will not be satisfied out of the sales proceeds unless securing payment of any loans assumed by Buyer and (b) assumed loans will not be in default. If any representation of Seller in this contract is untrue on the Closing Date, Seller will be in default.

20. FEDERAL TAX REQUIREMENTS: If Seller is a "foreign person," as defined by applicable law, or if Seller fails to deliver an affidavit to Buyer that Seller is not a "foreign person," then Buyer shall withhold from the sales proceeds an amount sufficient to comply with applicable tax law and deliver the same to the Internal Revenue Service together with appropriate tax forms. Internal Revenue Service regulations require filing written reports if currency in excess of specified amounts is received in the transaction.

21. NOTICES: All notices from one party to the other must be in writing and are effective when mailed to, hand-delivered at, or transmitted by facsimile or electronic transmission as follows:

To Buyer at: ____________________	**To Seller at:** ____________________
____________________	____________________
____________________	____________________
____________________	____________________
Telephone: ( ) ____________	Telephone: ( ) ____________
Facsimile: ( ) ____________	Facsimile: ( ) ____________
E-mail: ____________________	E-mail: ____________________

FIGURE 11.28 (CONTINUED)

TREC 20-7

Contract Concerning ____ Page 7 of 8 02-13-06
(Address of Property)

22. **AGREEMENT OF PARTIES:** This contract contains the entire agreement of the parties and cannot be changed except by their written agreement. Addenda which are a part of this contract are (Check all applicable boxes):

- ❑ Third Party Financing Condition Addendum
- ❑ Seller Financing Addendum
- ❑ Loan Assumption Addendum
- ❑ Buyer's Temporary Residential Lease
- ❑ Seller's Temporary Residential Lease
- ❑ Addendum for Sale of Other Property by Buyer
- ❑ Addendum for Seller's Disclosure of Information on Lead-based Paint and Lead-based Paint Hazards as Required by Federal Law
- ❑ Addendum for Property Subject to Mandatory Membership in an Owners' Association
- ❑ Environmental Assessment, Threatened or Endangered Species and Wetlands Addendum
- ❑ Addendum for "Back-Up" Contract
- ❑ Addendum for Coastal Area Property
- ❑ Addendum for Property Located Seaward of the Gulf Intracoastal Waterway
- ❑ Addendum for Release of Liability on Assumption of FHA, VA, or Conventional Loan Restoration of Seller's Entitlement for VA Guaranteed Loan
- ❑ Other (list): ______________________________

23. **TERMINATION OPTION:** For nominal consideration, the receipt of which is hereby acknowledged by Seller, and Buyer's agreement to pay Seller $______________ (Option Fee) within 2 days after the effective date of this contract, Seller grants Buyer the unrestricted right to terminate this contract by giving notice of termination to Seller within _____ days after the effective date of this contract. If no dollar amount is stated as the Option Fee or if Buyer fails to pay the Option Fee within the time prescribed, this paragraph will not be a part of this contract and Buyer shall not have the unrestricted right to terminate this contract. If Buyer gives notice of termination within the time prescribed, the Option Fee will not be refunded; however, any earnest money will be refunded to Buyer. The Option Fee ❑will ❑will not be credited to the Sales Price at closing. **Time is of the essence for this paragraph and strict compliance with the time for performance is required.**

24. **CONSULT AN ATTORNEY:** Real estate licensees cannot give legal advice. READ THIS CONTRACT CAREFULLY. If you do not understand the effect of this contract, consult an attorney BEFORE signing.

Buyer's Attorney is: ______________________	Seller's Attorney is: ______________________
______________________	______________________
Telephone: ( )	Telephone: ( )
Facsimile: ( )	Facsimile: ( )
E-mail:	E-mail:

EXECUTED the _____day of ____________________, 20____ (EFFECTIVE DATE). (BROKER: FILL IN THE DATE OF FINAL ACCEPTANCE.)

______________________	______________________
Buyer	Seller
______________________	______________________
Buyer	Seller

The form of this contract has been approved by the Texas Real Estate Commission. TREC forms are intended for use only by trained real estate licensees. No representation is made as to the legal validity or adequacy of any provision in any specific transactions. It is not intended for complex transactions. Texas Real Estate Commission, P.O. Box 12188, Austin, TX 78711-2188, 1-800-250-8732 or (512) 459-6544 (http://www.trec.state.tx.us) TREC NO. 20-7. This form replaces TREC NO. 20-6.

TREC NO. 20-7

FIGURE 11.28 (CONTINUED)

TREC 20-7

Contract Concerning ______________________________ Page 8 of 8 02-13-06
(Address of Property)

BROKER INFORMATION AND RATIFICATION OF FEE

Listing Broker has agreed to pay Other Broker ____________________ of the total sales price when Listing Broker's fee is received. Escrow Agent is authorized and directed to pay Other Broker from Listing Broker's fee at closing.

Other Broker — License No.	Listing Broker — License No.
represents ❑ Buyer only as Buyer's agent ❑ Seller as Listing Broker's subagent	represents ❑ Seller and Buyer as an intermediary ❑ Seller only as Seller's agent
Associate — Telephone	Listing Associate — Telephone
Broker's Address	Listing Associate's Office Address — Facsimile
City — State — Zip	City — State — Zip
Facsimile	Email Address
Email Address	Selling Associate — Telephone
	Selling Associate's Office Address — Facsimile
	City — State — Zip
	Email Address

OPTION FEE RECEIPT

Receipt of $______________ (Option Fee) in the form of ____________________ is acknowledged.

Seller or Listing Broker ____________________ Date ____________________

CONTRACT AND EARNEST MONEY RECEIPT

Receipt of ❑Contract and ❑$______________ Earnest Money in the form of ______________ is acknowledged.

Escrow Agent: ______________________ Date: ______________

By: ______________________ Email Address ______________

Address ______________________ Telephone (_____) ______________

City State Zip ______________________ Facsimile: (_____) ______________

TREC NO. 20-7

FIGURE 11.29

TREC 40-3

12-10-07

EQUAL HOUSING OPPORTUNITY

PROMULGATED BY THE TEXAS REAL ESTATE COMMISSION (TREC)

THIRD PARTY FINANCING CONDITION ADDENDUM

TO CONTRACT CONCERNING THE PROPERTY AT

→ 12656 Rolling Waves Lane Galveston, TX
(Street Address and City)

Buyer shall apply promptly for all financing described below and make every reasonable effort to obtain approval for the financing (Financing Approval). Buyer shall furnish all information and documents required by lender for Financing Approval. Financing Approval will be deemed to have been obtained when (1) the terms of the loan(s) described below are available and (2) lender determines that Buyer has satisfied all of lender's financial requirements (those items relating to Buyer's assets, income and credit history). If Buyer cannot obtain Financing Approval, Buyer may give written notice to Seller within 20 days after the effective date of this contract and this contract will terminate and the earnest money will be refunded to Buyer. **If Buyer does not give such notice within the time required, this contract will no longer be subject to Financing Approval. Time is of the essence for this paragraph and strict compliance with the time for performance is required.**

NOTE: Financing Approval does not include approval of lender's underwriting requirements for the Property, as specified in Paragraph 4.A.(1) of the contract.

Each note must be secured by vendor's and deed of trust liens.

CHECK APPLICABLE BOXES:

→ ☒ A. CONVENTIONAL FINANCING:

☒ (1) A first mortgage loan in the principal amount of $ 349,000 (excluding any financed PMI premium), due in full in 30 year(s), with interest not to exceed 7 % per annum for the first 30 year(s) of the loan with Loan Fees (loan origination, discount, buy-down, and commitment fees) not to exceed 2 % of the loan.

☐ (2) A second mortgage loan in the principal amount of $__________(excluding any financed PMI premium), due in full in __________year(s), with interest not to exceed ______% per annum for the first __________year(s) of the loan with Loan Fees (loan origination, discount, buy-down, and commitment fees) not to exceed ________% of the loan.

☐ B. TEXAS VETERANS LOAN: A loan(s) from the Texas Veterans Land Board of $__________ for a period in the total amount of _____years at the interest rate established by the Texas Veterans Land Board.

☐ C. FHA INSURED FINANCING: A Section __________ FHA insured loan of not less than $__________ (excluding any financed MIP), amortizable monthly for not less than _______years, with interest not to exceed _______% per annum for the first ______year(s) of the loan with Loan Fees (loan origination, discount, buy-down, and commitment fees) not to exceed _________ % of the loan. As required by HUD-FHA, if FHA valuation is unknown, *"It is expressly agreed that, notwithstanding any other provision of this contract, the purchaser (Buyer) shall not be obligated to complete the purchase of the Property described herein or to incur any penalty by forfeiture of earnest money deposits or otherwise unless the purchaser (Buyer) has been given in accordance with HUD/FHA or VA requirements a written statement issued by the Federal Housing Commissioner, Department of Veterans Affairs, or a Direct Endorsement Lender setting forth the appraised value of the Property of not less than $__________. The purchaser (Buyer) shall have the privilege and option of proceeding with consummation of the contract without regard to the amount of the*

FIGURE 11.29 (CONTINUED)

TREC 40-3

Third Party Financing Condition Addendum Concerning Page 2 of 2 12-10-07

➔ 12656 Rolling Waves Lane Galveston, TX
(Address of Property)

appraised valuation. The appraised valuation is arrived at to determine the maximum mortgage the Department of Housing and Urban Development will insure. HUD does not warrant the value or the condition of the Property. The purchaser (Buyer) should satisfy himself/herself that the price and the condition of the Property are acceptable."
NOTE: HUD 92564-CN "For Your Protection: Get a Home Inspection" must be attached to this Addendum.

❑ D. VA GUARANTEED FINANCING: A VA guaranteed loan of not less than $________________ (excluding any financed Funding Fee), amortizable monthly for not less than________years, with interest not to exceed_________% per annum for the first ________year(s) of the loan with Loan Fees (loan origination, discount, buy-down, and commitment fees) not to exceed _________% of the loan.

VA NOTICE TO BUYER: "*It is expressly agreed that, notwithstanding any other provisions of this contract, the Buyer shall not incur any penalty by forfeiture of earnest money or otherwise or be obligated to complete the purchase of the Property described herein, if the contract purchase price or cost exceeds the reasonable value of the Property established by the Department of Veterans Affairs. The Buyer shall, however, have the privilege and option of proceeding with the consummation of this contract without regard to the amount of the reasonable value established by the Department of Veterans Affairs."*

If Buyer elects to complete the purchase at an amount in excess of the reasonable value established by VA, Buyer shall pay such excess amount in cash from a source which Buyer agrees to disclose to the VA and which Buyer represents will not be from borrowed funds except as approved by VA. If VA reasonable value of the Property is less than the Sales Price, Seller may reduce the Sales Price to an amount equal to the VA reasonable value and the sale will be closed at the lower Sales Price with proportionate adjustments to the down payment and the loan amount.

Buyer hereby authorizes any lender to furnish to the Seller or Buyer or their representatives information relating only to the status of Financing Approval of Buyer.

______________________	______________________
Buyer	Seller
______________________	______________________
Buyer	Seller

This form has been approved by the Texas Real Estate Commission for use with similarly approved or promulgated contract forms. Such approval relates to this form only. TREC forms are intended for use only by trained real estate licensees. No representation is made as to the legal validity or adequacy of any provision in any specific transactions. It is not intended for complex transactions. Texas Real Estate Commission, P.O. Box 12188, Austin, TX 78711-2188, 1-800-250-8732 or (512) 459-6544 (http://www.trec.state.tx.us) TREC No. 40-3. This form replaces TREC No. 40-2.

TREC NO. 40-3

FIGURE 11.30

TREC 36-4

PROMULGATED BY THE TEXAS REAL ESTATE COMMISSION (TREC) 02-13-06

EQUAL HOUSING OPPORTUNITY

ADDENDUM FOR PROPERTY SUBJECT TO MANDATORY MEMBERSHIP IN AN OWNERS' ASSOCIATION

(NOT FOR USE WITH CONDOMINIUMS)

ADDENDUM TO CONTRACT CONCERNING THE PROPERTY AT

→ 12656 Rolling Waves Lane Galveston, TX

(Street Address and City)

→ Sandy Dunes Homeowners' Association

(Name of Owners' Association)

A. SUBDIVISON INFORMATION: "Subdivision Information" means: (i) the restrictions applying to the subdivision, (ii) the bylaws and rules of the Owners' Association, and (iii) a resale certificate, all of which were provided by the Owners' Association in compliance with Section 207.003 of the Texas Property Code.

(Check only one box):

→ ☒ 1. Within 15 days after the effective date of the contract, Seller shall at Seller's expense deliver the Subdivision Information to Buyer. If Buyer does not receive the Subdivision Information, Buyer may terminate the contract at any time prior to closing and the earnest money will be refunded to Buyer. If Seller delivers the Subdivision Information, Buyer may terminate the contract for any reason within 7 days after Buyer receives the Subdivision Information or prior to closing, whichever first occurs, and the earnest money will be refunded to Buyer.

☐ 2. Buyer has received and approved the Subdivision Information before signing the contract.

☐ 3. Buyer does not require delivery of the Subdivision Information.

If Seller becomes aware of any material changes in the Subdivision Information, Seller shall immediately give notice to Buyer. Buyer may terminate the contract prior to closing by giving written notice to Seller if: (i) any of the Subdivision Information provided was not true; or (ii) any material adverse change in the Subdivision Information occurs prior to closing, and the earnest money will be refunded to Buyer.

→ **B. FEES:** Buyer shall pay any Owners' Association fees resulting from the transfer of the Property not to exceed $ 100 and Seller shall pay any excess.

NOTICE TO BUYER REGARDING REPAIRS BY THE OWNERS' ASSOCIATION: The Owners' Association may have the sole responsibility to make certain repairs to the Property. If you are concerned about the condition of any part of the Property which the Owners' Association is required to repair, you should not sign the contract unless you are satisfied that the Owners' Association will make the desired repairs.

Buyer	Seller
Buyer	Seller

The form of this addendum has been approved by the Texas Real Estate Commission for use only with similarly approved or promulgated forms of contracts. Such approval relates to this contract form only. TREC forms are intended for use only by trained real estate licensees. No representation is made as to the legal validity or adequacy of any provision in any specific transactions. It is not intended for complex transactions. Texas Real Estate Commission, P.O. Box 12188, Austin, TX 78711-2188, 1-800-250-8732 or (512) 459-6544 (http://www.trec.state.tx.us) TREC No. 36-4. This form replaces TREC No. 36-3.

TREC NO. 36-4

FIGURE 11.31

TREC 28-1

PROMULGATED BY THE TEXAS REAL ESTATE COMMISSION (TREC) 04-23-07

EQUAL HOUSING OPPORTUNITY

ENVIRONMENTAL ASSESSMENT, THREATENED OR ENDANGERED SPECIES, AND WETLANDS ADDENDUM

TO CONTRACT CONCERNING THE PROPERTY AT

→ 12656 Rolling Waves Lane Galveston, TX

(Address of Property)

→ ☒ A. ENVIRONMENTAL ASSESSMENT: Buyer, at Buyer's expense, may obtain an environmental assessment report prepared by an environmental specialist.

☐ B. THREATENED OR ENDANGERED SPECIES: Buyer, at Buyer's expense, may obtain a report from a natural resources professional to determine if there are any threatened or endangered species or their habitats as defined by the Texas Parks and Wildlife Department or the U.S. Fish and Wildlife Service.

☐ C. WETLANDS: Buyer, at Buyer's expense, may obtain a report from an environmental specialist to determine if there are wetlands, as defined by federal or state law or regulation.

→ Within 20 days after the effective date of the contract, Buyer may terminate the contract by furnishing Seller a copy of any report noted above that adversely affects the use of the Property and a notice of termination of the contract. Upon termination, the earnest money will be refunded to Buyer.

Buyer	Seller
Buyer	Seller

This form has been approved by the Texas Real Estate Commission for use with similarly approved or promulgated contract forms. Such approval relates to this form only. TREC forms are intended for use only by trained real estate licensees. No representation is made as to the legal validity or adequacy of any provision in any specific transactions. It is not suitable for complex transactions. Texas Real Estate Commission, P.O. Box 12188, Austin, TX 78711-2188, 1-800-250-8732 or (512) 459-6544 (http://www.trec.state.tx.us) TREC No. 28-1. This form replaces TREC No. 28-0.

TREC No. 28-1

FIGURE 11.32

TREC 33-1

EQUAL HOUSING OPPORTUNITY

PROMULGATED BY THE TEXAS REAL ESTATE COMMISSION (TREC) 04-23-07

ADDENDUM FOR COASTAL AREA PROPERTY

(SECTION 33.135, TEXAS NATURAL RESOURCES CODE)

TO CONTRACT CONCERNING THE PROPERTY AT

→ 12656 Rolling Waves Lane Galveston, TX

(Address of Property)

NOTICE REGARDING COASTAL AREA PROPERTY

1. The real property described in and subject to this contract adjoins and shares a common boundary with the tidally influenced submerged lands of the state. The boundary is subject to change and can be determined accurately only by a survey on the ground made by a licensed state land surveyor in accordance with the original grant from the sovereign. The owner of the property described in this contract may gain or lose portions of the tract because of changes in the boundary.

→ 2. The seller, transferor, or grantor has no knowledge of any prior fill as it relates to the property described in and subject to this contract except: None ________________.

3. State law prohibits the use, encumbrance, construction, or placing of any structure in, on, or over state-owned submerged lands below the applicable tide line, without proper permission.

4. The purchaser or grantee is hereby advised to seek the advice of an attorney or other qualified person as to the legal nature and effect of the facts set forth in this notice on the property described in and subject to this contract. Information regarding the location of the applicable tide line as to the property described in and subject to this contract may be obtained from the surveying division of the General Land Office in Austin.

Buyer	Seller
Buyer	Seller

This form has been approved by the Texas Real Estate Commission for use with similarly approved or promulgated contract forms. Such approval relates to this form only. TREC forms are intended for use only by trained real estate licensees. No representation is made as to the legal validity or adequacy of any provision in any specific transactions. It is not suitable for complex transactions. Texas Real Estate Commission, P.O. Box 12188, Austin, TX 78711-2188, 1-800-250-8732 or (512) 459-6544 (http://www.trec.state.tx.us) TREC No. 33-1. This form replaces TREC No. 33-0.

TREC No. 33-1

FIGURE 11.33

TREC 34-3

PROMULGATED BY THE TEXAS REAL ESTATE COMMISSION (TREC) 12-10-07

EQUAL HOUSING OPPORTUNITY

ADDENDUM FOR PROPERTY LOCATED SEAWARD OF THE GULF INTRACOASTAL WATERWAY

(SECTION 61.025, TEXAS NATURAL RESOURCES CODE)

TO CONTRACT CONCERNING THE PROPERTY AT

→ 12656 Rolling Waves Lane Galveston, TX

(Address of Property)

DISCLOSURE NOTICE CONCERNING LEGAL AND ECONOMIC RISKS OF PURCHASING COASTAL REAL PROPERTY NEAR A BEACH

WARNING: THE FOLLOWING NOTICE OF POTENTIAL RISKS OF ECONOMIC LOSS TO YOU AS THE PURCHASER OF COASTAL REAL PROPERTY IS REQUIRED BY STATE LAW.

- READ THIS NOTICE CAREFULLY. DO NOT SIGN THIS CONTRACT UNTIL YOU FULLY UNDERSTAND THE RISKS YOU ARE ASSUMING.
- BY PURCHASING THIS PROPERTY, YOU MAY BE ASSUMING ECONOMIC RISKS OVER AND ABOVE THE RISKS INVOLVED IN PURCHASING INLAND REAL PROPERTY.
- IF YOU OWN A STRUCTURE LOCATED ON COASTAL REAL PROPERTY NEAR A GULF COAST BEACH, IT MAY COME TO BE LOCATED ON THE PUBLIC BEACH BECAUSE OF COASTAL EROSION AND STORM EVENTS.
- AS THE OWNER OF A STRUCTURE LOCATED ON THE PUBLIC BEACH, YOU COULD BE SUED BY THE STATE OF TEXAS AND ORDERED TO REMOVE THE STRUCTURE.
- THE COSTS OF REMOVING A STRUCTURE FROM THE PUBLIC BEACH AND ANY OTHER ECONOMIC LOSS INCURRED BECAUSE OF A REMOVAL ORDER WOULD BE SOLELY YOUR RESPONSIBILITY.

The real property described in this contract is located seaward of the Gulf Intracoastal Waterway to its southernmost point and then seaward of the longitudinal line also known as 97 degrees, 12', 19" which runs southerly to the international boundary from the intersection of the centerline of the Gulf Intracoastal Waterway and the Brownsville Ship Channel. If the property is in close proximity to a beach fronting the Gulf of Mexico, the purchaser is hereby advised that the public has acquired a right of use or easement to or over the area of any public beach by prescription, dedication, or presumption, or has retained a right by virtue of continuous right in the public since time immemorial, as recognized in law and custom.

The extreme seaward boundary of natural vegetation that spreads continuously inland customarily marks the landward boundary of the public easement. If there is no clearly marked natural vegetation line, the landward boundary of the easement is as provided by Sections 61.016 and 61.017, Natural Resources Code.

Much of the Gulf of Mexico coastline is eroding at rates of more than five feet per year. Erosion rates for all Texas Gulf property subject to the open beaches act are available from the Texas General Land Office.

State law prohibits any obstruction, barrier, restraint, or interference with the use of the public easement, including the placement of structures seaward of the landward boundary of the easement. OWNERS OF STRUCTURES ERECTED SEAWARD OF THE VEGETATION LINE (OR OTHER APPLICABLE EASEMENT BOUNDARY) OR THAT BECOME SEAWARD OF THE VEGETATION LINE AS A RESULT OF PROCESSES ARE SUBJECT TO A LAWSUIT BY THE STATE OF TEXAS TO REMOVE THE STRUCTURES.

The purchaser is hereby notified that the purchaser should: (1) determine the rate of shoreline erosion in the vicinity of the real property; and (2) seek the advice of an attorney or other qualified person before executing this contract or instrument of conveyance as to the relevance of these statutes and facts to the value of the property the purchaser is hereby purchasing or contracting to purchase.

Buyer	Seller
Buyer	Seller

This form has been approved by the Texas Real Estate Commission for use with similarly approved or promulgated contract forms. Such approval relates to this form only. TREC forms are intended for use only by trained real estate licensees. No representation is made as to the legal validity or adequacy of any provision in any specific transactions. It is not suitable for complex transactions. Texas Real Estate Commission, P.O. Box 12188, Austin, TX 78711-2188, 1-800-250-8732 or (512) 459-6544 (http://www.trec.state.tx.us) TREC No. 34-3. This form replaces TREC No. 34-2.

TREC No. 34-3

■ TRANSACTION 9 (SEE FIGURE 11.34)

For the final practice transaction, you will play the role of the listing agent who has just received an offer on one of your listings. In preparation for presenting it to the Seller, you review it carefully and find several errors. Some of the errors are minor; however, some of them are rather serious. When you find an error, simply circle it and be prepared to discuss what should have been done differently. Check your work against the form in the answer key for this transaction.

FIGURE 11.34

TREC 20-7

02-13-06

EQUAL HOUSING OPPORTUNITY

PROMULGATED BY THE TEXAS REAL ESTATE COMMISSION (TREC)

ONE TO FOUR FAMILY RESIDENTIAL CONTRACT (RESALE)

NOTICE: Not For Use For Condominium Transactions

1. PARTIES: Carol Anne Porter (Seller) agrees to sell and convey to Mary Ying Chow et al Charles Yang Chow (Buyer) and Buyer agrees to buy from Seller the Property described below.

2. PROPERTY:

A. LAND: Lot 128 Block 17, Section of Shady Hills Addition, City of Lakeview, County of Smith, Texas, known as 12690 Pinehall Court 76544 (address/zip code), or as described on attached exhibit.

B. IMPROVEMENTS: The house, garage and all other fixtures and improvements attached to the above-described real property, including without limitation, the following **permanently installed and built-in items,** if any: all equipment and appliances, valances, screens, shutters, awnings, wall-to-wall carpeting, mirrors, ceiling fans, attic fans, mail boxes, television antennas and satellite dish system and equipment, heating and air-conditioning units, security and fire detection equipment, wiring, plumbing and lighting fixtures, chandeliers, water softener system, kitchen equipment, garage door openers, cleaning equipment, shrubbery, landscaping, outdoor cooking equipment, and all other property owned by Seller and attached to the above described real property.

C. ACCESSORIES: The following described related accessories, if any: window air conditioning units, stove, fireplace screens, curtains and rods, blinds, window shades, draperies and rods, controls for satellite dish system, controls for garage door openers, entry gate controls, door keys, mailbox keys, above ground pool, swimming pool equipment and maintenance accessories, and artificial fireplace logs.

D. EXCLUSIONS: The following improvements and accessories will be retained by Seller and removed prior to delivery of possession: Swing set in the backyard is to be included in the sale.

The land, improvements and accessories are collectively referred to as the "Property".

3. SALES PRICE:

A. Cash portion of Sales Price payable by Buyer at closing................. $ 20,000.00

B. Sum of all financing described below (excluding any loan funding fee or mortgage insurance premium).. $ 280,000.00

C. Sales Price (Sum of A and B)... $ 300,000.00

4. FINANCING: The portion of Sales Price not payable in cash will be paid as follows: (Check applicable boxes below)

☒ A. THIRD PARTY FINANCING: One or more third party mortgage loans in the total amount of $ 280,000.00 (excluding any loan funding fee or mortgage insurance premium).

(1) Property Approval: If the Property does not satisfy the lenders' underwriting requirements for the loan(s), this contract will terminate and the earnest money will be refunded to Buyer.

(2) Financing Approval: (Check one box only)

☐ (a) This contract is subject to Buyer being approved for the financing described in the attached Third Party Financing Condition Addendum.

☐ (b) This contract is not subject to Buyer being approved for financing and does not involve FHA or VA financing.

☐ B. ASSUMPTION: The assumption of the unpaid principal balance of one or more promissory notes described in the attached TREC Loan Assumption Addendum.

☐ C. SELLER FINANCING: A promissory note from Buyer to Seller of $________, secured by vendor's and deed of trust liens, and containing the terms and conditions described in the attached TREC Seller Financing Addendum. If an owner policy of title insurance is furnished, Buyer shall furnish Seller with a mortgagee policy of title insurance.

5. EARNEST MONEY: Upon execution of this contract by both parties, Buyer shall deposit $ 1,000.00 as earnest money with Safe and Secure Title Company, as escrow agent, at 2800 South Island Drive, Suite 250, Lakeview, TX 76544 (address). Buyer shall deposit additional earnest money of $ 5,000.00 with escrow agent within 10 days after the effective date of this contract. If Buyer fails to deposit the earnest money as required by this contract, Buyer will be in default.

6. TITLE POLICY AND SURVEY:

A. TITLE POLICY: Seller shall furnish to Buyer at ☐Seller's ☒Buyer's expense an owner policy of title insurance (Title Policy) issued by Safe and Secure Title Company (Jane Washington) (Title Company) in the amount of the Sales Price, dated at or after closing, insuring Buyer

Initialed for identification by Buyer_____ _____ and Seller _____ _____ TREC NO. 20-7

FIGURE 11.34 (CONTINUED)

TREC 20-7

against loss under the provisions of the Title Policy, subject to the promulgated exclusions (including existing building and zoning ordinances) and the following exceptions:

(1) Restrictive covenants common to the platted subdivision in which the Property is located.
(2) The standard printed exception for standby fees, taxes and assessments.
(3) Liens created as part of the financing described in Paragraph 4.
(4) Utility easements created by the dedication deed or plat of the subdivision in which the Property is located.
(5) Reservations or exceptions otherwise permitted by this contract or as may be approved by Buyer in writing.
(6) The standard printed exception as to marital rights.
(7) The standard printed exception as to waters, tidelands, beaches, streams, and related matters.
(8) The standard printed exception as to discrepancies, conflicts, shortages in area or boundary lines, encroachments or protrusions, or overlapping improvements. Buyer, at Buyer's expense, may have the exception amended to read, "shortages in area".

B. COMMITMENT: Within 20 days after the Title Company receives a copy of this contract, Seller shall furnish to Buyer a commitment for title insurance (Commitment) and, at Buyer's expense, legible copies of restrictive covenants and documents evidencing exceptions in the Commitment (Exception Documents) other than the standard printed exceptions. Seller authorizes the Title Company to deliver the Commitment and Exception Documents to Buyer at Buyer's address shown in Paragraph 21. If the Commitment and Exception Documents are not delivered to Buyer within the specified time, the time for delivery will be automatically extended up to 15 days or the Closing Date, whichever is earlier.

C. SURVEY: The survey must be made by a registered professional land surveyor acceptable to the Title Company and any lender. (Check one box only)

☒ (1) Within 5 days after the effective date of this contract, Seller shall furnish to Buyer and Title Company Seller's existing survey of the Property and a Residential Real Property Affidavit promulgated by the Texas Department of Insurance (Affidavit). If the existing survey or Affidavit is not acceptable to Title Company or Buyer's lender, Buyer shall obtain a new survey at ☐ Seller's ☐ Buyer's expense no later than 3 days prior to Closing Date. If Seller fails to furnish the existing survey or Affidavit within the time prescribed, Buyer shall obtain a new survey at Seller's expense no later than 3 days prior to Closing Date.

☐ (2) Within _______ days after the effective date of this contract, Buyer shall obtain a new survey at Buyer's expense. Buyer is deemed to receive the survey on the date of actual receipt or the date specified in this paragraph, whichever is earlier.

☐ (3) Within _______ days after the effective date of this contract, Seller, at Seller's expense shall furnish a new survey to Buyer.

D. OBJECTIONS: Buyer may object in writing to defects, exceptions, or encumbrances to title: disclosed on the survey other than items 6A(1) through (7) above; disclosed in the Commitment other than items 6A(1) through (8) above; or which prohibit the following use or activity: Late night Tupperware parties _______________.

Buyer must object not later than (i) the Closing Date or (ii) 7 days after Buyer receives the Commitment, Exception Documents, and the survey, whichever is earlier. Buyer's failure to object within the time allowed will constitute a waiver of Buyer's right to object; except that the requirements in Schedule C of the Commitment are not waived. Provided Seller is not obligated to incur any expense, Seller shall cure the timely objections of Buyer or any third party lender within 15 days after Seller receives the objections and the Closing Date will be extended as necessary. If objections are not cured within such 15 day period, this contract will terminate and the earnest money will be refunded to Buyer unless Buyer waives the objections.

E. TITLE NOTICES:

(1) ABSTRACT OR TITLE POLICY: Broker advises Buyer to have an abstract of title covering the Property examined by an attorney of Buyer's selection, or Buyer should be furnished with or obtain a Title Policy. If a Title Policy is furnished, the Commitment should be promptly reviewed by an attorney of Buyer's choice due to the time limitations on Buyer's right to object.

(2) MANDATORY OWNERS' ASSOCIATION MEMBERSHIP: The Property ☐ is ☐ is not subject to mandatory membership in an owners' association. If the Property is subject to mandatory membership in an owners' association, Seller notifies Buyer under §5.012, Texas Property Code, that, as a purchaser of property in the residential community in which the Property is located, you are obligated to be a member of the owners' association. Restrictive covenants governing the use and occupancy of the Property and a dedicatory instrument governing the establishment, maintenance, and operation of this residential community have been or will be recorded in the Real Property Records of the county in which the Property is located. Copies of the restrictive covenants and dedicatory instrument may be obtained from the county clerk. You are obligated to pay

FIGURE 11.34 (CONTINUED)

TREC 20-7

Contract Concerning 12690 Pinehall Court Lakeview, 76544 Page 3 of 8 02-13-06
(Address of Property)

assessments to the owners' association. The amount of the assessments is subject to change. Your failure to pay the assessments could result in a lien on and the foreclosure of the Property. If Buyer is concerned about these matters, the TREC promulgated Addendum for Property Subject to Mandatory Membership in an Owner's Association should be used.

(3) STATUTORY TAX DISTRICTS: If the Property is situated in a utility or other statutorily created district providing water, sewer, drainage, or flood control facilities and services, Chapter 49, Texas Water Code, requires Seller to deliver and Buyer to sign the statutory notice relating to the tax rate, bonded indebtedness, or standby fee of the district prior to final execution of this contract.

(4) TIDE WATERS: If the Property abuts the tidally influenced waters of the state, §33.135, Texas Natural Resources Code, requires a notice regarding coastal area property to be included in the contract. An addendum containing the notice promulgated by TREC or required by the parties must be used.

(5) ANNEXATION: If the Property is located outside the limits of a municipality, Seller notifies Buyer under §5.011, Texas Property Code, that the Property may now or later be included in the extraterritorial jurisdiction of a municipality and may now or later be subject to annexation by the municipality. Each municipality maintains a map that depicts its boundaries and extraterritorial jurisdiction. To determine if the Property is located within a municipality's extraterritorial jurisdiction or is likely to be located within a municipality's extraterritorial jurisdiction, contact all municipalities located in the general proximity of the Property for further information.

(6) PROPERTY LOCATED IN A CERTIFICATED SERVICE AREA OF A UTILITY SERVICE PROVIDER: Notice required by §13.257, Water Code: The real property, described in Paragraph 2, that you are about to purchase may be located in a certificated water or sewer service area, which is authorized by law to provide water or sewer service to the properties in the certificated area. If your property is located in a certificated area there may be special costs or charges that you will be required to pay before you can receive water or sewer service. There may be a period required to construct lines or other facilities necessary to provide water or sewer service to your property. You are advised to determine if the property is in a certificated area and contact the utility service provider to determine the cost that you will be required to pay and the period, if any, that is required to provide water or sewer service to your property. The undersigned Buyer hereby acknowledges receipt of the foregoing notice at or before the execution of a binding contract for the purchase of the real property described in Paragraph 2 or at closing of purchase of the real property.

(7) PUBLIC IMPROVEMENT DISTRICTS: If the Property is in a public improvement district, §5.014, Property Code, requires Seller to notify Buyer as follows: As a purchaser of this parcel of real property you are obligated to pay an assessment to a municipality or county for an improvement project undertaken by a public improvement district under Chapter 372, Local Government Code. The assessment may be due annually or in periodic installments. More information concerning the amount of the assessment and the due dates of that assessment may be obtained from the municipality or county levying the assessment. The amount of the assessments is subject to change. Your failure to pay the assessments could result in a lien on and the foreclosure of your property.

7. PROPERTY CONDITION:

A. ACCESS,INSPECTIONS AND UTILITIES: Seller shall permit Buyer and Buyer's agents access to the Property at reasonable times. Buyer may have the Property inspected by inspectors selected by Buyer and licensed by TREC or otherwise permitted by law to make inspections. Seller at Seller's expense shall turn on existing utilities for inspections.

B. SELLER'S DISCLOSURE NOTICE PURSUANT TO §5.008, TEXAS PROPERTY CODE (Notice): (Check one box only)

☐ (1) Buyer has received the Notice.

☐ (2) Buyer has not received the Notice. Within ______ days after the effective date of this contract, Seller shall deliver the Notice to Buyer. If Buyer does not receive the Notice, Buyer may terminate this contract at any time prior to the closing and the earnest money will be refunded to Buyer. If Seller delivers the Notice, Buyer may terminate this contract for any reason within 7 days after Buyer receives the Notice or prior to the closing, whichever first occurs, and the earnest money will be refunded to Buyer.

☒ (3) The Seller is not required to furnish the notice under the Texas Property Code.

C. SELLER'S DISCLOSURE OF LEAD-BASED PAINT AND LEAD-BASED PAINT HAZARDS is required by Federal law for a residential dwelling constructed prior to 1978.

D. ACCEPTANCE OF PROPERTY CONDITION: Buyer accepts the Property in its present condition; provided Seller, at Seller's expense, shall complete the following specific repairs and treatments: Any lender required repairs with a cost not to exceed $2,500.

E. LENDER REQUIRED REPAIRS AND TREATMENTS: Unless otherwise agreed in writing, neither party is obligated to pay for lender required repairs, which includes treatment for wood

Initialed for identification by Buyer______ ______ and Seller _______ ______ TREC NO. 20-7

FIGURE 11.34 (CONTINUED)

TREC 20-7

Contract Concerning 12690 Pinehall Court Lakeview, 76544 Page 4 of 8 02-13-06
(Address of Property)

destroying insects. If the parties do not agree to pay for the lender required repairs or treatments, this contract will terminate and the earnest money will be refunded to Buyer. If the cost of lender required repairs and treatments exceeds 5% of the Sales Price, Buyer may terminate this contract and the earnest money will be refunded to Buyer.

F. COMPLETION OF REPAIRS AND TREATMENTS: Unless otherwise agreed in writing, Seller shall complete all agreed repairs and treatments prior to the Closing Date. All required permits must be obtained, and repairs and treatments must be performed by persons who are licensed or otherwise authorized by law to provide such repairs or treatments. At Buyer's election, any transferable warranties received by Seller with respect to the repairs and treatments will be transferred to Buyer at Buyer's expense. If Seller fails to complete any agreed repairs and treatments prior to the Closing Date, Buyer may do so and receive reimbursement from Seller at closing. The Closing Date will be extended up to 15 days, if necessary, to complete repairs and treatments.

G. ENVIRONMENTAL MATTERS: Buyer is advised that the presence of wetlands, toxic substances, including asbestos and wastes or other environmental hazards, or the presence of a threatened or endangered species or its habitat may affect Buyer's intended use of the Property. If Buyer is concerned about these matters, an addendum promulgated by TREC or required by the parties should be used.

H. RESIDENTIAL SERVICE CONTRACTS: Buyer may purchase a residential service contract from a residential service company licensed by TREC. If Buyer purchases a residential service contract, Seller shall reimburse Buyer at closing for the cost of the residential service contract in an amount not exceeding $ 500.00 . Buyer should review any residential service contract for the scope of coverage, exclusions and limitations. **The purchase of a residential service contract is optional. Similar coverage may be purchased from various companies authorized to do business in Texas.**

8. **BROKERS' FEES:** All obligations of the parties for payment of brokers' fees are contained in separate written agreements.

9. **CLOSING:**

A. The closing of the sale will be on or before September 22, 20 06, or within 7 days after objections made under Paragraph 6D have been cured or waived, whichever date is later (Closing Date). If either party fails to close the sale by the Closing Date, the non-defaulting party may exercise the remedies contained in Paragraph 15.

B. At closing:

(1) Seller shall execute and deliver a general warranty deed conveying title to the Property to Buyer and showing no additional exceptions to those permitted in Paragraph 6 and furnish tax statements or certificates showing no delinquent taxes on the Property.

(2) Buyer shall pay the Sales Price in good funds acceptable to the escrow agent.

(3) Seller and Buyer shall execute and deliver any notices, statements, certificates, affidavits, releases, loan documents and other documents required of them by this contract, the Commitment or law necessary for the closing of the sale and the issuance of the Title Policy.

C. Unless expressly prohibited by written agreement, Seller may continue to show the Property and receive, negotiate and accept back up offers.

D. All covenants, representations and warranties in this contract survive closing.

10. **POSSESSION:** Seller shall deliver to Buyer possession of the Property in its present or required condition, ordinary wear and tear excepted: ☒ upon closing and funding ☐ according to a temporary residential lease form promulgated by TREC or other written lease required by the parties. Any possession by Buyer prior to closing or by Seller after closing which is not authorized by a written lease will establish a tenancy at sufferance relationship between the parties. **Consult your insurance agent prior to change of ownership and possession because insurance coverage may be limited or terminated. The absence of a written lease or appropriate insurance coverage may expose the parties to economic loss.**

11. **SPECIAL PROVISIONS:** (Insert only factual statements and business details applicable to the sale. TREC rules prohibit licensees from adding factual statements or business details for which a contract addendum, lease or other form has been promulgated by TREC for mandatory use.)

1. Buyer must have a response to this contract by 5:00 P.M. August 1, 2006.
2. This contract is subject to appraisal.
3. Buyer may bill seller for cleaning if property is not clean at possession.
4. Seller is to stay in the house 48 hours after closing and funding.
5. Buyer has the right to terminate this contract if the property has termites.

FIGURE 11.34 (CONTINUED)

TREC 20-7

Contract Concerning 12690 Pinehall Court Lakeview, 76544 Page 5 of 8 02-13-06
(Address of Property)

12. SETTLEMENT AND OTHER EXPENSES:

A. The following expenses must be paid at or prior to closing:

(1) Expenses payable by Seller (Seller's Expenses):

(a) Releases of existing liens, including prepayment penalties and recording fees; release of Seller's loan liability; tax statements or certificates; preparation of deed; one-half of escrow fee; and other expenses payable by Seller under this contract.

(b) Seller shall also pay an amount not to exceed $ as agreed later to be applied in the following order: Buyer's Expenses which Buyer is prohibited from paying by FHA, VA, Texas Veterans Housing Assistance Program or other governmental loan programs, and then to other Buyer's Expenses as allowed by the lender.

(2) Expenses payable by Buyer (Buyer's Expenses):

(a) Loan origination, discount, buy-down, and commitment fees (Loan Fees).

(b) Appraisal fees; loan application fees; credit reports; preparation of loan documents; interest on the notes from date of disbursement to one month prior to dates of first monthly payments; recording fees; copies of easements and restrictions; mortgagee title policy with endorsements required by lender; loan-related inspection fees; photos; amortization schedules; one-half of escrow fee; all prepaid items, including required premiums for flood and hazard insurance, reserve deposits for insurance, ad valorem taxes and special governmental assessments; final compliance inspection; courier fee; repair inspection; underwriting fee; wire transfer fee; expenses incident to any loan; and other expenses payable by Buyer under this contract.

B. Buyer shall pay Private Mortgage Insurance Premium (PMI), VA Loan Funding Fee, or FHA Mortgage Insurance Premium (MIP) as required by the lender.

C. If any expense exceeds an amount expressly stated in this contract for such expense to be paid by a party, that party may terminate this contract unless the other party agrees to pay such excess. Buyer may not pay charges and fees expressly prohibited by FHA, VA, Texas Veterans Housing Assistance Program or other governmental loan program regulations.

13. PRORATIONS: Taxes for the current year, interest, maintenance fees, assessments, dues and rents will be prorated through the Closing Date. The tax proration may be calculated taking into consideration any change in exemptions that will affect the current year's taxes. If taxes for the current year vary from the amount prorated at closing, the parties shall adjust the prorations when tax statements for the current year are available. If taxes are not paid at or prior to closing, Buyer shall pay taxes for the current year.

14. CASUALTY LOSS: If any part of the Property is damaged or destroyed by fire or other casualty after the effective date of this contract, Seller shall restore the Property to its previous condition as soon as reasonably possible, but in any event by the Closing Date. If Seller fails to do so due to factors beyond Seller's control, Buyer may (a) terminate this contract and the earnest money will be refunded to Buyer (b) extend the time for performance up to 15 days and the Closing Date will be extended as necessary or (c) accept the Property in its damaged condition with an assignment of insurance proceeds and receive credit from Seller at closing in the amount of the deductible under the insurance policy. Seller's obligations under this paragraph are independent of any other obligations of Seller under this contract.

15. DEFAULT: If Buyer fails to comply with this contract, Buyer will be in default, and Seller may (a) enforce specific performance, seek such other relief as may be provided by law, or both, or (b) terminate this contract and receive the earnest money as liquidated damages, thereby releasing both parties from this contract. If, due to factors beyond Seller's control, Seller fails within the time allowed to make any non-casualty repairs or deliver the Commitment, or survey, if required of Seller, Buyer may (a) extend the time for performance up to 15 days and the Closing Date will be extended as necessary or (b) terminate this contract as the sole remedy and receive the earnest money. If Seller fails to comply with this contract for any other reason, Seller will be in default and Buyer may (a) enforce specific performance, seek such other relief as may be provided by law, or both, or (b) terminate this contract and receive the earnest money, thereby releasing both parties from this contract.

16. MEDIATION: It is the policy of the State of Texas to encourage resolution of disputes through alternative dispute resolution procedures such as mediation. Any dispute between Seller and Buyer related to this contract which is not resolved through informal discussion ☐ will ☒ will not be submitted to a mutually acceptable mediation service or provider. The parties to the mediation shall bear the mediation costs equally. This paragraph does not preclude a party from seeking equitable relief from a court of competent jurisdiction.

17. ATTORNEY'S FEES: The prevailing party in any legal proceeding related to this contract is entitled to recover reasonable attorney's fees and all costs of such proceeding incurred by the prevailing party.

Initialed for identification by Buyer______ ______ and Seller _______ ______ TREC NO. 20-7

FIGURE 11.34 (CONTINUED)

TREC 20-7

Contract Concerning 12690 Pinehall Court Lakeview, 76544 Page 6 of 8 02-13-06
(Address of Property)

18. ESCROW:

A. ESCROW: The escrow agent is not (i) a party to this contract and does not have liability for the performance or nonperformance of any party to this contract, (ii) liable for interest on the earnest money and (iii) liable for the loss of any earnest money caused by the failure of any financial institution in which the earnest money has been deposited unless the financial institution is acting as escrow agent.

B. EXPENSES: At closing, the earnest money must be applied first to any cash down payment, then to Buyer's Expenses and any excess refunded to Buyer. If no closing occurs, escrow agent may require payment of unpaid expenses incurred on behalf of the parties and a written release of liability of escrow agent from all parties.

C. DEMAND: Upon termination of this contract, either party or the escrow agent may send a release of earnest money to each party and the parties shall execute counterparts of the release and deliver same to the escrow agent. If either party fails to execute the release, either party may make a written demand to the escrow agent for the earnest money. If only one party makes written demand for the earnest money, escrow agent shall promptly provide a copy of the demand to the other party. If escrow agent does not receive written objection to the demand from the other party within 15 days, escrow agent may disburse the earnest money to the party making demand reduced by the amount of unpaid expenses incurred on behalf of the party receiving the earnest money and escrow agent may pay the same to the creditors. If escrow agent complies with the provisions of this paragraph, each party hereby releases escrow agent from all adverse claims related to the disbursal of the earnest money.

D. DAMAGES: Any party who wrongfully fails or refuses to sign a release acceptable to the escrow agent within 7 days of receipt of the request will be liable to the other party for liquidated damages of three times the amount of the earnest money.

E. NOTICES: Escrow agent's notices will be effective when sent in compliance with Paragraph 21. Notice of objection to the demand will be deemed effective upon receipt by escrow agent.

19. REPRESENTATIONS: Seller represents that as of the Closing Date (a) there will be no liens, assessments, or security interests against the Property which will not be satisfied out of the sales proceeds unless securing payment of any loans assumed by Buyer and (b) assumed loans will not be in default. If any representation of Seller in this contract is untrue on the Closing Date, Seller will be in default.

20. FEDERAL TAX REQUIREMENTS: If Seller is a "foreign person," as defined by applicable law, or if Seller fails to deliver an affidavit to Buyer that Seller is not a "foreign person," then Buyer shall withhold from the sales proceeds an amount sufficient to comply with applicable tax law and deliver the same to the Internal Revenue Service together with appropriate tax forms. Internal Revenue Service regulations require filing written reports if currency in excess of specified amounts is received in the transaction.

21. NOTICES: All notices from one party to the other must be in writing and are effective when mailed to, hand-delivered at, or transmitted by facsimile or electronic transmission as follows:

To Buyer at:	**To Seller at:**
c/o David Goldberg	
17405 West Drive	
Lakeview, TX 76544	
Telephone: (409) 234-7869	Telephone: ( )
Facsimile: (409) 234-2345	Facsimile: ( )
E-mail: dgoldberg@realty.net	E-mail: caponthego@aol.com

Initialed for identification by Buyer_____ _____ and Seller _____ _____ TREC NO. 20-7

FIGURE 11.34 (CONTINUED)

TREC 20-7

Contract Concerning 12690 Pinehall Court Lakeview, 76544 Page 7 of 8 02-13-06
(Address of Property)

22. AGREEMENT OF PARTIES: This contract contains the entire agreement of the parties and cannot be changed except by their written agreement. Addenda which are a part of this contract are (Check all applicable boxes):

- ❑ Third Party Financing Condition Addendum
- ❑ Seller Financing Addendum
- ❑ Loan Assumption Addendum
- ❑ Buyer's Temporary Residential Lease
- ❑ Seller's Temporary Residential Lease
- ❑ Addendum for Sale of Other Property by Buyer
- ❑ Addendum for Seller's Disclosure of Information on Lead-based Paint and Lead-based Paint Hazards as Required by Federal Law
- ❑ Addendum for Property Subject to Mandatory Membership in an Owners' Association
- ❑ Environmental Assessment, Threatened or Endangered Species and Wetlands Addendum
- ❑ Addendum for "Back-Up" Contract
- ❑ Addendum for Coastal Area Property
- ❑ Addendum for Property Located Seaward of the Gulf Intracoastal Waterway
- ❑ Addendum for Release of Liability on Assumption of FHA, VA, or Conventional Loan Restoration of Seller's Entitlement for VA Guaranteed Loan
- ❑ Other (list): ______

23. TERMINATION OPTION: For nominal consideration, the receipt of which is hereby acknowledged by Seller, and Buyer's agreement to pay Seller $ 1,000.00 (Option Fee) within 2 days after the effective date of this contract, Seller grants Buyer the unrestricted right to terminate this contract by giving notice of termination to Seller within 5 working days after the effective date of this contract. If no dollar amount is stated as the Option Fee or if Buyer fails to pay the Option Fee within the time prescribed, this paragraph will not be a part of this contract and Buyer shall not have the unrestricted right to terminate this contract. If Buyer gives notice of termination within the time prescribed, the Option Fee will not be refunded; however, any earnest money will be refunded to Buyer. The Option Fee ❑ will ☒ will not be credited to the Sales Price at closing. **Time is of the essence for this paragraph and strict compliance with the time for performance is required.**

24. CONSULT AN ATTORNEY: Real estate licensees cannot give legal advice. READ THIS CONTRACT CAREFULLY. If you do not understand the effect of this contract, consult an attorney BEFORE signing.

Buyer's	Seller's
Attorney is: None chosen at this time.	Attorney is: None chosen at this time.
Telephone: ( )	Telephone: ( )
Facsimile: ( )	Facsimile: ( )
E-mail:	E-mail:

EXECUTED the 2nd day of August , 20 06 (EFFECTIVE DATE).
(BROKER: FILL IN THE DATE OF FINAL ACCEPTANCE.)

Buyer Mary Ying Chow	Seller Carol Anne Porter
Buyer Charles Yang Chow	Seller

The form of this contract has been approved by the Texas Real Estate Commission. TREC forms are intended for use only by trained real estate licensees. No representation is made as to the legal validity or adequacy of any provision in any specific transactions. It is not intended for complex transactions. Texas Real Estate Commission, P.O. Box 12188, Austin, TX 78711-2188, 1-800-250-8732 or (512) 459-6544 (http://www.trec.state.tx.us) TREC NO. 20-7. This form replaces TREC NO. 20-6.

TREC NO. 20-7

FIGURE 11.34 (CONTINUED)

TREC 20-7

Contract Concerning 12690 Pinehall Court Lakeview, 76544 Page 8 of 8 02-13-06
(Address of Property)

BROKER INFORMATION AND RATIFICATION OF FEE

Listing Broker has agreed to pay Other Broker 3.500% of the total sales price when Listing Broker's fee is received. Escrow Agent is authorized and directed to pay Other Broker from Listing Broker's fee at closing.

Mary Ying Chow 0346521 Other Broker License No.	Lakeview Realty 0165996 Listing Broker License No.
represents ☐ Buyer only as Buyer's agent ☒ Seller as Listing Broker's subagent	represents ☒ Seller and Buyer as an intermediary ☐ Seller only as Seller's agent
Mary Ying Chow (409) 347-8874 Associate Telephone	Paul S. Brown (409) 236-8686 Listing Associate Telephone
2 Second Street Broker's Address	3 Third Street (409) 555-3333 Listing Associate's Office Address Facsimile
Lakeview TX 76544 City State Zip	Lakeview TX 76544 City State Zip
(409) 233-7777 Facsimile	isellit@realty.pro Email Address
marychow@msn.com Email Address	N/A (N/A) Selling Associate Telephone
	N/A (N/A) Selling Associate's Office Address Facsimile
	N/A N/A N/A City State Zip
	N/A Email Address

OPTION FEE RECEIPT

Receipt of $ N/A (Option Fee) in the form of N/A is acknowledged.

Seller or Listing Broker ____________ Date ____________

CONTRACT AND EARNEST MONEY RECEIPT

Receipt of ☒ Contract and ☒ $ 5,000.00 Earnest Money in the form of Check #1542 is acknowledged.

Escrow Agent: Safe and Secure Title Company Date: ____________

By: ____________ safeandsecure@title.com
Email Address

2800 South Island Drive, Suite 250 Telephone (409) 456-4567
Address

Lakeview TX 76544 Facsimile: (409) 456-4568
City State Zip

HOMEWORK QUIZ

The following quiz does not have an answer key included with the answer keys in Appendix B. Students who are using this book as the basis for a correspondence course should record and submit their answers to their course provider as instructed by the provider. The student will submit his or her answers for the Homework Quiz at the end of each chapter and for each transaction in Chapter 11.

Multiple-Choice Questions

1. In transaction 1, the correct amount to enter on line 3A of the contract is

   a. $106,000.
   b. $96,000.
   c. $19,200.
   d. $21,200.

2. If the effective date for transaction 1 is March 30, the option period will end at the close of what day?

   a. April 7
   b. April 6
   c. April 10
   d. A date not listed above

3. In transaction 2, the correct number of days to enter in paragraph 6D is

   a. 3.
   b. 5.
   c. 7.
   d. 10.

4. The correct amount to enter in line 3B of the contract for transaction 2 is

   a. $180,000.
   b. $36,000.
   c. $72,000.
   d. $162,000.

5. In transaction 3, Seller will receive notices

   a. through her attorney.
   b. through her listing agent.
   c. directly to her at her place of employment.
   d. directly to her at her home address only.

6. The Buyers in transaction 4 would like possession at closing and funding; however, they agree to let the Seller remain in possession through the 4th day following funding. The parties
   a. can write the details of the arrangement in paragraph 11 of the contract.
   b. must use the TREC 15-4.
   c. must use the TREC 16-4.
   d. must hire an attorney to draft a special addendum to address the arrangement.

7. To delete the title policy exclusion relating to discrepancies, conflicts, and shortages in area or boundaries in transaction 5, the parties will need to write in paragraph 11 that the
   a. Buyer will pay the additional 5 percent title policy premium.
   b. Seller will pay the additional 5 percent title policy premium.
   c. Buyer will pay the additional 15 percent title policy premium.
   d. Seller will pay the additional 15 percent title policy premium.

8. The parties in transaction 5 agree to mediate any dispute that might arise between them that cannot be resolved by informal discussion. In paragraph 16, they also agree to
   a. have the Seller pay for the mediation services.
   b. have the Buyer pay for the mediation services.
   c. equally split the cost of any mediation services.
   d. have the listing broker provide mediation services.

9. In transaction 5, the salesperson will enter what in paragraph 3B?
   a. \$895,000
   b. \$10,000
   c. \$2,500 × 350 acres
   d. None or N/A

10. The Seller's attorney's name to be noted in paragraph 24 is
    a. Harry Hawkeye.
    b. Sarah Listalot.
    c. Michael Holmes.
    d. Gordon Robinson.

CHAPTER TWELVE 12

Estimating Seller Net and Buyer Move-In

Buyers and Sellers are interested in the bottom line and expect the real estate license holder to give a reasonably accurate estimate of those bottom-line numbers. To be able to provide this information to the client or customer, the license holder should be comfortable with calculating closing costs, prepaids, and lender-required reserve deposits. License holders must be familiar with HUD's Uniform Settlement Statement that must be used in all transactions covered by the RESPA rules. These rules cover the vast majority of transactions structured with the TREC-promulgated forms we have been studying.

To estimate the costs accurately, do the following:

- Carefully examine the purchase agreement
- Know the typical charges incurred with the particular type of financing involved in the transaction
- Obtain a title insurance rate card
- Generate accurate numbers for the ad valorem taxes, homeowners' association maintenance fee, and homeowners' insurance policy premium

Most title insurance companies provide real estate license holders with charts to use in estimating closing costs. For our example, we will use the HUD form. Using this form for estimating purposes means your client or customer will be familiar with it when it is presented in its final form at closing. And familiarity with the form contributes to a smoother closing experience.

One of the most commonly encountered transactions involves a Buyer purchasing a single-family, previously occupied home with funds obtained from a 90 percent conventional loan. Transaction 8 in Chapter 11 of this book fits the description of *typical* and is used for this example. In our example, we round all line items to the nearest dollar. Rounding is acceptable for giving estimates. Exact numbers must be used at closing.

THE SELLER'S SIDE

The listing agent will be concerned with accurately estimating the bottom line for the Seller. To do this, begin by itemizing the applicable costs on the back of the statement. In Transaction 8, the Seller has charges at the following lines:

703	**Commission** (using a commission rate of 7%) Sales Price of $387,800 × 0.07 = $27,146	$27,146
1107	**Attorney's Fee** Preparation of General Warranty Deed and Release	$130
1110	**Owners' Title Insurance Policy Premium** Calculated on sale price using title insurance rate card; using current rate card	$2,885
1111	**Escrow Fee** Determined by title company	$75
1113	**Messenger** Determined by title company	$45
1201	**Recording Fees** Release of lien	$20

Enter these numbers in the column labeled "Paid from Seller's Funds at Settlement" on the back of the Uniform Settlement Statement. Total the column and enter your total on the front of the Uniform Settlement Statement at line 502.

On the front of the Uniform Settlement Statement, enter the contract Sales Price at line 401. The Seller paid the homeowners' association maintenance fee of $660 on January 1. We use a closing date of April 4 and need to prorate the homeowners' association maintenance fee with the Seller paying through the day of closing as stipulated in paragraph 13 of the contract. The Seller has had the benefit of January 1 through April 4. The Buyer will reimburse the Seller for the remaining portion of the year.

To calculate the amount involved, we shall use a "banker's year" of 360 days. For the remaining days in April, we subtract the closing date from 30.

April		May–December	Days Due
30 days – 4 = 26	+	240 (30 × 8)	= 266

The annual fee of $660 is divided by 360 days and multiplied by the days due to calculate the amount the Buyer will be charged and the Seller will be credited at lines 409 and 109.

$$\$660 \div 360 \text{ days} \times 266 \text{ days due} = \$488 \text{ (rounded)}$$

The Seller has an outstanding loan balance of $86,000 after the April 1 payment has been made. The loan is at 8 percent interest and has no prepayment penalty. To calculate the payoff to enter at line 504, calculate four days of interest and add it to the principal balance outstanding.

$$\text{Loan amount } \$86{,}000 \times 008 = \$6{,}880 \text{ annual interest}$$
$$\$6{,}880 \div 360 \text{ days} \times 4 \text{ days due} = \$76 \text{ (rounded)}$$
$$\$86{,}000 + \$76 = \$86{,}076 \text{ total payoff}$$

Paragraph 13 also calls for the ad valorem taxes to be prorated through the day of closing, April 4. The annual tax bill for the Property is $5,648. To prorate this tax bill, count the days from January 1 through April 4, calculate the dollar amount of tax per day and calculate the total amount of tax that will be charged to the Seller at line 510 and credited to the Buyer at line 210.

Jan		Feb		Mar		Apr	
30	+	30	+	30	+	4	= 94 days due
Annual tax	÷	360	=	$ per day	×	days due	= lines 510 and 210
$5,648	÷	360	=	$15.69	×	94	= $1,475 (rounded)

Now you may total all lines in the 400 series and enter your total at lines 420 and 601. Total all lines in the 500 Series and enter your total at lines 520 and 602. Subtract line 602 from line 601 and enter your answer at line 603. Check the box that indicates cash "To" the Seller at line 603 and you are ready to give a solid, accurate estimate to your Seller client.

THE BUYER'S SIDE

Again, begin on the back of the statement. The purchase agreement and a title company closing cost estimating sheet with typical numbers are invaluable tools.

The 800 series of line items relate to costs associated with the Buyer's new loan.

1201 **Recording Fees**
Paid to the county clerk's office to record the Deed of Trust ($35) and the General Warranty Deed ($23). $58

1204 **Tax Service Fee** $115

1301 **Survey** $325
Every Buyer should require a survey prior to closing. Lenders require a survey as part of the loan package.

Enter these numbers in the column labeled "Paid from the Borrower's Funds at Settlement" on the back of the Uniform Settlement Statement. Total the column and enter your total on the front of the Uniform Settlement Statement at line 103.

On the front of the Uniform Settlement Statement, enter the contract sale price at line 101. At line 201, enter the earnest money recited in paragraph 5 on the purchase agreement, and enter the amount from paragraph 3B on line 202. The prorated items should be entered on lines 109 (maintenance fee) and 210 (property tax). You are now ready to total the borrower's side.

Total all lines in the 100 series and enter the number at line 120 and at line 301. Total all lines in the 200 series and enter the number at line 220 and at line 302. To accurately estimate the amount the Buyer will need to bring to the closing in the form of a cashier's check, subtract line 302 from line 301 and enter the difference at line 303. Check the box that indicates cash "From" the borrower. Check your completed statement with the answer key in Appendix B.

For a further discussion of finding your way through and completing a closing statement, we recommend Chapter 14 in *Mastering Real Estate Math*, Seventh Edition, by Ralph Tamper and published by Dearborn™ Real Estate Education. Chapter 13 of the same book will help you prorate taxes, interest, insurance, homeowners' association maintenance fees, and rents.

Good luck and happy selling!

FIGURE 12.1

Uniform Settlement Statement

A. **Settlement Statement**

U.S. Department of Housing and Urban Development

OMB Approval No. 2502-0265

B. Type of Loan			
1. ☐ FHA 2. ☐ FmHA 3. ☐ Conv. Unins. 4. ☐ VA 5. ☐ Conv. Ins.	6. File Number:	7. Loan Number:	8. Mortgage Insurance Case Number:

C. Note: This form is furnished to give you a statement of actual settlement costs. Amounts paid to and by the settlement agent are shown. Items marked "(p.o.c.)" were paid outside the closing; they are shown here for informational purposes and are not included in the totals.

D. Name & Address of Borrower:	E. Name & Address of Seller:	F. Name & Address of Lender:

G. Property Location:	H. Settlement Agent:	
	Place of Settlement:	I. Settlement Date:

J. Summary of Borrower's Transaction		K. Summary of Seller's Transaction	
100. Gross Amount Due From Borrower		**400. Gross Amount Due To Seller**	
101. Contract sales price		401. Contract sales price	
102. Personal property		402. Personal property	
103. Settlement charges to borrower (line 1400)		403.	
104.		404.	
105.		405.	
Adjustments for items paid by seller in advance		**Adjustments for items paid by seller in advance**	
106. City/town taxes to		406. City/town taxes to	
107. County taxes to		407. County taxes to	
108. Assessments to		408. Assessments to	
109.		409.	
110.		410.	
111.		411.	
112.		412.	
120. Gross Amount Due From Borrower		**420. Gross Amount Due To Seller**	
200. Amounts Paid By Or In Behalf Of Borrower		**500. Reductions In Amount Due To Seller**	
201. Deposit or earnest money		501. Excess deposit (see instructions)	
202. Principal amount of new loan(s)		502. Settlement charges to seller (line 1400)	
203. Existing loan(s) taken subject to		503. Existing loan(s) taken subject to	
204.		504. Payoff of first mortgage loan	
205.		505. Payoff of second mortgage loan	
206.		506.	
207.		507.	
208.		508.	
209.		509.	
Adjustments for items unpaid by seller		**Adjustments for items unpaid by seller**	
210. City/town taxes to		510. City/town taxes to	
211. County taxes to		511. County taxes to	
212. Assessments to		512. Assessments to	
213.		513.	
214.		514.	
215.		515.	
216.		516.	
217.		517.	
218.		518.	
219.		519.	
220. Total Paid By/For Borrower		**520. Total Reduction Amount Due Seller**	
300. Cash At Settlement From/To Borrower		**600. Cash At Settlement To/From Seller**	
301. Gross Amount due from borrower (line 120)		601. Gross amount due to seller (line 420)	
302. Less amounts paid by/for borrower (line 220)	( )	602. Less reductions in amt. due seller (line 520)	( )
303. Cash ☐ From ☐ To Borrower		**603. Cash ☐ To ☐ From Seller**	

Section 5 of the Real Estate Settlement Procedures Act (RESPA) requires the following: • HUD must develop a Special Information Booklet to help persons borrowing money to finance the purchase of residential real estate to better understand the nature and costs of real estate settlement services; • Each lender must provide the booklet to all applicants from whom it receives or for whom it prepares a written application to borrow money to finance the purchase of residential real estate; • Lenders must prepare and distribute with the Booklet a Good Faith Estimate of the settlement costs that the borrower is likely to incur in connection with the settlement. These disclosures are manadatory.

Section 4(a) of RESPA mandates that HUD develop and prescribe this standard form to be used at the time of loan settlement to provide full disclosure of all charges imposed upon the borrower and seller. These are third party disclosures that are designed to provide the borrower with pertinent information during the settlement process in order to be a better shopper.

The Public Reporting Burden for this collection of information is estimated to average one hour per response, including the time for reviewing instructions, searching existing data sources, gathering and maintaining the data needed, and completing and reviewing the collection of information.

This agency may not collect this information, and you are not required to complete this form, unless it displays a currently valid OMB control number.

The information requested does not lend itself to confidentiality.

Previous editions are obsolete

Page 1 of 2

form **HUD-1** (3/86)
ref Handbook 4305.2

FIGURE 12.1 (CONTINUED)

Uniform Settlement Statement

L. Settlement Charges	Paid From Borrowers Funds at Settlement	Paid From Seller's Funds at Settlement
700. Total Sales/Broker's Commission based on price $ @ % =		
Division of Commission (line 700) as follows:		
701. $ to		
702. $ to		
703. Commission paid at Settlement		
704.		
800. Items Payable In Connection With Loan		
801. Loan Origination Fee %		
802. Loan Discount %		
803. Appraisal Fee to		
804. Credit Report to		
805. Lender's Inspection Fee		
806. Mortgage Insurance Application Fee to		
807. Assumption Fee		
808.		
809.		
810.		
811.		
900. Items Required By Lender To Be Paid In Advance		
901. Interest from to @$ /day		
902. Mortgage Insurance Premium for months to		
903. Hazard Insurance Premium for years to		
904. years to		
905.		
1000. Reserves Deposited With Lender		
1001. Hazard insurance months@$ per month		
1002. Mortgage insurance months@$ per month		
1003. City property taxes months@$ per month		
1004. County property taxes months@$ per month		
1005. Annual assessments months@$ per month		
1006. months@$ per month		
1007. months@$ per month		
1008. months@$ per month		
1100. Title Charges		
1101. Settlement or closing fee to		
1102. Abstract or title search to		
1103. Title examination to		
1104. Title insurance binder to		
1105. Document preparation to		
1106. Notary fees to		
1107. Attorney's fees to		
(includes above items numbers:)		
1108. Title insurance to		
(includes above items numbers:)		
1109. Lender's coverage $		
1110. Owner's coverage $		
1111.		
1112.		
1113.		
1200. Government Recording and Transfer Charges		
1201. Recording fees: Deed $; Mortgage $; Releases $		
1202. City/county tax/stamps: Deed $; Mortgage $		
1203. State tax/stamps: Deed $; Mortgage $		
1204.		
1205.		
1300. Additional Settlement Charges		
1301. Survey to		
1302. Pest inspection to		
1303.		
1304.		
1305.		
1400. Total Settlement Charges (enter on lines 103, Section J and 502, Section K)		

Previous editions are obsolete Page 2 of 2 form **HUD-1** (3/86) ref Handbook 4305.2

GLOSSARY

abstract (of title) A full summary of all recorded documents, recorded at the county courthouse, that may affect title to a given parcel of real estate; addressed in paragraph 6 of the TREC-promulgated contracts.

acceptance An expression of intent to be bound by the terms and conditions of an offer. To bind the agreement, the acceptance must be communicated to the person making the offer. An offer pertaining to real estate must be made in writing and accepted in writing.

accessory An item identified as part of the sale in paragraph 2 of the TREC-promulgated contract forms that does not meet the test of a fixture; defined in paragraph 2 of the TREC-promulgated contract forms.

acknowledgment A formal declaration made by a person signing a document to a duly authorized public official that the document was signed by the signor of his own free will. Documents must be acknowledged to be admissible for public recording.

addendum An addition or amendment to a contract; the contract must reference the addendum, and the addendum must reference the contract; listed in paragraph 22 of the TREC-promulgated contracts.

addition Another name for a platted subdivision; identified in paragraph 2 of the TREC-promulgated contract forms.

after Later than; in the TREC-promulgated contract forms, the counting of days is from the day after the date of signing or execution and does not include the day the document is signed.

affidavit A Residential Real Property Affidavit promulgated by the Texas Department of Insurance (see paragraph 6C of the TREC Form 20-7).

amendment A revision or change to a contract; the TREC contracts may be amended by using the TREC Form 39-6, Amendment.

annex (annexation) To add or attach to a municipality. The possibility is addressed in paragraph 6E(5) of the TREC-promulgated contract forms.

arbitration An alternative, nonjudicial, dispute resolution approach that submits the dispute to a selected third party who renders a decision that may or may not be binding upon the parties.

assign To transfer one's legal rights to another party.

assessments For periods prior to closing, additional taxes, penalties, or interest (see paragraph 13B of the TREC Form 20-7).

assumption To take on personal liability for a legal obligation made by another person.

attorney-in-fact A legally competent and neutral party who is authorized by another to act in his or her place as a fiduciary.

backup contract A secondary contract; a contract in which the contracting parties recognize the existence of a superior contract between one of the parties and a third party; created by use of the TREC-promulgated Form 11-6, Addendum for "Back-Up Contract.

baron sole An unmarried man

bilateral contract A contractual agreement in which each party agrees to perform or forbear in exchange for the other party's promise to perform or forebear.

breach (of contract) Nonperformance of the legal terms of a valid contract.

broker One who is licensed by the state to serve as a special agent to a buyer or seller in a real estate transaction.

Broker-Lawyer Committee In Texas, a statutorily created group of six brokers and six lawyers who draft and recommend forms for promulgation by the Real Estate Commission.

broker's fee The compensation (commission) charged by a broker for professional services rendered; addressed in paragraph 8 of the TREC-promulgated contracts.

business detail A point of agreement in a contract that does not define legal rights and remedies.

buyer's agent A broker who represents the interests of the buyer and acts as the buyer's special agent.

Buyer's Expenses Expenses payable by buyer; see paragraph 12A(2) of the TREC Form 20-7.

casualty loss A financial loss caused by physical damage to the improvements on a parcel of real estate; remedies for a casualty loss are identified in paragraph 14 of the TREC-promulgated contract forms.

chain of title A history of the succession of ownership of a parcel of land.

closing The consummation of a real estate transaction when the seller (grantor) delivers title to the buyer (grantee) and the buyer delivers consideration to the seller.

closing costs Expenses paid at closing in addition to the purchase price of the property; paragraph 12 of the TREC-promulgated contracts identifies who is responsible for paying various closing costs.

Closing Date A date established by the contracting parties or within seven days after objections made under paragraph 6D have been cured or voided, whichever date is later (see paragraph 9A of the TREC Form 20-7).

Commitment A commitment for title insurance (see paragraph 6B of the TREC Form 20-7).

competent party A party who has legal capacity to enter into a binding contract.

condominium documents The enabling and governing documents that create and guide the operations of a condominium project. Chapter 82 of the Texas Property Code establishes the statutory requirements to create a condominium.

consideration Something of value given by one party in exchange for something of value from another; money for a promise, money for money, a promise for a promise.

contingency A contractual provision that requires completion of a defined act before the contract is binding; the buyer, for example, must be approved for a loan before the buyer is obligated to perform and close the transaction.

contract A legally enforceable agreement between two parties to do (performance) or not to do (forbearance) a particular act.

contract for deed A purchase agreement that provides for deferred delivery of the title to the buyer (vendee) after the seller (vendor) has received all of the deferred payments due to be paid as the full consideration tendered for the property; identified as Executory Contract for Conveyance in section 5.061 of the Texas Property Code.

conventional Third party financing that is neither insured or guaranteed by an agency of government. Third party lending is addressed in paragraph 4 of the TREC-promulgated contracts with conventional financing terms being defined in the TREC Form 40-3, Third Party Financing Condition Addendum.

cooperating broker The broker who brings the buyer to the transaction who may be functioning as either a subagent of the listing broker or a buyer's agent.

counteroffer An offer made in response to an unacceptable offer.

declaration The recorded document that legally establishes a condominium.

deed restriction A provision placed in deeds, usually by the developer of a subdivision, that controls future use of the property; also called a restrictive covenant.

default *See* breach of contract.

disclosure A revelation of known facts; section 5.008 of the Texas Property Code requires sellers of previously occupied single-family residences to disclose material facts about the physical condition of the property.

dual agent A broker who has received the informed consent of both the seller and the buyer to represent both of the parties in a real estate transaction under common law principles rather than functioning as an intermediary as defined by statute.

earnest money The initial and additional cash deposits tendered by the prospective buyer of real property to show good faith. Earnest money and additional earnest money are addressed in paragraph 5 of the TREC-promulgated contracts and in the TREC Form 11-6, Addendum for "Back-Up" Contract.

Effective Date The date on which the offeree accepts the offer and the offeror is notified of the acceptance. The Statute of Frauds requires that the offer and acceptance be written; the notification may be verbal. The TREC contract forms call for the broker to fill in the effective date.

endangered species Certain fish, animal, and plant life that the federal government has determined to be in danger of extinction.

enforceable contract An agreement that meets all of the legal requirements to create a binding contract.

entitlement The portion of a VA-guaranteed loan that is guaranteed to the lender if the veteran defaults on the loan.

escrow The act of putting money and documents in the care of a third, disinterested party until certain conditions are met. Paragraph 18 of the TREC-promulgated contracts addresses the responsibilities of the escrow agent.

Et ux. And wife.

Et vir. And husband.

Exception Documents Legible copies of restrictive covenants and documents evidencing exceptions in the commitment (see paragraph 6B of the TREC Form 20-7).

Exclusions Items of real or personal property that are not to be included in the conveyance of the property as defined in paragraph 2 of the TREC-promulgated contract forms.

executed contract A contract that has been fully performed. Also used to identify the effective date of the contract when all parties have signed and the offeror has been notified of the acceptance of the offer.

executory contract A contract that is in the process of being performed.

exhibit A document that is attached to a contract to provide documentation supporting something in the principal document; for example, a metes-and-bounds legal description attached to a purchase agreement.

extraterritorial jurisdiction (ETJ) The property lo-cated outside of the limits of a municipality that is subject to annexation. Section 5.011 of the Texas Property Code requires that purchase agreements must contain a statutory notice that property located outside of the city may be in a city's ETJ and subject to annexation.

femme sole An unmarried woman.

FHA The federal agency under HUD that insures home loans to make loanable funds available to lower income buyers.

fiduciary A legal relationship between two persons who agree that one party will act on behalf of the other party, subject to the principal's direction and control.

forbearance Refraining from taking action.

four corners doctrine The legal requirement that courts interpret the provisions of a contract in the context of the entire agreement; also called the *four corners rule*.

fraud An act of deceit intended to cause someone to part with money or enter into a contract that he or she would not have entered into if the decision had been based on truth and accurate information.

funding When the seller receives the proceeds from the sale.

funding fee The fee charged by the Department of Veterans Affairs to guarantee a veteran's loan.

general warranty deed The most widely used deed in Texas; a deed that warrants the title free of encumbrances back to the sovereign of the soil. Paragraph 9B of the TREC-promulgated contracts calls for the seller to deliver title at closing by executing and delivering a general warranty deed.

hazard insurance Insurance to indemnify a property owner against financial loss in the event of a casualty loss.

incompetent party One who does not have the legal capacity to enter into a legally binding contract; a minor, or one who is under the influence of alcohol or other mind altering substances, or one who has been declared mentally incompetent by a court.

informal property description A street address.

improvements Physical additions and fixtures added to land.

intermediary A broker who has been authorized in writing, by the parties to a purchase agreement, to represent both parties following statutory provisions defined in section 1101.559 of the Texas Real Estate License Act.

lawful objective A lawful purpose.

lease A contract that transfers possessory rights from the holder of the fee simple estate to a tenant.

legal description A property description that is of such certainty and accuracy that one can go to it and identify it; a description that is acceptable to the courts; a reference to a recorded plat or a metes-and-bounds description.

lessee The tenant identified in a lease.

lessor The landlord or property owner identified in a lease.

license holder One who holds a valid Texas broker or salesperson license.

liquidated damages Monetary damages to be paid by agreement of the parties in the contract when a default occurs.

listing broker The broker who represents the interests of the property owner and acts as the seller's special agent.

Loan Fees Loan origination, discount, buydown, and commitment fees (see paragraph 12A(2)(a) of the TREC 20-7.

mediation A forum in which an impartial person, the mediator, facilitates communication between parties to promote reconciliation, settlement, or understanding among the parties.

mineral rights Rights to subsurface land and its profits.

MIP See mortgage insurance premium.

money damages Monetary damages awarded by a court when a party defaults and causes a financial loss to the nondefaulting party.

mortgage insurance premium (MIP) The cost to purchase the insurance issued by FHA to protect the lender's interest in the event of borrower default (see paragraph 12B of the TREC 20-7).

mortgagee The lender.

mortgagee's title policy A policy that protects the lender's interest in the event of a failure of title.

mortgagor The borrower.

mutual agreement A meeting of the minds between parties to a contract when no fraud, misrepresentation, or undue influence has been present in the negotiations.

mutual assent Mutual agreement.

notice Information that may be required by the terms of a contract. The effective delivery of notices is defined in paragraph 21 of the TREC-promulgated contract forms.

note A promise to pay.

novation The substitution of a new contract for an existing one or the substitution of a new party to an existing obligation.

offer One of the three components of a valid contract—offer, acceptance, and notification of the acceptance. Offers involving real property interests should always be in writing.

offeree The one to whom the offer is directed.

offeror The one who makes an offer.

option A contractual right that obligates the seller to sell but gives the buyer the unrestricted right to proceed or terminate within a defined time frame and at an agreed upon price. To be valid in Texas, the buyer must deliver valuable consideration (money) to the seller and time is of the essence.

owner's title policy An insurance policy that indemnifies a property owner against financial loss in the event of a title failure.

parol evidence rule Evidence that is outside and separate from the written contractual agreement and that is not admissible into court.

parties The signatories to a contract.

performance A contractual agreement or promise to do a particular act.

PMI *See* private mortgage insurance.

possession To take occupancy.

prepaids Expense items related to the ownership of a property that are paid in advance, such as loan interest from the date of closing to the first of the next month, the first year's hazard insurance premium plus two additional months to establish the reserve impound account, and the prorated tax amount received from the seller plus an additional two months to be deposited in the reserve impound account.

prevailing party The one who wins in a lawsuit; see paragraph 17 of the TREC-promulgated contract forms for a list of what said party is entitled to receive.

principals The parties to a contract; the buyer and the seller, or the tenant and the landlord.

private mortgage insurance (PMI) The insurance that the borrower must acquire to protect the interest of the lender in the event of borrower default on a greater than 80 percent LTV-ratio conventional loan (see paragraph 12B of the TREC Form 20-7).

promulgated Forms published by the Texas Real Estate Commission for mandatory use by licensees assisting buyers and sellers.

ratification The confirmation of an act already performed.

reasonable time A fair length of time, as determined by the court, for the performance of contractual obligations.

recorded Placed in the public records of the county in which the property is located.

release A document that relieves a person from any further legal obligations.

remedy Something used to correct a wrong.

resale certificate A document issued by a homeowners' association that certifies the requirements that the restrictive covenants and association rules impose upon the owner of the property.

residential service contract The statutory name for the contract that limits the owner's financial exposure in the event of a malfunction of the property being purchased; commonly referred to as a home warranty. The companies that issue these contracts are licensed and regulated by the Texas Real Estate Commission.

Real Estate Settlement Procedures Act (RESPA) A federal law that addresses closing procedures for residential transactions that are financed with a federally related loan.

restrictive covenant *See* deed restrictions.

rollback tax A tax that is assessed on Texas property when agriculturally exempted property is converted from agricultural use to another use.

Sales Price Sum of A, cash portion of the Sales Price payable by buyer at closing, and B, the sum of all financing described in paragraph 4 (see paragraph 3 of the TREC Form 20-7).

seller financing A transaction in which the seller receives part of the consideration as a note secured by a mortgage as part of the consideration. The details of the seller financing are addressed in the TREC Form 26-5, Seller Financing Addendum.

seller's agent The broker representing the owner's interest as a special agent; the listing broker.

seller's expenses Expenses payable by seller (see paragraph 12A(1) of the TREC Form 20-7).

settlement Closing of the transaction.

Statute of Frauds A state law that requires certain documents and agreements be reduced to writing to be enforceable in a court of law.

subagent A broker who brings a buyer customer to the real estate transaction.

subdivision Land that is divided into two or more parcels to be sold separately.

subject to A clause setting forth any contingencies or special conditions.

survey The process of determining and measuring land areas and boundaries to identify easements and encroachments.

temporary lease A leasehold estate that lasts for no more than 90 days.

tenant at sufferance A tenancy that exists when a party is in possession of the premises after the legal right to occupy those premises has expired.

termination The act of terminating or bringing to an end. Contract termination may occur by completion of the objective, a change in the law, death or insanity of the parties, expiration, mutual agreement, condemnation or destruction of the property, or bankruptcy of either party.

third party financing Financing that involves someone other than the seller of the property; may be conventional or government backed.

tidewaters Waters subject to the changing tides in the Gulf of Mexico.

time is of the essence The contracting parties agree that strict adherence to the time frames recited in the contract is an essential part of their agreement.

timely presentation Texas real estate licensees are required to present all offers to the client immediately.

title commitment A document furnished by a title company that establishes the conditions under which the title company will issue an owner's policy of title insurance.

title policy An owner policy of title insurance (see paragraph 6A of the TREC 20-7).

TREC Texas Real Estate Commission.

TRELA The real estate license act, Chapter 1101 of Texas Occupations Code.

unenforceable A contract that was valid but for a variety of possible reasons may no longer be enforced.

unilateral contract A contract that requires one party to complete a performance before the other party is obligated to act; for example, a seller is not obligated to pay a brokerage fee until the agent produces a ready, willing, and able buyer.

unimproved property A parcel of land that does not have improvements, fixtures, and accessories.

VA The Department of Veterans Affairs.

VA-funding fee The fee charged to a veteran by the Department of Veterans Affairs when a VA-guaranteed loan is originated; a fee charged to reduce the cost of administering the VA-loan guarantee program to the American taxpayer.

valid An agreement that meets all of the legal requirements of a contract.

valuable consideration Money.

Vernon's Texas Civil Statutes State laws that do not fall into one of the state's legal codes.

void The absence of something.

voidable A contract that may be set aside at the sole option of one of the contracting parties.

waive To give up or voluntarily surrender a legal right.

warranty A promise or a covenant.

wetlands Land areas protected by the U.S. government that have groundwater at or near the surface enough of the year to constitute swamps and marshlands.

will An instrument that conveys the real and personal property of a deceased person to a named beneficiary; a devisor conveys a devise (real property) to a devisee.

APPENDIX A

Quick Study Review and Practice Exam

QUICK STUDY REVIEW

According to the terms of the TREC-promulgated contract forms:

1. How many days does the Seller have to cure the timely Buyer objections to title? ______________________________

____

2. How many days does the title company have to furnish, on behalf of the Seller, the title commitment to the Buyer? ______________________________

____

3. How many days prior to closing does the Buyer or Seller have to obtain a new survey if the existing survey is not acceptable and approved by the title company? ______________________________

____

4. The closing paragraph calls for the closing of the transaction to occur on or before a date specified by the parties or within how many days after title objections have been cured? ______________________________

____

5. If the Seller's disclosure form is delivered to the Buyer after the effective date of the contract, for how many days after it is received does the Buyer have the unrestricted right to terminate the purchase agreement?

____

6. What is included in the definition of Loan Fees? ______________

____

7. How many days may the contract be extended to complete repairs caused by a casualty loss after the effective date of the contract? ______________

8. Once a purchase contract has been executed and title has been opened, may a Seller continue to show the Property to prospective Buyers and negotiate backup offers? ______________

____

9. Who pays the taxes and maintenance fees for the actual day of closing?

____

10. If one party makes written demand of the title company for the earnest money, how many days must the title company wait after giving notice by certified mail to the other party before it can release the money to the demanding party? ______________

11. Should the Seller's disclosure notice be referenced and added to the purchase agreement as an addendum? ______________

12. Who drafts the promulgated contracts? ______________

13. How many brokers sit on the Broker-Lawyer Committee? ______________

14. When should a Buyer or Seller consult an attorney? ______________

____

15. What two blanks must be completed to have a valid termination option?

____

____

16. If the effective date of the contract is the 15th of the month, when will the option period end if the agreement calls for a 7-day option period?

____

17. The lead-based paint addendum must be added to contracts for the purchase of homes built prior to what year? _______________

____

18. When must a Seller permit access for the Buyers to have the Property inspected by licensed inspectors? _______________

____

19. Who fills in the date of final acceptance after the offeror has been notified of the acceptance? _______________

20. Who pays for the owners' policy of title insurance? _______________

____

21. The Buyer may terminate the contract, even if the Seller is willing to pay the cost of repairs, when the cost of lender-required repairs exceeds what amount? _______________

22. If repairs are needed in order to complete the transactions, by whom must they be performed? _______________

23. If the Seller fails to complete any agreed repairs and treatments prior to the closing date, may the Buyer do so and receive reimbursement from the Seller at closing? _______________

24. What is the maximum number of days for which a Sellers' or Buyers' temporary lease may be used? _______________

25. What kind of a deed will the Seller execute and deliver to the Buyer at closing? _______________

26. If the parties agree to submit any dispute to an alternative dispute resolution procedure such as mediation, who will pay the cost? _______________

27. Where is the obligation of the parties for payment of broker's fees defined?

____

28. How shall the Buyer pay the Sales Price? ______________________________

____

29. Who is responsible for the expense related to releasing existing liens at closing?______________________________

30. Who will pay a required private mortgage insurance (PMI) premium?

____

31. What three things are collectively referred to as the Property?__________

____

____

32. For the most commonly used reference to a recorded plat type of legal description, what key element of the description has no blank provided?

____

33. In what paragraph do you find the words *time is of the essence*? __________

____

34. If the title company is unable to deliver the commitment for title insurance within the time frame defined in the contract, is an extension to that time frame possible? ______________________________

35. If a title policy is to be furnished, who should promptly review the commitment?______________________________

36. Where in the promulgated contract form would a Buyer itemize specific repairs that the Buyer wants completed at the Seller's expense prior to closing? ______________________________

37. Must municipal building permits be obtained by Sellers for repairs to be completed prior to closing? ______________________________

38. Unless otherwise agreed in writing, who is obligated to pay for lender required repairs? ______________________________

39. If a casualty loss occurs after the effective date of the contract and the Seller is unable to restore the Property prior to closing, the Buyer may accept an assignment of the Seller's insurance proceeds. What is the Buyer to receive in addition to the assignment? ______________________________

____

40. A Buyer defaults and releases the earnest money to the Seller as liquidated damages; can the Seller seek additional money damages from the court?

____

41. Does the fact that the parties agree to submit a dispute to an alternative dispute resolution procedure, such as mediation, preclude a party from seeking equitable relief from a court of competent jurisdiction? ______________

42. Does the escrow agent have any liability for the performance or nonperformance of any party to the contract? ______________________________

43. Is the option fee automatically credited to the Sales Price if the Buyer proceeds with the closing of the sale? ______________________________

44. Are there any limitations on the reasons for which a Buyer may terminate during the option period? ______________________________

____

45. What is the status of the termination option when the Buyer pays the Seller no money? ______________________________

____

46. What should a Buyer or Seller do if they do not understand the legal effect of any provision of the contract? ______________________________

____

47. Does a standard Texas Policy of Title Insurance insure against discrepancies, conflicts, or shortages in area or boundary lines? ______________

48. Whose responsibility is it to determine if the Property is located within a municipality's extraterritorial jurisdiction and may now or at a later time be subject to annexation? ______________________________

49. What Texas statute requires the Seller to notify the Buyer that the Property is situated in a utility or other statutorily created district providing water, sewer, drainage, or flood control facilities and services? ______________

____

50. When Seller financing is used to purchase the Property, who is responsible for furnishing the Seller with a mortgagee policy of title insurance?

____

PRACTICE EXAM

1. When should a party consult legal counsel?

   a. Before signing a contract
   b. Before making loan application
   c. Before tendering any money
   d. Anytime prior to closing

2. Which is *NOT* listed as part of the defined real estate in the Property paragraph of the TREC Form 20-7, One to Four Family Residential Contract (Resale)?

   a. Shrubbery
   b. Refrigerator
   c. Ceiling fans
   d. Satellite dish

3. The dollar amount entered in the Sales Price paragraph of the TREC Form 20-7, One to Four Family Residential Contract (Resale), excludes

   a. the cash portion of the transaction amount payable at closing.
   b. any financed private mortgage insurance (PMI).
   c. the earnest money.
   d. the Buyer's prepaids and Loan Fees.

4. What is the first consideration recited in the promulgated purchase contracts?

   a. The earnest money
   b. The Sales Price
   c. The Option Fee
   d. The exchange of promises in the Parties paragraph

5. If a Seller fails to provide the Buyer with the OP-H Form, Seller's Disclosure of Property Condition, as required by section 5.008 of the Texas Property Code, what is the status of the purchase contract?

   a. Unenforceable
   b. Void
   c. Voidable at the option of the Buyer
   d. Valid and enforceable

6. Which is acceptable language for the Special Provisions paragraph in the TREC-promulgated contract forms?

   a. Time is of the essence
   b. Buyer will do a walk-through
   c. Seller will pay for the survey
   d. Buyer will pay for the owners' title policy

7. The Property Condition paragraph gives the Buyer the right to personally inspect the Property

   a. during the period between contract and closing at any time of the buyer's choosing.
   b. in the period of time between contract and closing at reasonable times.
   c. when the Seller is present only.
   d. on any day between 9 AM and 10 PM.

8. Before what event do the TREC rules require that a real estate license holder advise a Buyer in writing to get an abstract examined by an attorney of the Buyer's choice or obtain an owners' title insurance policy?

   a. At first contact
   b. Prior to signing an agreement to purchase
   c. Prior to closing
   d. At the first face-to-face meeting

9. An offer becomes a binding contract when

   a. the last party has signed and the other party has been notified.
   b. the signed contract has been delivered to the title company.
   c. there is a meeting of the minds and earnest money tendered.
   d. one party states verbally that the written offer is accepted.

10. The maximum tenancy that may be addressed in the TREC Form 15-4, Seller's Temporary Residential Lease, or the TREC Form 16-4, Buyer's Temporary Lease, is

    a. 180 days.
    b. 90 days.
    c. 48 hours.
    d. 72 hours.

11. Which addendum contains the words *time is of the essence*?

    a. TREC 26-5, Seller Financing Addendum
    b. TREC OP-H, Seller's Disclosure of Property Condition
    c. TREC 11-6, Addendum for "Back-Up" Contract
    d. TREC 33-1, Addendum for Coastal Area Property

12. The TREC Form OP-H, Seller's Disclosure of Property Condition,

    a. is promulgated for mandatory use.
    b. is published for voluntary use.
    c. addresses many more items than the form published by the Texas Association of REALTORS®.
    d. does not need to be provided by a Seller selling his or her own house.

13. According to the standard wording in the Title Policy and Survey paragraph of the sales contract, utility easements created by the dedication deed and plat of the subdivision in which the Property is located

    a. are not a basis for raising objections to title.
    b. are basis for raising objections to title.
    c. permit the lender only to raise objections to title.
    d. require that a licensed Texas attorney raise objections on behalf of a party to the contract.

14. The TREC rules permit an agent to *NOT* present an offer to the Seller

    a. if the Seller, after entering into a contract to sell the Property, instructs the agent in writing not to present further offers.
    b. under no circumstances because the agent may never withhold an offer.
    c. if the Seller, after entering into a contract to sell the Property, instructs the agent verbally not to present further offers.
    d. when common business sense dictates otherwise.

15. Which is *NOT* an essential element of a contract for the purchase of a one- to four-family residential resale property?

    a. Competent parties
    b. Consideration
    c. Offer and acceptance
    d. Earnest money

16. In the *Parties* paragraph of a residential resale contract, which is the appropriate way to identify a Buyer who is a widow?

    a. Mary Beth Smith, an unmarried person
    b. Mary Beth Smith, as separate property
    c. Mary Beth Smith, tenant in common
    d. Mary Beth Smith, et al. and ux.

17. Which is the *BEST* example of a unilateral contract?

    a. A residential purchase agreement
    b. A residential lease
    c. An option to purchase
    d. Listing agreement

18. When a closing occurs on June 5th, who will pay the property tax attributable to June 5th according to the provisions of the standard wording in the TREC-promulgated contract forms?

    a. The Buyer pays for June 5.
    b. The Seller pays for June 5.
    c. The parties split the cost for June 6.
    d. The cost is prorated based on the hour of closing.

19. Which would *NOT* be listed as an addendum to a TREC-promulgated contract form?
    a. TREC Form OP-K, Information About Brokerage Services
    b. TREC Form 12-2, Addendum for Release of Liability on Assumption of FHA, VA or Conventional Loan/Restriction of Seller's Entitlement
    c. TREC Form 16-4, Buyer's Temporary Residential Lease
    d. TREC Form 34-3, Addendum for Property Located Seaward of the Gulf Intracoastal Waterway

20. When may a potential purchaser's offer to buy real estate be withdrawn?
    a. Only after the Seller has turned it down
    b. At any time if no earnest money was tendered
    c. At any time prior to Seller acceptance and notification
    d. At any time prior to opening title

21. Which is *NOT* addressed by a TREC-promulgated contract?
    a. Assumption of an FHA-insured loan
    b. A purchase using Seller financing
    c. A purchase using a contract for deed
    d. The purchase of a fee simple town house

22. Who is responsible for filling in the date of final acceptance on the TREC-promulgated purchase contracts?
    a. Broker
    b. Seller
    c. Buyer
    d. Last party to sign

23. What are promulgated forms?
    a. Forms written by the TREC and then published by the Broker-Lawyer Committee for mandatory use by license holders
    b. Forms written by the Broker-Lawyer Committee and then published by the TREC for mandatory use by license holders
    c. Forms written and issued by the Texas legislature for mandatory use by license holders
    d. Forms written and issued by the TREC for recommended use by license holders

24. What is a legal proceeding brought by a party to a contract against another party to compel action called for in the agreement?
    a. A suit for injunction
    b. A suit for specific performance
    c. A motion for release
    d. A writ of forbearance

25. After receipt of the commitment, how many days does the Buyer have to raise objections?

    a. 10
    b. Number of days as agreed to by the contracting parties
    c. 5
    d. 20

26. Which items might meet the test of a fixture but *NOT* be a part of the real estate because it is leased rather than owned by the Seller?

    a. Permanently installed air-conditioning equipment
    b. Built-in cleaning equipment
    c. Certain lighting fixtures
    d. Water-treatment systems

27. Every TREC contract must have *AT LEAST* how many TREC addenda incorporated into the agreement?

    a. One
    b. None
    c. Two
    d. Three

28. Who is required to pay for the lender-required repairs according to the standard wording in the Property Condition paragraph (paragraph 7E) of the TREC Form 20-7, One to Four Family Residential Contract (Resale)?

    a. Neither Buyer nor Seller
    b. Buyer
    c. Seller
    d. Buyer and Seller equally

29. A Buyer must sign the TREC Form OP-H, Seller's Disclosure of Property Condition, as required by section 5.008 of the Texas Property Code and incorporate it as an addendum to the purchase agreement.

    a. True
    b. False

30. All representations made by either party in a TREC-promulgated contract form will

    a. survive closing.
    b. continue for two years.
    c. terminate as of the closing date.
    d. continue for 90 days.

31. How much additional title insurance premium will be charged to delete the standard exception in a Texas Owners' Title Policy for a single-family residential property relating to the standard exception "as to discrepancies, conflicts, shortages in area or boundary lines, encroachment or protrusions, or overlapping improvements"?

    a. An amount established by the state
    b. 10% of the Sales Price
    c. 5% of the loan value
    d. 10% of the published premium

32. When may a Seller continue to show the Property to prospects after a purchase agreement has been signed unless agreed otherwise in writing?

    a. Throughout the term of the executory contract
    b. During the option period only
    c. Only upon receiving written permission from the Buyer
    d. Only until after title objections have been cured

33. According to the preprinted language, what type of deed is to be used at closing to convey the title to real property that is being sold using a TREC-promulgated contract form?

    a. Quitclaim
    b. Bargain and sale
    c. Special warranty
    d. General warranty

34. Financing or assumption approval is deemed to have been obtained when the lender determines that the Buyer has satisfied all of the lender's financial requirements such as Buyer's net worth, income, and creditworthiness.

    a. True
    b. False

35. Anything that is addressed in one of the TREC addenda can adequately and legally be set down in the Special Provisions paragraph (paragraph 11) if so desired by a license holder rather than using the addendum

    a. True
    b. False

36. The sum entered on the first line of the Sales Price paragraph of TREC-promulgated contracts excludes the Buyer's closing costs and prepaids.

    a. True
    b. False

37. An agent may explain the general content, factual statements, and business details contained in the promulgated forms so long as the agent does *NOT* give legal advice.

    a. True
    b. False

38. Who shall be entitled to collect reasonable attorney's fees if a legal proceeding is brought under or with relation to a TREC-promulgated contract?

    a. Buyer
    b. Seller
    c. Listing broker
    d. Prevailing party

39. When the Buyer makes a request to the Seller to amend a contract during the option period and the Seller fails to respond, what is the status of the contract two days after the option period has expired?

    a. The contract is null and void because the request to amend serves as adequate notice that the Buyer does not wish to proceed.
    b. The contract is enforceable and the Buyer is obligated to complete the transaction under the original terms and conditions.
    c. The option period is automatically extended until the Seller responds.
    d. The contract incorporates the Buyer's requested changes and moves to closing because the Seller did not object to the changes.

40. When may the general public use the promulgated forms?

    a. Only when they have the services of an attorney
    b. Only when they have the services of a real estate broker
    c. At no time
    d. At any time

41. According to the provisions of the Notices paragraph in the TREC-promulgated contracts, all notices from one party to the other are valid only when physically delivered to the party who is the recipient of the notice.

    a. True
    b. False

42. How many days does the Seller have to cure objections to title after the Buyer or third party lender has timely delivered objections to the Seller when using the residential resale contract?

    a. 5
    b. 7
    c. 10
    d. 15

43. If a Buyer decides to terminate a contract within the option period, where and how must the promulgated TREC Form 38-1, Notice of Termination of Contract, be delivered?

    a. To the listing agent
    b. As specified in *Notices* paragraph
    c. To the title company
    d. All of the above

44. When a Buyer is purchasing a home that was built prior to 1978, how many days *MUST* be given to the Buyer to have the Property evaluated for the presence of lead-based paint or lead hazards?

    a. 5
    b. 10
    c. 15
    d. 20

45. The fee that the Seller is to pay to the listing broker is *ALWAYS* stated in and made a part of the purchase agreement when using the TREC-promulgated forms.

    a. True
    b. False

46. The TREC-promulgated contract forms require that the Buyer *ALWAYS* pay the loan origination fee.

    a. True
    b. False

47. Who promulgates forms for mandatory use by license holders?

    a. Texas legislature
    b. Broker-Lawyer Committee
    c. Texas Real Estate Commission
    d. Texas Association of REALTORS®

48. Federal law dictates that an addendum addressing the possible presence of lead-based paint and lead-based paint hazards be attached to the purchase agreement when the house being sold was built before

    a. 1972.
    b. 1978.
    c. 1977.
    d. 1979.

49. How many contract forms are currently promulgated by the TREC?

    a. Seven
    b. Six
    c. Nine
    d. Ten

50. According to the standard wording in the Property Condition paragraph of the TREC Form, 20-7, One to Four Family Residential Contract (Resale), who is responsible for paying the fees involved for turning on utilities for inspections and reinspections?

    a. Buyer
    b. Seller
    c. Whoever's name is filled in the blank
    d. Party who wants to have inspections done

51. If the effective date on a contract is April 26 and it grants the Buyer an option period of 11 days, on what date at midnight will the option period end?

    a. May 10
    b. May 6
    c. May 7
    d. May 8

52. If a Buyer fails to deposit additional earnest money as called for in the Earnest Money paragraph (paragraph 5), the Buyer is in default and subject to the provisions in the default paragraph.

    a. True
    b. False

APPENDIX B

ANSWER KEY

Chapter 1

1. c
2. d
3. b
4. b
5. d
6. b
7. c
8. b
9. d
10. b

Chapter 2

1. d
2. a
3. b
4. a
5. d
6. b
7. b
8. c
9. b
10. d

Chapter 3

1. c
2. b
3. a
4. d
5. c
6. b
7. a
8. b
9. c
10. d
11. d
12. d
13. c
14. c
15. b
16. b
17. a
18. a
19. b
20. c

Chapter 4

1. c
2. b
3. a
4. b
5. b

Chapter 5

1. c
2. a
3. d
4. b
5. b
6. a
7. b
8. d
9. c
10. b

Chapter 6

Scenario 1

Contract paragraph

3A. $340,000
3B. $None or N/A
3C. $340,000

4 ☐ A. $________
A(2). ☐(a)
☐(b)
☐ B.
☐ C. $________

12A(1)(b). $None or N/A

Scenario 2

Contract paragraph

3A. $49,800
3B. $199,200
3C. $249,000

4 ☒ A. $199,200
A(2). ☒ (a)
☐(b)
☐ B.
☐ C. $________

12A(1)(b). $None or N/A

Scenario 2

12-10-07

EQUAL HOUSING OPPORTUNITY

PROMULGATED BY THE TEXAS REAL ESTATE COMMISSION (TREC)

THIRD PARTY FINANCING CONDITION ADDENDUM

TO CONTRACT CONCERNING THE PROPERTY AT

____

(Street Address and City)

Buyer shall apply promptly for all financing described below and make every reasonable effort to obtain approval for the financing (Financing Approval). Buyer shall furnish all information and documents required by lender for Financing Approval. Financing Approval will be deemed to have been obtained when (1) the terms of the loan(s) described below are available and (2) lender determines that Buyer has satisfied all of lender's financial requirements (those items relating to Buyer's assets, income and credit history). If Buyer cannot obtain Financing Approval, Buyer may give written notice to Seller within 20 days after the effective date of this contract and this contract will terminate and the earnest money will be refunded to Buyer. **If Buyer does not give such notice within the time required, this contract will no longer be subject to Financing Approval. Time is of the essence for this paragraph and strict compliance with the time for performance is required.**

NOTE: Financing Approval does not include approval of lender's underwriting requirements for the Property, as specified in Paragraph 4.A.(1) of the contract.

Each note must be secured by vendor's and deed of trust liens.

CHECK APPLICABLE BOXES:

☒ A. CONVENTIONAL FINANCING:

☒ (1) A first mortgage loan in the principal amount of $ 199,200 (excluding any financed PMI premium), due in full in 15 year(s), with interest not to exceed 6.5 % per annum for the first 15 year(s) of the loan with Loan Fees (loan origination, discount, buy-down, and commitment fees) not to exceed 1 % of the loan.

☐ (2) A second mortgage loan in the principal amount of $__________(excluding any financed PMI premium), due in full in ______year(s), with interest not to exceed ______% per annum for the first ______year(s) of the loan with Loan Fees (loan origination, discount, buy-down, and commitment fees) not to exceed ______% of the loan.

☐ B. TEXAS VETERANS LOAN: A loan(s) from the Texas Veterans Land Board of $__________ for a period in the total amount of _____years at the interest rate established by the Texas Veterans Land Board.

☐ C. FHA INSURED FINANCING: A Section __________ FHA insured loan of not less than $__________ (excluding any financed MIP), amortizable monthly for not less than ______years, with interest not to exceed ______% per annum for the first ______year(s) of the loan with Loan Fees (loan origination, discount, buy-down, and commitment fees) not to exceed ______ % of the loan. As required by HUD-FHA, if FHA valuation is unknown, *"It is expressly agreed that, notwithstanding any other provision of this contract, the purchaser (Buyer) shall not be obligated to complete the purchase of the Property described herein or to incur any penalty by forfeiture of earnest money deposits or otherwise unless the purchaser (Buyer) has been given in accordance with HUD/FHA or VA requirements a written statement issued by the Federal Housing Commissioner, Department of Veterans Affairs, or a Direct Endorsement Lender setting forth the appraised value of the Property of not less than $__________. The purchaser (Buyer) shall have the privilege and option of proceeding with consummation of the contract without regard to the amount of the*

Initialed for identification by Buyer____ ____ and Seller____ ____ TREC NO. 40-3

____
(Address of Property)

appraised valuation. The appraised valuation is arrived at to determine the maximum mortgage the Department of Housing and Urban Development will insure. HUD does not warrant the value or the condition of the Property. The purchaser (Buyer) should satisfy himself/herself that the price and the condition of the Property are acceptable."

NOTE: HUD 92564-CN "For Your Protection: Get a Home Inspection" must be attached to this Addendum.

☐ D. VA GUARANTEED FINANCING: A VA guaranteed loan of not less than $________________ (excluding any financed Funding Fee), amortizable monthly for not less than________years, with interest not to exceed_________% per annum for the first ________year(s) of the loan with Loan Fees (loan origination, discount, buy-down, and commitment fees) not to exceed _________% of the loan.

VA NOTICE TO BUYER: "*It is expressly agreed that, notwithstanding any other provisions of this contract, the Buyer shall not incur any penalty by forfeiture of earnest money or otherwise or be obligated to complete the purchase of the Property described herein, if the contract purchase price or cost exceeds the reasonable value of the Property established by the Department of Veterans Affairs. The Buyer shall, however, have the privilege and option of proceeding with the consummation of this contract without regard to the amount of the reasonable value established by the Department of Veterans Affairs."*

If Buyer elects to complete the purchase at an amount in excess of the reasonable value established by VA, Buyer shall pay such excess amount in cash from a source which Buyer agrees to disclose to the VA and which Buyer represents will not be from borrowed funds except as approved by VA. If VA reasonable value of the Property is less than the Sales Price, Seller may reduce the Sales Price to an amount equal to the VA reasonable value and the sale will be closed at the lower Sales Price with proportionate adjustments to the down payment and the loan amount.

Buyer hereby authorizes any lender to furnish to the Seller or Buyer or their representatives information relating only to the status of Financing Approval of Buyer.

________________________	________________________
Buyer	Seller
________________________	________________________
Buyer	Seller

Scenario 3

Contract paragraph

3A. $17,640
3B. $158,760
3C. $176,400

4 ☒ A. $158,760
A(2). ☐ (a)
☒ (b)
☐ B.
☐ C. $________

12A(1)(b). $1,500

Scenario 3

12-10-07

EQUAL HOUSING OPPORTUNITY

PROMULGATED BY THE TEXAS REAL ESTATE COMMISSION (TREC)

THIRD PARTY FINANCING CONDITION ADDENDUM

TO CONTRACT CONCERNING THE PROPERTY AT

____

(Street Address and City)

Buyer shall apply promptly for all financing described below and make every reasonable effort to obtain approval for the financing (Financing Approval). Buyer shall furnish all information and documents required by lender for Financing Approval. Financing Approval will be deemed to have been obtained when (1) the terms of the loan(s) described below are available and (2) lender determines that Buyer has satisfied all of lender's financial requirements (those items relating to Buyer's assets, income and credit history). If Buyer cannot obtain Financing Approval, Buyer may give written notice to Seller within N/A days after the effective date of this contract and this contract will terminate and the earnest money will be refunded to Buyer. **If Buyer does not give such notice within the time required, this contract will no longer be subject to Financing Approval. Time is of the essence for this paragraph and strict compliance with the time for performance is required.**

NOTE: Financing Approval does not include approval of lender's underwriting requirements for the Property, as specified in Paragraph 4.A.(1) of the contract.

Each note must be secured by vendor's and deed of trust liens.

CHECK APPLICABLE BOXES:

☒ A. CONVENTIONAL FINANCING:

☒ (1) A first mortgage loan in the principal amount of $ 158,760 (excluding any financed PMI premium), due in full in 30 year(s), with interest not to exceed 6.75 % per annum for the first 3 year(s) of the loan with Loan Fees (loan origination, discount, buy-down, and commitment fees) not to exceed 1 % of the loan.

☐ (2) A second mortgage loan in the principal amount of $__________(excluding any financed PMI premium), due in full in __________year(s), with interest not to exceed ______% per annum for the first __________year(s) of the loan with Loan Fees (loan origination, discount, buy-down, and commitment fees) not to exceed ________% of the loan.

☐ B. TEXAS VETERANS LOAN: A loan(s) from the Texas Veterans Land Board of $__________ for a period in the total amount of _____years at the interest rate established by the Texas Veterans Land Board.

☐ C. FHA INSURED FINANCING: A Section ______________ FHA insured loan of not less than $______________ (excluding any financed MIP), amortizable monthly for not less than ________years, with interest not to exceed _______% per annum for the first ______year(s) of the loan with Loan Fees (loan origination, discount, buy-down, and commitment fees) not to exceed _________ % of the loan. As required by HUD-FHA, if FHA valuation is unknown, *"It is expressly agreed that, notwithstanding any other provision of this contract, the purchaser (Buyer) shall not be obligated to complete the purchase of the Property described herein or to incur any penalty by forfeiture of earnest money deposits or otherwise unless the purchaser (Buyer) has been given in accordance with HUD/FHA or VA requirements a written statement issued by the Federal Housing Commissioner, Department of Veterans Affairs, or a Direct Endorsement Lender setting forth the appraised value of the Property of not less than $______________. The purchaser (Buyer) shall have the privilege and option of proceeding with consummation of the contract without regard to the amount of the*

____
(Address of Property)

appraised valuation. The appraised valuation is arrived at to determine the maximum mortgage the Department of Housing and Urban Development will insure. HUD does not warrant the value or the condition of the Property. The purchaser (Buyer) should satisfy himself/herself that the price and the condition of the Property are acceptable."
NOTE: HUD 92564-CN "For Your Protection: Get a Home Inspection" must be attached to this Addendum.

❑ D. VA GUARANTEED FINANCING: A VA guaranteed loan of not less than $________________ (excluding any financed Funding Fee), amortizable monthly for not less than________years, with interest not to exceed_________% per annum for the first ________year(s) of the loan with Loan Fees (loan origination, discount, buy-down, and commitment fees) not to exceed _________% of the loan.

VA NOTICE TO BUYER: "*It is expressly agreed that, notwithstanding any other provisions of this contract, the Buyer shall not incur any penalty by forfeiture of earnest money or otherwise or be obligated to complete the purchase of the Property described herein, if the contract purchase price or cost exceeds the reasonable value of the Property established by the Department of Veterans Affairs. The Buyer shall, however, have the privilege and option of proceeding with the consummation of this contract without regard to the amount of the reasonable value established by the Department of Veterans Affairs."*

If Buyer elects to complete the purchase at an amount in excess of the reasonable value established by VA, Buyer shall pay such excess amount in cash from a source which Buyer agrees to disclose to the VA and which Buyer represents will not be from borrowed funds except as approved by VA. If VA reasonable value of the Property is less than the Sales Price, Seller may reduce the Sales Price to an amount equal to the VA reasonable value and the sale will be closed at the lower Sales Price with proportionate adjustments to the down payment and the loan amount.

Buyer hereby authorizes any lender to furnish to the Seller or Buyer or their representatives information relating only to the status of Financing Approval of Buyer.

______________________	______________________
Buyer	Seller
______________________	______________________
Buyer	Seller

Scenario 4

Contract paragraph

3A. $43,500
3B. $391,500
3C. $435,000

4 ☒ A. $391,500
A(2). ☒ (a)
☐ (b)
☐ B.
☐ C. $________

12A(1)(b). $None or N/A

Scenario 4

12-10-07

EQUAL HOUSING OPPORTUNITY

PROMULGATED BY THE TEXAS REAL ESTATE COMMISSION (TREC)

THIRD PARTY FINANCING CONDITION ADDENDUM

TO CONTRACT CONCERNING THE PROPERTY AT

____

(Street Address and City)

Buyer shall apply promptly for all financing described below and make every reasonable effort to obtain approval for the financing (Financing Approval). Buyer shall furnish all information and documents required by lender for Financing Approval. Financing Approval will be deemed to have been obtained when (1) the terms of the loan(s) described below are available and (2) lender determines that Buyer has satisfied all of lender's financial requirements (those items relating to Buyer's assets, income and credit history). If Buyer cannot obtain Financing Approval, Buyer may give written notice to Seller within 20 days after the effective date of this contract and this contract will terminate and the earnest money will be refunded to Buyer. **If Buyer does not give such notice within the time required, this contract will no longer be subject to Financing Approval. Time is of the essence for this paragraph and strict compliance with the time for performance is required.**

NOTE: Financing Approval does not include approval of lender's underwriting requirements for the Property, as specified in Paragraph 4.A.(1) of the contract.

Each note must be secured by vendor's and deed of trust liens.

CHECK APPLICABLE BOXES:

☒ A. CONVENTIONAL FINANCING:

☒ (1) A first mortgage loan in the principal amount of $ 348,000 (excluding any financed PMI premium), due in full in 30 year(s), with interest not to exceed 6.75 % per annum for the first 30 year(s) of the loan with Loan Fees (loan origination, discount, buy-down, and commitment fees) not to exceed 1 % of the loan.

☒ (2) A second mortgage loan in the principal amount of $ 43,500 (excluding any financed PMI premium), due in full in 15 year(s), with interest not to exceed 7.5 % per annum for the first 15 year(s) of the loan with Loan Fees (loan origination, discount, buy-down, and commitment fees) not to exceed N/A % of the loan.

☐ B. TEXAS VETERANS LOAN: A loan(s) from the Texas Veterans Land Board of $_______ for a period in the total amount of _____ years at the interest rate established by the Texas Veterans Land Board.

☐ C. FHA INSURED FINANCING: A Section _________ FHA insured loan of not less than $_________ (excluding any financed MIP), amortizable monthly for not less than _______ years, with interest not to exceed _______ % per annum for the first ______ year(s) of the loan with Loan Fees (loan origination, discount, buy-down, and commitment fees) not to exceed _________ % of the loan. As required by HUD-FHA, if FHA valuation is unknown, *"It is expressly agreed that, notwithstanding any other provision of this contract, the purchaser (Buyer) shall not be obligated to complete the purchase of the Property described herein or to incur any penalty by forfeiture of earnest money deposits or otherwise unless the purchaser (Buyer) has been given in accordance with HUD/FHA or VA requirements a written statement issued by the Federal Housing Commissioner, Department of Veterans Affairs, or a Direct Endorsement Lender setting forth the appraised value of the Property of not less than $_____________. The purchaser (Buyer) shall have the privilege and option of proceeding with consummation of the contract without regard to the amount of the*

Third Party Financing Condition Addendum Concerning Page 2 of 2 12-10-07

____
(Address of Property)

appraised valuation. The appraised valuation is arrived at to determine the maximum mortgage the Department of Housing and Urban Development will insure. HUD does not warrant the value or the condition of the Property. The purchaser (Buyer) should satisfy himself/herself that the price and the condition of the Property are acceptable."

NOTE: HUD 92564-CN "For Your Protection: Get a Home Inspection" must be attached to this Addendum.

❑ D. VA GUARANTEED FINANCING: A VA guaranteed loan of not less than $__________ (excluding any financed Funding Fee), amortizable monthly for not less than________years, with interest not to exceed_________% per annum for the first ________year(s) of the loan with Loan Fees (loan origination, discount, buy-down, and commitment fees) not to exceed _________% of the loan.

VA NOTICE TO BUYER: "*It is expressly agreed that, notwithstanding any other provisions of this contract, the Buyer shall not incur any penalty by forfeiture of earnest money or otherwise or be obligated to complete the purchase of the Property described herein, if the contract purchase price or cost exceeds the reasonable value of the Property established by the Department of Veterans Affairs. The Buyer shall, however, have the privilege and option of proceeding with the consummation of this contract without regard to the amount of the reasonable value established by the Department of Veterans Affairs."*

If Buyer elects to complete the purchase at an amount in excess of the reasonable value established by VA, Buyer shall pay such excess amount in cash from a source which Buyer agrees to disclose to the VA and which Buyer represents will not be from borrowed funds except as approved by VA. If VA reasonable value of the Property is less than the Sales Price, Seller may reduce the Sales Price to an amount equal to the VA reasonable value and the sale will be closed at the lower Sales Price with proportionate adjustments to the down payment and the loan amount.

Buyer hereby authorizes any lender to furnish to the Seller or Buyer or their representatives information relating only to the status of Financing Approval of Buyer.

______________________ Buyer	______________________ Seller
______________________ Buyer	______________________ Seller

Scenario 5

Contract paragraph

3A. $2,600
3B. $112,400
3C. $115,000

4 ☒ A. $112,400
A(2). ☒ (a)
☐ (b)
☐ B.
☐ C. $________

12A(1)(b). $1,950

Scenario 5

12-10-07

EQUAL HOUSING OPPORTUNITY

PROMULGATED BY THE TEXAS REAL ESTATE COMMISSION (TREC)

THIRD PARTY FINANCING CONDITION ADDENDUM

TO CONTRACT CONCERNING THE PROPERTY AT

____

(Street Address and City)

Buyer shall apply promptly for all financing described below and make every reasonable effort to obtain approval for the financing (Financing Approval). Buyer shall furnish all information and documents required by lender for Financing Approval. Financing Approval will be deemed to have been obtained when (1) the terms of the loan(s) described below are available and (2) lender determines that Buyer has satisfied all of lender's financial requirements (those items relating to Buyer's assets, income and credit history). If Buyer cannot obtain Financing Approval, Buyer may give written notice to Seller within 20 days after the effective date of this contract and this contract will terminate and the earnest money will be refunded to Buyer. **If Buyer does not give such notice within the time required, this contract will no longer be subject to Financing Approval. Time is of the essence for this paragraph and strict compliance with the time for performance is required.**

NOTE: Financing Approval does not include approval of lender's underwriting requirements for the Property, as specified in Paragraph 4.A.(1) of the contract.

Each note must be secured by vendor's and deed of trust liens.

CHECK APPLICABLE BOXES:

☐ A. CONVENTIONAL FINANCING:

☐ (1) A first mortgage loan in the principal amount of $ ____________ (excluding any financed PMI premium), due in full in ________ year(s), with interest not to exceed ______% per annum for the first ________year(s) of the loan with Loan Fees (loan origination, discount, buy-down, and commitment fees) not to exceed ________% of the loan.

☐ (2) A second mortgage loan in the principal amount of $____________(excluding any financed PMI premium), due in full in ___________year(s), with interest not to exceed ______% per annum for the first ____________year(s) of the loan with Loan Fees (loan origination, discount, buy-down, and commitment fees) not to exceed ________% of the loan.

☐ B. TEXAS VETERANS LOAN: A loan(s) from the Texas Veterans Land Board of $____________ for a period in the total amount of _____years at the interest rate established by the Texas Veterans Land Board.

☒ C. FHA INSURED FINANCING: A Section 203(b) FHA insured loan of not less than $ 112,400 (excluding any financed MIP), amortizable monthly for not less than 30 years, with interest not to exceed 5.75 % per annum for the first 30 year(s) of the loan with Loan Fees (loan origination, discount, buy-down, and commitment fees) not to exceed 2 % of the loan. As required by HUD-FHA, if FHA valuation is unknown, *"It is expressly agreed that, notwithstanding any other provision of this contract, the purchaser (Buyer) shall not be obligated to complete the purchase of the Property described herein or to incur any penalty by forfeiture of earnest money deposits or otherwise unless the purchaser (Buyer) has been given in accordance with HUD/FHA or VA requirements a written statement issued by the Federal Housing Commissioner, Department of Veterans Affairs, or a Direct Endorsement Lender setting forth the appraised value of the Property of not less than $ 115,000 . The purchaser (Buyer) shall have the privilege and option of proceeding with consummation of the contract without regard to the amount of the*

Third Party Financing Condition Addendum Concerning

Page 2 of 2 12-10-07

____
(Address of Property)

appraised valuation. The appraised valuation is arrived at to determine the maximum mortgage the Department of Housing and Urban Development will insure. HUD does not warrant the value or the condition of the Property. The purchaser (Buyer) should satisfy himself/herself that the price and the condition of the Property are acceptable."
NOTE: HUD 92564-CN "For Your Protection: Get a Home Inspection" must be attached to this Addendum.

❑ D. VA GUARANTEED FINANCING: A VA guaranteed loan of not less than $______________ (excluding any financed Funding Fee), amortizable monthly for not less than________years, with interest not to exceed_________% per annum for the first ________year(s) of the loan with Loan Fees (loan origination, discount, buy-down, and commitment fees) not to exceed _________% of the loan.

VA NOTICE TO BUYER: "*It is expressly agreed that, notwithstanding any other provisions of this contract, the Buyer shall not incur any penalty by forfeiture of earnest money or otherwise or be obligated to complete the purchase of the Property described herein, if the contract purchase price or cost exceeds the reasonable value of the Property established by the Department of Veterans Affairs. The Buyer shall, however, have the privilege and option of proceeding with the consummation of this contract without regard to the amount of the reasonable value established by the Department of Veterans Affairs."*

If Buyer elects to complete the purchase at an amount in excess of the reasonable value established by VA, Buyer shall pay such excess amount in cash from a source which Buyer agrees to disclose to the VA and which Buyer represents will not be from borrowed funds except as approved by VA. If VA reasonable value of the Property is less than the Sales Price, Seller may reduce the Sales Price to an amount equal to the VA reasonable value and the sale will be closed at the lower Sales Price with proportionate adjustments to the down payment and the loan amount.

Buyer hereby authorizes any lender to furnish to the Seller or Buyer or their representatives information relating only to the status of Financing Approval of Buyer.

___________________________	___________________________
Buyer	Seller
___________________________	___________________________
Buyer	Seller

Scenario 6

Contract paragraph

3A. $15,600
3B. $62,400
3C. $78,000

4 ☒ A. $62,400
A(2). ☒ (a)
☐ (b)
☐ B.
☐ C. $________

12A(1)(b). $1,100

Scenario 6

12-10-07

EQUAL HOUSING OPPORTUNITY

PROMULGATED BY THE TEXAS REAL ESTATE COMMISSION (TREC)

THIRD PARTY FINANCING CONDITION ADDENDUM

TO CONTRACT CONCERNING THE PROPERTY AT

____

(Street Address and City)

Buyer shall apply promptly for all financing described below and make every reasonable effort to obtain approval for the financing (Financing Approval). Buyer shall furnish all information and documents required by lender for Financing Approval. Financing Approval will be deemed to have been obtained when (1) the terms of the loan(s) described below are available and (2) lender determines that Buyer has satisfied all of lender's financial requirements (those items relating to Buyer's assets, income and credit history). If Buyer cannot obtain Financing Approval, Buyer may give written notice to Seller within 30 days after the effective date of this contract and this contract will terminate and the earnest money will be refunded to Buyer. **If Buyer does not give such notice within the time required, this contract will no longer be subject to Financing Approval. Time is of the essence for this paragraph and strict compliance with the time for performance is required.**

NOTE: Financing Approval does not include approval of lender's underwriting requirements for the Property, as specified in Paragraph 4.A.(1) of the contract.

Each note must be secured by vendor's and deed of trust liens.

CHECK APPLICABLE BOXES:

❑ A. CONVENTIONAL FINANCING:

❑ (1) A first mortgage loan in the principal amount of $ __________________ (excluding any financed PMI premium), due in full in _________ year(s), with interest not to exceed ______% per annum for the first ________year(s) of the loan with Loan Fees (loan origination, discount, buy-down, and commitment fees) not to exceed ________% of the loan.

❑ (2) A second mortgage loan in the principal amount of $__________________(excluding any financed PMI premium), due in full in ___________year(s), with interest not to exceed ______% per annum for the first ____________year(s) of the loan with Loan Fees (loan origination, discount, buy-down, and commitment fees) not to exceed ________% of the loan.

❑ B. TEXAS VETERANS LOAN: A loan(s) from the Texas Veterans Land Board of $_____________ for a period in the total amount of _____years at the interest rate established by the Texas Veterans Land Board.

❑ C. FHA INSURED FINANCING: A Section _________________ FHA insured loan of not less than $__________________ (excluding any financed MIP), amortizable monthly for not less than _______years, with interest not to exceed _______% per annum for the first ______year(s) of the loan with Loan Fees (loan origination, discount, buy-down, and commitment fees) not to exceed _________ % of the loan. As required by HUD-FHA, if FHA valuation is unknown, *"It is expressly agreed that, notwithstanding any other provision of this contract, the purchaser (Buyer) shall not be obligated to complete the purchase of the Property described herein or to incur any penalty by forfeiture of earnest money deposits or otherwise unless the purchaser (Buyer) has been given in accordance with HUD/FHA or VA requirements a written statement issued by the Federal Housing Commissioner, Department of Veterans Affairs, or a Direct Endorsement Lender setting forth the appraised value of the Property of not less than $__________________. The purchaser (Buyer) shall have the privilege and option of proceeding with consummation of the contract without regard to the amount of the*

____
(Address of Property)

appraised valuation. The appraised valuation is arrived at to determine the maximum mortgage the Department of Housing and Urban Development will insure. HUD does not warrant the value or the condition of the Property. The purchaser (Buyer) should satisfy himself/herself that the price and the condition of the Property are acceptable."
NOTE: HUD 92564-CN "For Your Protection: Get a Home Inspection" must be attached to this Addendum.

☒ D. VA GUARANTEED FINANCING: A VA guaranteed loan of not less than $ 62,400 (excluding any financed Funding Fee), amortizable monthly for not less than 30 years, with interest not to exceed 7.25 % per annum for the first 30 year(s) of the loan with Loan Fees (loan origination, discount, buy-down, and commitment fees) not to exceed 1 % of the loan.

VA NOTICE TO BUYER: "*It is expressly agreed that, notwithstanding any other provisions of this contract, the Buyer shall not incur any penalty by forfeiture of earnest money or otherwise or be obligated to complete the purchase of the Property described herein, if the contract purchase price or cost exceeds the reasonable value of the Property established by the Department of Veterans Affairs. The Buyer shall, however, have the privilege and option of proceeding with the consummation of this contract without regard to the amount of the reasonable value established by the Department of Veterans Affairs."*

If Buyer elects to complete the purchase at an amount in excess of the reasonable value established by VA, Buyer shall pay such excess amount in cash from a source which Buyer agrees to disclose to the VA and which Buyer represents will not be from borrowed funds except as approved by VA. If VA reasonable value of the Property is less than the Sales Price, Seller may reduce the Sales Price to an amount equal to the VA reasonable value and the sale will be closed at the lower Sales Price with proportionate adjustments to the down payment and the loan amount.

Buyer hereby authorizes any lender to furnish to the Seller or Buyer or their representatives information relating only to the status of Financing Approval of Buyer.

Buyer	Seller
Buyer	Seller

Scenario 7

Contract paragraph 3A. $28,000
3B. $130,000
3C. $158,000

4 ☐ A. $________
A(2). ☐ (a)
☐ (b)
☒ B.
☒ C. $30,000

12A(1)(b). $None or N/A

Scenario 7

PROMULGATED BY THE TEXAS REAL ESTATE COMMISSION (TREC) 04-23-07

EQUAL HOUSING OPPORTUNITY

LOAN ASSUMPTION ADDENDUM
TO CONTRACT CONCERNING THE PROPERTY AT

____
(Address of Property)

A. CREDIT DOCUMENTATION. To establish Buyer's creditworthiness, Buyer shall deliver to Seller within ___3___ days after the effective date of this contract ☒ credit report ☒ verification of employment, including salary ☒ verification of funds on deposit in financial institutions ☒ current financial statement and ☐ ______________________________.
Buyer hereby authorizes any credit reporting agency to furnish copies of Buyer's credit reports to Seller at Buyer's sole expense.

B. CREDIT APPROVAL. If the credit documentation described in Paragraph A is not delivered within the specified time, Seller may terminate this contract by notice to Buyer within 7 days after expiration of the time for delivery, and the earnest money will be paid to Seller. If the credit documentation is timely delivered, and Seller determines in Seller's sole discretion that Buyer's credit is unacceptable, Seller may terminate this contract by notice to Buyer within 7 days after expiration of the time for delivery and the earnest money will be refunded to Buyer. If Seller does not terminate this contract within the time specified, Seller will be deemed to have approved Buyer's creditworthiness.

C. ASSUMPTION. Buyer's assumption of an existing note includes all obligations imposed by the deed of trust securing the note.

☒ (1) The unpaid principal balance of a first lien promissory note payable to _Chase Manhattan Mortgage Company_ which unpaid balance at closing will be $ _100,000_. The total current monthly payment including principal, interest and any reserve deposits is $ _786_. Buyer's initial payment will be the first payment due after closing.

☐ (2) The unpaid principal balance of a second lien promissory note payable to ______________ ______________ which unpaid balance at closing will be $ ______________. The total current monthly payment including principal, interest and any reserve deposits is $ ______________. Buyer's initial payment will be the first payment due after closing.

If the unpaid principal balance of any assumed loan as of the Closing Date varies from the loan balance stated above, the ☒ cash payable at closing ☐ Sales Price will be adjusted by the amount of any variance. If the total principal balance of all assumed loans varies in an amount greater than $500 at closing, either party may terminate this contract and the earnest money will be refunded to Buyer unless the other party elects to pay the excess of the variance.

D. LOAN ASSUMPTION TERMS. Buyer may terminate this contract and the earnest money will be refunded to Buyer if the noteholder requires:

(1) payment of an assumption fee in excess of $ ________ in C(1) or $ ________ in C(2) and Seller declines to pay such excess, or

(2) an increase in the interest rate to more than ______% in C(1) or ______% in C(2), or

(3) any other modification of the loan documents.

E. CONSENT BY NOTEHOLDER. If the noteholder fails to consent to the assumption of the loan, either Seller or Buyer may terminate this contract by notice to the other party and the earnest money will be refunded to the Buyer.

F. SELLER'S LIENS. Unless Seller is released from liability on any assumed note, a vendor's lien and deed of trust to secure assumption will be required. The vendor's lien will automatically be

Initialed for identification by Buyer______________ and Seller___________ TREC NO. 41-1

Loan Assumption Addendum Concerning Page 2 of 2 04-23-07

____
(Address of Property)

released on delivery of an executed release by noteholder.

G. TAX AND INSURANCE ESCROW. If noteholder maintains an escrow account for ad valorem taxes, casualty insurance premiums or mortgage insurance premiums, Seller shall transfer the escrow account to Buyer without any deficiency. Buyer shall reimburse Seller for the amount in the transferred accounts.

NOTICE TO BUYER: If you are concerned about the possibility of future adjustments, monthly payments, interest rates or other terms, do not sign the contract without examining the notes and deeds of trust.

NOTICE TO SELLER: Your liability to pay the notes assumed by Buyer will continue unless you obtain a release of liability from the noteholders. If you are concerned about future liability, you should use the TREC Release of Liability Addendum.

Buyer	Seller
Buyer	Seller

This form has been approved by the Texas Real Estate Commission for use with similarly approved or promulgated contract forms. Such approval relates to this form only. TREC forms are intended for use only by trained real estate licensees. No representation is made as to the legal validity or adequacy of any provision in any specific transactions. It is not suitable for complex transactions. Texas Real Estate Commission, P.O. Box 12188, Austin, TX 78711-2188, 1-800-250-8732 or (512) 459-6544 (http://www.trec.state.tx.us) TREC No. 41-1. This form replaces TREC No. 41-0.

PROMULGATED BY THE TEXAS REAL ESTATE COMMISSION (TREC) 12-04-06

EQUAL HOUSING OPPORTUNITY

SELLER FINANCING ADDENDUM

TO CONTRACT CONCERNING THE PROPERTY AT

____

(Address of Property)

A. CREDIT DOCUMENTATION. To establish Buyer's creditworthiness, Buyer shall deliver to Seller within ___3___ days after the effective date of this contract, ☒ credit report ☒ verification of employment, including salary ☒ verification of funds on deposit in financial institutions ☒ current financial statement and ☐ ____.
Buyer hereby authorizes any credit reporting agency to furnish copies of Buyer's credit reports to Seller at Buyer's sole expense.

B. CREDIT APPROVAL. If the credit documentation described in Paragraph A is not delivered within the specified time, Seller may terminate this contract by notice to Buyer within 7 days after expiration of the time for delivery, and the earnest money will be paid to Seller. If the credit documentation is timely delivered, and Seller determines in Seller's sole discretion that Buyer's credit is unacceptable, Seller may terminate this contract by notice to Buyer within 7 days after expiration of the time for delivery and the earnest money will be refunded to Buyer. If Seller does not terminate this contract, Seller will be deemed to have approved Buyer's creditworthiness.

C. PROMISSORY NOTE. The promissory note (Note) described in Paragraph 4 of this contract payable by Buyer to the order of Seller will bear interest at the rate of ___7___% per annum and be payable at the place designated by Seller. Buyer may prepay the Note in whole or in part at any time without penalty. Any prepayments are to be applied to the payment of the installments of principal last maturing and interest will immediately cease on the prepaid principal. The Note will contain a provision for payment of a late fee of 5% of any installment not paid within 10 days of the due date. Matured unpaid amounts will bear interest at the rate of 1½% per month or at the highest lawful rate, whichever is less. The Note will be payable as follows:

☐ (1) In one payment due ______________________ after the date of the Note with interest payable ☐ at maturity ☐ monthly ☐ quarterly. (check one box only)

☒ (2) In monthly installments of $ ___500___ ☐ including interest ☒ plus interest (check one box only) beginning ___first of the month___ after the date of the Note and continuing monthly thereafter for ___60___ months when the balance of the Note will be due and payable.

☐ (3) Interest only in monthly installments for the first __________ month(s) and thereafter in installments of $______________ ☐ including interest ☐ plus interest (check one box only) beginning ________________ after the date of the Note and continuing monthly thereafter for ________ months when the balance of the Note will be due and payable.

D. DEED OF TRUST. The deed of trust securing the Note will provide for the following:

(1) PROPERTY TRANSFERS: (check one box only)

☐ (a) Consent Not Required: The Property may be sold, conveyed or leased without the consent of Seller, provided any subsequent buyer assumes the Note.

☒ (b) Consent Required: If all or any part of the Property is sold, conveyed, leased for a period longer than 3 years, leased with an option to purchase, or otherwise sold (including any contract for deed), without Seller's prior written consent, which consent may be withheld in Seller's sole discretion, Seller may declare the balance of the Note

Initialed for identification by Buyer____________ and Seller__________

Seller Financing Addendum Concerning Page 2 of 2 12-04-06

____
(Address of Property)

to be immediately due and payable. The creation of a subordinate lien, any conveyance under threat or order of condemnation, any deed solely between buyers, or the passage of title by reason of the death of a buyer or by operation of law will not entitle Seller to exercise the remedies provided in this paragraph.

NOTE: *Under (a) or (b), Buyer's liability to pay the Note will continue unless Buyer obtains a release of liability from Seller.*

(2) TAX AND INSURANCE ESCROW: (check one box only)

☐ (a) Escrow Not Required: Buyer shall furnish Seller, before each year's ad valorem taxes become delinquent, evidence that all ad valorem taxes on the Property have been paid. Buyer shall annually furnish Seller evidence of paid-up casualty insurance naming Seller as a mortgagee loss payee.

☒ (b) Escrow Required: With each installment Buyer shall deposit in escrow with Seller a pro rata part of the estimated annual ad valorem taxes and casualty insurance premiums for the Property. Buyer shall pay any deficiency within 30 days after notice from Seller. Buyer's failure to pay the deficiency will be a default under the deed of trust. Buyer is not required to deposit any escrow payments for taxes and insurance that are deposited with a superior lienholder. The casualty insurance must name Seller as a mortgagee loss payee.

(3) PRIOR LIENS: Any default under any lien superior to the lien securing the Note will be a default under the deed of trust securing the Note.

______________________ ______________________
Buyer Seller

______________________ ______________________
Buyer Seller

The form of this contract has been approved by the Texas Real Estate Commission for use with similarly approved or promulgated contract forms. TREC forms are intended for use only by trained real estate licensees. No representation is made as to the legal validity or adequacy of any provision in any specific transactions. It is not intended for complex transactions. Texas Real Estate Commission, P.O. Box 12188, Austin, TX 78711-2188, 1-800-250-8732 or (512) 459-6544 (http://www.trec.state.tx.us) TREC No. 26-5. This form replaces TREC No. 26-4.

TREC NO. 26-5

Chapter 7

1. d
2. d
3. c
4. b
5. b
6. b
7. a
8. b
9. a
10. b

Chapter 8

1. 20 days, paragraph 6B
2. 15 days, paragraph 6D
3. 3 days, paragraph 6C (1)
4. As agreed, paragraph 5
5. 7 days, paragraph 7B (2)
6. 7 days, paragraph 9A
7. 15 days, paragraph 14
8. As agreed, paragraph 6C (3)
9. As agreed, paragraph 6C (2)
10. 15 days, paragraph 18C
    Exercise: Help for Sarah
    – June 28
11. As agreed, paragraph 23
12. As agreed, paragraph 6D

Chapter 9

1. b
2. d
3. d
4. c
5. b
6. d
7. b
8. b
9. b
10. a

Chapter 10

1. b
2. c
3. b
4. c
5. a

Chapter 11

Transaction 1

Page 1 of 8

1.	Seller:	Isabelle Gertrude Gerhard, a single person	
	Buyer:	John Paul Gordon and wife Mary Anne Gordon	
2.	A.	Lot:	6
		Block:	10
		Addition:	Section 1 of Windswept
		City:	Houston
		County:	Harris
		Address:	2615 Pleasure Point Drive 77084
	D.	Exclusions:	draperies in the master bedroom
3.	A. Cash portion:		$19,200
	B. Sum of financing:		$76,800
	C. Sales Price:		$96,000

4. Check box A: ☒ A.

   Total loans (same as 3B): $76,800

   Check box (2)(a): ☒ (a)

5. Earnest money: $10,000

   Escrow agent: No Cloud Title Company

   Address: 1700 South Main, Houston, TX 77001

   Additional earnest money: N/A

   Days for additional earnest money: N/A

6. Check Seller's box: ☒ Seller's

   Issued by: No Cloud Title Company

Page 2 of 8

Enter address at top of page: 2615 Pleasure Point Drive, Houston, TX 77084

6. continued . . .

   C. Check box (2): ☒ (2)

   Number of days: 20

   D. Prohibited uses: None

   Days to object: 9

   E(2) Check box "is": ☒ is

Page 3 of 8

Enter address at top of page: 2615 Pleasure Point Drive, Houston, TX 77084

7. B. Check box (1): ☒ (1)

   D. Repairs: None

Page 4 of 8

Enter address at top of page: 2615 Pleasure Point Drive, Houston, TX 77084

7. continued . . .

   H. Amount: N/A

9. A. Closing: Enter a date 30 days from today

10. Possession: ☒ upon closing and funding

11. Special provisions: None

Page 5 of 8
Enter address at top of page: 2615 Pleasure Point Drive, Houston, TX 77084

12. A(1)(b): None
16. Check "will": ☒ will

Page 6 of 8
Enter address at top of page: 2615 Pleasure Point Drive, Houston, TX 77084

21. Addresses, telephone, facsimile, and e-mails are to be provided by student.

Page 7 of 8
Enter address at top of page: 2615 Pleasure Point Drive, Houston, TX 77084

22. Check the following addenda:

    ☒ Third Party Financing Condition Addenda

    ☒ Addendum for Property Subject to Mandatory Membership in an Owner's Association

    ☒ Environmental Assessment, Threatened or Endangered Species and Wetlands Addendum

23. Option fee: $300

    Option days: 7

    Option fee: ☒ will

24. Buyer's attorney: None chosen at this time

    Seller's attorney: None chosen at this time

Page 8 of 8
Enter address at top of page: 2615 Pleasure Point Drive, Houston, TX 77084

Broker Information and Ratification of Fee

Listing broker will pay other broker 3% of the total Sales Price.

Other broker: Buyer's Broker Realty License No. 1234567

Represents: ☒ Buyer only as Buyer's agent

Listing broker: Smooth Sales Realty Company License No. 7657321

Represents: ☒ Seller only as Seller's agent

Names of associates, telephone numbers, addresses, facsimiles, and e-mails are to be provided by the student.

Option Fee Receipt

Amount: $300

In form of: personal check #4567

Date: today's date

Contract and Earnest Money Receipt

Check box for contract: ☒ Contract

Earnest money: $10,000

In form of: personal check # 4566

Escrow agent: No Cloud Title Company

Addresses, telephone, facsimile, and e-mails are to be provided by student.

Transaction 2

Page 1 of 8

1. Seller: Thomas Arnold Smith and wife Molly Bea Smith

   Buyer: John Charles Wayne and wife Sharon Sidekick Wayne

2. A. Lot: 7

   Block: 7

   Addition: Shady Acres

   City: Bellaire

   County: Harris

   Address: 3510 Mimosa Lane 77404

   D. Exclusions: None

3. A. Cash portion: $18,000

   B. Sum of financing: $162,000

   C. Sales Price: $180,000

4. Check box A: ☒ A.

   Total loans (same as 3B): $162,000

   Check box (2)(a): ☒ (a)

5. Earnest money: $4,000

   Escrow agent: Protective Title Company

	Address:		2000 West Road, Houston, TX 77087
	Additional earnest money:		$4,000
	Days for additional earnest money:		30
6.	Check Seller's box:		☒ Seller's
	Issued by:		Protective Title Company

Page 2 of 8

Enter address at top of page: 510 Mimosa Lane, Bellaire, TX 77404

6. continued . . .

C.	Check box (1):	☒ (1)
	Number of days:	3
	Check box	☒ Buyer's expense
D.	Prohibited uses:	NA
	Days to object:	7
E(2)	Check box "is":	☒ is

Page 3 of 8

Enter address at top of page: 510 Mimosa Lane, Bellaire, TX 77404

7.	B.	Check box (1):	☒ (1)
	D.	Repairs:	None

Page 4 of 8

Enter address at top of page: 510 Mimosa Lane, Bellaire, TX 77404

7. continued . . .

	H.	Amount:	$325.00
9.	A.	Closing:	Enter a date 40 days from today
10.	Possession:		☒ upon closing and funding
11.	Special provisions:		A. Buyers may do a walk-through during the four hours prior to closing. B. End of special provisions

Page 5 of 8

Enter address at top of page: 510 Mimosa Lane, Bellaire, TX 77404

12. A(1)(b) $810.00

16. Check "will": ☒ will

Page 6 of 8

Enter address at top of page: 510 Mimosa Lane, Bellaire, TX 77404

21. Addresses, telephone, facsimile, and e-mails are to be provided by student.

Page 7 of 8

Enter address at top of page: 510 Mimosa Lane, Bellaire, TX 77404

22. Check the following addenda:

    ☒ Third Party Financing Condition Addenda

    ☒ Addendum for Seller's Disclosure of Information on Lead-based Paint and Lead-based Paint Hazards as Required by Federal Law

23. Option fee: $400

    Option days: 10

    Option fee: ☒ will

24. Buyer's attorney: None chosen at this time

    Seller's attorney: None chosen at this time

Page 8 of 8

Enter address at top of page: 510 Mimosa Lane, Bellaire, TX 77404

Broker Information and Ratification of Fee

Listing broker will pay other broker N/A of the total Sales Price.

Other broker: N/A License No. N/A

Listing broker: Sarah Listalot License No. 0234567

Represents: ☒ Seller only as Seller's agent

Names of associates, telephone numbers, addresses, facsimiles, and e-mails are to be provided by the student.

Option Fee Receipt

Amount: $400

In form of: personal check #787

Date: today's date

Contract and Earnest Money Receipt

Check box for contract: ☒ Contract

Earnest money: $4,000

In form of: personal check #788

Escrow agent: Protective Title Company

Addresses, telephone, facsimile, and e-mails are to be provided by student.

Transaction 3

Page 1 of 8

1. Seller: Susan Helen Seller, a single person

   Buyer: Henry Arnold Homebuyer and wife Hanna Sue Homebuyer

2. A. Lot: N/A

   Block: N/A

   Addition: See attached metes-and-bounds description exhibit "A"

   City: N/A

   County: Harrison

   Address: 42 Pleasure Lake Drive, Podunk 77072

   D. Exclusions: Water softener and security system

3. A. Cash portion: $25,200

   B. Sum of financing: $100,800

   C. Sales Price: $126,000

4. Check box A: ☒ A.

   Total loans (same as 3B): $100,800

   Check box (2)(a): ☒ (a)

5. Earnest money: $1,500

   Escrow agent: Buyer's Choice Title Company

   Address: 1910 West Drive, Podunk, TX 77072

   Additional earnest money: N/A

   Days for additional earnest money: N/A

6.	Check Buyer's box:	☒ Buyer's
	Issued by:	Buyer's Choice Title Company

Page 2 of 8
Enter address at top of page: 42 Pleasure Lake Drive, Podunk 77072

6. continued . . .

C.	Check box (2):	☒ (2)
	Number of days:	15
D.	Prohibited uses:	None
	Days to object:	7
E.(2)	Check box "is not":	☒ is not

Page 3 of 8
Enter address at top of page: 42 Pleasure Lake Drive, Podunk 77072

7.	B.	Check box (1):	☒ (1)
	D.	Repairs:	Repair the septic system and bring it up to current county code

Page 4 of 8
Enter address at top of page: 42 Pleasure Lake Drive, Podunk 77072

7. continued . . .

	H.	Amount:	N/A
9.	A.	Closing:	Enter a date 30 days from today
10.	Possession:		☒ upon closing and funding
11.	Special provisions:		A. Seller to provide a county inspection certificate on the septic system B. End of special provisions

Page 5 of 8
Enter address at top of page: 42 Pleasure Lake Drive, Podunk 77072

12.	A(1)(b):	N/A
16.	Check "will":	☒ will

Page 6 of 8

Enter address at top of page: 42 Pleasure Lake Drive, Podunk 77072

21. Addresses, telephone, facsimile, and e-mails are to be provided by student.

Page 7 of 8

Enter address at top of page: 42 Pleasure Lake Drive, Podunk 77072

22. Check the following addenda:

    ☒ Third Party Financing Condition Addenda

23. Option fee: N/A

    Option days: N/A

24. Buyer's attorney: Michael Phelps
    2225 High Street
    Podunk, TX 77071

    Student to provide telephone, facsimile, and e-mail.

    Seller's attorney: None chosen at this time

Page 8 of 8

Enter address at top of page: 42 Pleasure Lake Drive, Podunk 77072

Broker Information and Ratification of Fee

Listing broker will pay other broker 3.5% of the total Sales Price.

Other broker: Happy Buyer Realty License No. 0234567

Represents: ☒ Seller as listing broker's subagent

Listing broker: Seller's Choice Realty Services License No. 0654321

Represents: ☒ Seller only as Seller's agent

Names of Associates, telephone numbers, addresses, facsimiles, and e-mails are to be provided by the student.

Option Fee Receipt

Amount: N/A

In form of: N/A

Date: N/A

Contract and Earnest Money Receipt

Check box for contract: ☒ Contract

Earnest money: $1,500

In form of: personal check #1245

Escrow agent: Buyer's Choice Title Company

Addresses, telephone, facsimile, and e-mails are to be provided by student.

Transaction 4

Page 1 of 8

1. Seller: Freddie Mac, a single person

   Buyer: Victor Vet and wife Victoria Vet

2. A. Lot: 64

   Block: 83

   Addition: Section 2 of Friendly Hills

   City: Austin

   County: Travis

   Address: 2365 Veterans Boulevard 78711

   D. Exclusions: None

3. A. Cash portion: $15,600

   B. Sum of financing: $62,400

   C. Sales Price: $78,000

4. Check box A: ☒ A.

   Total loans (same as 3B): $62,400

   Check box (2)(a): ☒ (a)

5. Earnest money: $1,000

   Escrow agent: Buyer's Choice Title Company

   Address: 2698 Texas Street, Austin, TX 78711

   Additional earnest money: N/A

   Days for additional earnest money: N/A

6. Check Seller's box: ☒ Seller's

   Issued by: Buyer's Choice Title Company

Page 2 of 8

Enter address at top of page: 2365 Veterans Boulevard, Austin 78711

6. continued . . .

	C.	Check box (3):	☒ (3)
		Number of days:	10
	D.	Prohibited uses:	None
		Days to object:	3
	E(2).	Check box "is":	☒ is

Page 3 of 8

Enter address at top of page: 2365 Veterans Boulevard, Austin 78711

7.	B.	Check box (2):	☒ (2)
		Days to deliver:	3
	D.	Repairs:	None

Page 4 of 8

Enter address at top of page: 2365 Veterans Boulevard, Austin 78711

7. continued . . .

	H.	Amount:	N/A
9.	A.	Closing:	October 20, current year
10.	Possession:		☒ according to a temporary residential lease form
11.	Special provisions:		None

Page 5 of 8

Enter address at top of page: 2365 Veterans Boulevard, Austin 78711

12.	A(1)(b):	$1,100
16.	Check "will":	☒ will

Page 6 of 8

Enter address at top of page: 2365 Veterans Boulevard, Austin 78711

21. Addresses, telephone, facsimile, and e-mails are to be provided by student.

Page 7 of 8
Enter address at top of page: 2365 Veterans Boulevard, Austin 78711

22. Check the following addenda:

    ☒ Third Party Financing Condition Addenda

    ☒ Seller's Temporary Residential Lease

    ☒ Addendum for Sale of Other Property by Buyer

    ☒ Addendum for Seller's Disclosure of Information on Lead-based Paint and Lead-based Paint Hazards as Required by Federal Law

23. Option fee: $200

    Option days: 8

    Option fee: ☒ will

24. Buyer's attorney: None chosen at this time

    Seller's attorney: None chosen at this time

Page 8 of 8
Enter address at top of page: 2365 Veterans Boulevard, Austin 78711

Broker Information and Ratification of Fee

Listing broker will pay other broker 2.75% of the total Sales Price.

Other broker: Peter Finch Realty License No. 0487234

Represents: ☒ Seller as listing broker's subagent

Listing broker: Friendly Agent Company License No. 0654321

Represents: ☒ Seller only as Seller's agent

Names of associates, telephone numbers, addresses, facsimiles, and e-mails are to be provided by the student.

Option Fee Receipt

Amount: $200

In form of: cash

Date: today's date

Contract and Earnest Money Receipt

Check box for contract: ☒ Contract

Earnest money: $1,000

In form of: personal check #2355

Escrow agent: Buyer's Choice Title Company

Addresses, telephone, facsimile, and e-mails are to be provided by student.

Transaction 5

Page 1 of 8

1. Seller: Samuel Jay Johnson, a single person
   Buyer: Thomas J. Swanson and wife Sarah J. Swanson
2. A. Lot: 6
   Block: 8
   Addition: Happily-Ever-After
   City: Waco
   County: McLennan
   Address: 15630 Paradise Avenue 76710
   D. Exclusions: None
3. A. Cash portion: $48,500
   B. Sum of financing: $25,000
   C. Sales Price: $73,500
4. Check box C: ☒ C.
   Loan amount: $25,000
5. Earnest money: $2,000
   Escrow agent: Secure Title Company
   Address: 7000 West Road, Waco, TX 76710
   Additional earnest money: N/A
   Days for additional earnest money: N/A
6. Check Seller's box: ☒ Seller's
   Issued by: Secure Title Company

Page 2 of 8
Enter address at top of page: 15630 Paradise Avenue, Waco 76710

6. continued . . .

C.	Check box (3):	☒ (3)
	Number of days:	10
D.	Prohibited uses:	N/A
	Days to object:	10
E(2).	Check box "is not":	☒ is not

Page 3 of 8
Enter address at top of page: 15630 Paradise Avenue, Waco 76710

7.	B.	Check box (1):	☒ (1)
	D.	Repairs:	None

Page 4 of 8
Enter address at top of page: 15630 Paradise Avenue, Waco 76710

7. continued . . .

	H.	Amount:	N/A
9.	A.	Closing:	May 27, current year
10.	Possession:		☒ upon closing and funding
11.	Special provisions:		A. Buyer to pay additional premium for deletion of exception #8 in paragraph 6A B. End of special provisions

Page 5 of 8
Enter address at top of page: 15630 Paradise Avenue, Waco 76710

12.	A(1)(b):	N/A
16.	Check "will":	☒ will

Page 6 of 8
Enter address at top of page: 15630 Paradise Avenue, Waco 76710

21. Addresses, telephone, facsimile, and e-mails are to be provided by student.

Page 7 of 8

Enter address at top of page: 15630 Paradise Avenue, Waco 76710

22. Check the following addenda:

 ☒ Seller Financing Addendum

 ☒ Environmental Assessment, Threatened or Endangered Species and Wetlands Addendum

23. Option fee: $150

 Option days: 10

 Option fee: ☒ will not

24. Buyer's attorney: None chosen at this time

 Seller's attorney: None chosen at this time

Page 8 of 8

Enter address at top of page: 15630 Paradise Avenue, Waco 76710

Broker Information and Ratification of Fee

Listing broker will pay other broker N/A of the total Sales Price.

Other broker: N/A License No. N/A

Listing broker: Smooth Sails Realty Company License No. 0234567

Represents: ☒ Seller only as Seller's agent

Names of associates, telephone numbers, addresses, facsimiles, and e-mails are to be provided by the student.

Option Fee Receipt

Amount: $150

In form of: personal check #123

Date: today's date

Contract and Earnest Money Receipt

Check box for contract: ☒ Contract

Earnest money: $2,000

In form of: personal check #122

Escrow agent: Secure Title Company

Addresses, telephone, facsimile, and e-mails are to be provided by student.

Transaction 6

Page 1 of 9

1. Seller: Fannie Phyllis Farmer, a single person
   Buyer: William Robert Richman and wife Mae Bea Richman
2. A. County: Pecos
   Described: See attached metes and bounds property description "Exhibit A"
   Known as: 2520 Farmer Road, Pecos, TX 78789
   E. Exclusions: None
   F. Reservations: 50% of oil and gas interests.
3. A. Cash portion: $895,000
   B. Sum of financing: $-0-
   C. Sales Price: $895,000
   D. Sales Price: ☒ will be adjusted
   Adjustment: $2,500 per acre
   Notice within 10 days
   Adjustments to: ☒ 3A

Page 2 of 9
Enter address at top of page: 2520 Farmer Road, Pecos, TX 78789

5. Earnest money: $100,000
   Escrow agent: Pecos County Abstract Company
   Address: 800 Main Street, Pecos, TX 70180
   Additional earnest money: N/A
   Days for additional earnest money: N/A
6. A. Issued by: N/A

Page 3 of 9
Enter address at top of page: 2520 Farmer Road, Pecos, TX 78789

6. continued . . .
   C. Check box (3): ☒ (3)
   Number of days: 20

D. Prohibited uses: N/A

Days to object: 7

E. Exception documents: N/A

F. Surface leases: N/A

Page 4 of 9

Enter address at top of page: 2520 Farmer Road, Pecos, TX 78789

6. continued . . .

G(7). Check "is not" : ☒ is not

7. B. Check box (1): ☒ (1)

D. Repairs: N/A

Page 5 of 9

Enter address at top of page: 2520 Farmer Road, Pecos, TX 78789

7. continued . . .

I. Residential Service Contract: N/A

J. Government Programs: N/A

9. A. Closing: December 23, current year

10. Possession: ☒ upon closing and funding

Special provisions: A. Seller is to provide buyer an abstract within 30 days after the effective date of this contract. B. End of special provisions

Page 6 of 9

Enter address at top of page: 2520 Farmer Road, Pecos, TX 78789

12. A(1)(b): NA

Page 7 of 9

Enter address at top of page: 2520 Farmer Road, Pecos, TX 78789

16. Check "will": ☒ will

21. Addresses, telephone, facsimile, and e-mails are to be provided by student.

Page 8 of 8
Enter address at top of page: 2520 Farmer Road, Pecos, TX 78789

22. Check the following addenda:

☒ Addendum for Seller's Disclosure of Information on Lead-based Paint and Lead-based Paint Hazards as Required by Federal Law

☒ Environmental Assessment, Threatened or Endangered Species and Wetlands Addendum

23. Option fee: N/A

Option days: N/A

24. Buyer's attorney: Ronald Hawkeye Redundant

Student to supply address, telephone, facsimile, and e-mail.

Seller's attorney: None chosen at this time

Page 9 of 9
Enter address at top of page: 2520 Farmer Road, Pecos, TX 78789

Ratification of fee: $10,000

Broker Information and Agreement for Payment of Broker's Fee

Other broker: Richard Hutchinson License No. 0234567

Represents: ☒ Buyer only as Buyer's agent

Listing broker: Hilton Charles License No. 0127643

Represents: ☒ Seller only

Names of associates, telephone numbers, addresses, facsimiles, and e-mails are to be provided by the student.

Option Fee Receipt

Option fee: N/A

In form of: N/A

Contract and Earnest Money Receipt

Check box for contract: ☒ Contract

Earnest money: $100,000

In form of: Check #1234

Escrow agent: Pecos Abstract Company

Addresses, telephone, facsimile, and e-mails are to be provided by student.

Transaction 7

Page 1 of 8

1. Seller: Peter Paul Pastor and wife Sarah Sue Pastor
   Buyer: Bernie Bryan Buyer and wife Beverly Barbara Buyer
2. A. Unit: 623
   Building: B
   Project: Freedom Flats Phase II
   City: Corpus Christi
   County: Nueces
   Parking: 1654 and 1658
   Address: 1215 Market Street, Apartment 623, 78411
   Exclusions: None
   B. Declaration: Check box (1) ☒ (1)
   C. Resale certificate: Check box (1) ☒ (1)
3. A. Cash portion: $103,192
   B. Sum of financing: $265,008
   C. Sales Price: $368,200

Page 2 of 8
Enter address at top of page: 1215 Market Street, Apartment 623, Corpus Christi 78411

4. Check box B: ☒ B.
5. Earnest money: $2,000
   Escrow agent: Buyer's Choice Title Company
   Address: 301 Seafront Drive, Corpus Christi, 78411
   Additional earnest money: N/A
   Days for additional earnest money: N/A
6. Check Buyer's box: ☒ Buyer's
   Issued by: Buyer's Choice Title Company
   C. Prohibited uses: None
   Days to object: 5

Page 3 of 8

Enter address at top of page: 1215 Market Street, Apartment 623, Corpus Christi 78411

7. B. Check box (1): ☒ (1)

   D. Repairs: Replace garbage disposal in kitchen and broken faucet in bathroom

Page 4 of 8

Enter address at top of page: 1215 Market Street, Apartment 623, Corpus Christi 78411

7. continued . . .

   H. Amount: N/A

9. A. Closing: June 16, current year

10. Possession: ☒ upon closing and funding

11. Special provisions: A. Seller will deliver a copy of the note and deed of trust to buyer within 3 days of the effective date of this contract.
    B. Copies of all other documents Buyer will sign at closing will be delivered to Buyer at least 48 hours prior to closing.

12. A(1)(b): None

Page 5 of 8

Enter address at top of page: 1215 Market Street, Apartment 623, Corpus Christi 78411

   12(3) Association transfer fee paid by: ☒ Buyer

16. Check "will": ☒ will

Page 6 of 8

Enter address at top of page: 1215 Market Street, Apartment 623, Corpus Christi 78411

21. Addresses, telephone, facsimile, and e-mails are to be provided by student.

Page 7 of 8

Enter address at top of page: 1215 Market Street, Apartment 623, Corpus Christi 78411

22. Check the following addenda:

    ☒ Loan Assumption Addendum

    ☒ Addendum for "Back-up" Contract

    ☒ Addendum for Property Located Seaward of the Gulf Intracoastal Waterway

    ☒ Addendum for Coastal Area Property

    ☒ Addendum for Release of Liability on Assumption of FHA, VA, or Conventional Loan Restoration of Seller's Entitlement for VA Guaranteed Loan

23. Option fee: N/A

    Option days: N/A

24. Buyer's attorney: None chosen at this time

    Seller's attorney: Michael Holmes

    Student is to provide telephone, facsimile, and e-mail.

Page 8 of 8

Enter address at top of page: 1215 Market Street, Apartment 623, Corpus Christi 78411

Broker Information and Ratification of Fee

Listing broker will pay other broker 3.25% of the total Sales Price.

Other broker: Downhome Realty License No. 0234567

Represents: ☒ Seller as listing broker's subagent

Listing broker: Skyline Realty License No. 0379428

Represents: ☒ Seller only as Seller's agent

Names of associates, telephone numbers, addresses, facsimiles, and e-mails are to be provided by the student.

Option Fee Receipt

Amount: N/A

In form of: N/A

Contract and Earnest Money Receipt

Check box for contract: ☒ Contract

Earnest money: $2,000

In form of: personal check #1776

Escrow agent: Buyer's Choice Title Company

Addresses, telephone, facsimile, and e-mails are to be provided by student.

Transaction 8

Page 1 of 8

1. Seller: Russell Alan Janes and wife Anna Marie Janes
   Buyer: Peter Paul Prospect and wife Pricilla Bea Prospect
2. A. Lot: 6
   Block: 6
   Addition: Section 2 of Sandy Dunes
   City: N/A
   County: Galveston
   Address: 12656 Rolling Waves Lane, Galveston 77573
   D. Exclusions: leased security system
3. A. Cash portion: $38,800
   B. Sum of financing: $349,000
   C. Sales Price: $387,800
4. Check box A: ☒ A.
   Total loans (same as 3B): $349,000
   Check box (2)(a): ☒ (a)
5. Earnest money: $25,000
   Escrow agent: Buyer's Choice Title Company
   Address: 200 Seaview Drive, Galveston, TX 77573
   Additional earnest money: N/A
   Days for additional earnest money: N/A
6. Check Seller's box: ☒ Seller's
   Issued by: Buyer's Choice Title Company

Page 2 of 8

Enter address at top of page: 12656 Rolling Waves Lane, Galveston 77573

6. continued . . .

C.	Check box (2):	☒ (2)
	Number of days:	10
D.	Prohibited uses:	N/A
	Days to object:	2
E(2).	Check box "is":	☒ is

Page 3 of 8

Enter address at top of page: 12656 Rolling Waves Lane, Galveston 77573

7. B. Check box (1): ☒ (1)

 D. Repairs: None

Page 4 of 8

Enter address at top of page: 12656 Rolling Waves Lane, Galveston 77573

7. continued . . .

 H. Amount: N/A

9. A. Closing: April 4, current year

10. Possession: ☒ upon closing and funding

11. Special provisions: A. Seller is to leave bedspread that matches the drapes in the master bedroom.
B. Buyer is to pay $100 homeowners' association transfer fee.
C. All closing documents will be available to Buyer 48 hours prior to closing.
D. Buyers may do a walk-through in the 4 hours prior to closing.
E. The leased security system is to be removed prior to closing.

Page 5 of 8

Enter address at top of page: 12656 Rolling Waves Lane, Galveston 77573

12. A(1)(b): N/A

16. Check "will": ☒ will

Page 6 of 8

Enter address at top of page: 12656 Rolling Waves Lane, Galveston 77573

21. Addresses, telephone, facsimile, and e-mails are to be provided by student.

Page 7 of 8

Enter address at top of page: 12656 Rolling Waves Lane, Galveston 77573

22. Check the following addenda:

    ☒ Third Party Financing Condition Addendum

    ☒ Addendum for Property Subject to Mandatory Membership in an Owner's Association

    ☒ Environmental Assessment, Threatened or Endangered Species and Wetlands Addendum

    ☒ Addendum for Coastal Area Property

    ☒ Addendum for Property Located Seaward of the Gulf Intracoastal Waterway

23. Option fee: $500

    Option days: 5

    Option fee: ☒ will

24. Buyer's attorney: Rachel Review

    Student to provide address, telephone, facsimile, and e-mail.

    Seller's attorney: None chosen at this time

Page 8 of 8

Enter address at top of page: 12656 Rolling Waves Lane, Galveston 77573

Broker Information and Ratification of Fee

Listing broker will pay other broker N/A of the total Sales Price.

Other broker: N/A License No. N/A

Listing broker: Smooth Sales Realty Company License No. 0987654

Represents: ☒ Seller and Buyer as Intermediary

Names of associates, telephone numbers, addresses, facsimiles, and e-mails are to be provided by the student.

Option Fee Receipt

Amount: $500

In form of: personal check #1432

Date: today's date

Contract and Earnest Money Receipt

Check box for contract: ☒ Contract

Earnest money: $25,000

In form of: personal check #1431

Escrow agent: Buyer's Choice Title Company

Addresses, telephone, facsimile, and e-mails are to be provided by student.

Transaction 9

NOTE: CORRECTIONS ARE IN BOLD.

Page 1 of 8

1. Seller: Carol Anne Porter, **a single person**

   Buyer: Mary Ying Chow **and husband** Charles Yang Chow

2. A. Lot: 128

   Block: 17

   Addition: Section 4 of Shady Hills

   City: Lakeview

   County: Smith

   Address: 12690 Pinehall Court, 76544

   D. Exclusions: **None**

3. A. Cash portion: $20,000

   B. Sum of financing: $280,000

   C. Sales Price: $300,000

4. Check box A: ☒ A.

   Total loans (same as 3.B.): $280,000

   Check box (2)(a): ☒ (a)

5. Earnest money: $1,000

   Escrow agent: Safe and Secure Title Company

   Address: 2800 South Island Drive, Suite 250
Lakeview, TX 76544

Additional earnest money: $5,000

Days for additional earnest money: 10

6. Check Seller's box: ☒ Seller's

Issued by: No Cloud Title Company

Page 2 of 8

Enter address at top of page: 12690 Pinehall Court, Lakeview, TX 76544

6. continued . . .

C. Check box (1): ☒ (1)

Number of days: 5

New survey paid by: **Seller or Buyer**

D. Prohibited uses: Late night Tupperware parties

Days to object: 7

E(2). **Check box "is" or "is not"**

Page 3 of 8

Enter address at top of page: 12690 Pinehall Court, Lakeview, TX 76544

7. B. **Check box (1): ☒ (1)**

D. Repairs: **None**

Page 4 of 8

Enter address at top of page: 12690 Pinehall Court, Lakeview, TX 76544

7. continued . . .

H. Amount: $500

9. A. Closing: September 22, current year

10. Possession: ☒ upon closing and funding

11. Special provisions:

A. REMOVE. This should be in a cover letter and referred to as an offer.

B. REMOVE. Agents should not structure "subject to" provisions.

C. REMOVE. Provision is unclear and in the Seller's temporary lease.

D. REMOVE. Use the Seller's temporary residential lease.

E. REMOVE. Addressed in Paragraph 23.

ADD: Seller to leave swing set in the backyard.

ADD: Mary Ying Chow holds a Texas real estate broker's license.

Page 5 of 8
Enter address at top of page: 12690 Pinehall Court, Lakeview, TX 76544

12. A(1)(b): **Enter some specific amount**
16. Check "will not": ☒ will not

Page 6 of 8
Enter address at top of page: 12690 Pinehall Court, Lakeview, TX 76544

Page 7 of 8
Enter address at top of page: 12690 Pinehall Court, Lakeview, TX 76544

23. Option fee: $1,000
    Option days: 5 **Remove the word "working"**
    Option fee: ☒ will not
24. Buyer's attorney: None chosen at this time
    Seller's attorney: None chosen at this time
    The effective date should not be filled in at this time.

Page 8 of 8
Enter address at top of page: 12690 Pinehall Court, Lakeview, TX 76544

Broker Information and Ratification of Fee

Listing broker will pay other broker 3.5% of the total Sales Price.

Other broker: Mary Ying Chow License No. 0346531

Represents: ☒ **Buyer only as Buyer's agent**

Listing broker: Lakeview Realty License No. 0165996

Represents: ☒ **Seller only as Seller's agent**

Names of Associates, telephone numbers, addresses, facsimiles, and e-mails are to be provided by the student.

Option Fee Receipt

Amount: **$1,000**

In form of: **personal check #456**

Date: today's date

Contract and Earnest Money Receipt

Check box for contract: ☒ Contract

Earnest money: $1,000

In form of: personal check # 457

Escrow agent: Safe and Secure Title Company

Addresses, telephone, facsimile, and e-mails are to be provided by student.

Appendix A Contract Content Review

1. 15 [6D]
2. 20 [6B]
3. 3 [6C(1)]
4. 7 [9]
5. 7 [7B(2)]
6. Origination, discount, buy-down, commitment [12A(2)(a)]
7. 15 [14]
8. Yes [9C]
9. Seller [13]
10. 15 [18]
11. No
12. The Texas Broker-Lawyer Committee
13. 6
14. Before signing the contract [24]
15. Amount of fee, number of days [23]
16. At midnight on the 22nd [16, 17, 18, 19, 20, 21, 22]
17. 1978 [7C]
18. At reasonable times [7A]
19. Broker [In space provided immediately above signature lines for Buyer and Seller]
20. As agreed by the parties [6A]
21. 5% [7E]
22. Persons licensed or otherwise authorized by law to provide such repairs or treatments [7F]
23. Yes [7F]
24. 90 days [TREC Form 15-3 or TREC Form 16-3]
25. General Warranty Deed [9B(1)]
26. Costs will be shared equally [16]
27. In separate agreements between the parties and their brokers [8]
28. In good funds acceptable to the escrow agent [9B(2)]
29. The Seller [12A(1)]
30. The Buyer [12B]
31. Land, improvements, accessories [2]
32. Section number [2A]
33. Termination Option [23]
34. Yes–15 days [6B]
35. An attorney of the Buyer's choice [6E(1)]
36. 7D
37. Yes [7F]
38. Neither party [7E]
39. A credit at closing for the amount of the deductible under the insurance policy [14]
40. No, acceptance of earnest money releases both parties from the obligations of the contract [15]
41. No [16]
42. No [18]
43. No, the parties must make an election [23]
44. No, it is an unrestricted right to terminate [23]
45. There is no option [23]
46. Consult an attorney prior to signing [24]
47. No [6A(8)]
48. Section 5.001 of the Texas Property Code requires the Seller to tell the Buyer to investigate [6E(5)]
49. Chapter 49, Texas Water Code [6E(3)]
50. The Buyer [TREC Form 26-5]

Practice Exam

1. a
2. b
3. b
4. d
5. c
6. b
7. b
8. b
9. a
10. b
11. c
12. b
13. a
14. a
15. d
16. a
17. c
18. b
19. a
20. c
21. c
22. a
23. b
24. b
25. b
26. d
27. b
28. a
29. b
30. a
31. a
32. a
33. d
34. a
35. b
36. a
37. a
38. d
39. b
40. d
41. b
42. d
43. b
44. b
45. b
46. b
47. c
48. b
49. b
50. b
51. c
52. a

Uniform Settlement Statement

A. Settlement Statement — **U.S. Department of Housing and Urban Development** — OMB Approval No. 2502-0265

B. Type of Loan	6. File Number:	7. Loan Number:	8. Mortgage Insurance Case Number:
1. ☐ FHA 2. ☐ FmHA 3. ☐ Conv. Unins. 4. ☐ VA 5. ☒ Conv. Ins.			

C. Note: This form is furnished to give you a statement of actual settlement costs. Amounts paid to and by the settlement agent are shown. Items marked "(p.o.c.)" were paid outside the closing; they are shown here for informational purposes and are not included in the totals.

D. Name & Address of Borrower: 232-36-3775	E. Name & Address of Seller: 492-56-6667	F. Name & Address of Lender:
Peter Paul Prospect, et ux Priscilla Bea Prospect 654 Broadway Galveston	Russell Alan James, et ux Anna Marie James 12656 Rolling Waves Lane Galveston	Deep Pocket Mortgage Company 6000 Money Lane Galveston, Texas

G. Property Location:	H. Settlement Agent:	
12656 Rolling Waves Lane Galveston, Texas 77573	Buyer's Choice Title Company	
	Place of Settlement: Galveston, Texas	I. Settlement Date: April 4

J. Summary of Borrower's Transaction		K. Summary of Seller's Transaction	
100. Gross Amount Due From Borrower		**400. Gross Amount Due To Seller**	
101. Contract sales price	*	401. Contract sales price	*
102. Personal property		402. Personal property	
103. Settlement charges to borrower (line 1400)	*	403.	*
104. Option fee paid	*<500>	404. Option fee received	*<500>
105.		405.	
Adjustments for items paid by seller in advance		**Adjustments for items paid by seller in advance**	
106. City/town taxes to		406. City/town taxes to	
107. County taxes to		407. County taxes to	
108. Assessments to		408. Assessments to	
109. Maintenance fee 4/4-12/31	*	409. Maintenance fee 4/4-12/31	*
110.		410.	
111.		411.	
112.		412.	
120. Gross Amount Due From Borrower	*	**420. Gross Amount Due To Seller**	*
200. Amounts Paid By Or In Behalf Of Borrower		**500. Reductions In Amount Due To Seller**	
201. Deposit or earnest money	*	501. Excess deposit (see instructions)	
202. Principal amount of new loan(s)	*	502. Settlement charges to seller (line 1400)	*
203. Existing loan(s) taken subject to		503. Existing loan(s) taken subject to	
204.		504. Payoff of first mortgage loan	*
205.		505. Payoff of second mortgage loan	
206.		506.	
207.		507.	
208.		508.	
209.		509.	
Adjustments for items unpaid by seller		**Adjustments for items unpaid by seller**	
210. City/town taxes 1/1 through 4/4	*	510. City/town taxes 1/1 through 4/4	*
211. County taxes to		511. County taxes to	
212. Assessments to		512. Assessments to	
213.		513.	
214.		514.	
215.		515.	
216.		516.	
217.		517.	
218.		518.	
219.		519.	
220. Total Paid By/For Borrower		**520. Total Reduction Amount Due Seller**	
300. Cash At Settlement From/To Borrower		**600. Cash At Settlement To/From Seller**	
301. Gross Amount due from borrower (line 120)		601. Gross amount due to seller (line 420)	
302. Less amounts paid by/for borrower (line 220)	( )	602. Less reductions in amt. due seller (line 520)	( )
303. Cash ☐ From ☐ To Borrower		**603. Cash ☐ To ☐ From Seller**	

Section 5 of the Real Estate Settlement Procedures Act (RESPA) requires the following: • HUD must develop a Special Information Booklet to help persons borrowing money to finance the purchase of residential real estate to better understand the nature and costs of real estate settlement services; • Each lender must provide the booklet to all applicants from whom it receives or for whom it prepares a written application to borrow money to finance the purchase of residential real estate; • Lenders must prepare and distribute with the Booklet a Good Faith Estimate of the settlement costs that the borrower is likely to incur in connection with the settlement. These disclosures are manadatory.

Section 4(a) of RESPA mandates that HUD develop and prescribe this standard form to be used at the time of loan settlement to provide full disclosure of all charges imposed upon the borrower and seller. These are third party disclosures that are designed to provide the borrower with pertinent information during the settlement process in order to be a better shopper.

The Public Reporting Burden for this collection of information is estimated to average one hour per response, including the time for reviewing instructions, searching existing data sources, gathering and maintaining the data needed, and completing and reviewing the collection of information.

This agency may not collect this information, and you are not required to complete this form, unless it displays a currently valid OMB control number.

The information requested does not lend itself to confidentiality.

L. Settlement Charges

	Paid From Borrowers Funds at Settlement	Paid From Seller's Funds at Settlement
700. Total Sales/Broker's Commission based on price $ @ % =		
Division of Commission (line 700) as follows:		
701. $ to		
702. $ to		
703. Commission paid at Settlement		*
704.		
800. Items Payable In Connection With Loan		
801. Loan Origination Fee 1 % of new loan (rounded)	*	
802. Loan Discount 1 % of new loan (rounded)	*	
803. Appraisal Fee to	*	
804. Credit Report to	*	
805. Lender's Inspection Fee		
806. Mortgage Insurance Application Fee to 1/2% of new loan	*	
807. Assumption Fee Amortization schedule		
808.	*	
809.		
810.		
811.		
900. Items Required By Lender To Be Paid In Advance		
901. Interest from 4/4 to 5/1 @$ /day	*	
902. Mortgage Insurance Premium for months to		
903. Hazard Insurance Premium for 1 year years to	*	
904. years to		
905.		
1000. Reserves Deposited With Lender		
1001. Hazard insurance 2 months@$ per month	*	
1002. Mortgage insurance months@$ per month		
1003. City property taxes 7 months@$ per month (rounded)	*	
1004. County property taxes months@$ per month		
1005. Annual assessments months@$ per month		
1006. months@$ per month		
1007. months@$ per month		
1008. months@$ per month		
1100. Title Charges		
1101. Settlement or closing fee to		
1102. Abstract or title search to		
1103. Title examination to		
1104. Title insurance binder to		
1105. Document preparation to For note and deed of trust	*	
1106. Notary fees to		
1107. Attorney's fees to For deed and release		*
(includes above items numbers:)		
1108. Title insurance to		
(includes above items numbers:)		
1109. Lender's coverage $	*	
1110. Owner's coverage $		*
1111.	*	*
1112.		
1113.	*	*
1200. Government Recording and Transfer Charges		
1201. Recording fees: Deed $Borrower ; Mortgage $Borrower ; Releases $ Seller	*	*
1202. City/county tax/stamps: Deed $; Mortgage $		
1203. State tax/stamps: Deed $; Mortgage $		
1204. Tax service fee	*	
1205.		
1300. Additional Settlement Charges		
1301. Survey to ABC Survey Company	*	
1302. Pest inspection to		
1303.		
1304.		
1305.		
1400. Total Settlement Charges (enter on lines 103, Section J and 502, Section K)	*	*

APPENDIX C

Web Site Resources

Rather than cut down more trees and increase the number of pages and the cost of this book, we provide Appendix C to assist you in locating and reviewing relevant statutory provisions. All Texas statutes are available on the State of Texas Web site.

Go to: *www.capitol.state.tx.us*

Under Legislative resources, click on Texas Statutes. Scroll down to locate the following relevant provisions:

Example: Occupations Code for licensing statutes

Property Code

Title 2, Chapter 5, Section 5.008
5.011
5.012

Title 7, Chapters 81–82, Condominiums
Title 8, Chapters 91–93, Landlord and Tenant

OTHER WEB SITES OF INTEREST

Vernon's Texas Civil Statutes	Residential Service Contract Act
Water Code	Chapter 40 regarding utility service districts
Texas Natural Resources Code	Chapter 33, 135 regarding tidewater-influenced land

For assistance with financing questions, the following sites can be very useful:

www.Fanniemae.com
www.Freddiemac.com
www.Ginniemae.gov
www.HUD.gov
www.VA.gov

INDEX

NOTE: Page references in italics refer to figures.